Kent English Reprints

THE RENAISSANCE

General Editor, Hilton Landry

VIRTVTE DVCE, COMITE FORTVNA.

Sir Philip Sidney
The Countess of Pembroke's Arcadia
Introduction by Carl Dennis

George Puttenham
The Arte of English Poesie
Introduction by Baxter Hathaway

THE
COVNTESSE
OF PEMBROKES
ARCADIA,

WRITTEN BY SIR PHILIPPE
SIDNEI.

Introduction by Carl Dennis

THE KENT STATE UNIVERSITY PRESS

A Facsimile Reproduction

Facsimile reproduction of the 1891 photographic facsimile of the original 1590 edition published in a limited edition by Kegan Paul, Trench, Trubner and Co., Ltd., and edited by H. Oskar Sommer.

Standard Book Number 87338-043-6 cloth bound/87338-044-4 soft bound
Library of Congress Catalog Number 78-85106
Manufactured in the United States of America
Designed by Merald Wrolstad

INTRODUCTION

hen Sidney rewrote the old version of the *Arcadia* in the early 1580's, he turned a conventional pastoral romance into a much loftier genre of prose fiction. Though he preserved the pastoral setting, he heightened the style, ennobled the central characters, and broadened the scope of the work by adding to the original subject of love an investigation of right rule and knightly service. To call the resulting work a prose epic, as many modern critics have done, seems therefore to have some justification. It is true that the book's structure seems at times to be based less on the unitary plot of the classical epic than on the complex interweavings of the chivalric and pastoral romance, and that romantic love is given a more central position than in any Greek or Roman epic. But the linear simplicity of the old version suggests that the complexity of the revision was introduced less to subscribe to the demands of pastoral romance than to gain epic magnificence; and this departure from unitary structure, as well as the emphasis on romantic love, finds sanction in Renaissance theories of the epic and in the practice of Sidney's contemporary Ariosto.

To call the *Arcadia* an epic is not simply to assign it an external label but to suggest that the work has to be approached with the seriousness given to a comprehensive treatment of moral problems. When in the *Defense*

Sidney insists upon the instructive power of literature,
it is to the classical epics that he resorts most often for
particular examples. For him they are the poems that
explore the meaning of human conduct most fully and
forcefully. To determine what the *Arcadia* actually has
to say about love, rule, and knightly service is therefore
a useful task for anyone interested in understanding
Renaissance conceptions of the moral life. Though
Sidney's revision was left unfinished, the work as it
stands makes a serious and coherent statement.

I

Though the *Arcadia* is properly called an epic, its chief
subject is that of the pastoral romance, love between man
and woman; and in his treatment of the topic Sidney relies
on the pastoral setting. In the leisurely pastoral world,
where man and woman have few public duties, love can be
made a full-time occupation. The writer is enabled by the
idealized and removed setting to treat love exclusively
without the incursion of other problems that would naturally be expected in more realistic surroundings. The usual
statement that emerges about love in the pastoral
romances is that its course does not run smooth. The
lovers meet external obstacles in the form of mistaken
identities, cruel parents, and jealous rivals, all of which
keep them painfully separated until, after many reversals,
they are finally united. In an external way the plot of the
Arcadia conforms to this pattern. In Books I and II the
two noble princes, Pyrocles and Musidorus, are kept apart
from the two noble princesses, Philocles and Pamela, by
the ladies' parents. King Basilius takes his family into
rustic retirement and forbids the approach of all male suit-

ors, fearing a dark prophecy concerning evil sons-in-law; and then he and his queen, Gynecia, fall in love with Musidorus. To gain access to the ladies the knights assume disguises, Pyrocles that of the Amazon, Zelmane; Musidorus that of the humble shepherd, Dorus; and these disguises become obstacles in their courtship. In Book III the lovers are divided by the greed of an aunt and the love of a rival knight. Cecropia abducts Zelmane, Pamela, and Philoclea, and presses her son Amphialus on the princesses; Amphialus courts Philoclea and refuses to free her. But though the external obstacles of the *Arcadia* are similar to those of other romances, the work is distinctive in its treatment of love; for by individualizing and contrasting its protagonists, it develops a comprehensive view of the nature of good love and the difficulties involved in asserting it.

The pattern of contrast between characters is defined by the opposition between two physical settings, by the contrast between the active world of aspiring minds and complex social forms from which the princes enter Arcadia, and the retired, peaceful pastoral world peopled by gentle souls who live content with a life of simplicity. Both realms possess their own positive modes of life. The busy public world is no mere foil for the peacefulness of the country life; the pastoral world is no mere critique of the excesses of public strife, although for the modern reader Arcadian life may at first appear extremely remote from his own daily existence. Modern critics who insist on the seriousness of pastoral works have often tended to defend them against the charge of being escape literature by treating the pastoral world as a literary device for analysing certain problems of the complex active life, as a means of working them out

in a simplified microcosm. The protagonist of the
pastoral romance is seen as coming from the busy
chivalric world into an idealized and abstracted world
which helps him clarify his emotional problems and
enables him to return educated and refreshed to take
up his former life. The danger of this approach is that
it exalts the pastoral genre by depreciating the viability
of the pastoral world. It gives that world value as a means
of clarifying moral issues, but it refuses to regard it as a
mature alternative to the life of heroic action. This
approach is particularly unprofitable when applied to
Sidney's *Arcadia*. For, as I hope to show, Sidney seriously
evaluates both modes of life, basing the central oppositions between his characters on the opposition
between the two worlds.

The critic who has studied the pastoral tradition of
the *Arcadia* most thoroughly, Walter Davis, has tried to
combine the conception of the pastoral as a microcosm
with the conception of the pastoral as a way of life by
distinguishing three worlds in the *Arcadia:* the outer
world of action and heroic strife, the contrasting peaceful Arcadian countryside, and the inmost circle of the
Arcadian court, which functions for Mr. Davis as a
kind of "microcosm where virtues and vices are simplified and heightened."[1] This three-fold division allows
Mr. Davis to emphasize the contrast between Arcadian
life and life in the rest of Greece, between the realms of
contemplation and action, while insisting on the universal
application of events surrounding the Arcadian Court.
But since most of the action occurs around the "micro-
cosmic" court, the initial opposition of the two worlds is
left behind, never integrated into his analysis of the
characters' virtues and vices. Mr. Davis does argue

cogently that most Renaissance pastorals do describe three distinct realms, the inmost center usually being a holy shrine or dwelling-place of the gods, the source of value for the outer world from which the hero of the romance receives his enlightenment and regeneration. But at the center of the *Arcadia*, as Mr. Davis admits, there is no holy shrine but a human court which should order the concerns of the pastoral kingdom. Indeed, it is Basilius's recourse to a holy oracle that causes his foolish retirement into the forest. The pastoral kingdom is most stable, it would seem, when its ruler regards himself as an autonomous agent, relying on no forces above and beyond him.

The reader of the *Arcadia* might do well to approach its pastoral world as the home of a particular way of life which is the natural expression of one kind of character. The exact label we give to this life should be chosen with some care. As the realm of unaspiring minds Arcadia might be called the land of contemplation, as opposed to the other lands of ambitious activity; but the term "contemplation" is not very accurate. The Arcadians are not engaged in holy meditation or in creating works of the intellect (except casual pastoral exercises), but in the laborious activity of love. And the good lover in the *Arcadia* must possess those virtues of clear judgment and emotional fidelity which are demanded by the nobly active knight and ruler. Nor can we limit the activity in Arcadia to love. Just as love plays a central part in the lives of people outside Arcadia, so the problems of rule and war have to be met by the Arcadians. Still, the unassuming Arcadians are characteristically different from the aspiring minds in other countries and approach all their activities in a different way. Perhaps we may call the contrast of the outer world and Arcadia the opposition of civilization and nature, a contrast based partly on two different physical settings but going beyond environment to character. The civilized life is that of a populous, complex, cultured, and ambitious community. Its members are trained to respect the laws of social order which give society beauty and coherence, and are urged to dedicate themselves to nurturing their natural gifts of mind and body for the service of their society. The natural life is that of a sparsely-populated, simple, unsophisticated, and humble community. Its members need little self-discipline because their characters are intrinsically subdued. They fulfil themselves by exercising their natural gifts of humility and emotional warmth in simple personal relations. Not all the Arcadians have natural temperaments, nor all outsiders civilized temperaments; but the realms they live in help to define and embody an opposition that is central to all the characters of the *Arcadia,* one that divides not only the king and queen, the princes, and the princesses, but most of the minor characters as well. In trying to understand what Sidney has to say about love in the *Arcadia*, we have to ask how well love is established and maintained by representatives of the two modes of life.

The contrast is perhaps most apparent in the princesses. Philoclea, in her simplicity, her humility, her warmth, and her natural innocence, is associated with nature. Pamela, in her wisdom, her self-respect, her emotional control, and her queenly sense of her own high estate, is associated with civilization. As Kalander says in describing the princesses to the two knights, there is "more sweetnesse in Philoclea but more majestie in Pamela; . . . [Philoclea is] so humble that she will put all pride out of countenance; . . . Pamela of high thoughts, who avoides not pride with not knowing her excellencies, but by making that one of her excellencies to be voide of pride" (pages 11 -12)[2]. The natural virtues of unqualified openness and self-forgetfulness are here juxtaposed with the more civilized virtues of internal discipline and respect for strict hierarchical distinctions.

Both women appear to be introduced as perfections of their kinds, but where love is concerned both their kinds have possible flaws. The danger for the woman of nature is that her feelings may lead her judgment astray, causing her to confuse her lover's sex and need with his merit. Thus she may love someone not worth loving. The danger for the woman of civilization, if she is able to maintain a strict control over her emotions, is that her respect for form and degree may cause her to judge men solely by external standards of rank and wealth. Thus she may confuse good fortune with good character. Both the princesses are given their special tests in love by the disguises which their lovers are forced to assume in order to court them. Philoclea, wooed by Pyrocles disguised as the Amazon, Zelmane, must fall in love with someone she thinks to be a woman. In this situation she cannot be led by immediate impulse and sexual attraction. Her love, if it develops at all, must proceed from friendship founded on respect. And this is the progress it eventually follows. Its development, as described in Book II, Chapter 4, is a gradual, logical process:

[Zelmane's] being a noble straunger had bred a kind of heed-full attention; her coming to that lonely place . . . a willingnes of conversation; her wit and behavior, a liking and silent admiration; at length the excellency of her natural gifts, joined

with the extreme shewes she made of most devout honouring
Philoclea, (carrying thus in one person the only two bands of
good will, lovelines and lovingnes) brought forth in her hart
a yeelding to a most friendly affection.   (Page 115^V)

Only when the friendship is established, and "liking
[Zelmane's] manners [has bred] good-wil," do her
emotions come to the foreground and "good-wil [be-
comes] the chiefe cause of her liking her manners"
(page 115^V). Her falling in love with Zelmane is not a
complete proof of her character, since it does not tell
us if she can resist false appeals to her emotions; but
it does show us that a woman in the natural mode can
achieve noble love, can love true "lovelines."

Pamela, wooed by Musidorus disguised as the lowly
shepherd, Dorus, must fall in love with someone from
the lowest class on the social scale. She must see the
man beneath the rank. Like Philoclea, she passes the
trial completely, gradually overcoming her respect for
forms as she sees repeated evidences of Dorus's noble
love and virtue. Pamela's falling in love does not mean
that she gives up her old values. It means simply that
she is able to embody social values in their highest form;
respecting moral worth she proves the worth of the civilized mode of love. Though she loves Dorus, she is not
willing to marry him until she discovers his true station.
To do otherwise would overturn social hierarchy. "The
judgment of the world," she tells Dorus when he pro-
poses, "stands upon matter of fortune" (page 107^V).
And she expresses her love, as does Philoclea, in the
way best suited to her character. Philoclea admits her
love as Shakespeare's Juliet does, with an artless openness that gives up all attempts at ingenuity. Pamela's

courtship is formal. She demands that Dorus maintain respectful humility, and he woos her indirectly by pretending to praise her serving maid, Mopsa, a piece of sophistication both lovers delight in. Similarly each woman protects herself from her lover's over-ardent advances by the means peculiar to her character. Philoclea accepts Zelmane's kisses but fends off further freedoms by an appeal to his sense of responsibility. Pamela accepts no advances at all and indignantly castigates Dorus's impudence. Each woman, then, consistently maintains her special beauty: Philoclea, the beauty of simplicity; Pamela, the beauty of elegance. Together they serve to vindicate the nobility of the way of nature and the way of civilization.

The two princes represent two parallel masculine kinds of love. As young knights fresh from their first military adventures, neither knows the ways of love until he enters Arcadia; but their responses to love differ because they represent contrasting knightly types. Pyrocles, as his name indicates, is the more emotional man. He has already led a rebellion of the Helots, and when he enters Arcadia he falls in love at once with the mere picture of Philoclea. To his impetuosity in love he adds an appreciation of the peacefulness and beauty of Arcadia that allows us to associate him with the mode of nature. Musidorus, with his keen sense of knightly dignity and social duty, is the man of civilization. Castigating the love-stricken Pyrocles, he condemns love as anti-social, effeminate madness, the "basest and fruitlessest of all passions, . . . engendered betwixt lust and idlenes" (pages 52-52^V). Since the noble masculine representatives of nature and civilization are more extreme, they demand more severe tests, tests that may help to soften and round their characters. When both knights fall in love, the disguises they assume are signs and trials of their ability to adapt their characters to the experience of love. Passionate Pyrocles must disguise himself as a woman; he must become more passive, retiring and controlled. Proud Musidorus must assume the disguise of a lowly shepherd, the humblest position on the social scale; he must be an extreme of submission and obedience. The princes' final success in love is a vindication of both their characters. Pyrocles's passion channels into a courtship of quiet restraint. He learns to speak by the eye, and not by violent action. Musidorus's proud social-consciousness widens to include respect for the nobility of love.

Though love tries and softens the princes, each loves in the way that befits him. Pyrocles courts not by his wit but by his loving gestures, by being simple and open. If his disguise as a woman softens his impetuousity, it also befits his warmer temperament. Musidorus on the other hand, carries out his courtship through a somewhat conventional Petrarchan submission to the will of an exalted woman, and takes a delight in the rigid hierarchy which the convention demands and in the sophisticated indirection of his speeches to Mopsa. The careers of the princes, like the careers of the princesses, affirm both the way of nature and the way of civilization.

By the end of Book II, the lovers have proved their natures and established love of the highest quality. In the third book this worthy love is tested for durability. The lovers are proven by misfortune and must keep faith despite suffering. Cecropia captures Zelmane, Pamela, and Philoclea; and first cajoles, then threatens, and then tortures the princesses in an attempt to force one to marry Amphialus and so secure for herself Basilius's kingdom. By their resistance both the princesses prove their fidelity, each in the mode of her character. Philoclea's soft feelings prove unshakable once having been given to Pyrocles. She resists Amphialus's warm appeals to her compassion and Cecropia's appeal to domestic comfort and the delights of motherhood. Pamela, more sophisticated than her sister, has more temptations. After Cecropia has failed to entice her by insisting on Amphialus's love and high estate, and the temptations of the flesh are beaten off "with the Majestie of Vertue," she tries by artful arguments to undermine Pamela's faith in all established morality (page 265). Preaching a doctrine of relativistic naturalism, she maintains that there are no divine laws, that common values are the "bugbeares of opinions" set up to keep the ignorant from their faults, and that God is a man-created notion originating in fear of the unseen (page 280). Her moral is that one should strive for worldly pleasure and not endanger his natural felicity by vain devotion to chimerical supernatural ends. Pamela's answer of outraged virtue, which immediately cows Cecropia, articulates her belief in an ordered world that underlies her commitment to civilization. It is a long proof that the world is governed by an all-wise, all-good God whose existence and excellence are proved by the harmony of the world. "Perfect order, perfect beautie, perfect constancie," she asserts, "[are not] the children of Chaunce" (page 282). Although this intellectual proof could not be understood by simple Philoclea, Philoclea's emotions are her guides to true value; and her fidelity is the final triumph of nature as Pamela's is the final triumph of civilization.

In asserting the existence of God-given absolute
moral law, Pamela's speech provides the central pre-
supposition of the treatment of love in the *Arcadia*.
Noble love is an absolute good for which man must
strive. It not only gives happiness; it demands fidelity.
Even if the love cannot end in temporal union, those
who keep faith can be comforted because their fidelity
puts them in harmony with eternal law.

The nobility of the love achieved by the princes and
princesses is emphasized by the contrast it presents to
the ignoble love of Basilius and Gynecia for Zelmane, an
attachment which proves to be one of the most serious
obstacles to the young lovers. Though Zelmane is
worthy of love, the love of the king and queen perverts
the code of civilization in being adulterous, and perverts nature in being directed towards their children's
contemporary. The quality of their love differs, however; for the king's character belongs to nature and the
queen's to civilization. Basilius is the father of Philoclea.
He is loved rather than revered; he is sweet and open
rather than wise and severe. His love for Zelmane grows
out of his naturally warm temper rather than from a
sudden fit of passion, and is presented as dotage rather
than emotional chaos. The harmless witlessness of his
love is seen most clearly in his inability to pierce
Zelmane's disguise and realize that he loves no woman
at all.

Regal Gynecia, on the other hand, is the mother of
Pamela. Daughter of the king of Cyprus rather than a
native Arcadian, she is "of great wit and . . . of more
princely vertues then her husband," as Kalander tells
the princes. But though like Pamela in her "wisdome,
greatnesse, [and] nobilitie," she lacks her daughter's

"constant temper"; for she is "of so working a minde
and so vehement spirits . . . it was happie shee tooke a
good course, for otherwise the results would have been
terrible" (pages 11ᵛ and 12). Her nature, then, is built
on conflict and she must maintain her basic allegiance
to the pole of civilization only by constant repression of
her strong emotions. When she falls in love with
Zelmane her control is broken. Her wit enables her to
understand her self-betrayal, but it proves too weak to
assert itself. All that she can do is decide to follow out
her passion despite all consequences, declaring, like
Macbeth and Satan, that "in shame there is no comfort
but to be beyond all bounds of shame" (page 99). In
this way Gynecia becomes more "terrible" than
Basilius. When the naturally emotional man like Basilius
is irrational, his character simply lacks limits. But when
the regal woman like Gynecia lets her emotions control
her, her character is completely subverted; her actions
become extreme because she has left behind all the intrinsic guides of her nature.

Much of the artistry of Books I and II consists in
presenting specific parallel actions of the young lovers
and old lovers so that they comment indirectly upon
each other. At times the relations seem external. Love
laments succeed each other so quickly that the reader is
first impressed by the simple comedy of repetition.
Gynecia's complaint for Zelmane is interrupted by the
sound of Zelmane's lament for Philoclea. The queen's
suit to Zelmane is interrupted by Basilius's love song for
Zelmane. And when Zelmane escapes her suitors, she
runs into Dorus, who confesses his love for Pamela.
Love plays the music of Arcadia and all men dance.
More often, however, the parallelism also works to

point out the differences in quality between the young
love and the old. The contrast between the externally
similar laments of Gynecia and Philoclea for Zelmane
is perhaps the most obvious. Both women go out alone
into the woods, confess that they have yielded themselves
up to love despite their resistance to it, and feel that the
love has betrayed their former purity. Both women ad-
dress a heavenly body in attempting to justify themselves, Gynecia the sun and Philoclea the moon. But
Gynecia's sun is the light of truth and she hates its
beams because they seem to expose to herself the desires
she knows to be evil. She recognizes "wild ravenous
beastes" within her which the soft nature of Arcadia
does not hold (page 98$^\text{v}$). Philoclea's moon is the Diana
to whom she vowed virginity as a child, when engaged
in her "wooddie devotion" (page -118). Her change is
from innocent childhood to innocent womanhood, and
the strange new passions that finally possess her are
sanctioned not only "by the comminalitie of Passions
but agreed unto by her most noble Thoughts" (page 116).
Her simple, natural woody devotion, then, is opposed
to the wilderness of Gynecia's heart. Basilius and
Musidorus are also specifically contrasted as lovers.
The love-stricken king dances grotesquely before
Zelmane in the delusion that he is still green and vigorous.
Musidorus performs before Pamela by displaying his
perfect skill in riding, subduing high animal spirits to
his own will. Thus although Philoclea is associated with
nature and Musidorus with civilization, the nobility of
both their loves is affirmed by the defects of the king
and queen.

Besides serving as foils to the young lovers, Basilius
and Gynecia, in obstructing the fruition of their child-

ren's love, introduce the subsidiary theme of the *Arcadia,* the power of fortune. The theme receives its fullest development in Book III, when the princesses are abducted by Cecropia, who is like Gynecia in her perverted intellect and passion, but who is prompted by greed rather than by love, and who is too godless ever to question the rightness of her actions. Though the abduction of Pamela and Philoclea allows the young lovers to pass the test of constancy, it also teaches them about the limitations of the human will and the need for patience in suffering. Sidney does not write his epic merely to give examples of virtues and vices. He tries to describe honestly the restrictions imposed on all human effort by circumstance, to present without falsification the mysterious relation of virtue and happiness. And he shows no simple-minded faith in the doctrine that love conquers all, that a good will can overcome all obstacles. The lovers in Book III are placed in an unfortunate situation in which no one can help his friend. Zelmane must watch helplessly what she thinks to be the execution of Philoclea, and keeps herself from suicide only by the vague hope of revenge. Musidorus is outside the castle, and his heroic attempts as the Black Knight to make entrance prove unsuccessful. In such a position the only alternatives seem to be suicide or senseless suffering. Proud Pamela inclines to suicide because she cannot bear the indignity of her helplessness, of their being, as she says, "balls to injurious Fortune" (page 353). "Hope," she affirms, "is the fawning traitour of the minde, while under colour of friendship, it robbes it of his chiefe force of resolution" (page 353). Zelmane's answer shows a more mature stoicism: "While [time] may bring foorth any good, doo not barre your selfe thereof; for then would be time to die nobly when you cannot live nobly" (page 353ᵛ). Ineffectual suffering, in other words, is never an indignity when endured for principle. Circumstances may limit noble action to standing firm and waiting. Although Zelmane's faith in life is later justified, and she is given the chance to meet force with action, the stoic moral is not altered. What we do is the result of will; what happens to us is the result of outside forces. Virtue lies in the hands of men; happiness is a gift of fortune. And no heavenly consolation is offered, since the *Arcadia* presents a pagan world. The unfortunate must find their sole comfort in their fidelity to principle.

The extended suffering of the protagonists in Book III gives the *Arcadia* a somberness not present in the first two books and develops new aspects of the meaning of nobility. As E.M.W. Tillyard points out, the somberness is new because never before has an evil character like Cecropia held for so long such complete power over the fortunes of the noble characters.[3] Her viciousness, it is true, comes as no surprise. Book I ends with an episode in which she attempts to kill the princesses by having a wild lion and wild bear released in their vicinity. Book II ends with her servants inciting a riot among the shepherds that threatens the life of the entire court. Yet both these dangers are immediately overcome. The princes kill the animals and quiet the mob. In Book III the princes must submit, for a time, to greater powers. The notion of heroic nobility is extended because the active virtues of strength and courage, which are displayed particularly by the princes in the minor episodes of Book II, are now completed by the virtues of spiritual patience and endurance in suffering. The task is harder for the princes than for the princesses since men are by nature more active than women, and their success is prepared for by their previous discipline during courtship, which tested their powers of self-control and so gave them the necessary preliminary education for their final trial.

Sidney's making passive endurance an essential quality of heroism allows us to place the *Arcadia* in the tradition of the Renaissance Christian epic, which reaches its final form in *Paradise Lost*. This tradition redefines the classical heroic qualities of wisdom and fortitude in more spiritual terms.[4] This not only means that honor, courage, and pride give way to stoic endurance, but also that trial and suffering are the results of noble commitments. Where the classical hero is often tried simply by his ability to endure the blows of fate and chance, the Christian epic hero is tried by constant temptation towards a bad choice, so that his endurance is resistance of evil and fidelity to the good. In the *Arcadia* the princes might not seem to subscribe fully to this ideal, since their suffering is not complicated by overt temptation. Yet their pain is caused by love, and love itself is a choice to go beyond stoic self-sufficiency, to subject one's happiness to the goddess Fortuna. In the princesses the Christian epic role is fulfilled completely. Cecropia's temptations to make them reject their love, her appeals to physical comfort, to the vitality of nature, to pride in beauty and state, are a prototype of Archimago's temptation of Guyon in Book II of the *Faerie Queene,* of Comus's appeal to the Lady in *Comus,* of Satan's temptation of Eve in *Paradise Lost,* and of Satan's temptation of the Son in *Paradise Regained.* The temptation in the *Arcadia* does not have the cosmic rami-

fications that it has in Milton's epics, because the fate of
mankind does not rest upon the choice of the protagonists.
But the resistance of the princesses is given an heroic
glory because Cecropia becomes almost demonic in her
godless atheism, an emissary of Satan's Kingdom like
Comus and Archimago. The simple problem of fidelity
to one's love is given a religious dimension that makes the
right choice one of salvation or damnation.

The consciousness of Sidney's attempt to ennoble
his four protagonists, to make them models of love and
suffering, is particularly evident when the reader of the
Arcadia is familiar with the "old" *Arcadia.* Book III is entirely new. In the old version, instead of the capture and
captivity of Zelmane and the princesses, we find the
elopement of Musidorus and Pamela. And in order to
divert Pamela's guards, Musidorus uses comic ruses
worthy of a fabliau, sending the shepherd Dametas to
dig for a treasure, sending his wife Mopsa to town to look
for Dametas (whom Musidorus accuses of adultery),
and sending their daughter Mopsa up a tree to await the
coming of Apollo, who is to grant all her wishes. And
Dorus is never completely schooled in humility. In the
final version when he attempts to embrace Pamela and
is castigated for his impudence, he is so humbled by her
reproach that he wanders for weeks in the forest and
does not appear again until he is disguised as the Black
Knight. In the old version he attempts to rape Pamela
as she lies asleep unprotected, is prevented only by the
attack of rustic rabble, and never really repents his
attempt. Pyrocles and Philoclea are also of lower dignity
in the old version. After getting Basilius and Gynecia to
lie together under the delusion that they are sleeping
with Zelmane, Pyrocles takes advantage of the time to

solicit the favours of Philoclea. And Philoclea yields to him instead of appealing to his sense of responsibility as she does in the revision. Natural love here is uncontrolled and does not lie within the limits of social law. When the two lovers are imprisoned, they are not held in a fortress by a cruel enemy but locked in Philoclea's bedroom by irate shepherds. And they look upon their suicide not as a means of escaping the indignities of mindless fortune, but as a way of avoiding the shame of trial and punishment which their action entails. When Sidney rewrote the *Arcadia,* then, he reconceived the characters of its heroes to make them the examplars of the highest kinds of love.

In vindicating and exalting its four protagonists, the *Arcadia* presents a view of love that is large and tolerant. Good love requires deep respect and strong feeling for worthy objects and an unflinching loyalty to them, but it can be reached by different characters through different modes, through the way of civilization or the way of nature. The tolerance of this love ethic is best appreciated when it is contrasted to the more common hierarchical scheme presented in a work like Book III of the *Faerie Queene,* the next English epic of love. Britomart, who represents true love, cannot embrace the qualities of Pamela and Philoclea. She is like Pamela in her self-respect and commitment to principle, but her power lacks the graces of wit and eloquence. In these respects Belphoebe is closer to Pamela, but Belphoebe is clearly defective since her virginal pride prevents her from loving any man. On the other hand Britomart does not have Philoclea's natural humility and warmth. In these respects Amoretta is closer to Philoclea, but Amoretta is also presented as defective. Her natural education in the Garden of Adonis has left her spirit undisciplined so that she is not completely able to subdue lust. Sidney's conception of good love, then, is broader than Spenser's. Both writers believe in absolutes, but Sidney believes that one may keep faith to them in more than one form. To modern readers, who have seen naturalists and rationalists in their most strident and exclusive forms, Sidney's tolerance is particularly refreshing.

In his attempt to make his epic of love comprehensive, Sidney introduces a variety of lovers outside the main plot who illustrate various degrees of worth and unworthiness in love, or who develop the relations of love and circumstance. Three peripheral stories of love are told in Book I, and the tales which princes and princesses tell about unhappy lovers in Book II, when taken with the related tales of knightly exploits, comprise almost a third of the entire *Arcadia.* The use of many personages seems to result in part from Sidney's belief in the fixity of human character. No figure in the *Arcadia* undergoes change, though many are tested under trial to reaffirm their initial positions. Different kinds of love, therefore, instead of being presented as stages in the development of one relation, must be embodied, if presented at all, in different agents. Where Milton makes Adam and Eve progress from love to selfishness to renewed love, Sidney gives each degree of love a separate exemplar. The kind of comprehensiveness that results may seem to the modern reader to be achieved at the expense of structural unity and narrative vigor. In Book II the love stories told by the central figures are so numerous and complexly interwoven that they bring the main plot to a standstill, leaving it lost in a welter of events to which it is not immediately related.

But though in practice Sidney's structural principle seems unwieldy, in theory it is an attempt to give coherence to a large mass of material, to give the work the unity of action which Sidney demands in the *Defense.* Sidney takes as his model not the Italian epic of Ariosto, in which several stories are woven together without subordination, but the classical epic, in which one main action is augmented with minor episodes. Kenneth Myrick has shown us that in the proliferation of episodes Sidney has special sanction from the Italian critic Minturno, who gives the episode an important place in the epic form as the means to increase the magnificence and variety of the action.[5] If the unity which this device is designed to preserve is not always maintained in the *Arcadia,* the attempt seems clear enough. Sidney wants to write a coherent work which achieves an epic magnitude in its treatment of its major themes. His main plot, with its disguises and intrigue, is already so complicated that to introduce into it a host of minor lovers would be to risk incoherence. By the use of stories told by the protagonists, or by brief incursions of lesser figures into the main story, he attempts to keep the progress of the work simple while developing the full implications of his subject. The tales slow the action but they are at least thematically relevant.

The three episodes of love in Book I, the tales of Argulus and Parthenia, Amphialus and Helena, and Philantius and Artesia, introduce the central concerns of the work. The story of Argulus and Parthenia is a miniature version of the central plot. The union of two perfect lovers is prevented by the greed and spite of a parent who, like Cecropia, knows no limits to her corrupt will, and who tries to cow her daughter by threats of force and by false

logic. The separation of the lovers following Parthenia's
being disfigured by her rejected suitor is analogous to the
capture of the princesses; and the final union perhaps
looks forward to the union of the protagonists, as the
death of Parthenia's mother upon the frustration of her
plans anticipates Cecropia's self-destruction. The story
also serves a dramatic function. Told by Kalander's
steward to Musidorus, it introduces Musidorus to the
workings of love. Coming from a world of strife and action
to a land of pastoral ease, and resisting, unlike Pyrocles,
the value of love, Musidorus is told a story of the noblest
lovers that should help prepare him for his ultimate
submission to Pamela.

Before he falls in love, his education is furthered by
hearing from Queen Helena the story of Amphialus,
which introduces in pure form the subject of love and
fortune to be elaborated completely in Book III, in
which Amphialus assumes major importance. Acting as
a pleader for his friend Philoxenus in his suit to Helena,
Amphialus only succeeds in awakening love for himself.
His friend suspects treachery and Amphialus, in
defending himself against Philoxenus, accidently kills
him. Philoxenus's father, who has raised Amphialus
from childhood, dies in grief. From the story as it
stands no general moral can be drawn but that fortune
and love are often opposed; that circumstances may
turn good intentions into disaster. For Musidorus the
story is particularly relevant, for he soon learns that
the actions of his best friend seem as unpredictable as
chance. Finding that Pyrocles has been driven by love to
a course of disguise and concealment, he sees that
human will can be an agent of fortune:

Heretofore [he complains to absent Pyrocles] I have accused

the sea, condemned the Pyrats, and hated my evill fortune, that deprived me of thee; But now thy self is the seá, which drounes my comfort, thy selfe is the Pirat that robbes thy selfe of me: Thy owne will becomes my evill fortune. (Page 40ᵛ).

"Thy owne will becomes my evill fortune" might serve as the motto of Amphialus and Helena. Amphialus finds that unwanted love turns a friend against him; Helena finds that she loves a man who disdains her. Musidorus is linked symbolically to the miseries of Amphialus when he dons Amphialus's cast-off armor. The incident serves as an immediate anticipation of his yielding up his own will to Pamela, and looks forward to the sufferings of all the protagonists for love in Book III.

When the flawed love of the king and queen for Zelmane begins to hinder the courtship of the princes, the central action is interrupted by the appearance of Philantius and Artesia, a pair whose defects compliment those of Basilius and Gynecia. Instead of love without reason and order, they embody ceremony without emotion, a perversion peculiar to the civilized mode of life. Like the princes the pair are strangers to Arcadia, but unlike the princes they cannot be made amenable to the country because they are incapable of love. Philantius's universal challenge to the knights of the world on behalf of his mistress's beauty is the result of an empty compliment made in flippant courtliness which was taken literally by Artesia out of spite and pride. That formalistic Philantius should finally be unseated in simple Arcadia is a comment on his moral inadequacies and an affirmation of the pastoral life; and the victory of Zelmane is in part the triumph of a mature form of natural love over a perverted form of civilized love. Disciplined feeling triumphs over empty form. But Musidorus's equal zeal in taking up Philantius's challenge, and his unceremonious mutilation of Philantius's shield in his desire to defend Pamela, indicate that the best formal lover is also opposed to the love that only exists in external ritual.

When in Book II the princes find their love reciprocated, and the jealousy of Gynecia becomes more desperate, the central story assumes a slightly darker cast which is reflected in the many tales of unhappy love told by the protagonists. The book begins with Gynecia's vow to satisfy her passion even if it means doing away with Philoclea, is interrupted by the incursion of Amphialus, who has become Zelmane's rival in love for Philoclea, and ends with a rebellion stirred up by Philoclea that almost topples the state. The minor love stories exemplify varieties of foolish, false, or ill-starred passion. Three of the five tales of love, the stories of Erona and Antiphilus, Dido and Pamphilus, and Andromena and the king of Iberia, illustrate the contrasting flaws of defective natural and civilized love. Two women and one man, Erona, Dido, and Iberia, love without judgment a person not worth loving; one woman and two men, Andromena, Antiphilus, and Pamphilus, use craft without love to satisfy their lust and greed. The different proportion of men and women assigned to the two kinds of defects probably reflects Sidney's subscription to the Renaissance belief that women tend to be emotional and passive and men more thoughtful and aggressive.

The tale of Erona, begun by Philoclea and finished by Basilius, depicts the excess to which the natural woman, like Philoclea, is most liable, unrestrained passion for an unworthy man. Good love for Sidney is

not a spontaneous and indiscriminate overflowing of
the heart without regard to the worth of the object.
Erona loves unworthily by casting the pearl of her love
before a swine. Her fall is prepared for by her proud
ignorance, by her contempt for the power of love. Where
innocent Philoclea makes an unrealistic vow of virginity
to Diana, Erona goes further and impiously rejects the
divinity of Cupid. When love finally comes to her, she is
therefore completely unprepared, without any means to
control it. Philoclea's love develops slowly and logically;
Erona's is sudden and mad. Her beloved, Antiphilus,
is not only a man of low degree and base character,
but incapable of love, as his name suggests, marrying
only for money and later attempting to abandon her for
another wife. No woman in the *Arcadia* is more faithful
than Erona once she has given her heart, and no man is
less capable of returning affection than the crafty
Antiphilus.

The opposition of unwise passion and designing craft
is varied slightly in the story of Dido and Pamphilus.
Dido and the eight other ladies whom Pyrocles finds
torturing Pamphilus are essentially over-credulous
women who have been seduced by false rhetoric into
loving a man of no worth. And Pamphilus is a man of
shrewd wit who lies for pleasure, ingeniously defending
his promiscuity as a quest for ever-higher embodiments
of beauty. But Dido is more sophisticated than Erona,
and is partly seduced by false values of civilization, by
the polish of Pamphilus's eloquence and by the coyness
of his courtship. And her anger at his infidelity stems
in part from his statement that she has lost her beauty,
which for her is the "scorne of al scornes" (page 185).
If her heart is too open, her mind is too small. Similarly

Pamphilus represents not only heartless craft but sheer lust, impersonal lechery that uses all women as delight for his body. Where Antiphilus ("anti-love") uses the pretenses of love to gain the externals of rank, Pamphilus ("all-love") uses the trappings of civilized rhetoric to advance his lechery.

In the third tale of defective love, the story of Andromena and the king of Iberia, we return to a simple opposition of heartless craft and mindless affection that we found in the tale of Erona and Antiphilus; but now the roles are assigned to opposite sexes. The king of Iberia is an uxorious husband, blindly trusting his untrustworthy wife and giving over to her complete control of the kingdom. Queen Andromena marries only for power. In her political ambition she is like Cecropia, but she follows Gynecia in using her position to serve her unnatural sexual passion, first attempting to make her step-son Plangus remain her lover after she has married his father, later attempting the double seduction of Pyrocles and Musidorus when they are guests in her husband's castle. When her son Palladius is accidentally killed as she pursues the escaping princes, her remorse and suicide cause us to look back to the self-destruction of Parthenia's mother, and forward to the death of Amphialus's mother, Cecropia – to the ends of women whose intelligence serves their passions.

Two minor figures in Book II, Plangus and the original Zelmane, stand outside the love stories already considered, since their misfortunes do not arise from any moral defect in asserting the mode of nature or the mode of civilization, from any thoughtless warmth or heartless policy, but from the mere force of circumstances. Their stories are overbalanced in bulk by tales of imperfect love, but the story of Plangus is given special emphasis by being broken up to frame the other tales. We hear of Plangus first in Chapter xii, when Zelmane reads his lament against fortune, which Basilius has recorded. Subsequent chapters tell us of the cruel plots which his own step-mother, Andromena, uses against him; but not until the last chapter of Book II is his lament explained as the record of his seemingly hopeless love for Erona. His love is a worthy passion for a worthy woman, but it brings him only suffering because fate is against him. Erona loves and marries the base Antiphilus; and when both are captured by their enemy Artaxia, Plangus is commanded by Erona to work for the release of his rival. When Antiphilus is executed, Artexia refuses to allow Plangus to fight for Erona's release. He must bring Musidorus and Pyrocles as her champions. Since they appear to have vanished from Greece, his task seems impossible. Fate allows him neither to receive the love he deserves nor to relieve the suffering of his beloved by direct intervention. No action is left for him, as his name suggests, but complaint. The burden of his recorded lament, that the gods are completely indifferent to human suffering, may appear the extreme statement of a grieving lover; but from what we are told of his predicament, no character in the *Arcadia* has a better right to believe it. This lament, it should be noticed, immediately follows the only appearance of luckless Amphialus in Book II, in which he is shown as having fallen hopelessly in love with Philoclea, who has already given her heart to Zelmane. The pains of Plangus at the hands of cruel fate serve as an anticipatory analogue for the pains which Amphialus is to suffer for worthy love in Book III.

The female counterpart of Plangus is the true Zelmane, a ward in the court of Plangus's father. Though she is loved by Plangus's worthy step-brother, Palladius, she falls in love with Pyrocles. Her beloved is eminently virtuous, but the choice is unfortunate because she feels Pyrocles too exalted to love her, and she pines away disguised as his page Diaphantus, not declaring her identity and her passion till on her death bed. Her unfortunate career is made to comment directly on the careers of Pyrocles and Musidorus, because the princes, following her dying wish, take the names of Diaphantus and Palladius when they land in Greece, Pyrocles also taking Zelmane's true name when he disguises himself as an Amazon. As part of a tale of fate's cruelty to lovers, the names serve as prophetic emblems of the princes' stoic suffering in Book III.

When in Book III Sidney turns to deal elaborately with the relation of love and fortune, ill-starred Amphialus, only briefly mentioned in Book II, assumes major importance in the central action. It is for his sake that his mother Cecropia captures and imprisons the princesses and Zelmane. And by petitioning Philoclea rather than attempting to secure her release, he becomes a party to his mother's plans. Fortune is particularly hard on him. Since the princes and princesses have established true reciprocal relations, their suffering is a test of their fidelity. They are given the opportunity to ennoble their love by resisting weakness and despair, and are comforted by their commitment to absolute values. But Amphialus's love for Philoclea is not returned and therefore he cannot choose between fidelity and betrayal. His love is remarkable in its intensity, but it would be better for him and for Philoclea if he could resist it. And it is particularly self-defeating since the more he presses his love on Philoclea, the more he alienates her. Fortune has seen to it that he must choose between her happiness and his own; to make her happy he must make himself miserable. Caught in such a dilemma Amphialus proves too weak to resolve the problem. In his gentlemanly courtesy he refuses to force Philoclea's will and orders the captives treated with respect; but his love is too passionate to allow their departure. His misfortune is compounded by the fact that his mother tries to force the situation by torturing the princesses. And when she falls to her death as Amphialus pursues her along the ramparts, Amphialus, attempting suicide, is forced to acknowledge his own love as the cause of general calamity. The final statement made on Amphialus's life by Helena, that it illustrates how nature grinds down its best men, does not seem too exaggerated. Even if we make allowances for her grief, we can conclude only that some men are born to live unfortunate lives.

The final lesson imparted by Sidney's treatment of fortune is tolerance. If some men are ruined while others are only tested, and if the tests are themselves unequal, we must learn to make allowances. In this way the theme of fortune's injustice compliments the positive tolerance demanded by the contrasting moral success of the four protagonists, a success which affirms that the highest kind of nobility in love may be achieved either through the way of civilization or the way of nature.

II

Love is the major subject of the *Arcadia,* but related problems of rule and knightly service are also given extensive treatment. Basilius is the king of Arcadia as well as a lover; his country is visited by knights like Musidorus, Pyrocles, and Plangus, who have long histories of martial exploits involving kings and other knights, and the telling of these histories takes up more than half of Book II; and in Book III the country undergoes a civil war which brings about critical problems of knightly loyalty. This extension of the subject matter does not make the *Arcadia* merely more comprehensive; it enables the work to treat the more complicated moral problems that arise when a man faces an apparent conflict of duties.

The problems of rule come first to the reader's attention, since it is King Basilius's sudden departure from his court into the forest that brings about the problems of love for the protagonists and forces the princes to woo in disguise. This retreat is doubtless unwise and unkingly. It is motivated by a superstitious fear of a dark Sibylline prophecy; and it only serves to make disturbances more probable, since as Basilius's good general, Philanax, contends, it is foolish to "deprive your selfe of government for feare of loosing your government" (page 15). Inevitably it results in an insurrection of the shepherds who are left without the security of royal control. But though the evils of the withdrawal are clear, one must guard against hasty conclusions about their final significance. It would be wrong, for example, to look upon the story as a rejection of the quiet pastoral life of Arcadia for a life of energetic authority like that represent-

ed by Pyrocles's father, King Euarchus, the model ruler
for the tales narrated in Book II. Actually there are
two modes of kingship, as there are two modes of love.
Each has its special virtues and its potential flaws.

We have already seen Basilius representing the natural
mode as a private man and a lover. His easy, quiet
nature also determines the way he governs. Near the
beginning of Book I Kalander describes him to the princes
as a ruler distinguished by simplicity and kindness,
and contrasts him with the king of the more awesome,
forceful qualities of the civilized mode:

He excells in nothing so much, as in the zealous love of his
people, wherein he doth not only passe al his owne fore-
goers, but as I thinke al the princes living. Whereof the
cause is, that though he exceed not in the vertues which get
admiration; as depth of wisdome, height of courage and
largenesse of magnificence, yet is hee notable in those whiche
stirre affection, as trueth of worde, meekenesse, courtesie,
mercifulness, and liberalitie. (Pages 11-11^V)

This opposition of virtues of admiration and virtues of
affection is almost exactly the distinction made between
Pamela and Philoclea, and indicates that Basilius, at
least before he retreats, has represented the model
qualities of the natural king. The role of ruler no doubt
requires more rigor than the role of lover, and "affection"
may seem to be a weak means of control; but Arcadia is
a small, peaceful country whose inhabitants have very
limited desires. In other words, it is a land which is
introduced as fulfilling all the conventional expectations
about the good pastoral life. Here is how Kalander
describes it to the princes:

This countrie Arcadia among all the provinces of Greece,

hath ever beene had in singular reputation: partly for the sweetnesse of the ayre, and other natural benefites, but principally for the well tempered minds of the people, who (finding that the shining title of glorie so much affected by other nations, doth in deed helpe little to the happinesse of life) are the onely people, which as by their Justice and providence geve neither cause nor hope to their neyghbours to annoy them, so are they not sturred with false praise to trouble others quiet, thinking it a small reward for the wasting of their owne lives in ravening, that their posteritie should long after saie, they had done so. (Page 11)

Both Basilius and Arcadia, then, are of the natural mode, and so are perfectly suited for each other. When Book I opens Basilius has been governing Arcadia well for thirty years.

Ideal perfection of the civilized mode of rule is completely embodied in Euarchus, King of Macedon. He is introduced in Book II, Chapter vi, as the first character in Zelmane's narrative, and is the standard by which all the kings spoken of later are judged. He excels in wisdom, courage, and magnificence rather than in Basilius's meekness and mercifulness. His quality is "greatness," and since he is a good king, this means the good use of great power. Pyrocles describes his father as "a prince that indeed especially measured his greatnesse by his goodnesse; and if for any thing he loved greatnesse, it was because therein he might exercise his goodnes" (page 126^{v}). He stirs in his subjects more awe and admiration than affection, and is capable of practicing severity when it is demanded for the general good. And indeed it is demanded the moment he assumes the throne, for the situation in Macedon is the reverse of that in Arcadia. Instead of finding a happy, gentle people under venerable law, he finds political chaos left by an ambitious oligarchy, the antinomy of right rule. It has used its power to exploit its subjects for its own benefit, and so has created a general revulsion against authority. Euarchus is the perfect king for the situation. By harsh measures he establishes order and then rules by love, when, as Zelmane says, "an awfull feare, ingendred by justice, did make that love most lovely" (page 127ᵛ). Since the people by nature have strong desires and aspiring minds, unlike the humble Arcadians, the king keeps his country ordered by exercising constant moral discipline, "making his life the example of his lawes" (page 127ᵛ). In every way, then, his hierarchical civilized rule provides an ideal complement to the rule of the natural mode.

Both the natural and civilized king, like the corresponding lovers, have potential flaws. Those of the natural king are perhaps more obvious. In his simplicity the Arcadian ruler may be unable to formulate consciously the moral principles which he instinctively follows. Thus in periods of stress he tends to abandon common sense and rational law for irrational guides. His simplicity may also make him a poor judge of character; a bias against civilization may cause him to confuse true plainness with simple-minded crudeness. And in his love of gentleness he may overlook the fact that the civil order is based on discipline; his excessive leniency may promote unrest. It is no surprise that Basilius, who is a defective lover in nature's mode, shows such defects as a king. He consults the oracle because he lacks faith in his own wisdom, virtue, and good government. When the oracle appears ominous he tries to meet the threat by abandoning the order he has established rather than by asserting it more vigorously. Nor does he show trust in the virtues of his daughters when he sets guards over them. And the rustic guards he appoints, Dametas, Miso, and Mopsa, are too ignorant, pleasure-loving, and childish to perform their offices well. Finally, in assuming that his general, Philanax, will be able to keep the country in order, he shows an over-confidence in the Arcadians's ability to govern themselves. His actions as a king are as unwise as his love for Zelmane.

But Basilius's failure as a king should not be regarded as Sidney's rejection of the natural mode of rule any more than his failure as a lover implies a rejection of the natural mode of love. It indicates simply that the Arcadian ruler is liable to err. Yet the situation does differ from the love plot in that while there are normative natural lovers, no king completely embodies the values of the natural mode. The most important reason for this want is that Arcadia has only one king, and Arcadia is the only country in which the natural mode of rule is possible. Since Sidney wants to treat both the complete and partial natural king, he must combine them in one character; and so Basilius's past rule is presented as idyllic and his present rule as irrational. It is also true that the first nobleman we meet in Arcadia, Kalander, serves in part as a surrogate for the ideal Arcadian king. He is Basilius's wise, elderly, trusted counsellor; and his house and household are described as vindications of the Arcadian way of life, where simplicity does not mean simple-mindedness, and stateliness may be obtained without magnificence: The house it selfe was built of faire and strong stone, not affecting so much any extraordinarie kinde of finenes, as an honorable representing of a firme statelines. The lightes, doores and staires, rather directed to the use of the guest, then to the eye of the Artificer: and yet as the one cheefly heeded, so the other not neglected; each place handsome without curiositie, and homely without lothsomnes. (Page 8)

This house, moreover, is not unique. It is one of many dotting the land, which are arranged in a "civil wildnes" where "all [are] scattered, no two being one by th'other, and yet not so far off as that it barred mutual succour" (page 7). In abandoning his court Basilius has chosen "wildness" without "civility" and thus not affirmed fully the values of his own country.

Where the faulty Arcadian king is guilty of love without firmness, the faulty civilized king is guilty of severity without love, or tyranny. Both the natural virtues and natural vices are embodied in Basilius; but the civilized virtues and vices are separated. The norms are presented in Euarchus, and the perversions in the figures of the tyrant kings whom the princes meet on their travels related in Book II. The motives prompting the kings to tyranny are many, but they are consistently base. The natural king may allow his prudence to be subverted by an honest though ill-conceived tenderheartedness; but the civilized king, for Sidney, becomes cruel not through some perverted sense of justice but through the more simple flaw of lovelessness. The kings of Phrygia and Pontus, whose descriptions follow that of Euarchus, are cases in point. Phrygia's king is a victim of psychopathic "melancholy" (page 134^v), oppressing his subjects through mad fears and suspicions; but his paranoia is a moral defect. He is a tyrant because he has no concern for his people, and he lacks love because he thinks all men as vicious as he is. When

Pyrocles is shipwrecked on his land, he immediately suspects a plot to deprive him of his kingdom, attributing to Pyrocles his own low cunning; and at the first sign of his soldiers' unwillingness to execute Pyrocles, he flees away fearing treason. Trapped in his tiny world of cabals and *Realpolitik,* he perverts the mode of civilized rule because he cannot conceive of power apart from aggressive self-aggrandizement. But the king of Pontus represents the worst perversion of civilized rule, since he does not respect his subjects even enough to fear them. Nor does he merely exploit them to fill his treasury. He looks upon them simply as sources of entertainment, killing off his friends in "wanton crueltie" when he grows weary of them and punishing "not so much for hate or anger, as because he [feels] not the smart of punishment" (page 139). His counsellor rounds out the list of perversions by adding to the melancholy that fears men and the wantonness that plays with them the jealousy that hates all men's happiness.

No subtle statement is being made about the failure of the tyrant kings. They are bad rulers because they are not concerned with the well-being of their people. Their defects are more reprehensible than the defects of the natural king who fails from weak judgment, or from a strong love of his people being overcome by a stronger desire for self-protection. But the defects of both kinds of kings, though different in quality, have the same political result, the subversion of order. Oppression brings rebellion; lack of discipline brings insurrection. The most extreme form of tyranny, the enslavement of an originally free people by a conquering invader, instanced in the episode of the Helots and Lacedemonians in Book I, leads to civil war. The retirement of Basilius leads to the uprising of the rustic rabble described at the end of Book II. Viewed as a treatise on revolt, these contrasting incidents seem to oppose the justified fight for freedom against bad rulers with an unjustified clamor for partial interests against a good ruler. The revolt of the Helots, which topples grinding oppression, springs rather from "the generalnes of the cause then [from] any artificiall practise" (page 25). The rustic rebellion against Basilius, the revolt of natural inferiors with petty and contradictory aims, springs partly from the craft of the rabble-rouser, Clinias, who is in the pay of Cecropia and feeds the ignorant rabble with false complaints. But if the rustic revolt is unjustified, it is partly explained by Basilius's incompetence, by his failure to provide guidance. Thus the more excusable human faults in a king lead to the more frightening form of political chaos. The righteous anger of the wronged is less to be feared than the petty passions of the unguided.

The problems of the natural ruler receive Sidney's more sympathetic and prolonged attention; for they show not simply how bad traits lead to bad politics, as in the case of the tyrant, but how the best qualities can become political liabilities. The open simplicity of the natural ruler does not have to fall into simple-mindedness for it to be a potential danger; it need only be placed in the world of intrigue which flourishes outside Arcadia. Such a situation is first fully presented in Book II in an episode concerning the king Paphlagonia, which follows the princes' adventure with the king of Pontus. The tale is familiar to the reader as the source of the underplot of *King Lear*. Plexirtus, the evil, ambitious, bastard son, tells his father the king, that his brother, Leonatus, is plotting treason. The king banishes Leonatus; the bastard son begins to

take control of the kingdom, and eventually blinds his
father and throws him out to wander, until he is found and
comforted by Leonatus. In so far as the king is guilty,
his crime is credulity. He succumbs to the false rhetoric of
Plexirtus. Yet one cannot call the episode a sharp criticism
of the natural defect, since its emotional weight falls upon
the cunning of the bastard and not upon the king's simplicity. And this impression of almost unavoidable error is
deepened as the tale develops. For when faithful Leonatus
finally gains the throne he is deceived by Plexirtus's false
repentance and allows him to return to court. This
leniency, a noble virtue in a natural ruler, almost causes
his own ruin, since, as we later learn (Chapter xxiii),
Plexirtus resumes his plotting to take over the kingdom
and attempts to kill his brother. Here we seem to have a
case of an Arcadian gentleness in a situation demanding
the shrewdness and severity of a Euarchus. Fate has
mismatched ruler and subject.

This topic of the misplaced natural ruler receives its
final development in Book III of the *Arcadia,* where
Basilius is faced with difficulties that are not produced
entirely by his own foibles. His negligence has caused
insubordination in a naturally peaceful people, but he
cannot be held responsible for the evil character of his
sister, Cecropia. It is true that his retirement has left
his daughters vulnerable to her attack, and that faith in
simplicity has caused inept guardians to be appointed;
but by rights Cecropia should not be in Arcadia at all.
She has a cruel, ambitious mind which is out of place
in that simple country. She is deviant fact produced by
a harsh fate, and an Arcadian king is not best equipped
to handle such an anomaly. It may be easy to over-
emphasize Basilius's unfortunate failure, since Book III

is not concerned so much with rule as with the testing
of the lovers and the problems of knightly loyalty; and
most of Basilius's fighting is managed by Philanax,
who conducts the siege with as much skill and prowess
as the circumstances allow. But towards the end of the
book, two important military decisions are forced upon
Basilius, and in both instances his Arcadian character
leads him to make the wrong choice over the advice
of his general. First, after weeks of fighting, he decides
to withdraw the siege when Cecropia threatens to kill
his daughters. This choice, though prompted by under-
standable emotions, is unwise; for as Philanax points
out, "A Prince of judgment ought not to consider what
his enimies promise, or threaten, but what the promisers and threatners in reason wil do" (page 324^V).
Similarly, when the enemy general Anaxius wants to
force marriage terms with Pamela, Basilius rejects
Philanax's sound advice to refuse to bargain and to press
the attack. Instead he consults the oracle again, fleeing to
"devotion" because he lacks "resolution" (page 354).
Certainly some of this irresolution results from Basilius's
defects rather than from necessary characteristics of the
natural king; and it is also true that the Arcadian Philanax
makes all the right decisions. But Philanax is as much an
anomaly in Arcadia as Cecropia; for in his rational stern-
ness he seems to be the perfect product of Euarchus's
Macedon. And the man who is described as best fulfilling
the Arcadian values, Kalander, supports Basilius against
Philanax when the question of lifting the siege is raised,
since he judges not by military wits but by his deep love
for the princesses. This is not a case of a good and bad
counsellor vying for a king's favor, it is rather a case of
two excellent men, one representing the best qualities of

the natural mode of rule, and one representing the best of the civilized mode, advising a natural king in a situation that demands the civilized response. In itself good Arcadian kingship is one norm of right rule, with a simple beauty that is different in quality from Euarchus's magnificence. But the conditions that help sustain it are extremely rare and fragile. One Cecropia can cause a calamity. Because Book III is unfinished we cannot be certain about the final government of Arcadia. Perhaps Euarchus would have been called upon to help restore order. Surely if Arcadia is to maintain stability in its present form it will have to live under the protection of a strong civilized power.

In making Arcadian government more fragile than civilized government, Sidney's treatment of rule seems to differ slightly from his treatment of love; for both kinds of love are equally vindicated under the severest trial. The artless simplicity that promotes full personal relations cannot always achieve the same success in politics, which demands more practical wit than commitment. The claims of society may seem to oppose the immediate claims of personal emotion. But the relation of love and rule is still very close, and their dependency can be seen clearly when both activities are exercised in the same person. Rulers in the *Arcadia,* whether Arcadian or civilized, are often lovers; and the question arises whether or not the claims of these roles are in harmony. That they may conflict in some form is suggested by the career of Basilius, since the king's doting love for Zelmane serves to distract him from his political duties. But, as we have seen, both his rule and his love are defective, and their opposition therefore does not work against the notion that good rule and good love can be asserted simultaneously. Indeed, when we look at the episodes in which Sidney tries to work out the problem, it appears that the two activities do not conflict when asserted in their best forms.

The question is explored most elaborately in two of the most important episodes of Book II, the story of Erona and Antiphilus, and the story of Plangus's parents. These stories differ in structure from the three stories about rule already discussed, since they are not told in unbroken sequence but are interrupted by the main plot. Begun by the princes and finished later by Zelmane, they are woven into the major love story in a way that suggests their complex subject. Both are stories of how love causes bad rule; but in both cases the love is as imperfect as the government. The conflict is produced not by a harsh universe which refuses to allow two goods to be asserted at once, but by the imperfections of the agents.

The story of Erona's love for Antiphilus has already been treated as an illustration of misplaced love, but it also shows how bad love makes for bad rule, since Erona's passion upsets her kingdom. Her father has offered her in marriage to King Tiridates of Armenia, who "desire[s] her more than the joyes of heaven" (page 159^V); and her refusal in favor of her nurse's son not only causes her father's death but also the invasion of her country by Tiridates, who tries to force the marriage and is prevented only by the intervention of Pyrocles and Musidorus. Erona looks upon her trials romantically as the result of fortune's cruelty to lovers; and her marriage to Antiphilus appears to be the happy end of a romance, with the princes as the heroes who have helped a maiden in distress. But the second

part of the story, told by Pyrocles in the last chapter of
Book II, exposes the meanness of Antiphilus and his
plans to marry Queen Artaxia. Here it becomes clear
that the initial opposition is not between romantic
love and the demands of statecraft but between wrong
love and right rule. The duties are in conflict only because the love is irrational. A similar point is made on
a lower moral plane in the case of Antiphilus's desire
to marry Artaxia. Antiphilus wants to marry only from
political ambition, and this mockery of love proves to
be his political downfall. Artaxia, who is Tiridates'
sister, lures her suitor to his death. Love and authority
conflict here because both are hollow.

The same point is made in the tale of Plangus's
parents. Like Erona, the king of Iberia loves an unworthy object and in so doing undermines right rule.
Blindly loving his wife, he gives control of his kingdom
to a lecherous and ambitious intriguer. And like the
career of Antiphilus, Andromena's suicide shows in its
lowest terms the inevitable political self-destruction
entailed by base love; for her scheming brings death to
her son, the prince to whom she has expected to
bequeath her power. It is true that Andromena's career,
like Erona's, provides only negative evidence for the
harmony of good rule and good love; but the point is
also made positively in a digression towards the end
of the tale, in which Pyrocles describes Queen Helena
of Corinth, who has sent knights to the Iberian jousts.
Helena is Andromena's opposite, for she is not only a
good ruler who disciplines a rebellious people, but a
queen who succeeds in making love a tool for social
harmony. She leads her gentlewomen in chastity until
her court becomes a "marriage place of Love and

Vertue" (page 195). As a good ruler and a good lover, her passion for Amphialus, though unrequited, is a faithful love for a worthy object. As Zelmane comments, "What doth better become wisdome then to discerne what is worthy the loving? what more agreable to goodnes, then to love it so discerned?" (page 195ᵛ). If her fortune causes her to be unhappy in love, it does not jeopardize her rule. The two goods are not exclusive.

In emphasizing the possible harmony of love and rule, the *Arcadia* presents a clement universe. Although harsh fortune darkens much of the work, the commitments of the characters do not appear to be in inevitable conflict with each other. This generalization cannot be asserted confidently until the relation of love and knightly loyalty is examined; but if it holds here too, it would help support the tolerance of the *Arcadia's* ethical system, which allows the necessary activities of life to be asserted both through the mode of civilization and the mode of nature.

III

Though the subject of knightly service receives its fullest development in Book III, where the civil war forces a choice of loyalties, it is sketched in skeletal form by some of the princes' tales in Book II. Musidorus and Pyrocles are models of knightly heroism and dedicate themselves early in their career "to seeke exercises of their vertue, thinking it not so worthy to be brought to heroycall effects by fortune or necessitie, like Ulysses and Aeneas, as by ones owne choice and working" (page 141ᵛ). Since Pyrocles is a lover in the natural mode and Musidorus in the civilized mode, one might expect the

same contrast to be evident in their early chivalric
adventures. But the distinction in these initial exploits
is somewhat blurred. Musidorus does tell tales most
concerned with order and right rule while Zelmane tells
Philoclea stories most concerned with love; but both
princes appear in both groups of stories, and their
actions do not appear significantly different. This
similarity is due in part to the nature of chivalry itself.
Love and rule are moral necessities in either the simplest
or most complex form of life; but chivalry is called into
being by social wrong, by oppression which is the particular defect of civilization. The knights therefore receive
their special training in arms from the model civilized
ruler, Euarchus, who is Pyrocles' father and Musidorus'
uncle. Only from him can they learn skills necessary for
subduing perverted ambitions.

But although there is only one mode of knighthood,
its highest form is defined as the union of energy and
form, emotion and control; and its defects are those to
which both the civilized and the natural modes of
behavior are liable, false values and emotional blindness.
Knighthood, like love and rule, consists of a set of noble
loyalties: loyalty to one's fellow knights, or friendship;
loyalty to one's lord, or fealty; and loyalty to humanity in
general, or courtesy. When a knight has bad values and
no loyalty he uses his relations to serve himself. When a
knight has loyalty and no wisdom, he may energetically
serve bad causes. The treacherous knight is more despic-
able, but the irrational knight may be just as harmful.

Noble friendship is presented in the relation of
Pyrocles and Musidorus. The opening chapter of the
Arcadia describes Musidorus as wanting to commit
suicide because he thinks his friend drowned; and in

more than people. When perverted by emotion the discourteous knight places his own irrational notions of honor above the needs of others. These defects are sketched peripherally in Book II in two adventures befalling Pyrocles after his encounter with Dido in Chapter xviii, the episodes dealing with Chremes and Anaxius. Dido's father, Chremes, is the victim of a morbid stinginess, the meanest civilized perversion. Though Pyrocles has saved his daughter, he entertains the prince with the most niggardly hospitality; and then attempts to betray him to his enemy, Artaxia, for a reward. Opposed to him is Anaxius, a man of great courage but completely unwilling to acknowledge the dignity of any man but himself. When Pyrocles breaks off their duel to help Dido, Anaxius accuses him of cowardice, since his own notion of dignity is emotional satisfaction rather than useful service. He is more frank and open than Chremes but he is just as morally blind.

This bare skeleton of models and parallel deviations, which is only sketched in Book II, is given flesh in the action of Book III. Amphialus here becomes the central figure. We have already seen him as an example of the unluckiest of lovers, the man most tried by fortune in a book where all the protagonists are unfortunate. As the leader of the forces in rebellion against Basilius he is also a rebel, and so plays a major part in the work's final definition of knightly service and its resolution of the relation of service and love. In his adamant refusal to return the princesses to Basilius he shows himself an imperfect knight, since he violates the key duty of fealty to a good king. Yet his love for Philoclea is so clearly sincere, and his knightly virtues are so many, that he serves, initially at least, as a model knight.

Within the microcosm of Cecropia's castle he combines the best of civilization and nature, blending wisdom
and commitment, refinement and courage, and is contrasted first with crafty Clinias, and then with lawless
Anaxius.

Amphialus is a wise and skilful general. He provisions
his castle, trains his troops, selects the best men for each
post, and in all things "instruct[s] by example [rather]
then precept" (page 258ᵛ), a description echoing the
account of Euarchus's methods. In this way he meets and
surpasses cunning Clinias on his own ground of knowledge, since Clinias' wit cannot structure and civilize a
state, but rather works only for treachery through
deception, as his attempt to stir the shepherds to rebellion has demonstrated. But with his wisdom Amphialus
also has great emotional strength and courage which
Clinias lacks completely. Amphialus is the heroic leader
of battle, the killer of scores, who rejoices in danger.
Clinias is half a man and less than half a soldier since he
has no natural warmth. We are told that in the first battle
"only Clinias and Amphialus did exceed the bounds of
mediocrity, the one in his naturall coldnesse of cowardise,
the other in heate of courage" (page 266). These obvious
differences are driven home in the parallel jousts in
which the two men engage. Amphialus initiates the
jousts "to keepe his valure in knowledge by some private
acte, since publique policie restrayned him" (page 285ᵛ);
and his victories are triumphs of skill, courage, and
courtesy won in the high chivalric manner that extends
pardon to those who fight for "love of Honour or honour
of his Love" (page 286). When Clinias jousts bathetically
with Dametas, on the other hand, he displays not only
complete cowardice but complete discourtesy, cringing

at the slightest resistance, and striking when his opponent appears beaten. Since Clinias has no emotional warmth, he is tied to Amphialus only by the fragile bond of expediency; and the humiliation of his exposure in the joust and his subsequent fear of expulsion are enough to cause him to plot Amphialus's murder and the release of the princesses. The sisters' refusal to become involved in the plot involves a recognition not only of the baseness of Clinias but of the essential nobility of their cousin Amphialus. They recognize a difference between a man who betrays his lord from selfish fear and a man who is insubordinate from true love.

The paragraph describing the execution of Clinias is followed by an account of the arrival of Anaxius, who breaks through Basilius's lines and enters the castle. The two men are so antinomous that they never could have been housed under the same roof. Anaxius, as the passionate man, cannot serve well because he cannot govern his own will. He has no equal in strength and daring, but his honor, as we have seen, is not based on a reasoned sense of true loyalty, but on revenging chimerical slights to his own dignity. He suggests very strongly Shakespeare's Hotspur, for whom he was perhaps the original. "No man," we are told, "[was] more tenderly sensible in any thing offred to himselfe, which in the farthest-fette construction might be wrested to the name of wrong; no man, that in his own actions could worse distinguish between Valour and Violence" (page 304ᵛ). He joins Basilius's forces "never taking paines to examine the quarrell, like a man whose will was his God, and his hand his lawe" (page 305). It is true that Amphialus is lawless in his insubordination towards Basilius, but he is at least aware of the problem.

and is impelled by love and not by irrational pride.
Since Anaxius's pride will not let him acknowledge
another's equality, he is a poor friend. He once saved
Amphialus's life, finding him "unknowen in a great
danger; . . . whereupon, loving his own benefite, began
to favor him" (page 304ᵛ). Thus whereas Amphialus
respects Anaxius for his courage and service, Anaxius
likes Amphialus because Amphialus is obliged to him.
The incompleteness of his character is evident also in
his disdain for all civilized refinements. He almost angers
"the courteous Amphialus" by his comment that love is
a dotage for a "peevish paltrie sex" (page 305ᵛ); and he
is only bored by the musical entertainment which
Amphialus arranges for him on the night of his arrival.
Like Hotspur, he likes "no musick but the neighing of
horses, the sound of trumpets, and the cries of yeelding
persons" (page 306ᵛ). He never enters a formal joust,
and on the battlefield his pride alone keeps him from
savagery, while his two brothers, less proud and even
more willful, murder wounded soldiers. Later they attempt to rape the princesses, whom Amphialus has tried
to protect from all discourtesy, while Anaxius does not
force his crude wooing of Pamela only because he thinks
he deserves grateful submission. Anaxius, then, is the
antinomy of cold Clinias; and though more admirable, he
is in the end a more powerful force of disorder.

Amphialus is the normative center of his own troops;
but he must eventually be compared unfavorably to
Philanax, Basilius's true general, who is devoted to his
king and leads the siege of the castle with courage and
wisdom. Amphialus's motives for rebellion are not
base, but his disloyalty to Basilius impairs his knighthood
and forces him into circumstances that cause him re-

peatedly to commit chivalric discourtesies. In order to win adherents to his cause he must lie about his motives and traduce Philanax's character. He jousts in the high manner of courtesy, but he kills noble Argulus against his own will. And though he offers friendship to Argulus he cannot obtain it, since, as Argulus comments, he has valor but wants "justice" (page 292). Despite his respect for women, he kills Parthenia when she jousts disguised as a knight; and later he indirectly causes the death of his mother who falls from the battlements as he pursues her. Even the treachery of Clinias is partly his responsibility, as Pamela points out, since his initial rebellion has taught rebellion to his men. In denying one aspect of knightly service, then, Amphialus is forced to impair all elements. Knighthood cannot be asserted piecemeal. When his attempted suicide allows Anaxius to assume the control of the castle, the disorder latent in his initial rebellion becomes dominant.

But Amphialus denies knightly service for love, and his career in Book III involves the important question of whether the world demands a choice between goods, or whether it clemently allows love and fealty to be asserted simultaneously. For Amphialus a choice seems necessary and love seems best. "Love," he tells Argulus, "justifieth the unjustice you lay unto me [and] dooth also animate me against all daungers" (pages 292-292$^\text{v}$). This kind of statement suggests that he sees himself as a romantic hero who rejects all ties in order to defend his mistress against those who would bear her away. But his case is the obverse of a position like Lancelot's in the Castle Joyous, since his own mistress rejects him, his enemies are her friends, and her accepted lover is imprisoned with her in the castle. No real conflict of

loyalties exist because Philoclea has given him no love
to which he must be loyal. And no matter how true his
love is, the "injustice" is to Philoclea as well as to
Basilius. The opposition between love and fealty is
therefore blurred, since the central conflict results from
his placing his own wants above his mistress's happiness.
Because of this reversal of the common romance
situation, Amphialus's Petrarchan humility before
Philoclea strikes the reader's ears with heavy irony. In
his first interview he kneels and proclaims that "in her
hands the ballance of his life or death [doth] stande, . . .
she being . . . the mistresse of his life, and he her eternall
slave" (page 254). In literal terms Philoclea is his captive
and he her master, so that the reader is forced by the
discrepancy to doubt the quality of Amphialus's humility.
And the doubt is increased in this interview when
Amphialus is compared to "the poore woman, who
loving a tame Doe she had above all earthly things, . . .
is constrained at length by famine . . . to kill the Deare
to sustaine her life" (page 254^V). This strangely ap-
petitive simile suggests that Amphialus's emotional
needs outweigh his altruism. He tries to explain his
position to Philoclea by asserting, "I finde my selfe
most willing to obey you, . . . but alas, that Tyrant
Love (which now possesseth the holde of all my life and
reason) will no way suffer it" (page 255); but the
equivocation of this excuse is exposed when he later
tells Cecropia that he will never force Philoclea because
"lust may well be a tyrant, but true-love where it is
indeed, is a servant" (page 313). Amphialus's love, then,
is divided against itself. It is imperfect because it lacks
the complete respect necessary to obey the beloved's
wishes. Its imperfection rather than its intensity brings

it into conflict with Amphialus's duty as a loyal knight. To this extent the world of the *Arcadia* is clement. Like love and rule, love and knightly service can be asserted simultaneously in their highest forms, while the debasement of one implies the debasement of the other.

The career of Amphialus might seem to suggest that the balance between civilized and natural elements in the good knight is very precarious. One good emotion not properly structured leads to a series of actions that force a partial betrayal of all loyalties. But Zelmane and Musidorus are fighters in this book as well as lovers, and are given martial roles which in some ways help to vindicate the stability of their contrasting personalities. As the Black Knight, Musidorus fights for Basilius and Pamela simultaneously. His proud civilized character learns that right may not always be immediately victorious, but he alone is given the distinction of defeating Amphialus in a joust, though both men are severely wounded. His victory suggests that he is a fuller man than Amphialus, that his love and his fealty are more complete and hence more forceful. In the same way impulsive Pyrocles not only learns to curb emotion and suffer passively, but is eventually given the opportunity to fight with Anaxius and display his greater maturity. His killing Anaxius's brothers is a sign of the order he has imposed on his own emotional nature, and though the fight between him and Anaxius is left unfinished, broken off in the middle of a sentence, he would probably have been victorious for the same reasons. Both fight for love, Anaxius for his brothers and Pyrocles for Philoclea; but their duel is the fight of "rage against resolution, fury against vertue, confidence against courage, [and] pride against noblenesse" (page 359). In knighthood as in love the protagonists assert their characters ideally.

The martial conflict that pervades Book III almost makes us forget that we are still in Arcadia, where such warfare is an anomaly. We have already seen that this new problem of insurrection is not met effectively by Basilius, the natural king. It is also true that no Arcadian knights have the capacity to subdue it. Philanax comes closest to being a perfect general, but he is out-voted by Basilius and Kalander, and his being captured by Amphialus and saved only at the intercession of Philoclea, suggests his inadequacy. The fact that the princes, the model knights, are Macedonians, trained by Euarchus, might suggest the faultiness of Arcadian education and the incompleteness of the simple Arcadian life. Nor can Amphialus's many martial accomplishments be taken as an indication of the possibilities of Arcadian chivalry; for though he is Basilius's nephew, he has been raised and trained in Corinth. But before we criticize Arcadia for wanting chivalry, two important distinctions must be made.

First of all we must distinguish between the Arcadian forest and the Arcadian court. It can be argued that when Basilius leaves his court for the forest, he not only makes a political mistake but also chooses an inferior way of life. Sidney makes no attempt, for example, to associate the shepherd's life with the life of religious and phil-osophical contemplation. There is no shepherd who could be called a shepherd-poet or a shepherd-philosopher. We do meet the elegant Strephon and Claius in the beginning of the work, but we never see them again; and the chief rustic figure, the head of the shepherds, Dametas, is a coward, a braggart, and a boor.

To see how Sidney might have exalted the life of complete retirement had he wished, we have only to consider the figure of Colin in Book VI of the *Faerie Queene*. As the shepherd poet, Colin is given the unique privilege of seeing the dance of the graces, and is thus alone able to transmit the necessary refinements to society. And Spenser's chief shepherd is not a Dametas, but the retired courtier, Meliboeus, who gives a persuasive defense of living the lowly quiet life among one's sheep.

Sidney's criticism of the shepherd's life can also be found outside the *Arcadia* in his only other work of prose fiction, the masque called "The Lady of May," which contrasts the active life of the forester, Therion, with the passive life of the shepherd, Espilus. Therion is an energetic lover who occasionally loses his temper; Espilus is a quiet lover, who spends his time "feeding his sheepe sitting under some sweete bush." The May Lady must choose between "the many deserts and many faults of Therion [and] the verie small deserts and no faults of Espilus."[6] When the opposition is put like this, and the distinction is made not between different kinds of life but between degrees of vigor, the forester seems to be superior. And Queen Elizabeth's choice of Espilus is probably only an indication of the novelty of Sidney's presentation, since the Queen is following the traditional association of the shepherd with the high life of Christian contemplation. But it would be wrong to assume that the poem rejects the simple life for complex civilization. The opposition is between lumpish passivity and sprightly service. The shepherd is described as being richer than the forester, and the forester's life is described as being quiet, simple, and retired, though more active. Moreover, when we turn to the *Arcadia*, we find that the favorite sport of the model Arcadian nobleman, Kalander, is the vigorous activity of hunting, and that he gives the princes specific advice about the importance of such exercise:

Then went they together abroad, the good Kalander enter-taining them with pleasaunt discoursing, howe well he loved the sporte of hunting when he was a young man, how much in the comparison thereof he disdained all chamber delights. . . . "O," saide he, "you will never live to my age, without you kepe your selves in breath with exercise, and in hart with joyfullnes: too much thinking doth consume the spirits: and oft it falles out, that while one thinkes too much of his doing, he leaves to doe the effect of his thinking. (Pages 39-39^V, misnumbered as 71-71^V)

Though contemplative retirement is rejected, just as is pastoral crudeness, the best Arcadians can combine activity with quiet just as Kalander's house combines elegance with simplicity. This hunting episode is later contrasted with a description of Basilius's hawking (page 113^V); for Basilius, the defective natural king, who chooses wildness in his weakness, naturally indulges in a less energetic sport. The crude life of the shepherd is criticized, but the best Arcadian life is affirmed.

Even with this distinction in mind, however, one must admit that the Arcadian nobleman is not specially trained in war and martial deeds. But in evaluating chivalry we must make the distinction between what is good about knightly service and what is only harsh necessity. It seems clear that martial life, as presented in Book III, is not completely glorified. The jousts initiated by the Corinthian-trained Amphialus are the pinnacles of elegance in their elaborate furniture and brilliant displays of courage and dexterity. But they accomplish nothing and cause the death of many good men. The siege produces the greatest acts of heroism on both sides, but even the first skirmish soon degenerates into butchery. Each general kills reluctantly an innocent young knight. Amphialus kills Agenor, Philanax's brother, who is "of all that armie the most beautifull, . . . full of jollitie in conversation, and lately growne a Lover" (page 267). Amphialus tries to spare him, but his lance splinters and Agenor dies "not onely a suddaine but a fowle death, leaving scarsely any tokens of his former beautie" (page 267^v). Philanax, moved by this death, kills Amphialus's squire, Ismenus, and "could have wished the blow ungiven, when he saw him fall like a faire apple, which some uncurteous bodie, breaking his bowe, should throw downe before it were ripe" (page 270^v). "Uncurteous" is a key word here, because it suggests that in the heat of battle no one is able to maintain his full knightly dignity. The whole skirmish is described as a progression from glamor to ugliness:

At the first, though it were terrible, yet Terror was deckt so bravelie with rich furniture, guilte swords, shining armours, pleasant pensils, that the eye with delight had scarce leasure to be afraide: But now all universally defiled with dust, bloud, broken armours, mangled bodies, tooke away the maske, and sette foorth Horror in his owne horrible manner. (Pages 271-271^v)

Knightly service is itself noble, but when tested by force, as it must be, it implies necessary brutality. If Arcadia is not prepared for such a test, it is because the Arcadians themselves demand no such heroism in order to be peaceful. If stronger knights are needed in Arcadia, as

a stronger king may be needed, the need is not produced
by the quality of the Arcadian life but by the harshness
of circumstance and the incursions into Arcadia of
aspiring minds.

   Once we make a distinction between the Arcadian
forest and court, and between the demands of fortune
and the intrinsic qualities of Arcadia, Sidney's treatment of the pastoral world appears more sympathetic
than Spenser's. The pastoral world of both is fragile,
but Sidney writes a pastoral romance which treats the
natural life in all its forms and gives Arcadia the
autonomy of a separate country; while Spenser's pastoral
world is only presented as a digression from Calidore's
true quest. And though it is praised, it is only a retired
part of Faerie land, under the rule of Gloriana, the
source of civilized values. This difference of attitude to
the pastoral world results from different moral systems.
For Spenser the great enemy to ordered life is mutability, which externally takes the form of leveling time
and within the society takes the form of the betrayal
of human relations. Fidelity is therefore the most necessary of virtues. Thus Calidore, as the knight of courtesy,
is distinguished by a respect for all men and a general
faith in human nature; and his enemy is the Blatant Beast,
malicious slander, which undermines our faith in each
other and breaks the bonds of human relations. In Book
I, where the subject is treated in religious terms, the chief
sin of Red Cross is loss of faith in Una, the true religion;
and the urgent need of faith is insisted upon by Una's
being presented not as an invincible figure of authority
(like the Truth of *Piers Plowman)* but as a fragile
woman with many enemies and in desperate need of support. In such a world, where social ties are always

threatening to come apart, any mode of life, like the pastoral, which is detached by its nature from the more complex order of society, can be tolerated only because it offers society special services, and cannot be looked upon as a worthy choice for most men. For Sidney, on the other hand, the dangers of mutability are not so formidable. There are deceivers like Plexirtus and Pontus who betray others for low ambitions, but there are also emotional men like Tydeus and Telenor whose faith is blind and immovable. When the emotions are not controlled, they are fixed permanently on objects not worthy of fidelity, or in the more subtle case of Amphialus, they are fixed on a worthy object with such passion that the good of the object is endangered. Since the social bonds are more stable, pastoral retirement does not imply a betrayal of society. It represents a way of life with qualities distinct from those of civilization but not opposed to them. By placing his story in a pastoral country, ruled by its own king, Sidney is able to give this mode of life, which requires special conditions for its expression, complete representation. Arcadia becomes the home of a particular kind of personality with its own forms of action, of a mode of life which contrasts with and complements civilized values, and which proves equally successful, with some qualifications, in fulfilling the ethical norms of love, rule, and knightly service.

IV

Although I hope that the preceding interpretation has demonstrated the consistency and maturity of the *Arcadia*, I do not expect a reader who found the work tedious before to find it suddenly exciting. One might legitimately claim that the book engaged his wits but cooled his feelings. The structure of the work alone might be enough to dampen the interest of many readers; even devotees of the *Arcadia* must find Book II a severe trial of their fidelity, with its mass of complicated subplots that almost bury the central action. Perhaps only a radical change of literary fashion could make the *Arcadia* as popular as it was when it first appeared. We would have to learn to get as much aesthetic delight in the representation of static hierarchies as we get now from rising and falling action, suspense, and dramatic climax. To be more accurate, we would have to be able to appreciate both kinds of plots at once; for the *Arcadia* offers an interesting example in aesthetic history of a transitional work that is eclectic and experimental in its structure. Book I displays the slow-moving quiet of the classical pastoral; Book II, in mapping out the static hierarchies of good and bad rule, is medieval in its motionlessness; and Book III, with its fast pace and ever-heightening suspense, anticipates the romantic plot we know today. One wonders if the structure of the *Arcadia* is uneven partly because Sidney could not decide whether he was ancient, medieval, or modern.

If the reader can overcome his objections to the structure of the *Arcadia,* he may find a more formidable obstacle to appreciation in its style. No elaborate analysis of style is necessary here. Critics have described it accurately and fully. But some of its obvious shortcomings for modern taste may be briefly mentioned. First of all, many passages are spoiled for us by an over abundance of tropes and word schemes which seem to cover over the subject at hand with a thick layer of rhetoric. The first sentence can serve as well as any to remind us of some characteristic devices:

It was in the time that the earth begins to put on her new aparrel against the approch of her lover, and that the Sun running a most even course becums an indifferent arbiter betweene the night and the day; when the hopelesse shepheard Strephon was come to the sandes, which lie against the Island of Cithera; where viewing the place with a heavy kinde of delight, and sometimes casting his eyes to the Ileward, he called his friendly rivall, the pastor Claius unto him, and setting first downe in his darkened countenance a dolefull copie of what he would speake: "O, my Claius," said he, "hether we are now come to pay the rent, for which we are so called unto by over-busie Remembrance, Remembrance, restlesse Remembrance, which claymes not onlely this dutie of us, but for it will have us forget our selves." (Pages 1-1^V)

If we put our minds to it we might work out a justification for the figures used here. We could begin by making the general point that Sidney is trying to dignify his style with the ornament that befits an epic, and that he maturely rejects the false dignity of latinate diction popular at the time for figures of thought like metaphor and personification. We then might point out the function of particular figures. The personification of spring as a lover seems appropriate to a work that makes love its central subject; the figure of the sun as an arbiter may suggest the complimentary oppositions on which the book

works; the comparison of the shepherd's face to a painting may emphasize the dignified control of the shepherd's
emotion; and the comparison of grief to rent may point
out the fitness and propriety of the shepherds' suffering. But the presence of all these figures in a single
sentence calls our attention away from the subject at
hand to the style itself, and this impression of self-
conscious stylistics is deepened when we observe the
host of other embellishments in the same sentence:
the oxymoron in "heavy kinde of delight"; the allitera-
tion of "hopelesse," "shepheard," "Strephon," and
"sandes," of "darkened" and "dolefull," of "rent" and
"Remembrance"; the assonance of "lie," "island,"
"Cithera," "kinde," "eyes," and "Ileward"; and the
three-fold repetition of "Remembrance." The modern
reader wants more matter with less art. In a passage
like this Sidney seems to be the victim of his times
in wanting to dignify his language with classical
eloquence without a proper regard for the demands
of the subject, making too mechanical an association
of certain tropes with sublimity. One has to defend
the *Arcadia* here not by justifying the rhetoric but by
pointing out the many passages in which the narrative
is relatively vigorous and unadorned.

  The most characteristic aspect of Sidney's style is
its sentence structure, its use of very long sentences
composed of members that are not closely bound to one
central clause. The sentence quoted above is a good
example. It consists of at least three grammatical units
connected by the conjunctions "where" and "and,"
with the aid of a few participial phrases, all of which
have almost no force of subordination or coordination.
The sentence therefore might be described as being

"loose" as opposed to "periodic". But the term would not do justice to the other obvious fact about its structure, the presence of parallel constructions within the loosely bound units. Thus the main clause of the first section is modified by two parallel adjective clauses, and that of the second by two balanced participial clauses. The resulting sentence tends to have both the flexibility of the loose sentence and some of the formality of the balanced period. The combination has been praised by George Philip Krapp as a respectable attempt to create a smooth narrative style that possesses epic dignity.[7] Surely Sidney deserves credit for avoiding the temptations of Euphuism. Figures of strict balance, like isocolon, parison, and paramoion, which Lyly and his followers had worked to death, are used only sparingly in the *Arcadia;* and often the parallelism is subdued by an intervening clause, or by slight variations in the length and structure of similar clauses. Sidney also wisely avoids the Ciceronian period, which is unsuitable for narrative prose because of its heavy subordination. The qualities which his loose but ordered sentence comes to affirm are the virtues which the noble characters of the *Arcadia* affirm – spontaneity and discipline, commitment and control. Yet when all justice is done to the Arcadian sentence, few readers will deny that the pattern is adhered to so strictly that it soon palls. For the first few chapters the sentences may sound stately and flowing. But after a hundred pages they begin to sound too long, too loose, and too precious. Perhaps it is asking too much to expect that a writer who has created a new style for a single work to practice it with flexibility and moderation.

What will hold the reader today to a study of the *Arcadia* is not any great aesthetic sophistication but the maturity of its presentation of the problems of life. Its view is basically tragic. Though the world it presents does not force its heroes to choose between mutually exclusive goods, does not oppose the claims of love with the claims of rule or knightly service, it insists on the inevitability of suffering. It does not cater to our modern "apostles of psychological maturity," as Walter Kaufman calls them,[8] who believe we can have all things that make man happy if we avoid childish fear, aggression, and remorse. In the *Arcadia* the forces of chance, time, and death are effective everywhere in making good men miserable. Consolation to the unfortunate is offered neither in the prospect of happiness in some future life nor in the prospect of eventual happiness on earth. If they know joy it must be in the painful triumph of the stoic who hopes that his actions and sufferings are in harmony with some unseen external order or with the highest laws of his own nature.

Perhaps the special appeal that the moral attitudes of the *Arcadia* make to today's reader lies in the warm tolerance of its ethical system, a system that sanctions two constrasting ways of carrying out the activities of life. These two modes of action, the way of nature and the way of civilization, can easily be renamed to apply to important divisions between modern moral attitudes. The virtues of nature — warmth, commitment, and artless spontaneity — might be called, on the secular level, romantic virtues; the virtues of civilization — discipline, social-consciousness, and a keen sense of moral hierarchy — might be called classic. When lifted to the level of religion by a sense of the service of God, the virtues of nature correspond to the qualities of *agape* which Anders Nygren, in his *Agape and Eros,* finds described in the words of Jesus and Paul, and which Kierkegaard celebrates in his *Works of Love:* a spontaneous giving based not on the worth of the recipient but on inner necessity. When the virtues of civilization are presented in religious terms, they correspond to the virtues upheld by Hebraists from the time of the Prophets to our own day: a love based on a keen sense of human worth and the dignity of judging and being judged. That aspects of both approaches to morality can find mansions in Sidney's house is a tribute to his breadth of mind, especially since Sidney does not blur their differences or overlook their perversions of undisciplined commitment and heartless formality. In an age of contentious moralists, the reader should warmly welcome such bracing and embracing tolerance.

State University of New York at Buffalo June, 1970.

Carl Dennis

[1] Walter R. Davis, "A Map of Arcadia: Sidney's Romance in Its Tradition," in Walter R. Davis and Richard A. Lanham, *Sidney's Arcadia* (New Haven, 1965), p. 38.

[2] The text is numbered by leaves rather than by pages, the lefthand page or back of the leaf being unnumbered. To refer to this page, the verso, in this introductory essay, the number of the obverse page will be printed with a raised v. Thus what would be page 12 of a modern text is referred to here as page 11^v.

[3] E. M. W. Tillyard, *The English Epic and Its Backgrounds* (New York, 1966), p. 298.

[4] For a useful discussion of the Christian hero in the Renaissance epic see Burton O. Kurth, *Milton and Christian Heroism,* University of California Publications, English Studies, XX (Berkeley, 1959).

[5] See Kenneth Myrick, *Sir Philip Sidney as a Literary Craftsman* (Cambridge, Mass., 1935), Chapters iv and v.

[6] Albert Feuillerat ed., *The Prose Works of Sir Philip Sidney,* 4 vols. (Cambridge, 1962), II, 211-212.

[7] George Philip Krapp, *The Rise of English Literary Prose* (New York, 1915), pp. 374-376.

[8] Walter Kaufman, *The Faith of a Heretic* (New York, 1963), p. 294

A NOTE ON THE TEXT

I have chosen the printed text of 1590 to be the text of this edition of the *Arcadia* because it is more authentic and coherent than the composite edition of 1593. The later text was obtained by the editors, adding to the 1590 edition the last three books of the unrevised original *Arcadia*. This addition completes the story but undermines the internal logic of Sidney's incomplete revision. It makes no attempt to resolve the martial struggles of Book III, toward which the entire action of the revision leads, dismissing the conflict in a sentence. And the love story which it appends violates the seriousness of Sidney's revision and betrays the nobility of its protagonists. (See the Introduction, pages xxii-xxiii). It is true that the two least noble actions of the princes in Book III of the original *Arcadia,* Musidorus's attempted rape of Pamela, and Pyrocles's seduction of Philoclea, were omitted when the book was added to the revision; but since the events that are dependent on these acts remain unaltered, the story is forced and inconsistent. The trial that concludes Book V becomes morally meaningless since the heroes have committed no crimes that deserve condemnation. And the events which precede the trial, the capture of the three protagonists, their laments against fate, and their contemplation of suicide, have already been given much loftier forms in Book III of the revision.

The only serious argument that has been offered in favor of the composite edition has been of the kind made by C. S. Lewis in his chapter on Sidney in *English Literature in the Sixteenth Century* (Oxford, 1954). To the "literary historian," Lewis contends, " '*The Arcadia*' must mean the composite text of 1593; it and it alone, is the book which lived; Shakespeare's book, Charles I's book, Milton's book, Lamb's book, our own book long before we heard of textual criticism. If the recovery of the cancelled version is to prevent our looking steadily at the text which really affected the English mind, it will have been a disaster" (page 333). This argument is misleading in two respects. First of all it is an exaggeration to say that the *Arcadia* "really affected the English mind." The book was almost totally neglected in the eighteenth and nineteenth centuries, and in earlier times the major writers who were most deeply influenced by it, Shakespeare and Spenser, could have read the edition of 1590 just as easily as that of 1593. Secondly, the principle of historical sanction is a treacherous guide for textual criticism. Using this guide one might defend Tate's emendation of *King Lear* because it was applauded by intelligent readers for one hundred and fifty years. Surely our first responsibility is to Sidney's work, not to the time-honored graftings of his editors. How Sidney planned to end his revised *Arcadia* is a question that cannot now be answered. If one avoids speculating on the unknowable, and concentrates on examining the revision that Sidney left us, he will be impressed by its fundamental coherence.

The text of this edition has been reproduced photographically from H. Oskar Sommer's facsimile edition of the *Arcadia* of 1590 (London: Kegan Paul, Trench, Trubner and Co., 1891). Because Sommer's text is a photographic facsimile and retains all of the printing peculiarities of the first edition, a word or two of explanation may be in order here for the reader who is unfamiliar with Elizabethan printing conventions.[1] As far as the lettering is concerned, the reader will notice first of all that *s* is used only at the end of words, the "long *s*," *f*, being used in all other positions. Secondly, the capital letter *I* is used for the modern *I* and *J*, and the capital *V* for the modern *U* and *V*. And finally, although the four letters *i, j, u,* and *v* occur in lower-case type, *j* is used only when preceded by *i*, or in Roman numerals; and *u* and *v* are not used according to their pronunciation but according to their position in the word, *v* occurring at the beginning of a word and *u* in all other positions.

The spelling, it will be noticed, is haphazard, the same word often being spelled in different ways on the same page; and the punctuation, though more standardized, tends to be much heavier than modern usage demands, indicating not only syntactical connections but also rhetorical pauses. Two oddities of spelling and punctuation deserve special mention, the use of the tilde and the use of quotation marks. The tilde above a letter indicates the omission of an *m* or *n;* thus "then" may be written as "thẽ." Quotation marks here are not used to indicate direct quotation but to point out sententious remarks, and they are printed in the margin rather than at the precise beginning and end of the remark to which they call attention.

I would like to conclude this note by acknowledging the useful criticism I have received on my introductory essay from four careful readers: my former teachers, Josephine Miles and Norman Rabkin; my friend, John Gardner; and my collegue, Victor Doyno. I am greatly indebted to them all. Finally, I want to thank the Institutional Funds Committee of the Faculty of Arts and Letters of the State University of New York at Buffalo for a grant which helped make possible the publication of this edition.

[1]For a short, lucid discussion of these conventions see Ronald B. McKerrow, *An Introduction to Bibliography for Literary Students* (Oxford, 1928), pp. 309-318.

TO MY DEARE LADIE
AND SISTER, THE COVN-
TESSE OF PEMBROKE.

Ere now haue you (moſt deare, and moſt worthy to be moſt deare Lady) this idle worke of mine: which I fear (like the Spiders webbe) will be thought fitter to be ſwept away, then worn to any other purpoſe. For my part, in very trueth (as the cruell fathers among the Greekes, were woont to doo to the babes they would not foſter) I could well find in my harte, to caſt out in ſome deſert of forgetfulnes this child, which I am loath to

A3   *fa-*

father. But you defired me to doo it, and your defire, to my hart is an abfolute com-mandement. Now, it is done onelie for you, onely to you: if you keepe it to your felfe, or to fuch friendes, who will weigh errors in the ballaunce of good will, I hope, for the fathers fake, it will be par-doned, perchance made much of, though in it felfe it haue deformities. For in-deede, for feuerer eyes it is not, being but a trifle, and that triflinglie handled. Your deare felfe can beſt witnes the maner, be-ing done in loofe fheetes of paper, moſt of it in your prefence, the reſt, by fheetes, fent vnto you, as faſt as they were done. In fumme, a young head, not fo well ſtayed as I would it were, (and fhall be when God will) hauing many many fancies begot-ten in it, if it had not ben in fome way de-liuered, would haue growen a monſter, & more forie might I be that they came in,

then

then that they gat out. But his chiefe safetie, shalbe the not walking abroad; & his chiefe protection, the bearing the liuerye of your name; which (if much much good will do not deceaue me) is worthy to be a sactuary for a greater offender. This say I, because I knowe the vertue so; and this say I, because it may be euer so; or to say better, because it will be euer so. Read it then at your idle tymes, and the follyes your good iudgement wil finde in it, blame not, but laugh at. And so, looking for no better stuffe, then, as in an Haberdashers shoppe, glasses, or feathers, you will continue to loue the writer, who doth excedinglie loue you; and most most hartelie praies you may long liue, to be a principall ornament to the familie of the Sidneis.

Your louing Brother

Philip Sidnei.

*T*He *diuision and summing of the Chapters was not of Sir* Philip Sidneis *dooing, but aduentured by the ouer-seer of the print, for the more ease of the* Readers. *He therfore submits himselfe to their iudgement, and if his labour answere not the worthines of the booke, desireth pardon for it. As also if any defect be found in the Eclogues, which although they were of Sir* Phillip Sidneis *writing, yet were they not perused by him, but left till the worke had bene finished, that then choise should haue bene made, which should haue bene taken, and in what manner brought in. At this time they haue bene chosen and disposed as the ouer-seer thought best.*

THE COVNTESSE OF
PEMBROKES ARCADIA WRIT-
TEN BY SIR PHILIP
SIDNEI.

THE FIRST BOOKE.

CHAP. I.

¹ The sheperdish complaints of the absented louers Strephon *and* Claius. *² The second shipwrack of* Pyrocles *and* Musidorus. *Their strange sauing, ³ enterview, and ⁴ parting.*

IT was in the time that the earth begins to put on her new aparrel against the approch of her louer, and that the Sun rūning a most euē course becums an indifferent arbiter betweene the night and the day; when the hopelesse shepheard *Strephon* was come to the sandes, which lie against the Island of Cithera; where viewing the place with a heauy kinde

of

of delight, and fometimes cafting his eyes to the Ile-ward, he called his friendly riuall, the paftor *Claius* vnto him, and fetting firft downe in his darkened counte-nance a dolefull copie of what he would fpeake: O my *Claius*, faid he, hether we are now come to pay the rent, for which we are fo called vnto by ouer-bufie Remem-brance, Remembrance, reftleffe Remembrance, which claymes not onely this dutie of vs, but for it will haue vs forget our felues. I pray you when wee were amid our flocke, and that of other fhepeheardes fome were running after their fheep ftrayed beyond their bounds, fome delighting their eyes with feeing them nibble vp-on the fhort and fweete graffe, fome medicining their ficke ewes, fome fetting a bell for an enfigne of a fheep-ifh fquadron, fome with more leafure inuenting new games of exercifing their bodies & fporting their wits: did Remembrance graunt vs any holiday, eyther for paftime or deuotion, nay either for neceffary foode or naturall reft? but that ftill it forced our thoughts to worke vpõ this place, where we laft (alas that the word laft fhould fo long laft) did gaze our eyes vpon her e-uer florifhing beautie: did it not ftill crie within vs? Ah you bafe minded wretches, are your thoughts fo deep-ly bemired in the trade of ordinary worldlings, as for refpect of gaine fome paultry wooll may yeeld you, to let fo much time paffe without knowing perfectly her eftate, efpecially in fo troublefome a feafon? to leaue that fhore vnfaluted, from whence you may fee to the Ifland where fhe dwelleth? to leaue thofe fteps vnkif-fed wherein *Vrania* printed the farewell of all beautie? Wel then, Remembraunce commaunded, we obeyed, and here we finde, that as our remembrance came euer

cloathed

cloathed vnto vs in the forme of this place, so this place
giues newe heate to the feauer of our languishing remembrance. Yonder my *Claius, Vrania* lighted, the verie horse (me thought) bewayled to be so disburdned :
and as for thee, poore *Claius,* when thou wentst to help
her downe, I saw reuerence and desire so deuide thee,
that thou didst at one inftant both blushe and quake,
and in stead of bearing her, weart ready to fall downe
thy selfe. There shee sate, vouchsafing my cloake (then
most gorgeous) vnder her : at yonder rifing of the
ground she turned her selfe, looking backe toward her
woonted abode, and because of her parting bearing
much sorrow in hir eyes, the lightsomnes whereof had
yet so naturall a cherefulnesse, as it made euen sorrow
seeme to smile; at that turning she spake vnto vs all, opening the cherrie of hir lips, & Lord how greedily mine
eares did feed vpon the sweete words she vttered? And
here she laide her hand ouer thine eyes, when shee saw
the teares springing in them, as if she would conceale
them from other, and yet her selfe feele some of thy sorrow : But woe is me, yonder, yonder, did she put her
foote into the boate, at that inftant as it were deuiding
her heauenly beautie, betweene the Earth and the Sea.
But when she was imbarked, did you not marke how
the windes whiftled, & the seas daunft for ioy, how the
failes did swel with pride, and all because they had *Vrania?* O *Vrania,* blessed be thou *Vrania,* the sweeteft faire-
nesse and faireft sweetnesse : with that worde his voice
brake so with sobbing, that he could say no further; and
Claius thus answered. Alas my *Strephon* (said he) what
needes this skore to recken vp onely our losses ? What
doubt is there, but that the light of this place doth call

our thoughtes to appeare at the court of affection, held
by that racking steward, Remembraunce? Aswell may
sheepe forget to feare when they spie woolues, as wee
can misse such fancies, when wee see any place made
happie by her treading. Who can choose that saw her
but thinke where she stayed, where she walkt, where she
turned, where she spoke? But what is all this? truely
no more, but as this place serued vs to thinke of those
thinges, so those thinges serue as places to call to memorie more excellent matters. No, no, let vs thinke
with confideration, and confider with acknowledging,
and acknowledge with admiration, and admire with
loue, and loue with ioy in the midst of all woes: let vs
in such forte thinke, I say, that our poore eyes were so
inriched as to behold, and our low hearts so exalted as
to loue, a maide, who is such, that as the greatest thing
the world can shewe, is her beautie, so the least thing
that may be prayfed in her, is her beautie. Certainely
as her eye-lids are more pleasant to behold, then two
white kiddes climing vp a faire tree, and browfing on
his tendrest braunches, and yet are nothing, compared
to the day-shining starres contayned in them; and as
her breath is more sweete then a gentle South-west
wind, which comes creeping ouer flowrie fieldes and
shaddowed waters in the extreeme heate of summer,
and yet is nothing, compared to the hony flowing
speach that breath doth carrie: no more all that our
eyes can see of her (though when they haue seene her,
what else they shall euer see is but drie stuble after clo-
uers grasse) is to bee matched with the flocke of vnspeakeable vertues laid vp delightfully in that best builded folde. But in deede as wee can better confider the

funnes beautie, by marking how he guildes thefe waters, and mountaines them by looking vpon his owne
face, too glorious for our weake eyes : fo it may be our
conceits (not able to beare her fun-ftayning excellencie) will better way it by her workes vpon fome meaner fubiect employed. And alas, who can better witneffe that then we, whofe experience is grounded vpon feeling: hath not the onely loue of her made vs (being filly ignorant fhepheards) raife vp our thoughts
aboue the ordinary leuell of the worlde, fo as great
clearkes do not difdaine our conference: hath not the
defire to feeme worthie in her eyes made vs when o-
thers were fleeping, to fit vewing the courfe of heauens: when others were running at bafe, to runne o-
uer learned writings: when other marke their fheepe,
we to marke our felues: hath not fhee throwne reafon
vpon our defires, and, as it were giuen eyes vnto *Cupid?*
hath in any, but in her, loue-fellowfhip maintained
friendfhip betweene riuals, and beautie taught the beholders chaftitie: He was going on with his praifes,
but *Strephon* bad him ftay, & looke: & fo they both perceaued a thing which floted drawing nearer and nearer
to the banke; but rather by the fauourable working of
the Sea, then by any felfe induftrie. They doubted a
while what it fhould be; till it was caft vp euen hard before the: at which time they fully faw that it was a man:
Wherupon running for pitie fake vnto him, they found
his hands (as it fhould appeare, conftanter frends to his
life then his memorie) faft griping vpon the edge of a
fquare fmall coffer, which lay all vnder his breaft : els in
him felfe no fhew of life, fo as the boord feemed to bee
but a beere to carry him a land to his Sepulchre. So

B 3 drew

drew they vp a young man of so goodly shape and well pleasing fauour, that one would think death had in him a louely countenance; and, that though he were naked, nakednes was to him an apparrell. That sight increased their compassion, and their compassion called vp their care; so that lifting his feete aboue his head, making a great deale of salt water to come out of his mouth, they layd him vpon some of their garments, and fell to rub and chafe him, till they brought him to recouer both breath the seruant, & warmth the companion of liuing. At length, opening his eyes, he gaue a great groane, (a dolefull note but a pleasaunt dittie) for by that, they found not onely life, but strength of life in him. They therefore continued on their charitable office, vntil (his spirits being well returned,) hee (without so much as thanking them for their paines) gate vp, and looking round about to the vttermost lymittes of his sight, and crying vpon the name of *Pyrocles*, nor seeing nor hearing cause of comfort: what (said he) and shall *Musidorus* liue after *Pyrocles*? therewithall hee offered wilfully to cast destruction & himselfe againe into the sea : a strange sight to the shepheards, to whom it seemed, that before being in apparance dead had yet saued his life, and now comming to his life, shoulde be a cause to procure his death; but they ranne vnto him, and pulling him backe, (then too feeble for them) by force stickled that vnnatural fray. I pray you (said he) honest men, what such right haue you in me, as not to suffer me to doe with my self what I list? and what pollicie haue you to bestow a benefite where it is counted an iniury? They hearing him speake in Greek (which was their naturall language) became the more tender hearted towards him; and considering
dering

dering by his calling and looking, that the losse of some
deare friend was great cause of his sorow; told him they
were poore men that were bound by course of humanitie to preuent so great a mischiefe; and that they wisht
him, if opinion of some bodies perishing bred such desperate anguish in him, that he should be comforted by
his owne proofe, who had lately escaped as apparant
danger as any might be. No, no (said hee) it is not for
me to attend so high a blissefulnesse: but since you take
care of mee, I pray you finde meanes that some Barke
may be prouided, that will goe out of the hauen, that .f
it be possible we may finde the body farre farre too precious a foode for fishes: and for the hire (said he) I haue
within this casket, of value sufficient to content them.
Claius presently went to a Fisherman, & hauing agreed,
with him, and prouided some apparrell for the naked
stranger, he imbarked, and the Shepheards with him;
and were no sooner gone beyond the mouth of the hauen, but that some way into the sea they might discerne
(as it were) a stayne of the waters colour, and by times
some sparkes and smoke mounting thereout. But the
young man no sooner saw it, but that beating his brest,
he cried, that there was the beginning of his ruine, intreating them to bend their course as neere vnto it as
they could: telling, how that smoake was but a small
relique of a great fire, which had driue both him & his
friend rather to committe themselues to the cold mercie of the sea, then to abide the hote crueltie of the fire:
and that therefore, though they both had abandoned
the ship, that he was (if any where) in that course to be
met withall. They steared therefore as neere thetherward as they could: but when they came so neere as

B 4.   their

their eies were ful mafters of the obiect, they faw a fight full of piteous ftrangenes: a fhip, or rather the carkas of the fhippe, or rather fome few bones of the carkas, hulling there, part broken, part burned, part drowned: death hauing vfed more then one dart to that deftructi-on. About it floted great ftore of very rich thinges, and many cheftes which might promife no leffe. And a-midft the precious things were a number of dead bo-dies, which likewife did not onely teftifie both eleméts violence, but that the chiefe violence was growen of humane inhumanitie: for their bodies were ful of grifly wounds, & their bloud had (as it were) filled the wrinc-kles of the feas vifage: which it feemed the fea woulde not wafh away, that it might witnes it is not alwaies his fault, when we condemne his crueltie: in fumme, a de-feate, where the conquered kept both field and fpoile: a fhipwrack without ftorme or ill footing: and a waft of fire in the midft of water.

But a litle way off they faw the maft, whofe proude height now lay along; like a widdow hauing loft her make of whom fhe held her honor: but vpon the maft they faw a yong man (at leaft if he were a man) bearing fhew of about 18. yeares of age, who fate (as on horf-back) hauing nothing vpon him but his fhirt, which be-ing wrought with blew filk & gold; had a kind of refem-blance to the fea: on which the fun (then neare his We-fterne home) did fhoote fome of his beames. His haire (which the young men of Greece vfed to weare very long) was ftirred vp & down with the wind, which fee-med to haue a fport to play with it, as the fea had to kiffe his feet; himfelfe full of admirable beautie, fet foorth by the ftrangenes both of his feate & gefture: for, holding

his

his head vp full of vnmoued maieſtie, he held a ſworde
aloft with his faire arme, which often he waued about
his crowne as though he would threaten the world in
that extremitie. But the fiſhermen, when they came ſo
neere him, that it was time to throwe out a rope, by
which hold they might draw him, their ſimplicity bred
ſuch amaſement, & their amaſement ſuch a ſuperſtitiõ,
that (aſſuredly thinking it was ſome God begotten betweene *Neptune* and *Venus*, that had made all this terrible ſlaughter) as they went vnder ſayle by him, held vp
their hands, and made their prayers. Which when *Muſidorus* ſawe, though he were almoſt as much rauiſhed
with ioy, as they with aſtoniſhment, he lept to the Ma-
riner, and tooke the rope out of his hande and (ſaying,
doeſt thou liue, and arte well? who anſwered, thou
canſt tell beſt, ſince moſt of my well beyng ſtandes in
thee,) threwe it out, but alreadie the ſhippe was paſt
beyond *Pyrocles :* and therefore *Muſidorus* could doo
no more but perſwade the Mariners to caſt about a-
gaine, aſſuring them that hee was but a man, although
of moſt diuine excellencies, and promiſing great re-
wardes for their paine.

  And now they were alreadie come vpon the ſtaies;
when one of the ſaylers deſcried a Galley which came
with ſayles and oares directlie in the chaſe of them;
and ſtreight perceaued it was a well knowne Pirate,
who hunted not onely for goodes but for bodies of
menne, which hee imployed eyther to bee his Galley
ſlaues, or to ſell at the beſt market. Which when the
Maiſter vnderſtood, he commaunded forthwith to ſet
on all the canuaſſe they could, and flie homeward, leauing in that ſort poore *Pyrocles* ſo neere to be reskewed.

But what did not *Mufidorus* fay? what did he not offer
to perfwade them to venture the fight? But feare
ftanding at the gates of their eares, put back all perfwafions: fo that hee had nothing to accompanie
Pyrocles, but his eyes; nor to fuccour him, but his wi-
fhes. Therefore praying for him, and cafting a long
look that way he faw the Galley leaue the purfuite of
them, & turne to take vp the fpoiles of the other wrack:
and laftly he might well fee them lift vp the yong man;
and alas (faid he to himfelfe) deere *Pyrocles* fhall that
bodie of thine be enchayned? fhall thofe victorious
handes of thine be commaunded to bafe offices? fhall
vertue become a flaue to thofe that be flaues to vici-
oufnes? Alas, better had it bene thou hadft ended nobly thy noble daies: what death is fo euill as vnworthy
feruitude? But that opinion foone ceafed when he faw
the gallie fetting vpon an other fhip, which held long
and ftrong fight with her: for then he began afrefh to
feare the life of his friende, and to wifh well to the Pirates whome before he hated, leaft in their ruyne hee
might perifh. But the fifhermen made fuch fpeed into
the hauen, that they abfented his eyes from beholding
the iffue: where being entred, he could procure neither them nor any other as then to put themfelues into the fea: fo that beyng as full of forrow for being vnable to doe any thing, as voide of counfell how to doe
any thing, befides, that ficknefle grew fomething vpon
him, the honeft fhepheards *Strephon* and *Claius* (who
being themfelues true friends, did the more perfectly
iudge the iuftnefle of his forrowe) aduife him, that he
fhould mitigate fomwhat of his woe, fince he had gotten an amendment in fortune, being come from affured

red perſuaſion of his death, to haue no cauſe to diſpaire of his life. as one that had lamented the death
of his ſheepe, ſhould after know they were but ſtrayed,
would receiue pleaſure though readily hee knew not
where to finde them.

CHAP. 2.

1 *The paſtors comfortes to the wracked* Muſidorus. 2 *His
paſſage into Arcadia. The deſcriptions of* 3 *Laconia,*
4 *Arcadia,* Kalanders 5 *perſon,* 6 *houſe, and* 7 *entertainement to* Muſidorus *, now called* Palladius. *His*
8 *ſicknes, recouery,* 9 *and perfections.*

Ow ſir (ſaide they) thus for our
ſelues it is. Wee are in profeſſion   1
but ſhepheards, and in this countrie of Laconia little better then
ſtrangers, and therefore neither in
skill, nor habilitie of power greatly
to ſtead you. But what we can preſent vnto you is this: Arcadia, of
which countrie wee are, is but a little way hence, and
euen vpon the next confines.

There dwelleth a Gentleman, by name *Kalander*,
who vouchſafeth much fauour vnto vs: A man who   5
for his hoſpitalitie is ſo much haunted, that no newes
ſturre, but comes to his eares; for his vpright dealing ſo
beloued of his neighbours, that he hath many euer readie to doe him their vttermoſt ſeruice, and by the great
good will our Prince beares him, may ſoone obtaine
the vſe of his name and credit, which hath a principall
ſwaie,

ſwaie,not only in his owne Arcadia but in al theſe coũ-
tries of *Peloponneſus : and* (which is worth all) all theſe
things giue him not ſo much power,as his nature giues
him will to benefit : ſo that it ſeemes no Muſicke is ſo
ſweet to his eare as deſerued thankes . To him we will
bring you,& there you may recouer againe your helth,
without which you cãnot be able to make any diligent
ſearch for your friend:and therefore but in that reſpect,
you muſt labour for it.Beſides,we are ſure the cõfort of
curteſie,& eaſe of wiſe counſell ſhall not be wanting.

2   *Muſidorus*(who beſides he was meerly vnacquainted
in the coũtrie had his wits aſtoniſhed with ſorow)gaue
eaſie conſent to that,frõ which he ſaw no reaſon to diſ-
agree: & therefore (defraying the Mariners with a ring
beſtowed vpon thẽ) they tooke their iourney together
through *Laconia;Claius* & *Strephon* by courſe carying his
cheſt for him,*Muſidorus* only bearing in his coũtenance
euidẽt marks of a ſorowfulmind ſupported with a weak
bodie, which they perceiuing,& knowing that the violence of ſorow is not at the firſt to be ſtriuẽ withal:(being like a mighty beaſt,ſoner tamed with folowing,thã
ouerthrowẽ by withſtãding) they gaue way vnto it for
that day & the next;neuer troubling him , either with
asking queſtions,or finding fault with his melãcholie,
but rather fitting to his dolor dolorous diſcourſes of
their own & other folks misfortunes. Which ſpeeches,
thogh they had not a liuely entrãce to his ſeces ſhut vp
in ſorow , yet like one half aſleep,he toke hold of much
of the matters ſpoken vnte him,ſo as a man may ſay,ere
ſorow was aware , they made his thoughts beare away
ſomething els beſide his own ſorow,which wrought ſo
in him, that at lẽgth he grew cõtent to mark their ſpeeches,then to maruel at ſuch wit in ſhepheardes, after to
like

like their company,& laftly to vouchfafe conferēce: fo
that the 3. day after, in the time that the morning did
ftrow rofes & violets in the heauenly floore againft the
cōming of the Sun,the nightingales(ftriuing one with
the other which coulde in moft dainty variety recount
their wrong-caufed forow) made thē put of their fleep,
& rifing frō vnder a tree(which that night had bin their
pauiliō)they went on their iorney,which by & by wel-
comed *Mufidorus* eyes(wearied with the wafted foile of
Laconia)with delightfull profpects. There were hilles
which garnifhed their proud heights with ftately trees:
hūble valleis,whofe bafe eftate femed cōforted with re-
frefhing of filuer riuers:medows,enameld with al forts
of ey-pleafing floures:thickets, which being lined with
moft pleafāt fhade,were witneffed fo to by the chereful
depofitiō of many wel-tuned birds: each pafture ftored
with fheep feeding with fober fecurity, while the prety
lābs with bleting oratory craued the dams cōfort: here
a fhepheards boy piping, as though he fhould neuer be
old:there a yong fhepherdeffe knitting,and withall finging, & it feemed that her voice cōforted her hands to
work,& her hāds kept time to her voices mufick. As for
the houfes of the coutry (for many houfes came vnder
their eye)they were all fcattered, no two being one by
th'other,& yet not fo far off as that it barred mutual fuc-
cour:a fhew, as it were,of an accōpanable folitarines,&
of a ciuil wildnes. I pray you(faid *Mufidorus*, then firft
vnfealing his long filent lips)what coūtries be thefe we
paffe through,which are fo diuers irr fhew, the one wā-
ting no ftore,th'other hauing no ftore but of want.

　　The country(anfwered *Claius*)where you were caft a
fhore, & now are paft through,is Laconia,not fo poore
by the barrennes of the foyle (though in it felfe not
　　　　　　　　　　　　　　　　　passing

4

3

paſſing fertill) as by a ciuill warre, which being theſe two yeares within the bowels of that eſtate, betweene the gentlemen & the peaſants (by them named *Helots*) hath in this ſorte as it were disfigured the face of nature, and made it ſo vnhoſpitall as now you haue found it: the townes neither of the one ſide nor the other, willingly opening their gates to ſtrangers, nor ſtrangers willingly entring for feare of being miſtaken.

4   But this countrie (where now you ſet your foote) is Arcadia: and euen harde by is the houſe of *Kalander* whether we lead you: this countrie being thus decked with peace, and (the childe of peace) good husbandrie. Theſe houſes you ſee ſo ſcattered are of men, as we two are, that liue vpon the commoditie of their ſheepe: and therefore in the diuiſion of the Arcadian eſtate are termed ſhepheards; a happie people, wanting litle, becauſe they deſire not much. What cauſe then, ſaid *Muſidorus*, made you venter to leaue this ſweete life, and put your ſelfe in yonder vnpleaſant and dangerous realme? Garded with pouertie (anſwered *Strephon*) & guided with loue: But now (ſaid *Claius*) ſince it hath pleaſed you to aske any thing of vs whoſe baſenes is ſuch as the very knowledge is darknes: geue vs leaue to know ſomthing of you, & of the young man you ſo much lament, that at leaſt we may be the better inſtructed to enforme *Kalander*, and he the better know how to proportion his entertainment. *Muſidorus* (according to the agreement betweene *Pyrocles* and him to alter their names) anſwered, that he called himſelf *Palladius*, and his friend *Daiphantus*; but till I haue him againe (ſaid he) I am in deed nothing: and therefore my ſtorie is of nothing, his entertainement (ſince ſo good a man he is) cannot be ſo

lowe

lowe as I account my eftate: and in fumme,the fumme
of all his curtefie may be to helpe me by fome meanes
to feeke my frend .

They perceiued he was not willing to open himfelfe further,and therefore without further queftioning 6
brought him to the houfe: about which they might fee
(with fitte confideration both of the ayre, the profpect,
and the nature of the ground) all fuch neceffarie addi-
tions to a great houfe, as might well fhewe, *Kalander*
knew that prouifion is the foundation of hofpitalitie,
and thrift the fewell of magnificence . The houfe it
felfe was built of faire and ftrong ftone, not affecting fo
much any extraordinarie kinde of finenes , as an honorable reprefenting of a firme ftatelines . The lightes,
doores and ftaires , rather directed to the vfe of the
gueft, then to the eye of the Artificer : and yet as the
one cheefly heeded , fo the other not neglected ; each
place handfome without curiofitie , and homely without lothfomnes : not fo daintie as not to be trode on,
nor yet flubberd vp with good felowfhippe : all more
lafting then beautifull,but that the confideration of the
exceeding laftingneffe made the eye beleeue it was exceeding beautifull . The feruants not fo many in number, as cleanlie in apparell, and feruiceable in behauiour, teftifying euen in their countenaunces , that their
maifter tooke afwell care to be ferued,as of the that did
ferue . One of them was forth-with readie to welcome
the fhepheards, as men,who though they were poore,
their maifter greatly fauoured : and vnderftanding by
them , that the young man with them was to be much
accounted of, for that they had feene tokens of more
then common greatnes,how fo euer now eclipfed with
fortune.

fortune : He ranne to his mafter, who came prefentlie foorth, and pleafantly welcomming the fhepheardes, but efpecially applying him to *Mufidorus*, *Strephon* priuately told him all what he knew of him, and particularly that hee found this ftranger was loath to be knowen.

7   No faid *Kalander* (fpeaking alowd)I am no herald to enquire of mens pedegrees, it fufficeth me if I know their vertues:which(if this young mans face be not a falfe witnes) doe better apparrell his minde,then you haue done his body. While hee was fpeaking, there came a boy in fhew like a Merchants prentice, who taking *Strephon* by the fleeue,deliuered him a letter written ioyntly both to him and *Claius* from *Vrania:* which they no fooner had read, but that with fhort leaue-taking of *Kalander* (who quickly gheft and fmiled at the matter) and once againe (though haftely) recommending the yong man vnto him,they went away, leauing *Mufidorus* euen lothe to part with them, for the good conuerfation he had of them,& obligation he accounted himfelfe tied in vnto them : and therefore,they deliuering his cheft vnto him, he opened it, and would haue prefented the with two very rich iewels, but they abfolutelie refufed them, telling him they were more then enough rewarded in the knowing of him, and without herkening vnto a replie (like men whofe harts difdained all defires but one) gate fpeedely away, as if the letter had brought wings to make them flie.But by that fight *Kalander* foone iudged that his gueft was of no meane calling; and therefore the more refpectfullie entertaining him, *Mufidorus* found his ficknes (which the fight, the fea, and late trauell had layd vpon him)

growe

grow greatly : fo that fearing fome fuddaine accident, he deliuered the cheft to *Kalander* ; which was full of moft pretious ftones, gorgeoufly & cunningly fet in diuerfe maners, defiring him he would keep thofe trifles, and if he died, he would beftow fo much of it as was needfull, to finde out and redeeme a young man, naming himfelfe *Daiphantus*, as then in the handes of Laconia pirates.

But *Kalander* feeing him faint more and more, with carefull fpeede conueyed him to the moft cōmodious lodging in his houfe : where being poffeft with an extreeme burning feuer, he cōtinued fome while with no great hope of life : but youth at length got the victorie of ficknefle, fo that in fix weekes the excellencie of his returned beautie was a credible embaffadour of his health; to the great ioy of *Kalander* : who, as in this time he had by certaine friendes of his that dwelt neare the Sea in Meffenia, fet foorth a fhippe and a galley to feeke and fuccour *Daiphantus* : fo at home did hee omit nothing which he thought might eyther profite or gratifie *Palladius*.

For hauing found in him (befides his bodily giftes beyond the degree of Admiration) by dayly difcourfes which he delighted him felfe to haue with him, a mind of moft excellent compofition (a pearcing witte quite voide of oftentation, high erected thoughts feated in a harte of courtefie, an eloquence as fweete in the vttering, as flowe to come to the vttering, a behauiour fo noble, as gaue a maieftie to aduerfitie : and all in a man whofe age could not be aboue one & twenty yeares,) the good old man was euen enamoured with a fatherly loue towards him ; or rather became his feruaunt by

C the

the bondes ſuch vertue laid vpon him ; once hee acknowledged him ſelfe ſo to be , by the badge of diligent attendance.

CHAP. 3.

The ¹ pictures of Kalanders dainty garden-houſe. His narra-
tion of the ² Arcadian eſtate, ³ the King, ⁴ the Queene,
⁵ their two daughters , and ⁶ their gardians , with their
qualities, which is the ground of all this ſtorie.

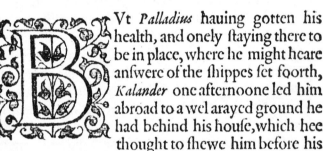

Vt *Palladius* hauing gotten his
health, and onely ſtaying there to
be in place, where he might heare
anſwere of the ſhippes ſet foorth,
Kalander one afternoone led him
abroad to a wel arayed ground he
had behind his houſe, which hee
thought to ſhewe him before his
going, as the place him ſelfe more then in any other delighted : the backeſide of the houſe was neyther field,
garden, nor orchard ; or rather it was both fielde, garden , and orcharde : for as ſoone as the deſcending of
the ſtayres had deliuered them downe , they came into a place cunninglie ſet with trees of the moſte taſt-
pleaſing fruites : but ſcarcelie they had taken that into
their conſideration, but that they were ſuddainely ſtept
into a delicate greene, of each ſide of the greene a thic-
ket bend , behinde the thickets againe newe beddes of
flowers, which being vnder the trees , the trees were to
them a Pauilion, and they to the trees a moſaical floore:
ſo that it ſeemed that arte therein would needes be delightfull

lightfull by counterfaiting his enemie error, and making order in confusion.

In the middeſt of all the place, was a faire ponde,
whoſe ſhaking chriſtall was a perfect mirrour to all the
other beauties, ſo that it bare ſhewe of two gardens;
one in deede, the other in ſhaddowes: and in one of
the thickets was a fine fountaine made thus. A naked
Venus of white marble, wherein the grauer had vſed
ſuch cunning, that the naturall blew veines of the marble were framed in fitte places, to ſet foorth the beautifull veines of her bodie. At her breſt ſhe had her babe
Æneas, who ſeemed (hauing begun to ſucke) to leaue
that, to looke vpon her fayre eyes, which ſmiled at the
babes follie, the meane while the breaſt running. Hard
by was a houſe of pleaſure builte for a Sommer retiring
place, whether *Kalander* leading him, he found a ſquare
roome full of delightfull pictures, made by the moſt
excellent workeman of Greece. There was *Diana*
when *Actæon* ſawe her bathing, in whoſe cheekes the
painter had ſet ſuch a colour, as was mixt betweene
ſhame & diſdaine: & one of her fooliſh Nymphes, who
weeping, and withal lowring, one might ſee the work-
man meant to ſet forth teares of anger. In another table
was *Atalanta*; the poſture of whoſe lims was ſo liuelie
expreſſed, that if the eyes were the only iudges, as they
be the onely ſeers, one would haue ſworne the very picture had runne. Beſides many mo, as of *Helena*, *Om-
phale*, *Iole*: but in none of them all beautie ſeemed to
ſpeake ſo much as in a large table, which contained a
comely old man, with a lady of midle age, but of excellét beautie; & more excellét would haue bene deemed,
but that there ſtood betweene thé a yong maid, whoſe

wonderfulneſſe tooke away all beautie from her, but that, which it might ſeeme ſhee gaue her backe againe by her very ſhadow. And ſuch differéce, being knowne that it did in deed counterfeit a perſon liuing, was there betweene her and al the other, though Goddeſſes, that it ſeemd the skill of the painter beſtowed on the other new beautie, but that the beautie of her beſtowed new skill of the painter. Though he thought inquiſitiuenes an vncomely gueſt, he could not chooſe but aske who ſhe was, that bearing ſhew of one being in deed, could with natural gifts go beyond the reach of inuentiõ. *Ka-lander* anſwered, that it was made by *Philoclea*, the yon-ger daughter of his prince, who alſo with his wife were conteined in that Table: the painter meaning to repre-ſent the preſent condition of the young Ladie, who ſtood watched by an ouer-curious eye of her parents: & that he would alſo haue drawne her eldeſt ſiſter, eſte-med her match for beautie, in her ſhepheardiſh attire; but that the rude clown her gardiã would not ſuffer it: nether durſt he aske leaue of the Prince for feare of ſuſ-pitiõ. *Palladius* perceaued that the matter was wrapt vp in ſome ſecreſie, and therefore would for modeſtie de-maund no further : but yet his countenance could not but with dumme Eloquence deſire it: Which *Kalander* perceauing, well ſaid he, my deere gueſt, I know your minde, and I will ſatisfie it : neyther will I doo it like a niggardly anſwerer, going no further then the boundes of the queſtion, but I will diſcouer vnto you, aſwell that wherein my knowledge is common with others, as that which by extraordinarie means is deliuered vn-to me: knowing ſo much in you, though not long ac-quainted, that I ſhall find your eares faithfull treaſurers.

So

So then fitting downe in two chaires, and fometimes cafting his eye to the picture, he thus fpake.

This countrie Arcadia among all the prouinces of Greece, hath euer beene had in fingular reputation: partly for the fweetneffe of the ayre, and other natural benefites, but principally for the well tempered minds of the people, who (finding that the fhining title of glorie fo much affected by other nations, doth in deed helpe little to the happineffe of life) are the onely people, which as by their Iuftice and prouidence geue neither caufe nor hope to their neyghbours to annoy them, fo are they not fturred with falfe praife to trouble others quiet, thinking it a fmall reward for the wafting of their owne liues in rauening, that their pofteritie fhould long after faie, they had done fo. Euen the Mufes feeme to approue their good determinatiō, by chofing this countrie for their chiefe repairing place, & by beftowing their perfections fo largely here, that the very fhepheards haue their fancies lifted to fo high conceits, as the learned of other nations are content both to borrow their names, and imitate their cunning.

Here dwelleth, and raigneth this Prince (whofe picture you fee) by name *Bafilius*, a Prince of fufficient skill to gouerne fo quiet a countrie, where the good minds of the former princes had fet down good lawes, and the well bringing vp of the people doth ferue as a moft fure bond to hold thē. But to be plaine with you, he excels in nothing fo much, as in the zealous loue of his people, wherein he doth not only paffe al his owne fore-goers, but as I thinke al the princes liuing. Wherof the caufe is, that though he exceed not in the vertues which get admiration; as depth of wifdome, height of

courage

courage and largenesse of magnificence, yet is hee notable in thofe whiche ftirre affection, as trueth of worde, meekeneffe, courtefie, mercifulneffe, and liberalitie.

4 He being already well ftriken in yeares, maried a young princes, named *Gynecia*, daughter to the king of Cyprus, of notable beautie, as by her picture you fee: a woman of great wit, and in truth of more princely vertues, then her husband: of moft vnfpotted chaftitie, but of fo working a minde, and fo vehement fpirits, as a man may fay, it was happie fhee tooke a good courfe : for otherwife it would haue beene terrible.

5 Of thefe two are brought to the worlde two daughters, fo beyonde meafure excellent in all the gifts allotted to reafonable creatures, that wee may thinke they were borne to fhewe, that Nature is no ftepmother to that fex, how much fo euer fome men (fharpe witted onely in euill fpeaking) haue fought to difgrace them. The elder is named *Pamela*; by many men not deemed inferiour to her fifter: for my part, when I marked them both, me thought there was (if at leaft fuch perfections may receyue the worde of more) more fweetneffe in *Philoclea*, but more maieftie in *Pamela* : mee thought loue plaide in *Philocleas* eyes, and threatned in *Pamelas* : me thought *Philocleas* beautie onely perfwaded, but fo perfwaded as all harts muft yeelde : *Pamelas* beautie vfed violence, and fuch violence as no hart could refift : and it feemes that fuch proportion is betweene their mindes; *Philoclea* fo bafhfull as though her excellencies had ftolne into her before fhee was aware: fo humble, that fhe will put all pride out of countenance: in fumme, fuch proceeding as will ftirre hope,

but

but teach hope good māners. *Pamela* of high thoughts, who auoides not pride with not knowing her excellencies, but by making that one of her excellencies to be voide of pride; her mothers wifdome, greatneffe, nobilitie, but (if I can ghefle aright) knit with a more conftant temper. Now then, our *Bafilius* being fo publickly happie as to be a Prince, and fo happie in that happineffe as to be a beloued Prince, and fo in his priuate bleffed as to haue fo excellent a wife, and fo ouerexcellent children, hath of late taken a courfe which yet makes him more fpoken of then all thefe bleffings. For, hauing made a iourney to Delphos, and fafely returned, within fhor. fpace hee brake vp his court, and retired himfelfe, his wife, and children into a certaine Forreft hereby, which hee calleth his defert, where in (befides a houfe appointed for ftables and lodgings for certaine perfons of meane calling, who do all houfhold feruices,) hee hath builded two fine lodges. In the one of them him felfe remaines with his younger daughter *Philoclea*, which was the caufe they three were matched together in this picture, without hauing any other creature liuing in that lodge with him.

Which though it bee ftraunge, yet not fo ftraunge, 6 as the courfe he hath taken with the princeffe *Pamela*, whom hee hath placed in the other lodge : but how thinke you accopanied? truly with none other, but one *Dametas*, the moft arrant doltifh clowne, that I thinke euer was without the priuiledge of a bable, with his wife *Mifo*, and daughter *Mopfa*, in whome no witt can deuife anie thing wherein they maie pleafure her, but to exercife her patience, and to ferue for a foile of her perfections. This loutifh clowne is fuch, that

C 4 you

you neuer ſaw ſo ill fauourd a viſar, his behauiour ſuch, that he is beyond the degree of ridiculous ; and for his apparrel, euen as I would wiſh him : *Miſo* his wife , ſo handſome a beldame, that onely her face and her ſplay-foote haue made her accuſed for a witch ; onely one good point ſhe hath, that ſhe obſerues *decorū*, hauing a froward mind in a wretched body. Betweene theſe two perſonages (who neuer agreed in any humor, but in diſ-agreeing) is iſſued forth miſtreſſe *Mopſa*, a fitte woman to participate of both their perfections : but becauſe a pleaſant fellow of my acquaintance ſet forth her praiſes in verſe, I will only repeate them, and ſpare mine owne tongue, ſince ſhe goes for a woman . Theſe verſes are theſe, which I haue ſo often cauſed to be ſong, that I haue them without booke.

What length of verſe can ſerue braue Mopſas *good to ſhow ?*
Whoſe vertues ſtrange, & beuties ſuch, as no mā thē may know
Thus ſhrewdly burdned thē, how cā my Muſe eſcape? (*ſhape.*
The gods muſt help, and pretious things muſt ſerue to ſhew her
Like great god Saturn *faire, and like faire* Venus *chaſte:*
As ſmothe as Pan, *as* Iuno *milde, like goddeſſe* Iris *faſte.*
With Cupid *ſhe fore-ſees, and goes god* Vulcans *pace:*
And for a taſt of all theſe gifts, ſhe ſteales god Momus *grace.*
Her forhead iacinth like, her cheekes of opall hue,
Her twinkling eies bedeckt with pearle, her lips as Saphir *blew:*
Her haire like Crapal-ſtone, *her mouth O heauenly wyde ;*
Her skin like burniſht gold, her hands like ſiluer vre vntryde.
As for her parts vnknowne, which hidden ſure are beſt :
Happie be they which well beleeue, & neuer ſeeke the reſt.

Now

Now truely hauing made thefe defcriptions vnto you, me thinkes you fhould imagine that I rather faine fome pleafant deuife,then recount a truth,that a Prince (not banifhed from his own wits) could poffibly make fo vnworthie a choife. But truely (deare gueft) fo it is, that Princes (whofe doings haue beene often foothed with good fucceffe) thinke nothing fo abfurde, which they cannot make honourable. The beginning of his credite was by the Princes ftraying out of the way, one time he hunted, where meeting this fellow,and asking him the way;& fo falling into other queftiõs,he found fome of his aunfwers (as a dog fure if he could fpeake, had wit enough to defcribe his kennell)not vnfenfible, & all vttered with fuch rudenes, which he enterpreted plainneffe(though there be great difference betweene them) that *Bafilius* conceauing a fodaine delight,tooke him to his Court,with apparant fhew of his good opi- nion : where the flattering courtier had no fooner takē the Princes minde, but that there were ftraight reafons to confirme the Princes doing, & fhadowes of vertues found for *Dametas*. His filence grew wit,his bluntneffe integritie,his beaftly ignorance vertuous fimplicitie: & the Prince (according to the nature of great perfons,in loue with that he had done himfelfe) fancied, that his weakneffe with his prefence would much be mended. And fo like a creature of his owne making,he liked him more and more,and thus hauing firft giuen him the of- fice of principall heardman , laftly , fince he tooke this ftrange determination, he hath in a manner put the life of himfelfe and his children into his hands.Which au- thoritie (like too great a fayle for fo fmall a boate) doth fo ouer-fway poore *Dametas*, that if before he were a
good

good foole in a chamber, he might be allowed it now
in a comedie: So as I doubt me (I feare mee in d eede)
my maſter will in the end(with his coſt)finde, t hat his
office is not to make men,but to vſe men as,men are;no
more then a horſe will be taught to hunt, or an aſſe to
mannage. But in ſooth I am afraide I haue geu en your
eares too great a ſurfette, with the groſſe diſco urſes of
that heauie peece of fleſh. But the zealous gree fe I con-
ceue to ſee ſo great an error in my Lord,hath made me
beſtow more words, then I confeſſe ſo baſe a ſubiect
deſerueth.

CHAP. 4.

The [1] *cauſe of* Baſilius *his diſcourting.* [2] Philanax *his diſ-*
ſwaſiue letter. [3] Baſilius *his priuiledged companie.* [4] *Foure*
cauſes why old men are diſcourſers. [5] *The ſtate,the skil,and*
exerciſe of the Arcadian *ſhepheards.*

T Hus much now that I haue tolde
you,is nothing more then in effect
any Arcadian knowes. But what
moued him to this ſtrange ſolitarines hath bin imparted(as I thinke)
but to one perſon liuing. My ſelfe
cã cõiecture, & in deed more then
coniecture, by this accident that I will tell you : I haue
an onely ſonne, by name *Clitophon,*who is now abſent,
preparing for his owne mariage,which I meane ſhortly
ſhalbe here celebrated. This ſonne of mine (while the
Prince kept his Court) was of his bed-chamber; now
ſince the breaking vp thereof, returned home, and
ſhewed me(among other things he had gathered) the
coppy

coppy which he had taken of a letter : which when the prince had read,he hadlaid in a window,presuming no body durſt looke in his writings:but my ſonne not on-ly tooke a time to read it,but to copie it.In trueth I bla-med *Clitophon* for the curioſitie, which made him break his duetie in ſuch a kind,whereby kings ſecrets are ſub-ieƈ to be reuealed: but ſince it was done,I was content to take ſo much profite, as to know it. Now here is the letter, that I euer ſince for my good liking, haue caried about me:which before I read vnto you,I muſt tell you from whom it came. It is a noble-man of this countrie, named *Philanax*, appointed by the Prince, Regent in this time of his retiring,and moſt worthie ſo to be: for, there liues no man,whoſe excellent witte more ſimplie imbraſeth integritie, beſides his vnfained loue to his maſter,wherein neuer yet any could make queſtion, ſa-uing,whether he loued *Baſilius* or the Prince better: a rare temper,while moſt men either ſeruile-ly yeeld to al appetites,or with an obſtinate auſteritie looking to that they fanſie good, in effeƈ negleƈ the Princes perſon. This then being the man,whom of all other (and moſt worthie)the Prince cheefly loues,it ſhould ſeeme (for more then the letter I haue not to gheſſe by) that the Prince vpon his returne from Delphos,(*Philanax* then lying ſick)had written vnto him his determination , ri-ſing(as euidently appeares) vpon ſome Oracle he had there receaued:whereunto he wrote this anſwere.

Philanax his letter to Baſilius.

Moſt redouted & beloued prince,if aſwel it had plea-ſed you at your going to Delphos as now , to haue

vſed

vsed my humble seruice, both I should in better sea-
son, and to better purpose haue spoken : and you (if
my speech had preuayled) should haue beene at this
time, as no way more in danger , so much more in quietnes; I would then haue said, that wisdome and vertue
be the only destinies appointed to mã to follow, whéce
we ought to seeke al our knowledge, since they be such
guydes as cannot faile; which, besides their inward cõfort, doo lead so direct a way of proceeding , as either
prosperitie must ensue; or, if the wickednes of the world
should oppresse it, it can neuer be said, that euil hapneth
to him, who falles accompanied with vertue : I would
then haue said, the heauenly powers to be reuerenced,
and not searched into ; & their mercies rather by prayers to be sought, then their hidden councels by curiositie . These kind of soothsayers (since they haue left vs
in our selues sufficient guides)to be nothing but fansie,
wherein there must either be vanitie, or infalliblenes, &
so, either not to be respected , or not to be preuented.
But since it is weakenes too much to remember what
should haue beene done, and that your commandemét
stretcheth to know what is to be done, I do (most deare
Lord)with humble boldnes say, that the maner of your
determination dooth in no sort better please me , then
the cause of your going . These thirtie yeares you haue
so gouerned this Region , that neither your Subiectes
haue wanted iustice in you, nor you obediéce in them;
& your neighbors haue found you so hurtlesly strong,
that they thought it better to rest in your friendshippe,
then make newe triall of your enmitie . If this then
haue proceeded out of the good constitution of your
state, and out of a wise prouidence, generally to preuent
all

all thofe things, which might encober your happines :
why fhould you now feeke newe courfes, fince your
owne enfample comforts you to continue, and that it
is to me moft certaine (though it pleafe you not to tell
me the very words of the Oracle) that yet no deftinie,
nor influence whatfoeuer, can bring mans witte to a
higher point, then wifdome and goodnes? Why fhould
you depriue your felfe of gouernment, for feare of loofing your gouernment ? like one that fhould kill himfelfe for feare of death ? nay rather, if this Oracle be to
be accouted of, arme vp your courage the more againft
it: for who wil ftick to him that abandones himfelfe?
Let your fubiects haue you in their eyes ; let them fee
the benefites of your iuftice dayly more and more ; and
fo muft they needes rather like of prefent fureties, then
vncertaine changes. Laftly, whether your time call you
to liue or die, doo both like a prince. Now for your fecond refolution ; which is, to fuffer no worthie prince
to be a fuiter to either of your daughters, but while you
liue to keep the both vnmaried ; &, as it were, to kill the
ioy of pofteritie, which in your time you may enioy:
moued perchance by a mif-underftoode Oracle : what
fhall I fay, if the affection of a father to his owne children, cannot plead fufficietly againft fuch fancies? once
certaine it is, the God, which is God of nature, doth neuer teach vnnaturalnes : and euen the fame minde hold
I touching your banifhing them from companie, leaft, I
know not what ftrange loues fhould follow: Certainly
Sir, in my ladies, your daughters, nature promifeth nothing but goodnes, and their education by your fatherly care, hath beene hetherto fuch, as hath beene moft fit
to reftraine all euill : geuing their mindes vertuous delights,

lights, and not greeuing them for want of wel-ruled libertie. Now to fall to a ſodain ſtraightning them, what
can it doo but argue ſuſpition, a thing no more vnpleaſant, then vnſure, for the preſeruing of vertue? Leaue
womens minds, the moſt vntamed that way of any: ſee
whether any cage can pleaſe a bird? or whether a dogge
growe not fiercer with tying? what dooth ic[ealouſie, but
ſtirre vp the mind to thinke, what it is from which they
are reſtrayned? for they are treaſures, or things of great
delight, which men vſe to hide, for the aptneſſe they
haue to catch mens fancies: and the thoughtes once a-
waked to that, harder ſure it is to keepe thoſe thoughts
from accompliſhment, then it had been before to haue
kept the minde (which being the chiefe part, by this
meanes is defiled) from thinking. Laſtly, for the recommending ſo principall a charge of the Princeſſe *Pamela*,
(whoſe minde goes beyond the gouerning of many
thouſands ſuch) to ſuch a perſon as *Dametas* is (beſides
that the thing in it ſelf is ſtrange) it comes of a very euil
ground, that ignorance ſhould be the mother of faithfulnes. O no; he cannot be good, that knowes not why
he is good, but ſtands ſo farre good, as his fortune may
keepe him vnaſſaied: but comming once to that, his
rude ſimplicitie is either eaſily changed, or eaſily decci-
ued: & ſo growes that to be the laſt excuſe of his fault,
which ſeemed to haue been the firſt foundation of his
faith. Thus farre hath your commaundement and my
zeale drawn me; which I, like a man in a valley that may
diſcern hilles, or like a poore paſſenger that may ſpie a
rock, ſo humbly ſubmit to your gracious conſideration,
beſeeching you againe, to ſtand wholy vpon your own
vertue, as the ſureſt way to maintaine you in that you
are, and to auoyd any euill which may be imagined.

By

By the contents of this letter you may perceiue, that the caufe of all, hath beene the vanitie which poffeffeth many, who(making a perpetuall manfion of this poore baiting place of mans life)are defirous to know the certaintie of things to come; wherein there is nothing fo certaine, as our continual vncertaintie. But what in particular points the oracle was, in faith I know not: nether (as you may fee by one place of *Philanax* letter)he himfelfe diftinctly knew. But this experience fhewes vs, that *Bafilius* iudgement, corrupted with a Princes fortune, hath rather heard then followed the wife (as I take it) counfell of *Philanax.* For, hauing loft the fterne of his gouernment, with much amazement to the people, among whom many ftrange bruits are receiued for currant, and with fome apparance of daunger in refpect of the valiant *Amphalus*, his nephew , & much enuy in the ambitious number of the Nobilitie againft *Philanax*, to fee *Philanax* fo aduaunced, though (to fpeake fimply) he deferue more the as many of vs as there be in Arcadia: the prince himfelf hath hidden his head, in fuch fort as I told you, not fticking plainly to cofeffe, that he means not(while he breathes) that his daughters fhal haue any hufbad, but keep the thus folitary with him: wher he **3** giues no other body leue to vifit him at any time, but a certain prieft, who being excellent in poetrie, he makes him write out fuch thinges as he beft likes. he being no les delightful in couerfatio, the needfull for deuotio, & about twety fpecified fhepheards, in who(fome for exercifes, & fome for Eglogs)he taketh greater recreatio.

And now you know as much as my felf: wherin if I **4** haue held you ouer long, lay hardly the fault vpon my olde age, which in the very difpofition of it is talkatiue: whether it be(faid he fmiling)that nature loues to

exer-

exercife that part moft,which is leaft decayed, and that
is our tongue:or,that knowledge being the only thing
whereof we poore old men can brag, we cannot make
it knowen but by vtterance: or, that mankinde by all
meanes feeking to eternize himfelfe fo much the more,
as he is necre his end,dooth it not only by the children
that come of him,but by fpeeches and writings recommended to the memorie of hearers and readers. And
yet thus much I wil fay for my felfe,that I haue not laid
thefe matters,either fo openly,or largely to any as your
felfe: fo much (if I much fayle not) doo I fee in you,
which makes me both loue and truft you. Neuer may
he be old, anfwered *Palladius*,that dooth not reuerence
that age,whofe heauines,if it waie downe the frayl and
flefhly ballance, it as much lifts vp the noble and fpiri-
tuall part: and well might you haue alledged another
reafon,that their wifdome makes them willing to profite others. And that haue I receiued of you, neuer to
be forgotten,but with vngratefulnes. But among many
ftrange conceits you tolde me,which haue fhewed effects in your Prince, truly euen the laft, that he fhould
conceiue fuch pleafure in fhepheards difcourfes,would
not feeme the leaft vnto me, fauing that you told me at
the firft, that this countrie is notable in thofe wits, and
that in deed my felfe hauing beene brought not onely
to this place, but to my life, by *Strephon* and *Claius*, in
their conference found wits as might better become
fuch fhepheards as *Homer* fpeakes of,that be gouernors
of peoples, then fuch fenatours who hold their councell in a fhepecoate: for them two (faid *Kalander*) efpecially *Claius*, they are beyond the reft by fo much, as
learning commonlie doth adde to nature: for,hauing
                                                    neglected

neglected their wealth in refpect of their knowledge,
they haue not fo much empayred the meaner, as they
bettered the better . Which all notwithftanding, it
is a fporte to heare howe they impute to loue, whiche
hath indewed their thoughts (faie they) with fuche a
ftrength.

But certainely, all the people of this countrie from
high to lowe, is giuen to thofe fportes of the witte, fo
as you would wonder to heare how foone euen children will beginne to verfifie. Once, ordinary it is a-
mong the meaneft forte, to make Songes and Dia-
logues in meeter, either loue whetting their braine. or
long peace hauing begun it, example and emulation
amending it. Not fo much, but the clowne *Dametas*
will ftumble fometimes vpon fome Songs that might
become a better brayne : but no forte of people fo excellent in that kinde as the paftors; for their liuing ftanding but vpon the looking to their beaftes, they haue
eafe, the Nurfe of Poetrie. Neither are our fhepheards
fuch, as (I heare) they be in other countries; but they
are the verie owners of the fheepe, to which eyther
themfelues looke, or their children giue daylie atten-
daunce. And then truely, it would delight you vnder
fome tree, or by fome riuers fide (when two or three
of them meet together) to heare their rurall mufe, how
pretely it will deliuer out, fometimes ioyes, fometimes
lamentations, fometimes chalengings one of the o-
ther, fometimes vnder hidden formes vttering fuch
matters, as otherwife they durft not deale with . Then
they haue moft commonly one, who iuogeth the price
to the beft doer, of which they are no leffe gladde, then
great Princes are of triumphes: and his parte is to fette

D   downe

downe in writing all that is saide, saue that it may be, his pen with more leasure doth polish the rudenesse of an vnthought-on songe. Now the choise of all (as you may well thinke) either for goodnesse of voice, or pleasantnesse of wit, the Prince hath : among whom also there are two or three straungers, whom inwarde melancholies hauing made weery of the worldes eyes, haue come to spende their liues among the countrie people of *Arcadia* ; & their conuersation being well approued, the prince vouchsafeth them his presence, and not onely by looking on, but by great courtesie and liberalitie, animates the Shepheardes the more exquisitely to labour for his good liking. So that there is no cause to blame the Prince for somtimes hearing them; the blame-worthinesse is, that to heare them, he rather goes to solitarinesse, then makes them come to companie. Neyther doo I accuse my maister for aduauncing a countriman, as *Dametas* is, since God forbid, but where worthinesse is (as truely it is among diuers of that fellowship) any outward lownesse should hinder the hiest rayfing, but that he would needes make election of one, the basenesse of whose minde is such, that it sinckes a thousand degrees lower, then the basest bodie could carrie the most base fortune : Which although it might bee aunswered for the Prince, that it is rather a trust hee hath in his simple plainnesse, then any great aduauncement, beyng but chiefe heardman: yet all honest hartes feele, that the trust of their Lord goes beyond all aduauncement. But I am euer too long vppon him, when hee crosseth the waie of my speache, and by the shaddowe of yonder Tower, I see it is a fitter time, with our supper to pay the duties we

owe

owe to our ſtomacks, thē to break the aire with my idle
diſcourſes: And more witte I might haue learned of
Homer (whome euen now you mentioned) who neuer entertayned eyther gueſtes or hoſtes with long
ſpeaches, till the mouth of hunger be throughly ſtopped. So withall he roſe, leading *Palladius* through the
gardeine againe to the parler, where they vſed to ſuppe;
Palladius aſſuring him, that he had alreadie bene more
fed to his liking, then hee could bee by the skilfulleſt
trencher-men of *Media*.

CHAP. 5.

The ¹ *ſorow of* Kalander *for his ſonne* Clitophon. *The*
  ² *ſtorie of* Argalus *and* Parthenia, *their* ³ *perfeƈtions,*
  their ⁴ *loue, their* ⁵ *troubles, her* ⁶ *impoyſoning,* ⁷ *his*
  rare conſtancie, ⁸ *her ſtraunge refuſall,* ⁹ *their patholo-*
  gies, her ¹⁰ *flight, his* ¹¹ *reuenge on his riuall the miſ-*
  chieſe-worker Demagoras, *then Captaine of the re-*
  bell Helots, *who* ¹² *take him, and* ¹³ Clitophon *that*
  ſought to helpe him: but ¹⁴ *both are kept aliue by their*
  new captaine.

Vt beeing come to the ſupping
place, one of *Kalanders* ſeruaunts
rounded in his eare; at which (his
collour chaungyng) hee retired
him ſelfe into his chamber; commaunding his men diligentlie to
waite and attend vpon *Palladius*,
and to excuſe his abſence with
ſome neceſſarie buſines he had preſentlie to diſpatch.

D 2   Which

Which they accordinglie did, for ſome fewe dayes
forcing theſelues to let no change appeare: but though
they framed their countenaunces neuer ſo cunningly,
Palladius perceaued there was ſome il-pleaſing accidént
fallen out. Whereupon, being againe ſet alone at ſup-
per, he called to the Steward, and deſired him to tell
him the matter of his ſuddaine alteration : who after
ſome trifling excuſes, in the endé confeſſed vnto him,
that his maiſter had receiued newes, that his ſonne before the daie of his neere marriage, chaunſt to be at a
battaile, which was to be fought betweene the Gentle-
menne of Lacedæmon and the *Helots :* who winning
the victorie, hee was there made priſoner, going to
deliuer a friend of his taken pryſoner by the *Helots*;
that the poore young Gentleman had offered great
raunſome for his life : but that the hate thoſe payſaunts
conceaued agaynſt all Gentlemen was ſuche, that e
uerie houre hee was to looke for nothing, but ſome
cruell death : which hether-vnto had onely beene delayed by the Captaines vehement dealing for him,
who ſeemed to haue a hart of more manlie pittie then
the reſt. Which loſſe had ſtricken the old Gentleman
with ſuch ſorrowe, as if aboundance of teares did not
ſeeme ſufficiently to witneſſe it, he was alone retyred,
tearing his bearde and hayre, and curſing his old age,
that had not made his graue to ſtoppe his eares from
ſuch aduertiſements : but that his faithfull ſeruaunts
had written in his name to all his friends, followers,
and tenants (*Philanax* the gouernour refuſing to deale
in it, as a priuate cauſe, but yet giuing leaue to ſeeke
their beſt redreſſe, ſo as they wronged not the ſtate
of Lacedæmon) of whom there were now gathered

vpon

vpon the frontiers good forces, that he was sure would spende their liues by any way, to redeeme or reuenge *Clitophon*. Now sir (said he) this is my maisters nature, though his grief be such, as to liue is a griefe vnto him, & that euen his reason is darkened with sorrow; yet the lawes of hospitality (long and holily obserued by him) giue still such a sway to his proceeding, that he will no waie suffer the straunger lodged vnder his roofe, to receyue (as it were) any infection of his anguish, especially you, toward whom I know not whether his loue, or admiration bee greater. But *Palladius* could scarce heare out his tale with patience: so was his hart torne in peeces with compassion of the case, liking of *Kalanders* noble behauiour, kindnesse for his respect to himwarde, and desire to finde some remedie, besides the image of his deerest friend *Daiphantus*, whom he iudged to suffer eyther a like or a worse fortune: therefore rising from the boorde, he desired the steward to tell him particularly, the ground, and euent of this accident, because by knowledge of many circumstaunces, there might perhaps some waie of helpe be opened. Whereunto the Steward easilie in this sorte condiscended.

My Lord (said he) when our good king *Basilius*, with better successe then expectation, tooke to wife (euen in his more then decaying yeares) the faire yong princes *Gynecia*; there came with her a young Lord, cousin german to her selfe, named *Argalus*, led hether, partly with the loue & honour of his noble kinswomã, partly with the humour of youth, which euer thinkes that good, whose goodnes he secs not: & in this court he receiued so good encrease of knowledge, that after some yeares

ſpent, he ſo manifeſted a moſt vertuous mind in all his
actions, that *Arcadia* gloried ſuch a plant was tranſ-
ported vnto them, being a Gentleman in deede moſt
rarely accompliſhed, excellentlie learned, but without all vayne glory: friendly, without factiouſhes: valiaunt, ſo as for my part I thinke the earth hath no man
that hath done more heroicall actes then hee; how ſoeuer now of late the fame flies of the two princes of
Theſſalia and *Macedon*, and hath long done of our noble prince *Amphialus*: who in deede, in our partes is
onely accounted likely to match him: but I ſay for my
part, I thinke no man for valour of minde, and habilitie of bodie to bee preferred, if equalled to *Argalus*;
and yet ſo valiant as he neuer durſt doo any bodie iniurie: in behauiour ſome will ſay euer ſadde, ſurely ſober, and ſomewhat giuen to muſing, but neuer vncourteous; his worde euer ledde by his thought, and followed by his deede; rather liberall then magnificent,
though the one wanted not, and the other had euer
good choiſe of the receiuer: in ſumme (for I perceiue
I ſhall eaſily take a great draught of his praiſes, whom
both I and all this countrie loue ſo well) ſuch a man
was (and I hope is) *Argalus*, as hardly the niceſt eye
can finde a ſpot in, if the ouer-vehement conſtancie of
yet ſpotles affection, may not in harde wreſted conſtru-
ctions be counted a ſpot: which in this manner began
that worke in him, which hath made bothe him, and it
ſelfe in him, ouer all this country famous. My maiſters
ſonne *Clitophon* (whoſe loſſe giues the cauſe to this diſcourſe, and yet giues me cauſe to beginne with *Argalus*, ſince his loſſe proceedes from *Argalus*) beyng a
young Gentleman, as of great birth (being our kings
ſiſters

fifters fonne) fo truely of good nature, and one that can fee good and loue it, haunted more the companie of this worthie *Argalus*, then of any other: fo as if there were not a friendfhip (which is fo rare, as it is to bee doubted whether it bee a thing in deede, or but a worde) at leaft there was fuch a liking and friendlines, as hath brought foorth the effectes which you fhall heare. About two yeares fince, it fo fell out, that hee brought him to a great Ladies houfe, fifter to my maifter, who had with her, her onely daughter, the faire *Parthenia*; faire in deede (fame I thinke it felfe daring not to call any fayrer, if it be not *Helena* queene of *Corinth*, and the two incomparable fifters of *Arcadia*) and that which made her faireneffe much the fayrer, was, that it was but a faire embaffadour of a moft faire minde, full of wit, and a wit which delighted more to iudge it felfe, then to fhowe it felfe: her fpeach being as rare as pretious; her filence without fullenneffe; her modeftie without affectation; her fhamefaftnes without ignorance: in fumme, one, that to praife well, one muft firft fet downe with himfelfe, what it is to be excellent: for fo fhe is.

I thinke you thinke, that thefe perfections meeting, 4 could not choofe but find one another, and delight in that they found; for likenes of manners is likely in reafon to drawe liking with affection: mens actions doo not alwaies croffe with reafon: to be fhort, it did fo in deed. They loued, although for a while the fire therof (hopes winges being cut of) were blowen by the bellowes of difpaire, vpon this occafion.

There had beene a good while before, and fo conti- 5 nued, a futer to this fame lady, a great noble mã, though of Laconia, yet neere neighbour to *Parthenias* mother, named *Demagoras*: A man mightie in riches & power, and proude thereof, ſtubbornly ſtout, louing no bodie but him ſelfe, and for his owne delights ſake *Parthenia*: and purſuing vehemently his deſire, his riches had ſo guilded ouer all his other imperfections, that the olde Ladie (though contrarie to my Lord her brothers minde) had giuen her conſent; and vſing a mothers authoritie vpon her faire daughter, had made her yeeld thereunto, not becauſe ſhee liked her choiſe, but becauſe her obedient minde had not yet taken vppon it to make choyſe; and the daie of their aſſurance drew neere, when my young Lord *Clitophon* brought this noble *Argalus*, perchaunce principallie to ſee ſo rare a ſight, as *Parthenia* by all well iudging eyes was iudged.

But though fewe dayes were before the time of aſſurance appointed, yet loue that ſawe hee had a great iourney to make in ſhorte time, haſted ſo him ſelfe, that before her worde could tie her to *Demagoras*, her harte hath vowed her to *Argalus*, with ſo gratefull a receipte in mutuall affection, that if ſhee deſired aboue all thinges to haue *Argalus*, *Argalus* feared nothing but to miſſe *Parthenia*. And now *Parthenia* had learned both liking and miſliking, louing and lothing, and out of paſſion began to take the authoritie of iudgement; in ſo much, that when the time came that *Demagoras* (full of proude ioy) thought to receaue the gifte of her ſelfe, ſhee with woordes of reſolute refuſall (though with teares ſhewing ſhe was ſorie ſhe muſt refuſe) aſſured her mother, ſhe would firſt be bedded in her graue, then wedded to *Demagoras*. The chaunge was no more

more ſtraunge, then vnpleaſant to the mother: who
beyng determinately (leaſt I ſhoulde ſay of a great Lady,wilfully) bent to marrie her to *Demagoras*, tryed all
wayes which a wittie and hard-harted mother could
vſe, vpon ſo humble a daughter · in whome the onely reſiſting power was loue. But the more ſhee aſſaulted, the more ſhee taught *Parthenia* to defende: and
the more *Parthenia* defended, the more ſhe made her
mother obſtinate in the aſſault: who at length finding,
that *Argalus* ſtanding betweene them, was it that moſt
eclipſed her affection from ſhining vpon *Demagoras*,
ſhe ſought all meanes how to remoue him,ſo much the
more, as he manifeſted himſelf an vnremoueable ſuiter
to her daughter: firſt,by imploying him in as many dãgerous enterpriſes, as euer the euill ſtepmother *Iuno* recommended to the famous *Hercules :* but the more his
vertue was tried, the more pure it grew, while all the
things ſhe did to ouerthrow him, did ſet him vp vpon
the height of honor; inough to haue moued her harte,
eſpecially to a man euery way ſo worthy as *Argalus*:but
ſhe ſtrugling againſt all reaſon,becauſe ſhe would haue
her will, and ſhew her authoritie in matching her with
Demagoras,the more vertuous *Argalus* was, the more
ſhe hated him: thinking her ſelfe conquered in his cõ-
queſts, and therefore ſtill imploying him in more and
more dangerous attempts:meane while,ſhe vſed all extremities poſſible vpon her faire daughter, to make her
geue ouer her ſelfe to her direction. But it was hard to
iudge,whether he in doing,or ſhe in ſuffering, ſhewed
greater conſtancie of affection: for, as to *Argalus* the
world ſooner wanted occaſions, then he valour to goe
thorow them ; ſo to *Parthenia*,malice ſooner ceaſed,the
her

her vnchanged patience. Laftly, by treafons, *Demagoras* and fhe would haue made away *Argalus* : but hee with prouidence & courage fo paft ouer all, that the mother tooke fuch a fpitefull grief at it, that her hart brake withall, and fhe died.

6　　But then, *Demagoras* affuring himfelfe, that now *Parthenia* was her owne, fhe would neuer be his, and receiuing as much by her owne determinate anfwere, not more defiring his owne happines, then enuying *Argalus*, whom he faw with narrow eyes, euen ready to enioy the perfection of his defires; ftrengthning his conceite with all the mifchieuous counfels which difdayned loue, and enuious pride could geue vnto him; the wicked wretch (taking a time that *Argalus* was gone to his countrie, to fetch fome of his principall frendes to honour the mariage, which *Parthenia* had moft ioyfully confented vnto,) the wicked *Demagoras* (I fay) defiring to fpeake with her, with vnmercifull force, (her weake armes in vaine refifting) rubd all ouer her face a moft horrible poyfon: the effect whereof was fuch, that neuer leaper lookt more vgly thē fhe did: which done, hauing his men & horfes ready, departed away in fpite of her feruāts, as redy to reuenge as they could be, in fuch an vnexpected mifchiefe. But the abhominablenes of this fact being come to my L. *Kalander*, he made fuch meanes, both by our kings interceffion, & his own, that by the king, & Senat of Lacedæmō, *Demagoras* was vpon paine of death, banifhed the countrie: who hating the punifhment, where he fhould haue hated the fault, ioynde himfelfe, with al the powers he could make, vnto the *Helots*, lately in rebellion againft that ftate: and they (glad to haue a man of fuch authority among thē) made

made him their general: & vnder him haue committed
diuers the moſt outragious villanies, that a baſe multi-
tude(full of deſperate reuenge)can imagine.

But within a while after this pitifull faſt committed   7
vpon *Parthenia*, *Argalus* returned(poore gentleman)ha-
uing her faire image in his heart, and alredy promiſing
his eies the vttermoſt of his felicitie, when they (no
bodie els daring to tell it him) were the firſt meſſen-
gers to themſelues of their owne misfortune. I meane
not to moue paſſions with telling you the griefe of
both, when he knew her, for at firſt he did not, nor at
firſt knowledge could poſſibly haue Vertues aide ſo
ready, as not euen weakly to lament the loſſe of ſuch a
iewell, ſo much the more, as that skilful men in that arte
aſſured it was vnrecouerable: but within a while, trueth
of loue(which ſtill held the firſt face in his memorie) a
vertuous conſtancie, and euen a delight to be conſtant,
faith geuen, and inward worthines ſhining through the
fouleſt miſtes, tooke ſo full holde of the noble *Argalus*,
that not onely in ſuch comfort which witty arguments
may beſtow vpon aduerſitie, but euen with the moſt a-
boundant kindneſſe that an eye-rauiſhed louer can expreſſe, he laboured both to driue the extremity of ſorow
from her, & to haſten the celebration of their mariage:
wherunto he vnfainedly ſhewed himſelf no leſſe chere-
fully earneſt, then if ſhe had neuer been diſinherited of
that goodly portion, which nature had ſo liberally bequeathed vnto her: and for that cauſe deferred his intēded reuenge vpon *Demagoras*, becauſe he might continually be in her preſence; ſhewing more huble ſeruice-
ablenes, and ioy to content her, then euer before.

But as he gaue this rare enſaple, not to be hoped for of   8
any

any other, but of an other *Argalus:* ſo of the other ſide, ſhe tooke as ſtrange a courſe in affection: for, where ſhe deſired to enioy him, more then to liue ; yet did ſhe o-uerthrow both her owne deſire, and his, and ir ¬o ſorte would yeeld to marry him; with a ſtrange encounter of loues affects, and effects: that he by an affection ſprong from exceſſiue beautie, ſhould delight in horrible foul-neſſe; and ſhe, of a vehement deſire to haue him, ſhould kindly buyld a reſolution neuer to haue him: for trueth is, that ſo in heart ſhe loued him, as ſhe could not finde in her heart he ſhould be tied to what was vnworthy of his preſence.

9   Truely Sir, a very good Orator might haue a fayre field to vſe eloquence in, if he did but onely repeate the lamentable, and truely affectionated ſpeeches, while he coniured her by remembrance of her affection, & true oathes of his owne affection, not to make him ſo vn-happy, as to think he had not only loſt her face, but her hart; that her face, when it was fayreſt, had been but as a marſhall, to lodge the loue of her in his minde; which now was ſo well placed, as it needed no further help of any outward harbinger : beſeeching her, euen with teares, to know, that his loue was not ſo ſuperficial, as to go no further then the skin; which yet now to him was moſt faire, ſince it was hers : how could hee be ſo vn-gratefull, as to loue her the leſſe for that, which ſhe had onely receiued for his ſake? that he neuer beheld it, but therein he ſaw the louelines of her loue towarde him: proteſting vnto her, that he would neuer take ioy of his life, if he might not enioy her, for whom principally he was glad he had life . But (as I heard by one that ouer-heard them) ſhe (wringing him by the hand) made no
other

other anſwere but this:my Lord(ſaid ſhe)God knowes
I loue you:if I were Princeſſe of the whole world , and
had,withal,al the bleſſings that euer the world brought
forth, I ſhould not make delay,to lay my ſelſe,& them,
vnder your feete : or if I had continued but as I was,
though (I muſt côfcſſe)far vnworthy of you,yet would
I,(with too great a ioy for my hart to think of)haue accepted your vouchſaſing me to be yours, & with faith
and obedience would haue ſupplied all other defects.
But firſt let me be much more miſerable then I am , ere
I match *Argalus* to ſuch a *Parthenia*:Liue happy,dearc
Argalus,I geue you full libertie,and I beſeech you take
it;and I aſſure you I ſhall reioyce (whatſoeuer become
of me) to ſee you ſo coupled,as may be fitte , both for
your honor,and ſatisfaction. With that ſhe burſt out in
crying and weeping , not able longer to conteine her
ſelfe from blaming her fortune,and wiſhing her owne
death.

But *Argalus* with a moſt heauie heart ſtill purſuing 10
his deſire,ſhe fixt of mind to auoid further intreatie , &
to flie all companie;which(euen of him) grew vnpleaſant vnto her;one night ſhe ſtole away: but whether,as
yet is vnknowen,or in deede what is become of her.

Argalus ſought her long, and in many places : at 11
length(deſpairing to finde her,and the more he deſpai-
red,the more enraged) weerie of his life,but firſt determining to be reuenged of *Demagoras* , hee went alone
diſguyſed into the chiefe towne held by the *Helots :*
where comming into his preſence , garded about by
many of his ſouldiers,he could delay his fury no lôger
for a fitter time: but ſetting vpon him , in deſpight of a
great many. that helped him , gaue him diuers mortall
wounds,

wounds, and himſelf (no queſtion) had been there pre-
12 ſently murthered, but that *Demagoras* himſelfe deſired
he might be kept aliue; perchaunce with intention to
feed his owne eyes with ſome cruell execution to bee
layd vpon him, but death came ſoner then he lookt for;
yet hauing had leiſure to appoint his ſucceſſor, a young
man, not long before deliuered out of the priſon of the
King of *Lacedæmon*, where hee ſhould haue ſuffered
death for hauing ſlaine the kings Nephew: but him he
named, who at that time was abſent, making roades vpon the *Lacedemonians*, but being returned, the reſt of
the *Helots*, for the great liking they conceiued of that
yong man, (eſpecially becauſe they had none among
themſelues to whom the others would yeeld) were cōtent to ſollow *Demagoras* appointment. And well hath
it ſucceded with them, he hauing ſince done things beyond the hope of the yongeſt heads; of whom I ſpeak
the rather, becauſe he hath hetherto preſerued *Argalus*
aliue, vnder pretence to haue him publiquely, and with
exquiſite tormentes executed, after the ende of theſe
warres, of which they hope for a ſoone and proſperous
iſſue.

　　And he hath likewiſe hetherto kept my young Lord
13 *Clitophon* aliue, who (to redeme his friend) went with
certaine other noble-men of *Laconia*, and forces gathered by them, to beſiege this young and new ſucceſſor:
but he iſſuing out (to the wonder of all men) defeated
14 the *Laconians*, ſlew many of the noble-men, & tooke
Clitophon priſoner, whom with much a doo he keepeth
aliue: the *Helots* being villanouſly cruell; but he tempe-
reth thē ſo, ſometimes by folowing their humor, ſometimes by ſtriuing with it, that hetherto hee hath ſaued
both

both their liues, but in different eſtates; *Argalus* being kept in a cloſe & hard priſon , *Clitophon* at ſome libertie. And now Sir, though (to ſay the truth) we can promiſe our ſelues litle of their ſafeties, while they are in the *Helots* hands, I haue deliuered all I vnderſtande touching the loſſe of my Lords ſonne, & the cauſe therof: which, though it was not neceſſarie to *Clitophons* caſe , to be ſo particularly told, yet the ſträgenes of it, made me think it would not be vnpleſant vnto you.

CHAP. 6.

1 Kalanders *expedition againſt the* Helots. 2 *Their eſtate.* 3 Palladius *his ſtratageme againſt them:* 4 *which pre-uayleth.* 5 *T he* Helots *reſiſtance, diſcomfiture, and* 6 *re-enforce by the returne of their new captaine* 7 *The com-bat and* 8 *enterknowledge of* Daiphantus *&* Palladius, *and by their* 9 *meanes a peace , with* 10 *the releaſe of* Ka-lander *and* Clitophon.

Alladius thanked him greatly for it, being euen paſſionatly delighted with hearing ſo ſtraunge an acci-dēt of a knight ſo famous ouer the world, as *Argalus*, with whome he had himſelfe a long deſire to meet: ſo had fame poured a noble emu-lation in him, towards him. But thē (wel bethinking himſelf) he called for armour, 1 deſiring them to prouide him of horſe & guide, and ar-med al ſauing the head, he wet vp to *Kaläder*, whom he found lying vpó the groūd, hauing euer ſince baniſhed
both

both sleepe and foode, as enemies to the mourning which passion persvaded him was reasonable. But *Palladius* raysed him vp, saying vnto him No more, no more of this,my Lord *Kalander*; let vs labour to finde, before wee lament the losse : you know my selfe misse one,who,though he be not my sonne,I would disdayn the fauour of life after him : but while there is hope left,let not the weaknes of sorow, make the strength of it languish: take comfort,and good successe will folow. And with those wordes, comfort seemed to lighten in his eyes, and that in his face and gesture was painted victorie, Once, *Kalanders* spirits were so reuiued withal, that(receiuing some sustenance, and taking a litle rest) he armed himselfe,and those few of his seruants he had left vnsent,and so himself guyded *Palladius* to the place vpon the frontiers: where alredy there were assembled betwene three and four thousand men,all wel disposed (for *Kalanders* sake)to abide any perill:but like men dis-used with a long peace,more determinate to doo, then skilfull how to doo: lusty bodies , and braue armours: with such courage,as rather grew of despising their eni-mies , whom they knew not, then of any confidence for any thing, which in them selues they knew;but nei-ther cunning vse of their weapons , nor arte shewed in their marching, or incamping . Which *Palladius* soone perceiuing, he desired to vnderstand(as much as could be deliuered vnto him)the estate of the *Helots*.

2   And he was answered by a man well acquainted with the affaires of Laconia, that they were a kinde of people,who hauing been of old, freemen and possessi-oners,the Lacedemonians had conquered them , and layd,not onely tribute,but bondage vpon them:which

they

they had long borne ; till of late the *Lacedæmonians*
through greedineſſe growing more heauie then they
could beare, and through contempt leſſe carefull how
to make them beare, they had with a generall conſent
(rather ſpringing by the generalnes of the cauſe, then
of any artificiall practiſe) ſet themſelues in armes, and
whetting their courage with reuenge, and grounding
their reſolutiō vpon deſpaire, they had proceeded with
vnloked-for ſucces: hauing already takē diuers Towns
and Caſtels, with the ſlaughter of many of the gentrie;
for whom no ſex nor age could be accepted for an excuſe. And that although at the firſt they had fought
rather with beaſtly furie, then any ſouldierly diſcipline,
practiſe had now made then comparable to the beſt
of the *Lacedæmonians*; & more of late then euer; by reaſon, firſt of *Demagoras* a great Lord, who had made him
ſelf of their partie, and ſince his death, of an other Captaine they had gotten, who had brought vp their ignorance, and brought downe their furie, to ſuch a meane
of good gouernment, and withall led them ſo valou-
rouſlie, that (beſides the time wherein *Clitophon* was
taken) they had the better in ſome other great cōflicts:
in ſuch wiſe, that the eſtate of *Lacedæmon* had ſent vnto
them, offering peace with moſt reaſonable and honorable conditions. *Palladius* hauing gotten this generall knowledge of the partie againſt whom, as hee had
already of the party for whom he was to fight, he went
to *Kalander*, and told him plainlie, that by playne force
there was ſmall apparaunce of helping *Clitophon*: but
ſome deuice was to be taken in hand, wherein no leſſe
diſcretion then valour was to be vſed.

Whereupon, the councel of the chiefe men was cal- 3
E   led

led, and at laft, this way *Palladius* (who by fome experience, but efpeciallie by reading Hiftories, was acquainted with ftratagemes) inuented, and was by all
the reft approoued : that all the men there fhoulde
dreffe themfelues like the pooreft forte of the people
in *Arcadia*, hauing no banners, but bloudie fhirtes
hanged vpon long ftaues, with fome bad bagge pipes
in ftead of drumme and fife, their armour they fhould
afwell as might be, couer, or at leaft make them looke
fo ruftilie, and ill-fauouredly as might well become
fuch wearers; and this the whole number fhould doo,
fauing two hundred of the beft chofen Gentlemen,
for courage and ftrength, whereof *Palladius* him felfe
would be one, who fhould haue their armes chayned,
and be put in cartes like prifoners. This being performed according to the agreement, they marched on towards the towne of *Cardumila* where *Clitophon* was captiue; and being come two houres before Sunne-fet
within vewe of the walles, the *Helots* alreadie defcry-
ing their number, and beginning to found the Alla-
rum, they fent a cunning fellow, (fo much the cunnin-
ger as that he could maske it vnder rudenes) who with
fuch a kind of Rhetorike, as weeded out all flowers of
Rhetorike, deliuered vnto the *Helots* affembled together, that they were countrie people of *Arcadia*, no leffe
oppreffed by their Lords, & no leffe defirous of liberty
then they, & therfore had put themfelues in the field, &
had alreadie (befides a great number flaine) taken nine
or ten skore Gentlemen prifoners, who they had there
well & faft chained. Now becaufe they had no ftrong
retiring place in *Arcadia*, & were not yet of number e
nough to keepe the fielde againft their Princes forces,
they

they were come to them for succor; knowing, that daily more & more of their qualitie would flock vnto thē,
but that in the mean time, left their Prince should pursue thē, or the *Lacedæmonian* King & Nobilitie(for the
likenes of the cause)fall vpon them, they desired that if
there were not roome enough for them in the towne,
that yet they might encampe vnder the walles, and for
surety haue their prisoners (who were such mē as were
euer able to make their peace)kept within the towne.

The *Helots* made but a short consultatiō, being glad **4**
that their contagion had spread it selfe into *Arcadia*,
and making account that if the peace did not fall out
betweene them and their King, that it was the best way
to set fire in all the parts of *Greece*; besides their greedi-
nesse to haue so many Gentlemen in their handes, in
whose raunsoms they already meant to haue a share, to
which hast of concluding, two thinges wel helped; the
one, that their Captaine with the wisest of them, was at
that time absent about confirming or breaking the
peace, with the state of *Lacedæmon* : the second, that o-
uer-many good fortunes began to breed a proude reck-
lesnesse in them : therefore sending to view the campe,
and finding that by their speach they were *Arcadians*,
with whom they had had no warre, neuer suspecting a
priuate mans credite could haue gathered such a force,
and that all other tokens witnessed them to be of the
lowest calling (besides the chaines vpon the Gentlemen) they graunted not onely leaue for the prisoners,
but for some others of the companie, and to all, that
they might harbour vnder the walles. So opened they
the gates, and receiued in the carts; which being done,
and *Palladius* seing fit time, he gaue the signe, and sha-

king

king of their chaynes; (which were made with ſuch
arte, that though they ſeemed moſt ſtrong and faſt,
he that ware them might eaſily looſe them) drew their
ſwordes hidden in the cartes, and ſo ſetting vpon the
ward, made them to flie eyther from the place, or
from their bodies, and ſo giue entrie to all the force
of the *Arcadians*,beforethe *Helots* could make any head
to reſiſt them.

    But the *Helots* being men hardened againſt daun-
gers, gathered as(well as they could)together in the
market place, and thence would haue giuen a ſhrewd
welcome to the *Arcadians*, but that *Palladius* (blaming
thoſe that were ſlow, hartning thē that were forward,
but eſpecially with his owne enſample leading them)
made ſuch an impreſſion into the ſquadron of the *Helots*, that at firſt the great bodie of them beginning to
ſhake, and ſtagger; at length,euery particular bodie recommended the protection of his life to his feet.Then
Kalander cried to go to the priſon, where he thought
his ſonne was,but *Palladius* wiſht him (firſt ſcouring the
ſtreates) to houſe all the *Helots*, and make themſelues
maiſters of the gates.

    But ere that could be accompliſhed, the *Helots* had
gotten new hart, and with diuers ſortes of ſhot from
corners of ſtreats, and houſe windowes, galled them;
which courage was come vnto them by the returne of
their Captain;who though he brought not many with
him(hauing diſperſt moſt of his companies to other of
his holds)yet meeting a great nūber rūning out of the
gate, not yet poſſeſt by the *Arcadians*, he made them
turne face,& with banners diſplayed,his Trumpet giue
the lowdeſt teſtimonie he could of his returne, which

once

once heard, the reſt of the *Helots* which were otherwiſe
ſcattered, bent thetherward, with a new life of reſolution : as if their Captaine had beene a roote, out of
which (as into braunches)their courage had ſprong.
Then began the fight to grow moſt ſharpe, and the encounters of more cruell obſtinacie. The *Arcadians* fighting to keepe that they had wonne, the *Helots* to recouer what they had loſt. The *Arcadians*, as in an vnknowne place, hauing no ſuccour but in their handes;
the *Helots*, as in their own place, fighting for their li-
uings, wiues, & children. There was victory & courage
againſt reuenge and deſpaire: ſafety of both ſides being
no otherwiſe to be gotten, but by deſtruction.

    At length, the left winge of the *Arcadians* began to
looſe ground; which *Palladius* ſeeing, he ſtreight thruſt
himſelfe with his choiſe bande againſt the throng that
oppreſſed thē, with ſuch an ouerflowing of valour, that
the Captaine of the *Helots* (whoſe eies ſoone iudged
of that wherwith thēſelues were gouerned)ſaw that he
alone was worth al the reſt of the *Arcadians*. Which he
ſo wondred at, that it was hard to ſay, whether he more
liked his doings, or miſliked the effects of his doings :
but determining that vpon that caſt the game lay, and
diſdaining to fight with any other, ſought onely to
ioine with him: which minde was no leſſe in *Palladius*,
hauing eaſily marked, that he was as the firſt mouer of
al the other handes. And ſo their thoughts meeting in
one point, they conſented (though not agreed) to trie
each others fortune: & ſo drawing themſelues to be the
vttermoſt of the one ſide, they began a combat, which
was ſo much inferior to the battaile in noiſe and number, as it was ſurpaſſing it in brauery of fighting, & (as it

were)delightful terriblenes.Their courage was guided
with skill,and their skill was armed with courage; neither did their hardinesse darken their witte, nor their
witte coole their hardines : both valiant, as men despising death; both confident,as vnwonted to be ouercome; yet doutefull by their present feeling ,and re-
spectfull by what they had already seene. Their feete
stedy,their hands diligent,their eyes watchfull,& their
harts resolute. The partes either not armed,or weakly armed,were well knowen , and according to the
knowledge should haue bene sharpely visited , but that
the aunswere was as quicke as the obiection. Yet some
lighting; the smarte bred rage , and the rage bred
smarte againe : till both sides beginning to waxe faint,
and rather desirous to die accompanied, then hopeful
to liue victorious, the Captaine of the *Helots* with a
blow , whose violence grew of furie,not of strength,or
of strength proceeding of furie , strake *Palladius* vpon
the side of the head,that he reelde astonied : and withall the helmet fell of, he remayning bare headed : but
other of the *Arcadians* were redie to shield him from
any harme might rise of that nakednes.

8   But little needed it, for his chiefe enemie in steed of
pursuing that aduauntage , kneeled downe, offering
to deliuer the pommell of his sworde,in token of yeelding,with all speaking aloud vnto him,that he thought
it more libertie to be his prisoner , then any others generall. *Palladius* standing vppon him selfe, and mis-
doubting some craft , and the *Helots* (that were next
their captaine) wauering betweene looking for some
stratageme, or fearing treason , What, saide the captaine,hath *Palladius* forgotten the voice of *Daiphantus?*

By

By that watche worde *Palladius* knew that it was his
onely friende *Pyrocles*, whome he had loft vpon the
Sea, and therefore both moft full of wonder, fo to be
mett, if they had not bene fuller of ioye then wonder, caufed the retraite to be founded, *Daiphantus* by
authoritie, and *Palladius* by perfuafion; to which helped well the little aduauntage that was of eyther fide:
and that of the *Helots* partie their Captaines behauiour had made as many amazed as fawe or heard of
it: and of the *Arcadian* fide the good olde *Kalan-*
der ftriuing more then his old age could atchieue, was
newly taken prifoner. But in deede, the chiefe par-
ter of the fraye was the night, which with her blacke
armes pulled their malicious fightes one from the o-
ther. But he that tooke *Kalander*, meant nothing leffe
then to faue him, but onelie fo long, as the Captaine
might learne the enemies fecrets: towardes whom he
led the old Gentleman, when he caufed the retreit to
be founded: looking for no other deliuerie from that
captiuitie, but by the painfull taking away of all paine:
when whome fhould he fee nexte to the Captaine
(with good tokens how valiantly he had fought that
daie againft the *Arcadians*) but his fonne *Clitophon*?
But nowe the Captaine had caufed all the principall
Helots to be affembled, as well to deliberate what they
had to do, as to receiue a meffage from the *Arcadians*:
Amóg whom *Palladius* vertue (befides the loue *Kalan-*
der bare him) hauing gotté principall authoritie, he had
perfuaded them to feeke rather by parley to recouer
the Father and the Sonne, then by the fword: fince the
goodnes of the Captain affured him that way to fpeed,
and his value (wherewith he was of old acquainted

E 4　　　　made

made him thinke any other way dangerous. This therfore was donne in orderly manner, giuing them to vnderſtand, that as they came but to deliuer *Clitophon*, ſo
offering to leaue the footing they already had in the
towne, to goe away without any further hurte, ſo as
they might haue the father, & the ſonne without raunſome deliuered. Which conditions beyng heard and
conceaued by the *Helots*, *Daiphantus* perſwaded them
without delay to accept them. For firſt (ſayd he) ſince
the ſtrife is within our owne home, if you looſe, you
looſe all that in this life can bee deare vnto you : if you
winne, it will be a blouddy victorie with no profite, but
the flattering in our ſelues that ſame badde humour of
reuenge. Beſides, it is like to ſtirre *Arcadia* vppon vs,
which nowe, by vſing theſe perſons well, maie bee
brought to ſome amitie. Laſtly, but eſpecially, leaſt the
king and nobility of *Laconia* (with whom now we haue
made a perfect peace) ſhould hope, by occaſion of this
quarrell to ioyne the *Arcadians* with them, & ſo breake
of the profitable agreement alreadie concluded. In
ſumme, as in al deliberations (waying the profite of the
good ſucceſſe with the harme of the euill ſucceſſe) you
ſhall find this way moſt ſafe and honorable.

10   The *Helots* aſmuch moued by his authoritie, as perſwaded by his reaſons, were content therewith. Wher-
vpon, *Palladius* tooke order that the *Arcadians* ſhould
preſently march out of the towne, taking with them
their priſoners, while the night with mutual diffidence
might keepe them quiet, and ere day came they might
be well on of their way, and ſo auoid thoſe accidents
which in late enemies, a looke, a word, or a particular
mans quarel might engéder. This being on both ſides
concluded

concluded on, *Kalander* and *Clitophon* who now (with
infinite ioy did knowe each other) came to kisse the
hands and feet of *Daiphantus* : *Clitophon* telling his father, how *Daiphantus* (not without danger to himselfe)
had preserued him from the furious malice of the *Helots* :& euen that day going to conclude the peace (least
in his absence he might receiue some hurt) he had taken him in his companie, and geuen him armour, vpon
promise he should take the parte of the *Helots*; which he
had in this fight perfourmed, little knowing that it was
against his father: but (said *Clitophon*) here is he, who (as
a father)hath new-begotten me, and (as a God)hath saued me from many deaths, which already laid hold on
me: which *Kalander* with teares of ioy acknowledged
(besides his owne deliuerance) onely his benefite. But
Daiphantus, who loued doing well for it selfe, and not
for thanks, brake of those ceremonies, desiring to know
how *Palladius* (for so he called *Musidorus*) was come into that companie, & what his present estate was: whereof receiuing a brief declaration of *Kalander*, he sent him
word by *Clitophon*, that he should not as now come vnto him, because he held himselfe not so sure a master of
the *Helots* minds, that he would aduenture him in their
power, who was so well knowen with an vnfriendly acquaintance; but that he desired him to return with *Kalander*, whether also he within few daies (hauing dispat-
ched himselfe of the *Helots*) would repaire. *Kalander*
would needes kisse his hande againe for that promise,
protesting, he would esteme his house more blessed thē
a temple of the gods, if it had once receiued him. And
then desiring pardon for *Argalus* *Daiphantus* assured
them that hee woulde die, but hee woulde bring him,

(though

(though till the kept in close prison, indeed for his safetie, the *Helots* being so animated against him as els hee could not haue liued) and so taking their leaue of him, *Kalander*, *Clitophon*, *Palladius* and the rest of the *Arcadians* swearing that they would no further in any sorte molest the *Helots*, they straight way marched out of the towne, carying both their dead and wounded bodies with them; and by morning were alreadie within the limits of *Arcadia*.

CHAP. 7,

The articles of peace betwene the Lacedæmonians *&* Helots, *Daiphātus his departure frõ the* Helots *with* Argalus *to* Kalanders *house.* *The offer of a straunge Lady to* Argalus *his refusal, and who she was.*

He *Helots* of the other side shutting their gates, gaue them selues to burye their dead, to cure their woundes, and rest their weeried bodies: till (the next day bestowing the chereful vse of the light vpon them) *Daiphantus* making a generall conuocation spake vnto them in this manner. We are first (said he) to thanke the Gods, that (further then wee had either cause to hope; or reason to imagine) haue deliuered vs out of this gulfe of daunger, wherein we were alredie swallowed. For all being lost, (had they had not directed,

my

my return fo iuft as they did) it had bene too late to recouer that, which being had,we could not keep. And
had I not happened to know one of the principall men
among them,by which meanes the truce beganne betweene vs,you may eafily conceiue, what little reafon
we haue to think,but that either by fome fupplie out of
Arcadia, or from the Nobilitie of this Country (who
would haue made fruites of wifdome grow out of this
occafion,) wee fhould haue had our power turned to
ruine,our pride to repentance and forow. But now the
ftorme,as it fell out,fo it ceafed: and the error committed, in retaining *Clitophon* more hardly then his age or
quarrell deferued, becomes a fharply learned experience, to vfe in other times more moderation.

Now haue I to deliuer vnto you the conclufion be- 1
tween the Kings with the Nobilitie of *Lacedæmon,* and
you; which is in all points as your felues defired:afwell
for that you would haue graunted, as for the affurance
of what is graunted. The Townes and Fortes you prefently haue,are ftill left vnto you,to be kept either with
or without garrifon, fo as you alter not the lawes of
the Countrie, and pay fuch dueties as the reft of the
Laconians doo. Your felues are made by publique
decree,free men, and fo capable both to giue and receiue voice in election of Magiftrates. The diftinction
of names betweene *Helots* and *Lacedæmonians* to bee
quite taken away, and all indifferently to enioy both
names and priuiledges of *Laconians.* Your children to
be brought vp with theirs in *Spartane* difcipline: and fo
you (framing your felues to be good members of that
eftate) to bee hereafter fellowes, and no longer feruaunts.

Which

which conditions you see, cary in themselues no more
contentation then assuraunce. For this is not a peace
which is made with them, but this is a peace by which
you are made of them. Lastly, a forgetfulnes decreed of
of all what is past, they shewing themselues glad to haue
so valiant men as you are, ioyned with them : so that
you are to take mindes of peace, since the cause of war
is finished; and as you hated them before like oppres-
sours, so now to loue them as brothers; to take care of
their estate because it is yours, and to labour by vertuous doing, that the posteritie may not repent your ioyning. But now one Article onely they stood vpon,
which in the end I with your commissioners haue a-
greed vnto, that I should no more tarry here, mistaking
perchaunce my humor, and thinking me as sedicious
as I am young, or els it is the king *Amiclas* procuring, in
respect that it was my il hap to kil his nephew *Eurileon*;
but how soeuer it be, I haue condiscended. But so will
not wee cryed almost the whole assemblie, councelling
one an other, rather to trye the vttermost euent, then
to loose him by whō they had beene victorious. But he
as well with generall orations, as particular dealing
with the men of most credit, made them throughly see
how necessary it was to preferree such an opportunity
before a vaine affection; but yet could not preuaile, til
openly he sware, that he would (if at any time the *Lacedæmonians* brake this treatie) come back againe, and be
their captaine.

2   So then after a few dayes, setling them in perfect order, hee tooke his leaue of them, whose eyes bad him
farwell with teares, & mouthes with kissing the places
where he stept, and after making temples vnto him as

to a demi-God: thinking it beyond the degree of humanitie to haue a witt so farre ouergoing his age, and such dreadful terror proceed from so excellent beutie. But he for his sake obtayned free pardon for *Argalus*, whom also (vppon oath neuer to beare armes againſt the *Helots*) he deliuered: and taking onely with him certaine principall Iewells of his owne, he would haue parted alone with *Argalus*, (whose countenaunce well ſhewed, while *Parthenia* was loſt he counted not himſelfe deliuered) but that the whole multitude would needs gard him into *Arcadia.* Where again leauing the all to lament his departure, he by enquirie gotte to the wel-knowne houſe of *Kalander*: There was he receiued with louing ioye of *Kalander*, with ioyfull loue of *Palladius*, with humble (though doulful) demeanor of *Argalus* (whom ſpecially both he and *Palladius* regarded) with gratefull ſeruiſablenes of *Clitophon*, and honourable admiration of all. For being now well veiwed to haue no haire of his face, to witnes him a man, who had done acts beyond the degree of a man, and to looke with a certaine almoſt baſhefull kinde of modeſtie, as if hee feared the eyes of men, who was vnmooued with ſight of the moſt horrible countenaunces of death; and as if nature had miſtaken her woorke to haue a *Marſes* heart in a *Cupides* bodye: All that beheld him (and al that might behold him, did behold him) made their eyes quicke meſsengers to their minds, that there they had ſeene the vttermoſt that in mankind might be ſeene. The like wonder *Palladius* had before ſtirred, but that *Daiphantus*, as younger and newer come, had gotten now the aduantage in the moyſt & fickle impreſsion of eye-ſight. But while all

men

men (sauing poore *Argalus*) made the ioy of their eyes speake for their harts towards *Daiphantus*: Fortune (that belike was bid to that banket, & ment then to play the good fellow) brought a pleasaut aduenture among the.

3　It was that as they had newly dined, there came in to *Kalander* a meſſenger, that brought him word, a young noble Lady, neere kinſwoman to the fair *Helen* Queene of *Corinth*; was come thether, and deſired to be lodged in his houſe. *Kalander* (moſt glad of ſuch an occaſion) went out, and all his other worthie gueſts with him, ſauing onely *Argalus*, who remained in his chamber, deſirous that this company were once broken vp, that he might goe in his ſolitarie queſt after *Parthenia*. But when they met this Lady; *Kalander* ſtreight thought he ſawe his neece *Parthenia*, and was about in ſuch familiar ſorte to haue ſpoken vnto her: But ſhe in graue and honorable manner giuing him to vnderſtand that he was miſtaken, he halfe aſhamed, excuſed himſelfe with the exceeding likenes was betwene them, though indeede it ſeemed that his Lady was of the more pure and daintie complexion; ſhee ſaid, it might very well be, hauing bene many times taken one for an other. But aſſoone as ſhe was brought into the houſe, before ſhe would reſt her, ſhe deſired to ſpeake with *Argalus* publickly, who ſhe heard was in the houſe. *Argalus* came in haſtely, and as haſtelie thought as *Kalander* had done, with ſodaine chaunges of ioye into ſorrow. But ſhe whē ſhe had ſtayd their thoughts with telling them her name, and qualitie in this ſort ſpake vnto him. My Lord *Argalus*, ſayd ſhe, being of late left in the court of Queene *Helen* of *Corinth*, as chiefe in her abſence (ſhe being vpō ſome occaſion gone thēce) there

there came vnto me the Lady *Parthenia*,ſo diſguyſed,as
I thinke Greece hath nothing ſo ougly to behold. For
my part, it was many dayes, before with vehement
oathes, and ſome good prooues, ſhe could make me
thinke that ſhe was *Parthenia*. Yet at laſt finding certen-
ly it was ſhe, and greatly pitying her misfortune, ſo
much the more, as that all men had euer told me, (as
now you doo)of the great likenes betweene vs,I tooke
the beſt care I could of herıand of her vnderſtood the
whole tragicall hiſtorie of her vndeſerued aduenture:
and therewithall,of that moſt noble conſtancie in you
my Lord *Argalus*: which whoſoeuer loues not, ſhewes
himſelfe to be a hater of vertue, and vnworthie to liue
in the ſocietie of mankind. But no outward cheriſhing
could ſalue the inward ſore of her minde, but a fewe
dayes ſince ſhee died : before her death earneſtly deſiring,and perſwading me,to thinke of no husbande but
of you; as of the onely man in the world worthie to be
loued;with-all, ſhe gaue me this Ring to deliuer you;
deſiring you, & by the authoritie of Ioue cõmaunding
you, that the affection you bare her you ſhould turne
to me: aſſuring you, that nothing can pleaſe her ſoule
more, then to ſee you and me matched together.Now
my L.though this office be not(perchance) ſutable to
my eſtate nor ſex,who ſhuld rather looke to be deſired;
yet, an extraordinarie deſert requires an extraordinarie
proceding: and therfore I am come(with faithfull loue
built vpõ your worthines)to offer my ſelf,& to beſeech
you to accept the offer:& if theſe noble gētlemē preſēr
will ſay it is great folly,let thē withal,ſay it is great loue.
And then ſhe ſtaid, earneſtly attending *Argalus* his anſwere,who(firſt making moſt hartie ſighes do ſuch ob-
ſequies as he could,to *Parthenia*)thus anſwered her.

L.ſa

4 Madame (faid he) infinitely bound am I vnto you, for this, no more rare, then noble courtefie; but moft bound for the goodnes I perceiue you fhewed to the lady *Parthenia*, (with that the teares ranne downe his eyes;but he followed on)and as much as fo vnfortunat a man,fitte to be the fpectacle of miferie, can doo you feruice; determine you haue made a purchafe of a flaue (while I liue) neuer to fayle you. But this great matter you propofe vnto me,wherein I am not fo blind,as not to fee what happines it fhould be vnto mee; Excellent Ladie,know,that if my hart were mine to giue,you before al other, fhould haue it;but *Parthenias* it is,though dead: there I began,there I end all matter of affection: I hope I fhall not long tarry after her,with whofe beautie if I had onely been in loue,I fhould be fo with you, who haue the fame beautie: but it was *Parthenias* felfe I loued,and loue;which no likenes can make one,no cõmaundement diffolue,no foulnes defile, nor no death finifh. And fhall I receiue (faid fhe) fuch difgrace,as to be refufed? Noble Ladie(faid he) let not that harde word be vfed;who know your exceeding worthinefse farre beyond my defert: but it is onely happinefse I refufe,fince of the onely happines I could and can defire, I am refufed.

5 He had fcarce fpoken thofe words, when fhe ranne to him,and imbrafing him, Why then *Argalus* (faide fhe) take thy *Parthenia*; and *Parthenia* it was in deede. But becaufe forow forbad him too foon to beleeue,fhe told him the trueth,with all circumftances; how being parted alone,meaning to die in fome folitarie place, as fhe hapned to make her complaint,the Queen *Helen* of *Corinth* (who likewife felt her part of miferies) being
then

then walking alſo alone in that louely place, heard
her, and neuer left, till ſhe had knowen the whole diſcourſe. Which the noble Queene greatly pittying, ſhe
ſent her to a Phiſition of hers, the moſt excellent man
in the worlde, in hope he could helpe her: which in
ſuch ſorte as they ſaw perfourmed, and ſhe taking with
her of the Queenes ſeruaunts, thought yet to make this
triall, whether he would quickly forget his true *Parthe-*
nia, or no. Her ſpeach was confirmed by the *Corinthian*
Gentlemen, who before had kept her counſell, and *Ar-*
galus eaſily perſwaded to what more then ten thouſand
yeares of life he deſired: and *Kalander* would needes
haue the mariage celebrated in his houſe, principallie
the longer to hold his deare gueſtes, towardes whom
he was now (beſides his owne habite of hoſpitalitie)
carried with loue and dutie: & therfore omitted no ſeruice that his wit could inuent, and his power miniſter.

CHAP. 8.

The aduentures¹ firſt of Muſidorus, ² *then of* Pyrocles *ſince*
their ſhipwracke, to their meeting.³ The mariage of Argalus *and* Parthenia.

Vt no waie he ſawe he could ſo
much pleaſure them, as by leauing
the two friends alone, who being
ſhruncke aſide to the banqueting
houſe where the pictures were;
there *Palladius* recounted vnto
him, that after they had both abã-
doned the burning ſhip (& either

F   of

of them taken some thing vnder him the better to sup-
porte him to the shore) he knew not how, but either
with ouer-labouring in the fight and sodaine colde,or
the too much receauing of salt water,he was past himselfe : but yet holding fast(as the nature of dying men
is to doo) the chest that was vnder him, he was cast on
the sandes , where he was taken vp by a couple of
Shepherds, and by them brought to life againe, and
kept from drowning him selfe, when he despaired of
his safetie. How after hauing failed to take him into
the fisher boate, he had by the Shepheards persuasion
come to this Gentlemans house;where being daunge-
rouslie sicke, he had yeelded to seeke the recouery of
health,onely for that he might the sooner go seeke the
deliuerie of *Pyrocles* : to which purpose *Kalander* by
some friends of his in *Messenia*, had alreadie set a ship
or two abroad, when this accident of *Clitophons* taking had so blessedly procured their meeting. Thē did
he set foorth vnto him the noble entertainement and
careful cherishing of *Kalander* towards him,& so vpon
occasiō of the pictures present deliuered with the frank-
nesse of a friends tongue,as neere as he could,word by
word what *Kalander* had told him touching the strange
storie(with al the particularities belonging) of *Arcadia*,
which did in many sortes so delight *Pyrocles* to heare;
that he would needs haue much of it againe repeated,
and was not contented till *Kalander* him selfe had answered him diuers questions.

2 But first at *Musidorus* request,though in brief māner,
his mind much running vpō the strange storie of *Arcadia*,he did declare by what course of aduētures.he was
come to make vp their mutuall happinesse in meeting.
                                                    When

When (cofin, faid he) we had ftript our felues, and were
both leapt into the Sea, and fwom a little toward the
fhoare, I found by reafon of fome wounds I had, that I
fhould not be able to get the lande, and therefore turned backe againe to the maft of the fhippe, where you
found me, affuring my felfe, that if you came aliue
to the fhore, you would feeke me ; if you were loft, as
I thought it as good to perifhe as to liue, fo that place
as good to perifh in as an other. There I found my
fworde among fome of the fhrowds, wifhing (I muft
confeffe) if I died, to be found with that in my hand,
and withall wauing it about my head, that faylers by
it might haue the better glimpfe of me. There you
miffing me, I was taken vp by Pyrates, who putting
me vnder boorde prifoner, prefentlie fett vppon another fhippe, and mainteining a long fight, in the
ende, put them all to the fworde. Amongft whom
I might heare them greatlie prayfe one younge man,
who fought moft valiantlie, whom (as loue is carefull, and misfortune fubiect to doubtfulnes) I thought
certainely to be you. And fo holding you as dead,
from that time till the time I fawe you, in trueth I
fought nothing more then a noble ende, which perchance made me more hardie then otherwife I would
haue bene. Triall whereof came within two dayes
after : for the Kinges of *Lacedæmon* hauing fett out
fome Galleys, vnder the charge of one of their Ne-
phews to skowre the Sea of the Pyrates, they met with
vs, where our Captaine wanting men, was driuen
to arme fome of his prifoners, with promife of libertie for well fighting : among whom I was one, and
being boorded by the Admirall, it was my fortune to

kil

kil *Eurileon* the Kings nephew: but in the end they preuailed, & we were all takē priſoners: I not caring much
what became of me (onely keeping the name of *Daiphantus*, according to the reſolution you know is betweene vs,) but beyng laid in the iayle of *Tenaria*, with
ſpeciall hate to me for the death of *Eurileon*, the popular ſort of that towne conſpired with the *Helots*, and ſo
by night opened them the gates; where entring and
killing all of the gentle and riche faction, for honeſtie
ſake brake open all priſons, and ſo deliuered me; and
I mooued with gratefulneſſe, and encouraged with
careleſneſſe of life, ſo behaued my ſelfe in ſome conflictes they had in fewe dayes, that they barbarouſlie
thinking vnſenſible wonders of mee, and withall ſo
much they better truſting mee, as they heard I was
hated of the Kinge of *Lacedæmon*, (their chiefe Cap-
tayne beyng ſlaine as you knowe by the noble *Argalus*, who helped therevnto by his perſwaſion) hauing borne a great affection vnto me, and to auoyde
the daungerous emulation whiche grewe among the
chiefe, who ſhould haue the place, and all ſo affected,
as rather to haue a ſtraunger then a competitour, they
elected mee, (God wotte little prowde of that dignitie,) reſtoring vnto mee ſuch thinges of mine as being
taken firſt by the pyrates, and then by the *Lacedæmonians*, they had gotten in the ſacke of the towne. Now
being in it, ſo good was my ſucceſſe with manie victories, that I made a peace for them to their owne
liking, the verie daie that you deliuered *Clitophon*,
whom I with much adoo had preſerued. And in my
peace the King *Amiclas* of *Lacedæmon* would needes
haue mee banniſhed, and depriued of the dignitie
where-

whereunto I was exalted: which (and you may fee
howe much you are bounde to mee) for your fake
I was content to fuffer, a newe hope rifing in mee,
that you were not dead: and fo meaning to trauaile
ouer the worlde to feeke you ; and now here (my
deere *Mufidorus*) you haue mee. And with that(embracing and kiffinge each other) they called *Kalander*, of whom *Daiphantus* defired to heare the full ftorie, which before hee had recounted to *Palladius*, and
to fee the letter of *Philanax*, which hee read and well
marked.

But within fome daies after, the marriage betweene
Argalus and the faire *Parthenia* beyng to be celebrated, *Daiphantus* and *Palladius* felling fome of their iewels, furnifhed themfelues of very faire apparell, meaning to doo honour to their louing hofte ; who as
much for their fakes, as for the marriage, fet foorth
each thing in moft gorgeous manner. But all the coſt
beftowed did not fo much enrich, nor all the fine dec-
kinges fo much beautifie, nor all the daintie deuifes
fo much delight, as the faireneffe of *Parthenia*, the
pearle of all the maydes of *Mantinæa*: who as fhee
went to the Temple to bee maried, her eyes themfelues feemed a temple, wherein loue and beautie were
married: her lippes, although they were kepte clofe
with modeft filence, yet with a pretie kinde of naturall fwelling, they feemed to inuite the gueftes that
lookt on them; her checkes blufhing, and withal when
fhee was fpoken vnto, a little fmilyng, were like rofes,
when their leaues are with a little breath ftirred: her
hayre being layed at the full length downe her backe,
bare fhewe as if the voward fayled, yet that would

conquer.

conquere. *Daiphantus* marking her, O *Iupiter* (said he
speaking to *Palladius*) how happens it, that Beautie is
onely confined to *Arcadia*? But *Palladius* not greatly attending his speach, some daies were continued in the
solemnising the marriage, with al conceipts that might
deliuer delight to mens fancies.

CHAP. 9.

Pyrocles *his inclination to loue.* ² *His, and* Musidorus
disputation thereabouts ³ *broken of by* Kalander.

Vt such a chaunge was growen in
Daiphantus, that (as if cheerefulnesse had bene tediousnesse, and
good entertainement were turnd
to discourtesie) he would euer get
him selfe alone, though almost
when he was in compani ne was
alone, so little attention he gaue to
any that spake vnto him: euen the colour and figure of
his face began to receaue some alteration ; which he
shewed little to heede : but euerie morning earlie going abroad, either to the garden, or to some woods towards the desert, it seemed his only comfort was to be
without a cóforter. But long it could not be hid from
Palladius, whom true loue made redy to marke, & long
knowledge able to marke; & therfore being nowgrowê
weary of his abode in *Arcadia*, hauing informed himselfe fully of the strength & riches of the coûtry, of the
nature of the people, and manner of their lawes ; and,

leing

feing the courte could not be vifited, prohibited to
all men, but to certaine fheapheardifh people, he greatly defired a fpeedy returne to his own countrie, after
the many mazes of fortune he had troden. But perceauing this great alteration in his friend, he thought firft
to breake with him thereof, and then to haften his returne; whereto he founde him but fmally enclined:
whereupon one day taking him alone with certaine
graces and countenances, as if he were difputing with
the trees, began in this manner to fay vnto him.
A mind wel trayned and long exercifed in vertue (my **2**
fweete and worthy cofin) doth not eafily chaunge any
courfe it once vndertakes, but vpon well grounded &
well wayed caufes. For being witnes to it felfe of his
owne inward good, it findes nothing without it of fo
high a price, for which it fhould be altered . Euen
the very countenaunce and behauiour of fuch a man
doth fhew forth Images of the fame conftancy , by
maintaining a right harmonie betwixt it and the inward good , in yeelding it felfe futable to the vertuous refolution of the minde. This fpeech I direct
to you (noble friend *Pyrocles*) the excellencie of whofe
minde and well chofen courfe in vertue, if I doo not
fufficiently know , hauing feene fuch rare demonftra-
tions of it, it is my weakenes, and not your vnworthines . But as in deede I know it, and knowing
it, moft dearely loue both it; and him that hath it;
fo muft I needs faye, that fince our late comming
into this country, I haue marked in you , I will not fay
an alteratiõ, but a relenting truely, & a flacking of the
maine career, you had fo notably begon, & almoft performed

formed ; and that in ſuch ſorte, as I cannot finde ſufficient reaſon in my great loue toward you how to allow it ; for (to leaue of other ſecreter argumcnts which
my acquaintaunce with you makes me eaſily finde)
this in effect to any manne may be manyfeſt , that
whereas you were wont in all places you came ,
to giue your ſelfe vehemently to the knowledge
of thoſe thinges which might better your minde;
to ſeeke the familiaritye of excellent men in learning
and ſouldiery : and laſtly, to put all theſe thinges in
practiſe both by continuall wiſe proceedinge, and
worthie enterpriſes, as occaſion fell for them ; you
now leaue all theſe things vndone : you let your minde
fal aſleepe : beſide your countenaunce troubled (which
ſurely comes not of vertue; for vertue like the cleare
heauen, is without cloudes) and laſtly you ſubiect your
ſelfe to ſolitarines, the ſlye enimie , that doth moſt ſe-
parate a man from well doing . *Pyrocles* minde was
all this while ſo fixed vpon another deuotion, that he
no more attentiuely marked his friends diſcourſe, then
the childe that hath leaue to playe, markes the laſt part
of his leſson ; or the diligent Pilot in a daungerous
tempeſt doth attend the vnſkilful words of a paſſinger :
yet the very ſound hauing imprinted the general point
of his ſpeech in his hart, pierced with any miſlike of
ſo deerely an eſteemed friend, and deſirous by degrees
to bring him to a gentler conſideration of him, with a
ſhamefaſt looke (witneſſing he rather could not helpe,
then did not know his fault) anſwered him to this purpoſe . Excellent *Muſidorus*, in the praiſe you gaue me in
the beginning of your ſpech, I eaſily acknowledge the
force of your good will vnto mee, for neither coulde
you

you haue thought fo well of me, if extremitie of loue
had not made your iudgement partiall, nor you could
haue loued me fo intierlie, if you had not beene apt to
make fo great (though vndeferued) iudgements of me;
and euen fo muft I fay to thofe imperfections, to which
though I haue euer through weaknes been fubiect, yet
you by the daily meding of your mind haue of late bin
able to looke into them, which before you could not
difcerne; fo that the chaunge you fpeake of, falles not
out by my impairing, but by your betring. And yet vnder the leaue of your better iudgement, I muft needes
fay thus much, my deere cofin, that I find not my felfe
wholye to be condemned, becaufe I do not with continuall vehemecy folow thofe knowledges, which you
call the bettering of my minde; for both the minde it
felfe muft (like other thinges) fometimes be vnbent,
or elfe it will be either weakned, or broken: And thefe
knowledges, as they are of good vfe, fo are they not all
the minde may ftretch it felfe vnto : who knowes whether I feede not my minde with higher thoughts. Tru-
lie as I know not all the particularities, fo yet I fee
the bounds of all thefe knowledges: but the workings
of the minde I finde much more infinite, then can be
led vnto by the eye, or imagined by any, that diftract
their thoughts without themfelues. And in fuch contemplation, or as I thinke more excellent, I enioye my
folitarines; and my folitarines perchaunce is the nurfe
of thefe contemplations. Eagles we fee fly alone; and
they are but fheepe, which alvvaies heard together; co-
demne not therefore my minde fomtime to enioy it
felfe; nor blaine not the taking of fuch times as ferue
moft fitte for it. And alas, deere *Mufidorus*, if I be fadde,
vvho

who knowes better then you the iuſt cauſes I haue of
ſadnes? And here *Pyrocles* ſodainly ſtopped, like a man
vnſatiſſied in himſelfe, though his witte might wel haue
ſerued to haue ſatiſſied another. And ſo looking with
a countenaunce, as though he deſired he ſhould know
his minde without hearing him ſpeake, and yet deſirous to ſpeake, to breath out ſome part of his inward
euill, ſending againe new blood to his face, he continued his ſpeach in this manner. And Lord (dere coſin,
ſaid he) doth not the pleaſauntnes of this place carry in
it ſelfe ſufficienr reward for any time loſt in it? Do you
not ſee how all things conſpire together to make this
coũtry a heauenly dwelling? Do you not ſee the graſſe
how in colour they excell the Emeralds, euerie one
ſtriuing to paſſe his fellow, and yet they are all kept of
an equal height? And ſee you not the reſt of theſe beautifull flowers, each of which would require a mans wit
to know, and his life to expreſſe? Do not theſe ſtately
trees ſeeme to maintaine their floriſhing olde age with
the onely happines of their ſeat, being clothed with a
continuall ſpring, becauſe no beautie here ſhould euer
fade? Doth not the aire breath health, which the Birds
(delightfull both to eare and eye) do dayly ſolemnize
with the ſweet cõſent of their voyces? Is not euery *eccho*
therof a perfect Muſicke? and theſe freſh and delightful
brookes how ſlowly they ſlide away, as loth to leaue
the company of ſo many things vnited in perfection?
and with how ſweete a murmure they lament their
forced departure? Certainelie, certainely, coſin, it muſt
needes be that ſome Goddeſſe enhabiteth this Region, who is the ſoule of this ſoile: for neither is any,
leſſe then a Goddeſſe, worthie to be ſhrined in ſuch
a heap of pleaſures: nor any leſſe thẽ a Goddeſſe, could
haue

haue made it fo perfect a plotte of the celeftiall dwellings. And fo ended with a deep figh, rufully cafting his
eye vpon *Mufidorus*, as more defirous of pittie thē plea-
ding. But *Mufidorus* had all this while helde his looke
fixed vpon *Pyrocles* countenance; and with no leffe louing attention marked how his words proceeded from
him: but in both thefe he perceiued fuch ftrange diuer-
fities, that they rather increafed new doubts, then gaue
him ground to fettle any iudgement : for, befides his
eyes fometimes euen great with teares, the oft chāging
of his colour, with a kind of fhaking vnftayednes ouer
all his body, he might fee in his countēnace fome great
determinatiō mixed with feare ; and might perceiue in
him ftore of thoughts, rather ftirred then digefted ; his
words interrupted continually with fighes (which ferued as a burthen to each fentence) and the tenor of his
fpeech (though of his wōted phrafe) not knit together
to one conftāt end, but rather diffolued in it felfe, as the
vehemencie of the inwarde paffion preuayled : which
made *Mufidorus* frame his aunfwere neereft to that humor, which fhould fooheft put out the fecret. For, hauing in the beginning of *Pyrocles* fpeech which defēded
his folitarines, framed in his minde a replie againft it, in
the praife of honourable action, in fhewing that fuch a
kind of cōtēplatiō is but a glorious title to idlenes; that
in actiō a man did not onely better himfelf, but benefit
others; that the gods would not haue deliuered a foule
into the body, which hath armes & legges, only inftru-
mēts of doing, but that it wer intēded the mind fhould
imploy thē; & that the mind fhould beft know his own
good or euill, by practife : which knowledge was the
onely way to increafe the one, and correct the other:
befides many other argumentes, which the plentiful-
neffe of the matter yeelded to the fharpnes of his wit.

When he found *Pyrocles* leaue that, and fall into ſuch an affected praiſing of the place, he left it likewiſe, and ioyned with him therein: becauſe he found him in that humor vtter more ſtore of paſſion; and euen thus kindly embraſing him, he ſaid: Your words are ſuch (noble couſin) ſo ſweetly and ſtrongly handled in the praiſe of ſolitarineſſe, as they would make me likewiſe yeeld my ſelfe vp into it, but that the ſame words make me know, it is more pleaſant to enioy the companie of him that can ſpeake ſuch words, then by ſuch wordes to be perſwaded to follow ſolitarines. And euen ſo doo I giue you leaue (ſweet *Pyrocles*) euer to defend ſolitarines; ſo long, as to defende it, you euer keep companie. But I maruell at the exceſſiue praiſes you giue to this countrie; in trueth it is not vnpleaſant: but yet if you would returne into *Macedon*, you ſhould ſee either many heauens, or find this no more then earthly. And euē *Tempe* in my *Theſſalia*, (where you & I to my great happineſſe were brought vp together) is nothing inferiour vnto it. But I think you will make me ſee, that the vigor of your witte can ſhew it ſelfe in any ſubiect: or els you feede ſometimes your ſolitarines with the conceites of the Poets, whoſe liberall pennes can as eaſilie trauaile ouer mountaines, as molehils: and ſo like wel diſpoſed men, ſet vp euery thing to the higheſt note; eſpecially, when they put ſuch words in the mouths of one of theſe fantaſticall mind-infected people, that children & Muſitiãs cal Louers. This word, Louer, did no leſſe pearce poore *Pyrocles*, then the right tune of muſicke toucheth him that is ſick of the *Tarantula*. There was not one part of his body, that did not feele a ſodaine motion, while his hart with panting, ſeemed to daunce to the ſounde of

that

that word;yet after some pause(lifting vp his eyes a litle
from the ground, and yet not daring to place them in
the eyes of *Musidorus*)armed with the verie coūtenance
of the poore prisoner at the barr,whose aunswere is nothing but guiltie:with much a do he brought forth this
question.And alas,saide he, deare cosin,what if I be
not so much the Poet (the freedome of whose penne
canne exercise it selfe in any thing) as euen that miserable subiect of his conning, whereof you speake?
Now the eternall Gods forbid (mainely cryed out
Musidorus) that euer my eare should be poysoned with
so euill newes of you . O let me neuer know that any
base affectiō shuld get any Lordship in your thoughts.
But as he was speaking more,*Kalander* came,and brake
of their discourse,with inuiting thē to the hunting of a
goodly stagge,which beeing harbored in a wood therby,he hoped would make them good sporte,and driue
away some part of *Daiphantus* melancholy. They condiscended,& so going to their lodgings, furnished thē
selues as liked them *Daiphantus* writing a fevv vvordes
vvhich he left in a sealed letter against their returne.

CHAP. 10.

Kalanders *hunting.* ¹ Daiphantus *his close departure,* ²
and letter ³ Palladius *his care,and* ⁴ *quest after him,*
⁵ *accompanied with* Clitophon. ⁶ *His finding and*
taking on Amphilus *his armor* ⁷ *Their encounter*
with Queene Helens *attendants.* ⁸ *Her mistaking* Palladius.

Hen went they together abroad, the good
Kalander entertaining thē, with pleasaunt
discoursing,howe well he loued the sporte
of hunting vvhen he was a young man,
hovv

how much in the comparison thereof he difdained all
chamber delights ; that the Sunne (how great a iornie
foeuer he had to make) could neuer preuent him with
earlines,nor the Moone(with her fober countenance)
diffwade him from watching till midnight for the
deeres feeding O,faide he, you vvill neuer liue to my
age, vvithout you kepe your felues in breath vvith exercife,and in hart vvith ioyfullnes :too much thinking
doth confume the fpirits:& oft it falles out,that vvhile
one thinkes too much of his doing, he leaues to doe
the effect of his thinking . Then fpared he not to remember how much *Arcadia* was chaunged fince his
youth:actiuitie &good felowfhip being nothing in the
price it was then held in,but according to the nature of
the old growing world,ftill worfe & worfe.The would
he tell them ftories of fuch gallaunts as he had knowen:
and fo with pleafant com pany beguiled the times haft,
and fhortned the wayes length, till they came to the
fide of the wood, where the houndes were in couples
ftaying their comming,but with a whining Accent crauing libertie : many of them in colour and marks fo refembling , that it fhowed they were of one kinde.
The huntfmen handfomely attired in their greene liueries , as though they were children of Sommer,
with ftaues in their hands to beat the guiltleffe earth,
when the houndes were at a fault, and with hornes a-
bout their neckes to founde an alarum vpon a fillie fugitiue . The houndes were ftraight vncoupled, and
ere long the Stagge thought it better to truft the nimblenes of his feete, then to the flender fortification of
his lodging: but euen his feete betrayed him;for howfoeuer they went, they themfelues vttered themfelues
to the fent of their enimies ; who one taking it of an
other

other, and fometimes beleeuing the windes aduertife-ments, fometimes the view of (their faithfull councel-lors) the huntfmen, with open mouthes then denoun-ced warre, when the warre was alreadie begun. Their crie being compofed of fo well forted mouthes, that a-ny man would perceiue therein fome kind of proporti-on, but the skilfull woodmen did finde a mufick. Then delight and varietie of opinion drew the horfinen fun-drie wayes; yet cheering their houndes with voyce and horn, kept ftill (as it were) together. The wood feemed to confpire with them againft his own citizens, difper-fing their noife through all his quarters; and euen the Nimph *Echo* left to bewayle the loffe of *Narciffus*, and became a hunter. But the Stagge was in the end fo hot-ly purfued, that (leauing his flight) he was driuen to make courage of defpaire; & fo turning his head, made the hounds (with change of fpeech) to teftifie that he was at bay : as if from hotte purfuite of their enemie, they were fodainly come to a parley.

But *Kalander* (by his skill of coafting the Countrey) was among the firft that came in to the befiged Deere; whom when fome of the younger fort would haue kil-led with their fwordes, he woulde not fuffer: but with a Croffebowe fent a death to the poore beaft, who with teares fhewed the vnkindneffe he tooke of mans crueltie.

But by the time that the whole companie was affem-bled, and that the Stagge had beftowed himfelfe libe-rally among them that had killed him, *Daiphantus* was mift, for whom *Palladius* carefully enquiring, no newes could be giuen him, but by one that fayd, he thought
he

he was returned home ; for that he markt him , in the chiefe of the hunting , take a by way, which might lead to *Kalanders* houſe. That anſwer for the time ſatisfying, and they hauing perfourmed all dueties, as well for the Stagges funeral, as the hounds triumph, they returned: ſome talking of the fatnes of the Deeres bodie; ſome of the fairenes of his head; ſome of the hounds cunning; ſome of their ſpeed; and ſome of their cry: til comming home (about the time that the candle begins to inherit the Suns office) they found *Daiphantus* was not to bee found. Whereat *Palladius* greatly maruailing, and a day or two paſſing, while neither ſearch nor inquirie could help him to knowledge, at laſt he lighted vpon the letter, which *Pyrocles* had written before hee went a hunting, and left in his ſtudie among other of his writings. The letter was directed to *Palladius* himſelfe , and conteyned theſe words.

3   My onely friend , violence of loue leades me into ſuch a courſe, wherof your knowledge may much more vexe you, then help me. Therefore pardon my concealing it from you, ſince : if I wrong you, it is in reſpect I beare you . Returne into *Theſſalia,* I pray you , as full of good fortune, as I am of deſire: and if I liue, I will in ſhort time follow you; if I die, loue my memorie.

4   This was all, and this *Palladius* read twiſe or thriſe ouer. Ah (ſaid he) *Pyrocles,* vvhat meanes this alteratiõ? vvhat haue I deſerued of thee , to be thus baniſhed of thy counſels ? Heretofore I haue accuſed the ſea , condemned the Pyrats , and hated my euill fortune , that depriued me of thee; But now thy ſelf is the ſea, vvhich drounes my comfort , thy ſelfe is the Pirat that robbes thy ſelfe of me: Thy ovvne vvill becomes my euill for-

tune

tune. Thē turned he his thoughts to al forms of gheſſes
that might light vpon the purpoſe and courſe of *Pyro-*
cles : for he was not ſo ſure by his wordes, that it was
loue, as he was doubtful where the loue was. One time
he thought, ſome beautie in *Laconia* had layed hold of
his eyes; an other time he feared, that it might be *Par-*
thenias excellencie, which had broken the bands of all
former reſolution. But the more he thought, the more
he knew not what to thinke, armies of obiections riſing againſt any accepted opinion.

Then as carefull he was what to doo himſelfe : at 5
length determined, neuer to leaue ſeeking him, till his
ſearch ſhould be either by meeting accōpliſhed, or by
death ended. Therfore (for all the vnkindneſſe bearing
tender reſpect, that his friends ſecrete determination
ſhould be kept from any ſuſpition in others) he went
to *Kalander*, and told him, that he had receaued a meſſage from his friend, by which he vnderſtood he was
gone backe againe into *Laconia*, about ſome matters
greatly importing the poore men, whoſe protection he had vndertaken, and that it was in any ſorte fit
for him, to follow him, but in ſuch priuate wiſe, as not
to be knowne, and that therefore he would as then bid
him farewell : arming him ſelfe in a blacke armour, as
either a badge, or prognoſtication of his mind : and taking onely with him good ſtore of monie, and a fewe
choiſe iewels, leauing the greateſt number of them, &
moſt of his apparell with *Kalander* : which he did partly
to giue the more cauſe to *Kalander* to expect their return, & ſo to be the leſſe curiouſly inquiſitiue after thē :
and partly to leaue thoſe honorable thankes vnto him,
for his charge & kindnes, which he knew he would no
other way receaue. The good old man hauing nei-

ther reafon to diffuade , nor hope to perfuade , receaued the things,with mind of a keeper,not of an owner;
but before he went , defired he might haue the happines, fully to know what they were : which he faid , he
had euer till then delaid, fearing to be any way impor-
tune : but now he could not be fo much an enemie to
his defires as any longer to imprifon thē in filence. *Palladius* tolde him that the matter was not fo fecrete , but
that fo worthie a friend deferued the knowledge , and
fhuld haue it as foone as he might fpeak with his friéd:
without whofe confent (becaufe their promife bound
him otherwife) he could not reueale it : but bad him
hold for moft affured, that if they liued but a while,he
fhould find that they which bare the names of *Daiphātus* and *Palladius*,would giue him & his caufe to thinke
his noble courtefie wel imploied.*Kalāder* would preffe
him no further : but defiring that he might haue leaue
to go, or at leaft to fende his fonne and feruaunts with
him, *Palladius* brake of all ceremonies , by telling him;
his cafe ftood fo , that his greateft fauour fhould be in
making left adoo of his parting. Wherewith *Kalander*
knowing it to be more cumber then courtefie,toftriue,
abftained from further vrging him,but not from hartie
mourning the loffe of fo fweet a conuerfation.

6   Onely *Clitophon* by vehement importunitie obteyned to go with him, to come againe to *Daiphantus*,
whom he named and accoūted his Lord. And in fuch
priuate guife departed *Palladius*,though hauing a com-
paniō to talke with all,yet talking much more with vnkindneffe. And firft they went to *Mantinæa*; whereof
becaufe *Parthenia* was , he fufpected there might be
fome caufe of his abode . But finding there no newes
of him he went to *Tegæa, Ripa, Eniſpæ, Stimphalus,* and
                                                    Pheneus,

Pheneus, famous for the poifonous *Stygian* water, and through all the reft of *Arcadia*, making their eyes, their eares, and their tongue ferue almoft for nothing, but that enquirie. But they could know nothing but that in none of thofe places he was knowne. And fo went they, making one place fucceed to an other, in like vncertaintie to their fearch, manie times encountring ftrange aduétures, worthy to be regiftred in the roulles of fame; but this may not be omitted. As they paft in a pleafant valley, (of either fide of which high hils lifted vp their beetle-browes, as if they would ouer looke the pleafantnes of their vnder-profpect) they were by the daintines of the place, & the wearines of thefelues, inuited to light frō their horfes; & pulling of their bits, that they might fomething refrefh their mouths vpon the graffe (which plentifully grewe, brought vp vnder the care of thofe wel fhading trees,) they thefelues laid thē downe hard by the murmuring muficke of certain waters, which fpouted out of the fide of the hils, and in the bottome of the valley, made of many fprings a pretie brooke, like a common-wealth of many families: but when they had a while harkened to the perfuafion of fleepe, they rofe, and walkt onward in that fhadie place, till *Clitiphon* efpied a peece of armour, & not far of an other peece: and fo the fight of one peece teaching him to looke for more, he at length found all, with headpeece & fhield, by the deuife whereof, which was he ftreight knew it to be the armour of his coufin, the noble *Amphialus*. Wherupon (fearing fome incóuenience hapned vnto him) he told both his doubte, and his caufe of doubte to *Palladius*, who (confidering therof) thought beft to make no longer ftay, but to follow on: leaft perchance fome violēce

were offered to ſo worthy a Knight,whom the fame of
the world ſeemed to ſet in ballance with any Knight liuing. Yet with a ſodaine conceipt,hauing long borne
great honour to the name of *Amphialus*, *Palladius*
thought beſt to take that armour, thinking thereby to
learne by them that ſhould know that armour,ſome
newes of *Amphialus*,& yet not hinder him in the ſearch
of *Daiphantus* too.So he by the help of *Clitophon* quickly put on that armour,whereof there was no one piece
wanting, though hacked in ſome places, bewraying
ſome fight not long ſince paſſed.It was ſome-thing too
great, but yet ſerued well enough.

8   And ſo getting on their horſes, they trauailed but a
little way, when in opening of the mouth of the valley
into a faire field, they met with a coach drawne with
foure milke-white horſes,furniſhed all in blacke,with a
black a more boy vpo euery horſe,they al apparelled in
white,the coach it ſelf very richly furniſhed in black &
white. But before they could come ſo neere as to diſcerne what was within, there came running vpõ them
aboue a doſen horſmen, who cried to thẽ to yeeld thẽ-
ſelues priſoners, or els they ſhould die. But *Palladius*
hot accuſtomed to grant ouer the poſſeſſiõ of him ſelf
vpon ſo vniuſt titles, with ſword drawne gaue them ſo
rude an anſwer, that diuers of thẽ neuer had breath to
reply again: for being wel backt by *Clitophon*,& hauing
an excellẽt horſe vnder him,when he was ouerpreſt by
ſome,he auoided them,and ere th'other thought of it,
puniſhed in him his fellowes faults : and ſo, ether with
cunning or with force, or rather with a cunning force,
left none of them either liuing, or able to make his life
ſerue to others hurt. Which being done,he approched
the coach,aſſuring the black boies they ſhould haue no
                                                    hurt

hurt,who were els readie to haue run away, &looking
into the coach, he foūd in the one end a Lady of great
beautie, & such a beautie, as shewed forth the beames
both of wisdome & good nature, but al as much darkened,as might be,with sorow. In the other,two Ladies,
(who by their demeanure shewed well, they were but
her seruants) holding before them a picture ; in which
was a goodly Gētleman(whom he knew not)painted,
hauing in their faces a certaine waiting sorrow, their
eies being infected with their mistres weeping

But the chiefe Ladie hauing not so much as once 9
heard the noise of this cōflict(so had sorow closed vp al
the entries of her mind,&loue tied her seces to that beloued picture) now the shadow of him falling vpō the
picture made her cast vp her eie, and seeing the armour
which too wel she knew,thinking him to be *Amphialus*
the Lord of her desires,(bloud cōming more freely into her cheekes,as though it would be bold,& yet there
growing new againe pale for feare)with a pitiful looke
(like one vniustly condēned) My Lord *Amphialus*(said
she)you haue enough punished me:it is time for cruelty to leaue you,& euil fortune me;if not I pray you, (&
to graunt,my praier fitter time nor place you can haue)
accomplish the one euen now,& finish the other.With
that, sorrow impatient to be slowly vttered in her ofte
staying speeches,poured it selfso fast in teares, that *Palladius* could not hold her longer in errour, but pulling
of his helmet,Madame(said he)I perceaue you mistake
me:I am a stranger in these parts,set vpon(without any
cause giuē by me)by some of your seruants, whom because I haue in my iust defence euill entreated, I came
to make my excuse to you,whom seing such as I doo,I
find greater cause, why I should craue pardon of you.

When

When she saw his face, & heard his speech, she looked out of the coach, and seing her men, some slaine, some lying vnder their dead horses, and striuing to get from vnder them, without making more account of the matter, Truely (said she) they are well serued that durst lift vp their armes against that armour. But Sir Knight, (said she) I pray you tell me, how come you by this armour? for if it be by the death of him that owed it, then haue I more to say vnto you. *Palladius* assured her it was not so; telling her the true manner how he found it. It is like enough (said she) for that agrees with the manner he hath lately vsed. But I beseech you Sir (said she) since your prowes hath bereft me of my cōpany : let it yet so farre heale the woundes it selfe hath giuen, as to garde me to the next towne. How great so euer my businesse be fayre Ladie (said he) it shall willingly yeeld to so noble a cause : But first euen by the fauour you beare to the Lorde of this noble armour, I coniure you to tell me the storie of your fortune herein, lest hereafter when the image of so excellent a Ladie in so straunge a plight come before mine eyes, I condemne my selfe of want of consideration in not hauing demaunded thus much. Neither aske I it without protestation, that wherein my sworde and faith may auaile you, they shall binde themselues to your seruice. Your coniuration, fayre Knight (said she) is too strong for my poore spirite to disobey, and that shall make me (without any other hope, my ruine being but by one vnrelieueable) to graunt your wil herein : and to say the truth, a straunge nicenesse were it in me to refraine that from the eares of a person representing so much worthinesse, which I am glad euen to rockes and woods to vtter.

CHAP.

CHAP. 11.

The story of Queene Helen ` Philoxenus *her suiter* : Amphialus *an intercessor for his friende*. ` *His praises,* ` *birth, and* ` *education*. ` *Her loue wonne to himselfe* ` *His refusall and departure* ` Philoxenus *wronge-rage against him*. ` ` *Their fight*. ` ` *The death of sonne and father*. ` ` Amphialus *his sorrow and detestation of the* Queene. ` ` *A new onset on* Palladius *for* Amphialus *his Armour* : ` ` *whose griefe is amplified by meeting his dead frends dog*. ` ` Palladius *his parting with* Helen *and* Clitophon.

Now you then that my name is *Helen*, Queene by birth : and hetherto possession of the faire Citie and territorie of *Corinth*. I can say no more of my selfe, but beloued of my people : and may iustly say, beloued, since they are content to beare with my absence, and folly. But I being left by my fathers death, and accepted by my people, in the highest degree, that countrie could receiue ; assoone, or rather, before that my age was ripe for it ; my court quickely swarmed full of suiters ; some perchaunce louing my state, others my person, but once I know all of them, howsoeuer my possessions were in their harts, my beauty (such as it is) was in their mouthes ; many strangers of princely and noble blood, and all of mine owne country, to whom ether birth or vertue gaue courage to avowe so high a desire.

G 4   Among

2   Among the reft, or rather before the reft, was the Lord *Philoxenus,*fonne and heire to the vertuous noble man *Timotheus* : which *Timotheus* was a man both in power, riches, parentage,and (which paffed all thefe) goodnes, and (which followed all thefe) loue of the people, beyond any of the great men of my countrie.Now this fonne of his I muft fay truly,not vnworthy of fuch a father, bending himfelfe by all meanes of feruifeablenes to mee,and fetting foorth of himfelfe to win my fauour,wan thus farre of mee, that in truth I leffe mifliked him then any of the reft : which in fome proportion my countenaunce deliuered vnto him. Though I muft proteft it was a verie falfe embaffadour, if it deliuered at all any affection,whereof my hart was vtterly void,I as then efteeming my felfe borne to rule, & thinking foule fcorne willingly to fubmit my felfe to be ruled.

3   But whiles *Philoxenus* in good forte purfued my fauour,and perchaunce nourifhed himfelfe with ouer much hope, becaufe he found I did in fome forte acknowledge his valew, one time among the reft he brought with him a deare friend of his. With that fhe loked vpon the picture before her, & ftraight fighed,& ftraight teares followed,as if the Idol of dutie ought to be honoured with fuch oblations, and the her fpeach ftaied the tale,hauing brought her to that loke,but that looke hauing quite put her out of her tale.But *Palladius* greatly pitying fo fweete a forrow in a Ladie,whom by fame he had already knowen,and honoured,befought her for her promife fake, to put filence fo longe vnto her moning,til fhe had recounted the reft of this ftory.

4   Why faid fhe, this is the picture of *Amphialus*: what neede I fay more to you: what eare is fo barbarous but

hath

hath hard of *Amphialus?* who follows deeds of Armes, but euery where findes monumēt of *Amphialus?* who is courteous, noble, liberall, but he that hath the example before his eyes of *Amphialus?* where are all heroicall parts, but in *Amphialus?* O *Amphialus* I would thou were not so excellent, or I would I thought thee not so excellent, and yet would I not, that I would so: with that she wept againe, til he againe folliciting the conclusion of her story. Then must you (said she) know the story of *Amphialus:* for his will is my life, his life my history: and indeed, in what can I better employ my lippes, then in speaking of *Amphialus?*

This knight then whose figure you see, but whose mind can be painted by nothing, but by the true shape of vertue, is brothers sonne to *Basilius* King of *Arcadia,* and in his childhood esteemed his heir: till *Basilius* in his olde yeeres marrying a young and a faire Lady, had of her those two daughters, so famous for their perfection in beauty: which put by their young cosin from that expectation. Whereupon his mother (a woman of a hauty hart, being daughter to the King of *Argos*, either disdaining, or fearing, that her sonne should liue vnder the power of *Basilius* sent him to that Lorde *Timotheus* (betwene whom and her dead husband ther had passed streight bands of mutuall hospitality to be brought vp in company with his sonne *Philoxenus?*

A happie resolution for *Amphialus*, whose excellent nature was by this meanes trayned on with as good education, as any Princes sonne in the world could haue, which otherwise it is thought his mother (farre vnworthie of such a sonne) would not haue giuer him. The good *Timotheus*) no lesse louing him
then

then his owne ſonne : well they grew in yeeres; and
ſhortly occaſions fell aptly to trie *Amphialus*, and all
occaſions were but ſteppes for him to clime fame by.
Nothing was ſo hard, but his valour ouercame: which
yet ſtill he ſo guided with true vertue, that although no
man was in our parts ſpoken of but he, for his māhood,
yet, as though therein he excelled him ſelfe, he was cō-
monly called the courteous *Amphialus* . An endleſſe
thing it were for me to tell, how many aduentures (terrible to be ſpoken of) he atchieued : what monſters,
what Giants, what conqueſt of countries : ſometimes
vſing policy, ſome times force, but alwaies vertue, well
followed, and but followed by *Philoxenus* : betweene
whom, and him, ſo faſt a friendſhip by education was
knit , that at laſt *Philoxenus* hauing no greater matter to
employ his frindſhip in, then to winne me, therein deſired, and had his vttermoſt furtheraunce: to that purpoſe brought he him to my court, where truly I may
iuſtly witnes with him , that what his wit could con-
ceiue(and his wit can conceaue as far as the limits of
reaſon ſtretch) was all directed to the ſetting forwarde
the ſuite of his friend *Philoxenus:* my eares could heare
nothing from him, but touching the worthines of *Philoxenus*, and of the great happines it would be vnto me
to haue ſuch a husband : with many arguments, which
God knowes, I cannot well remember becauſe I did
not much beleeue.

For why ſhould I vſe many circūſtances to come to
that where alredy I am, and euer while I liue muſt continue? In fewe wordes, while he pleaded for an other,
he wanne me for himſelfe: if at leaſt(with that ſhe ſigh-
ed) he would account it a winning , for his fame
had ſo framed the way to my mind, that his preſence

so full of beauty, sweetnes, and noble conuersation, had entred there before he vouchsafed to call for the keyes. O Lord, how did my soule hang at his lippes while he spake! O when he in feeling maner would describe the loue of his frend, how well (thought I) dooth loue betweene those lips! when he would with daintiest eloquence stirre pitie in me toward *Philoxenus*, why sure (said I to my selfe) *Helen*, be not afraid, this hart cannot want pitie: and when he would extol the deeds of *Philoxenus*, who indeede had but waited of him therin, alas (thought I) good *Philoxenus*, how euil doth it become thy name to be subscribed to his letter? What should I say? nay, what should I not say (noble knight) who am not ashamed, nay am delighted, thus to expresse mine owne passions?

Dayes paste; his eagernes for his friende neuer decreased, my affection to him euer increased. At length, in way of ordinarie courtesie, I obteined of him (who suspected no such matter) this his picture, the only *Amphialus*, I feare that I shall euer enioy: and growen bolder, or madder, or bould with madnes, I discouered my affection vnto him. But, Lord, I shall neuer forget, how anger and courtesie, at one instant appeared in his eyes, when he heard that motion: how with his blush he taught me shame. In summe, he left nothing vnassayed, which might disgrace himselfe, to grace his frend; in sweet termes making me receiue a most resolute refusal of himselfe. But when he found that his presence did far more perswade for himselfe, then his speeche could doo for his frend, he left my court: hoping, that forgetfulnesse (which commonly waits vpon absence) woulde make roome for his friende: to whome he woulde not vtter thus much (I thinke) for a kinde feare not to grieue him, or perchance (though he cares little for me) of a certaine honorable grateſulnes, nor yet to diſcourſe ſo much of my ſecrets : but as it ſhould ſeeme, meant to trauell into farre countreyes, vntill his friends affection either ceaſed, or preuayled.

9 But within a while, *Philoxenus* came to ſee how onward the fruites were of his friends labour, when (as in trueth I cared not much how he tooke it) he found me ſitting, beholding this picture, I know not with how affectionate countenãce, but I am ſure with a moſt affectionate mind. I ſtraight found ielouſie and diſdaine tooke hold of him: and yet the froward paine of mine owne harte made me ſo delight to puniſh him, whom I eſteemed the chiefeſt let in my way, that when he with humble geſture, and vehement ſpeeches, ſued for my fauor, I told him, that I would heare him more willingly, if he would ſpeake for *Amphialus*, as well as *Amphialus* had done for him : he neuer anſwered me, but pale and quaking, went ſtraight away ; and ſtraight my heart miſgaue me ſome euill ſucceſſe : and yet though I had authoritie inough to haue ſtayed him (as in theſe fatall things it falles out, that the hie-working powers make ſecond cauſes vnwittingly acceſſarie to their determinations) I did no further but ſent a foot-man of mine (whoſe faithfulnes to me I well knew) from place to place to follow him, and bring me word of his proceedings: which (alas) haue brought foorth that which I feare I muſt euer rewe.

10 For he had trauailed ſcarſe a dayes iorney out of my Countrey, but that (not farre from this place) he ouertooke *Amphialus*, who (by ſuccouring a diſtreſſed Lady) had bene here ſtayed: and by and by called him to fight

fight with him, protefting that one of the two fhould die : you may eafily iudge how ftraunge it was to *Amphialus*, whofe hart could accufe it felfe of no fault, but too much affection toward him, which he (refufing to fight with him) would faine haue made *Philoxenus* vnderftand, but (as my feruant fince tolde me) the more *Amphialus* went back, the more he followed, calling him Traytor, and coward, yet neuer telling the caufe of this ftrange alteration. Ah *Philoxenus* (faide *Amphialus*) I know I am no Traytor, and thou well knoweft I am no coward: but I pray thee content thy felfe with this much, and let this fatisfie thee, that I loue thee, fince I beare thus much of thee, but he leauing words drew his fworde, and gaue *Amphialus* a great blow or two, which but for the goodnes of his armour would haue flaine him ; and yet fo farre did *Amphialus* containe himfelfe, ftepping afide, and faying to him, Well *Philoxenus*, and thus much villany am I content to put vp, not any longer for thy fake (whom I haue no caufe to loue, fince thou doft iniure me, and wilt not tell me the caufe) but for thy vertuous fathers fake, to whom I am fo much bound. I pray thee goe away, and conquer thy owne paffions, and thou fhalt make me foone yeeld to be thy feruant.

But he would not attend his wordes, but ftill ftrake fo fiercely at *Amphialus*, that in the end (nature preuailing aboue determination) he was faine to defend him felfe, and with-all to offend him, that by an vnluckye blow the poore *Philoxenus* fell dead at his feete, hauing had time onely to fpeake fome wordes, whereby *Amphialus* knew it was for my fake : which when *Amphialus*

phialus sawe, he forthwith gaue such tokens of true felt sorrow; that as my seruant said, no imagination could conceiue greater woe. But that by and by, an vnhappie occasion made *Amphialus* passe himselfe in sorrow: for *Philoxenus* was but newly dead, when there comes to the same place, the aged and vertuous *Timotheus*, who (hauing heard of his sonnes sodaine and passionate manner of parting from my Court) had followed him as speedily as he could; but alas not so speedily, but that he foũd him dead before he could ouer take him. Though my hart be nothing but a stage for Tragedies; yet I must confesse, it is euen vnable to beare the miserable representation thereof: knowing *Amphialus* and *Timotheus* as I haue done. Alas what sorrow, what amasement, what shame was in *Amphialus*, when he saw his deere foster father, find him the killer of his onely sonne? In my hart I know, he wished mountaines had laine vpon him, to keepe him from that meeting. As for *Timotheus*, sorow of his sonne and (I thinke principally) vnkindnes of *Amphialus* so deuoured his vitall spirits that able to say no more but *Amphialus*, *Amphialus*, haue I? he sancke to the earth, and presently dyed.

12   But not my tongue though daily vsed to complaints; no nor if my hart (which is nothing but sorrow) were turned to tonges, durst it vnder-take to shew the vnspeakeablenes of his griefe. But (because this serues to make you know my fortune,) he threw away his armour, euen this which you haue now vpon you, which at the first sight I vainely hoped, he had put on againe; and thẽ (as ashamed of the light) he ranne into the thickest of the woods, laméting, & euen crying out so pityfully, that my seruant, (though of a fortune not

not vfed to much tendernes) could not refraine weeping when he tolde it me. He once ouertooke him,but
Amphialus drawing his fword, which was the only part
of his armes(God knowes to what purpofe) he caried
about him,threatned to kill him if he folowed him,and
withall,bad him deliuer this bitter meffage,that he wel
inough foûd,I was the caufe of al this mifchiefe:& that
if I were a man,he would go ouer the world to kill me:
but bad me affure my felfe, that of all creatures in the
world,he moft hated me . Ah Sir knight(whofe eares I
think by this time are tyred with the rugged wayes of
thefe misfortunes)now way my cafe,if at left you know
what loue is.For this caufe haue I left my country,pu-
ting in hazard how my people wil in time deale by me,
aduéturing what perils or difhonors might enfue, only
to folow him,who proclaimeth hate againft me,and to
bring my neck vnto him,if that may redeem my trefpas
& affuage his fury.And now fir(faid fhe)you haue your
requeft, I pray you take paines to guide me to the next
town,that there I may gather fuch of my company a-
gaine,as your valor hath left me. *Palladius* willingly cô-
difcéded:but ere they began to go,there cam *Clitophon*,
who hauing bene fomething hurt by one of them, had
purfued him a good way: at length ouertaking him , &
ready to kill him, vnderftood they were feruants to the
faire Queene *Helen*, and that the caufe of this enterprife
was for nothing,but to make *Amphialus* prifoner, who
they knew their miftreffe fought,for fhe concealed her
forow,nor caufe of her forow from no body.

But *Clitophon*(very forie for this accident)came back 13
to comfort the Queene, helping fuch as were hurt , in
the beft fort that he could,& framing frêdly côftruciôs

of

of this raſhly vndertaken enmitie, when in comes ano-
ther(till that time vnſeene) all armed, with his beuer
downe, who firſt looking round about vpon the companie, as ſoone as he ſpied *Palladius*, he drew his ſword,
and making no other prologue, let flie at him. But *Palladius*(ſorie for ſo much harm as had alredy happened)
ſought rather to retire, and warde, thinking he might
be ſome one that belonged to the faire Queene, whoſe
caſe in his harte he pitied. Which *Clitophon* ſeeing, ſtept
betweene them, asking the new come knight the cauſe
of his quarrell; who anſwered him, that he woulde kill
that theefe, who had ſtollen away his maſters armour,
if he did not reſtore it. With that *Palladius* lookt vpon
him, and ſawe that he of the other ſide had *Palladius*
owne armour vpon him: truely(ſaid *Palladius*)if I haue
ſtolne this armour, you did not buy that: but you ſhall
not fight with me vpon ſuch a quarrell, you ſhall haue
this armour willingly, which I did onely put on to doo
honor to the owner. But *Clitophon* ſtraight knewe by
his words and voyce, that it was *Iſmenus*, the faithfull &
diligent Page of *Amphialus*: and therefore telling him
that he was *Clitophon*, and willing him to acknowledge
his error to the other, who deſerued all honour, the
yong Geutleman pulled of his head-peece, and (lighting)went to kiſſe *Palladius* hands; deſiring him to pardon his follie, cauſed by extreame griefe, which eaſilie
might bring foorth anger. Sweete Gentleman (ſaidé
Palladius) you ſhall onely make me this amendes, that
you ſhal cary this your Lords armour from me to him,
and tell him from an vnknowen knight (who admires
his worthines) that he cannot caſt a greater miſte ouer
his glory, thē by being vnkind to ſo excellēt a princeſſe

as

as this Queene is. *Ismenus* promised he would, as soone
as he durst find his maister: and with that went to doo
his dutie to the Queene, whom in all these encounters
astonishment made hardy; but assoone as she saw *Ismenus* (looking to her picture) *Ismenus* (said she) here is
my Lord, where is yours? or come you to bring me
some sentence of death from him? if it be so, welcome
be it. I pray you speake; and speake quickly. Alas Madame, said *Ismenus*, I haue lost my Lorde, (with that
teares came vnto his eyes) for assoone as the vnhappie
combate was concluded with the death both of father
and sonne, my maister casting of his armour, went his
way: forbidding me vpō paine of death to follow him.

Yet diuers daies I followed his steppes; till lastly I
found him, hauing newly met with an excellent Spaniel, belonging to his dead companion *Philoxenus*. The
dog streight fawned on my maister for old knowledge:
but neuer was there thing more pittifull then to heare
my maister blame the dog for louing his maisters murtherer, renewing a fresh his cōplaints, with the dumbe
counceller, as if they might cōfort one another in their
miseries. But my Lord hauing spied me, rase vp in such
rage, that in truth I feared he would kill me: yet as then
he said onely, if I would not displease him, I should not
come neere him till he sent for me: too hard a cōmaun-
dement for me to disobey: I yeelded, leauing him onely waited on by his dog, and as I thinke seeking out the
most solitarie places, that this or any other country can
graunt him: and I returning where I had left his armour, found an other in steed thereof, & (disdaining I
must confesse that any should beare the armour of the
best Knight liuing) armed my selfe therein to play the

H   foole

foole,as euē now I did. Faire *Ismenus* (said the Queen)
a fitter meſſenger could hardly be to vnfold my Tragedie : I ſee the end,I ſee my ende.

15   With that (ſobbing)ſhe deſired to be conducted to
the next towne, where *Palladius* left her to be waited
on by *Clitophon*,at *Palladius* earneſt entreatie,who deſired alone to take that melancholy courſe of ſeeking his
friend: & therefore changing armours again with *Ismenus*(who went withal to a caſtle belonging to his maſter)he cōtinued his queſt for his friend *Daiphantus*.

CHAP. 12.

1 Palladius *after long ſearch of* Daiphantus, *lighteth on an*
Amazon *Ladie.* 2 *Her habite,* 3 *ſong,* 4 *and who ſhe
was.* 5 *Obiections of the one againſt women,and loue of
them.* 6 *The anſwcres of the other for them both.*
7 *Their paſsionate concluſion in relenting kindneſſe.*

SO directed he his courſe to *Laconia*, aſwell among the *Helots* , as
Spartans. There indeed he found
his fame flouriſhing , his monument engraued in Marble, and yet
more durable in mens memories ;
but the vniuerſall lamenting his
abſented preſence , aſſured him of
his preſent abſence. Thence into the *Elean* prouince,
to ſee whether at the Olympian games (there celebrated) he might in ſuch concourſe bleſſe his eyes with
ſo deſired an encounter : but that huge and ſportfull
aſſemblie grewe to him a tedious lonelineſſe , eſteeming

ming no bodie founde, fince *Daiphantus* was loft. Afterward he paffed through *Achaia* and *Sicyonia*, to the *Corinthians*, prowde of their two Seas, to learne whether by the ftreight of that *Isthmus*, it was poffible to know of his paffage. But finding euerie place more dumbe then other to his demaunds, and remembring that it was late-taken loue, which had wrought this new courfe, he returned againe (after two months trauaile in vaine) to make frefhe fearche in *Arcadia*; fo much the more, as then firft he bethought him felfe of the picture of *Philoclea* (in refembling her he had once loued) might perhaps awake againe that fleeping paffion. And hauing alreadie paft ouer the greateft part of *Arcadia*, one day comming vnder the fide of the pleafaunt mountaine *Menalus*, his horfe (nothing guiltie of his inquifitiueneffe) with flat tiring taught him, that difcrete ftayes make fpeedie iourneis. And therefore lighting downe, and vnbrideling his horfe, he him felfe went to repofe him felfe in a little wood he fawe thereby. Where lying vnder the protection of a fhadie tree, with intention to make forgetting fleepe comfort a forrowfull memorie, he fawe a fight which perfwaded, and obteyned of his eyes, that they would abide yet a while open. It was the appearing of a Ladie, who becaufe fhe walked with her fide toward him, he could not perfectly fee her face; but fo much he might fee of her, that was a furetie for the reft, that all was excellent.

Well might he perceaue the hanging of her haire in faireft quátitie, in locks, fome curled, & fome as it were forgotten, with fuch a careleffe care, & an arte fo hiding arte, that fhe feemed fhe would lay them for a paterne,

H ?   whether

whether nature fimply, or nature helped by cunning, be more excellent : the reft whereof was drawne into a coronet of golde richly fet with pearle; and fo ioyned all ouer with gold wiers, and couered with feathers of diuers colours, that it was not vnlike to an helmet, fuch a glittering fhew it bare, & fo brauely it was held vp frō the head. Vpon her bodie fhe ware a doublet of skie colour fattin, couered with plates of gold, & as it were nailed with pretious ftones, that in it fhe might feeme armed; the nether parts of her garment was fo full of ftuffe, & cut after fuch a fafhion, that though the length of it reached to the ankles, yet in her going one might fometimes difcerne the fmal of her leg, which with the foot was dreffed in a fhort paire of crimfon veluet buf-kins, in fome places open (as the ancient manner was) to fhew the fairenes of the skin. Ouer all this fhe ware a certaine mantell, made in fuch manner, that comming vnder the right arme, and couering moft of that fide, it had no faftning of the left fide, but onely vpon the top of the fhoulder : where the two endes met, and were clofed together with a very riche iewell : the deuife wherof (as he after faw) was this: a *Hercules* made in lit-tle fourme, but a diftaffe fet within his hand as he once was by *Omphales* commaundement with a worde in Greeke, but thus to be interpreted, *Neuer more va-liant* . On the fame fide, on her thigh fhee ware a fword, which as it witneffed her to be an *Amazon*, or one following that profeffion, fo it feemed but a need-les weapon, fince her other forces were without with-ftanding. But this Ladie walked out-right, till he might fee her enter into a fine clofe arbour : it was of trees whofe branches fo louingly interlaced one the other,

that

that it could refift the ftrógeft violence of eye-fight;but
fhe went into it by a doore fhe opened; which moued
him as warely as he could to follow her,and by and by
he might heare her fing this fong,with a voice no leffe
beautifull to his eares, then her goodlineffe was full of
harmonic to his eyes.

Ransformd in shew, but more transformd in minde,　　3
　I ceafe to ftriue with double conqueft foild :
For (woe is me) my powers all I finde
With outward force, and inward treafon fpoild.

For from without came to mine eyes the blowe,
Whereto mine inward thoughts did faintly yeeld;
Both thefe confpird poore Reafons ouerthrówe;
Falfe in my felfe, thus-haue I loft the field.

Thus are my eyes ftill Captiue to one fight:
Thus all my thoughts are flaues to one thought ftill:
Thus Reafon to his feruants yeelds his right;
Thus is my power transformed to your will.
　What maruaile then I take a womans hew,
　Since what I fee, thinke, know is all but you ?

The dittie gaue him fome fufpition, but the voice　4
gaue him almoft affurance, who the finger was. And
therefore boldly thrufting open the dore, and entring
into the arbour, he perceaued in deed that it was *Pyro-*
cles thus difguifed, wherewith not receauing fo much
ioy to haue found him,as griefe fo to haue found him,
amazedly looking vpon him (as *Apollo* is painted when
he faw *Daphne* fodainly turned into a Laurell) he was
　　　　　H 3　　　　　　　　not

not able to bring forth a worde . So that *Pyrocles* (who had as much shame , as *Musidorus* had sorrow) rising to him, would haue formed a substantiall excuse ; but his infinuation being of blushinge , and his diuision of sighes,his whole oration stood vpon a short narration, what was the caufer of this Metamorphosis ? But by that time *Musidorus* had gathered his spirites together, and yet casting a gastfull countenaunce vpon him (as if he would coniure some strange spirits)he thus spake vnto him.

5   And is it possible,that this is *Pyrocles*,the onely yong Prince in the world,formed by nature, and framed by education,to the true exercise of vertue? or is it indeed some *Amazon* that hath counterfeited the face of my friend,in this fort to vexe me ? for likelier sure I would haue thought it, that any outwarde face might haue bene difguifed,then that the face of fo excellēt a mind coulde haue bene thus blemished . O sweete *Pyrocles*, separate your selfe a little (if it be possible) from your selfe , and let your owne minde looke vpon your owne proccedings : so shall my wordes be needlesse, and you best instructed . See with your selfe , how fitt it will be for you in this your tender youth , borne fo great a Prince , and of fo rare, not onely expectation , but proofe, desired of your olde Father , and wanted of your natiue countrie , now fo neere your home, to diuert your thoughts from the way of goodnesse;to loofe, nay to abuse your time. Lastly to ouerthrow all the excellent things you haue done , which haue filled the world with your fame ; as if you should drowne your ship in the long desired hauen , or like an ill player,should marre the last act of his Tragedie.

                                                    Remem-

Remember(for I know you know it) that if we wil be men, the reasonable parte of our soule, is to haue absolute commaundement; againſt which if any ſenſuall weaknes ariſe, we are to yeelde all our ſounde forces to the ouerthrowing of ſo vnnaturall a rebellion, wherein how can we wante courage, ſince we are to deale againſt ſo weake an aduerſary, that in it ſelfe is nothinge but weakeneſſe? Nay we are to reſolue,that if reaſon direct it, we muſt doo it,and if we muſt doo it, we will doo it; for to ſay I cannot, is childiſh,and I will not, womaniſh.And ſee how extremely euery waye you endaunger your minde; for to take this womanniſh habit (without you frame your behauiour accordingly) is wholy vaine : your behauiour can neuer come kindely from you, but as the minde is proportioned vnto it. So that you muſt reſolue, if you will playe your parte to any purpoſe, whatſoeuer peeuiſh affections are in that ſexe, ſoften your hart to receiue them, the very firſt downe-ſteppe to all wickednes : for doo not deceiue your ſelfe, my deere coſin, there is no man ſodainely excellentlie good, or extremely euill, but growes either as hee holdes himſelfe vp in vertue, or lets himſelf ſlide to vitiouſnes. And let vs ſee, what power is the aucthor of all theſe troubles:forſooth loue, loue,a paſſion,and the baſeſt and fruitleſſeſt of all paſſions:feare breedeth wit, Anger is the cradle of courage : ioy openeth and enhableth the hart: ſorrow, as it cloſeth, ſo it draweth it inwarde to looke to the correcting of it ſelfe ; and ſo all generally haue power towards ſome good by the direction of right Reaſon. But this baſtarde Loue (for in deed the name of Loue is moſt vnworthylie

applied

applie to so hatefull a humour) as it is engendered betwixt lust and idlenes; as the matter it workes vpon is
nothing; but a certaine base weakenes , which some
gentle fooles call a gentle hart;as his adioyned companions be vnquietnes , longings , fond comforts , faint
discomforts, hopes, ieloulies, vngrounded rages, caus-
lelfe yeeldings ; so is the hiest ende it aspires vnto, a
litle pleasure with much paine before,and great repentaunce after . But that end how endlelfe it runs to infinite euils , were fit inough for the matter we speake of,
but not for your eares , in whome indeede there is so
much true disposition to vertue : yet thus much of his
worthie effects in your selfe is to be seen, that(besides
your breaking lawes of hospitality with *Kalander* and
of friendlhip with me) it vtterly subuerts the course of
nature , in making reason giue place to sense , & man
to woman. And truely I thinke heere-vpon it first gatte
the name of Loue : for indeede the true loue hath that
excellent nature in it , that it doth transform the very
essence of the louer into the thing loued, vniting, and
as it were incorporating it with a secret & inward working . And herein do these kindes of loue imitate the
excellent;for as the loue of heauen makes one heauenly,the loue of vertue , vertuous ; so doth the loue of
the world make one become worldly,and this effeminate loue of a woman ,doth so womanilh a man , that
(if he yeeld to it) it will not onely make him an *Ama-*
zon;but a launder, a diftaff-spinner;or what so euer o-
ther vile occupation their idle heads ca imagin,& theii
weake hands performe.Therefore (to trouble you no
longer with my tedious but louing words) if either
you remember what you are , what you haue bene , or
what

what you muſt be: if you côſider what it is, that moued
you, or by what kinde of creature you are moued, you
ſhall finde the cauſe ſo ſmall, the effeƈ ſo daungerous,
your ſelfe ſo vnworthie to runne into the one, or to be
driuē by the other, that I doubt not I ſhall quickly haue
occaſion rather to praiſe you for hauing conquered it,
then to giue you further counſell, how to doo it.

But in *Pyrocles* this ſpeech wrought no more, but 6
that he, who before he was eſpied, was afraid; after, being perceiued, was aſhamed, now being hardly rubd
vpon, lefte both feare and ſhame, and was moued to
anger. But the exceeding good will he bare to *Muſidorus* ſtriuing with it, he thus, partely to ſatisfie him, but
principally to looſe the reines to his owne motions,
made him anſwere. Coſin, whatſouer good diſpoſition
nature hath beſtowed vpon me, or howſoeuer that diſpoſition hath bene by bringing vp côfirmed, this muſt
I confeſſe, that I am not yet come to that degree of wiſdome, to thinke light of the ſexe, of whom I haue my
life; ſince if I be any thing (which your friendſhip rather
finds, thē I acknowledge) I was to come to it, born of a
womã, & nurſed of a womã. And certēly (for this point
of your ſpeach doth neereſt touch me) it is ſtrãge to ſee
the vnman-like cruelty of mākind; who not côtent with
their tyrãnous ãbition, to haue brought the others vertuous patience vnder them (like to childiſh maiſters)
thinke their maſterhood nothing, without doing in-
iniury to them, who (if we will argue by reaſon) are
framed of nature with the ſame parts of the minde for
the exerciſe of vertue, as we are. And for example, euen
this eſtate of *Amazons*, (which I now for my greateſt
honor do ſeek to counterfaite) doth well witnes, that if
generally the ſwetnes of their diſpoſitiõs did not make
them

them fee the vainneffe of thefe thinges, which we ac-
cópt glorious, they nether want valor of mind,nor yet
doth their fairnes take away their force.And truely we
men,and praiers of men,fhould remember,that if we
haue fuch exceliécies, it is reafon to thinke them excellent creatures , of whom we are : fince a Kite neuer
brought forth a good flying Hauke.But to tel you true,
as I thinke it fuperfluous to vfe any wordes of fuch a
fubiect,which is fo praifed in it felfe , as it needes no
praifes ; fo withall I feare left my conceate(not able to
reach vnto them) bring forth wordes,which for their
vnworthines may be a difgrace vnto thé I fo inwardly
honor . Let this fuffice,that they are capable of vertue:
& vertue(ye your felues fay)is to be loued,& I too tru-
ly:but this I willingly cófeffe,that it likes me much better,when I finde vertue in a faire lodging, then when I
am bound to feeke it in an ill fauoured creature, like a
pearle in a dounghill . As for my fault of being an vnciuill gueft to *Kalander* , if you could feele what an inward gueft my felfe am hoft vnto : ye would thinke it
very excufeable,in that I rather performe the ducties
of an hoft,then the ceremonies of a gueft. And for my
breaking the lawes of friendfhippe with you,(which I
would rather dye, then effectually doo) truely,I could
finde in my hart to aske you pardon for it,but that your
handling of me giues me reafon to my former dealing . And here *Pyrocles* ftayed , as to breath himfelfe,
hauing bene tranfported with a litle vehemency , becaufe it feemed him *Mufidorus* had ouer-bitterly glaun-
fed againft the reputation of woman-kinde : but then
quieting his countenance (afwell as out of an vnquiet
mind it might be)he thus proceeded on: And poore

                                                    Loue

Loue(said he)deare cosin,is little beholding vnto you, since you are not contented to spoile it of the honor of the highest power of the mind,which notable mē haue attributed vnto it; but ye deiect it below all other passi-ons,in trueth somewhat strangely;since,if loue receiue any disgrace,it is by the company of these passions you preferre before it. For those kinds of bitter obiections (as,that lust,idlenes, and a weak harte, shoulde be,as it were, the matter and forme of loue)rather touch me, deare *Musidorus*,then loue : But I am good witnesse of mine own imperfections,& therefore will not defende my selfe:but herein I must say , you deale contrary to your self:for if I be so weak,then can you not with rea-son stir me vp as ye did,by remēbrance of my own ver-tue:or if indeed I be vertuous,thē must ye cōfesse, that loue hath his working in a vertuous hart : & so no dout hath it, whatsoeuer I be:for if we loue vertue, in whom shal we loue it but in a vertuous creature?without your meaning be,I should loue this word *vertue*,where I see it written in a book.Those troblesome effects you say it breedes,be not the faults of loue,but of him that loues; as an vnable vessel to beare such a licour:like euill eyes, not able to look on the Sun;or like an ill braine,soonest ouerthrowē with best wine. Euen that heauenly loue you speake of,is accōpanied in some harts with hopes, griefs,longings, & dispaires.And in that heauēly loue, since ther are two parts,the one the loue it self,th'other the excellency of the thing loued; I,not able at the first leap to frame both in me, do now(like a diligent work-man)make ready the chiefe instrument,and first part of that great worke,which is loue it self;which whē I haue a while practised in this sort,then you shall see me turn

it

it to greater matters. And thus gently you may (if it pleafe you) think of me. Neither doubt ye,becaufe I weare a womans apparell, I will be the more womannifh,fince,I affure you(for all my apparrel) there is nothing I defire more, then fully to proue my felfe a man in this enterprife. Much might be faid in my defence, much more for loue,and moft of all for that diuine creature, which hath ioyned me and loue togcther. But thefe difputations are fitter for quiet fchooles,then my troubled braines,which are bent rather in deeds to performe, then in wordes to defende the noble defire which poffeffeth me. O Lord (faide *Mufidorus*) how fharp-witted you are to hurt your felfe? No(anfwered he)but it is the hurt you fpeake of, which makes me fo fharp-witted. Euen fo(faid *Mufidorus*) as euery bafe occupation makes one fharp in that practife, and foolifh in all the reft. Nay rather(anfwered *Pyrocles*) as each excellent thing once well learned, ferues for a meafure of all other knowledges. And is that become (faid *Mufidorus*)a meafure for other things,which neuer receiued meafure in it felfe? It is counted without meafure (anfwered *Pyrocles*,)becaufe the workings of it are without meafure: but otherwife, in nature it hath meafure, fince it hath an end allotted vnto it. The beginning being fo excellent,I would gladly know the end. Enioying,anfwered *Pyrocles*,with a great figh. O (faid *Mufidorus*) now fet ye foorth the bafenes of it: fince if it ende in enioying, it fhewes all the reft was nothing. Ye miftake me(anfwered *Pyrocles*)I fpake of the end to which it is directed; which end ends not, no fooner then the life. Alas, let your owne braine dif-enchaunt you (faid *Mufidorus*.)My hart is toc farre poffeffed(faid *Pyrocles*.)

But

But the head giues you direction. And the hart giues me life; aunſwered *Pyrocles*.

But *Muſidorus* was ſo greeued to ſee his welbeloued friend obſtinat, as he thought, to his owne deſtruction, that it forced him with more then accuſtomed vehemency, to ſpeake theſe words; Well, well, (ſaide he) you liſt to abuſe your ſelfe; it was a very white and red vertue, which you could pick out of a painterly gloſſe of a viſage: Confeſſe the truth; and ye ſhall finde , the vtmoſt wasbut beautie; a thing, which though it be in as great excellencye in your ſelfe as may be in any, yet I am ſure you make no further reckning of it, then of an outward fading benefite Nature beſtowed vpon you. And yet ſuch is your want of a true grounded vertue, which muſt be like it ſelfe in all points , that what you wiſely account a trifle in your ſelfe, you fondly become a ſlaue vnto in another. For my part I now proteſt I haue left nothing vnſaid , which my wit could make me know, or my moſt entier friendſhip to you requires of me; I do now beſech you euen for the loue betwixt vs (if this other loue haue left any in you towards me) and for the remembraunce of your olde careful father (if you can remeber him that forget your ſelf) laſtly for *Pyrocles* owne ſake (who is now vpon the point of falling or riſing) to purge your ſelfe of this vile infection; other wiſe giue me leaue , to leaue of this name of friendſhp, as an idle title of a thing which cannot be, where vertue is aboliſhed. The length of theſe ſpeaches before had not ſo much cloied *Pyrocles*, though he were very vnpatient of long deliberations, as the laſt farewel of him he loued as his owne life, did wound his ſoule, thinking him ſelfe afflicted, he was the apter to con-

ceiue

ceiue vnkindneſſe deepely : infomuch , that ſhaking
his head , and deliuering ſome ſhewe of teares, he thus
vttered his griefes. Alas (ſaid he) prince *Muſidorus*, how
cruelly you deale with me; if you ſeeke the victory, take
it ; and if ye liſte , triumph . Haue you all the reaſon of
the world, and with me remaine all the imperfections ;
yet ſuch as I can no more lay from me, then the Crow
can be perſwaded by the Swanne to caſt of all his black
fethers . But truely you deale with me like a Phiſition,
that ſeeing his patient in a peſtilent feuer , ſhould chide
him , in ſteede of miniſtring helpe, and bid him be ſick
no more ; or rather like ſuch a friend , that viſiting his
friend condemned to perpetuall priſon ; and loaden
with greeuous fetters, ſhould will him to ſhake of his
fetters, or he wuld leaue him. I am ſicke , & ſicke to the
death; I am a priſoner, neither is any redreſſe, but by her
to whom I am ſlaue . Now if you liſt to leaue him that
loues you in the hieſt degree : But remember euer to
cary this with you , that you abandon your friend in
his greateſt extremity.

And herewith the deepe wound of his loue being rubbed afreſh with this new vnkindnes, begã (as it
were) to bleed again, in ſuch ſort that he was not hable
to beare it any longer , but guſhing out aboundance
of teares , and croſſing his armes ouer his woefull hart,
as if his teares had beene out-flowing blood , his
armes an ouer-preſſing burthen , he ſuncke downe to
the ground, which ſodaine traunce went ſo to the hart
of *Muſidorus*. that falling down by him & kiſſing the we-
ping eyes of his friend, he beſought him not to make
account of his ſpeach; which if it had bene ouer vehe-
mcnt

ment, yet was it to be borne withall, becaufe it came
out of a loue much more vehement; that he had not
thought fancie could haue receiued fo deep a wound:
but now finding in him the force of it, hee woulde
no further contrary it; but imploy all his feruice to
medicine it, in fuch fort, as the nature of it required.
But euen this kindnes made *Pyrocles* the more melte in
the former vnkindnes, which his manlike teares well
fhewed, with a filent look vpō *Mufidorus*, as who fhould
fay, And is it poffible that *Mufidorus* fhould threaten to
leaue me? And this ftrooke *Mufidorus* minde and fenfes
fo dumbe too, that for griefe being not able to fay any
thing, they refted, with their eyes placed one vpon another, in fuch fort, as might well paint out the true paffion of vnkindnes to be neuer aright, but betwixt them
that moft dearely loue.

And thus remayned they a time; till at length, *Mufi-*
dorus embrafing him, faid, And will you thus fhake of
your friend? It is you that fhake me of (faide *Pyrocles*)
being for my vnperfectnes vnworthie of your friend
fhippe. But this (faid *Mufidorus*) fhewes you more vnperfect, to be cruell to him, that fubmits himfelfe vnto
you; but fince you are vnperfect (faid he fmiling) it is
reafon you be gouerned by vs wife and perfect men.
And that authoritie will I beginne to take vpon me,
with three abfolute cōmandements: The firft, that you
increafe not your euill with further griefes: the fecond,
that you loue her with all the powers of your mind: &
the laft cōmandemēt fhalbe, ye cōmand me to do what
feruice I can, towards the attaining of your defires. *Py-*
rocles hart was not fo oppreffed with the mighty paffiōs
of

of loue and vnkindnes, but that it yeelded to some
mirth at this commaundement of *Musidorus*, that he
should loue : so that something cleering his face from
his former shewes of griefe; Wel(said he)deare cousin,
I see by the well choosing of your commandementes,
that you are fitter to be a Prince, then a Counseller: and
therfore I am resolued to imploy all my endeuour to o-
bey you; with this condition, that the comandementes
ye commaund me to lay vpon you, shall onely be, that
you continue to loue me, and looke vpon my imperfections, with more affection then iudgemēt. Loue you?
(said he)alas, how can my hart be seperated from the
true imbrasing of it, without it burst, by being too full
of it? But(said he)let vs leaue of these flowers of newe
begun frendship: and now I pray you againe tel me; but
tell it me fully, omitting no circumstance, the storie of
your affections both beginning, and proceeding: assuring your selfe, that there is nothing so great, which I
will feare to doo for you: nor nothing so small which I
will disdaine to doo for you. Let me therfore receiue a
cleere vnderstāding, whrch many times we misse, while
those things we account small, as a speech, or a look are
omitted, like as a whole sentence may faile of his con-
gruitie, by wanting one particle. Therefore betweene
frends, all must be layd open, nothing being superflu-
ous, nor tedious. You shalbe obeyed(said *Pyrocles*)and
here are we in as fitte a place for it as may be; for this ar-
bor no body offers to come into but my selfe; I vsing it
as my melancholy retiring place, and therefore that
respect is born vnto it; yet if by chāce any should come,
say that you are a seruant sent from the Q. of the *Amazons* to seeke me, and then let me alone for the rest. So
sate they downe, and *Pyrocles* thus said.

CHAP.

CHAP. 13.

¹ How Pyrocles *fell in loue with* Philoclea. *² His counsell
and course therein . ³ His disguising into* Zelmane.
⁴ Her meeting with Damætas, *⁵* Basilius, *⁶ the Queene
and her daughters, & their speaches. ⁷ Her abode there
ouer entreated; ⁸ and the place thereof described.*

Ousin (saide hee) then began the
fatall ouerthrowe of all my libertie, when walking among the
pictures in *Kalanders* house, you
your selfe deliuered vnto mee
what you had vnderstood of *Philoclea* , who muche resembling
(though I must say much surpas-
sing) the Ladie *Zelmane,* whom too well I loued: there
were mine eyes infected, & at your mouth did I drinke
my poison . Yet alas so sweete was it vnto me , that I
could not be contented, til *Kalander* had made it more
and more strong with his declaratió . Which the more
I questioned, the more pittie I conceaued of her vnworthie fortune : and when with pittie once my harte
was made tender, according to the aptnesse of the humour, it receaued quickly a cruell impression of that
wonderful passió which to be definde is impossible, because no wordes reach to the strange nature of it: they
onely know it, which inwardly feele it, it is called loue.
Yet did I not (poore wretch) at first know my disease,
thinking it onely such a woonted kind of desire, to see
rare sights; & my pitie to be no other, but the fruits of a

I   gentle

gentle nature. But euē this arguing with my selfe came of further thoughts; & the more I argued, the more my thoughts encreased. Desirous I was to see the place where she remained, as though the *Architecture* of the lodges would haue bene much for my learning; but more desirous to see her selfe, to be iudge, forsooth, of the painters cūning. For thus at the first did I flatter my selfe, as though my wound had bene no deeper : but when within short time I came to the degree of vncertaine wishes, and that the wishes grew to vnquiet longings, when I could fix my thoughts vpō nothing, but that within little varying, they should end with *Philoclea* : when each thing I saw, seemed to figure out some parts of my passions; whē euen *Parthenias* faire face became a lecture to me of *Philocleas* imagined beautie; when I heard no word spoken, but that me thought it caried the sum of *Philocleas* name : then indeed, then I did yeeld to the burthen, finding my selfe prisoner, before I had leasure to arme my selfe; & that I might well, like the spaniel, gnaw vpon the chaine that ties him, but I should sooner marre my teeth, then procure liberty.

2   Yet I take to witnesse the eternall spring of vertue, that I had neuer read, heard, nor seene any thing; I had peuer any tast of Philosophy, nor inward feeling in my selfe, which for a while I did not call for my succour. But (alas) what resistance was there, when ere long my very reason was (you will say corrupted) I must needs confesse, conquered; and that me thought euen reason did assure me, that all eies did degenerate from their creation, which did not honour such beautie? Nothing in trueth could holde any plea with it, but the reuerent friendship I bare vnto you. For as it went

against

againſt my harte to breake any way from you, ſo did I feare more then anie aſſault to breake it to you:finding (as it is indeed) that to a hart fully reſolute, counſaile is tedious, but reprehenſion is lothſome : & that there is nothing more terrible to a guilty hart, then the eie of a reſpected friĕd. This made me determine with my ſelf, (thinking it a leſſe fault in friĕdſhip to do a thing without your knowledge, then againſt your wil) to take this ſecret courſe : Which conceit was moſt builded vp in me, the laſt day of my parting and ſpeaking wɪth you; whĕ vpŏ your ſpeach with me,& my but naming loue, (when els perchaŭce I would haue gone further)I ſaw your voice & coutenance ſo chaunge, as it aſſured me, my reuealing it ſhould but purchaſe your griefe with my cumber:& therfore(deere *Muſidorus*)euĕ ran away frŏ thy wel knowne chiding:for hauing writtĕ a letter, which I know not whether you found or no, & taking my chiefe iewels with me, while you were in the middeſt of your ſport,I got a time(as I think) vnmarked,to ſteale away, I cared not whether ſo I mighr ſcape you: & ſo came I to *Ithonia* in the prouince of *Meſſenia*;wher lying ſecret I put this in practiſe which before I had deuiſed. For remĕbring by *Philanax* his letter,& *Kalăders* ſpeech,how obſtinatcly *Baſilius* was determined not to mary his daughters,& therfore fearing,leſt any publike dealing ſhould rather increaſe her captiuitie, then further my loue; Loue(the refiner of inuentiŏ)had put in my head thus to diſguiſe my ſelf,that vnder that maske I might (if it were poſſible,) get acceſſe, and what acceſſe could bring forth,commit to fortune & induſtry: determining to beare the countenance of an *Amazon*. Therfore in the cloſeſt manet I could,naming my ſelfe

Zelmane, for that deere Ladies fake, to whofe memorie I am fo much bound, I caufed this apparell to be made, and bringing it neere the lodges, which are harde at hand, by night, thus dreffed my felfe, refting till occafion might make me found by them, whom I fought: which the next morning hapned as well, as my owne plot could haue laide it. For after I had runne ouer the whole petigree of my thoughts, I gaue my felfe to fing a little, which as you know I euer delighted in, fo now efpecially, whether it be the nature of this clime to ftir vp Poeticall fancies, or rather as I thinke, of loue; whofe fcope being pleafure, will not fo much as vtter his griefes, but in fome forme of pleafure.

4   But I had fong very little, when (as I thinke difpleafed with my bad mufike) comes mafter *Dametas* with a hedging bill in his hand, chafing, and fwearing by the patable of *Pallas*, & fuch other othes as his rufticall brauery could imagine; & whē he faw me, I affure you my beauty was no more beholding to him thē my harmony; for leaning his hands vpon his bil, & his chin vpon his hāds, with the voice of one that plaieth *Hercules* in a play, but neuer had his fancie in his head, the firft word he fpake to me, was, am not I *Dametas?* why am not I *Dametas?* he needed not name him felfe: for *Kalanders* defcription had fet fuch a note vpō him, as made him very notable vnto me, and therefore the height of my thoughts would not difcend fo much as to make him any anfwer, but continued on my inward difcourfes: which (he perchaunce witnes of his owne vnworthines, & therefore the apter to thinke him felfe contēned) tooke in fo hainous manner, that ftanding vpō his tip-toes, and ftaring as though he would haue a mote pulled

pulled out of his eie, Why (said he) thou womã, or boy,
or both, what soeuer thou be, I tell thee here is no
place for thee, get thee gone, I tell thee it is the Princes
pleasure, I tell thee it is *Dametas* pleasure. I could not
choose, but smile at him, seeing him looke so like an
Ape that had newly taken a purgation; yet taking my
selfe with the maner, spake these wordes to my selfe:
O spirite (saide I) of mine, how canst thou receaue a-
nie mirth in the midst of thine agonies, and thou mirth
how darest thou enter into a minde so growne of late
thy professed enemie? Thy spirite (saide *Dametas*)
doost thou thinke me a spirite? I tell thee I am *Basilius* officer, and haue charge of him, and his daughters. O onely pearle (said I sobbing) that so vile an
oyster should keepe thee? By the combe-case of *Diana*
(sware *Dametas*) this woman is mad: oysters, and
pearles? doost thou thinke I will buie oysters? I tell
thee once againe get thee packing, and with that lifted
vp his bill to hit me with the blunt ende of it: but indeede that put me quite out of my lesson, so that I forgat al *Zelmanes-ship*, and drawing out my sworde, the
basenesse of the villaine yet made me stay my hande,
and he (who, as *Kalander* tolde me, from his childe-
hood euer feared the blade of a sworde) ran backe,
backward (with his hands aboue his head) at left twentie paces, gaping and staring, with the verie grace (I
thinke) of the clownes, that by *Latonas* prayers were
turned into Frogs. At length staying, finding himselfe without the compasse of blowes, he fell to a fresh
scolding, in such mannerlie manner, as might well
shewe he had passed through the discipline of a Ta-
uerne. But seeing me walke vp and downe, without

I 3   marking

marking what he saide, he went his way (as I perceiued after) to *Basilius*: for within a while he came vnto mee, bearing in deed shewes in his countenaunce of an honest and well-minded gentleman, and with as much courtesie, as *Dametas* with rudenesse saluting me, Faire Lady (saide he) it is nothing strange, that such a solitary place as this should receiue solitary persons; but much do I maruaile, how such a beauty as yours is, should be suffered to be thus alone. I (that now knew it was my part to play) looking with a graue maiestie vpon him, as if I found in my selfe cause to be reuerenced. They are neuer alone (saide I) that are accompanied with noble thoughts. But those thoughts (replied *Basilius*) cānot in this your lonelines neither warrant you from suspition in others, nor defend you from melancholy in your selfe. I then shewing a mislike that he pressed me so farre, I seeke no better warraunt (saide I) then my owne conscience, nor no greater pleasures, then mine owne contentation. Yet vertue seekes to satisfie others, (saide *Basilius*.) Those that be good (saide I,) and they wil be satisfied as long as they see no euill. Yet will the best in this country, (said *Basilius*) suspect so excellent a beauty being so weakely garded. Then are the best but starke nought, (aunswered I) for open suspecting others, comes of secrete condemning themselues; But in my countrie (whose manners I am in all places to maintaine and reuerence) the generall goodnes (which is nourished in our harts) makes euery one thinke the strength of vertue in an other, whereof they finde the assured foundation in themselues. Excellent Ladie (said he) you praise so greatly, (and yet so wisely) your coūtry, that I must needes desire to know what the nest is, out of which such Byrds doo flye.

You

You muſt firſt deſerue it (ſaid I) before you may obtaine it. And by what meanes(ſaide *Baſilius*) ſhall I deſerue to know your eſtate ? By letting me firſt knowe
yours(aunſwered I.)To obey you(ſaid he)I will doe it,
although it were ſo much more reaſon, yours ſhould be
knowen firſt, as you doo deſerue in all points to be
preferd .Know you(faire Lady)that my name is *Baſilius*, vnworthily Lord of this coutry: the reſt, either fame
hath brought to your eares, or(if it pleaſe you to make
this place happie by your preſence)at more leaſure you
ſhall vnderſtand of me. I that from the beginning aſſured my ſelfe it was he, but would not ſeeme I did ſo, to
keepe my grauitie the better , making a peece of reuerēce vnto him, Mighty Prince(ſaid I)let my not knowing you ſerue for the excuſe of my boldnes, and the little reuerence I doe you, impute it to the manner of
my coutry, whch is the inuincible Lande of the *Amazons*; My ſelfe neece to *Senicia* , Queene thereof, line-
ally deſcended of the famous *Pentheſilea*, ſlaine by the
bloody hand of *Pyrrhus*. I hauing in this my youth
determined to make the worlde ſee the *Amazons* excellencies , aſwell in priuate, as in publicke
vertue, haue paſſed ſome daungerous aduentures in
diuers coutries : till the vnmercifull Sea depriued me
of my company : ſo that ſhipwrack caſting me not far
hence, vncertaine wandring brought me to this place.
But *Baſilius*(who now began to taſt that , which
ſince he hath ſwallowed vp, as I will tell you) fell to
more cunning intreating my aboad, then any greedy
hoſt would vſe to well paying paſſingers. I thought nothing could ſhoot righter at the mark of my deſires; yet
had I learned alredy ſomuch, that it was aganſt my womanhood

manhoode to be forward in my owne wishes. And
therefore he (to proue whither intercessions in fitter
mouths might better preuaile) commaunded *Dametas*
to bring forth-with his wife and daughters thether;
three Ladies, although of diuers, yet all of excellent
beauty.

6   His wife in graue Matronlike attire, with countenaunce and gesture sutable, and of such fairnes (being
in the strengh of her age) as if her daughters had not
bene by, might with iust price haue purchased admiration; but they being there, it was enough that the
most dainty eye would thinke her a worthy mother of
such children. The faire *Pamela*, whose noble hart I
finde doth greatly disdaine, that the trust of her vertue
is reposed in such a louts hands as *Dametas*, had yet to
shew an obedience, taken on a shepeardish apparell,
which was but of Russet cloth cut after their fashion,
with a straight body, open brested, the nether parte
ful of pleights, with long and wide sleeues: but beleeue
me she did apparell her apparell, and with the precious-
nes of her body made it most sumptuous. Her haire at
the full length, wound about with gold lace, onely by
the comparison to see how farre her haire doth excell
in colour: betwixt her breasts (which sweetly rase vp
like two faire Mountainets in the pleasaunt valley of
Tempe) there honge a very riche *Diamond* set but in a
blacke horne, the worde I haue since read is this; *yet still
my selfe*. And thus particularly haue I described them,
because you may know that mine eyes are not so partiall, but that I marked them too. But when the ornament of the Earth, the modell of heauen, the Triumphe of Nature, the light of beauty, Queene of
Loue

Loue,yoũg *Philoclea* appeared in her Nimphe-like apparell, fo neare nakednes, as one might well difcerne
part of her perfeƈtions; & yet fo apparelled,as did ſhew
ſhe kept beſt ſtore of her beuty to her felf: her haire (alas
too poore a word,why ſhould I not rather call thē her
beames)drawē vp into a net, able to take *Iupiter* when
he was in the forme of an Eagle; her body (O ſweet body) couered with a light taffeta garment, fo cut, as the
wrought ſmocke came through it in many places,
inough to haue made your reſtraind imaginatiõ haue
thought what was vnder it: with the caſt of her blacke
eyes; blacke indeed,whether nature fo made them,that
we might be the more able to behold & bear their wõ-
derfull ſhining,or that ſhe, (goddeſſe like)would work
this miracle in her felfe, in giuing blacknes the price a-
boue all beauty. Then (I fay)indeede me thought the
Lillies grew pale for enuie,the rofes me thought bluſhed to fee fweeter rofes in her cheekes, & the apples me
thought,fell downe frõ the trees, to do homage to the
apples of her breaſt; Then the cloudes gaue place,that
the heauẽs might more freſhly ſmile vpõ her; at the left
the cloudes of my thoughts quite vaniſhed : and my
fight(then more cleere and forcible then euer) was fo
fixed there,that(I imagine) I ſtood like a well wrought
image,with fome life in ſhew,but none in praƈtife. And
fo had I beene like inough to haue ſtayed long time,
but that *Gynecia* ſtepping betweene my fight and the
onely *Philoclea*, the chaunge of obieƈt made mee recouer my fenſes : fo that I coulde with reaſonable
good manner receiue the falutation of her, and of the
the Princeſſe *Pamela*,doing thē yet no further reuerẽce
　　　　　　　　　　　　　　　　　　　then

then one Prince vseth to another. But when I came
to the neuer-inough praised *Philoclea*, I could not but
fall downe on my knees, and taking by force her hand,
and kissing it(I must confesse)with more then womanly ardency, Diuine Lady, (saide I) let not the worlde,
nor these great princes maruaile, to se me(contrary to
my manner) do this especiall honor vnto you, since all
both men and women, do owe this to the perfection
of your beauty. But she blushing (like a faire morning
in Maye)at this my singularity, and causing me to rise,
Noble Lady, (saide she) it is no maruaile to see your
iudgement mistaken in my beauty, since you beginne
with so great an errour, as to do more honour vnto me
then to them, whom I my selfe owe all seruice. Rather
(answered I with a bowed downe countenaunce)that
shewes the power of your beauty, which forced me to
do such an errour, if it were an errour. You are so well
acquainted(saide she sweetely, most sweetely smiling,)
with your owne beautie, that it makes you easilie fall
into the discourse of beauty. Beauty in me? (said I truely sighing) alas if there be any, it is in my eyes, which
your blessed presence hath imparted vnto them:
7 But then(as I thinke)*Basilius* willing her so do, Well
(saide she)I must needs confesse I haue heard that it is
a great happines to be praised of them that are most
praise worthie; And well I finde that you are an inuincible *Amazon*, since you will ouercome, though in a
wrong matter. But if my beauty be any thing, then let
it obtaine thus much of you , that you will remaine
some while in this cōpanie, to ease your owne trauail,
and our solitarines. First let me dye(said I)before any
word spoken by such a mouth, should come in vaine.
                                                                    And

And thus with some other wordes of entertaining, was my staying concluded, and I led among them to the lodge ; truely a place for pleasantnes, not vnfitte to flatter solitarinesse ; for it being set vpon such an vnsensible rising of the ground , as you are come to a prety height before almost you perceiue that you ascend , it giues the eye lordship ouer a good large circuit, which according to the nature of the coūtry, being diuersified betwene hills and dales, woods and playnes, one place more cleere, and the other more darksome, it seemes a pleasant picture of nature, with louely lightsomnes and artificiall shadowes . The Lodge is of a yellow stone, built in the forme of a starre ; hauing round about a garden framed into like points : and beyond the gardein, ridings cut out , each aunswering the Angles of the Lodge: at the end of one of them is the other smaller Lodge , but of like fashion ; where the gratious *Pamela* liueth : so that the Lodge seemeth not vnlike a faire *Comete*, whose taile stretcheth it selfe to a starre of lesse greatnes.

CHAP. 14.

The deuises of the first banket to Zelmane. *Her crosses in loue,* by the loue of *Basilius and* Gynecia *The conclusion between* Musidorus *and* Zelmane.

O *Gynecia* her selfe bringing me to my Lodging, anone after I was inuited and brought downe to suppe with them in the gardein, a place not fairer in naturall ornaments, then artificiall inuentions: wherein is

is a banquetting houfe among certaine pleafant trees,
whofe heads feemed curled with the wrappings about
of Vine branches. The table was fet neere to an excellent water-worke; for by the cafting of the water in
moft cunning maner,it makes (with the fhining of the
Sunne vpon it)a perfect rainbow, not more pleafant to
the eye then to the mind,fo fenfibly to fee the proof of
the heauenly *Iris*.There were birds alfo made fo finely,
that they did not onely deceiue the fight with their figure,but the hearing with their fongs; which the watrie inftruments did make their gorge deliuer. The table at which we fate, was round, which being faft to
the floore whereon we fate,and that deuided from the
reft of the buildings (with turning a vice, which *Bafilius* at firft did to make me fport)the table,and we about
the table, did all turne rounde, by meanes of water
which ranne vnder, and carried it about as a Mille.
But alas, what pleafure did it to mee, to make diuers
times the full circle round about, fince *Philoclea*(being
alfo fet)was carried ftill in equall diftance from me,and
that onely my eyes did ouertake her; which when the
table was ftayed, and wee beganne to feede, dranke
much more eagerlie of her beautie, then my mouth
did of any other licour. And fo was my common
fenfe deceiued (being chiefly bent to her) that as I
dranke the wine, and withall ftale a looke on her, me
feemed I tafted her delicioufneffe. But alas, the one
thirfte was much more inflamed,then the other quenched. Sometimes my eyes would lay themfelues open
to receiue all the dartes fhe did throwe,fomtimes cloze
vp with admiration, as if with a contrary fancie, they
woulde preferue the riches of that fight they had
gotten,

gotten, or caſt my lidde as curtaines ouer the image of beautie, her preſence had painted in them. True it is, that my Reaſon (now growen a ſeruant to paſſion) did yet often tel his maſter, that he ſhould more moderatly vſe his delight. But he, that of a rebell was become a Prince, diſdayned almoſt to allow him the place of a Counſeller: ſo that my ſenſes delights being too ſtróg for any other reſolution, I did euen looſe the raines vnto them: hoping, that (going for a woman) my lookes would paſſe, either vnmarked, or vnſuſpected.

Now thus I had (as me thought) well playd my firſt acte, aſſuring my ſelfe, that vnder that diſguiſment, I ſhould find opportunitie to reueal my ſelf to the owner of my harte. But who would thinke it poſſible (though I feele it true) that in almoſt eight weekes ſpace, I haue liued here (hauing no more companie but her parents, and I being familiar, as being a woman, and watchfull, as being a louer) yet could neuer finde opportunitie to haue one minutes leaſure of priuie conference: the cauſe whereof is as ſtrange, as the effects are to me miſerable. And (alas) this it is.

At the firſt ſight that *Baſilius* had of me (I think *Cupid* hauing headed his arrows with my misfortune) he was ſtriken (taking me to be ſuch as I profeſſe) with great affectió towards me, which ſince is growen to ſuch a doting loue, that (till I was faine to gette this place, ſometimes to retire vnto freely) I was euen choaked with his tedioufnes. You neuer ſaw fourſcore yeares daunce vp and downe more liuely in a young Louer: now, as fine in his apparrell, as if he would make me in loue with a cloake; and verſe for verſe with the ſharpeſt-witted Louer in *Arcadia*. Doo you not think that this is a ſallet of

worm·

woormwood,while mine eyes feede vpon the *Ambro-*
sia of *Philocleas* beauty.

But this is not all; no this is not the worst; for he
(good man) were easy enough to be dealt with: but (as
I thinke) Loue and mischeefe hauing made a wager,
which should haue most power in me, haue set *Gynecia*
also on such a fire towardes me, as will neuer (I feare)
be quenched but with my destruction. For she (being
a woman of excellent witte, and of strong working
thoughts) whether she suspected me by my ouer-vehement showes of affection to *Philoclea* (which loue forced me vnwisely to vtter; while hope of my maske foolishly incouraged me) or that she hath take some other
marke of me, that I am not a woman: or what deuil it is
hath reuealed it vnto her, I know not; but so it is, that al
her countenances, words and gestures, are miserable
portraitures of a desperate affection. Whereby a man
may learne, that these auoydings of companie, doo but
make the passions more violent, when they meete
with fitte subiects. Truely it were a notable dumb shew
of *Cupids* kingdome, to see my eyes (languishing with
ouer-vehement longing) direct themselues to *Philoclea:*
& *Basilius* as busie about me as a Bee, & indeed as cumbersome; making such suits to me, who nether could if I
would; nor would if I could, helpe him: while the terrible witte of *Gynecia*, carried with the beere of violent
loue, runnes thorow vs all. And so ielious is she of my
loue to her daughter, that I could neuer yet beginne to
open my mouth to the vneuitable *Philoclea*, but that
her vnwished presence gaue my tale a coclusion, before
it had a beginning.

And surely if I be not deceiued, I see such shewes of
liking,

liking, and (if I bee acquainted with paſſions) of almoſt a paſſionate liking in the heauenly *Philoclea*, towardes me , that I may hope her eares would not ab-
horre my diſcourſe. And for good *Baſilius*, he thought
it beſt to haue lodged vs together , but that the eternall hatefulnes of my deſtinie, made *Gynecias* ielouſie
ſtoppe that,and all other my bleſſings. Yet muſt I confeſſe,that one way her loue doth me pleaſure : for ſince
it was my fooliſh fortune, or vnfortunate follie, to be
knowen by her,that keepes her from bewraying me to
Baſilius . And thus (my *Muſidorus*) you haue my Tragedie played vnto you by my ſelfe , which I pray the
gods may not in deede prooue a Tragedie. And there
he ended, making a full point of a hartie ſigh.

  Muſidorus recōmended to his beſt diſcourſe,all which 5
Pyrocles had told him. But therein he found ſuch intri-
catenes,that he could ſee no way to lead him out of the
maze;yet perceiuing his affection ſo grounded, that ſtriuing againſt it, did rather anger then heale the wound,
and rather call his friendſhippe in queſtion , then giue
place to any friendly councell. Well (ſaid he) deare coſin, ſince it hath pleaſed the gods to mingle your other
excellencies with this humor of loue , yet happie it is,
that your loue is imployed vpon ſo rare a woman : for
certainly, a noble cauſe dooth eaſe much a grieuous
caſe. But as it ſtands now, nothing vexeth me,as that I
cānot ſee wherein I can be ſeruiſable vnto you. I deſire
no greater ſeruice of you (āſwered *Pyrocles*)thē that you
remayn ſecretly in this country, & ſome-times come to
this place ; either late in the night, or early in the morning,where you ſhal haue my key to ēter,bicauſe as my
for-

fortune, eyther amendes or empaires. I may declare
it vnto you, and haue your counſell and furtheraunce:
& hereby I will of purpoſe lead her, that is the prayſe,
and yet the ſtaine of all womankinde, that you may
haue ſo good a view, as to allowe my iudgement: and
as I can get the moſt conuenient time, I wil come vnto you; for though by reaſon of yonder wood you
cannot ſee the Lodge; it is harde at hande. But now,
(ſaid ſhe) it is time for me to leaue you, and towardes
euening wee will walke out of purpoſe hetherward,
therefore keepe your ſelfe cloſe in that time. But *Muſidorus* bethinking him ſelfe that his horſe might happen to bewray them, thought it beſt to returne for that
day, to a village not farre of, and diſpatching his horſe
in ſome ſorte, the next day early to come a foote thither, and ſo to keepe that courſe afterward, which *Pyrocles* very well liked of. Now farewell deere couſin
(ſaid he) from me, no more *Pyrocles*, nor *Daiphantus*
now, but *Zelmane*: *Zelmane* is my name, *Zelmane* is
my title, *Zelmane* is the onely hope of my aduauncement. And with that word going out, and ſeeing that
the coaſt was cleare, *Zelmane* diſmiſſed *Muſidorus*, who
departed as full of care to helpe his friend, as before
he was to diſſwade him.

CHAP. 15.

Zelmane

Eimane returned to the Lodge, where (inflamed by *Philoclea*, watched by *Gynecia*, and tired by *Bafilius*) fhe was like a horfe, defirous to runne, and miferablie fpurred, but fo fhort rainde, as he cannot ftirre forward : *Zelmane* fought occafion to fpeake with *Philoclea*; *Bafilius* with *Zelmane*; and *Gynecia* hindered them all. If *Philoclea* hapned to figh (and figh fhe did often) as if that figh were to be wayted on, *Zelmane* fighed alfo; whereto *Bafilius* and *Gynecia* foone made vp foure parts of forow . Their affection increafed their conuerfation; and their conuerfation increafed their affection. The refpect borne bredde due ceremonies; but the affection fhined fo through them, that the ceremonies feemed not ceremonious. *Zelmanes* eyes were (like children afore fweet meate) eager, but fearefull of their ill-pleafing gouernors. Time in one inftant, feeming both fhort, and long vnto them: fhort, in the pleafingnes of fuch prefence: long, in the ftay of their defires.

But *Zelmane* fayled not to intice them all many times abroad, becaufe fhe was defirous her friend *Mufidorus* (neere whom of purpofe fhe ledde them) might haue full fight of them. Sometimes angling to a little Riuer neere hand, which for the moifture it beftowed vpon rootes of fome flourifhing Trees, was rewarded with their fhadowe. There would they fitte downe, & pretie wagers be made betweene *Pamela* and *Philoclea*, which could fooneft beguile filly fifhes; while *Zelmane* protefted, that the fitte pray for them was hartes of Princes. She alfo had an angle in her hand; but the taker was fo

K   taken,

taken, that fhe had forgotten taking. *Basilius* in the meane time would be the cooke him felfe of what was fo caught,& *Gynecia* fit ftil , but with no ftil penfifneffe. Now fhe brought them to fee a feeled Doue, who the blinder fhe was, the higher fhe ftraue·. Another time a Kite, which hauing a gut cunningly pulled out of her, and fo let flie, called all the Kites in that quarter, who (as oftentimes the worlde is deccaued) thinking her profperous when indeed fhe was wounded, made the poore Kite find,that opinion of riches may welbe dangerous.

3   But thefe recreations were interrupted by a delight of more gallant fhew ; for one euening as *Basilius* returned from hauing forced his thoughts to pleafe themfelues in fuch fmall conquefts,there came a fhepheard, who brought him word that a Gentlemã defired leaue to do a meffage from his Lord vnto him. *Basilius* granted;wherupon the Gentleman came, and after the dutifull ceremonies obferued , in his maifters name tolde him,that he was fent from *Phalātus* of *Corinth*,to craue licence , that as he had done in many other courts, fo he might in his prefence defie all *Arcadian* Knights in the behalfe of his miftres beautie,who would befides, her felfe in perfon be prefent, to giue euident proofe what his launce fhould affirme. The conditions of his chalenge were,that the defendant fhould bring his miftreffe picture, which being fet by the image of *Artefia* (fo was the miftreffe of *Phalantus* named) who in fix courfes fhould haue better of the other , in the iudgement of *Basilius*,with him both the honors and the pictures fhould remaine . *Basilius* (though he had retired him felfe into that folitarie dwelling , with intention

to

to auoid,rather then to accept any matters of drawing
company; yet becauſe he would entertaine *Zelmane,*
(that ſhe might not think the time ſo gainefull to him,
loſſe to her) graunted him to pitch his tent for three
dayes, not farre from the lodge, and to proclayme his
chalenge, that what *Arcadian* Knight (for none els
but vpon his perill was licenſed to come) woulde defende what he honored againſt *Phalantus,*ſhould haue
the like freedome of acceſſe and returne.

This obteyned and publiſhed,*Zelmane* being deſi- 4
rous to learne what this *Phalantus* was, hauing neuer
knowne him further then by report of his owne good,
in ſomuch as he was commonly called, The faire man
of armes, *Baſilius* told her that he had had occaſion by
one very inward with him, to knowe in parte the diſcourſe of his life, which was, that he was baſtard-bro-
ther to the faire *Helen* Queene of *Corinth,* and deerly e-
ſteemed of her for his exceeding good parts,being ho-
norablie courteous, and wrongleſly valiaunt, conſi-
derately pleaſant in conuerſation,& an excellent courtier without vnfaithfulnes; who (finding his ſiſters vn-
perſwadeable melancholy,thorow the loue of *Amphialus*) had for a time left her court,and gone into *Laconia*: where in the warre againſt the *Helots*, he had
gotté the reputatió of one,that both durſt & knew.But
as it was rather choiſe thé nature, that led him to matters of armes,ſo as ſoon as the ſpur of honor ceaſed, he
willingly reſted in peaceable delightes, being beloued
in all cópanies for his louely qualities, & (as a má may
terme it) cunning cherefulnes, wherby to the Prince
& Court of *Laconia,*none was more agreable thé *Phalantus*: and he not giuen greatly to ſtruggle with his
K 2   owne

owne difpofition, followed the gentle currant of it, hauing a fortune fufficient to content, & he content with a fufficient fortune. But in that court he fawe, and was acquainted with this *Artefia* whofe beautie he now defendes, became her feruant, faid him felfe, and perchaunce thought him felfe her louer. But certainly, (faid *Bafilius*) many times it falles out, that thefe young companiōs make tnemfelues beleeue they loue at the firft liking of a likely beautie; louing, becaufe they will loue for want of other bufineffe, not becaufe they feele indeed that diuine power, whicn makes the heart finde a reafon in paffion: and fo (God knowes) as inconftantly leane vpon the next chaunce that beautie caftes before them. So therefore taking loue vppon him like a fafhion, he courted this Ladie *Artefia*, who was as fit to paie him in his owne monie as might be. For fhe thinking fhe did wrong to her beautie if fhe were not prowde of it, called her difdaine of him chaftitie, and placed her honour in little fetting by his honouring her: determining neuer to marrie, but him, whome fhe thought worthie of her: and that was one, in whome all worthineffe were harboured And to this conceipt not onely nature had bent her, but the bringing vp fhe receaued at my fifter in lawe *Cecropia*, had confirmed her: who hauing in her widowhood taken this young *Artefia* into her charge; becaufe her Father had bene a deare friend of her dead husbandes, and taught her to thinke that there is no wifdome but in including heauen & earth in ones felf: and that loue, courtefie, gratefulneffe, friendfhip, and all other vertues are rather to be taken on, then taken in ones felfe: And fo good difcipline fhe found of her,

that

that liking the fruits of her owne planting, she was côtent (if so her sonne could haue liked of it) to haue wished her in marriage to my Nephew *Amphialus*. But I
thinke that desire hath lost some of his heate, since she
hath knowne, that such a Queene as *Helen* is, doth offer so great a price as a kingdome, to buie his fauour; for
if I be not deceaued in my good sister *Cecropia*, shee
thinks no face so beautifull, as that which lookes vnder
a crowne. But *Artesia* indeede liked well of my Nephew *Amphialus*; for I câ neuer deeme that loue, which
in hauty harts proceeds of a desire onely to please, and
as it were, peacock themselues; but yet she hath shewed
vehemencie of desire that way, I thinke, becaufe all her
desires be vehemêt, in so much that she hath both placed her onely brother (a fine youth called *Ismenus*) to
be his squire, and her selfe is content to waite vpon
my sister, till she may see the vttermost what she may
worke in *Amphialus*: who being of a melancholie
(though I must needes saye courteous and noble)
mind, seems to loue nothing lesse then Loue: & of late
hauing through some aduenture, or inwarde miscon-
tentment, withdrawne him selfe frô any bodies knowledge, where he is: *Artesia* the easier condiscended
to goe to the court of *Laconia*, whether she was sent
for by the Kinges wife, to whome she is somewhat
allied.

And there after the war of the *Helots*, this Knight *Phalantus*, (at least for tongue-delight) made him selfe her
seruaunt, and she so little caring, as not to showe miflike thereof, was content onely to be noted to haue a
notable seruaunt. For truely one in my court neerely
acquainted with him, within these few dayes made me

₴ pleasaunt description of their loue, while he with cheerefull lookes would speake sorowfull words, vsing the phrase of his affection in so high a stile, that *Mercurie* would not haue wooed *Venus* with more magnificent Eloquence : but els neyther in behauiour, nor action, accusing in him selfe anie great trouble in minde, whether he sped or no. And she of the other side, well finding howe little it was, and not caring for more, yet taught him, that often it falleth out but a foolishe wittinesse, to speake more then one thinkes.

5   For she made earnest benefite of his iest, forcing him in respect of his promise, to doo her suche seruice, as were both cumbersome and costly vnto him, while he stil thought he went beyond her, becau̇se his harte did not commit the idolatrie . So that lastlie, she (I thinke) hauing in minde to make the fame of her beautie an oratour for her to *Amphialus*, (perswading her selfe perhaps, that it might fall out in him, as it dothe in some that haue delightfull meate before them, and haue no stomacke to it, before other folkes prayse it) she tooke the aduauntage one daye vppon *Phalantus* vnconscionable praysinges of her, and certaine cast-awaie vowes howe much he would doo for her sake, to arrest his woord assoone as it was out of his mouth, and by the vertue thereof to charge him to goe with her thorow all the courts of *Greece*, & with the chalenge now made, to giue her beauty the principality ouer all other. *Phalantus* was entrapped, and saw round about him, but could not get out . Exceedinglie perplexed he was (as he confest to him that tolde mee the tale) not for doubt hee had of him selfe (for

indeed

indeede he had litle caufe, being accounted, with his
Launce efpecially (whereupon the challenge is to be
tryed)as perfect as any that *Greece* knoweth;but becaufe
he feared to offend his fifter *Helen*,and with all (as he
faid)he could not fo much beleeue his loue,but that he
might thinke in his hart (whatfoeuer his mouth affirmed)that both fhe,my daughters,and the faire *Parthenia*(wife to a moft noble Gentleman,my wiues neere
kinfman) might far better put in their clayme for that
prerogatiue . But his promife had bound him prentice,
and therfore it was now better with willingnes to purchafe thankes,then with a difcontented doing to haue
the paine,and not the reward : and therefore wenr on,
as his faith, rather then loue,did lead him.

And now hath he already paffed the courts of *Laco- 6
nia*,*Elis*,*Argos* and *Corinth* : and(as many times it hap-
pẽs)that a good pleader makes a bad caufe to preuaile;
fo hath his Lawnce brought captiues to the triumph of
Artefias beauty , fuch, as though *Artefia* be among the
faireft,yet in that company were to haue the prehemi-
nence:for in thofe courts many knights (that had bene
in other far countries)defẽded fuch as they had feene,
and liked in their trauaile : but their defence had bene
fuch; as they had forfayted the picture of their Ladies,
to giue a forced falfe teftimonie to *Artefias* excellencie.
And now laftly is he come hether,where he hath leaue
to trye his fortune. But I affure you, if I thought it not
in dew & true côfideratiõ an iniurious feruice & chur-
lifh curtefie,to put the danger of fo noble a title in the
deciding of fuch a dãgerles côbat,I would make yong
mafter *Phalantus* know,that your eyes can fharpẽ a blũt

Launce

Launce, and that age, which my graye haires (onely gotten by the louing care of others) make feeme more then it is, hath not diminifhed in me the power to pro-tect an vndeniable verity. With that he buftled vp him-felfe, as though his harte would faine haue walked a-broad. *Zelmane* with an inwarde fmiling gaue him outward thanks, defiring him to referue his force for worthier caufes.

CHAP. 16.

1 Phalantus *and* Artefias *pompous entraunce.* 2 *The pain-ted mufter of an eleuen conquered beauties.*

S O paffing their time according to their woont, they wayted for the cóming of *Phalantus*, who the next morning hauing alredy caufed his tents to be pitched, neere to a faire tree hard by the Lodge, had vp-pon the tree made a fhield to bee hanged vp, which the defendant fhould ftrike, that woulde call him to the mainteyning his challendge. The *Imprefa* in the fhield, was a heauen full of ftarres, with a fpeech fignifying, that it was *the beauty which gaue it the praife.*

Himfelfe came in next after a triumphant chariot, made of Carnatió veluet inriched with purle & pearle, wherein *Artefia* fat, drawne by foure winged horfes with artificiall flaming mouths, and fiery winges, as if fhe had newly borrowed them of *Phæbus*. Before her marched, two after two, certaine footemé pleafantly at-tired, who betweene them held one picture after another

other of them that by *Phalantus* well running had loſt
the prize in the race of beauty, and at euery pace they
ſtayed, turning the pictures to each ſide, ſo leaſurely,
that with perfect iudgement they might be diſcerned.

The firſt that came in (folowing the order of the time   1
wherein they had bene wonne) was the picture of *Andromana*, Queene of *Iberia*; whom a *Laconian* Knight
hauing ſometime (and with ſpeciall fauour) ſerued,
(though ſome yeares ſince retourned home) with more
gratefulnes then good fortune defended. But therein
Fortune had borrowed witte; for indeede ſhe was not
cōparable to *Arteſia*; not becauſe ſhe was a good deale
elder (for time had not yet beene able to impoueriſh
her ſtore thereof) but an exceeding red haire with ſmall
eyes, did (like ill companions) diſgrace the other aſſembly of moſt commendable beauties.

Next after her was borne the counterfaite of the   2
princeſſe of *Elis*, a Lady that taught the beholders no
other point of beauty, but this, that as lyking is, not alwaies the child of beauty, ſo whatſoeuer likcth, is beautyfull; for in that viſage there was nether Maieſtie,
grace, fauour, nor faireneſſe; yet ſhe wanted not a ſeruaunt that woulde haue made her fairer then the faire
Arteſia. But he wrote her praiſes with his helmet in the
duſt, and left her picture to be as true a witnes of his
ouerthrow, as his running was of her beauty.

After her was the goodly *Artaxia*, great Q. of *Arme-   3
nia*, a Lady vpon whom nature beſtowed, & wel placed
her delightful colours; & withal, had proportioned her
without any fault, quickly to be diſcouered by the ſenſes, yet altogether ſeemed not to make vp that harmony, that *Cupid* delights in; the reaſō wherof might ſeem
a manniſh countenance, which ouerthrew that louely
ſweetenes,

ſweetnes, the nobleſt power of womankinde, farre fitter to preuàile by parley, then by battell.

4　Of a farre contrary conſideratiō was the repreſentation of her that next followed, which was *Erona* Queenē of *Licia*, who though of ſo browne a haire, as no man ſhould haue iniuried it to haue called it blacke, and that in the mixture of her cheeks the white did ſo much ouercome the redde (though what was, was very pure) that it came neare to palenes, and that her face was a thought longer then the exacte *Symmetrians* perhaps would allow; yet loue plaid his part ſo well, in euerie part, that it caught holde of the iudgement, before it could iudge, making it firſt loue, & after acknowledge it faire, for there was a certaine delicacie, which in yeelding, conquered; & with a pitiful looke made one find cauſe to craue helpe himſelfe.

5　After her came two Ladies, of noble, but not of royall birth: the former was named *Baccha*, who though very faire, and of a fatnes rather to allure, then to miſlike, yet her breſts ouer-familiarly laide open, with a mad countenaunce about her mouth, betweene ſimpring & ſmyling, her head bowed ſomwhat down, ſeemed to lāguiſh with ouer-much idlenes, with an inuiting look caſt vpward, diſſwading with too much perſwading, while hope might ſeem to ouercome deſire.

6　The other (whoſe name was written *Leucippe*) was of a fine daintines of beauty, her face carying in it a ſober ſimplicitie; like one that could do much good, & ment no hurt, her eyes hauing in them ſuch a cheerefulnes, as nature ſeemed to ſmile in them: though her mouth and cheekes obeyed that prety demurenes which the more one markes, the more one woulde iudge the poore ſoule apt to beleue; & therfore the more pitie

to

to deceiue her.

Next came the Queene of *Laconia*, one that seemed 7 borne in the confines of beauties kingdome: for all her lineaméts were neither perfect possessions thereof, nor absent strangers thereto: but she was a Queene, and therefore beautyfull.

But she that followed, conquered indeed with being 8 conquered; & might well haue made all the beholders waite vpó her triumph, while her selfe were led captiue. It was the excellétly-faire Queene *Helen*, whose Iacinth haire curled by nature, & intercurled by arte (like a fine brooke through goldé sads) had a rope of faire pearles, which now hiding, now hidden by the haire, did as it were play at fast or loose, each with other, mutually giuing & receiuing riches. In her face so much beautie & fauour expressed, as if *Helen* had not bene knowé, some would rather haue iudged it the painters exercise, to shew what he could do, thé coúterfaiting of any liuing patterne: for no fault the most fault finding wit could haue foúd, if it were not, that to the rest of the body the face was somewhat too little: but that little was such a sparke of beauty, as was able to enflame a world of loue. For euery thing was full of a choyce finenes, that if it wáted any thing in maiestie, it supplied it with increase of pleasure; & if at the first it strake not admiration, it rauished with delight. And no indifferét soule there was, which if it could resist fró subiecting it selfe to make it his princesse, that would not lóg to haue such a playfelow. As for her attire, it was costly and curious, though the look (fixt with more sadnes thé it seemed nature had bestowed to any that knew her fortune) bewraied, that as she vsed those ornaméts, not for her self, but to preuaile with another, so she feared, that all would not serue.

Of

9   Of a farre differing (though esteemed equall) beautie, was the faire *Parthenia*, who next wayted on *Artesias* triumph, though farre better she might haue sitte in the throne. For in her euery thing was goodly, and stately; yet so, that it might seeme that great-mindednes was but the auncient-bearer to humblenes. For her great graie eye, which might seem full of her owne beauties, a large, and exceedingly faire forhead, with all the rest of her face and body, cast in the mould of Noblenes; was yet so attired, as might shew, the mistres thought it either not to deserue, or not to need any exquisite decking, hauing no adorning but cleanlines; and so farre from all arte, that it was full of carelesnesse : vnlesse that carelesnesse it selfe (in spite of it selfe) grew artificiall. But *Basilius* could not abstaine from praising *Parthenia*, as the perfect picture of a womanly vertue, and wiuely faithfulnes: telling withall *Zelmane*, how he had vnderstoode, that when in the court of *Laconia*, her picture (maintained by a certaine *Sycionian* Knight) was lost, thorow want, rather of valour, then iustice : her husband (the famous *Argalus*) would in a chafe haue gone and redeemed it with a new triall. But she (more sporting then sorrowing for her vndeserued champion) tolde her husbande, she desired to be beautifull in no bodies eye but his; and that she would rather marre her face as euill as euer it was, then that it should be a cause to make *Argalus* put on armour. Then would *Basilius* haue tolde *Zelmane*, that which she alredie knew, of the rare triall of their coupled affection : but the next picture made the mouth giue place to their eyes.

10   It was of a young mayd, which sate pulling out a thorne out of a Lambs foote, with her looke so attentiue

tiue vppon it, as if that little foote coulde haue bene
the circle of her thoughts; her apparell so poore, as it
had nothing but the infide to adorne it; a fhephooke
lying by her with a bottle vpon it. But with al that pouertie, beauty plaid the prince, and commanded as many harts as the greateft Queene there did. Her beautie
and her eftate made her quicklie to be knowne to be
the faire fhepheardeffe, *Vrania*, whom a rich knight called *Lacemon*, farre in loue with her, had vnluckely defended.

    The laft of all in place, becaufe laft in the time of   11
her being captiue, was *Zelmane*, daughter to the King
Plexirtus: who at the firft fight feemed to haue fome refembling of *Philoclea*, but with more marking (cōparing
it to the prefent *Philoclea*, who indeed had no paragon
but her fifter) they might fee, it was but fuch a likeneffe,
as an vnperfect glaffe doth giue; aunfwerable enough
in fome feitures, & colors, but erring in others. But *Zelmane* fighing, turning to *Bafilius*, Alas fir (faid fhe) here
be fome pictures which might better become the tōbes
of their Miftreffes, then the triumphe of *Artefia*. It is
true fweeteft Lady (faide *Bafilius*) fome of them be
dead, and fome other captiue: But that hath happened
fo late, as it may be the Knightes that defended their
beauty, knew not fo much : without we will fay (as in
fome harts I know it would fall out) that death it felfe
could not blot out the image which loue hath engrauē
in thē . But diuers befides thefe (faid *Bafilius*) hath *Phalantus* woon, but he leaues the reft, carying onely fuch,
who either for greatnes of eftate, or of beauty, may iuftly glorifie the glory of *Artefias* triumph.

                            CHAP.

CHAP. 17.

¹ *The ouerthrow of fiue* Arcadian *knights.* ² *The young ſhep-*
heards prettie challenge. ³ *What paſsions the ſixth knights*
foyle bredde in Zelmane. ⁴ Clitophon *hardly ouermat-*
ched by Phalantus. ⁵ *The ill arayed, & the black knights*
contention for prioritie againſt Phalantus. ⁶ *The halting*
knights complaint againſt the black knight. ⁷ Phalantus
fall by the ill furniſht knight. ⁸ *The croſſe-parting of* Phalantus *with* Arteſia, ⁹ *and who the victor was.*

Hus talked *Baſilius* with *Zelmane*,
glad to make any matter ſubiect to
ſpeake of, with his miſtreſſe, while
Phalantus in this pompous manner, brought *Arteſia* with her gē-
tlewomē, into one Tent, by which
he had another : where they both
wayted who would firſt ſtrike vpon the ſhielde, while
Baſilius the Iudge appointed ſticklers, and trumpets, to
whom the other ſhould obey. But non that day appeared, nor the next, till already it had conſumed halfe his
allowance of light; but then there came in a knight,
proteſting himſelfe as contrarie to him in minde, as he
was in apparrell. For *Phalantus* was all in white, hauing
in his baſes, and capariſon imbroidered a wauing water : at each ſide whereof he had nettings caſt ouer, in
which were diuers fiſhes naturally made, & ſo pretily,
that as the horſe ſtirred, the fiſhes ſeemed to ſtriue, and
leape in the nette.

But the other knight, by name *Neſtor*, by birth an *Ar-*
cadian,

cadian, & in affection vowed to the faire Shepherdesse,
was all in black, with fire burning both vpō his armour,
and horse. His *impresa* in his shield, was a fire made of
Iuniper, with this word, *More easie, and more sweete*. But
this hote knight was cooled with a fall, which at the
third course he receiued of *Phalantus*, leauing his picture to keepe companie with the other of the same
stampe; he going away remedilesly chafing at his rebuke. The next was *Polycetes*, greatly esteemed in *Arcadia*, for deedes he had done in armes: and much spoken
of for the honourable loue he had long borne to *Gynecia*; which *Basilius* himselfe was content, not onely to
suffer, but to be delighted with; he carried it in so honorable and open plainnes, setting to his loue no other
marke, then to do her faithfull seruice. But neither her
faire picture, nor his faire running, could warrant him
from ouerthrow, and her from becomming as then the
last of *Artesias* victories : a thing *Gynecias* vertues would
little haue recked at another time, nor then, if *Zelmane*
had not seene it. But her champion went away asmuch
discomforted, as discomfited. Then *Telamon* for *Polixe-
na*, & *Eurimelo* for *Elpine*, and *Leon* for *Zoana*; all braue
Knights, all faire Ladies, with their going down, lifted
vp the ballance of his praise for actiuitie, and hers for
fairenes.

Vpon whose losse as the beholders were talking,
there comes into the place where they ranne, a shepheard stripling (for his height made him more then a
boy, & his face would not allow him a mā) brown of cō-
plexiō (whether by nature, or by the Suns familiaritie)
but very louely withall; for the rest so perfectly proportioned, that Nature shewed, she dooth not like men
who

who flubber vp matters of meane account. And well might his proportion be iudged; for he had nothing vpon him but a paire of floppes, and vpon his bodie a Gote-fkinne, which he caft ouer his fhoulder, doing all things with fo pretie grace, that it feemed ignorance could not make him do amiffe, becaufe he had a hart to do well, holding in his right hand a long ftaffe, & fo cō-ming with a looke ful of amiable fiercenes, as in whom choller could not take away the fweetnes, he came to-wards the king, and making a reuerence (which in him was comely becaufe it was kindly) My liege Lord (faid he) I pray you heare a few words; for my hart wil break if I fay not my minde to you. I fee here the picture of *Vrania*, which (I cannot tell how, nor why) thefe men when they fall downe, they fay is not fo faire as yonder gay woman. But pray God, I may neuer fee my olde mother aliue, if I think fhe be any more match to *Vra-nia*, then a Goate is to a fine Lambe; or then the Dog that keepes our flock at home, is like your white Grei-hounde, that pulled down the Stagge laft day.

And therefore I pray you let me be dreft as they be, and my hart giues me, I fhall tumble him on the earth: for indeede he might afwell fay, that a Couflip is as white as a Lillie: or els I care not let him come with his great ftaffe, and I with this in my hand, and you fhall fee what I can doo to him. *Bafilius* fawe it was the fine fhepheard *Lalus*, whom once he had afore him in Pa-ftorall fportes, and had greatly delighted in his wit full of prety fimplicitie, and therefore laughing at his ear-neftneffe, he bad him be content, fince he fawe the pi-ctures of fo great Queenes, were faine to follow their champions fortune. But *Lalus* (euen weeping ripe)
went

went among the reſt, longing to ſee ſome bodie that would reuenge *Vrania* wronge; and praying hartely for euery bodie that ran againſt *Phalantus*, then began to feele pouerty, that he could not ſet him ſelfe to that triall. But by and by, euen when the Sunne (like a no-ble harte) began to ſhew his greateſt countenaunce in his loweſt eſtate, there came in a Knight, called *Phebi-lus*, a Gentleman of that coutry, for whom hatefull for-tune had borrowed the dart of Loue, to make him mi-ſerable by the ſight of *Philoclea*. For he had euen from her infancie loued her, and was ſtriken by her, before ſhe was able to knowe what quiuer of arrowes her eyes caried; but he loued and diſpaired; and the more he diſpaired, the more he loued. He ſawe his owne vnworthines, and thereby made her excellencie haue more terrible aſpect vpon him: he was ſo ſecrete there-in, as not daring to be open, that to no creature he e-uer ſpake of it, but his hart made ſuch ſilent complaints within it ſelfe, that while all his ſenſes were attentiue thereto, cunning iudges might perceaue his minde. ſo that he was knowne to loue though he denied, or ra-ther was the better knowne, becauſe he denied it. His armour and his attire was of a Sea couler, his *Im-preſa*, the fiſhe called *Sepia*, which being in the nette caſtes a blacke inke about it ſelfe, that in the darke-neſſe thereof it may eſcape: his worde was, *Not ſo.* *Philocleas* picture with almoſt an idolatrous magnifi-cence was borne in by him. But ſtreight ielouſie was a harbinger for diſdaine in *Zelmanes* harte, when ſhe ſawe any (but her ſelfe) ſhould be auowed a cham-pion for *Philoclea*: in ſomuch that ſhe wiſht his ſhame, till ſhe ſawe him ſhamed: for at the ſecond courſe he

L was

was ſtriken quite from out of the ſaddle,ſo full of grief,
and rage withall , that he would faine with the ſworde
haue reuenged it: but that being contrary to the order
ſet downe,*Baſilius* would not ſuffer;ſo that wiſhing him
ſelfe in the bottome of the earth, he went hiſway , leauing *Zelmane* no leſſe angry with his los, thē ſhe would
haue beene with his victory . For if ſhe thought before
a riuals prayſe woulde haue angred her , her Ladies
diſgrace did make her much more forget what ſhe then
thought, while that paſſion raigned ſo much the more,
as ſhe ſaw a pretie bluſh in *Philoclea* cheekes bewray a
modeſt diſcontentment . But the night commaunded
truce for thoſe ſportes,& *Phalantus* (though intreated)
would not leaue *Arteſia* , who in no caſe would come
into the houſe, hauing(as it were)ſuckte of *Cecropias*
breath a mortall miſlike againſt *Baſilius*.

4   But the night meaſured by the ſhort ell of ſleepe,
was ſoone paſt ouer, and the next morning had giuen
the watchful ſtars leaue to take their reſt,when a trumpet ſummoned *Baſilius* to play his iudges parte : which
he did,taking his wife & daughters with him ; *Zelmane*
hauing lockt her doore , ſo as they would not trouble
her for that time: for already there was a Knight in the
fielde , readie to proue *Helen* of *Corinth* had receaued
great iniury,both by the erring iudgement of the chal-
lenger , and the vnlucky weakeneſſe of her former de-
fender . The new Knight was quickly knowne to be
Clitophon (Kaladers ſonne of *Baſilius* his ſiſter) by his armour,which al guilt,was ſo well hādled,that it ſhewed
like a glittering ſande and grauell , interlaced with ſiluer riuers : his deuice he had put in the picture of *Helen* which hee defended. It was the *Ermion* , with a
ſpeach

ſpeach that ſignified, *Rather dead then ſpotted*. But in
that armour ſince he had parted frō *Helen* (who would
no longer his companie, finding him to enter into
termes of affection,) he had performed ſo honourable
actiōs,(ſtil ſeeking for his two friends by the names of
Palladius and *Daiphatus*,) that though his face were couered, his being was diſcouered, which yet *Baſilius*
(which had brought him vp in his court) would not
ſeeme to do; but glad to ſee triall of him, of whom he
had heard very well,he commaunded the trumpets to
ſound; to which the two braue Knights obeying, they
performed their courſes, breaking their ſix ſtaues,with
ſo good,both skill in the hitting,& grace in the maner,
that it bred ſome difficulty in the iudgement. But *Baſilius* in the ende gaue ſentence againſt *Clitophon*,becauſe
Phalantus had broken more ſtaues vpō the head,& that
once *Clitophon* had receiued ſuch a blowe, that he had
loſt the raines of his horſe, with his head well nie touching the crooper of the horſe.But *Clitophon* was ſo angry with the iudgemēt, (wherin he thought he had receiued wrōg) that he omitted his duty to his Prince, &
vncle; and ſodainly went his way, ſtill in the queſt of
them,whom as then he had left by ſeeking : & ſo yeelded the field to the next commer.

Who comming in about two houres after, was no
leſſe marked then al the reſt before,becauſe he had nothing worth the marking. For he had neither picture,
nor deuice, his armour of as old a faſhion (beſides the
ruſtic pooreneſſe,) that it might better ſeeme a monument of his graundfathes courage : about his middle
he had in ſteede of baſes,a long cloake of ſilke, which
as vnhandſomely, as it needes muſt, became the wea-

rer : ſo that all that lookt on , meaſured his length on
the earth alreadie , ſince he had to meete one who
had bene victorious of ſo many gallants . But he went
on towardes the ſhielde , and with a ſober grace ſtrake
it ; but as he let his ſworde fall vpon it, another Knight,
all in blacke came ruſtling in , who ſtrake the ſhield almoſt aſſoone as he , and ſo ſtrongly, that he brake the
ſhield in two : the ill appointed Knight (for ſo the beholders called him) angrie with that, (as he accounted,) inſolent iniurie to himſelfe , hit him ſuch a ſound
blowe , that they that looked on ſaide , it well became
a rude arme. The other aunſwered him againe in the
ſame caſe , ſo that Launces were put to ſilence , the
ſwordes were ſo buſie.

But *Phalantus* angry of this defacing his ſhield, came
vpon the blacke Knight , and with the pommell of his
ſworde ſet fire to his eyes , which preſently was reuenged, not onely by the Blacke , but the ill apparelled
Knight , who diſdained another ſhould enter into his
quarrell , ſo as, who euer ſawe a matachin daunce to i-
mitate fighting , this was a fight that did imitate the
matachin : for they being but three that fought , euerie one had aduerſaries , ſtriking him, who ſtrooke the
third , and reuenging perhaps that of him , which he
had receaued of the other. But *Baſilius* riſing himſelfe
to parte them , the ſticklers authoritie ſcarſlie able to
perſwade cholerike hearers ; and parte them he did.

But before he could determine , comes in a fourth,
halting on foote, who complained to *Baſilius*, demaunding iuſtice on the blacke Knight , for hauing by force
taken away the picture of *Pamela* from him , whiche in
little forme he ware in a Tablet, and couered with
ſilke

filke had faftened it to his Helmet, purpoſing for want
of a bigger, to paragon the little one with *Arteſias*
length, not doubting but in that little quantitie, the
excellencie of that would ſhine thorow the weakeneſſe of the other: as the ſmalleſt ſtarre dothe thorow
the whole Element of fire. And by the way he had
met with this blacke Knight, who had (as he ſaid) robbed him of it. The iniurie ſeemed grieuous, but when
it came fully to be examined, it was found, that the halting Knight meeting the other, asking the cauſe of his
going thetherward, and finding it was to defend *Pame-*
las diuine beautie againſt *Arteſias*, with a prowde iollitie commaunded him to leaue that quarrell onely for
him, who was onely worthy to enter into it. But the
blacke Knight obeying no ſuch cōmandements, they
fell to ſuch a bickering, that he gat a halting, & loft his
picture. This vnderſtood by *Baſilius*, he told him he
was now fitter to looke to his owne bodie, then an o-
thers picture: & ſo (vncomforted therein) ſent him a-
way to learn of *Æſculapius* that he was not fit for *Venus.*
    But then the queſtion ariſing who ſhould be the for-
mer againſt *Phalantus*, of the blacke, or the ill apparelled Knight (who now had gotten the reputation of
ſome ſturdy loute, he had ſo well defended himſelfe)
of the one ſide, was alleged the hauing a picture
which the other wanted: of the other ſide, the firſt ſtriking the ſhield; but the concluſion was, that the ill apparelled Knight ſhould haue the precedence, if he deliuered the figure of his miſtreſſe to *Phalantus*; who aſ-
king him for it, Certainely (ſaid he) her liuelieſt picture,
(if you could ſee it) is in my hart, & the beſt cōpariſon
I could make of her, is of the Sunne & of all other the
heauenly

heauenly beauties. But becauſe perhappes all eyes cannot taſte the Diuinitie of her beautie, and would rather be dazeled, then taught by the light, if it bee not
clowded by ſome meaner thing ; know you then,
that I defend that ſame Ladie, whoſe image *Phebilus*
ſo feebly loſt yeſternight, and in ſteede of an other
(if you ouercome mee) you ſhall haue me your ſlaue
to carrie that image in your miſtreſſe triumphe. *Phalantus* eaſilie agreed to the bargaine, which alreadie he
made his owne.

7   But when it came to the triall, the ill apparelled
Knight chooſing out the greateſt ſtaues in all the ſtore,
at the firſt courſe gaue his head ſuch a remembraunce,
that he loſt almoſt his remembraunce, he himſelfe
receyuing the incounter of *Phalantus* without any extraordinarie motion. And at the ſeconde gaue him
ſuch a counterbuffe, that becauſe *Phalantus* was ſo
perfite a horſeman, as not to be driuen from the ſaddle, the ſaddle with broken girthes was driuen from
the horſe : *Phalantus* remaining angrie and amazed,
becauſe now being come almoſt to the laſt of his promiſed enterpriſe, that diſgrace befell him, which he had
neuer before knowne.

8   But the victorie being by the iudges giuen, and the
trumpets witneſſed to the ill apparelled Knight ; *Phalantus* diſgrace was ingrieued in lieu of comforte by
Arteſia ; who telling him ſhe neuer lookt for other,
bad him ſeeke ſome other miſtreſſe. He excuſing himſelfe, and turning ouer the fault to Fortune, Then let
that be your ill Fortune too (ſaide ſhe) that you haue
loſt me.

Nay truely Madame (ſaide *Phalantus*) it ſhall not
be

be ſo : for I thinke the loſſe of ſuch a Miſtreſſe will
prooue a great gaine : and ſo concluded; to the ſporte
of *Baſilius*, to ſee young folkes loue, that came in
maſkt with ſo great pompe, goe out with ſo little conſtancie . But *Phalantus* firſt profeſſing great ſeruice to
Baſilius for his curteous intermitting his ſolitary courſe
for his ſake, would yet conduct *Arteſia* to the caſtle of
Cecropia, whether ſhe deſired to goe : vowing in himſelfe, that neither hart, nor mouth-loue, ſhould euer a-
ny more intangle him. And with that reſolution he left
the company.

Whence all being diſmiſſed (among whom the black
knight wēt away repyning at his luck, that had kept him
frō winning the honor, as he knew he ſhuld haue don,
to the picture of *Pamela*) the ill apparelled knight (who
was only deſired to ſtay, becauſe *Baſilius* meant to ſhew
him to *Zelmane*) puld of his Helmet, & then was knowē
himſelfe to be *Zelmane*: who that morning (as ſhe told)
while the others were buſie, had ſtolne out to the Princes ſtable, which was a mile of frō the Lodge, had gotten a horſe (they knowing it was *Baſilius* pleaſure ſhe
ſhould be obeyed) & borrowing that homely armour
for want of a better, had come vpon the ſpur to redeem
Philocleas picture, which ſhe ſaid , ſhe could not beare,
(being one of that little wildernesſe-company) ſhould
be in captiuitie, if the cunning ſhe had learned in her
coūtrye of the noble *Amazons*, could withſtād it: & vnder that pretext faine ſhe would haue giuē a ſecret paſport to her affection. But this act painted at one inſtant
redneſſe in *Philocleas* face, and paleneſſe in *Gynecias*, but
broght forth no other coūtenāces but of admiratio, no
ſpeches but of cōmēdatiōs: al theſe few (beſides loue)

thinking

thinking they honoured them selues , in honouring
so accomplished a person as *Zelmane*: whom dayly they
sought with some or other sports to delight, for which
purpose *Basilius* had in a house not farre of, seruaunts,
who though they came not vncalled, yet at call were
redye.

CHAP. 18.

*₁ Musidorus disguised. ₂ His song. ₃ His loue, ₄ the cause
thereof. ₅ His course therein.*

ANd so many daies were spent, and
many waies vsed, while *Zelmane*
was like one that stoode in a tree
waiting a good occasió to shoot, &
Gynecia a blauncher, which kept the
deareſt deere from her. But the day
being come , which according to
an apointed course, the sheapheards were to asséble, &
make their paſtorall sports afore *Basilius*: *Zelmane* (fearing, left many eyes, and comming diuers waies, might
hap to spy *Musidorus*) went out to warne him thereof.

But before she could come to the Arbour, she sawe
walking from her-ward, a man in sheapperdish apparrel
who being in the sight of the Lodge it might seeme he
was allowed there . A lóg cloke he had on; but that caſt
vnder his right arme, wherein he held a shephooke, so
finely wrought, that it gaue a brauery to pouerty; & his
rayments, though they were meane, yet receiued they
hanſomnes by the grace of the wearer; though he himselfe

selfe went but a kinde of languishing pace, with his eies
somewhat cast vp to heauen , as though his fancyes
straue to mount higher; sometimes throwne downe to
the ground , as if the earth could not beare the burthens of his sorrowes; at length, with a lamētable tune,
he songe these fewe verses.

Come shepheards weedes, become your masters minde: 2
Yeld outward shew, what inward chance he tryes :
Nor be abasht, since such a guest you finde,
Whose strongest hope in your weake comfort lyes.

Come shepheards weedes, attend my woefull cryes :
Difuse your selues from sweete Menalcas *voice:*
For other be those tunes which sorrow tyes,
From those cleere notes which freely may reioyce.
    Than power out plaint, and in one word say this :
    Helples his plaint, who spoyles himselfe of blisse.

And hauing ended, he strake himselfe on the brest ;
saying, O miserable wretch, whether do thy destenies
guide thee : The voice made *Zelmane* hasten her pace
to ouertake him : which hauing done, she plainly perceaued that it was her deare friend *Musidorus*, whereat
maruailing not a little, she demaunded of him, whether
the Goddesse of those woods had such a powre to trãs-
forme euery body , or whether, as in all enterprises elsc
he had done, he meant thus to match her in this newe
alteration.

    Alas, (said *Musidorus*) what shall I say, who am loth 3
to say, and yet faine would haue said? I find indeed, that
all is but lip-wisdome , which wants experience. I now

(woe is me) do try what loue can doo: O *Zelmane*, who will resist it, must either haue no witte , or put out his eyes: can any man resist his creation ? certainely by loue we are made, and to loue we are made. Beasts onely cannot discerne beauty, and let them be in the role of Beasts that doo not honor it . The perfect friendship *Zelmane* bare him, and the great pitie she (by good triall) had of such cases, coulde not keepe her from smiling at him , remembring how vehemently he had cryed out against the folly of louers. And therefore a litle to punish him , Why how now deere cousin (said she) you that were last day so hie in Pulpit against louers, are you now become so meane an auditor? Remember that loue is a passion ; and that a woorthie mans reason must euer haue the masterhood . I recant, I recant (cryed *Musidorus*,) and withall falling downe prostrate, O thou celestial, or infernal spirit of Loue, or what other heauenly or hellish title thou list to haue (for effects of both I finde in my selfe) haue compassion of me , and let thy glory be as great in pardoning them that be submitted to thee, as in conquering those that were rebellious. No , no saide *Zelmane* , I see you well enough : you make but an enterlude of my mishaps, and doo but counterfaite thus, to make me see the deformitie of my passions : but take heede , that this iest do not one day turne to earnest. Now I beseech thee (saide *Musidorus* taking her fast by the hand) euen for the truth of our friendship , of which (if I be not altogether an vnhappy man) thou hast some rememberaunce, & by those sacred flames which (I know) haue likewise neerely touched thee ; make no iest of that, which hath so ernestly pearced me thorow, nor let that

be

be light to thee, which is to me ſo burdenous , that I am not able to beare it. *Muſidorus* both in words & behauiour, did ſo liuely deliuer out his inward grief, that *Zelmane* found indeede, he was thorowly woũded: but there roſe a new ielouſy in her minde, leſt it might be with *Philoclea*, by whom, as *Zelmane* thought, in right all hartes and eyes ſhould be inherited. And therefore deſirous to be cleered of that doubt, *Muſidorus* ſhortly (as in haſt and full of paſſionate perplexednes,) thus recounted his caſe vnto her.

The day (ſaid he) I parted from you, I being in mind **4** to returne to a towne, from whence I came hether, my horſe being before tired, would ſcarce beare me a mile hence: where being benighted, the light of a candle (I ſaw a good way of) guided me to a young ſhepheards houſe, by name *Menalcas*, who ſeing me to be a ſtraying ſträger, with the right honeſt hoſpitality which ſeemes to be harboured in the *Arcadian* breſts , & though not with curious coſtlines, yet with cleanly ſufficiencie, entertained me: and hauing by talke with him, found the manner of the countrie , ſomething more in particular, then I had by *Kalanders* report, I agreed to ſoiourne with him in ſecret, which he faithfully promiſed to obſerue. And ſo hether to your arbour diuers times repaired: & here by your meanes had the ſight (O that it had neuer bene ſo , nay , O that it might euer be ſo) of a Goddeſſe, who in a definite compaſſe can ſet forth infinite beauty. All this while *Zelmane* was racked with iealouſie . But he went on, For (ſaide he) I lying cloſe, and in truth thinking of you , and ſaying thus to my ſelfe, O ſweet *Pyrocles*, how art thou bewitched? where is thy vertue? where is the vſe of thy reaſon? how much
am.

am I inferior to thee in the ſtate of the mind? And yet
know I, that all the heauens cannot bring me to ſuch
thraldome. Scarcely, thinke I, had I ſpoken this word,
when the Ladies came foorth; at which ſight, I thinke
the very words returned back again to ſtrike my ſoule;
at leaſt, an vnmeaſurable ſting I felt in my ſelfe, that I
had ſpoken ſuch words. At which ſight? ſaid *Zelmane*,
not able to beare him any longer. O (ſayd *Muſidorus*)
I know your ſuſpition; No, no, baniſh all ſuch feare, it
was, it is, and muſt be *Pamela*. Then all is ſafe (ſayd *Zelmane*) proceede, deare *Muſidorus*. I will not (ſaid he)
impute it to my late ſolitarie life (which yet is prone to
affections) nor, to the much thinking of you (though
that cald the conſideratiō of loue into my mind, which
before I euer neglected) nor to the exaltation of *Venus*;
nor reuenge of *Cupid*; but euen to her, who is the Pla-
net, nay, the Goddeſſe, againſt which, the onely ſhielde
muſt be my Sepulchre. When I firſt ſaw her, I was preſently ſtriken, and I (like a fooliſh child, that when any
thing hits him, wil ſtrike himſelfe again vpon it) would
needs looke agrine; as though I would perſwade mine
eyes, that they were deceiued. But alas, well haue I
found, that Loue to a yeelding hart is a king; but to a
reſiſting, is a tyrant. The more with arguments I ſhaked
the ſtake, which he had planted in the grounde of my
harte, the deeper ſtill it ſanke into it. But what meane I
to ſpeake of the cauſes of my loue, which is as impoſſible to deſcribe, as to meaſure the backſide of heauen?
Let this word ſuffice, I loue.

And that you may know I doo ſo, it was I that came
in black armour to defende her picture, where I was
both preuented, and beaten by you. And ſo, I that waited

ted here to do you seruice, haue now my self most need of succor. But wherupon got you your self this aparrel? said *Zelmane*. I had forgotten to tel you (said *Musidorus*) though that were one principall matter of my speech; so much am I now master of my owne minde. But thus it happened: being returned to *Menalcas* house, full of tormenting desire, after a while faynting vnder the weight, my courage stird vp my wit to seeke for some releefe, before I yeelded to perish. At last this came into my head, that very euening, that I had to no purpose last vsed my horse and armour. I tolde *Menalcas*, that I was a *Thessalian* Gentle-man, who by mischaunce hauing killed a great fauorit of the Prince of that coūtry, was pursued so cruelly, that in no place, but either by fauour, or corruption, they would obtaine my destruction; and that therefore I was determined (till the fury of my persecutions might be asswaged) to disguise my selfe among the shephadrs of *Arcadia*, & (if it were possible) to be one of them that were allowed the Princes presence; Because if the woorst should fall, that I were discouered, yet hauing gotten the acquaintance of the Prince, it might happen to moue his hart to protect me. *Menalcas* (being of an honest dispositiō) pittied my case, which my face through my inward torment made credible; and so (I giuing him largely for it) let me haue this rayment, instructing me in all the particularities, touching himselfe, or my selfe, which I desired to know: yet not trusting so much to his constancie, as that I would lay my life, and life of my life, vpon it, I hired him to goe into *Thessalia* to a friend of mine, & to deliuer him a letter frō me; coniuring him to bring me as speedy an answeere as he could, because it imported

me

me greatly to know, whether certaine of my friendes
did yet poſſeſſe any fauour, whoſe interceſſiōs I might
vſe for my reſtitution. He willingly tooke my letter,
which being well ſealed, indeed conteyned other matter. For I wrote to my truſtie ſeruant *Calodoulus* (whom
you know)that aſſoone as he had deliuered the letter,
he ſhould keep him priſoner in his houſe, not ſuffering
him to haue cōference with any body, till he knewe
my further pleaſure: in all other reſpects that he ſhould
vſe him as my brother. And thus is *Menalcas* gone, and
I here a poore ſhepheard; more proud of this eſtate, thē
of any kingdom: ſo manifeſt it is, that the higheſt point
outward things can bring one vnto, is the contentmēt
of the mind: with which, no eſtate; without which, all
eſtates be miſerable. Now haue I choſen this day, becauſe (as *Menalcas* tolde me) the other ſhepheards are
called to make their ſports, and hope that you wil with
your credite, finde meanes to get me allowed among
them. You neede not doubt (anſwered *Zelmane*) but
that I will be your good miſtreſſe: marrie the beſt way
of dealing muſt be by *Dametas*, who ſince his blunt
braine hath perceiued ſome fauour the Prince dooth
beare vnto me (as without doubt the moſt ſeruile flatterie is lodged moſt eaſilie in the groſſeſt capacitie; for
their ordinarie conceite draweth a yeelding to their
greaters, and then haue they not witte to learne the
right degrees of duetie)is much more ſeruiceable vnto
me, then I can finde any cauſe to wiſh him. And therefore diſpaire not to winne him: for euery preſent occaſion will catch his ſenſes, and his ſenſes are maſters of
his ſillie mind; onely reuerence him, and reward him,
and with that bridle and ſaddle you ſhall well ride him.

O

O heauen and earth (said *Mufidorus*) to what a paffe are
our mindes brought, that from the right line of vertue,
are wryed to thefe crooked fhifts? But ô Loue, it is thou
that dooft it: thou changeft name vpó name; thou dif-
guifeft our bodies, and disfigureft our mindes. But in
deed thou haft reafon, for though the wayes be foule,
the iourneys end is moft faire and honourable.

CHAP. 19.

1 *The meanes of* Mufidorus *his apprentifage vnto* Dametas.
2 *The preparation and place of the Paftorals.* 3 *The Lyons
affault on* Philoclea, *and death by* Zelmane. 4 *The fhee
beares on* Pamela, *and death by* Dorus. 5 *The* Io Pæan
of Dametas, 6 *and his fcape from the beare.* 7 *The victors
praifes.* 8 *Whence thofe beafts were fent.*

N O more fweete *Mufidorus* (faid *Zelmane*) of thefe philofophies; for
here comes the very perfon of *Dametas*. And fo he did in deed, with
a fword by his fide, a forreft-bill on
his neck, and a chopping-knife vnder his girdle: in which prouided
forte he had euer gone, fince the
feare *Zelmane* had put him in. But he no fooner fawe
her, but with head and armes he laid his reuerence a-
fore her; inough to haue made any man forfweare all
courtefie. And then in *Bafilius* name, he did inuite her
to walke downe to the place, where that day they were
to haue the Paftoralles.

But

But when he spied *Musidorus* to be none of the shepheards allowed in that place, he would faine haue perswaded himselfe to vtter some anger, but that he durste
not; yet muttering, and champing, as though his cudde
troubled him; he gaue occasion to *Musidorus* to come
neare him, and feine this tale of his owne life: That he
was a younger brother of the shepheard *Menalcas*, by
name *Dorus*, sent by his father in his tender age to *A-*
thens, there to learne some cunning more then ordina-
ric, that he might be the better lik'd of the Prince: and
that after his fathers death, his brother *Menalcas* (latelie
gone thether to fetch him home) was also deceased:
where (vpon his death) he had charged him to seek the
seruice of *Dametas*, and to be wholy, and euer guyded
by him; as one in whose iudgement and integritie, the
Prince had singular confidence. For token whereof, he
gaue to *Dametas* a good summe of golde in redy coine,
which *Menelcas* had bequeathed vnto him, vpon condition he should receiue this poore *Dorus* into his seruice, that his mind and manner might grow the better
by his dayly example. *Dametas*, that of all manners of
stile could best conceiue of golden eloquence, being
withall tickled by *Musidorus* prayses, had his brayne so
turned, that he became slaue to that, which he, that
shewed to be his seruant, offered to giue him: yet for
countenance sake, he seemed very squeimish, in respect
of the charge he had of the Princesse *Pamela*. But such
was the secrete operation of the golde, helped with the
perswasion of the Amazon *Zelmane*, (who sayde it was
pittie so handsome a young man should be any where
els, then with so good a master) that in the ende he a-
greed (if that day he behaued himselfe so to the lyking
of

of *Basilius*, as he might be cõtented) that then he would receiue him into his seruice.

And thus went they to the Lodge, where they foũd *Gynecia* and her daughters ready to go to the field, to delight themselues there a while, vntill the shepheards comming: whether also taking *Zelmane* with them, as they went, *Dametas* told them of *Dorus*, and desired he might be accepted there that day, in steed of his brother *Menalcas*. As for *Basilius*, he staied behind to bring the shepherds, with whom he meant to cõfer, to breed the better *Zelmanes* liking (which he onely regarded) while the other beautifull band came to the faire field, appointed for the shepherdish pastimes. It was indeed a place of delight; for thorow the middest of it, there ran a sweete brooke, which did both hold the eye open with her azure streams, & yet seeke to close the eie with the purling noise it made vpon the pibble stones it ran ouer: the field it self being set in some places with roses, & in al the rest constantly preseruing a florishing greene; the Roses added such a ruddy shew vnto it, as though the field were bashfull at his owne beautie: about it (as if it had bene to inclose a *Theater*) grew such a sort of trees, as eyther excellency of fruit, statelines of grouth, continuall greennes, or poeticall fancies haue made at any time famous. In most part of which there had bene framed by art such pleasant arbors, that (one tree to tree, answering another) they became a gallery aloft from almost round about, which below gaue a perfect shadow, a pleasant refuge then from the cholericke looke of *Phœbus*.

In this place while *Gynecia* walked hard by them, carying many vnquiet cõtentions about her, the Ladies
M　　　　sate

ſate them downe, inquiring many queſtiõs of the ſhepheard *Dorus*; who (keeping his eie ſtill vpon *Pamela*) anſwered with ſuch a trembling voice, & abaſhed coūtenance, & oftentimes ſo far from the matter, that it was
ſome ſport to the young Ladies, thinking it want of e-
ducation, which made him ſo diſcountenaunced with
vnwoonted preſence. But *Zelmane* that ſaw in him the
glaſſe of her owne miſerie, taking the hande of *Philoclea*, and with burning kiſſes ſetting it cloſe to her lips
(as if it ſhould ſtande there like a hand in the margine
of a Booke, to note ſome ſaying worthy to be marked)
began to ſpeake theſe wordes. O Loue, ſince thou art
ſo changeable in mens eſtates, how art thou ſo conſtãt
in their torments? when ſodainly there came out of a
wood a monſtrous Lion, with a ſhe Beare not far from
him, of litle leſſe fiercenes, which (as they gheſt) hauing
bene huted in Foreſts far of, were by chaūce come thether, where before ſuch beaſtes had neuer bene ſeene.
Then care, not feare; or feare, not for themſelues, altered ſome thing the coūtenances of the two Louers,
but ſo, as any man might perceiue, was rather an aſſem-
bling of powers, then diſmaiednes of courage. *Philoclea*
no ſooner eſpied the Liõ, but that obeying the cõmandement of feare, ſhe lept vp, & ran to the lodge-waid,
as faſt as her delicate legs could carrie her, while *Dorus*
drew *Pamela* behind a tree, where ſhe ſtood quaking
like the Partridge, on which the Hawke is euē ready to
ſeaze. But the Lion (ſeing *Philoclea* run away) bent his
race to her-ward, & was ready to ſeaze him ſelfe on the
pray, when *Zelmane* (to whome daunger then was a
cauſe of dreadleſnes, all the cõpoſitions of her elemēts
being nothing but fierie) with ſwiftneſſe of deſire croſt
him,

him, and with force of affection ſtrake him ſuch a blow
vpon his chine, that ſhe opened al his body: wherwith
the valiant beaſt turning vpõ her with open iawes, ſhe
gaue him ſuch a thruſt thorow his breſt, that al the Liõ
could do, was with his paw to teare of the mantle and
ſleeue of *Zelmane*, with a little ſcratch, rather then a
wound; his death-blow hauing takē away the effect of
his force. But there withall he fell downe, & gaue *Zelmane* leaſure to take of his head, to carrie it for a preſent
to her Ladie *Philoclea*: who all this while (not knowing what was done behind her) kept on her courſe, like
Arethuſa when ſhe ran from *Alpheus*; her light apparell
being carried vp with the winde, that much of thoſe
beauties ſhe would at another time haue willingly hidden, was preſent to the ſight of the twiſe wounded *Zelmane*. Which made *Zelmane* not folow her ouer haſtily,
left ſhe ſhould too ſoone depriue her ſelfe of that pleaſure: But carying the Lions head in her hand, did not
fully ouertake her, till they came to the preſence of *Baſilius*. Nether were they lõg there, but that *Gynecia* came
thether alſo: who had bene in ſuch a traunce of muſing, that *Zelmane* was fighting with the Lion, before
ſhe knew of any Lions cōming: but then affection reſiſting, and the ſoone ending of the fight preuenting
all extremitie of feare, ſhe marked *Zelmanes* fighting.
And when the Lions head was of, as *Zelmane* ran after
Philoclea, ſo ſhe could not find in her hart but run after
Zelmane: ſo that it was a new ſight, Fortune had prepared to thoſe woods, to ſee theſe great perſonages
thus runne one after the other each carried forward
with an inwarde violence: *Philoclea* with ſuch feare,
that ſhe thought ſhe was ſtill in the Lions mouth:

M 2   *Zelmane*

Zelmane with an eager and impatient delight, *Gynecia*
with wings of Loue, flying they neither knew, nor cared to know whether. But now, being all come before *Basilius* amazed with this fight, and feare hauing
such possessiō in the faire *Philoclea*, that her bloud durst
not yet to come to her face, to take away the name of
palenesse from hec most pure whitenes, *Zelmane* kneeled down, and presented the Lions head vnto her. Only Ladie (said she) here see you the punishment of that
vnnatural beast, which cōtrary to her owne kind wold
haue wronged Princes bloud, guided with such traiterous eies, as durst rebell againſt your beauty. Happy am
I, and my beautie both (answered the sweete *Philoclea*
then blushing, for feare had bequeathed his roome
to his kinsman bashfulnes) that you excellent *Amaʒon*,
were there to teach him good manners . And euen
thankes to that beautie (answered *Zelmane*) which can
giue an edge to the bluntest swordes ? There *Philoclea*
told her father, how it had hapned : but as she had turned her eyes in her tale to *Zelmane*, she perceiued some
bloud vpō *Zelmanes* shoulder, so that starting with the
louely grace of pitty, she shewed it to her Father and
mother: who, as the nurse sometimes with ouer-much
kissing may forget to giue the babe sucke, so had they
with too much delighting, in beholding and prayfing
Zelmane, left of to marke whether she needed succour.
But then they ran both vnto her, like a father and mother to an onely childe, and (though *Zelmane* assured
them, it was nothing) would needes see it ; *Gynecia* hauing skill in surgery, an arte in those daies much esteemed, because it serued to vertuous courage, which euē
Ladies would (euē with the contēpt of courage) seeme
to

to cherifh . But looking vpon it (which gaue more inward bleeding woūds to *Zelmane*, for fhe might fometimes feele *Philocleas* touch, whiles fhe helped her mother) fhe found it was indeed of no great importance : yet applied fhe a pretious baulme vnto it, of power to heale a greater griefe.

But euen then, & not before, they remēbred *Pamela*, 4 & therefore *Zelmane* (thinking of her friend *Dorus*) was running back to be fatisfied, whē they might all fee *Pamela* cōming between *Dorus* & *Dametas*, hauing in her hād the paw of a Beare, which the fhepheard *Dorus* had newly prefented vnto her, defiring her to accept it, as of fuch a beaft, which though fhe deferued death for her prefumption, yet was her will to be efteemed, fince fhe could make fo fweet a choice. *Dametas* for his part came piping and dauncing, the merieft man in a parifh. But whē he came fo neere, as he might be heard of *Bafilius*, he would needs breake thorow his eares with this ioyfull fong of their good fucceffe.

NOw thanked be the great God Pan,   5
     which thus preferues my loued life :
Thanked be I that keepe a man,
     who ended hath this fearefull ftrife :
For if my man muft praifes haue,
     what then muft I that ke.pe the knaue ?

For as the Moone the eies doth pleafe,
     with gentle beames not hurting fight :
Yet hath fir Sunne the greateft praife,
     becaufe from him doth come her light :
So if my man muft praifes haue,
     what then muft I that keepe the knaue?

M 3   Being

4   Being al now come together, & all defirous to know
each others aduētures, *Pamelas* noble hart would needs
gratefully make knowne the valiāt mean of her fafety:
which (directing her fpeach to her mother) fhe did in
this māner. As foone(faid fhe)as ye were all run away,
and that I hoped to be in fafetie, there came out of the
fame woods a foule horrible Beare, which (fearing belike to deale while the Lion was prefent, as foone as he
was gone) came furioufly towardes the place where I
was, and this youug fhepheard left alone by me; I truly
(not guilty of any wifedome, which fince they lay to
my charge, becaufe they fay, it is the beft refuge againft
that beaft, but euē pure feare bringing forth that effect
of wifedome) fell downe flat of my face, needing not
coūterfait being dead, for indeed I was litle better. But
this fhepheard hauing no other weapon, but that knife
you fee, ftanding before the place where I lay, fo behaued him felfe, that the firft fight I had (when I thought
my felfe nearer *Charons* ferry,) was the fhepheard fhewing me his bloudy knife in token of victory. I pray you
(faide *Zelmane*, fpeaking to *Dorus*, whofe valour fhe was
carefull to haue manifefted) in what forte, fo ill wea-
poned, could you atchiue this enterprife? Noble Ladie (faide *Dorus*) the manner of thefe beaftes fighting
with any man, is to ftande vp vpon their hinder feete :
and fo this did, & being ready to giue me a fhrewd imbracement, I thinke, the God *Pan*, (euer carefull of the
chiefe bleffings of *Arcadia*) guided my hand fo iuft to
the hart of the beaft, that neither fhe could once touch
me, nor (which is the only matter in this worthy remē-
brāce) breed any dāger to the Princeffe. For my part, I
am rather (withall fubiected humblenes) to thanke her
excellencies, fince the duety thereunto gaue me harte
to

to faue my felfe, then to receiue thankes for a deede, which was her onely infpiring. And this *Dorus* fpake, keeping affection as much as he could, backe fiom cōming into his eyes and geftures. But *Zelmane* (that had the fame Character in her heart) could eafily difcerne it, and therefore to keepe him the longer in fpeach, defired to vnderfland the conclufion of the matter; and how the honeft *Dametas* was efcaped.

Nay (faid *Pamela*) none fhall take that office from my felfe, being fo much bound to him as I am, for my education. And with that word (fcorne borrowing the countenance of myrth) fomewhat fhe fmiled, and thus fpake on ⸴ When (faid fhe) *Dorus* made me affuredly perceiue, that all caufe of feare was paffed (the truth is) I was afhamed to finde my felfe alone with this fhepheard : and therefore looking about me, if I could fee any bodie; at length we both perceiued the gentle *Dametas*, lying with his breaft and head as farre as he could thruft himfelfe into a bufh: drawing vp his legges as clofe vnto him as hee coulde : for, like a man of a very kind nature, foone to take pittie of himfelfe, he was full refolued not to fee his owne death. And when this fhepheard pufhed him, bidding him to be of good cheere; it was a good while, ere we could perfwade him, that *Dorus* was not the beare : fo that he was faine to pull him out by the heeles, & fhew him the beaft, as deade as he could wifh it : which you may beleeue me, was a very ioyful fight vnto him. But then he forgate al curtefie, for he fel vpon the beaft, giuing it many a manfull wound: fwearing by much, it was not wel fuch beafts fhuld be fuffered in a cōmō welth. And then my gouernour, as full of ioy, as before of feare,

came

came dauncing and singing before vs as euen now you saw him. Well wel (said *Basilius*) I haue not chosen *Dametas* for his fighting, nor for his discoursing, but for his plainenesse and honestie, and therein I know he will not deceaue me.

7

But then he told *Pamela* (not so much because she should know it, as because he would tell it) the wonderfull act *Zelmane* had perfourmed, which *Gynecia* likewise spake off, both in such extremitie of praising, as was easie to be seene, the constructions of their speach might best be made by the Grammer rules of affection. *Basilius* told with what a gallant grace shee ranne with the Lyons head in her hand, like another *Pallas* with the spoiles of *Gorgon. Gynecia* sware, shee sawe the face of the young *Hercules* killing the *Nemean* Lion, & all with a gratefull assent confirmed the same praises: onely poore *Dorus* (though of equall desert, yet not proceeding of equall estate) should haue bene left forgotten, had not *Zelmane* againe with great admiration, begun to speake of him; asking, whether it were the fashion or no, in *Arcadia,* that sheepherds should performe such valorous enterprises. This *Basilius* (hauing the quicke sense of a louer) tooke, as though his Mistres had giuen a secret reprehension, that he had not shewed more gratefulnesse to *Dorus*; and therefore (as nymblie as he could) enquired of his estate, adding promise of great rewards : among the rest, offering to him, if he would exercise his courage in souldierie, he would commit some charge vnto him vnder his Lieutenant *Philanax.* But *Dorus* (whose ambition clymed by another stayre) hauing first answered touching his estate, that he was brother to the shepheard *Menalcas*; who

who

who among other, was wont to refort to the Princes
prefence,& excufed his going to fouldierie, by the vn-
aptneffe he found in himfelfe that way : he told *Bafilius*, that his brother in his laft teftament had willed him
to ferue *Dametas*; and therefore (for due obedience
thereunto) he would thinke his feruice greatly rewarded, if he might obtaine by that meane to liue in the
fight of his Prince, and yet practife his owne chofen
vocation. *Bafilius* (liking well his goodly fhape and
handfome manner) charged *Dametas* to receiue him
like a fonne into his houfe : faying, that his valour,
and *Dametas* truth would be good bulwarkes againft
fuch mifchiefes, as (he fticked not to fay) were threatned to his daughter *Pamela*.

    Dametas, no whit out of countenance with all that   2
had bene faid(becaufe he had no worfe to fal into then
his owne)accepted *Dorus:* and with all,telling *Bafilius*,
that fome of the fhepheards were come; demaunded
in what place he would fee their fports : who firft curious to know whether it were not more requifite for
Zelmanes hurt to reft, then fit vp at thofe paftimes; and
fhe (that felt no wound but one) earneftly defiring to
haue Paftorals, *Bafilius* commanded it fhould be at the
gate of the lodge : where the throne of the Prince being (according to the auncient manner) he made *Zelmane* fit betweene him & his wife therin, who thought
her felfe betweene drowning and burning : and the
two young Ladies of either fide the throne, and fo prepared their eyes and eares to bee delighted by the
fhepheards.

    But before al of them were affembled to begin their   8
fports,there came a fellow,who being out of breath (or

feeming

ſeeming ſo to be for haſte) with humble haſtines told
Baſilius, that his Miſtres, the Lady *Cecropia*, had ſent him
to excuſe the miſchance of her beaſtes ranging in that
dāgerous ſort, being happened by the folly of the keeper; who thinking himſelf able to rule them, had caried
them abroad, & ſo was deceiued: whom yet (if *Baſilius*
would puniſh for it) ſhe was readie to deliuer. *Baſilius*
made no other anſwere, but that his Miſtres if ſhee had
any more ſuch beaſtes, ſhould cauſe them to be killed:
and then he told his wife & *Zelmane* of it, becauſe they
ſhould not feare thoſe woods; as though they harbored ſuch beaſts, where the like had neuer bene ſeene.
But *Gynecia* tooke a further conceit of it, miſtruſting
Cecropia, becauſe ſhee had heard much of the diuelliſh
wickedneſſe of her heart, and that particularly ſhe did
her beſt to bring vp her ſonne *Amphialus* (being brothers ſonne to *Baſilius*) to aſpire to the crowne, as next
heire male after *Baſilius*; and therefore ſaw no reaſon,
but that ſhe might coniecture, it proceeded rather of
ſome miſchieuous practiſe, than of misfortune. Yet
did ſhe onely vtter her doubt to her daughters, thinking, ſince the worſt was paſt, ſhee would attend a further occaſion, leaſt ouer much haſte might ſeeme to
proceede of the ordinarie miſlike betweene ſiſters in
Lawe: onely they maruelled, that *Baſilius* looked no
further into it; who (good man) thought ſo much of
his late conceiued common wealth, that all other
matters were but digreſſions vnto him. But the ſhepheards were ready, and with wel handling themſelues,
called their ſenſes to attend their paſtimes.

The

The firſt Eclogues.

ASILIVS, becauſe *Zelmane* ſo would haue it, vſed the artificiall day of torches, to lighten the ſports their inuētions could miniſter. And yet becauſe many more ſhepheards were newly come, then at the firſt; he did in a gentle manner chaſtiſe the cowardiſe of the fugitiue ſhepheards: with making them (for that night) the Torch-bearers, and the others later come, he willed with all freedome of ſpeech and behauiour, to keepe their accuſtomed method. Which while they prepared to do, *Dametas,* who much diſdained (ſince his late authority) all his old companions, brought his ſeruant *Dorus* in good acquaintance and allowance of thē; & himſelfe ſtood like a directer ouer thē, with nodding, gaping, winking, or ſtamping ſhewing how he did like, or miſlike thoſe things he did not vnderſtand. The firſt ſports the ſhepheards ſhewed, were full of ſuch leapes & gambols, as being accorded to the Pipe (which they bare in their mouthes, euen as they daunced) made a right picture of their chiefe god *Pan,* and his companions the *Satyres.* Then would they caſt away their Pipes; and holding hand in hand, daunce as it were in a braule, by the onely cadence of their voices, which they would vſe in ſinging ſome ſhort coplets, whereto the one halfe beginning, the other halfe ſhould anſwere. As the one halfe ſaying,

We loue, and haue our loues rewarded.

The others would aunſwere.

We loue, and are no whit regarded.

The

The firſt againe.

We finde moſt ſweete affections ſnare,
With like tune it ſhould be as in quire ſent back againe.
That ſweete, but ſower deſpairefull care.
A third time likewiſe thus :
Who can deſpaire, whom hope doth beare?
The aunſwere.
And who can hope, that feeles deſpaire ?
Then all ioyning their voyces, and dauncing a faſter
meaſure, they would couclude with ſome ſuch words:
As without breath, no pipe doth moue,
No muſike kindly without loue.

Hauing thus varied both their ſongs and daunces
into diuers ſorts of inuentions ; their laſt ſport was one
of them to prouoke another to a more large expreſſing
of his paſſions: which *Lalus* (accounted one of the beſt
ſingers amongſt them) hauing marked in *Dorus* dauncing, no leſſe good grace & hanſome behauiour, then
extreame tokens of a trauelled minde ; began firſt with
his Pipe, and then with his voice, thus to chalenge *Do-*
rus, and was by him anſwered in the vnderwritten ſort.

Lalus and Dorus.

COme Dorus, *come, let ſongs thy ſorowes ſignifie:*
And if for want of vſe thy minde aſhamed is,
That verie ſhame with Loues high title dignifie.
No ſtile is held for baſe, where Loue well named is:
Ech eare ſuckes vp the words, a true loue ſcattereth,
And plaine ſpeach oft, then quaint phraſe, better framed is.

Nigh-

Nightingales ſeldome ſing, the Pie *ſtill chattereth:*   Dorus.
The wood cries moſt, before it throughly kindled be,
Deadly wounds inward bleed, ech ſleight ſore mattereth.
   Hardly they heard, which by good hunters ſingled be.
Shallow brookes murmure moſt, deep ſilent ſlide away,
Nor true loue loues thoſe loues with others mingled be.

   If thou wilt not be ſeene, thy face goe hide away,   Lalus.
Be none of vs, or els maintaine our faſhion :
Who frownes at others feaſtes, dooth better hide away.
   But if thou haſt a Loue, in that Loues paſsion,
I challenge thee by ſhew of her perfection,
Which of vs two deſerueth moſt compaſsion.

   Thy challenge great, but greater my protection :   Dorus.
Sing then, and ſee (for now thou haſt inflamed me)
Thy health too meane a match for my infection.
   No, though the heau'ns for high attempts haue blamed me,
Yet high is my attempt. O Muſe *hiſtorifie*
Her praiſe, whoſe praiſe to learne your skill hath framed me.

   Muſe hold your peace: but thou, my God Pan, *glorifie*   Lalus.
My Kalas *giftes: who with all gooa gifts filled is.*
Thy pipe, ô Pan, *ſhall helpe, though I ſing ſorilie.*
   A heape of ſweetes ſhe is, where nothing ſpilled is;
Who though ſhe be no Bee, *yet full of honie is :*
A Lillie *field, with plowe of* Roſe *which tilled is.*
   Milde as a Lambe, more daintie then a Conie is :
Her eyes my eyeſight is, her conuerſation
More gladde to me, then to a miſer monie is.
   What coye account ſhe makes of eſtimation ?
How niec to touch how all her ſpeeches peized be?

A Nimph thus turnde, but mended in tranſlation.

Dorus. Such Kala *is:* but ah, my fancies rayſed be
In one, whoſe name to name were high preſumption,
Since vertues all, to make her title, pleaſed be.

  O happie Gods, which by inward aſſumption
Enioy her ſoule, in bodies faire poſſeſſion,
And keep it ioynde, fearing your ſeates conſumption.

  How oft with raine of teares skies make confeſſion,
Their dwellers rapt with ſight of her perfection
From heau'nly throne to her heau'n vſe digreſſion?

  Of beſt things then what world can yeeld confection
To liken her? Decke yours with your compariſon:
She is her ſelfe, of beſt things the collection.

Lalus. How oft my dolefull Sire cried to me, tarrie ſonne
When firſt he ſpied my loue? how oft he ſaid to me,
Thou art no ſouldier fitte for Cupids garriſon?

  My ſonne, keepe this, that my long toyle hath laide to me:
Loue well thine owne: me thinkes, woolles whitenes paſſeth all:
I neuer found long loue ſuch wealth hath paide to me.

  This winde he ſpent: but when my Kala glaſſeth all
My ſight in her faire limmes, I then aſſure my ſelfe,
Not rotten ſheepe, but high crownes ſhe ſurpaſſeth all.

  Can I be poore, that her golde haire procure my ſelfe?
Want I white wooll, whoſe eyes her white skinne garniſhed?
Till I get her, ſhall I to keepe enure my ſelfe?

Dorus. How oft, when reaſon ſaw, loue of her harniſed
With armour of my hart, he cried, O vanitie,
To ſet a pearle in ſteele ſo meanely varniſhed?

  Looke to thy ſelfe; reach not beyond humanitie:

Her

Her minde,beames,state farre from thy weake wings banished:
And Loue,which louer hurts is inhumanitie.

   Thus Reason said: but she came, Reason vanished;
Her eyes so maistering me,that such obiection
Seemde but to spoyle the foode of thoughts long famished.

   Her peereles height my minde to high erection
Drawes vp;and if hope-fayling ende liues pleasure,
Of fayrer death how can I make election?

   Once my well-waiting eyes espied my treasure,   **Lalus.**
With sleeues turnde vp,loose haire,and brest enlarged,
Her fathers corne(mouing her faire limmes)measure.

   O cried I,of so meane worke be discharged :
Measure my case,how by thy beauties filling
With seede of woes my hart brimme-full is charged.

   Thy father bids thee saue,and chides for spilling.
Saue then my soule,spill not my thoughts well heaped,
No louely praise was euer got by killing.

   These bolde words she did heare,this fruite I reaped,
That she,whose looke alone might make me blessed,
Did smile on me,and then away she leaped.

   Once,ô sweete once,I saw with dread oppressed   **Dorus.**
Her whom I dread;so that with prostrate lying
Her length the earth in Loues chiefe clothing dressed.

   I saw that riches fall,and fell a crying;
Let not dead earth enioy so deare a couer,
But deck therewith my soule for your sake dying.

   Lay all your feare vpon your fearefull louer:
Shine eyes on me,that both our liues be guarded;
So I your sight,you shall your selues recouer.

   I cried,and was with open rayes rewarded :

                                      But.

But straight they fledde, summond by cruell honor,
Honor, the cause, desart is not regarded.

Lalus.
This mayde, thus made for ioyes, ô Pan bemone her,
That without loue she spends her yeares of loue :
So faire a fielde would well become an owner.
  And if enchantment can a harde hart moue,
Teach me what circle may acquaint her sprite,
Affections charmes in my behalfe to proue.
  The circle is my (round about her) sight:
The power I will inuoke dwelles in her eyes :
My charme should be, she haunt me day and night.

Dorus.
Farre other care, ô Muse, my sorrow tries,
Bent to such one, in whom, my selfe must say,
Nothing can mend that point that in her lies.
  What circle then in so rare force beares swaye ?
Whose sprite all sprites can spoile, raise, damne, or saue:
No charme holdes her, but well possesse she may;
  Possesse she doth, and makes my soule her slaue:
My eyes the bandes, my thoughts the fatall knot.
No thralles like them that inward bondage haue.

Lalus.
Kala at length conclude my lingring lotte :
Disdaine me not, although I be not faire .
Who is an heire of many hundred sheep
Doth beauties keep, which neuer Sunne can burne,
Nor stormes doo turne: fairenes serues oft to wealth.
Yet all my health I place in your good-will.
Which if you will (ô doo) bestow on me,
Such as you see, such still you shall me finde.
Constant and kind: my sheep your foode shall breed,

                                   Their

Their wooll your weede, I will you Musique yeeld
In flowrie fielde; and as the day begins
With twenty ginnes we will the small birds take,
And pastimes make, as Nature things hath made.
But when in shade we meet of mirtle bowes,
Then Loue allowes, our pleasures to enrich,
The thought of which doth passe all worldly pelfe.

Lady your selfe, whom nether name I dare,   Dorus.
And titles are but spots to such a worthe,
Heare plaints come forth from dungeon of my minde.
The noblest kinde reiects not others woes.
I haue no shewes of wealth : my wealth is you,
My beauties hewe your beames, my health your deeds;
My minde for weeds your vertues liuerie weares.
My foode is teares; my tunes waymenting yeeld :
Despaire my fielde; the flowers spirits warrs :
My day newe cares; my ginnes my daily sight,
In which do light small birds of thoughts orethrowne:
My pastimes none : time passeth on my fall :
Nature made all, but me of dolours made :
I finde no shade, but where my Sunne doth burne :
No place to turne; without, within it fryes :
Nor helpe by life or death who liuing dyes.

But if my Kala this my suite denies,   Lalus,
Which so much reason beares,
Let crowes picke out mine eyes, which saw too much :
If still her minde be such,
My earthy moulde will melte in watrie teares.

My earthy moulde doth melte in watrie teares,   Dorus.
N   *And*

And they againe resolue
To aire of sighes, sighes to the hartes fire turne,
Which doth to ashes burne :
So doth my life within it selfe dissolue,

Lalus.   *So doth my life within it selfe dissolue,*
That I am like a flower
New plucked from the place where it did breed,
Life showing, dead indeed :
Such force hath Loue aboue poore Natures power

Dorus.   *Such force hath Loue aboue poore Natures power,*
That I growe like a shade,
Which being nought seems somewhat to the eyen,
While that one body shine.
Oh he is mard that is for others made.

Lalus.   *Oh he is mard that is for others made.*
Which thought doth marre my piping declaration,
Thinking how it hath mard my shepheards trade.
Now my hoarse voice doth faile this occupation,
And others long to tell their loues condition:
Of singing take to thee the reputation.

Dorus.   *Of singing take to thee the reputation*
New friend of mine; I yeeld to thy habilitie :
My soule doth seeke another estimation.
But ah my Muse *I would thou hadst agilitie,*
To worke my Goddesse so by thy inuention,
On me to cast those eyes, where shine nobilitie.
Seen, and vnknowne; heard, but without attention.

This

THis Eclogue betwixt *Lalus* & *Dorus*, of euery one
of the beholders receiued great commendations.
When *Basilius* called to a yong shepheard, who nether
had daunced nor song with thē, but layne al this while
vpō the ground at the foot of a cypresse tree, in so deep
a melancholy, as though his mind were banished from
the place he loued, to be in prison in his body: & desired him he would begin some Eclogue, with some o-
ther of the shepheards, according to the accustomed
guise: or els declare the discourse of his owne fortune,
vnknowne to him; as being a straunger in that coūtry.
But he praied the King to pardon him, the time being
far too ioyful to suffer the rehersall of his miseries. Yet,
to satisfy *Basilius* some way, he sange this songe, he had
learned before he had subiected his thoughts to acknowledge no maister, but a mistresse.

AS I my little flocke on Ister banke
(A little flocke; but well my pipe they couthe)
Did piping leade, the Sunne already sanke
Beyond our worlde, and ere I got my boothe
Each thing with mantle black the night doth scothe;
 Sauing the glowe worme, which would curteous be
 Of that small light oft watching shepheards see.

The welkin had full niggardly enclosed
In cofer of dimme clowdes his siluer groates,
Icleped starres; each thing to rest disposed:
The caues were full, the mountaines voide of goates:
The birds eyes closde closed their chirping notes.
 As for the Nightingale woodmusiques King,
 It August was, he daynde not then to sing.

And

Amid my ſheepe, though I ſawe nought to feare
Yet (for I nothing ſawe) I feared ſore ;
Then fonde I which thing is a charge to beare
As for my ſheepe I dradded mickle more
Then euer for my ſelfe ſince I was bore :
 I ſate me downe : for ſee to goe ne could,
 And ſange vnto my ſheepe leſt ſtray they ſhould.

The ſonge I ſange old Lanquet *had me taught,*
Lanquet, *the ſhepheard beſt ſwift* Iſter *knewe,*
For clerkly reed, and hating what is naught,
For faithfull hart, cleane hands, and mouth as true :
With his ſweet skill my skilleſſe youth he drewe,
 To haue a feeling taſt of him that ſitts
 Beyond the heauen, far more beyond your witts.

He ſaid, the Muſique beſt thilke powers pleaſd
Was iumpe concorde betweene our wit and will:
Where higheſt notes to godlines are raiſd,
And loweſt ſinke not downe to iote of ill :
With old true tales he woont mine eares to fill,
 How ſheepheards did of yore, how now they thriue,
 Spoiling their flock, or while twixt the they ſtriue.

He liked me, but pitied luſtfull youth :
His good ſtrong ſtaffe my ſlippry yeares vpbore :
He ſtill hop'd well, becauſe he loued truth :
Till forſte to parte, with harte and eyes euen ſore,
To worthy Coriden *he gaue me ore.*
 But thus in okes true ſhade recounted he
 Which now in nights deepe ſhade ſheep heard of me.

Such

Such maner time there was (what time I n'ot)
When all this Earth, this damme or mould of ours
Was onely won'd with such as beastes begot :
Vnknowne as then were they that builded towers :
The cattell wild, or tame, in natures bowers
Might freely rome, or rest, as seemed them :
Man was not man their dwellings in to hem.

The beastes had sure some beastly pollicie :
For nothing can endure where order n'is.
For once the Lion by the Lambe did lie ;
The fearcfull Hinde the Leopard did kiffe :
Hurtles was Tygers pawe and Serpents hiffe.
This thinke I well, the beasts with courage clad
Like Senators a harmeles empire had.

At which whether the others did repine,
(For enuie harbreth most in feeblest hartes)
Or that they all to chaunging did encline,
(As euen in beasts their dames leaue chaunging parts)
The multitude to Ioue a suite empartes,
With neighing, blaying, braying, and barking,
Roring, and howling for to haue a King.

A King, in language theirs they said they would :
(For then their language was a perfect speech)
The birdes likewise with chirpes, and puing could
Cackling, and chattring, that of Ioue befeech.
Onely the owle still warnde them not to feech
So hastily that which they would repent :
But sawe they would, and he to deferts went.

Ioue

Ioue wiſely ſaid (for wiſedome wiſely ſayes)
O beaſts, take heed what you of me deſire.
Rulers will thinke all things made them to pleaſe
And ſoone forget the ſwincke due to their hire.
But ſince you will, part of my heau'nly fire
   I will you lende; the reſt your ſelues muſt giue,
   That it both ſeene and felte may with you liue.

Full glad they were and tooke the naked ſprite,
Which ſtreight the Earth yclothed in his claye :
The Lion, harte; the Ounce gaue actiue might;
The Horſe, good ſhape; the Sparrow, luſt to playe;
Nightingale, voice, entiſing ſonges to ſaye.
   Elephant gaue a perfect memorie:
   And Parot, ready tongue, that to applie.

The Foxe gaue craſtie; the Dog gaue flatterie;
Aſſe, pacience; the Mole, a working thought;
Eagle, high looke; Wolfe ſecrete crueltie :
Monkie, ſweet breath; the Cow, her faire eyes brought;
The Ermion, whiteſt skinne, ſpotted with nought;
   The ſheep, mild-ſeeming face; climing, the Beare;
   The Stagge did giue the harme eſchewing feare.

The Hare, her ſleights; the Cat, his melancholie;
Ante, induſtrie; and Connie, skill to builde;
Cranes, order; Storkes, to be appearing holie;
Cameleon, eaſe to chaunge; Ducke, eaſe to yelde;
Crocodile, teares, which might be falſely ſpilde :
   Ape great thing gaue, though he did mowing ſtand,
   The inſtrument of inſtruments, the hand .

Ech

Ech other beast likewise his present brings :
And (but they drad their Prince they ought should want)
They all consented were to giue him wings :
And aye more awe towards him for to plant,
To their owne worke this priuiledge they graunt,
   That from thenceforth to all eternitie,
   No beast should freely speake, but onely he.

Thus Man was made; thus Man their Lord became:
Who at the first, wanting, or hiding pride,
He did to beastes best vse his cunning frame ;
With water drinke, herbes meate, and naked hide,
And fellow-like let his dominion slide ;
   Not in his sayings saying I, but we :
   As if he meant his lordship common be.

But when his seate so rooted he had found,
That they now skilld not, how from him to wend ;
Then gan in guiltlesse earth full many a wound,
Iron to seeke, which gainst it selfe should bend,
To teare the bowels, that good corne should send.
   But yet the common Damme none did bemone ;
   Because (though hurt) they neuer heard her grone.

Then gan the factions in the beastes to breed ;
Where helping weaker sort, the nobler beastes,
(As Tygers, leopards, beares, and Lions seed)
Disdaind with this, in deserts sought their restes ;
Where famine rauine taught their hungrie chestes,
   That craftily he forst them to do ill,
   Which being done he afterwards would kill.

N 4

For murthers done, which neuer erſt was ſeene,
By thoſe great beaſtes, as for the weakers good,
He choſe themſelues his guarders for to bene,
Gainſt thoſe of might, of whom in feare they ſtood,
As horſe and dogge, not great, but gentle blood :
　Blith were the commons cattell of the fielde,
　Tho when they ſaw their foen of greatnes kilde.

But they or ſpent, or made of ſlender might,
Then quiekly did the meaner cattell finde,
The great beames gone, the houſe on ſhoulders light :
For by and by the horſe faire bitts did binde :
The dogge was in a coller taught his kinde.
　As for the gentle birds like caſe might rewe
　When falcon they, and goſſehauke ſaw in mewe.

Worſt fell to ſmalleſt birds, and meaneſt heard,
Whom now his owne, full like his owne he vſed.
Yet firſt but wooll, or fethers off he teard :
And when they were well vſde to be abuſed,
For hungrie teeth their fleſh with teeth he bruſed :
　At length for glutton taſte he did them kill :
　At laſt for ſport their ſillie liues did ſpill.

But yet ȏ man, rage not beyond thy neede :
Deeme it no gloire to ſwell in tyrannie.
Thou art of blood ; ioy not to ſee things bleede :
Thou feareſt death ; thinke they are loth to die.
A plaint of guiltleſſe hurt doth pierce the ſkie.
　And you poore beaſtes, in patience bide your hell,
　Or know your ſtrengths, and then you ſhall do well.

Thus

Thus did I sing, and pipe eight sullen houres
To sheepe, whom loue, not knowledge, made to heare,
Now fancies fits, now fortunes balefull flowers :
But then I homewards call'd my lambkins deare :
For to my dimmed eyes beganne t'appeare
   The night growne old, her blacke head waxen gray,
   Sure shepherds signe, that morne should soone fetch day.

A Ccording to the nature of diuerse eares, diuerse iudgements streight followed : some praising his voice, others his words fit to frame a pastorall stile, others the strangenes of the tale, and scanning what he shuld meane by it. But old *Geron* (who had borne him a grudge euer since in one of their Eclogues he had taken him vp ouer-bitterly) tooke hold of this occasion to make his reuenge, and said, He neuer saw thing worse proportioned, then to bring in a tale of he knew not what beastes at such a sport-meeting, when rather some song of loue, or matter for ioyfull melody was to be brought forth. But, said he, This is the right conceipt of young men, who thinke, then they speake wiseliest, when they cannot vnderstand themselues. But little did the melancholike shepherd regard either his dispraises, or the others praises, who had set the foundation of his honour there; where he was most despised. And therefore he returning againe to the traine of his desolate pensiuenesse, *Geron* inuited *Histor* to answere him in Eclogue-wise; who indeed hauing bene long in loue with the faire *Kala*, and now by *Lalus* ouergone; was growne into a detestation of marriage. But thus it was.

Geron

Geron. Hiſtor.

Gron. IN faith, good Hiſtor, long is your delay,
From holy marriage ſweete and ſureſt meane:
Our fooliſh luſt in honeſt rules to ſtay.
I pray thee doo to Lalus ſample leane:
Thou ſeeſt, how friske, and iolly now he is,
That laſt day ſeem'd, he could not chew a beane.
Beleeue me man, there is no greater bliſſe,
Then is the quiet ioy of louing wife;
Which who ſo wants, halfe of himſelfe doth miſſe.
Friend without change, playfellow without ſtrife,
Foode without fulnes, counſaile without pride,
Is this ſweet doubling of our ſingle life.

Hiſtor. No doubt to whom ſo good chance did betide,
As for to finde a paſture ſtrawed with golde,
He were a foole, if there he did not bide.
Who would not haue a Phœnix if he could?
The humming Waſpe, if it had not a ſtinge,
Before all flies the Waſpe accept I would.
But this bad world, few golden fieldes doth bring,
Phœnix but one, of Crowes we millions haue:
The Waſpe ſeemes gay, but is a combrous thing.
If many Kalaes our Arcadia gaue,
Lalus example I would ſoone enſue,
And thinke, I did my ſelfe from ſorrow ſaue.
But of ſuch wiues we finde a ſlender crew;
Shrewdnes ſo ſtirres, pride ſo puffes vp the hart,
They ſeldome ponder what to them is due.
With meager lookes, as if they ſtill did ſmart;

Puiling

Puiling, and whimpring, or elſe ſcolding flat,
Make home more paine then following of the cart.

  Ether dull ſilence, or eternall chat ;
Still contrarie to what her huſband ſayes ;
If he do praiſe the dog, ſhe likes the cat.

  Auſtere ſhe is, when he would honeſt playes ;
And gameſome then, when he thinkes on his ſheepe ;
She bids him goe, and yet from iorney ſtayes.

  She warre doth euer with his kinsfolke keepe,
And makes them fremb'd, who frinds by nature are,
Enuying ſhallow toyes with malice deepe.

  And if forſooth there come ſome new found ware,
The little coine his ſweating browes haue got,
Muſt goe for that, if for her lowres he care :

  Or els ; Nay faith, mine is the luckleſt lot,
That euer fell to honeſt woman yet :
No wife but I hath ſuch a man, God wot.

  Such is their ſpeech, who be of ſober wit ;
But who doo let their tongues ſhew well their rage,
Lord, what bywords they ſpeake, what ſpite they ſpit?

  The houſe is made a very lothſome cage,
Wherein the birde doth neuer ſing but cry ;
With ſuch a will as nothing can aſſwage.

  Dearely the ſeruants doo their wages buy,
Reuil'd for ech ſmall fault, ſometimes for none :
They better liue that in a gaile doo lie.

  Let other fowler ſpots away be blowne ;
For I ſeeke not their ſhame, but ſtill me thinkes,
A better life it is to lye alone.

   Who for ech fickle feare from vertue ſhrinkes,
Shall in his life embrace no worthy thing :

No mortall man the cuppe of suretie drinkes.

   The heau'ns doo not good haps in handfuls bring,
But let vs pike our good from out much bad :
That still our little world may know his king.

   But certainly so long we may be glad,
While that we doo what nature doth require,
And for th'euent we neuer ought be sad.

   Man oft is plag'de with aire, is burnt with fire,
In water dround, in earth his buriall is ;
And shall we not therefore their vse desire?

   Nature aboue all things requireth this,
That we our kind doo labour to maintaine ;
Which drawne-out line doth hold all humane blisse.

   Thy father iustly may of thee complaine,
If thou doo not repay his deeds for thee,
In granting vnto him a grandsires gaine.

   Thy common-wealth may rightly grieued be,
Which must by this immortall be preserued,
If thus thou murther thy posteritie.

   His very being he hath not deserued,
Who for a selfe-conceipt will that forbeare,
Whereby that being aye must be conserued.

   And God forbid, women such cattell were,
As you paint them : but well in you I finde,
No man doth speake aright, who speakes in feare.

   Who onely sees the ill is worse then blind.
These fiftie winters maried haue I beene ;
And yet finde no such faults in womankind.

   I haue a wife worthie to be a Queene,
So well she can command, and yet obay ;
In ruling of a house so well shee's seene.

   And yet in all this time, betwixt vs tway,

                                      We

We beare our double yoke with such consent,
That neuer paſt foule word, I dare well ſay.

   But theſe be your loue-toyes, which ſtill are ſpent
In lawleſſe games, and loue not as you ſhould,
But with much ſtudie learne late to repent.

   How well laſt day before our Prince you could
Blinde Cupids *workes with wonder teſtifie?*
Yet now the roote of him abaſe you would.

   Goe to, goe to, and Cupid *now applie*
To that where thou thy Cupid *maiſt auowe,*
And thou ſhalt finde, in women vertues lie.

   Sweete ſupple mindes which ſoone to wiſdome bowe
Where they by wiſdomes rule directed are,
And are not forſt fonde thraldome to allow.

   As we to get are fram'd, ſo they to ſpare:
We made for paine, our paines they made to cheriſh :
We care abroad, and they of home haue care.

   O Hiſtor, *ſeeke within thy ſelfe to flouriſh :*
Thy houſe by thee muſt liue, or els be gone :
And then who ſhall the name of Hiſtor *nouriſh?*

   Riches of children paſſe a Princes throne;
Which touch the fathers hart with ſecret ioy,
When without ſhame he ſaith, theſe be mine owne.

   Marrie therefore; for marriage will deſtroy
Thoſe paſsions which to youthfull head doo clime
Mothers and Nurſes of all vaine annoy.

ALl the aſſemblie laught at the luſtines of the old fe-
lowe, and eaſilie perceiued in *Hiſtor,* he liked *Lalus*
fortune better, then he loued his perſon. But *Baſilius*
to entermixe with theſe light notes of libertie, ſome
ſadder tune, ſet to the key of his own paſſion, not ſeeing
there

there *Strephon* or *Klaius*, (who called thence by *Vranias* letter, were both gone to continue their suite, like two true runners, both employing their beſt ſpeed, but not one hindring the other) he called to one *Lamō* of their acquaintance, and willed him to ſing ſome one of their ſongs; which he redily performed in this doble Seſtine.

Strephon.　　Klaius.

Strephon.　Y Ou Gote-heard Gods, that loue the graßie mountaines,
　　　　　　 You Nimphes that haunt the ſprings in pleaſant vallies,
　　　　　　 You Satyrs ioyde with free and quiet forreſts,
　　　　　　 Vouchſafe your ſilent eares to playning muſique,
　　　　　　 Which to my woes giues ſtill an early morning :
　　　　　　 And drawes the dolor on till wery euening.

Klaius.　 *O Mercurie, foregoer to the euening,*
　　　　　　 O heauenlie huntreſſe of the ſauage mountaines,
　　　　　　 O louelie ſtarre, entitled of the morning,
　　　　　　 While that my voice doth fill theſe wofull vallies,
　　　　　　 Vouchſafe your ſilent eares to plaining muſique,
　　　　　　 Which oft hath Echo tir'd in ſecrete forreſts.

Strephon.　*I that was once free-burges of the forreſts,*
　　　　　　 Where ſhade from Sunne, and ſports I ſought at euening,
　　　　　　 I that was once eſteem'd for pleaſant muſique,
　　　　　　 Am baniſht now among the monſtrous mountaines
　　　　　　 Of huge deſpaire, and foule afflictions vallies,
　　　　　　 Am growne a ſhrich-owle to my ſelfe each morning.

Klaius.　 *I that was once delighted euery morning,*
　　　　　　 Hunting the wilde inhabiters of forreſts,

　　　　　　　　　　　　　　　　　　　　　 I that

I that was once the musique of these vallies,
So darkened am, that all my day is euening,
Hart-broken so, that molehilles seeme high mountaines,
And fill the vales with cries in steed of musique.

Long since alas, my deadly Swannish musique
Hath made it selfe a crier of the morning,   Strephon.
And hath with wailing stregth clim'd highest mountaines:
Long since my thoughts more desert be then forrests:
Long since I see my ioyes come to their euening,
And state throwen downe to ouer-troden vallies.

Long since the happie dwellers of these vallies,   Klaius.
Haue praide me leaue my strange exclaiming musique,
Which troubles their dayes worke, and ioyes of euening:
Long since I hate the night, more hate the morning:
Long since my thoughts chase me like beasts in forrests,
And make me wish my selfe layd vnder mountaines.

Me seemes I see the high and stately mountaines,   Strephon.
Transforme themselues to lowe deiected vallies:
Me seemes I heare in these ill changed forrests,
The Nightingales doo learne of Owles their musique:
Me seemes I feele the comfort of the morning
Turnde to the mortall serene of an euening.

Me seemes I see a filthie clowdie euening,   Klaius.
As soon as Sunne begins to clime the mountaines:
Me seemes I feele a noysome sent, the morning
When I doo smell the flowers of these vallies:
Me seemes I heare, when I doo heare sweete musique,
The dreadfull cries of murdred men in forrests.

I wish

Strephon.
I wish to fire the trees of all these forrests;
I giue the Sunne a last farewell each euening ;
I curse the fidling finders out of Musicke :
With enuie I doo hate the loftie mountaines;
And with despite despise the humble vallies:
I doo detest night, euening, day, and morning.

Klaius.
Curse to my selfe my prayer is, the morning :
My fire is more, then can be made with forrests;
My state more base, then are the basest vallies:
I wish no euenings more to see, each euening;
Shamed I haue my selfe in sight of mountaines,
And stoppe mine eares, lest I growe mad with Musicke.

Strephon.
For she, whose parts maintainde a perfect musique,
Whose beautie shin'de more then the blushing morning,
Who much did passe in state the stately mountaines,
In straightnes past the Cedars of the forrests,
Hath cast me wretch into eternall euening,
By taking her two Sunnes from these darke vallies.

Klaius.
For she, to whom compar'd, the Alpes are vallies,
She, whose left word brings from the spheares their musique,
At whose approach the Sunne rose in the euening,
Who, where she went, bare in her forhead morning,
Is gone, is gone from these our spoyled forrests,
Turning to desarts our best pastur'de mountaines.

Strephon.
Klaius.
These mountaines witnesse shall, so shall these vallies,
These forrests eke, made wretched by our musique,
Our morning hymne is this, and song at euening.

Zel-

ZElmane feing no body offer to fill the ftage, as if her long reftrained conceits had new burft out of prifon, fhe thus defiring her voice fhould be accorded to nothing but *Philocleas* eares, laying faft holde on her face with her eyes, fhe fange thefe Sapphiques, fpeaking as it were to her owne Hope.

IF mine eyes can fpeake to doo harty errande,
Or mine eyes language fhe doo hap to iudge of,
So that eyes meffage be of her receaued,
　　　Hope we do liue yet.

But if eyes faile then, when I moft doo need them,
Or if eyes language be not vnto her knowne,
So that eyes meffage doo returne reiected,
　　　Hope we doo both dye.

Yet dying, and dead, doo we fing her honour;
So become our tombes monuments of her praife;
So becomes our loffe the triumph of her gayne;
　　　Hers be the glory.

If the fpheares fenfeleffe doo yet hold a mufique,
If the Swannes fweet voice be not heard, but at death,
If the mute timber when it hath the life loft,
　　　Yeldeth a lutes tune.

Are then humane mindes priuiledg'd fo meanly,
As that hatefull death can abridge them of powre,
With the vowe of truth to recorde to all worldes,
　　　That we be her fpoiles?

Thus

Thus not ending, endes the due praise of her praise;
Fleshly vaile consumes; but a soule hath his life,
Which is helde in loue, loue it is, that hath ioynde
Life to this our soule.

But if eyes can speake to doo harty errande,
Or mine eyes language she doo hap to iudge of,
So that eyes message be of her receaued,
Hope we doo liue yet.

WHat exclaiming praises *Basilius* gaue to *Zelmanes* songe, any man may ghesse, that knowes loue is better then a paire of spectacles to make euery thing seeme greater, which is scene through it : and then is it neuer tongue-tied, where fit commendation (whereof womankind is so licorous) is offered vnto it. Yea, he fel prostrate on the ground, and thanked the Gods, they had preserued his life so long, as to heare the very musique they themselues vsed, in an earthly body. But the wasting of the torches serued as a watch vnto them, to make them see the time waste; and therefore the King (though vnwilling) rose from the seate , which he thought excellently setled on the one side: and considering *Zelmanes* late hurte , perswaded her to take that farre-spent nights rest. And so of all sides they went to recommend themselues to the elder brother of death.

The end of the first Booke.

THE SECOND BOOKE
OF THE COVNTESSE OF
PEMBROKES ARCADIA.

CHAP. I.

The loue-complaintes [1] of Gynecia, *[2]* Zelmane, *[3] and* Bafilius. *[4] Her, [5] and his wooing of* Zelmane, *and her
fhifting of both, [6] to bemone her felfe*

N thefe *paftorall pa-*
ftimes a great number
of dayes wcre fent to
follow their flying pre-
deceffouis , while the
cup of poifon (which
was deepely tafted of
this noble companie)
had left no finewe of
theirs without mortal-
ly fearching into it ; yet
neuer manifefting his venomous worke , till once,
that the night(parting away angerly, that fhe could diftill no more fleepe into the eies of louers) had no fooner giuen place to the breaking out of the morning
light, and the Sunne beftowed his bcames vpon the
tops of the mountaines, but that the wofull *Gynecia*(to
whom reft was no eafe) had left her loathed lodging,
and gotten her felfe into the folitary places thofe de-

O 2   ferts

ſerts were full of, going vp and downe with ſuch vnquiet motions, as a grieued & hopeles mind is wont to
bring forth. There appeered vnto the eies of her iudgement the euils ſhe was like to run into, with ougly infamie waiting vpon them : ſhe felt the terrous of her
owne conſcience : ſhe was guilty of a long exerciſed
vertue, which made this vice the fuller of deformitie.
The vttermoſt of the good ſhe could aſpire vnto, was a
mortall wound to her vexedſpirits : and laſtly no ſmall
part of her euils was, that ſhe was wiſe to ſee her euils.
In ſo much, that hauing a great while throwne her
coūtenaunce ghaſtly about her (as if ſhe had called all
the powers of the worlde to witneſſe of her wretched
eſtate) at length caſting vp her watrie eyes to heauen,
O Sunne (ſaid ſhe) whoſe vnſpotted light directs the
ſteps of mortall mankind, art thou not aſhamed to impart the clearneſſe of thy preſence to ſuch a duſt-cree-
ping worme as I am ? O you heauens (which continually keepe the courſe allotted vnto you) can none of
your influences preuaile ſo much vpon the miſerable
Gynecia, as to make her preſerue a courſe ſo lōg embraced by her ? O deſerts, deſerts, how fit a gueſt am I for
you, ſince my hart can people you with wild rauenous
beaſtes, which in you are wanting ? O Vertue, where
dóoſt thou hide thy ſelfe ? or what hideous thing is
this which doth eclips thee? or is it true that thou weart
neuer but a vaine name, and no eſſentiall thing, which
haſt thus left thy profeſſed ſeruant, when ſhe had moſt
need of thy louely preſence? O imperfect proportio of
reaſon, which cā too much forſee, & too little preuent.
Alas, alas (ſaid ſhe) if there were but one hope for all
my paines, or but one excuſe for all my faultineſſe. But
wretch

wretch that I am, my torment is beyond all succour,& my euill deseruing doth exceed my euill fortune. For nothing els did my husband take this straunge resolutiõ to liue so solitarily : for nothing els haue the winds deliuered this straunge guest to my country : for nothing els haue the destinies reserued my life to this time, but that only I (most wretched I) should become a plague to my selfe, and a shame to womankind. Yet if my desire (how vninst so euer it be) might take effect, though a thousand deaths folowed it, and euery death were followed with a thousand shames; yet should not my sepulcher receiue me without some contentment. But alas, though sure I am, that *Zelmane* is such as can answere my loue ; yet as sure I am, that this disguising must needs come for some foretaké cóceipt. And then, wretched *Gynecia*, where cást thou find any smal groudplot for hope to dwel vpon ? No, no, it is *Philoclea* his hart is set vpon : it is my daughter I haue borne to supplant me . But if it be so, the life I haue giuen thee (vngratefull *Philoclea*) I will sooner with these handes bereaue thee of, then my birth shall glory, she hath bereaued me of my desires. In shame there is no cófort, but ,, to be beyond all bounds of shame.

Hauing spoké thus, she began to make a piteous war with hir faire haire, when she might heare (not far frõ her) an extremely doleful voice, but so suppressed with a kind of whispering note, that she could not conceaue the wordes distinctly . But (as a lamentable tune is the ,, sweetest musicke to a wofull mind) she drewe thether neere-away, in hope to find some cópaniõ of her misery. And as she passed on, she was stopped with a nuber of trees, so thickly placed together , that she was afraid she should (with rushing thorow) stop the speach of

the

the lamentable partie, which ſhe was ſo deſirous to vnderſtand . And therefore ſetting her downe as ſoftly
as ſhe could (for ſhe was now in diſtaunce to heare)
ſhe might firſt perceaue a Lute excellently well played
vpon, and then the ſame dolefull voice accompanying
it with theſe verſes.

IN vaine, mine Eyes, you labour to amende
   With flowing teares your fault of haſty ſight :
Since to my hart her ſhape you ſo did ſende;
   That her I ſee, though you did loſe your light.

In vaine, my Hart, now you with ſight are burnd,
   With ſighes you ſeeke to coole your hotte deſire:
Since ſighes (into mine inward fornace turnd)
   For bellowes ſerue to kindle more the fire.

Reaſon, in vaine (now you haue loſt my hart)
   My head you ſeeke, as to your ſtrongeſt forte :
Since there mine eyes haue played ſo falſe a parte,
   That to your ſtrength your foes haue ſure reſorte.
   Then ſince in vaine I find were all my ſtrife,
   To this ſtrange death I vainely yeeld my life.

The ending of the ſong ſerued but for a beginning of
new plaints, as if the mind (oppreſſed with too heauy a
burthē of cares) was faine to diſcharge it ſelf of al ſides,
& as it were, paint out the hideouſnes of the paine in al
ſortes of coulours. For the wofull perſon (as if the lute
had euill ioined with the voice) threw it to the ground
with ſuch like words : Alas, poore Lute, how much art
thou deceiu'd to think, that in my miſeries thou couldſt
eaſe my woes, as in my careles times thou was wont to
                                pleaſe

pleafe my fancies? The time is changed, my Lute, the
time is changed; and no more did my ioyfull minde
then receiue euery thing to a ioyful confideration, then
my carefull mind now makes ech thing taft like the bitter iuyce of care. The euill is inward, my Lute, the euill
is inward; which all thou dooft doth ferue but to make
me thinke more freely off, and the more I thinke, the
more caufe I finde of thinking, but leffe of hoping. And
alas, what is then thy harmony, but the fweete meats of
forrow? The difcord of my thoughts, my Lute, doth
ill agree to the concord of thy ftrings; therefore be not
afhamed to leaue thy mafter, fince he is not aftaide to
forfake himfelfe.

And thus much fpoke (in fteed of a conclufion) was 4
clofed vp with fo harty a groning, that *Gynecia* could not
refraine to fhew her felfe, thinking fuch griefes could
ferue fitly for nothing, but her owne fortune. But as fhe
came into the little Arbour of this forrowfull muficke,
her eyes meet with the eyes of *Zelmane*, which was the
party that thus had indited her felfe of miferie : fo that
either of them remained confufed with a fodaine aftonifhment. *Zelmane* fearing, leaft fhee had heard fome
part of thofe complaints, which fhee had rifen vp that
morning of purpofe, to breath out in fecret to her felfe.
But *Gynecia* a great while ftoode ftill, with a kind of dull
amafement, looking ftedfaftly vpon her : at length returning to fome vfe of her felfe, fhee began to afke *Zelmane*, what caufe carried her fo early abroad? But as if
the opening of her mouth to *Zelmane*, had opened fome
great flood-gate of forrow (wherof her heart could not
abide the violet iffue) fhe fanke to the ground, with her
hands ouer her face, crying vehemently, *Zelmane* helpe
me,

me, O *Zelmane* haue pittie on me. *Zelmane* ranne to
her, maruelling what fodaine ficknesse had thus pos-
fessed her: and beginning to afke her the caufe of her
paine, and offring her feruice to be imployed by her:
Gynecia opening her eyes wildly vpon her, pricked with
the flames of loue, and the torments of her owne confcience; O *Zelmane, Zelmane,*(faid fhe) dooft thou offer me phificke, which art my onely poyfon? Or wilt
thou doo me feruice, which haft alredie brought me
into eternall flauerie? *Zelmane* then knowing well at
what marke fhe fhot, yet loth to enter into it; Moft excellent Ladie (faid fhe) you were beft retire your felfe
into your lodging, that you the better may paffe this
fodaine fitte. Retire my felfe? (faid *Gynecia*) If I had
retyred my felfe into my felfe, when thou to me (vnfortunate gueft) cameft to draw me from my felfe; bleffed
had I beene, and no neede had I had of this counfaile.
But now alas, I am forced to flie to thee for fuccour,
whom I accufe of all my hurt; and make thee iudge of
my caufe, who art the onely author of my mifchiefe.
Zelmane the more aftonifhed, the more fhe vnderftood
her, Madam (faid fhe) whereof do you accufe me, that
I will not cleere my felfe? Or wherein may I fteed you,
that you may not command me? Alas, anfwered *Gy-*
necia, what fhall I fay more? Take pitty of me, O *Zel-*
mane, but not as *Zelmane,* and difguife not with me in
words, as I know thou dooft in apparell.

    Zelmane was much troubled with that word, finding
her felfe brought to this ftreight. But as fhee was thinking what to anfwere her; they might fee olde *Bafilius*
paffe harde by them, without euer feeing them: complayning likewife of loue verie frefhly; and ending his
com-

complaint with this fong, Loue hauing renewed both
his inuention, and voyce.

L Et not old age difgrace my high defire,
   O heauenly foule, in humaine fhape conteind :
Old wood inflam de, doth yeeld the braueft fire,
When yonger dooth in fmoke his vertue fpend.

Ne let white haires, which on my face doo grow,
   Seeme to your eyes of a difgracefull hewe :
Since whiteneffe doth prefent the fweeteft fhow,
Which makes all eyes doo honour vnto you.

Old age is wife and full of conftant truth ;
   Old age well ftayed from raunging humor liues :
Old age hath knowne what euer was in youth :
   Old age orecome, the greater honour giues.
   And to old age fince you your felfe afpire,
   Let not old age difgrace my high defire.

Which being done, he looked verie curioufly vpon
himfelfe, fometimes fetching a little fkippe, as if he had
faid, his ftrength had not yet forfaken him. But *Zelma-*
ne hauing in this time gotten leafure to thinke for an
anfwere; looking vpon *Gynecia*, as if fhe thought fhe did
her fome wrong : Madam (faid fhe) I am not acquainted with thofe words of difguifing, neither is it the
profeffion of an *Amazon*, neither are you a partie with
whom it is to be vfed. If my feruice may pleafe you,
imploy it, fo long as you do me no wrong in mifiudge-
ing of me. Alas *Zelmane* (faid *Gynecia*) I perceiue you
know ful little; how percing the eyes are of a true louer.
                         There

There is no one beame of thoſe thoughts you haue planted in me, but is able diſcerne a greater cloud then you doo goe in. Seeke not to conceale your ſelfe further from me, nor force not the paſſion of loue into violent extremities. Nowe was *Zelmane* brought to an exigent, when the king, turning his eyes that way thorow the trees, perceiued his wife and miſtres togither: ſo that framing the moſt louely countenance he could, he came ſtraightway towards them; and at the firſt word (thanking his wife for hauing entertained *Zelmane*,) deſired her ſhe would now returne into the lodge, becauſe hee had certaine matters of eſtate to impart to the Ladie *Zelmane*. The Queene (being nothing troubled with ielouſie in that point) obeyed the kings commaundement; full of raging agonies, and determinatly bent, that as ſhe would ſeeke all louing meanes to winne *Zelmane*, ſo ſhe would ſtirre vp terrible tragedies, rather then faile of her entent. And ſo went ſhe from them to the lodge-ward, with ſuch a battaile in her thoughts, and ſo deadly an ouerthrow giuen to her beſt reſolutions, that euen her bodie (where the fielde was fought) was oppreſſed withall: making a languiſhing ſickneſſe waite vpon the triumph of paſſion; which the more it preuailed in her, the more it made her ielouſie watchfull, both ouer her daughter, and *Zelmane*; hauing euer one of them entruſted to her owne eyes.

But as ſoone as *Baſilius* was ridde of his wiues preſence, falling downe on his knees, O Lady (ſaid he) which haſt onely had the power to ſtirre vp againe thoſe flames which had ſo long layn deade in me; ſee in me the power of your beautie; which can make
old

old age come to aſke counſaile of youth; and a Prince vncõquered, to become a ſlaue to a ſtranger. And whẽ you ſee that power of yours, loue that at leſt in me, ſince it is yours, although of me you ſee nothing to be loued. Worthy Prince (anſwered *Zelmane*,taking him vp from his kneeling) both your manner, and your ſpeech are ſo ſtraunge vnto me, as I know not how to anſwere it better then with ſilence. If ſilence pleaſe you (ſaid the king) it ſhal neuer diſpleaſe me, ſince my heart is wholly pledged to obey you: otherwiſe if you would vouchſafe mine eares ſuch happineſſe, as to heare you, they ſhall conuay your words to ſuch a mind, which is with the humbleſt degree of reuerẽce to receiue them. I diſdaine not to ſpeake to you (mightie Prince ſaid *Zelmane*,) but I diſdaine to ſpeake to any matter which may bring my honor into queſtion. And therewith, with a braue counterfeited ſcorne ſhe departed from the king; leauing him not ſo ſorie for his ſhort anſwere, as proud in himſelf that he had broken the matter. And thus did the king (feeding his minde with thoſe thoughts) paſſe great time in writing verſes, & making more of himſelfe, then he was wont to doo : that with a little helpe, he would haue growne into a prettie kind of dotage.

But *Zelmane* being ridde of this louing, but little-lo 6 ued company, Alas (ſaid ſhe) poore *Pyrocles*,was there euer one, but I, that had receiued wrong, and could blame no body? that hauing more then I deſire, am ſtill in want of that I woulde ? Truly Loue, I muſt needes ſay thus much on thy behalfe; thou haſt imployed my loue there, where all loue is deſerued; and for re-compence haſt ſent me more loue then euer I deſired.

But.

But what wilt thou doo *Pyrocles?* which way canſt thou finde to ridde thee of thy intricate troubles? To her whom I would be knowne to, I liue in darkeneſſe: and to her am reuealed, from whom I would be moſt ſecreat. What ſhift ſhall I finde againſt the diligent loue of *Baſilius?* what ſhield againſt the violent paſſions of *Gynecia?* And if that be done, yet how am I the neerer to quench the fire that conſumes me? Wel, well, ſweete *Philoclea*, my whole confidence muſt be builded in thy diuine ſpirit, which cannot be ignorant of the cruell wound I haue receiued by you.

CHAP. 2.

1 Dametas-*his enſtructing of* Dorus. 2 Zelmanes *diſcourſe to* Dorus *of her difficulties;* 3 *& his to her of his ſucceſſe in loue.* 4 *His loue-ſuits made to* Mopſa, *meant to* Pamela: *with their anſweres.*

Vt as ſicke folkes, when they are a-lone, thinke companie would relieue them, & yet hauing company do find it noyſome; changing willingly outward obiects, when indeed the euill is inward: So poore *Zelmane* was no more weery of *Baſilius,* then ſhe was of her ſelfe, when *Baſilius* was gone: and euer the more, the more ſhe turned her eyes to become her owne iudges. Tyred wherewith, ſhe longed to meete her friende *Dorus;* that vpon the ſhoulders of friendſhip ſhe might lay the burthen of ſorrow: and therefore went toward the other lodge: where among certaine Beeches ſhe found *Dorus,* apparelled in flanen, with a goats ſkin caſt vpon him, & a garland of Laurell

mixt

mixt with Cypres leaues on his head, wayting on his
maſter *Dametas*, who at that time was teching him how
with his ſheephooke to catch a wanton Lambe, & with
the ſame to caſt a litle clod at any one that ſtrayed out
of côpanie. And while *Dorus* was practiſing, one might
ſee *Dametas* hold his hand vnder his girdle behind him,
nodding from the waſt vpwards, & ſwearing he neuer
knew man go more aukewardly to worke: & that they
might talke of booke-learning what they would; but
for his part, he neuer ſaw more vnfeatlie fellowes, then
great clearks were.

But *Zelmanes* comming ſaued *Dorus* from further 2
chiding. And ſo ſhe beginning to ſpeake with him of
the number of his maſters ſheepe, and which Prouince
of *Arcadia* bare the fineſt wooll, drewe him on to follow her in ſuch countrie diſcourſes, till (being out of
Dametas hearing) with ſuch vehemencie of paſſion, as
though her harte would clime into her mouth, to take
her tongues office, ſhe declared vnto him, vpon what
briers the roſes of her affections grew: how time ſtill
ſeemed to forget her, beſtowing no one houre of comfort vpon her; ſhe remaining ſtil in one plight of ill fortune, ſauing ſo much worſe, as continuance of euill
dooth in it ſelfe increaſe euill. Alas my *Dorus* (ſaid ſhe)
thou ſeeſt how long and languiſhingly the weekes are
paſte ouer vs ſince our laſte talking. And yet am I the
ſame, miſerable I, that I was: onely ſtronger in longing, and weaker in hoping. Then fell ſhe to ſo pitifull
a declaration of the inſupportablenes of her deſires,
that *Dorus* eares (not able to ſhew what woundes that
diſcourſe gaue vnto them) procured his eyes with
teares to giue teſtimonie, how much they ſuffered for
                                                    her

her suffering: till paffion (a moft cumberfome gueft to it felfe)made *Zelmane* (the fooner to fhake it of) earne-ftly intreate *Dorus*, that he alfo(with like freedome of difcourfe)would beftow a Mappe of his little worlde, vpon her;that fhe might fee, whether it were troubled with fuch vnhabitable climes of colde defpaires, and hotte rages,as hers was. And fo walking vnder a fewe Palme trees, (which being louing in their own nature, feemed to giue their fhadow the willinglier, becaufe they held difcourfe of loue) *Dorus* thus entred to the defcription of his foitune.

3   Alas(faid he)deare Cofin,that it hath pleafed the high powers to throwe vs to fuch an eftate, as the one-ly entercourfe of our true friendfhippe, muft be a bar-tring of miferies. For my parte, I muft confeffe in-deede, that from a huge darkenes of forrowes, I am crept (I cannot fay to a lightfomnes, but) to a certain dawning, or rather, peeping out of fome poffibilitie of comfort: But woe is me, fo farre from the marke of my defires, that I rather thinke it fuch a light,as comes through a fmall hole to a dungeon, that the miferable caitife may the better remember the light, of which he is depriued: ot like a fcholler, who is onely come to that degree of knowledge,to finde him felfe vtterly ig-norant.

But thus ftands it with me: After that by your meanes I was exalted to ferue in yonder bleffed lodge, for a while I had,in the furnace of my agonies, this re-frefhing; that (becaufe of the feruice I had done in kil-ling of the Beare) it pleafed the Princeffe (in whom indeede ftatelines fhines through courtefie) to let fall fome gratious looke vpon me. Sometimes to fee my
ex-

exercifes, fometimes to heare my fonges. For my
parte, my harte woulde not fuffer me to omitte any
occafion, whereby I might make the incomparable
Pamela, fee how much extraordinarie deuotion I bare
to her feruice: and withall, ftraue to appeare more worthy in her fight; that fmall defert, ioyned to fo great affection, might preuaile fomething in the wifeft Ladie
But too well (alas) I founde, that a fhepheards feruice
was but confidered of as from a fhepheard, and the acceptation limitted to no further proportion, then of a
good feruant. And when my countenance had once
giuen notice, that there lay affection vnder it, I fawe
ftraight, Maiefty (fitting in the throne of Beautie) draw
foorth fuch a fworde of iuft difdaine, that I remayned
as a man thunder-ftriken; not daring, no not able, to
beholde that power. Now, to make my eftate knowen,
feemed againe impoffible, by reafon of the fufpitiouf-
nes of *Dametas*, *Mifo*, and my young Miftreffe, *Mopfa*. For, *Dametas* (according to the conftitution of a
dull head) thinkes no better way to fhewe him felfe
wife, then by fufpecting euery thing in his way.
Which fufpition *Mifo* (for the hoggifh fhrewdneffe of
her braine) and *Mopfa* (for a very vnlikely enuie fhe
hath ftumbled vpon, againft the Princeffes vnfpeake-
able beautie) were very gladde to execute. So that
I (finding my feruice by this meanes lightlie regarded, my affection defpifed, and my felfe vnknowen)
remayned no fuller of defire, then voyde of comfort
how to come to my defire. Which (alas) if thefe trees
could fpeak, they might well witneffe. For, many times
haue I ftoode here, bewailing my felfe vnto them:
many

many times haue I, leaning to yonder Palme, admired the bleſſednes of it, that coulde beare Loue without ſence of paine. Many times, when my maſters cattle came hether to chewe their cudde, in this freſh place, I might ſee the young Bull teſtifie his loue. But how? with proud lookes, and ioyfulnes. O wretched mankind (ſaid I then to my ſelfe) in whom witte (which ſhould be the gouerner of his welfare) becomes the traitor to his bleſſednes. Theſe beaſts, like children to nature, inherite her bleſſings quietly; we, like baſtards, are layd abroad, euen as foundlinges to be trayned vp by griefe and ſorrow. Their mindes grudge not their bodies comfort, nor their ſences are letted from enioying their obiects: we haue the impediments of honor, and the torments of conſcience. Truely in ſuch cogitatiōs haue I ſomtimes ſo long ſtood, that me thought my feete began to grow into the ground, with ſuch a darkenes and heauines of minde, that I might eaſilie haue bene perſwaded to haue reſigned ouer my very eſſence. But Loue, (which one time layeth burthens, another time giueth wings) when I was at the loweſt of my downward thoughts, pulled vp my harte to reméber, that nothing is atchieued before it be throughlie attempted; and that lying ſtill doth neuer goe forward: and that therefore it was time, now or neuer, to ſharpen my inuention, to pearce thorow the hardnes of this enterpriſe; neuer ceaſing to aſſemble al my conceites, one after the other; how to manifeſt both my minde and eſtate. Till at laſt, I lighted and reſolued on this way, which yet perchaunce you will think was a way rather to hide it.

4   I began to counterfeite the extremeſt loue towards
Mopſa,

Mopſa, that might be: and as for the loue, ſo liuely it was
indeed within me, (although to another ſubiect) that
litle I needed to counterfait any notable demonſtrations of it: and ſo making a contrariety the place of my
memory, in her fowlnes I beheld *Pamelas* fayreneſſe;
ſtill looking on *Mopſa*, but thinking on *Pamela*; as if I
ſaw my Sunne ſhine in a puddled water: I cryed out
of nothing but *Mopſa*: to *Mopſa* my attendance was
directed: to *Mopſa* the beſt fruites I coulde gather
were brought: to *Mopſa* it ſeemed ſtill that mine eye
conueyed my tongue. So that *Mopſa* was my ſaying; *Mopſa* was my ſinging; *Mopſa*, (that is onely
ſuteable in laying a foule complexion vpon a filthy fauour, ſetting foorth both in ſluttiſhneſſe) ſhe was the
load-ſtarre of my life, ſhe the bleſſing of mine eyes,
ſhe the ouerthrowe of my deſires, and yet the recompence of my ouerthrowe; ſhe the ſweetneſſe of my
harte, euen ſweetning the death, which her ſweetneſſe drew vpon me. In ſumme, what ſoeuer I thought
of *Pamela*, that I ſaide of *Mopſa*; whereby as I gatte
my maiſters good-will, who before ſpited me, fearing
leſt I ſhould winne the Princeſſe fauour from him, ſo
did the ſame make the Princeſſe be better content to
allow me her preſence: whether indeede it were, that
a certaine ſparke of noble indignation did riſe in her,
not to ſuffer ſuch a baggage to winne away any thing
of hers, how meanely ſoeuer ſhe reputed of it; or rather (as I thinke) my words being ſo paſſionate; and
ſhooting ſo quite contrarie from the markes of *Mopſaes* worthineſſe, ſhe perceiued well enough, whither
they were directed: and therefore being ſo maſked, ſhe
was contented, as a ſporte of witte to attend them.

               P   Where-

Whereupon one day determining to find fome means to tel (as of a third perfon) the tale of mine owne loue, and eftate, finding *Mopfa* (like a Cuckoo by a Nightingale) alone with *Pamela*, I came in vnto them, and with a face (I am fure) full of clowdy fancies, tooke a harpe, and fonge this fonge.

Since fo mine eyes are fubiect to your fight,
That in your fight they fixed haue my braine:
Since fo my harte is filled with that light,
That onely light doth all my life maintaine;

Since in fwecte you all goods fo richly raigne,
That where you are no wifhed good can want ;
Since fo your liuing image liues in me,
That in my felfe your felfe true loue doth plant ;
How can you him vnworthy then decree,
In whofe chiefe parte your worthes implanted be ?

The fong being ended, which I had often broken of in the middeft with grieuous fighes, which ouertooke euery verfe I fange, I let fall my harpe frõ me; & cafting my eie fometime vpon *Mopfa*, but fetting my fight principally vpon *Pamela*, And is it the onely fortune moft bewtiful *Mopfa* (faid I) of wretched *Dorus*, that fortune fhould be meafure of his mind? Am I onely he that becaufe I am in miferie, more miferie muft be laid vpon me? muft that which fhould be caufe of compaffion, become an argument of cruelty againft me? Alas excellent *Mopfa*, confider, that a vertuous Prince requires the life of his meaneft fubiect, and the heauenly

ly Sunne difdaines not to giue light to the fmalleft
worme. O *Mopfa, Mopfa,*if my hart could be as manifeft
to you, as it is vncomfortable to me, I doubt not the
height of my thoughts fhould well counteruaile the
lowneffe of my qualitie. Who hath not heard of the
greatnes of your eftate? who feeth not, that your eftate
is much excelled with that fweet vniting of al beauties,
which remaineth & dwelleth with you? who knowes
not, that al thefe are but ornamēts of that diuine fparke
within you, which being defcēded from heauen could
not els-where picke out fo fweete a manfion? But if
you will knowe what is the bande that ought to knit
all thefe excellencies together, it is a kinde of mercy-
fulneffe to fuch a one, as is in his foule deuoted to
thofe perfections. *Mopfa* (who already had had a certaine fmackring towardes me) ftood all this while with
her hand fometimes before her face, but moft cōmon-
ly with a certaine fpeciall grace of her owne, wagging
her lips, and grinning in fteede of fmiling: but all the
wordes I could get of her, was, wringing her wafte,
and thrufting out her chinne, In faith you ieft with
me: you are a merry man indeede. But the euer-plea-
fing *Pamela* (that well found the Comedie would be
marred, if fhe did not helpe *Mopfa* to her parte) was cotent to vrge a little further of me. Maifter *Dorus* (faid
the faire *Pamela*) me thinks you blame your fortune very wrongfully, fince the fault is not in Fortune, but in
you that cannot frame your felfe to your fortune: and
as wrongfully do require *Mopfa* to fo great a difparagement as to her Fathers feruaunt; fince fhe is not worthy to be loued, that hath not fome feeling of her
owne worthines. I ftaied a good while after her words,

in hope fhe would haue continued her fpeech (fo
great a delight I receaued in hearing her) but feeing
her fay no further, (with a quaking all ouer my body)
I thus anfwered her. Ladie, moft worthie of all dutie,
how falles it out that you in whom all vertue fhines,
will take the patronage of fortune, the onely rebellious handmaide againft vertue? Efpecially, fince before
your eyes, you haue a pittifull fpectacle of her wickedneffe, a forlorne creature, which muft remaine not
fuch as I am, but fuch as fhe makes me, fince fhe muft
be the ballance of worthineffe or difparagement. Yet
alas, if the condemned man (euen at his death) haue
leaue to fpeake, let my mortall wound purchafe thus
much confideration; fince the perfections are fuch in
the partie I loue, as the feeling of them cannot come
into any vnnoble hart; fhall that harte, which doth not
onely feele them, but hath all the working of his life
placed in them, fhall that hart I faie, lifted vp to fuch a
height, be counted bafe? O let not an excellent fpirit
doo it felfe fuch wrong, as to thinke, where it is placed, imbraced, and loued; there can be any vnworthineffe, fince the weakeft mift is not eafilier driuen a-
way by the Sunne, then that is chafed away with fo
high thoughts. I will not denie (anfwered the gratious *Pamela*) but that the loue you beare to *Mopfa*, hath
brought you to the confideration of her vertues, and
that confideration may haue made you the more vertuous, and fo the more worthie: But euen that then
(you muft confeffe) you haue receiued of her, and fo
are rather gratefully to thanke her, then to preffe any
further, till you bring fomething of your owne wherby to claime it. And truely *Dorus*, I muft in *Mopfaes*
behalfe

behalfe fay thus much to you, that if her beauties
haue fo ouertaken you, it becomes a true Loue to
haue your harte more fet vpon her good then your
owne, and to beare a tenderer refpect to her honour,
then your fatisfaction. Now by my hallidame, Madame (faid *Mopfa*, throwing a great number of fheeps
eyes vpon me) you haue euen touched mine owne
minde to the quicke, forfooth. I (finding that the pollicie that I had vfed, had at left wife procured thus
much happineffe vnto me, as that I might euen in my
Ladies prefence, difcouer the fore which had deepely
feftered within me, and that fhe could better conceaue my reafons applied to *Mopfa*, then fhe would
haue vouchfafed them, whileft her felfe was a partie)
thought good to purfue on my good beginning, v-
fing this fit occafion of *Pameleas* wit, and *Mopfaes* ignorance. Therfore with an humble pearcing eye, looking
vpon *Pamela*, as if I had rather bene cōdemned by her
mouth, then highly exalted by the other, turning my
felfe to *Mopfa*, but keeping mine eye where it was, faire
Mopfa (faid I) well doo I finde by the wife knitting together of your anfwere, that any difputatiō I can vfe is
afmuch too weake, as Ivnworthy. I find my loue fhalbe
proued no loue, without I leue to loue, being too vnfit
a veffell in whō fo high thoughts fhould be engraued.
Yet fince the Loue I beare you, hath fo ioyned it felf to
the beft part of my life, as the one cānot depart, but that
th'other will follow, before I feeke to obey you in making my laft paffage, let me know which is my vnworthines, either of minde, eftate, or both? *Mopfa* was about
to fay, in neither; for her hart I thinke tūbled with ouer
much kindneffe, when *Pamela* with a more fauourable

countenance thē before (finding how apt I was to fall
into diſpaire) told me, I might therein haue anſwered
my ſelfe; for beſides that it was graunted me, that the
inward feeling of *Mopſaes* perfectiōs had greatly beautified my minde, there was none could denie, but that
my minde and bodie deſerued great allowance. But
Dorus (ſayd ſhe) you muſt be ſo farre maiſter of your
loue, as to conſider, that ſince the iudgement of the
world ſtands vpon matter of fortune, and that the ſexe
of womankind of all other is moſt bound to haue re-
gardfull eie to mens iudgements,it is not for vs to play
the philoſophers, in ſeeking out your hidden vertues:
ſince that,which in a wiſe prince would be coūted wiſdome,in vs wil be taken for a light-grounded affectiō :
ſo is not one thing,one,done by diuers perſons.There
is no man in a burning feuer feeles ſo great contentmēt in cold water greedily receiued (which aſſoone as
the drinke ceaſeth,the rage reneweth)as poore I found
my ſoule refreſhed with her ſweetly pronoūced words;
& newly, & more violētly againe enflamed,aſſoone as
ſhe had cloſed vp her delightfull ſpeach, with no leſſe
wel graced ſilence.But remēbring in my ſelf that aſwell
the Souldier dieth which ſtandeth ſtill,as he that giues
the braueſt onſet:& ſeeing that to the making vp of my
fortune,there wanted nothing ſo much as the making
knowne of mine eſtate, with a face wel witneſſing how
deeply my ſoule was poſſeſſed,& with the moſt ſubmiſ-
ſiue behauior,that a thralled hart could expreſſe,euē as
my words had bene too thicke for my mouth, at lēgth
ſpake to this purpoſe.Alas,moſt worthy Princeſſe (ſaid
I)& do not then your owne ſweet words ſufficiētly teſtifie, that there was neuer mā could haue a iuſter actiō
againſt

againſt filthy fortune, thē I, ſince all other things being
granted me, her blindneſſe is my onely let? O heauēly
God, I would either ſhe had ſuch eyes as were able to
diſcerne my deſerts, or I were blind not to ſee the daily
cauſe of my miſfortune. But yet (ſaid I) moſt honoured
Lady, if my miſerable ſpeeches haue not already cloied
you, & that the verie preſence of ſuch a wretch become not hatefull in your eyes; let me reply thus much
further againſt my mortall ſentence, by telling you a
ſtorie, which happened in this ſame country long ſince
(for woes make the ſhorteſt time ſeeme long) where- ”
by you ſhall ſee that my eſtate is not ſo contemptible,
but that a Prince hath bene content to take the like vpon him, and by that onely hath aſpired to enioy a
mightie Princeſſe. *Pamela* gratiouſly harkened, and I
told my tale in this ſort

CHAP. 3.

Dorus-his tale of his owne ¹ *education,* ² *trauaile,* ³ *ena.noring,*
⁴ *metamorphoſing,* ⁵ *ſauing from ſea,* ⁶ *and being* Muſidorus. ⁷ *His octaue.* ⁸ *Pamelas and Mopſas anſwere to his ſuit.*
⁹ *His preſent to them;* ¹⁰ *and perplexitie in himſelfe.*

N the countrie of *Theſſalia,* (alas
why name I that accurſed country, which brings forth nothing,
but matters for tragedies? but
name it I muſt) in *Theſſalia* (I ſay)
there was (well may I ſay, there
was) a Prince (no, no Prince, whō
bondage wholly poſſeſſed; but

yet accounted a Prince, and) named *Mufidorus*. O *Mufi-dorus*, *Mufidorus*; but to what ferue exclamations, where there are no eares to receiue the founde? This *Mufi-dorus*, being yet in the tendreft age, his worthy father paied to nature (with a violent death) her laft dueties, leauing his childe to the faith of his friends, and the proofe of time : death gaue him not fuch pangs as the forefight-full care hee had of his filly fucceffour. And yet if in his forefight he could haue feene fo much, happie was that good Prince in his timely depar-ture, which barred him from the knowledge of his fonnes miferies, which his knowledge could neither haue preuented, nor relieued. The young *Mufidorus* (being thus, as for the firft pledge of the deftinies good will, depriued of his principall ftay) was yet for fome yeares after (as if the ftarres would breath themfelues for a greater mifchiefe) lulled vp in as much good luck, as the heedfull loue of his dolefull mother, and the flo-rifhing eftate of his country could breed vnto him.

2   But when the time now came, that miferie feemed to be ripe for him, becaufe he had age to know mifery, I thinke there was a confpiracy in all heauenly & earth-ly things, to frame fit occafion to leade him vnto it. His people (to whom all forraine matters in foretime were odious) beganne to wifh in their beloued Prince, ex-perience by trauaile : his deare mother (whofe eyes were held open, onely with the ioy of looking vpon him) did now difpenfe with the comfort of her wi-dowhead life, defiring the fame her fubiectes did, for the increafe of her fonnes worthineffe. And here-to did *Mufidorus* owne vertue (fee how vertue can be a minifter to mifchiefe) fufficiently prouoke him : for
indeed

indeed thus much I muſt ſay for him,although the like-
neſſe of our miſhaps makes me preſume to patterne my
ſelfe vnto him) that well-doing was at that time his
ſcope, from which no faint pleaſure could with-hold
him. But the preſent occaſion which did knit all this
togither, was his vncle the king of *Macedon*; who hauing lately before gottē ſuch victories, as were beyond
expectation, did at this time ſend both for the Prince
his ſonne (brought vp togither, to auoid the warres,
with *Muſidorus*) and for *Muſidorus* himſelfe, that his ioy
might be the more full, hauing ſuch partakers of it.
But alas, to what a ſea of miſeries my plaintfull toong
doth lead me; and thus out of breath, rather with that
I thought, then that I ſaid, I ſtayed my ſpeech, till *Pamela* ſhewing by countenance that ſuch was her pleaſure, I thus continued it. Theſe two young Princes to
ſatiſſie the king,tooke their way by ſea,towards *Thrace*,
whether they would needs go with a Nauie to ſuccour
him : he being at that time before *Bizantium* with a
mighty Army beſeeging it;where at that time his court
was. But when the conſpired heauens had gotten this
Subiect of their wrath vpon ſo fit a place as the ſea was,
they ſtreight began to breath out in boyſtrous windes
ſome part of their malice againſt him; ſo that with the
loſſe of all his Nauie, he onely with the Prince his coſin, were caſt a land, farre off from the place whether
their deſires would haue guided them. O cruell winds
in your vnconſiderate rages, why either beganne you
this furie, or why did you not end it in his end ? But
your cruelty was ſuch, as you would ſpare his life for
many deathfull torments. To tel you what pittiful miſhaps fell to the young Prince of *Macedon* his coſen, I
                                                ſhould

should too much fill your eares with ſtrange horrors;
neither will I ſtay vpon thoſe laborſome aduētures, nor
loathſome miſaduentures, to which, & through which
his fortune and courage conducted him; My ſpeach
haſtneth it ſelf to come to the ful-point of *Muſidorus* his
infortunes. For as we finde the moſt peſtilēt diſeaſes do
gather into themſelues al the infirmitie, with which the
body before was annoyed; ſo did his laſt miſery em-
bracein the extremitie of it ſelf all his former miſchiefes.

3   *Arcadia*, *Arcadia* was the place prepared to be the
ſtage of his endleſſe ouerthrow. *Arcadia* was, (alas well
might I ſay it is) the charmed circle, where all his ſpirits
for euer ſhould be enchaunted. For here (and no where
els) did his infected eyes make his minde know, what
power heauenly beauty hath to throw it downe to helliſh agonies. Here, here did he ſee the *Arcadian* Kings
eldeſt daughter, in whom he forthwith placed ſo all his
hopes of ioy, and ioyfull parts of his heart, that he left
in himſelfe nothing, but a maze of longing, and a dungeon of ſorrow. But alas what can ſaying make them
beleeue, whom ſeeing cannot perſwade? Thoſe paines
muſt be felt before they cā be vnderſtood; no outward
vtterance can command a conceipt. Such was as then
the ſtate of the King, as it was no time by direct meanes
to ſeeke her. And ſuch was the ſtate of his captiued wil,
as he could delay no time of ſeeking her.

  In this intangled caſe, he cloathed himſelfe in a ſhep-
4 heards weede, that vnder the baſeneſſe of that forme,
he might at leſt haue free acceſſe to feed his eyes with
that, which ſhould at length eate vp his hart. In which
doing, thus much without doubt he hath manifeſted,
that this eſtate is not alwayes to be reiected, ſince vnder

der that vaile there may be hidden things to be efteemed. And if he might with taking on a fhepherds look
caft vp his eyes to the faireft Princeffe Nature in that
time created; the like,nay the fame defire of mine need
no more to be difdained, or held for difgracefull. But
now alas mine eyes waxe dimme, my toong beginnes
to falter,and my hart to want force to help, either with
the feeling remembrance I haue, in what heape of miferies the caitife Prince lay at this time buried. Pardon
therfore, moft excellent Princeffe,if I cut off the courfe
of my dolorous tale, fince if I be vnderftood,I haue
faid enough, for the defence of my bafeneffe; and for
that which after might befall to that patterne of ill fortune, (the matters are monftrous for my capacitie) his
hatefull deftinies muft beft declare their owne workemanfhip.

Thus hauing deliuered my tale in this perplexed **5**
manner, to the end the Princeffe might iudge that he
ment himfelfe, who fpake fo feelingly; her aunfwere
was both ftrange,and in fome refpect comfortable.For
would you thinke it? fhe hath heard heretofore of vs
both,by meanes of the valiant prince *Plangus*, and particularly of our cafting away:which fhe(following my
owne ftile) thus delicately brought foorth. You haue
told(faid fhe) *Dorus*,a prettie tale;but you are much deceiued in the latter end of it. For the prince *Mufidorus*
with his cofen *Pyrocles* did both perifh vpon the coaft
of *Laconia*; as a noble gentleman, called *Plangus* (who
was well acquainted with the hiftorie) did affure my
father. O how that fpeach of hers did poure ioyes in
my hart?ô bleffed name(thought I)of mine,fince thou
haft bene in that toong, and paffed through thofe lips,
　　　　　　　　　　　　　　　　　　　　though

though I can neuer hope to approch them. As for *Hi-rocles* (said I) I will not denie it, but that he is perished: (which I said, least sooner suspition might arise of your being, then your selfe would haue it) and yet affirmed no lye vnto her, since I onely said, I would not deny it. But for *Musidorus* (said I) I perceiue indeed you haue neither heard or read the story of that vnhappy Prince; for this was the verie obiection, which that peereleſse Princesse did make vnto him, whē he sought to appeare such as he was before her wisdome: and thus as I haue read it faire written in the certaintie of my knowledge he might answere her, that indeed the ship wherein hē came, by a treason was perished, and therfore that *Plangus* might easily be deceaued: but that he himselfe was cast vpon the coast of *Laconia*, where he was taken vp by a couple of shepheards, who liued in those dayes famous; for that both louing one faire maide, they yet remained constant friends; one of whose songs not long since was song before you by the shepheard *Lamon*, and brought by them to a noble-mans house, neere *Mantinea*, whose sonne had a little before his mariage, bene taken prisoner, and by the helpe of this Prince, *Musidorus* (though naming himselfe by another name) was deliuered. Now these circumlocutions I did vse, because of the one side I knewe the Princesse would knowe well the parties I ment; and of the other, if I should haue named *Strephon*, *Claius*, *Kalander*, and *Clitophon*, perhappes it would haue rubd some coniecture into the heauie heade of Mistreſſe *Mopsa*.

And therfore (said I) most diuine Lady, he iustly was to argue against such suspitions; that the Prince might easily

eafily by thofe parties be fatisfied,that vpon that wraek
fuch a one was taken vp : and therefore that *Plangus*
might well erre. who knew not of anies taking vp a-
gaine:that he that was fo preferued, brought good tokens to be one of the two,chiefe of that wracked companie : which two fince *Plangus* knew to be *Mufidorus*
and *Pyrocles*,he muft needes be one of them, although
(as I faid)vpon a foretaken vowe , he was otherwife at
that time called. Befides, the Princeffe muft needes
iudge, that no leffe then a Prince durft vndertake fuch
an enterprife,which(though he might gette the fauour
of the Princeffe)he could neuer defend with leffe thē a
Princes power, againft the force of *Arcadia*. Laftly,
(faid he) for a certaine demonftration,he prefumed to
fhew vnto the Princeffe a marke he had on his face, as
I might(faid I)fhew this of my neck to the rare *Mopfa:*
and withall,fhewed my necke to them both, where(as
you know)there is a redde fpotte, bearing figure (as
they tell me)of a Lyons pawe, that fhe may afcertaine
her felfe,that I am *Menalcas* brother. And fo did he,be-
feeching her to fend fome one fhe might truft, into
Theffalia, fecretely to be aduertifed, whether the age,
the complexion, and particularly that notable figne,
did not fully agree with this Prince *Mufidorus*. Doo
you not know further (faide fhe, with a fetled counte
nance, not accufing any kind of inwarde motion) of
that ftorie. Alas no,(faid I)for euen here the Hiftorio-
grapher ftopped,faying, The reft belonged to Aftrolo-
gie. And therewith, thinking her filent imaginations
began to worke vpon fomewhat, to mollifie them (as
the nature of Mufick is to do)and withal,to fhew what
kind

kind of ſhepheard I was, I took vp my Harpe, and ſang theſe few verſes.

7   *MY ſheepe are thoughts, which I both guide and ſerue :*
    Their paſture is faire hilles of fruitleſſe Loue :
On barren ſweetes they feede, and feeding ſterue :
I waile their lotte, but will not other proue.
My ſheepehooke is wanne hope, which all vpholdes :
My weedes, Deſire, cut out in endleſſe foldes .
  What wooll my ſheepe ſhall beare, whiles thus they liue,
  In you it is, you muſt the iudgement giue.

And then, partly to bring *Mopſa* againe to the matter (leſt ſhe ſhould too much take heed to our diſcourſes) but principally, if it were poſſible, to gather ſome comfort out of her anſweares, I kneeled downe to the Princeſſe, and humblie beſought her to moue *Mopſa* in my behalfe, that ſhe would vnarme her hart of that ſteely reſiſtãce againſt the ſweet blowes of Loue: that ſince all her parts were decked with ſome particular ornamẽt; her face with beautie, her head with wiſdome, her eyes with maieſtie, her countenance with gracefulnes, her lippes with louelines, her tongue with victorie; that ſhe woulde make her hart the throne of pitie, being the moſt excellent rayment of the moſt excellent part.

8   *Pamela*, without ſhew either of fauour or diſdaine, either of heeding or neglecting what I had ſaid, turned her ſpeech to *Mopſa*, and with ſuch a voice and action,

as might fhewe fhe fpake of a matter which little did
concerne her, Take heede to your felfe (faide fhe)
*Mopfa,*for your fhepheard can fpeake well: but truely,
if he doo fully prooue himfelfe fuch as he faith, I mean,
the honeft fhepheard *Menalchas* his brother, and heire,
I know no reafon why you fhoulde thinke fcorne of
him. *Mopfa* though (in my confcience) fhe were e-
uen then farre fpent towards me, yet fhe anfwered her,
that for all my queint fpeeches, fhe would keepe her
honeftie clofe inough: And that as for the highe
way of matrimony, fhe would fteppe neuer a foote further, till my maifter her father had fpoken the whole
word him felfe, no fhe would not. But euer and anon
turning her muzzell toward me, fhe threwe fuch a profpect vpon me, as might well haue giuen a furfet to any
weake louers ftomacke. But Lord what a foole am I,
to mingle that driuels fpeeches among my noble
thoughts? but becaufe fhe was an Actor in this Tragedie, to geue you a ful knowledge, and to leaue nothing
(that I can remember) vnrepeated.

　Now the Princeffe being about to withdrawe her
felfe from vs, I tooke a Iewell, made in the figure of a 　**9**
Crab-fifh, which, becaufe it lookes one way and goes
another, I thought it did fitly patterne out my looking
to *Mopfa*, but bending to *Pamela:* The word about it
was, *By force, not choice*; and ftill kneeling, befought the
Princeffe that fhe would vouchfafe to giue it *Mopfa*,
and with the bleffednes of her hande to make acceptable vnto her that toye which I had founde, fol-
lowinge of late an acquaintaunce of mine at the
plowe. For (faydI) as the earth was turned vp, the
plow-fhare lighted vpon a great ftone: we puld that

vp

vp,& so found both that,and some other prety thinges which we had deuided betwixt vs.

10   *Mopsa* was benummed with ioy when the Princesse gaue it her:but in the Princesse I could finde no apprehension of what I either said or did, but with a calme carelesnesse letting each thing slide,iustly as we doo by their speeches, who neither in matter nor person doo any way belong vnto vs) which kind of colde temper, mixt with that lightning of her naturall maiestie, is of all others most terrible vnto me : for yet if I found she contemned me,I would desperatly labour both in fortune and vertue to ouercome it ; if she onely misdoubted me, I were in heauen ; for quickly I woulde bring sufficient assurance: lastly,if she hated me, yet I should know what passion to deale with; and either with infinitenes of desert I would take away the fewell from that fire ; or if nothing would serue, then I would giue her my hart-bloud to quench it. But this cruell quietnes, neither retiring to mislike, nor proceeding to fauour;gratious,but gratious still after one maner; all her courtesies hauing this engrauen in them, that what is done,is for vertues sake, not for the parties ; euer keeping her course like the Sun, who neither for our prayses,nor curses,will spare or stoppe his horses. This (I say)heauenlines of hers,(for how so euer my miserie is I cannot but so entitle it)is so impossible to reach vnto, that I almost begin to submitte my selfe to the tyrannie of despaire, not knowing any way of perswasiō, where wisdome seemes to be vnsensible. I haue appeared to her eyes,like my selfe, by a deuice I vsed with my master, perswading him,that we two might put on a certaine rich apparrel I had prouided,and so practise some
thing

thing on horſback before *Pamela*, telling him, it was apparell I had gotten for playing well the part of a King
in a Tragedie at *Athens*: my horſe indeed was it I had
left at *Menalcas* houſe, and *Dametas* got one by friendſhip out of the Princes ſtable. But how ſoeuer I ſhow, I
am no baſe bodie, all I doo is but to beate a rocke and
get ſome.

CHAP. 4.

Baſilius his hauking. ¹ *Gynecias hurte by* Dametas *ouer-
turning her coache.* ³ *Her ielouſie ouer* Zelmane. *Philoclea* ⁴ *louepaſſions,* ⁵ *vowe of chaſtitie,* ⁶ *reuocation,*
⁷ *lamentation.*

Vt as *Dorus* was about to tell further, *Dametas* (who came whiſt-
ling, & counting vpon his fingers
how many loade of hay his ſeuen-
teen fat oxen eat vp in a yeare) deſired *Zelmane* from the King that
ſhe would come into the lodge,
where they ſtayed for her. Alas
(ſaid *Dorus*, taking his leaue) the ſum is this, that you
may wel find you haue beate your ſorrow againſt ſuch
a wall, which with the force of rebound may wel make
your ſorrow ſtroger. But *Zelmane* turning her ſpeach to
Dametas, I ſhall grow (ſaid ſhe) skilfull in country matters, if I haue often conference with your ſeruaunt. In
ſooth (anſwered *Dametas* with a graceleſſe skorne) the
Lad may proue wel enough, if he ouerſoon thinke not
too well of himſelfe, and will beare away that he hea-

reth of his elders. And therewith as they walked to the other lodge, to make *Zelmane* find she might haue spét. her time better with him, he began with a wilde Methode to runne ouer all the art of husbandrie : especially imploying his tongue about well dunging of a fielde : while poore *Zelmane* yeelded her eares to those tedious strokes, not warding them so much as with any one answere, till they came to *Basilius*, and *Gynecia*, who attéded for her in a coach to carrie her abroad to see some sportes prepared for her. *Basilius* and *Gynecia* sitting in the one ende, placed her at the other, with her left side to *Philoclea*. *Zelmane* was moued in her minde, to haue kissed their feete for the fauour of so blessed a scate : for the narrownesse of the coach made them ioine from the foote to the shoulders very close together ; the truer touch wherof though it were barred by their enuious apparell, yet as a perfect Magnes, though put in an iuorie boxe, will thorow the boxe send forth his imbraced vertue to a beloued needle ; so this imparadised neighbourhood made *Zelmanes* soule cleaue vnto her, both thorow the iuory case of her body, and the apparell which did ouer-clowd it. All the bloud of *Zelmanes* body stirring in her, as wine will do when suger is hastely put into it, seeking to sucke the sweetnes of the beloued guest; her hart, like a lion new imprisoned, seeing him that restraines his libertie, before the grate; not panting, but striuing violently (if it had bene possible) to haue leapt into the lappe of *Philoclea*. But *Dametas*, euen then proceeding from being maister of a carte, to be doctor of a coach, not a little prowd in himselfe, that his whippe at that time guided the rule of *Arcadia*, draue the coach (the couer wherof

vhereof was made with fuch ioints, that as they might
(to auoid the weather) pull it vp clofe when they lifted, fo when they would they might put each ende
downe, and remaine as difcouered & open fighted as
on horfebacke) till vpon the fide of the forreft they
had both greyhounds, fpaniels, and hounds: whereof
the firft might feeme the Lords, the fecond the Gentlemen, and the laft the Yeomen of dogges; a caft
of Merlins there was befides, which flying of a
gallant height ouer certaine bufhes, would beate the
birdes (that rofe) downe vnto the bufhes, as Faul-
cons will doo wilde-foule ouer a riuer. But the fporte
which for that daie *Bafilius* would principallie fhewe
to *Zelmane*, was the mountie at a Hearne, which getting vp on his wagling winges with paine, till he was
come to fome height, (as though the aire next to the
earth were not fit for his great bodie to flie thorow)
was now growen to diminifh the fight of himfelf, & to
giue example to great perfons, that the higher they be,
the leffe they fhould fhow: whē a Ierfaulcon wascaft of
after her, who ftreight fpying where the pray was, fix-
ing her eie with defire, & guiding her wing by her eie,
vfed no more ftrēgth then induftry. For as a good buil-
der to a hie tower will not make his ftayre vpright, but
winding almoft the ful cōpaffe about, that the fteepnes
be the more vnfenfible: fo fhe, feing the towring of her
purfued chafe, went circkling, & cōpaffing about, rifing
fo with the leffe fence of rifing; & yet finding that way
fcantly ferue the greedines of her haft, as an ambitious
body wil go far out of the direct way, to win to a point
of height which he defires; fo would fhe (as it were)
turne taile to the Heron, & flie quite out another way,

but all was to returne in a higher pitche; which once gotten, fhe would either beate with cruell affaults the Heron, who now was driuen to the beft defence of force, fince flight would not ferue; or els clafping with him, come downe together, to be parted by the ouer-partiall beholders.

2   Diuers of which flights *Bafilius* fhewing to *Zelmane*, thus was the richeffe of the time fpent, and the day deceaffed before it was thought of, till night like a degenerating fucceffour made his departure the better remembred. And therefore (fo conftrained) they willed *Dametas* to driue homeward, who (halfe fleeping, halfe mufing about the mending of a vine-preffe) guided the horfes fo ill, that the wheele comming ouer a great ftub of a tree, it ouerturned the coach. Which though it fell violently vpon the fide where *Zelmane* & *Gynecia* fat, yet for *Zelmanes* part, fhe would haue bene glad of the fall, which made her beare the fweete burthen of *Philoclea*, but that fhe feared fhe might receaue fome hurt. But indeede neither fhe did, nor any of the reft, by reafon they kept their armes and legs within the coach, fauing *Gynecia*, who with the onely bruze of the fall had her fhoulder put out of ioinct; which though by one of the Faulkeners cunning, it was fet well againe, yet with much paine was fhe brought to the lodge; and paine (fetching his ordinary companion, a feuer with him) draue her to entertaine them both in her bedde.

3   But neither was the feuer of fuch impatient heate, as the inwarde plague-fore of her affection, nor the paine halfe fo noyfome, as the iealoufie fhe conceaued of her daughter *Philoclea*, left this time of her fickneffe
might

might giue apt occafion to *Zelmane*, whom fhe mifdoubted . Therefore fhe called *Philoclea* to her, and
though it were late in the night, commaunded her in
her eare to go to the other lodge, and fend *Mifo* to her,
with whom fhe would fpeake, and fhe lie with her fifter *Pamela*. The meane while *Gynecia* kepte *Zelmane*
with her, becaufe fhe would be fure, fhe fhould be out
of the lodge, before fhe licenced *Zelmane*. *Philoclea*
not skild in any thing better then obedience, went
quietly downe; and the Moone then full (not thinking skorne to be a torche-bearer to fuch beautie) guided her fteppes, whofe motions bare a minde, which
bare in it felfe farre more ftirring motions. And alas
(fweete *Philoclea*) how hath my penne till now forgot
thy paffions, fince to thy memorie principally all this
long matter is intended? pardon the flacknes to come
to thofe woes, which hauing caufed in others, thou
didft feele in thy felfe.

The fweete minded *Philoclea* was in their degree of 4
well doing, to whom the not knowing of euill ferueth
for a ground of vertue, and hold their inward powers
in better forme with an vnfpotted fimplicitie, then many, who rather cūningly feeke to know what goodnes
is, then willingly take into themfelues the following of
it. But as that fweet & fimple breath of heauenly goodneffe, is the eafier to be altered, becaufe it hath not paffed through the worldlie wickedneffe. nor feelingly
found the euill, that euill caries with it; fo now the Ladie *Philoclea* (whofe eyes and fenfes had receaued nothing, but according as the naturall courfe of each
thing required; which frō the tender youth had obedi
ently liued vnder her parents behefts, without framing

Q 3 . out

out of her own wil the fore-choſing of any thing)whẽ now ſhe came to appoint,wherin her iudgemẽt was to be practized,in knowing faultines by his firſt tokẽs,ſhe was like a yong faune, who cõming in the wind of the hunters, doth not know whether it be a thing or no to be eſchewed ; whereof at this time ſhe began to get a coſtly experience. For after that *Zelmane* had a while li-ued in the lodge with her, and that her onely being a noble ſtraunger had bred a kind of heedfull attention; her cõming to that lonely place (where ſhe had no bo-dy but her parents)a willingnes of conuerſatiõ; her wit & behauiour,a liking & ſilent admiration;at length the excellency of her natural gifts,ioined with the extreme ſhewes ſhe made of moſt deuout honouring *Philoclea*, (carying thus in one perſon the only two bãds of good will,louelines & louingnes)brought forth in her hart a yeelding to a moſt friẽdly affectiõ ; which when it had gotten ſo ful poſſeſſion of the keies of her mind, that it would receaue no meſſage frõ her ſenſes,without that affection were the interpreter; thẽ ſtreight grew an ex-ceeding delight ſtil to be with her, with an vnmeaſura-ble liking of al that *Zelmane* did:maters being ſo turned in her; that where at firſt,liking her manners did breed good-wil,now good-wil became the chiefe cauſe of li-king her manners : ſo that within a while *Zelmane* was not prized for her demeanure, but the demeanure was prized becauſe it was *Zelmanes*. Thẽ followed that moſt natural effect of cõforming ones ſelf to that,which ſhe did like,and not onely wiſhing to be her ſelfe ſuch an other in all thinges, but to ground an imitation vp-on ſo much an eſteemed authoritie : ſo that the next degree was to marke all *Zelmanes* dooings, ſpeeches,

and

and fashions, and to take them into herselfe, as a parterne of worthy proceeding. Which when once it was enacted, not onely by the comminaltie of Passions, but agreed vnto by her most noble Thoughts, and that by Reason it felf (not yet experienced in the issues of such matters) had granted his royall assent; then Friendship (a diligent officer) tooke care to see the statute thorowly.obserued. Then grew on that not onely she did imitate the sobernes of her countenance, the gracefulnesse of her speech, but euen their particular gestures: so that as *Zelmane* did often eye her, she would often eye *Zelmane*; & as *Zelmanes* eyes would deliuer a submissiue, but vehement desire in their looke, she, though as yet she had not the desire in her, yet should her eyes answere in like pearcing kindnesse of a looke. *Zelmane* as much as *Gynetias* iealousie would suffer, desired to be neere *Philoclea*; *Philoclea*, as much as *Gynecias* iealousie would suffer, desired to be neere *Zelmane*. If *Zelmane* tooke her hand, and softly strained it, she also (thinking the knots of friendship ought to bee mutuall) would (with a sweete fastnes) shew she was loth to part from it. And if *Zelmane* sighed, she would sigh also; whē *Zelmane* was sad, she deemed it wisdome, and therefore she would be sad too. *Zelmanes* languishing coūtenāce with crost armes, and sometimes cast-vp eyes, she thought to haue an excellent grace : and therefore she also willingly put on the same countenāce: til at the last (poore soule, ere she were aware) she accepted not onely the band, but the seruice; not only the signe, but the passion signified. For whether it were, that her wit in cōtinuāce did finde, that *Zelmanes* friendship was full of impatient desire, hauing more thē ordinarie limits, & therfore

she

Q 4

shee was content to second *Zelmane*, though her selfe
knew not the limits; or that in truth, true-loue (well
considered) haue an infectiue power. At last she fell in
acquaintance with loues harbinger, wishing. First she
would wish, that they two might liue all their liues togither, like two of *Dianas* Nimphes. But that wish, she
thought not sufficient, becaule she knew, there would
be more Nimphes besides them, who also would haue
their part in *Zelmane*. Thē would she wish, that she were
her sister, that such a natural band might make her more
speciall to her. But against that, she considered, that
though being her sister, if she happened to be married, she should be robbed of her. Then growne bolder, she would wish either her selfe, or *Zelmane* a man,
that there might succeed a blessed marriage betwixt
them. But when that wish had once displaied his en-
signe in her minde, then followed whole squadrons
of longings, that so it might be, with a maine battaile
of mislikings, and repynings against their creation,
that so it was not. Then dreames by night beganne to
bring more vnto her, then she durst wish by day, whereout making did make her know her selfe the better by
the image of those fancies. But as some diseases when
they are easie to be cured, they are hard to be knowne,
but when they grow easie to be knowne, they are almost impossible to be cured : so the sweete *Philoclea*,
while she might preuent it, she did not feele it, now she
felt it, when it was past preuenting; like a riuer, no ram-
piers being built against it, till alreadie it haue ouer-
flowed. For now indeed, Loue puld of his maske,
and shewed his face vnto her, and told her plainly, that
shee was his prisoner. Then needed she no more paint
her

her face with paffions; for paffions fhone thorow her
face; Then her rofie coulor was often encreafed with
extraordinarie blufhing: and fo another time, perfect
whiteneffe afcended to a degree of paleneffe; now hot,
then cold, defiring fhe knew not what, nor how, if fhe
knew what. Then her minde (though too late) by the
fmart was brought to thinke of the difeafe, and her
owne proofe taught her to know her mothers minde;
which (as no error giues fo ftrong affault, as that which
comes armed in the authoritie of a parent, fo) greatly
fortified her defires, to fee, that her mother had the
like defires. And the more iealous her mother was,
the more fhe thought the Iewell precious, which was
with fo many lookes garded. But that preuailing fo far,
as to keepe the two louers from priuate conference,
then began fhe to feele the fweetneffe of a louers folitarineffe, when freely with words and geftures, as if
Zelmane were prefent, fhee might giue paffage to her
thoughts, and fo as it were vtter out fome fmoke of
thofe flames, wherewith elfe fhe was not only burned,
but fmothered. As this night, that going from the one
lodge to the other by her mothers commandement,
with dolefull geftures and vncertaine paces, fhee did
willingly accept the times offer, to be a while alone: fo
that going a little afide into the wood; where manie
times before fhe had delighted to walke, her eyes were
faluted with a tuft of trees, fo clofe fet togither, as with
the fhade the moone gaue thorow it, it might breede
a fearefull kinde of deuotion to looke vpon it. But true
thoughts of loue banifh all vaine fancie of fuperftition. Full well fhe did both remember and like the
place; for there had fhe often with their fhade beguiled

led *Phœbus* of looking vpon her: There had ſhe enioyed her ſelfe often, while she was miſtreſſe of her ſelfe, and had no other thoughts, but ſuch as might ariſe out of quiet ſenſes.

5   But the principall cauſe that inuited her remembrance, was a goodly white marble ſtone, that should ſeeme had bene dedicated in ancient time to the *Siluan* gods: which she finding there a fewe dayes before *Zelmanes* comming, had written theſe words vpon it, as a teſtimonie of her mind, againſt the ſuſpition her captiuitie made her thinke ſhe liued in. The writing was this.

> *Y* *Ou liuing powres encloſed in ſtately ſhrine*
>   *Of growing trees; you rurall Gods that wield*
> *Your ſcepters here, if to your eares diuine*
> *A voice may come, which troubled ſoule doth yeld:*
>   *This vowe receaue, this vowe ô Gods maintaine;*
>   *My virgin life no ſpotted thought ſhall ſtaine.*
>
> *Thou pureſt ſtone, whoſe pureneſſe doth preſent*
> *My pureſt minde; whoſe temper hard doth ſhowe*
> *My tempred hart; by thee my promiſe ſent*
> *Vnto my ſelfe let after-liuers know.*
>   *No fancy mine, nor others wronge ſuſpect*
>   *Make me, ô vertuous Shame, thy lawes neglect.*
>
> *O Chaſtitie, the chiefe of heauenly lightes,*
> *Which makſt vs moſt immortall ſhape to weare,*
> *Holde thou my hart, eſtabliſh thou my ſprights:*
> *To onely thee my conſtant courſe I beare.*

Till

Till spotlesse soule vnto thy bosome flye,
Such life to leade, such death I vow to dye.

But now that her memorie serued as an accuser of 6
her change, and that her own hand-writing was there,
to beare testimony against her fall ; she went in among
those few trees, so closed in the toppes togither, as they
might seeme a little chappell : and there might she by
the help of the moone-light perceiue the goodly stone,
which serued as an altar in that wooddie deuotion. But
neither the light was enough to reade the words, and
the inke was alreadie foreworne, and in many places
blotted : which as she perceaued, Alas (said she) faire
Marble, which neuer receiuedst spot but by my writing, well do these blots become a blotted writer. But
pardon her which did not dissemble then, although she
haue chaunged since. Enioy, enioy the glorie of thy
nature, which can so constantly beare the markes of
my inconstancie. And herewith hiding her eyes with
her soft hand, there came into her head certaine verses,
which if she had had present commoditie, she would
haue adioyned as a retractation to the other. They
were to this effect.

MY words, in hope to blaze my stedfast minde,
This marble those, as of like temper knowne :
But loe, my words defaste, my fancies blinde,
Blots to the stone, shame to my selfe I finde :
  And witnesse am, how ill agree in one,
  A womans hand with constant marble stone.

My words full weake, the marble full of might ;

      My

My words in ſtore, the marble all alone;
My words blacke inke, the marble kindly white;
My words vnſeene, the marble ſtill in ſight,
May witneſſe beare, how ill agree in one,
A womans hand, with conſtant marble ſtone.

7   But ſeeing ſhe could not ſee meanes to ioyne as thē
this recantation to the former vow, (laying all her faire
length ynder one of the trees) for a while ſhe did nothing but turne vp and downe, as if ſhe had hoped
to turne away the fancie that maſtred her, and hid her
face, as if ſhe could haue hidden her ſelfe from her
owne fancies. At length with a whiſpring note to her
ſelfe; O me vnfortunate wretch (ſaid ſhe) what poyſonous heates be theſe, which thus torment me? How
hath the ſight of this ſtrange gueſt inuaded my ſoule?
Alas, what entrance found this deſire, or what ſtrength
had it thus to conquer me? Then, a cloud paſſing betweene her ſight and the moone, O *Diana* (ſaid ſhe) I
would either the cloud that now hides the light of my
vertue would as eaſily paſſe away, as you will quickly
ouercome this let; or els that you were for euer thus
darkned, to ſerue for an excuſe of my outragious folly.
Then looking to the ſtarres, which had perfitly as then
beautified the cleere ſkie: My parēts (ſaid ſhe) haue told
me, that in theſe faire heauenly bodies, there are great
hiddē deities, which haue their working in the ebbing
& flowing of our eſtates. If it be ſo, then (O you Stars)
iudge rightly of me, & if I haue with wicked intēt made
my ſelfe a pray to fancie, or if by any idle luſtes I framed my harte fit for ſuch an impreſſion, then let this
plague dayly encreaſe in me, till my name bee made
                                              odious

odious to womankind. But if extreame and vnresifta-
ble violence haue oppreffed me, who will euer do any
of you facrifice (ô you Starres) if you do not fuccour
me. No, no, you will not help me. No, no, you cannot
helpe me : Sinne muſt be the mother, and fhame the
daughter of my affeóion. And yet are thefe but childifh obieótions(fimple *Philoclea)* it is the impoffibilitie
that dooth torment me : for, vnlawfull defires are puniſhed after the effeó of enioying; but vnpoffible defires are puniſhed in the defire it felfe. O then, ô tenne
times vnhappie that I am, fince where in all other hope
kindleth loue; in me defpaire fhould be the bellowes of
my affeótion : and of all defpaires the moſt miferable,
which is drawen from impoffibilitie. The moſt couetous man longs not to get riches out of a groũd which
neuer can beare any thing; Why? becaufe it is impoffible. The moſt ambitious wight vexeth not his wittes
to clime into heauen; Why? becaufe it is impoffible.
Alas then, ô Loue, why dooſt thou in thy beautifull
fampler fette fuch a worke for my Defire to take out,
which is as much impoffible? And yet alas, why doo I
thus condemne my Fortune, before I heare what fhe
can fay for her felfe? What doo I, fillie wench, knowe
what Loue hath prepared for me? Doo I not fee my
mother, as well, at left as furiouflie as my felfe, loue *Zel-*
mane? And fhould I be wifer then my mother? Either
fhe fees a poffibilitie in that which I think impoffible,
or els impoffible loues neede not mifbecome me. And
doo I not fee *Zelmane* (who doth not thinke a thought
which is not firſt wayed by wifdome and vertue) dôth
not fhe vouchfafe to loue me with like ardour? I fee it,
her eyes dep ofe it to be true; what then? and if fhe can
loue

loue poore me, shall I thinke scorne to loue such a woman as *Zelmane*? Away then all vaine examinations of
why and how. Thou louest me, excellent *Zelmane*, and
I loue thee: and with that, embrasing the very grounde
whereon she lay, she said to her selfe (for euen to her
selfe she was ashamed to speake it out in words) O my
Zelmane, gouerne and direct me: for I am wholy giuen
ouer vnto thee.

CHAP. 5.

[1] *The bedfellow communication of* Philoclea *and* Pamela.
[2] *Pamelas narration of her shepheardes making loue,* [3] *of*
Dorus *and* Dametas *horsemanshippe,* [4] *of his hote pur-*
suite, and her colde acceptance. [5] *His letter.* [6] *Her relen-*
ting, [7] *and* Philocleas *sole complaint.*

I N this depth of muzes, and diuers
sorts of discourses, would she haue
rauingly remained, but that *Dametas* and *Miso* (who were rounde a-
bout to seeke her, vnderstanding
she was to come to their lodge that
night) came hard by her; *Dametas*
saying, That he would not deale in
other bodies matters; but for his parte, he did not like
that maides should once stirre out of their fathers houses, but if it were to milke a cow, or saue a chicken from
a kites foote, or some such other matter of importance.
And *Miso* swearing that if it were her daughter *Mopsa*,
she woulde giue her a lesson for walking so late, that
should make her keepe within dores for one fortnight.
But

But their iangling made *Philoclea* rife, and pretending
as though fhe had done it but to fport with them, went
with them (after fhe had willed *Mifo* to waite vpon her
mother) to the lodge; where (being now accuftomed
by her parents difcipline, as well as her fifter, to ferue
her felfe) fhe went alone vp to *Pamelas* chamber: where
meaning to delight her eies, and ioy her thoughts with
the fweet conuerfation of her beloued fifter, fhe found
her 'though it were in the time that the wings of night
doth blow fleep moft willingly into mortall creatures)
fitting in a chaire, lying backward, with her head almoft
ouer the back of it, & looking vpon a wax-cadle which
burnt before her; in one hand holding a letter, in the o-
ther her hand-kerchiefe. which had lately dronk vp the
teares of her eyes, leauing in fteed of them, crimfen cir-
cles, like redde flakes in the element, when the weather
is hotteft. Which *Philoclea* finding (for her eyes had
learned to know the hedges of forowes) fhe earneftlie
intreated to knowe the caufe thereof, that either fhe
might comforte, or accompanie her dolefull humor.
But *Pamela*, rather feeming forie that fhe had perceiued fo much, then willing to open any further, O my
Pamela (faid *Philoclea*) who are to me a fifter in nature
a mother in counfell, a Princeffe by the law of our cou-
trey, and which name (me thinke) of all other is the
deareft, a friend by my choice and your fauour, what
meanes this banifhing me from your counfels? Do you
loue your forrowe fo well, as to grudge me part of it?
Or doo you thinke I fhall not loue a fadde *Pamela*, fo
well as a ioyfull? Or be my eares vnwoorthie, or my
tongue fufpected? What is it (my fifter) that you fhould
conceale from your fifter, yea and feruant *Philoclea*?

                                                    Thefe

These wordes wanne no further of *Pamela*, but that telling her they might talke better as they lay together,
they impouerished their cloathes to inriche their bed,
which for that night might well scorne the shrine of
Venus: and there cherishing one another with deare,
though chaste embracements; with sweet, though cold
kisses; it might seeme that Loue was come to play him
there without darte; or that weerie of his owne fires, he
was there to refreshe himselfe betweene their sweete-
breathing lippes But *Philoclea* earnestly againe intreated *Pamela* to open her griefe ; who (drawing the cur-
tain, that the candle might not complaine of her blushing) was ready to speake: but the breath almost formed
into words, was againe stopt by her, and turned into
sighes. But at last, I pray you (said she) sweete *Philoclea*,
let vs talke of some other thing: & tell me whether you
did euer see any thing so ameded as our Pastoral sports
be, since that *Dorus* came hether ? O Loue, how farre
thou seest with blind eyes? *Philoclea* had straight found
her, and therefore to draw out more, In deed (said she)
I haue often wondred to my selfe how such excellecies
could be in so meane a person; but belike Fortune was
afraide to lay her treasures, where they should be staind
with so many perfections: onely I maruaile how he can
frame himselfe to hide so rare giftes vnder such a block
as *Dametas*. Ah (said *Pamela*) if you knew the cause: but
no more doo I neither; and to say the trueth: but Lord,
how are we falne to talke of this fellow? and yet indeed
if you were sometimes with me to marke him, while
Dametas reades his rusticke lecture vnto him (how to
feede his beastes before noone, where to shade them in
the extreame heate, how to make the manger hansome
                                                    for

for his oxen, when to vſe the goade, & when the voice: giuing him rules of a heardmã, though he pretẽded to make him a ſhepheard) to ſee all the while with what a grace (which ſeemes to ſet a crowne vpon his baſe e-ſtate) he can deſcend to thoſe poore matters, certainly you would: but to what ſerues this? no doubt we were better ſleepe then talke of theſe idle matters. Ah my *Pamela* (ſaid *Philoclea*) I haue caught you, the conſtant-nes of your wit was not wont to bring forth ſuch diſ-iointed ſpeeches: you loue, diſſemble no further. It is true (ſaid *Pamela*) now you haue it; and with leſſe adoo ſhould, if my hart could haue thoght thoſe words ſute-able for my mouth. But indeed (my *Philoclea*) take heed: for I thinke Vertue it ſelf is no armour of proofe againſt affection. Therfore learne by my example. Alas thought *Philoclea* to her ſelfe, your ſheeres come to late to clip the birds wings that already is flowne away.

But then *Pamela* being once ſet m the ſtreame of her Loue, went away a maine withall, telling her how his noble qualities had drawne her liking towardes him; but yet euer waying his meanenes, & ſo held continu-ally in due limits; till ſeeking m.ny meanes to ſpeake with her, & euer kept from it (as el becauſe ſhe ſhund it, ſeing and diſdaining his mind, as becauſe of her iea-lous iaylours) he had at length vſed the fineſt pollicie that might be in counterfaiting loue to *Mopſa*, & ſaying to *Mopſa* what ſoeuer he would haue her know: and in how paſſionate manner he had told his owne tale in a third perſon, making poore *Mopſa* beleue, that it was a matter fallen out many ages before. And in the end, be-cauſe you ſhal know my teares come not, neither of re-pẽtance nor miſery, who thinke you, is my *Dorus* fallen

R   out

2

out to be ? euen the Prince *Muſidorus*, famous ouer all *Aſia*, for his heroical enterprifes, of whom you remember how much good the ſtraunger *Plangus* told my father; he not being drowned (as *Plangus* thought) though his couſin *Pyrocles* indeed periſhed. Ah my ſiſter, if you had heard his words, or ſeene his geſtures, when he made me know what, and to whom his loue was, you would haue matched in your ſelfe (thoſe two rarely matched together) pittie and delight. Tell me deare ſiſter (for the gods are my witneſſes I deſire to doo vertuouſly) can I without the deteſtable ſtaine of vngratefulneſſe abſtaine from louing him, who (far exceeding the beautifulneſſe of his ſhape with the beautifulneſſe of his minde, and the greatneſſe of his eſtate with the greatneſſe of his actes) is content ſo to abaſe him ſelfe, as to become *Dametas* ſeruaunt for my ſake? you will ſay, but how know I him to be *Muſidorus*, ſince the handmaid of wiſdome is ſlow belief? That cóſideratió did not want in me, for the nature of deſire it ſelfe is no eaſier to receiue beliefe, then it is hard to ground belief. For as deſire is glad to embrace the firſt ſhew of comfort, ſo is deſire deſirous of perfect aſſuraunce: and that haue I had of him, not onely by neceſſary arguments to any of cómon ſenſe, but by ſufficient demonſtrations. Laſtly he would haue me ſend to *Theſſalia*: but truly I am not as now in mind to do my honorable Loue ſo much wrong, as ſo far to ſuſpect him: yet poor ſoule knowes he no other, but that I doo both ſuſpect, neglect, yea & deteſt him. For euery day he finds one way or other to ſet forth him ſelfe vnto me, but all are rewarded with like coldneſſe of acceptation.

3   A few daies ſince, he & *Dametas* had furniſhed théſelues

felues very richly to run at the ring before me. O how
mad a fight it was to fee *Dametas*, like rich Tiffew furd
with lambe skins? But ô how well it did with *Dorus* to
fee with what a grace he prefented him felfe before me
on horfeback, making maieftic wait vpon humblenes?
how at the firft, ftanding ftil with his eies bent vpô me,
as though his motiôs were chained to my looke, he fo
ftaide till I caufed *Mopfa* bid him doo fomething vpon
his horfe : which no fooner faid, but (with a kinde rather of quick gefture, then fhew of violéce) you might
fee him come towards me, beating the groûd in fo due
time, as no daunce can obferue better meafure. If you
remember the fhip we faw once, whê the Sea went hie
vpon the coaft of *Argos*; fo went the beaft : But he (as if
Cêtaurlike he had bene one peece with the horfe) was
no more moued, then one is with the going of his
owne legges : and in effeçt fo did he command him, as
his owne limmes, for though he had both fpurres and
wande, they feemed rather markes of foueraintie, then
inftruments of punifhment; his hand and legge (with
moft pleafing grace) commâding without threatning,
& rather remêbring then chaftifing, at left if fometimes
he did, it was fo ftolen, as neyther our eyes could difcerne it, nor the horfe with any chaunce did côplaine
of it, he euer going fo iuft with the horfe, either foorth
right, or turning, that it feemed as he borrowed the
horfes body, fo he lent the horfe his minde : in the
turning one might perceiue the bridle-hand fomthing
gently ftir, but indeed fo gently, as it did rather diftill
vertue, then vfe violence. Him felf (which me thinkes is
ftraunge) fhewing at one inftant both fteadines & nimblenes; fomtimes making him turne clofe to the groûd,

like a cat, when scratchingly she wheeles about after a mouse: sometimes with a little more rising before, now like a Rauen leaping from ridge to ridge, then like one of *Dametas* kiddes bound ouer the hillocks: and all so done, as neither the lustie kinde shewed any roughneſſe, nor the eaſier any idleneſſe: but ſtill like a well obeyed maiſter, whose becke is enough for a diſcipline, euer concluding ech thing he did with his face to me-wards, as if thence came not onely the beginning, but ending of his motions. The ſporte was to ſee *Dametas*, how he was toſt from the ſadle to the mane of the horſe, and thence to the ground, giuing his gay apparell almoſt as foule an outſide, as it had an inſide. But as before he had euer ſaid, he wanted but horſe & apparell to be as braue a courtier as the beſt, so now bruſed with proofe, he proclaimed it a folly for a man of wiſedome, to put himſelfe vnder the tuition of a beaſt; so as *Dorus* was fayne alone to take the Ringe. Wherein truely at leſt my womaniſh eyes could not diſcerne, but that taking his ſtaffe from his thigh, the deſcending it a little downe, the getting of it vp into the reſt, the letting of the point fall, and taking the ring was but all one motion, at leſt (if they were diuers motions) they did ſo ſtealingly ſlippe one into another, as the latter parte was euer in hande, before the eye could diſcerne the former was ended. Indeed *Dametas* found fault that he ſhewed no more ſtrength in ſhaking of his ſtaffe: but to my conceite the fine cleernes of bearing it was exceeding delightfull.

4 But how delightfull ſoeuer it was, my delight might well be in my ſoule, but it neuer went to looke out of the window to doo him any comfort. But how much
more

more I found reafon to like him, the more I fet all the
ftrength of mind to fupprefle it, or at left to conceale it.
Indeed I muft confefle, as fome Phyfitions haue tolde
me, that when one is cold outwardly, he is not inwardly; fo truly the colde afhes layed vpon my fire, did not
take the nature of fire from it. Full often hath my breft
fwollen with keeping my fighes imprifoned; full often haue the teares, I draue backe from mine eyes, turned backe to drowne my harte. But alas what did
that helpe poore *Dorus*? whofe eyes (being his diligent intelligencers) coulde carrie vnto him no other
newes, but difcomfortable. I thinke no day paft, but
by fome one inuention he would appeare vnto me to
teftifie his loue. One time he daunced the Matachine
daunce in armour (O with what a gracefull dexteritie?) I thinke to make me fee, that he had bene brought
vp in fuch exercifes: an ocher time he perfwaded his
maifter (to make my time feeme fhorter) in manner
of a Dialogue, to play *Priamus* while he plaide *Paris*.
Thinke (fweet *Philoclea*) what a *Priamus* we had: but
truely, my *Paris* was a *Paris*, and more then a *Paris*:
who while in a fauage apparell, with naked necke,
armes, and legges, he made loue to *Oenone*, you might
wel fee by his chaunged countenance, and true teares,
that he felte the parte he playde. Tell me (fweet *Philoclea*) did you euer fee fuch a fhepheard? tell me, did
you euer heare of fuch a Prince? And then tell me,
if a fmall or vnworthy affaulte haue conquered me.
Truely I would hate my life, if I thought vanitie led
me. But fince my parents deale fo cruelly with me, it
is time for me to truft fomething to my owne iudgement. Yet hetherto haue my lookes bene as I told you,

which

which continuing after many of these his fruitles trials, haue wrought such change in him, as I tell you true
(with that worde she laid her hand vpon her quaking
side) I doo not a little feare him. See what a letter this
is (then drewe she the curtaine and tooke the letter
from vnder the pillowe) which to daie (with an afflicted humblenesse) he deliuered me, pretending before
Mopsa, that I should read it vnto her, to mollifie (forfooth) her iron stomacke; with that she read the letter
containing thus much.

5 MOst blessed paper, which shalt kisse that hãd, whereto al blessednes is in nature a seruãt, do not yet difdain to cary with thee the woful words of a miser now
despairing: neither be afraid to appeare before her,
bearing the base title of the sender. For no sooner shal
that diuine hande touch thee, but that thy basenesse
shall be turned to most hie preferment. Therefore
mourne boldly my Inke; for while she lookes vpõ you,
your blacknes wil shine: crie out boldly my Lamẽtatiõ;
for while she reads you, your cries wil be musicke. Say
then (O happy messenger of a most vnhappy message)
that the too soone borne, too late dying creature,
which dares not speake, no not looke, no not scarcely
thinke (as from his miserable selfe, vnto her heauenly
highnesse) onely presumes to desire thee (in the time
that her eyes and voice doo exalt thee) to say, and in
this manner to say, not from him, O no, that were not
fit, but of him. Thus much vnto her sacred iudgement:
O you, the onely, the onely honour to women, to men
the onely admiration, you that being armed by Loue,
defie him that armed you, in this high estate wherein you haue placed me, yet let me remember him
to

to whom I am bound for bringing me to your presence; and let me remember him, who (since he is
yours, how meane so euer it be) it is reaso you haue an
account of him. The wretch (yet your wretch) though
with languishing steppes runnes fast to his graue, and
will you suffer a temple (how poorely-built soeuer, but
yet a temple of your deitie) to be rased? But he dyeth: it is most true, he dyeth; and he in whom you
liue, to obey you, dieth. Whereof though he plaine,
he doth not complaine: for it is a harme, but no
wrong, which he hath receiued. He dyes, because
in wofull language all his senses tell him, that such
is your pleasure: for since you will not that he liue,
alas, alas, what followeth, what followeth of the
most ruined *Dorus*, but his ende? Ende then, euill
destinyed *Dorus*, ende; and ende thou wofull letter,
end; for it suffiseth her wisedome to know, that her
heauenly will shalbe accomplished.

O my *Philoclea*, is hee a person to write these **6**
words? and are these words lightly to be regarded?
But if you had seene, when with trembling hand he
had deliuered it, how hee went away, as if he had
beene but the coffin that carried himselfe to his sepulcher. Two times I must confesse I was about to
take curtesie into mine eyes; but both times the former resolution stopt the entrie of it: so that he departed without obtaining any further kindnesse. But
he was no sooner out of the doore, but that I looo-
ked to the doore kindly; and truely the feare of him e-
uer since hath put me into such perplexitie, as now you
found me. Ah my *Pamela* (said *Philoclea*) leaue sorrow.
The riuer of your teares will soone loose his fountaine;

it is in your hand as well to ſtitch vp his life againe, as it was before to rent it. And ſo (though with ſelf-grieued mind) ſhe comforted her ſiſter, till ſleepe came to bath himſelfe in *Pamelaes* faire weeping eyes.

5 Which when *Philoclea* found, wringing her hands, O me (ſaid ſhe) indeed the onely ſubiect of the deſtinies diſpleaſure, whoſe greateſt fortunatenes is more vnfortunate, then my ſiſters greateſt vnfortunateneſſe. Alas ſhee weepes becauſe ſhe would be no ſooner happy; I weepe becauſe I can neuer be happie; her teares flow from pittie; mine from being too farre lower then the reach of pittie. Yet doo I not enuie thee, deare *Pamela*, I do not enuy thee: onely I could wiſh that being thy ſiſter in nature, I were not ſo farre off a kin in fortune.

CHAP. 6.

¹ The Ladies vpriſing, ² and interrogatories to Dorus *concerning* Pyrocles *and* Euarchus. *³ His hiſtoriologie of* Euarchus *kingly excellencies, ⁴ his entry on a moſt corrupt eſtate, ⁵ and reformation thereof by royall arts and actions. ⁶ His, and* Dorilaus *croſſe-mariage to ech others ſiſter, hauing by ech a ſonne; their mutuall defence, with* Dorilaus *death.*

Vt the darkeneſſe of ſorrow ouerſhadowing her mind, as the night did her eyes, they were both content to hide themſelues vnder the wings of ſleepe, till the next morning had almoſt loſt his name, before

fore the two sweet sleeping sisters awaked frō dreames,
which flattered them with more comfort, then their
waking could, or would consent vnto. For then they
were called vp by *Miso*; who hauing bene with *Gynecia*,
had receiued commaundement to be continually with
her daughters, and particularly not to let *Zelmane* and
Philoclea haue any priuate cōferēce, but that she should
be present to heare what passed. But *Miso* hauing now
her authoritie encreased, came with skowling eyes to
deliuer a slauering good morrow to the two Ladies,
telling them, it was a shame for them to marre their
complexions, yea and conditions to, with long lying
a bedde: & that, when she was of their age, she trowed,
she would haue made a handkerchiefe by that time of
the day. The two sweete Princes with a smiling silence
answered her entertainement, and obeying her direction, couered their daintie beauties with the glad clothes. But as soone as *Pamela* was readie (& sooner she
was then her sister) the agony of *Dorus* giuing a fit to
her selfe, which the words of his letter (liuely imprinted in her minde) still remembred her of, she called to
Mopsa, and willed her to fetch *Dorus* to speake with her:
because (she said) she woule take further iudgement of
him, before she would moue *Dametas* to graunt her
in mariage vnto him. *Mopsa* (as glad as of sweete-meate
to goe of such an arrant) quickly returned with *Dorus* to *Pamela*, who entended both by speaking with
him to giue some comfort to his passionate harte, and
withall to heare some part of his life past; which although fame had alreadie deliuered vnto her, yet she
desired in more particular certainties to haue it from
so beloued an historian. Yet the sweetnesse of vertues
disposition

disposition iealous, euen ouer it selfe, suffred her
not to enter abruptlie into questions of *Musidorus*
(whom she was halfe ashamed she did loue so well,
and more then halfe sorie she could loue no better)
but thought best first to make her talke arise of *Pyrocles*, and his vertuous father : which thus she did.

2   *Dorus* (said she) you told me the last day, that *Plangus*
was deceaued in that he affirmed the Prince *Musidorus*
was drowned : but withall, you confessed his cosen *Pyrocles* perished; of whom certainly in that age there was
a great losse, since (as I haue heard) he was a young
Prince, of whō al mē expected as much, as mans power
could bring forth, & yet vertue promised for him, their
expectation should not be deceaued. Most excellent
Ladie (said *Dorus*) no expectatiō in others, nor hope in
himselfe could aspire to a higher mark, thē to be thought
worthy to be praised by your iudgement, & made worthy to be praised by your mouth. But most sure it is, that
as his fame could by no meanes get so sweete & noble
an aire to flie in, as in your breath, so could not you
(leauing your selfe aside) finde in the world a fitter
subiect of commendation; as noble, as a long succession of royall ancestors, famous, and famous of victories
could make him: of shape most louely, and yet of mind
more louely; valiant, curteous, wise, what should I say
more ? sweete *Pyrocles*, excellent *Pyrocles*, what can my
words but wrong thy perfections, which I would to
God in some small measure thou hadst bequethed to
him that euer must haue thy vertues in admiration;
that masked at least in them, I might haue found some
more gratious acceptation? with that he imprisoned
his looke for a while vpon *Mopsa*, who thereupon
                                                    fell

fell into a verie wide fmiling. Truely (faid *Pamela*) *Do-rus* I like well your minde, that can raife it felfe out of fo bafe a fortune, as yours is, to thinke of the imitating fo excellent a Prince, as *Pyrocles* was. Who fhootes at the mid-day Sunne, though he be fure he fhall neuer hit the marke; yet as fure he is, he fhall fhoote higher, then who aymes but at a bufh. But I pray you *Do-rus* (faid fhe) tell me (fince I perceaue you are well acquainted with that ftorie) what Prince was that *Euar-chus* father to *Pyrocles*, of whom fo much fame goes, for his rightly royall vertues, or by what wayes he got that opinion. And then fo defcend to the caufes of his fending firft away from him, and then to him for that excellent fonne of his, with the difcourfe of his life and loffe: and therein you may (if you lift) fay fomething of that fame *Mufidorus* his cofen, becaufe, they going togither, the ftory of *Pyrocles* (which I onely defire) may be the better vnderftood.

Incomparable Lady (faid he) your commandement 3 doth not onely giue me the wil, but the power to obey you, fuch influence hath your excellencie. And firft, for that famous King *Euarchus*, he was (at this time you fpeake off) King of *Macedon*, a kingdome, which in elder time had fuch a foueraintie ouer all the prouinces of *Greece*, that euē the particular kings therin did acknowledge (with more or leffe degrees of homage) fome kind of fealty thereunto: as among the reft, euen this now moft noble (and by you ennobled) kingdome of *Arcadia*. But he, whē he came to his crowne, finding by his later anceftors either negligēce, or misfortune, that in fome ages many of thofe duties had bin intermitted, would neuer ftirre vp old titles (how apparant foeuer) where-

whereby the publike peace (with the losse of manie
not guiltie soules) should be broken; but contenting
himselfe to guide that shippe, wherein the heauens
had placed him, shewed no lesse magnanimitie in
daungerlesse despising, then others in daungerous affecting the multiplying of kingdomes : for the earth
hath since borne enow bleeding witnesses, that it was
no want of true courage. Who as he was most wise to
see what was best, and most iust in the perfourming
what he saw,& temperate in abstaining from any thing
any way contrary:so thinke I,no thought can imagine
a greater harte to see and contemne daunger, where
daunger would offer to make any wrongfull threatning vpon him. A Prince, that indeed especially measured his greatnesse by his goodnesse : and if for any
thing he loued greatnesse, it was, because therein he
might exercise his goodnes. A Prince of a goodly a-
spect,and the more goodly by a graue maiestie, wherewith his mind did decke his outward graces; strong of
body,and so much the stronger, as he by a well disciplined exercise taught it both to do, and suffer. Of age,so
as he was about fiftie yeares when his Nephew *Musidorus* tooke on such shepherdish apparell for the loue of
the worlds paragon, as I now weare.

    This King left Orphan both of father and mother,
(whose father & grandfather likewise had dyed yong)
he found his estate, when he came to age (which allowed his authoritie) so disioynted euen in the noblest
& strongest lims of gouernmēt,that the name of a King
was growne euē odious to the people, his autority hauing bin abused by those greatLords,& litle kings:who
in those betweene-times of raigning (by vniust fauouring.

ring thofe that were partially theirs,& oppreſſing them that woulde defende their libertie againſt them had brought in(by a more felt then feene maner of proceeding) the worſt kind of *oligarchie*; that is,whē men are gouerned in deede by a fewe,and yet are not taught to know what thofe fewe be,to whom they ſhould obey. For they hauing the power of kinges, but not the nature of kings,vſed the authority as men do their farms, of which they fee within a yeere they ſhal goe out: making the Kinges fworde ſtrike whom they hated, the Kings purfe reward whom they loued:and (which is worſt of all) making the Royall countenance ferue to vndermine the Royall foueraintie. For the Subiectes could taſte no fweeter fruites of hauing a King, then grieuous taxations to ferue vaine purpofes; Lawes made rather to finde faults,then to preuent faultes: the Court of a Prince rather deemed as a priuiledged place of vnbrideled licentioufnes, then as a biding of him, who as a father,ſhould giue a fatherly example vnto his people. Hence grew a very diſſolution of all eſtates, while the great men (by the nature of ambition neuer fatisfied)grew factious among themfelues: and the vnderlings,glad indeede to be vnderlings to them they hated leſt,to preferue them from fuch they hated moſt. Men of vertue fuppreſſed,leſt their ſhining ſhould diſcouer the others filthines ; and at length vertue it felfe almoſt forgotten,when it had no hopefull end whereunto to be directed;olde men long nuſled in corruption,fcorning them that would feeke reformation;yong men very fault-finding,but very faultie: and fo to newfanglenes both of manners, apparrell, and each thing
els

els, by the cuſtome of ſelfe-guiltie euill, glad to change
though oft for a worſe; marchandiſe abuſed, and ſo
townes decayed for want of iuſt and naturall libertie;
offices, euen of iudging ſoules, ſolde; publique defen-
ces negleċted; and in ſumme, (leſt too long I trouble
you) all awrie, and (which wried it to the moſt wrie
courſe of all) witte abuſed, rather to faine reaſon
why it ſhould be amiſſe, then how it ſhould be amen-
ded.

    In this, and a much worſe plight,then it is fitte to
trouble your excellent eares withal,did the King *Enar-*
chus finde his eſtate, when he tooke vpon him the regi-
ment: which by reaſon of the long ſtreame of abuſe,
he was forced to eſtabliſh by ſome euen extreme ſeue-
ritie, not ſo much for the very faultes themſelues,
(which he rather ſought to preuent then to puniſh.) as
for the faultie ones; who ſtrong, euen in their faultes,
ſcorned his youth, and coulde not learne to diſgeſt,
that the man which they ſo long had vſed to maſke
their owne appetites, ſhould now be the reducer of
them into order. But ſo ſoone as ſome fewe (but in
deede notable) examples, had thundred a duetie into
the ſubieċts hartes, he ſoone ſhewed, no baſenes of ſuſpition,nor the baſeſt baſenes of enuie, could any whit
rule ſuch a Ruler. But then ſhined foorth indeede all
loue among them, when an awfull feare, ingendred by
iuſtice, did make that loue moſt louely: his firſt & principall care being to appeare vnto his people, ſuch as he
would haue them be, & to be ſuch as he appeared; making his life the example of his lawes, as it were, his actions ariſing out of his deedes. So that within ſmall
time,

time,he wanne a fingular ſoue in his people, and engraffed fingular confidence. For how could they chuſe
but loue him, whom they found ſo truely to loue thē?
He euen in reaſon diſdayning, that they that haue
charge of beaſtes, ſhould loue their charge, and care
for them; and that he that was to gouerne the moſt excellent creature,ſhould not loue ſo noble a charge. And
therefore,where moſt Princes (ſeduced by flatterie to
builde vpon falſe grounds of gouernment)make them-
ſelues(as it were) another thing from the people; and
ſo count it gaine what they can get from them : and(as
if it were two counter ballances, that their eſtate goes
hieſt when the people goes loweſt) by a fallacie of argument thinking themſelues moſt Kinges, when the
ſubiect is moſt baſely ſubiected: he contrariwiſe, vertu-
ouſlie and wiſely acknowledging,that he with his people made all but one politike bodie, whereof himſelfe
was the head;euen ſo cared for them,as he woulde for
his owne limmes: neuer reſtrayning their liberty,with-
out it ſtretched to licenciouſnes,nor pulling from them
their goods, which they found were not imployed to
the purchaſe of a greater good : but in all his actions
ſhewing a delight to their welfare, broght that to paſſe,
that while by force he tooke nothing, by their loue he
had all. In ſumme (peereleſſe Princeſſe) I might as
eaſily ſette downe the whole Arte of gouernement, as
to lay before your eyes the picture of his proceedings.
But in ſuch ſorte he flouriſhed in the ſweete comforte
of dooing much good, when by an action of leauing
his Countrie, he was forced to bring foorth his vertue of magnanimitie, as before he had done of iuſtice.

He

6   He had onely one fifter, a Ladie (left I fhould too eafilie fall to partiall prayfes of her) of whom it may be iuftly faid, that fhe was no vnfit brāch to the noble ftock wherof fhe came. Her he had giuen in mariage to *Dori-laus*, Prince of *Theffalia*, not fo much to make a frēdfhip, as to cōfirm the frēdfhip betwixt their pofteritie, which betwene them, by the likenes of vertue, had been long before made : for certainly, *Dorilaus* could neede no amplifiers mouth for the higheft point of praife. Who hath not heard (faid *Pamela*) of the valiāt, wife, and iuft *Dorilaus*, whofe vnripe death doth yet (fo many yeares fince) draw teares frō vertuous eyes? And indeede, my father is wont to fpeak of nothing with greater admira-tion, then of the notable friendfhippe (a rare thing in Princes, more rare betwene Princes) that fo holily was obferued to the laft, of thofe two excellent men . But (faid fhe) goe on I pray you. *Dorilaus* (faid he) hauing maried his fifter, had his mariage in fhort time bleft (for fo are folke woont to fay, how vnhappie foeuer the children after grow) with a fonne, whom they named *Mufidorus:* of whom I muft needes firft fpeake before I come to *Pyrocles;* becaufe as he was borne firft, fo vpon his occafion grew (as I may fay accidentally) the others birth. For fcarcely was *Mufidorus* made partaker of this oft-blinding light, when there were found numbers of Southfayers, who affirmed ftrange & incredible things fhould be performed by that childe; whether the hea-uens at that time lifted to play with ignorant mankind, or that flatterie be fo prefumptuous, as euen at times to borow the face of Diuinitie . But certainly, fo did the boldnes of their affirmation accompanie the greatnes of what they did affirme (euen defcending to particularities,

rities, what kingdomes he should ouercome) that the King of *Phrygia* (who ouer-superstitiously thought him selfe touched in the matter) sought by force to destroy the infant, to preuent his after-expectations: because a skilful man (hauing compared his natiuity with the child) so told him. Foolish mā, either vainly fearing what was not to be feared, or not considering, that if it were a worke of the superiour powers, the heauens at length are neuer children. But so he did, & by the aid of the Kings of *Lydia* and *Crete* (ioining together their armies) inuaded *Thessalia*, & brought *Dorilaus* to some behind-hand of fortune, when his faithfull friend & brother *Euarchus* came so mightily to his succour, that with some enterchanging changes of fortune, they begat of a iust war, the best child, peace. In which time *Euarchus* made a crosse mariage also with *Dorilaus* his sister, & shortly left her with child of the famous *Pyrocles*, driuen to returne to the defence of his owne countrie, which in his absence (helped with some of the ill contented nobilitie) the mighty King of *Thrace*, & his brother, King of *Pannonia*, had inuaded. The successe of those warres was too notable to be vnknowne to your eares, to which it seemes all worthy fame hath glory to come vnto. But there was *Dorilaus* (valiantly requiting his friēds helpe) in a great battaile depriued of his life, his obsequies being no more solénifed by the teares of his partakers, thē the bloud of his enimies; with so pearcing a sorrow to the constant hart of *Euarchus*, that the newes of his sons birth could lighten his countenance with no shew of comfort, although al the comfort that might be in a child, truth it selfe in him forthwith deliuered. For what fortune onely southsayers foretold of *Musidorus*, that all men might see prognosticated in *Pyrocles*,

rocles,

*rocles;*both Heauens & Earth giuing tokés of the comming forth of an Heroicall vertue. The senate house of the planets was at no time to set, for the decreeing of perfectió in a man, as at that time all folkes skilful therin did acknowledge : onely loue was threatned , and promised to him,and so to his cousin, as both the tempest and hauen of their best yeares . But as death may haue preuented *Pyrocles* , so vnworthinesse must be the death to *Musidorus.*

CHAP. 7.

* *The education of* Pyrocles *&* Musidorus.* *Their friend-ship, * nauigation,* and first shipwracke.* *The straunge gratitude of two brothers to them , vpon their liberalitie to those two brothers.*

 Vt the mother of *Pyrocles* (shortly after her childe-birth)dying, was cause that *Euarchus* recommended the care of his only son to his sister ; doing it the rather because the warre continued in cruell heat, betwixt him & those euil neighbours of his. In which meane time those young Princes (the only comforters of that vertuous widow) grewe on so , that *Pyrocles* taught admiration to the hardest conceats : *Musidorus* (perchaunce because among his subiectes) exceedingly beloued : and by the good order of *Euarchus* (well perfourmed by his sister) they were so brought vp,that all the sparkes of vertue , which nature had kindled in the,were so blowne to giue forth their vttermost heate
that

that iuftly it may be affirmed, they enflamed the affections of all that knew thē. For almoft before they could
perfectly fpeake, they began to receaue cōceits not vnworthy of the beft fpeakers: excellent deuifes being v-
fed, to make euen their fports profitable; images of battailes, & fortificatiōs being then deliuered to their memory, which after, their ftronger iudgemēts might dif-
pens, the delight of tales being cōuerted to the knowledge of al the ftories of worthyPrinces, both to moue
them to do nobly, & teach them how to do nobly; the
beautie of vertue ftill being fet before their eyes, & that
taught them with far more diligent care, then Grāma-
tical rules, their bodies exercifed in all abilities, both of
doing and fuffring, & their mindes acquainted by degrees with daungers; & in fum, all bent to the making
vp of princely mindes: no feruile feare vfed towardes
them, nor any other violent reftraint, but ftil as to Princes: fo that a habite of commaunding was naturalized
in them, and therefore the farther from Tyrannie: Nature hauing done fo much for them in nothing, as that
it made them Lords of truth, whereon all the other
goods were builded.

Among which I nothing fo much delight to re-   2
count, as the memorable friendfhip that grewe betwixt the two Princes, fuch as made them more like
then the likeneffe of all other vertues, and made them
more neer one to the other, then the neerenes of their
bloud could afpire vnto; which I think grew the fafter,
and the fafter was tied betweene them, by reafon that
Mufidorus being elder by three or foure yeares, it was
neither fo great a difference in age as did take away the
delight in focietie, and yet by the difference there was

taken away the occasion of childish contentions; till
they had both past ouer the humour of such contentions. For *Pyrocles* bare reueréce ful of loue to *Musidorus*,
& *Musidorus* had a delight full of loue in *Pyrocles*. *Musidorus*, what he had learned either for body or minde,
would teach it to *Pyrocles* ; and *Pyrocles* was so glad to
learne of none, as of *Musidorus*: till *Pyrocles*, being come
to sixtene yeares of age, he seemed so to ouerrun his
age in growth, strength, and al things following it, that
not *Musidorus*, no nor any man liuing (I thinke) could
performe any action, either on horse, or foote, more
strongly, or deliuer that strength more nimbly, or become the deliuery more gracefully, or employ al more
vertuously. Which may well seeme wonderfull: but
wonders are no wonders in a wonderfull subiect.

3   At which time vnderstanding that the King *Euarchus*, after so many yeares warre, and the conquest of all
Pannonia, and almost *Thrace*, had now brought the cô-
clusion of al to the siege of *Bizantium* (to the raising of
which siege great forces were made) they would needs
fall to the practise of those vertues, which they before
learned. And therefore the mother of *Musidorus* nobly
yeelding ouer her owne affects to her childrens good
(for a mother she was in effect to thé both) the rather
that they might helpe her beloued brother, they brake
of all delayes; which *Musidorus* for his parte thought already had deuoured too much of his good time, but
that he had once graunted a boone (before he knew
what it was) to his deere friend *Pyrocles*; that he would
neuer seeke the aduentures of armes, vntil he might go
with him: which hauing fast boûd his hart (a true slaue
to faith) he had bid a tedious delay of following his
owne

owne humour for his friends fake, till now finding
him able euery way to go thorow with that kinde of
life, he was as defirous for his fake, as for his owne, to
enter into it. So therefore preparing a nauie, that they
might go like themfelues, and not onely bring the
comfort of their prefence, but of their power to their
deere parent *Euarchus*, they recommended themfelues to the Sea, leauing the fhore of *Theffalia* full of
teares and vowes; and were receiued thereon with fo
fmooth and fmiling a face, as if *Neptune* had as then
learned falfely to fawne on Princes. The winde was
like a feruaunt, wayting behind them fo iuft, that they
might fill the failes as they lifted; and the beft faylers
fhewing themfelues leffe couetous of his liberalitie,
fo tempered it, that they all kept together like a beautifull flocke, which fo well could obey their maifters
pipe: without fometimes, to delight the Princes eies,
fome two or three of them would ftriue, who could (either by the cunning of well fpending the windes
breath, or by the aduantageous building of their moo-
uing houfes) leaue their fellowes behind them in the
honour of fpeed: while the two Princes had leafure to
fee the practife of that, which before they had learned
by bookes: to confider the arte of catching the winde
prifoner, to no other ende, but to runne away with it;
to fee how beautie, and vfe can fo well agree together,
that of all the trinckets, where with they are attired,
there is not one but ferues to fome neceffary purpofe.
And (ô Lord) to fee the admirable power & noble effects of Loue, whereby the feeming infenfible Load-
ftone, with a fecret beauty (holding the fpirit of iron in
it) can draw that hard-harted thing vnto it, and (like a
S 3 vertuous

vertuous miſtreſſe) not onely make it bow it ſelfe, but with it make it aſpire to ſo high a Loue, as of the heauenly Poles; and thereby to bring foorth the nobleſt deeds, that the children of the Earth can boaſt of. And ſo the Princes delighting their côceats with côfirming their knowledge, ſeing wherein the Sea-diſcipline differed from Land-ſeruice, they had for a day & almoſt a whole night, as pleaſing entertainement, as the falſeſt hart could giue to him he meanes worſt to.

4   But by that the next morning began a little to make a guilden ſhewe of a good meaning, there aroſe euen with the Sun, a vaile of darke cloudes before his face, which ſhortly (like inck powred into water) had blacked ouer all the face of heauen; preparing (as it were) a mournefull ſtage for a Tragedie to be plaied on. For forthwith the windes began to ſpeake lowder, and as in a tumultuous kingdome, to thinke themſelues fitteſt inſtruments of commaundement; and blowing whole ſtormes of hayle and raine vpon them, they were ſooner in daunger, then they coulde almoſt bethinke themſelues of chaunge. For then the traiterous Sea began to ſwell in pride againſt the afflicted Naue, vnder which (while the heauen fauoured them) it had layne ſo calmely, making mountaines of it ſelfe, ouer which the toſſed and tottring ſhip ſhoulde clime, to be ſtreight carried downe againe to a pit of helliſh darkeneſſe; with ſuch cruell blowes againſt the ſides of the ſhippe (that which way ſoeuer it went, was ſtill in his malice) that there was left neither power to ſtay, nor way to eſcape. And ſhortly had it ſo diſſeuered the louing companie, which the daie before had tarried together, that moſt of them neuer met againe,
but

but were fwallowed vp in his neuer-fatiffied mouth.
Some indeed (as fince was knowne) after long wandring returned into *Theffalia*; other recouered *Bizan-*
tium, and ferued *Euarchus* in his warre. But in the fhip
wherein the Princes were (now left as much alone as
proud Lords be when fortune fails them) though they
employed all induftrie to faue themfelues, yet what
they did was rather for dutie to nature, then hope to e-
fcape. So ougly a darkeneffe, as if it would preuent the
nights comming, vfurped the dayes right: which (accompanied fometimes with thunders, alwayes with
horrible noyfes of the chafing winds)made the mafters
and pilots fo aftonifhed, that they knew not how to direct, and if they knew they could fcarcely (when they
directed) heare their owne whiftle. For the fea ftraue
with the winds which fhould be lowder,& the fhrouds
of the fhip with a ghaftful noife to them that were in it,
witneffed, that their ruine was the wager of the others
contention, and the heauen roaring out thunders the
more amazed them, as hauing thofe powers for enimies. Certainely there is no daunger carries with it
more horror, then that which growes in thofe flowing
kingdomes. For that dwelling place is vnnaturall to
mankind, and then the terriblleneffe of the continuall
motion, the diffolutiõ of the fare being from comfort,
the eye and the eare hauing ougly images euer before
it, doth ftill vex the minde, euen when it is beft armed
againft it. But thus the day paft (if that might be called
a day)while the cunningeft mariners were fo conquered by the ftorme, as they thought it beft with ftriking failes to yeelde to be gouerned by it: the valian-
teft feeling inward difmayedneffe, and yet the feare-
fulleft

fulleſt aſhamed fully to ſhew it, ſeeing that the Princes (who were to parte from the greateſt fortunes) did
in their countenances accuſe no point of feare, but
encouraging them to doo what might be done (putting their handes to euerie moſt painefull office)
taught them at one inſtant to promiſe themſelues
the beſt, and yet not to deſpiſe the worſt. But ſo
were they carryed by the tyrannie of the winde, and
the treaſon of the ſea, all that night, which the elder it was, the more wayward it ſhewed it ſelfe towards them : till the next morning (knowne to be
a morning better by the houre-glaſſe, then by the day
cleereneſſe) hauing runne fortune as blindly, as it
ſelfe euer was painted, leſt the concluſion ſhould not
aunſwere to the reſt of the play, they were driuen vpon a rocke : which hidden with thoſe outragious
waues, did, as it were, cloſely diſſemble his cruel mind,
till with an vnbeleeued violence (but to them that
haue tried it) the ſhippe ranne vpon it; and ſeeming
willinger to periſh then to haue her courſe ſtayed, re-
doubled her blowes, till ſhe had broken her ſelfe in
peeces; and as it were tearing out her owne bowels to
feede the ſeas greedineſſe, left nothing within it but
deſpaire of ſafetie, and expectation of a loathſome end.
There was to be ſeene the diuerſe manner of minds
in diſtreſſe: ſome ſate vpon the toppe of the poupe weeping and wailing, till the ſea ſwallowed them; ſome
one more able to abide death, then feare of death, cut
his owne throate to preuent drowning; ſome prayed,
and there wanted not of them which curſed, as if
the heauens could not be more angrie then they were.
But a monſtrous crie begotten of manie roaring

vowes

vowes, was able to infect with feare a minde that had not preuented it with the power of reason.

But the Princes vsing the passions of fearing euill, and desiring to escape, onely to serue the rule of vertue, not to abandon ones selfe, lept to a ribbe of the shippe, which broken from his fellowes, floted with more likelyhood to doo seruice, then any other limme of that ruinous bodie; vpon which there had gotten alreadie two brethren, well knowne seruants of theirs; and streight they foure were carryed out of sight, in that huge rising of the sea, from the rest of the shippe. But the peece they were on sinking by little and little vnder them, not able to support the weight of so manie, the brethren (the elder whereof was *Leucippus*, the younger *Nelsus*) shewed themselues right faithfull and gratefull seruants vnto them; gratefull (I say) for this cause: Those two gentlemen had bene taken prisoners in the great warre the king of *Phrygia* made vpon *Thessalia*, in the time of *Musidorus* his infancie; and hauing beene solde into another countrie (though peace fell after betweene these Realmes) could not be deliuered, because of their valor knowne, but for a farre greater summe, then either all their friends were able, or the Dowager willing to make, in respect of the great expences her selfe and people had bene put to in those warres; and so had they remained in prison about thirteene yeares, when the two young Princes (hearing speaches of their good deserts) found meanes both by selling all the Iewels they had of great price, and by giuing vnder their hands great estates when they should come to be Kings (which promises their vertue promised for them should be kept) to get

so

ſo much treaſure as redeemed them from captiuitie.
This remembred, and kindly remembred by theſe two
brothers, perchance helped by a naturall duetie to their
Princes blood, they willingly left holde of the boord,
committing themſelues to the ſeas rage, & euen when
they went to dye, themſelues praying for the Princes
liues. It is true, that neither the paine nor daunger, ſo
moued the Princes hartes as the tenderneſſe of that louing part, farre from glorie, hauing ſo few lookers on;
farre from hope of reward, ſince themſelues were ſure
to periſh.

CHAP. 8.

*Pyrocles caſt on the ſhore of Phrygia led priſoner to the
King. That ſuſpicious tyrant naturalized. His intent
to kill Pyrocles. Muſidorus-his eſcape from ſea, and
offer to dye for his friend. Their contention for death.
Preparation for Muſidorus execution. His ſtraunge deliuerie by Pyrocles, and a ſodaine mutinie. Their killing the bad King, and creating a better.*

Vt now of all the royal Nauie they
had left but one peece of one ſhip,
whereon they kept themſelues in
all trueth, hauing enterchaunged
their cares, while either cared for
other, ech comforting and councelling how to labour for the better, and to abide the worſe. But ſo
fell it out, that as they were carryed by the tide (which
there ſeconded by the ſtorme ran exceedingly ſwiftly)
Muſidorus

Mufidorus feeing (as he thought) *Pyrocles* not well vpon the boord, as he would with his right hand haue
helped him on better, he had no fooner vnfaftned his
hold, but that a waue forcibly fpoiled his weaker hand
of hold; and fo for a time parted thofe friends, each
crying to the other, but the noife of the fea drowned
their farewell. But *Pyrocles* (then carelefle of death, if it
had come by any meanes, but his owne) was fhort-
ly brought out of the feas furie to the lands comfort;
when (in my confcience I know) that comfort was but
bitter vnto him. And bitter indeed it fell out euen in it
felfe to be vnto him.

For being caft on land much brufed & beaten both
with the feas hard farewell, and the fhores rude welcome; and euen almoft deadly tired with the length of
his vncomfortable labour, as he was wall ing vp to difcouer fome bodie, to whom he might goe for reliefe,
there came ftreight running vnto him certaine, who
(as it was after knowne) by appointment watched
(with manie others) in diuerfe places along the coaft:
who laide handes of him, and without either queftioning with him, or fhewing will to heare him, (like
men fearefull to appeare curious) or which was worfe
hauing no regard to the hard plight he was in (being fo wette and weake) they carried him fome miles
thence, to a houfe of a principall officer of that countrie. Who with no more ciuilitie (though with much
more bufines then thofe vnder-fellowes had fhewed)
beganne in captious manner to put interrogatories
vnto him. To which he (vnufed to fuch entertainment)
did fhortlie and plainely aunfwere, what he was, and
how he came thither.

But

But that no fooner knowne, with numbers of armed men to garde him (for mifchiefe, not from mifchiefe) he was fent to the Kings ccurt, which as then was not aboue a dayes iourney off, with letters from that officer, containing his owne feruiceable diligence in difcouering fo great a perfonage; adding with all more then was true of his coniectures, becaufe he would endeare his owne feruice.

3   This country whereon he fell was *Phrygia*, and it was to the King thereof to whom he was fent, a Prince of a melancholy conftitution both of bodie and mind; wickedly fad, euer mufing of horrible matters; fufpecting, or rather condemning all men of euill, becaufe his minde had no eye to efpie goodneffe: and therefore accufing *Sycophantes*, of all men did beft fort to his nature; but therefore not feeming *Sycophantes*, becaufe of no euill they faid, they could bring any new or doubtfull thing vnto him, but fuch as alreadie he had bene apt to determine; fo as they came but as proofes of his wifedome : fearefull and neuer fccure; while the feare he had figured in his minde had any poffibilitie of euent. A tode-like retyredneffe, and clofeneffe of minde; nature teaching the odioufneffe of poyfon, and the daunger ef odioufneffe. Yet while youth lafted in him, the exercifes of that age, and his humour (not yet fullie difcouered) made him fomething the more frequentable, and leffe daungerous. But after that yeares beganne to come on with fome, though more feldome fhewes of a bloudie nature, and that the prophecie of *Mufidorus* deftinie came to his eares (deliuered vnto him, and receiued of him with the hardeft interpretation, as though his

his ſubiectes did delight in the hearing thereof.)
Then gaue he himſelfe indeede to the full currant of
his diſpoſition, eſpetially after the warre of *Theſſalia,*
wherein (though in trueth wrongly) he deemed, his
vnſucceſſings proceeded of their vnwillingnes to haue
him proſper: and then thinking him ſelfe contemned,
(knowing no countermine againſt contempt, but terror) began to let nothing paſſe which might beare the
colour of a fault, without ſharpe puniſhment: & when
he wanted faults, excellencie grew a fault; and it was
ſufficient to make one guiltie, that he had power to be
guiltie. And as there is no honor, to which impudent
pouertie cannot make it ſelfe ſeruiceable, ſo were there
enow of thoſe deſperate ambitious, who would builde
their houſes vpon others ruines, which after ſhoulde
fall by like practiſes. So as ſeruitude came mainly vpon
that poore people, whoſe deedes were not onely puniſhed, but words corrected, and euen thoughts by ſome
meane or other puld out of thē: while ſuſpitiō bred the
mind of crueltie, and the effectes of crueltie ſtirred a
new cauſe of ſuſpition. And in this plight (ful of watchfull fearefulnes) did the ſtorme deliuer ſweete *Pyrocles*
to the ſtormie minde of that Tyrant, all men that did
ſuch wrong to ſo rare a ſtranger (whoſe countenaunce
deſerued both pitie and admiration) condemning thēſelues as much in their hearts, as they did brag in their
forces.

But when this bloudy King knew what he was, and **4**
in what order he and his coſin *Muſidorus* (ſo much of
him feared) were come out of *Theſſalia,* aſſuredly thinking (becauſe euer thinking the worſt) that thoſe forces were prouided againſt him; glad of the periſhing
(as

(as he thought)of *Mufidorus*, determined in publique
fort to put *Pyrocles* to death . For hauing quite lofte the
way of noblenes,he ftraue to clime to the height of ter-
riblenes;and thinking to make all men adread, to make
fuch one an enemie,who would not fpare,nor feare to
kill fo great a Prince; and laftly,hauing nothing in him
why to make him his friend, thought,he woulde make
him away,for being his enemie. The day was appointed,and all things appointed for that cruell blow, in fo
folemne an order, as if they would fet foorth tyrány in
moft gorgeous decking. The Princely youth of inuincible valour , yet fo vniuftly fubiected to fuch outragious wrong, carrying himfelfe in all his demeanure fo
conftatly, abiding extremitie,that one might fee it was
the cutting away of the greateft hope of the world,and
deftroying vertue in his fweeteft grouth.

5   But fo it fell out that his death was preuented by a
rare example of friendfhippe in *Mufidorus:* who being
almoft drowned, had bene taken vp by a Fifherman
belonging to the kingdome of *Pontus*;and being there,
and vnderftanding the full difcourfe(as Fame was very
prodigall of fo notable an accident) in what cafe *Pyro-*
cles was; learning withall, that his hate was farre more
to him then to *Pyrocles*, he founde meanes to acquaint
him felfe with a noble-man of that Countrie,to whom
largely difcouering what he was, he found him a moft
fitte inftrument to effectuate his defire. For this nobleman had bene one, who in many warres had ferued
Euarchus, and had bene fo mind-ftriken by the beautie
of vertue in that noble King, that (though not borne
his Subiect) he euen profefte himfelfe his feruaunt.
His defire therefore to him was, to keepe *Mufidorus*
in a

in a ftrong Caftle of his, and then to make the King of *Phrygia* vnderftande, that if he would deliuer *Pyrocles*, *Mufidorus* woulde willingly put him felfe into his handes: knowing well, that how thirftie fo euer he was of *Pyrocles* bloud, he woulde rather drinke that of *Mufidorus*.

The Nobleman was loath to preferue one by the loffe of another, but time vrging refolution : the importunitie of *Mufidorus* (who fhewed a minde not to ouer-liue *Pyrocles*) with the affection he bare to *Euarchus*, fo preuayled, that he carried this ftrange offer of *Mufidorus*, which by that Tyrant was greedelie accepted.

And fo vpon fecuritie of both fides, they were 6 enterchanged. Where I may not omitte that worke of friendfhippe in *Pyrocles*, who both in fpeache and coûtenance to *Mufidorus*, well fhewed, that he thought himfelfe iniured, and not releeued by him : asking him, what he had euer feene in him, why he could not beare the extremities of mortall accidentes as well as any man? and why he fhoulde enuie him the glorie of fuffering death for his friendes caufe, and (as it were) robbe him of his owne poffeffion? But in this notable contention, (where the conqueft muft be the conquerers deftruction, and fafetie the punifhment of the conquered) *Mufidorus* preuayled : becaufe he was a more welcome prize to the vniufte King, that wifht none well, to them worfe then others, and to him worfte of all : and as chearefully going towardes, as *Pyrocles* went frowardly fromwarde his death, he was deliuered to the King, who could not be inough fure of him, without he fed his owne eies vpon
one,

one, whom he had begon to feare, as soone as the other began to be.

7   Yet becaufe he would in one acte, both make oftentation of his owne felicitie (into whofe hands his moft feared enemie was fallen)and withal cut of fuch hopes from his fufpected fubiects(when they fhould knowe certainly he was dead) with much more fkilful cruelty, and horrible folemnitie he caufed each thing to be prepared for his triumph of tyrannie. And fo the day being come,he was led foorth by many armed men(who often had beene the fortifiers of wickednes) to the place of execution:where comming with a mind comforted in that he had done fuch feruice to *Pyrocles*, this ftrange encounter he had.

8   The excelling *Pyrocles* was no fooner deliuered by the kings feruants to a place of liberty,then he bent his witte and courage,(and what would not they bring to paffe?)how ether to deliuer *Mufidorus*,or to perifh with him. And(finding he could get in that countrie no forces fufficient by force to refcue him) to bring himfelfe to die with him, (little hoping of better euent) he put himfelfe in poore rayment, and by the helpe of fome few crownes he tooke of that noble man,(who full of forrow, though not knowing the fecrete of his intent, fuffered him to goe in fuch order from him) he (euen he,born to the greateft expectation, and of the greateft bloud that any Prince might be)fubmitted himfelfe to be feruant to the executioner that fhould put to death *Mufidorus*: a farre notabler proofe of his friendfhip, confidering the height of his minde, then any death could be. That bad officer not fufpecting him, being araied fit for fuch an eftate,& hauing his beautie hidden

by

by many foule spots he artificially put vpon his face,
gaue him leaue not onely to weare a sworde himselfe,
but to beare his sworde prepared for the iustified murther. And so *Pyrocles* taking his time, when *Musidorus*
was vpon the scaffold (separated somewhat from the
rest,as allowed to say something) he stept vnto him; &
putting the sworde into his hande not bound (a point
of ciuility the officers vsed towards him, becaufe they
doubted no such enterprise) *Musidorus* (said he) die
nobly. In truth,neuer mã betweene ioy before knowledge what to be glad of, and feare after cõsidering his
case,had such a confusion of thoughts, as I had, when
I saw *Pyrocles,*so neare me But with that *Dorus* blushed,
and *Pamela* smiled : and *Dorus* the more blushed at her
smiling, and she the more smiled at his blushing ; because he had (with the remembraunce of that plight
he was in) forgotten in speaking of him selfe to vse the
third person But *Musidorus* turned againe her thoughts
from his cheekes to his tongue in this sorte : But (said
he) when they were with swordes in handes, not turning backs one to the other (for there they knew was
no place of defence) but making that a preseruation in
not hoping to be preserued, and now acknowledging
themselues subiect to death, meaning onely to do honour to their princely birth, they flew amongst thë all
(for all were enimies) & had quickly either with flight
or death,left none vpon the scaffolde to annoy them.
Wherein *Pyrocles* (the excellent *Pyrocles*) did such wonders beyonc beliefe, as was hable to leade *Musidorus* to
courage,though he had bene borne a coward . But indeed,iust rage & desperate vertue did such effects , that
the popular sorte of the beholders began to be almost

super-

ſuperſtitiouſly amazed, as at effectes beyond mortall power. But the King with angry threatnings from-out a window (where he was not aſhamed, the worlde ſhould behold him a beholder)cōmaunded his garde, and the reſt of his ſouldiers to haſten their death. But many of them loſt their bodies to looſe their ſoules, when the Princes grew almoſt ſo weary, as they were ready to be conquered with conquering.

But as they were ſtil fighting with weake armes, and ſtrong harts, it happened, that one of the ſouldiers (cōmaūded to go vp after his fellowes againſt the Princes) hauing receiued a light hurt, more wouded in his hart, went backe with as much diligence, as he came vp with modeſtie: which another of his fellowes ſeeing, to pike a thanke of the King, ſtrake him vpon the face, reuiling him, that ſo accompanied, he would runne away from ſo fewe. But he (as many times it falls out) onely valiant, when he was angrie, in reuenge thruſt him through : which with his death was ſtreight reuenged by a brother of his : and that againe requited by a fellow of the others. There began to be a great tumult amongſt the ſouldiers; which ſeene, and not vnderſtood by the people (vſed to feares but not vſed to be bolde in them) ſome began to crie treaſon; and that voice ſtreight multiplying it ſelfe, the King (O the cowardiſe of a guiltie conſcience) before any man ſet vpon him, fled away Where-with a bruit (either by arte of ſome well meaning men, or by ſuch chaunce as ſuch thinges often fall out by) ran from one to the other, that the King was ſlaine; wherwith certaine yong men of the braueſt minds, cried with lowde voice, Libertie; and encouraging the other Citizens to follow

them,

them, set vpon the garde, and souldiers as chiefe instruments of Tyrannie: and quickly, aided by the Princes,
they had left none of them aliue, nor any other in the
cittie, who they thought had in any sorte set his hand
to the worke of their seruitude, and (God knowes) by
the blindnesse of rage, killing many guiltles persons, either for affinity to the Tyrant, or enmitie to the tyrant-
killers. But some of the wisest (seeing that a popular licence is indeede the many-headed tyranny) preuailed
with the rest to make *Musidorus* their chiefe: choosing
one of them (because Princes) to defende them, and
him because elder and most hated of the Tyrant, and
by him to be ruled: whom foorthwith they lifted vp,
Fortune (I thinke) smiling at her worke therein, that
a scaffold of execution should grow a scaffold of coro-
nation.

But by and by there came newes of more certaine
truth, that the King was not dead, but fled to a strong
castle of his, neere had, where he was gathering forces
in all speed possible to suppresse this mutinie. But now
they had run themselues too farre out of breath, to go
backe againe the same carcer; and too well they knew
the sharpnesse of his memorie to forget such an iniury;
therefore learning vertue of necessitie, they continued
resolute to obey *Musidorus*. Who seing what forces
were in the citic, with them issued against the Tyrant,
while they were in this heat; before practises might be
vsed to disseuer them: & with them met the King, who
likewise hoping little to preuaile by time, (knowing
and finding his peoples hate) met him with little delay
in the field: where him selfe was slaine by *Musidorus*,
after he had seene his onely sonne (a Prince of great

T 2 courage

courage & beautie, but foſtred in bloud by his naughty
Father) ſlaine by the hand of *Pyrocles*. This victory obteined, with great, and truly not vndeſerued honour to
the two Princes, the whole eſtates of the country with
one conſent, gaue the crowne and all other markes of
ſoueraigntie to *Muſidorus*; deſiring nothing more, then
to liue vnder ſuch a gouernment, as they promiſed thēſelues of him.

11   But he thinking it a greater greatnes to giue a kingdome, then get a kingdome; vnderſtanding that there
was left of the bloud Roiall, & next to the ſucceſſiō, an
aged Gentleman of approued goodnes (who had gotten nothing by his couſins power, but danger frō him,
and odiouſnes for him) hauing paſt his time in modeſt
ſecrecy, & aſmuch from entermedling in matters of gouernment, as the greatneſſe of his bloud would ſuffer
him, did (after hauing receiued the full power to his
owne hands) reſigne all to the noble-mā: but with ſuch
conditions, & cautions of the conditions, as might aſſure the people (with aſmuch aſſurāce as worldly matters beare) that not onely that gouernour, of whom indeed they looked for al good, but the nature of the gouernment, ſhould be no way apt to decline to Tyrány.

CHAP. 9.

1 *The two brothers eſcape to the ſhore of* Pontus. 2 *Incōſtancy,*
3 *and enuie purtraied in the King & his Counſellor.* 4 *The
aduancement & ouerthrow by them of thoſe two brothers.*
5 *The reuenge thereof by the two Princes.* 6 *The cruelties of
two reuengefull Gyants, and their death by the Princes.*
7 *Their honours, and their honourable mindes.*

This

His dooing fet foorth no leffe his **1**
magnificéce,then the other act did
his magnanimitie : fo that greatly
prayfed of al,and iuftly beloued of
the newe King ,who in all both
wordes and behauiour protefted
him felfe their Tenaunt,or Liege-
man, they were drawne thence to
reuenge thofe two feruáts of theirs,of whofe memorable faith,I told you(moft excellét Princeffe)in willingly giuing themfelues to be drowned for their fakes: but
drowned indeed they were not, but gat with painefull
fwimming vpon a rocke:frö whence(after being come
as neere famifhing, as before drowning) the weather
breaking vp, they were brought to the maine lande of
Pontus;the fame coútry vpon which *Mufidorus* alfo was
fallen,but not in fo luckie a place.

For they were brought to the King of that country, **2**
a Tyrant alfo,not thorow fufpition,greedines,or vnre-
uégefulnes,as he of *Phrygia*,but (as I may terme it)of a
wanton crueltie:inconftant of his choife of friends, or
rather neuer hauing a friéd,but a playfellow; of whom
when he was wearie, he could not otherwife rid himfelf,thé by killing thé: giuing fomtimes prodigally,not
becaufe he loued them to whom he gaue, but becaufe
he lufted to giue:punifhing,not fo much for hate or anger,as becaufe he felt not the fmart of punifhment:de-
lighted to be flattered, at firft for thofe vertues which
were not in him, at length making his vices vertues
worthy the flattering : with like iudgement glorying,
when he had happened to do a thing well, as when he
had performed fome notable mifchiefe.

T 3   He

3   He chaūced at that time (for indeed long time none lafted with him) to haue next in vfe about him, a mā of the moft enuious difpofitiō, that (I think) euer infeɗed the aire with his breath : whofe eies could not looke right vpon any happie mā, nor eares beare the burthen of any bodies praife : cōtrary to the natures of al other plagues, plagued with others well being ; making happines the ground of his vnhappineffe, & good newes the argumēt of his forrow: in fum, a man whofe fauour no man could winne, but by being miferable.

4   And fo, becaufe thefe two faithfull feruants of theirs came in miferable forte to that Courte, he was apte inough at firft to fauour them ; and the King vnderftanding of their aduenture, (wherein they had fhewed fo conftant a faith vnto their Lordes) fuddainly falles to take a pride in making much of them, extolling them with infinite prayfes, and prayfing him felfe in his harte, in that he prayfed them. And by and by were they made great courtiers, and in the way of minions, when aduauncement (the moft mortall offence to enuy) ftirred vp their former friend, to ouerthrow his owne worke in them ; taking occafion vpon the knowledge (newly come to the court) of the late King of *Phrygia* deftroied by their two Lordes, who hauing bene a neere kinfman to this Prince of *Pontus*, by this enuious Coūcellour, partly with fufpition of praɗife, partly with glory of in-part reuēging his coufins death, the King was fuddainly turned, (and euery turne with him was a downe-fall) to locke them vp in prifon, as feruaunts to his enimies, whom before he had neuer knowne, nor (til that time one of his own fubieɗs had entertained and dealt for them) did euer take heed of.

But

But now earneft in euery prefent humour, and making
himfelfe braue in his liking, he was content to giue
them iuft caufe of offence, when they had power to
make iuft reuenge. Yet did the Princes fend vnto him
before they entred into war, defiring their feruants liberty. But hef velling in thier hublenes, (like a bubble
fwollen vp with a fmall breath., broken with a great)
forgetting, or neuer knowing humanitie, caufed their
heads to be ftriken off, by the aduice of his enuious
Councellor (who now hated them fo much the more,
as he forefaw the happines in hauing fuch, and fo fortunate mafters) and fent them with vnroyall reproches
to *Mufidorus* and *Pyrocles*, as if they had done traiteroufl-
ly, and not heroically in killing his tyrannicall Cofen.

But that iniurie went beyond al degree of reconcile-
ment; fo that they making forces in *Phrygia* (a kingdome wholy at their commandement, by the loue of
the people, and gratefulneffe of the King) they entred
his country; and wholy conquering it (with fuch deeds
as at left Fame faid were excellent) tooke the King; and
by *Mufidorus* commaundement (*Pyrocles* hart more enclined to pitie) he was flaine vpon the tombe of their
two true Seruants; which they caufed to be made for
them with royall expences, and notable workmanfhip
to preferue their deade liues. For his wicked Seruant
he fhould haue felt the like, or worfe, but that his
harte brake euen to death with the beholding the honour done to the deade carcaffes? There might *Py-*
rocles quietly haue enioyed that crowne, by all the
defire of that people, moft of whom had reuolted
vnto him: but he, finding a fifter of the late Kings
(a faire and well efteemed Ladie) looking for no-

thing more, then to be oppreſſed with her brothers ruines, gaue her in marriage to the noble man his fathers old friend, and endowed them with the crowne of that kingdome. And not content with thoſe publike actions, of princely, and (as it were) gouerning vertue, they did (in that kingdome and ſome other neere about) diuers acts of particular trials, more famous, becauſe more perilous. For in that time thoſe regions were full both of cruell monſters,& monſtrous men: all which in ſhort time by priuate combats they deliuered the countries of.

6   Among the reſt, two brothers of huge both greatneſſe & force, therefore commonly called giants, who kept théſelues in a caſtle ſeated vpon the top of a rocke, impregnable, becauſe there was no comming vnto it, but by one narrow path, where one mans force was able to keepe downe an armie. Theſe brothers had a while ſerued the King of *Pontus*, and in all his affaires (eſpecially of war,wherunto they were onely apt) they had ſhewed, as vncôquered courage, ſo a rude faithfulnes : being men indeed by nature apter to the faults of rage,then of deceipt;not greatly ambitious, more then to be well and vprightly dealt with; rather impatient of iniury, then delighted with more then ordinary curteſies;and in iniuries more ſenſible of ſmart or loſſe,then of reproch or diſgrace. Theſe men being of this nature (and certainely Iewels to a wiſe man,conſidering what indeed wonders they were able to performe) yet were diſcarded by that vnworthyPrince after many notable deſerts, as not worthy the holding. Which was the more euident to them; becauſe it ſodainly fell from an exceſſe of fauor,which (many examples hauing taught them)

them) neuer ftopt his race till it came to an headlong
ouerthrow: they full of rage, retyred themfelues vnto
this caftle. Where thinking nothing iufter thē reuenge,
nor more noble then the effects of anger, that (according to the nature) ful of inward brauery and fiercenes,
fcarcely in the glaffe of Reafon, thinkihg it felf faire, but
when it is terrible, they immediately gaue themfelues
to make all the countrie about them (fubiect to that
King) to fmart for their Lords folly: not caring how
innocent they were, but rather thinking the more innocent they were, the more it teftified their fpite,
which they defired to manifeft. And with vfe of euill,
growing more and more euill, they tooke delight in
flaughter, and pleafing themfelues in making others
wracke the effect of their power: fo that where in the
time that they obeyed a mafter, their anger was a feruiceable power of the minde to doo publike good; fo
now vnbridled, and blinde iudge of it felfe, it made
wickedneffe violent, and praifed it felfe in excellencie
of mifchiefe; almoft to the ruine of the countrie, not
greatly regarded by their careleffe and loueleffe king.
Till now thefe Princes finding them fo flefhed in crueltie, as not to be reclaimed, fecreatly vndertooke the
matter alone: for accompanied they would not haue
fuffered them to haue mounted; and fo thofe great fellowes fcornefully receiuing them, as foolifh birds falne
into their net, it pleafed the eternall iuftice to make thē
fuffer death by their hands: So as they were manifold-
ly acknowledged the fauers of that countrie.

It were the part of a verie idle Orator to fet forth the 7
numbers of wel-deuifed honors done vnto them: But
as high honor is not onely gotten and borne by paine,

and

and daunger, but muſt be nurſt by the like, or els va
niſheth as ſoone as it appeares to the world : ſo the naturall hunger thereof (which was in *Pyrocles*) ſuffered
him not to account a reſting ſeate of that, which euer
either riſeth, or falleth, but ſtill to make one action beget another ; whereby his doings might ſend his praiſe
to others mouthes to rebound againe true contentment to his ſpirite. And therefore hauing well eſtabli-
ſhed thoſe kingdomes, vnder good gouernours, and
rid them by their valure of ſuch giants and monſters,
as before time armies were not able to ſubdue, they
determined in vnknowne order to ſee more of the
world, & to imploy thoſe gifts eſteemed rare in them,
to the good of mankinde ; and therefore would themſelues (vnderſtanding that the King *Euarchus* was paſſed all the cumber of his warres) goe priuately to ſeeke
exerciſes of their vertue ; thinking it not ſo worthy, to
be brought to heroycall effects by fortune, or neceſſitie
(like *Vlyſſes* and *Aeneas*) as by ones owne choice, and
working. And ſo went they away from verie vnwilling
people to leaue them, making time haſte it ſelfe to be a
circumſtance of their honour, and one place witneſſe
to another of the truth of their doings. For ſcarcely
were they out of the côfines of *Pontus*, but that as they
ridde alone armed, (for alone they went, one ſeruing
the other) they mette an aduenture ; which though
not ſo notable for any great effect they perfourmed,
yet worthy to be remembred for the vn-vſed examples
therein, as well of true natural goodnes, as of wretched
vngratefulneſſe.

CHAP.

CHAP. 10.

[1] *The pitifull ſtate, and ſtorie of the* Paphalgonian *vnkinde
King, and his kind ſonne,* [2] *firſt related by the ſon,* [3] *then by
the blind father.* [4] *The three Princes aſsaulted by* Plexirtus
and his traine : [5] *aſsiſted by their King of* Pontus *and his
troupes.* [6] Plexirtus *ſuccoured and ſaued by two brothers,
that vertuouſly loued a moſt vicious man.* [7] *Beſeeged by the
new King,* [8] *he ſubmitteth, & is pardoned.* [9] *The two Princes depart to aide the Queene of* Lycia.

I T was in the kingdome of *Galacia,* [1]
the ſeaſon being (as in the depth
of winter) very cold, and as then
ſodainely growne to ſo extreame
and foule a ſtorme, that neuer any
winter (I thinke) brought foorth a
fowler child: ſo that the Princes
were euen compelled by the haile,
that the pride of the winde blew into their faces, to
ſeeke ſome ſhrowding place within a certaine hollow
rocke offering it vnto them, they made it their ſhield a-
gainſt the tempeſts furie. And ſo ſtaying there, till the
violence thereof was paſſed, they heard the ſpeach of a
couple, who not perceiuing them (being hidde within
that rude canapy) helde a ſtraunge and pitifull diſputation which made them ſteppe out; yet in ſuch ſort,
as they might ſee vnſeene. There they perceaued an a-
ged man, and a young, ſcarcely come to the age of a
man, both poorely arayed, extreamely weather-bea-
ten; the olde man blinde, the young man leading
him: and yet through all thoſe miſeries, in both theſe
seemed

seemed to appeare a kind of noblenesse, not sutable to that affliction. But the firstwords they heard, were these of the old man. Well *Leonatus* (said he) since I cannot perswade thee to lead me to that which should end my griefe, & thy trouble, let me now entreat thee to leaue me: feare not, my miserie cannot be greater then it is, & nothing doth become me but miserie; feare not the danger of my blind steps, I cannot fall worse then I am. And doo not I pray thee, doo not obstinately continue to infect thee with my wretchednes. But flie, flie from this region, onely worthy of me. Deare father (answered he) doo not take away from me the onely remnant of my happinesse : while I haue power to doo you seruice, I am not wholly miserable. Ah my sonne (said he, and with that he groned, as if sorrow straue to breake his harte,) how euill fits it me to haue such a sonne, and how much doth thy kindnesse vpbraide my wickednesse ? These dolefull speeches, and some others to like purpose (well shewing they had not bene borne to the fortune they were in,) moued the Princes to goe out vnto them, and aske the younger what they were. Sirs (answered he, with a good grace, and made the more agreable by a certaine noble kinde of piuousnes) I see well you are straungers, that know not our miserie so well here knowne, that no man dare know, but that we must be miserable. In deede our state is such, as though nothing is so needfull vnto vs as pittie, yet nothing is more daungerous vnto vs, then to make our selues so knowne as may stirre pittie. But your presence promiseth, that cruelty shall not ouer-runne hate. And ifit did, in truth our state is soncke below the degree of feare.

This

This old man (whom I leade) was lately rightfull **2**
Prince of this countrie of *Paphlagonia*, by the hard-harted vngratefulnes of a fonne of his, depriued, not onely of his kingdome (whereof no forraine forces were
euer able to fpoyle him) but of his fight, the riches
which Nature graūts to the pooreft creatures. Whereby, & by other his vnnaturall dealings, he hath bin driuen to fuch griefe, as euen now he would haue had me
to haue led him to the toppe of this rocke, thēce to caft
himfelfe headlong to death: and fo would haue made
me (who receiued my life of him) to be the worker of
his deftruction . But noble Gentlemen (faid he) if either of you haue a father, and feele what duetifull affection is engraffed in a fonnes hart, let me intreate you
to conuey this afflicted Prince to fome place of reft &
fecuritie. Amongft your worthie actes it fhall be none
of the leaft, that a King, of fuch might and fame, and fo
vniuftly oppreffed, is in any fort by you relieued.

But before they could make him anfwere, his father **3**
began to fpeake, Ah my fonne (faid he) how euill an
Hiftorian are you, that leaue out the chiefe knotte of all
the difcourfe ? my wickednes, my wickednes. And if
thou doeft it to fpare my eares, (the onely fenfe nowe
left me proper for knowledge) affure thy felfe thou doft
miftake me. And I take witneffe of that Sunne which
you fee (with that he caft vp his blinde eyes, as if he
would hunt for light,) and wifh my felfe in worfe cafe
then I do wifh my felfe, which is as euill as may be, if I
fpeake vntruely; that nothing is fo welcome to my
thoughts, as the publifhing of my fhame. Therefore
know you Gentlemen (to whom from my harte I wifh
that it may not proue ominous foretokē of misfortune

to

to haue mette with ſuch a miſer as I am) that whatſoeuer my ſonne(ô God, that trueth binds me to reproch
him with the name of my ſonne)hath ſaid, is true. But
beſides thoſe truthes, this alſo is true, that hauing had
in lawful mariage, of a mother fitte to beare royall children, this ſonne(ſuch one as partly you ſee, and better
ſhall knowe by my ſhorte declaration) and ſo enioyed
the expectations in the world of him, till he was growē
to iuſtifie their expectations (ſo as I needed enuie no
father for the chiefe comfort of mortalitie, to leaue an
other ones-ſelfe after me) I was caried by a baſtarde
ſonne of mine (if at leaſt I be bounde to beleeue the
words of that baſe woman my concubine, his mother)
firſt to miſlike, then to hate, laſtly to deſtroy, to doo my
beſt to deſtroy, this ſonne (I thinke you thinke) vnde-
ſeruing deſtruction. What waies he vſed to bring me to
it, if I ſhould tell you, I ſhould tedzouſly trouble you
with as much poyſonous hypocriſie, deſperate fraude,
ſmoothe malice, hidden ambition, & ſmiling enuie, as
in any liuing perſon could be harbored. But I liſt it not,
no remembrance, (no, of naughtines)delights me, but
mine own; & me thinks, the accuſing his traines might
in ſome manner excuſe my fault, which certainly I loth
to doo. But the concluſion is, that I gaue order to ſome
ſeruants of mine, whom I thought as apte for ſuch cha-
rities as my ſelfe, to leade him out into a forreſt, & there
to kill him.

But thoſe theeues (better natured to my ſonne
then my ſelfe)ſpared his life, letting him goe, to learne
to liue poorely : which he did, giuing himſelfe to
be a priuate ſouldier, in a countrie here by . But as he
was redy to be greatly aduaunced for ſome noble peeces

ces of seruice which he did, he hearde newes of me:
who (dronke in my affection to that vnlawfull and vnnaturall sonne of mine)suffered my self so to be gouerned by him, that all fauors and punishments passed by
him, all offices, and places of importance, distributed to
his fauourites; so that ere I was aware, I had left my self
nothing but the name of a King: which he shortly wearie of too, with many indignities (if any thing may be
called an indignity, which was laid vpon me)threw me
out of my seat, and put out my eies; and then(proud in
his tyrannie)let me goe, nether imprisoning, nor killing
me: but rather delighting to make me feele my miserie;
miserie indeed, if euer there were any; full of wretchednes, fuller of disgrace, and fullest of guiltines. And as
he came to the crowne by so vniust meanes, as vniustlie
he kept it, by force of stranger souldiers in *Cittadels*, the
nestes of tyranny, & murderers of libertie; disarming all
his own countrimen, that no man durst shew himself a
wel-willer of mine: to say the trueth(I think)few of the
being so (considering my cruell follie to my good
sonne, and foolish kindnes to my vnkinde bastard:)but
if there were any who fell to pitie of so great a fall, and
had yet any sparkes of vnstained duety left in them towardes me, yet durst they not shewe it, scarcely with
giuing me almes at their doores; which yet was the
onelie sustenaunce of my distressed life, no bodie
daring to shewe so much charitie, as to lende me a
hande to guide my darke steppes: Till this sonne
of mine (God knowes, woorthie of a more vertuous, and more fortunate father) forgetting my abhominable wrongs, not recking danger, & neglecting
the present good way he was in doing himselfe good,

came

came hether to doo this kind office you ſee him performe towards me, to my vnſpeakable griefe; not onely becauſe his kindnes is a glaſſe euē to my blind eyes,
of my naughtines, but that aboue all griefes, it greeues
me he ſhould deſperatly aduenture the loſſe of his ſoul-
deſeruing life for mine, that yet owe more to fortune
for my deſerts, as if he would cary mudde in a cheſt of
chriſtall. For well I know, he that now raigneth, how
much ſoeuer (and with good reaſon) he deſpiſeth me,
of all men deſpiſed; yet he will not let ſlippe any aduantage to make away him, whoſe iuſt title (ennobled by
courage and goodnes) may one day ſhake the ſeate of a
neuer ſecure tyrannie. And for this cauſe I craued of
him to leade me to the toppe of this rocke, indeede I
muſt confeſſe, with meaning to free him from ſo Ser-
pentine a companion as I am. But he finding what I
purpoſed, onely therein ſince he was borne, ſhewed
himſelfe diſobedient vnto me. And now Gentlemen,
you haue the true ſtorie, which I pray you publiſh to
the world, that my miſchieuous proceedinges may be
the glorie of his filiall pietie, the onely reward now left
for ſo great a merite. And if it may be, let me obtaine
that of you, which my ſonne denies me: for neuer was
there more pity in ſauing any, then in ending me; both
becauſe therein my agonies ſhall ende, and ſo ſhall you
preſerue this excellent young man, who els wilfully fo-
lowes his owne ruine.

4 The matter in it ſelf lamentable, lamentably expreſſed by the old Prince (which needed not take to himſelfe the geſtures of pitie, ſince his face could not put of
the markes thereof) greatly moued the two Princes to
compaſſion, which could not ſtay in ſuch harts as theirs
with-

without feeking remedie. But by and by the occafion was prefented: for *Plexirtus* (fo was the baftard called) came thether with fortie horfe, onely of purpofe to murder this brother; of whofe comming he had foone aduertifement, and thought no eyes of fufficient credite in fuch a matter, but his owne; and therefore came him felfe to be actor, and fpectator. And as foone as he came, not regarding the weake (as he thought) garde of but two men, commaunded fome of his followers to fet their handes to his, in the killing of *Leonatus*. But the young Prince (though not otherwife armed but with a fworde) how falfely foeuer he was dealt with by others, would not betray him felfe: but brauely drawing it out, made the death of the firft that affaulted him, warne his fellowes to come more wartly after him. But then *Pyrocles* and *Mufidorus* were quickly become parties (fo iuft a defence deferuing as much as old friendfhip) and fo did behaue them among that côpanie (more iniurious, then valiant) that many of them loft their liues for their wicked maifter.

Yet perhaps had the number of them at laft preuailed, if the King of *Pontus* (lately by them made fo) had not come vnlooked for to their fuccour. Who (hauing had a dreame which had fixt his imagination vehemently vpon fome great daunger, prefently to follow thofe two Princes whom he moft deerely loued) was come in all haft, following as well as he could their tracke with a hundreth horfes in that countrie, which he thought (confidering who then raigned) a fit place inough to make the ftage of any Tragedie.

But then the match had ben fo ill made for *Plexirtus*, that his ill-led life, & worfe gotten honour fhould haue

tumbled

tumbled together to deſtructió; had there not come in *Tydeus* & *Telenor*,with fortie or fiftie in their ſuit,to the defence of *Plexirtus*. Theſe two were brothers,of the nobleſt houſe of that country, brought vp frō their infancie with *Plexirtus* : men of ſuch proweſſe, as not to know feare in themſelues, and yet to teach it others that ſhould deale with them : for they had often made their liues triumph ouer moſt terrible daungers; neuer diſmayed,and euer fortunate ; and truely no more ſetled in their valure, then diſpoſed to goodneſſe and iuſtice,if either they had lighted on a better friend, or could haue learned to make friendſhip a child,and not the father of Vertue. But bringing vp (rather then choiſe)hauing firſt knit their minds vnto him, (indeed craftie inough , eyther to hide his faultes , or neuer to ſhew them, but when they might pay home) they willingly held out the courſe, rather to ſatisfie him,then al the world ; and rather to be good friendes , then good men : ſo as though they did not like the euill he did, yet they liked him that did the euill ; and though not councellors of the offence,yet protectors of the offender. Now they hauing heard of this ſodaine going out,with ſo ſmall a company, in a country full of euilwiſhing minds toward him(though they knew not the cauſe)followed him;till they found him in ſuch caſe as they were to venture their liues, or elſe he to looſe his: which they did with ſuch force of minde and bodie, that truly I may iuſtly ſay, *Pyrocles* & *Muſidorus* had neuer till then found any , that could make them ſo well repeate their hardeſt leſſon in the feates of armes. And briefly ſo they did,that if they ouercame not ; yet were they not ouercome ,but caried away that vngratefull
maiſter

maifter of theirs to a place of fecuritie; howfoeuer the
Princes laboured to the côtrary. But this matter being
thus far begun, it became not the conftãcie of the Princes fo to leaue it; but in all haft making forces both in
Pontus and *Phrygia*, they had in fewe dayes, lefte him
but only that one ftrong place where he was. For feare
hauing bene the onely knot that had faftned his people vnto him, that once vntied by a greater force, they
all fcattered from him; like fo many birdes, whofe cage
had bene broken.

In which feafon the blind King (hauing in the chief 7
cittie of his Realme, fet the crowne vpõ his fonne *Leo-*
natus head) with many teares (both of ioy and forrow)
fetting forth to the whole people, his owne fault & his
fonnes vertue, after he had kift him, and forft his fonne
to accept honour of him (as of his newe-become fubiect) eué in a moment died, as it fhould feeme: his hart
broken with vnkindnes & affliction, ftretched fo farre
beyond his limits with this exceffe of côfort, as it was
able no longer to keep fafe his roial fpirits. But the new
King (hauing no leffe louingly performed all duties to
him dead, then aliue) purfued on the fiege of his vnnatural brother, afmuch for the reuenge of his father, as
for the eftablifhing of his owne quiet. In which fiege
truly I cannot but acknowledge the proweffe of thofe
two brothers, then whom the Princes neuer found in
all their trauell two men of greater habilitie to performe, nor of habler skill for conduct.

But *Plexirtus* finding, that if nothing els, famin would 8
at laft bring him to deftructiõ, thought better by hûble-
nes to creepe, where by pride he could not march. For
certainely fo had nature formed him, & the exercife of

craft conformed him to all turnings of sleights, that though no mã had lesse goodnes in his soule then he, no man could better find the places whence argumẽts might grow of goodnesse to another: though no man felt lesse pitie, no man could tel better how to stir pitie: no mã more impudẽt to deny, where proofes were not manifest; no man more ready to confesse with a repenting mãner of aggrauating his owne euil, where denial would but make the fault fowler. Now he tooke this way, that hauing gotten a pasport for one (that pretended he would put *Plexirtus* aliue into his hãds) to speak with the King his brother, he him selfe (though much against the minds of the valiant brothers, who rather wished to die in braue defence) with a rope about his necke, barefooted, came to offer himselfe to the discretion of *Leonatus*. Where what submission he vsed, how cunningly in making greater the faulte he made the faultines the lesse, how artificially he could set out the torments of his owne cõscience, with the burdensome comber he had found of his ambitious desires, how finely seeming to desire nothing but death, as ashamed to liue, he begd life, in the refusing it, I am not cunning inough to be able to expresse : but so fell out of it, that though at first sight *Leonatus* saw him with no other eie, then as the murderer of his father; & anger already began to paint reuenge in many colours, ere long he had not only gotten pitie, but pardon, and if not an excuse of the fault past, yet an opinion of a future amẽdment: while the poore villaines (chiefe ministers of his wickednes, now betraied by the author therof,) were deliuered to many cruell sorts of death ; he so handling it, that it rather seemed, he had rather come into the defence

fence of an vnremediable mifchiefe already cómitted,
then that they had done it at firft by his confent.

In fuch fort the Princes left thefe recóciled brothers
(*Plexirtus* in all his behauiour carying him in far lower
degree of feruice, then the euer-noble nature of *Leona-*
tus would fuffer him) & taking likewife their leaues of
their good friend the King of *Pontus* (who returned to
enioy their benefite, both of his wife and kingdome)
they priuately went thence, hauing onely with them
the two valiant brothers, who would needs accópanie
them, through diuers places ; they foure dooing actes
more daungerous, though leffe famous, becaufe they
were but priuat chiualries : till hearing of the faire and
vertuous Queene *Erona* of *Lycia*, befieged by the puif-
fant King of *Armenia*, they bent themfelues to her fuccour, both becaufe the weaker (& weaker as being a Ladie,) & partly becaufe they heard the King of *Armenia*
had in his company three of the moft famous men liuing, for matters of armes, that were knowne to be in
the worlde. Whereof one was the Prince *Plangus*,
(whofe name was fweetened by your breath, peerleffe
Ladie, when the laft daie it pleafed you to mention
him vnto me) the other two were two great Princes
(though holding of him) *Barzanes* and *Euardes*, men
of Giant-like both hugenes and force: in which two efpecially, the truft the King had of victorie, was repofed.
And of them, thofe two brothers *Tydeus* and *Telenor*
(fufficient iudges in warlike matters) fpake fo high
commendations, that the two yong Princes had euen
a youthfull longing to haue fome triall of their vertue.
And therefore as foone as they were entred into *Lycia*
they ioyned théfelues with them that faithfully ferued

the poore Queene, at that time besieged : and ere long
animated in such sort their almost ouerthrowne harts,
that they went by force to relieue the towne, though
they were depriued of a great part of their strength by
the parting of the two brothers, who were sent for in
all hast to returne to their old friend and maister, *Plexirtus*: who (willingly hood-winking themselues from
seeing his faultes, and binding themselues to beleeue
what he said)often abused the vertue of courage to defend his fowle vice of iniustice. But now they were
sent for to aduaunce a conquest he was about; while
Pyrocles and *Musidorus* pursued the deliuerie of the
Queene *Erona*.

CHAP. II.

1 Dorus *his suite to* Pamela *interrupted by* Mopsas *waking.*
2 *The sisters going with* Zelmane *to wash themselues.*
3 *The pleasantnes of the riuer.* 4 *The pleasure* Zelmane
had in seeing them, vttered 5 *in speach,* 6 *and song.* 7 *She
led by a spaniel, to know, and hurte her noble riuall.* 8 *The
parting of that fraye.*

I Haue heard (said *Pamela*) that parte
of the story of *Plangus* whē he passed through this country : therfore
you may (if you list)passe ouer that
warre of *Eronaes* quarrell, lest if
you speake too much of warre matters, you should wake *Mopsa*, which
might happily breed a great broile.
1 He looked, and saw that *Mopsa* indeed sat swallowing
of

offleepe with opē mouth, making fuch a noife withal,
as no bodie could lay the ftealing of a nappe to her
charge. Whereupon, willing to vfe that occafion , he
kneeled downe,and with humble-hartedneffe,& harty
earneftnes printed in his graces, Alas (faid he) diuine
Lady, who haue wrought fuch miracles in me, as to
make a Prince (none of the bafeft) to thinke all princi-
palities bafe, in refpect of the fheephooke, which may
hold him vp in your fight ; vouchfafe now at laft to
heare in direct words my humble fute,while this dragō
fleepes, that keepes the golden fruite. If in my defire I
wifh,or in my hopes afpire,or in my imagination faine
to my felfe any thing which may be the leaft fpot to that
heauenly vertue,which fhines in all your doings;I pray
the eternal powers,that the words I fpeak may be deadly poyfons,while they are in my mouth,and that all my
hopes, all my defires, all my imaginations, may onely
worke their owne confufion. But if loue , loue of you,
loue of your vertues, feeke onely that fauour of you,
which becommeth that gratefulnes, which cānot mifbecome your excellencie, O doo not: He would haue
faid further,but *Pamela* calling aloud *Mopfa*, fhe fodainly ftart vp,ftaggering, and rubbing her eies,ran firft out
of the doore, and then backe to them, before fhe knew
how fhe went out, or why fhe came in againe : till at
length,being fully come to her little felfe,fhe afked *Pamela*, why fhe had called her.For nothing(faid *Pamela*)
but that you might heare fome tales of your feruants
telling:and therefore now(faid fhe) *Dorus* go on.

But as he (who found no fo good facrifice, as obe- 2
dience) was returning to the ftory of himfelfe,*Philoclea*
came in, & by and by after her,*Mifo*; fo as for that time
they

they were faine to let *Dorus* depart. But *Pamela*) delighted eué to preserue in her memory, the words of so wel a beloued speaker) repeated the whole substance to her sister, till their sober dinner being come an l gone, to recreate themselues something, (euen tyred with the noysomnes of *Misos* conuersation) they determyned to goe (while the heate of the day lasted) to bath themselues (such being the maner of the *Arcadian* nymphes often to doo) in the riuer of *Ladon*, and take with them a Lute, meaning to delight them vnder some shadow. But they could not stir, but that *Miso* with her daughter *Mopsa* was after them : and as it lay in their way to passe by the other lodge, *Zelmane* out of her window espied them, and so stale downe after them : which she might the better doo because that *Gynecia* was sicke, and *Basilius* (that day being his birth-day) according to his maner, was busie about his deuotions ; and therefore she went after, hoping to finde some time to speake with *Philoclea* : but not a word could she beginne, but that *Miso* would be one of the audience ; so that she was driuen to recommend thinking, speaking, and all, to her eyes, who diligently perfourmed her trust, till they came to the riuers side; which of all the riuers of *Greece* 3 had the price for excellent purenesse and sweetenesse, in so much as the verie bathing in it, was accoúted exceeding healthfull. It ranne vpon so fine and delicate a ground, as one could not easely iudge, whether the Riuer did more wash the grauell, or the grauel did purifie the Riuer ; the Riuer not running forth right, but almost continually winding, as if the lower streames would returne to their spring, or that the Riuer had a delight to play with itselfe. The banckes of either side

seeming

feeming armes of the louing earth, that faine would
embrace it; and the Riuer a wanton nymph which ftill
would ftirre from it: either fide of the bancke being
fringed with moft beautifull trees, which refifted the
funnes dartes from ouer-much pearcing the naturall
coldnes of the Riuer. There was the

But among
the reft a goodly *Cypres*, who bowing her faire head
ouer the water, it feemed fhe looked into it, and dreffed
her greene lockes, by that running Riuer. There the
Princeffes determining to bath themfelues, though it
was fo priuiledged a place, vpon paine of death, as no
bodie durft prefume to come thither, yet for the more
furety, they looked round about; and could fee nothing
but a water fpaniell, who came downe the riuer, fhewing that he hunted for a duck, & with a fnuffling grace,
difdaining that his fmelling force coulde not as well
preuaile thorow the water, as thorow the aire, & therefore wayting with his eye, to fee whether he could
efpie the duckes getting vp againe: but then a little below them failing of his purpofe, he got out of the riuer,
& fhaking off the water (as great men do their friends,
now he had no further caufe to vfe it) in-weeded himfelfe fo, as the Ladies loft the further marking his fport-
fulneffe: and inuiting *Zelmane* alfo to wafh her felfe
with them, and fhe excufing her felfe with hauing taken a late cold, they began by peece-meale to take a-
way the eclipfing of their apparell.

Zelmane would haue put to her helping hand, but fhe
was taken with fuch a quiuering, that fhe thought it
more wifedome to leane her felfe to a tree and looke
on, while *Mifo* and *Mopfa* (like a couple of forefwat
melters)

melters)were getting the pure siluer of their bodies out
of the vre of their garments. But as the rayments went
of to receaue kisses of the ground, *Zelmane* enuied the
happinesse of all, but of the smocke was euen iealous,
and when that was taken away too, and that *Philoclea*
remained (for her *Zelmane* onely marked) like a *Dya-*
mond taken from out the rocke, or rather like the Sun
getting from vnder a cloud, and shewing his naked
beames to the full vew, then was the beautie too much
for a patient sight, the delight too strong for a stayed
conceipt : so that *Zelmane* could not choose but runne,
to touch, embrace,and kisse her; But conscience made
her come to her selfe, & leaue *Philoclea*, who blushing,
and withall smiling, making shamefastnesse pleasant,
and pleasure shamefast, tenderly moued her feete, vnwonted to feele the naked ground, till the touch of the
cold water made a prettie kinde of shrugging come o-
uer her bodie, like the twinckling of the fairest among
the fixed stars. But the Riuer it selfe gaue way vnto her,
so that she was streight brest high; which was the deepest that there-about she could be : and when cold *La-*
don had once fully imbraced them, himselfe was no
more so cold to those Ladies, but as if his cold complexion had bene heated with loue, so seemed he to
play about euery part he could touch.

5   Ah sweete, now sweetest *Ladon* (said *Zelmane*) why
dost thou not stay thy course to haue more full tast of
thy happines? But the reason is manifest, the vpper
streames make such haste to haue their part of embracing,that the nether (though lothly) must needs giue
place vnto them. O happie *Ladon*, within whom she
is,vpon whom her beautie fals, thorow whom her eye
perceth.

perceth. O happie *Ladon*, which art now an vnperfect
mirror of al perfection, canſt thou euer forget the bleffednes of this impreſſion? if thou do, then let thy bed
be turned from fine grauel, to weeds & mudde; if thou
doo, let ſome vniuſt niggards make weres to ſpoile thy
beauty; if thou do, let ſome greater riuer fal into thee, to
take away the name of *Ladon.* Oh *Ladon*, happie *Ladon*,
rather ſlide then run by her, left thou ſhouldeſt make
her legs flippe from her; and then, O happy *Ladon*, who
would then cal thee, but the moſt curſed *Ladon?* But as
the Ladies plaid them in the water, ſomtimes ſtriking it
with their hands, the water (making lines in his face)
ſeemed to ſmile at ſuch beating, and with twentie bub-
bles, not to be content to haue the picture of their face
in large vpon him, but he would in ech of thoſe bub-
bles ſet forth the miniature of them.

But *Zelmane*, whoſe fight was gaine-ſaid by nothing **6**
but the tranſparent vaile of *Ladon*, (like a chamber
where a great fire is kept, though the fire be at one ſtay,
yet with the continuance continually hath his heate
encreaſed) had the coales of her affection ſo kindled
with wonder, and blowne with delight, that nowe all
her parts grudged, that her eyes ſhould doo more homage, then they, to the Princeſſe of them. In ſomuch
that taking vp the Lute, her wit began to be with a diuine furie inſpired; her voice would in ſo beloued an
occaſion ſecond her wit; her hands accorded the Lutes
muſicke to the voice; her panting hart daunced to the
muſicke; while I thinke her feete did beate the time;
while her bodie was the roome where it ſhould be
celebrated; her ſoule the Queene which ſhoulde be
delighted. And ſo togither went the vtterance and
the

the inuention, that one might iudge, it was *Philocleæ*
beautie which did ſpeedily write it in her eyes; or the
ſenſe thereof, which did word by word endite it in her
minde, whereto ſhe (but as an organ) did onely lend
vtterance. The ſong was to this purpoſe.

WHat toong can her perfections tell
   In whoſe each part all pens may dwell?
Her haire fine threeds of fineſt gould
In curled knots mans thought to hold:
But that her fore-head ſayes in me
A whiter beautie you may ſee.
Whiter indeed; more white then ſnow,
Which on cold winters face doth grow.
That doth preſent thoſe euen browes,
Whoſe equall line their angles bowes,
Like to the Moone when after chaunge
Her horned head abroad doth raunge:
And arches be to heauenly lids,
Whoſe winke ech bold attempt forbids.
For the blacke ſtarres thoſe Spheares containe
The matchleſse paire, euen praiſe doth ſtaine.
No lampe, whoſe light by Art is got,
No Sunne, which ſhines, and ſeeth not,
Can liken them without all peere,
Saue one as much as other cleere:
Which onely thus vnhappie be,
Becauſe themſelues they cannot ſee.
   Her cheekes with kindly claret ſpred.
Aurora like new out of bed,
Or like the freſh Queene-apples ſide,
Bluſhing at ſight of Phœbus *pride.*

Her

Her nose, her chinne pure iuorie weares :
No purer then the pretie eares.
So that therein appeares some blood,
Like wine and milke that mingled stood
In whose Incirclets if ye gaze,
Your eyes may tread a Louers maze.
But with such turnes the voice to stray,
No talke vntaught can finde the way.
The tippe no iewell needes to weare :
The tippe is iewell of the eare.

   But who those ruddie lippes can misse ?
Which blessed still themselues doo kisse.
Rubies, Cherries, and Roses new,
In worth, in taste, in perfitte hewe :
Which neuer part but that they showe
Of pretious pearle the double rowe,
The second sweetly-fenced warde,
Her heau'nly-dewed tongue to garde.
Whence neuer word in vaine did flowe.

   Faire vnder these doth stately growe,
The handle of this pretious worke,
The neck, in which strange graces lurke.
Such be I thinke the sumptuous towers
Which skill dooth make in Princes bowers.
So good a say inuites the eye,
A little downward to espie,
The liuelie clusters of her brests,
Of Venus *babe the wanton nests :*
Like pomels round of Marble cleere :
Where azurde veines well mixt appeere.
With dearest tops of porphyrie.

   Betwixt these two a way doth lie,

                             A way

A way more worthie beauties fame,
Then that which beares the Milkie *name.*
This leades into the ioyous field,
Which onely ſtill doth Lillies yeeld:
But Lillies ſuch whoſe natiue ſmell
The Indian odours doth excell.
Waſte it is calde, for it doth waſte
Mens liues, vntill it be imbraſte.

There may one ſee, and yet not ſee
Her ribbes in white all armed be.
More white then Neptunes *ſomie face,*
When ſtrugling rocks he would imbrace.

In thoſe delights the wandring thought
Might of each ſide aſtray be brought,
But that her nauel doth vnite,
In curious circle, buſie ſight :
A daintie ſeale of virgin-waxe,
Where nothing but impreſsion lackes.

Her bellie then gladde ſight doth fill,
Iuſtly entitled Cupids *hill.*
A hill moſt fitte for ſuch a maſter,
A ſpotleſſe mine of Alablaſter.
Like Alablaſter faire and ſleeke,
But ſoft and ſupple ſatten like.
In that ſweete ſeate the Boy doth ſport:
Loath, I muſt leaue his chiefe reſort.

„ *For ſuch a vſe the world hath gotten,*
„ *The beſt things ſtill muſt be forgotten.*

Yet neuer ſhall my ſong omitte
Thighes, for Ouids *ſong more fitte;*
Which flanked with two ſugred flankes,
Liſt vp their ſtately ſwelling bankes;

That

That Albion *cliues in whitenes paſſe:*
With hanches ſmooth as looking glaſſe.
   But bow all knees, now of her knees
My tongue doth tell what fancie ſees.
The knottes of ioy, the gemmes of loue,
Whoſe motion makes all graces moue.
Whoſe bought incau'd doth yeeld ſuch ſight,
Like cunning Painter ſhadowing white.
The gartring place with child-like ſigne,
Shewes eaſie print in mettall fine.
But then againe the fleſh doth riſe
In her braué calues, like chriſtall skies.
Whoſe Atlas *is a ſmalleſt ſmall,*
More white then whiteſt bone of all.
   Thereout ſteales out that round cleane foote
This noble Cedars *pretious roote :*
In ſhewe and ſent pale violets,
Whoſe ſteppe on earth all beautie ſets.
   But back vnto her back, my Muſe,
Where Ledas *ſwanne his feathers mewes,*
Along whoſe ridge ſuch bones are met,
Like comfits round in marchpane ſet.
   Her ſhoulders be like two white Doues,
Pearching within ſquare royall rooues,
Which leaded are with ſiluer skinne,
Paſsing the hate-ſport Ermelin.
And thence thoſe armes deriued are;
The Phœnix *wings are not ſo rare*
For faultleſſe length, and ſtaincleſſe hewe,
   Ah woe is me, my woes renewe;
Now courſe doth leade me to her hand,
Of my firſt loue the fatall band.

Where

Where whitenes dooth for euer ſitte :
Nature her ſelfe enameld it.
For there with ſtrange compact dooth lie
Warme ſnow,moyſt pearle,ſofte iuorie.
There fall thoſe Saphir-coloured brookes,
Which conduit-like with curious crookes,
Sweete Ilands make in that ſweete land.
As for the fingers of the hand,
The bloudy ſhaftes of Cupids *warre,*
With amatiſts they headed are.

　Thus hath each part his beauties part ,
But how the Graces doo impart
To all her limmes a ſpetiall grace,
Becomming euery time and place.
Which doth euen beautie beautifie,
And moſt bewitch the wretched eye .
How all this is but a faire Inne
Of fairer gueſtes,which dwell within.
Of whoſe high praiſe,and praiſefull bliſſe,
Goodnes the penne,heauen paper is.
The inke immortall fame dooth lende:
As I began,ſo muſt I ende.

　No tongue can her perfections tell,
In whoſe each part all tongues may dwel.

But as *Zelmane* was cōming to the latter end of her
ſoug ſhe might ſee the ſame water-ſpaniell which before had hūted,come and fetch away one of *Philoclea*
gloues ; whoſe fine proportion , ſhewed well what a
daintie gueſt was wont there to be lodged. It was a delight to *Zelmane* , to ſee that the dogge was therewith
delighted, and ſo let him goe a little way withall , who
quickly

quickly caried it out of fight among certaine trees and bufhes,which were very clofe together.But by & by he came againe,& amongft the raiments *(Mifo* and *Mopfa* being preparing fheets againft their comming out)the dog lighted vpon a little booke of foure or fiue leaues of paper,& was bearing that away to. But then *Zelmane* (not knowing what importace it might be of)ran after the dog,who going ftreight to thofe bufhes, fhe might fee the dog deliuer it to a Gentleman who fecretly lay there.But fhe haftily cóming in, the Gétleman rofe vp, & with a courteous(though fad) countenance prefented himfelfe vnto her.*Zelmanes* eies ftreight willed her mind to marke him: for fhe thought,in her life fhe had neuer feene a má of a more goodly prefence, in whom ftrong making tooke not away delicacie , nor beautie ferceneffe:being indeed fuch a right manlike man , as Nature often erring,yet fhewes fhe would faine make. But when fhe had a while (not without admiration) vewed him, fhe defired him to deliuer backe the gloue & paper,becaufe they were the Ladie *Philocleas*;telling him withall,that fhe would not willingly let thé know of his clofe lying in that prohibited place , while they were bathing théfelues ; becaufe fhe knew they would be mortally offended withall . Faire Ladie (anfwered he)the worft of the complaint is already paffed,fince I feele of my fault in my felf the punifhmét.But for thefe things I affure you,it was my dogs wanton boldneffe, not my prefumption. With that he gaue her backe the paper: But for the gloue (faid he) fince it is my Ladie *Philocleas*,giue me leaue to keepe it,fince my hart cánot perfuade it felfe to part from it . And I pray you tell the Lady (I ady indeed of all my defires) that owes it, that

X I

I will direct my life to honour this gloue with seruing her. O villain (cried out *Zelmane*, madded with finding an vnlooked-for Riuall, and that he would make her a messenger) dispatch (said she) and deliuer it, or by the life of her that owes it, I wil make thy soul (though too base a price) pay for it. And with that drewe out her sworde, which (*Amazon*-like) she euer ware about her. The Gentlemā retired himself into an open place frō a-mong the bushes; & thē drawing out his too, he offred to deliuer it vnto her, saying withall, God forbid I should vse my sworde against you, since (if I be not de-ceiued) you are the same famous *Amazon*, that both de-fended my Ladies iust title of beautie against the vali-ant *Phalantus*, & saued her life in killing the Lion: ther-fore I am rather to kisse your hands, with acknowled-ging my selfe boūd to obey you. But this courtesie was worse then a bastonado to *Zelmane*: so that againe with ragefull eyes she bad him defend himselfe, for no lesse then his life should answere it. A hard case (said he) to teach my sworde that lesson, which hath euer vsed to turne it self to a shield in a Ladies presence. But *Zelmane* harkening to no more wordes, began with such wittie furie to pursue him with blowes & thrusts, that Nature & Vertue commanded the Gentleman to looke to his safetie. Yet stil courtesie, that seemed incorporate in his hart, would not be perswaded by daunger to offer any offence, but only to stand vpon the best defensiue gard he could; somtimes going backe, being content in that respect to take on the figure of cowardise; sometime with strong and well-met wards; sometime cunning a-uoidings of his body; and sometimes faining some blowes, which himself puld backe before they needed

to be withſtood. And ſo with play did he a good while
fight againſt the fight of *Zelmane*, who (more ſpited
with that curteſie, that one that did nothing ſhould be
able to reſiſt her) burned away with choller any motions, which might grow out of her owne ſweet diſpoſitiō, determining to kill him if he fought no better; & ſo
redoubling her blowes, draue the ſtranger to no other
ſhift; then to warde, and go backe; at that time ſeeming
the image of innocencie againſt violence. But at length
he found, that both in publike and priuate reſpectes,
who ſtandes onely vpon defence, ſtands vpon no defence : For *Zelmane* ſeeming to ſtrike at his head, and
he going to warde it, withall ſtept backe as he was accuſtomed, ſhe ſtopt her blow in the aire, and ſuddenly
turning the point, ranne full at his breaſt; ſo as he was
driuen with the pommell of his ſworde (hauing no o-
ther weapon of defence) to beate it downe : but the
thruſt was ſo ſtrong, that he could not ſo wholy beate
it awaie, but that it met with his thigh, thorow which
it ranne. But *Zelmane* retiring her ſworde, and ſeeing
his bloud, victorious anger was conquered by the be-
fore-conquered pittie; and hartily ſorie, and euen aſhamed with her ſelfe ſhe was, conſidering how little he
had done, who well ſhe found could haue done more.
In ſo much that ſhe ſaid, truly I am ſorie for your hurt,
but your ſelfe gaue the cauſe, both in refuſing to deliuer the gloue, and yet not fighting as I knowe you
could haue done. But (ſaide ſhee) becauſe I perceaue you diſdayne to fight with a woman, it may
be before a yeare come about, you ſhall meete with
a neere kinſman of mine, *Pyrocles* Prince of *Macedon*,
and I giue you my worde, he for me ſhall maintaine

this

this quarell againſt you. I would (anſwered *Amphialus*)
I had many more ſuch hurtes to meete and know that
worthy Prince, whoſe vertue I loue & admire, though
my good deſtiny hath not bene to ſee his perſon.

But as they were ſo ſpeaking, the yong Ladies came,
to whõ *Mopſa* (curious in any thing, but her own good
behauiour) hauing followed & ſeene *Zelmane* fighting,
had cried, what ſhe had ſeene, while they were drying
themſelues, & the water (with ſome drops) ſeemed to
weepe, that it ſhould parte from ſuch bodies. But they
carefull of *Zelmane* (aſſuring themſelues that any *Arcadian* would beare reuerence to them) *Pamela* with a
noble mind, and *Philoclea* with a louing (haſtily hiding
the beauties, whereof Nature was prowde, and they
aſhamed) they made quicke worke to come to ſaue
Zelmane. But already they found them in talke, & *Zelmane* careful of his wound. But whẽ they ſaw him they
knew it was their couſin germain, the famous *Amphialus*; whom yet with a ſweete-graced bitternes they bla-
med for breaking their fathers commaundement, eſpecially while themſelues were in ſuch ſort retired. But
he craued pardon, proteſting vnto them that he had
onely bene to ſeeke ſolitary places, by an extreme melancholy that had a good while poſſeſt him, and guided to that place by his ſpaniell, where while the dog
hunted in the riuer, he had withdrawne himſelfe to pacifie with ſleepe his ouer-watched eyes : till a dreame
waked him, and made him ſee that whereof he had
dreamed, & withall not obſcurely ſignified that he felt
the ſmart of his owne doings. But *Philoclea* (that was
euen iealous of her ſelf for *Zelmane*) would needs haue
her gloue, and not without ſo mighty a loure as that
face

face could yeeld. As for *Zelmane* when she knew, it was
Amphialus, Lord *Amphialus* (said she) I haue lõg desired
to know you, heretofore I muſt confeſſe with more
good will, but ſtill with honoring your vertue, though
I loue not your perſon : & at this time I pray you let vs
take care of your wound, vpon cõdition you ſhal hereafter promiſe, that a more knightly combat ſhalbe performed betweene vs. *Amphialus* anſwered in honorable ſort, but with ſuch excuſing himſelfe, that more and
more accuſed his loue to *Philoclea*, & prouoked more
hate in *Zelmane*. But *Mopſa* had already called certaine
ſhepheards not far of (who knew & wel obſerued their
limits) to come and helpe to carrie away *Amphialus*,
whoſe wound ſuffered him not without daunger to
ſtraine it: and ſo he leauing himſelfe with them, departed from them, faſter bleeding in his hart, then at his
wound: which bound vp by the ſheetes, wherwith *Philoclea* had bene wrapped, made him thanke the wound,
and bleſſe the ſword for that fauour.

CHAP. 12.

How Baſilius *found* Plangus: *his lamẽtation.* *Philoclea
entreated by* Zelmane *to relate the ſtorie of* Erona.

HE being gone, the Ladies (with me-
ry anger talking, in what naked ſim
plicitie their couſin had ſeene thẽ)
returned to the lodge-warde: yet
thinking it too early (as long as
they had any day) to breake of ſo
pleaſing a company, with going to
performe a cuberſome obediẽce,

Zelmane

Zelmane inuited them to the little arbour, only reserued
for her, which they willingly did: and there sitting, *Pa-*
mela hauing a while made the lute in his láguage, shew
how glad it was to be touched by her fingers, *Zelmane*
deliuered vp the paper, which *Amphialus* had at first
yeelded vnto her: and seeing written vpon the back-
side of it, the complaint of *Plangus*, remembring what
Dorus had told her, and desiring to know how much
Philoclea knew of her estate, she tooke occasion in the
presenting of it, to aske whether it were any secret, or
no. No truely (answered *Philoclea*) it is but euen an
exercise of my fathers writing, vpon this occasion: He
was one day (somwhile before your comming hether)
walking abroade, hauing vs two with him, almost a
mile hence; and crossing a hie way, which comes from
the cittie of *Megalopolis*, he saw this Gentleman, whose
name is there written, one of the proprest and best-gra-
ced men that euer I sawe, being of middle age, and of
a meane stature. He lay as then vnder a tree, while his
seruaunts were getting fresh post-horses for him. It
might seeme he was tired with the extreme trauaile he
had taken, and yet not so tyred, that he forced to take
any rest; so hasty he was vpon his iourney: and withall so sorrowfull, that the very face thereof was painted in his face; which with pitifull motions, euen
groanes, teares, and passionate talking to him selfe,
moued my Father to fall in talke with him: who at
first not knowing him, answered him in such a desperate phrase of griefe, that my Father afterward tooke a
delight to set it downe in such forme as you see: which
if you read, what you doubt of, my sister and I are
hable to declare vnto you. *Zelmane* willingly opened
the

the leaues, and read it, being written Dialogue-wise in
this manner.

Plangus. Baſilius.

A *Las how long this pilgrimage doth laſt?*
 What greater ills haue now the heauens in ſtore,
To'couple comming harmes with ſorrowes paſt?
Long ſince my voice is hoarce, and throte is ſore,
 With cries to ſkies, and curſes to the ground,
 But more I plaine, I feele my woes the more.
Ah where was firſt that cruell cunning found,
 To frame of Earth a veſſell of the minde,
 Where it ſhould be to ſelfe-deſtruction bound?
What needed ſo high ſprites ſuch manſions blind?
 Or wrapt in fleſh what do they here obtaine,
 But glorious name of wretched humaine-kind?
Balles to the ſtarres, and thralles to Fortunes raigne;
 Turnd from themſelues, infected with their cage,
 Where death is feard, and life is held with paine.
Like players pla'ſt to fill a filthy ſtage,
 Where chaunge of thoughts one foole to other ſhewes,
 And all but ieſts, ſaue onely ſorrowes rage.
The child feeles that; the man that feeling knowes,
 With cries firſt borne, the preſage of his life,
 Where wit but ſcrues, to haue true taſt of woes.
A Shop of ſhame, a Booke where blots be riſe
 This bodie is : this boat ſo compoſed,
 As in it ſelfe to nouriſh mortall ſtrife.
So diuers be the Elements diſpoſed
 In this weake worke, that it can neuer be
 Made vniforme to any ſtate repoſed.
Griefe onely makes his wretched ſtate to ſee

X 4

(Euen like a toppe which nought but whipping moues)
This man, this talking beaſt, this walking tree.
Griefe is the ſtone which fineſt iudgement proues :
For who grieues not hath but a blockiſh braine,
Since cauſe of griefe no cauſe from life remoues.

Baſilius *How long wilt thou with monefull muſicke ſtaine*
The cheerefull notes theſe pleaſant places yeeld,
Where all good haps a perfeēt ſtate maintaine ?

Plangus *Curſt be good haps, and curſt be they that build*
Their hopes on haps, and do not make deſpaire
For all theſe certaine blowes the ſureſt ſhield.
Shall I that ſaw Eronaes *ſhining haire*
Torne with her hands, and thoſe ſame hands of ſnow
With loſſe of pureſt blood themſelues to teare?
Shall I that ſaw thoſe breſts, where beauties flow,
Swelling with ſighes, made pale with mindes diſeaſe,
And ſaw thoſe eyes (thoſe Sonnes) ſuch ſhoures to ſhew;
Shall I, whoſe eares her mournefull words did ſeaze,
Her words in ſyrup laid of ſweeteſt breath,
Relent thoſe thoughts, which then did ſo diſpleaſe?
No, no : Deſpaire my dayly leſſon ſaith,
And ſaith, although I ſeeke my life to flie,
Plangus *muſt liue to ſee* Eronaes *death.*
Plangus *muſt liue ſome helpe for her to trie,*
Though in deſpaire, ſo Loue enforceth me ;
Plangus *doth liue, and muſt* Erona *dye?*
Erona *dye? O heauen (if heauen there be)*
Hath all thy whirling courſe ſo ſmall effeēt ?
Serue all thy ſtarrie eyes this ſhame to ſee?
Let doltes in haſte ſome altars faire ereēt

To those high powers, which idly sit aboue,
 And vertue do in greatest need neglect.

O man, take heed, how thou the Gods do moue   **Basilius**
 To irefull wrath, which thou canst not resist.
 Blasphemous words the speaker vaine do proue.
Alas while we are wrapt in foggie mist
 Of our selfe-loue (so passions do deceaue)
 We thinke they hurt, when most they do assist.
To harme vs wormes should that high Iustice leaue
 His nature? nay, himselfe? for so it is.
 What glorie from our losse can he receaue?
But still our daʒeled eyes their way do misse,
 While that we do at his sweete scourge repine,
 The kindly way to beate vs to our blisse.
If she must dye, then hath she past the line
 Of lothsome dayes, whose losse how canst thou mone,
 That doost so well their miseries define?
But such we are with inward tempest blowne
 Of mindes quite contrarie in waues of will:
 We mone that lost, which had we did bemone.

And shall shee dye? shall cruell fier spill   **Plan**
 Those beames that set so many harts on fire?
 Hath she not force euen death with loue to kill?
Nay euen cold Death enflamde with hot desire
 Her to enioy, where ioy it selfe is thrall,
 Will spoile the earth of his most rich attire.
Thus Death becomes a riuall to vs all,
 And hopes with foule embracements her to get,
 In whose decay Vertues faire shrine must fall.
O Vertue weake, shall death his triumph set

Vpon thy ſpoiles, which neuer ſhould lye waſte?
Let Death firſt dye; be thou his worthy let.
By what eclipſe ſhall that Sonne be defaſte?
   What myne hath erſt throwne downe ſo faire a tower?
   What ſacriledge hath ſuch a ſaint diſgra'ſt ?
The world the garden is, ſhe is the flower
   That ſweetens all the place; ſhe is the gueſt
   Of rareſt price, both heau'n and earth her bower.
And ſhall (ô me) all this in aſhes reſt ?
   Alas, if you a Phœnix *new will haue*
   Burnt by the Sunne, ſhe firſt muſt build her neſt.
But well you know, the gentle Sunne would ſaue
   Such beames ſo like his owne, which might haue might
   In him, the thoughts of Phaëtons *damme to graue.*
Therefore, alas, you vſe vile Vulcans *ſpight,*
   Which nothing ſpares, to melt that Virgin-waxe
   Which while it is, it is all Aſias *light.*
O Mars, *for what doth ſerue thy armed axe?*
   To let that wit-old beaſt conſume in flame
   Thy Venus *child, whoſe beautie* Venus *lackes?*
O Venus *(if her praiſe no enuy frames,*
   In thy high minde) get her thy husbands grace.
Sweete ſpeaking oft a curriſh hart reclaimes.
O eyes of mine, where once ſhe ſaw her face,
   Her face which was more liuely in my hart ;
   O braine, where thought of her hath onely place;
O hand, which toucht her hand when ſhe did part;
   O lippes, that kiſt her hand with my teares ſprent;
   O toonge, then dumbe, not daring tell my ſmart;
O ſoule, whoſe loue in her is onely ſpent,
   What ere you ſee, thinke, touch, kiſſe, ſpeake, or loue,
   Let all for her, and vnto her be bent.

Thy wailing words do much my spirits moue,
  They vttred are in such a feeling fashion,
  That sorrowes worke against my will I proue.
Me-thinkes I am partaker of thy passion,
  And in thy case do glasse mine owne debilitie:
  Selfe-guiltie folke most prone to feele compassion.
Yet Reason saith, Reason should haue abilitie,
  To hold these worldly things in such proportion,
  As let them come or go with euen facilitie.
But our Desires tyrannicall extortion
  Doth force vs there to set our chiefe delightfulnes,
  Where but a baiting place is all our portion.
But still, although we faile of perfect rightfulnes,
  Seeke we to tame the childish superfluities :
  Let vs not winke though void of purest sightfulnes.
For what can breed more peeuish incongruities,
  Then man to yeeld to female lamentations?
  Let vs some grammar learne of more congruities.

Basilius.

If through mine eares pearce any consolation
  By wise discourse, sweete tunes, or Poets fiction ;
  If ought I cease these hideous exclamations,
While that my soule, she, she liues in affliction;
  Then let my life long time on earth maintained be,
  To wretched me, the last worst malediction.
Can I, that know her sacred parts restrained be,
  For any ioy, know fortunes vile displacing her,
  In morall rules let raging woes contained be ?
Can I forget, when they in prison placing her,
  With swelling hart in spite and due disdainfulnes
  She lay for dead, till I helpt with vnlasing her ?
Can I forget, from how much mourning plainfulnes

Plangus

With

With *Diamond in window-glasse she graued,*
Erona dye, and end thy ougly painefulnes?
Can I *forget in how straunge phrase she craued*
That quickly they would her burne, drowne, or smother,
As if by death she onely might be saued?
Then let me eke forget one hand from other:
Let me forget that Plangus *I am called:*
Let me forget I am sonne to my mother,
But if *my memory must thus be thralled*
To that strange stroke which conquer'd all my senses,
Can thoughts still thinking so rest vnappalled?

Basilius.   *Who still doth seeke against himselfe offences,*
What pardon can auaile? or who employes him
To hurt himselfe, what shields can be defenses?
Woe to poore man : ech outward thing annoyes him
In diuers kinds; yet as he were not filled,
He heapes in inward griefe, which most destroyes him .
Thus is our thought with paine for thistles tilled :
Thus be our noblest parts dryed vp with sorrow :
Thus is our mind with too much minding spilled.
One day layes vp stuffe of griefe for the morrow :
And whose good haps do leaue him vnprouided,
Condoling cause of friendship he will borrow.
Betwixt the good and shade of good diuided,
We pittie deeme that which but weakenes is :
So are we from our high creation slided.
But Plangus *lest I may your sicknesse misse*
Or rubbing hurt the sore, I here doo end.
The asse did hurt when he did thinke to kisse.

When

When *Zelmane* had read it ouer, marueyling verie much of the fpeeche of *Eronas* death, and therefore defirous to know further of it, but more defirous to heare *Philoclea* fpeake, Moft excellent Ladie (faid fhe) one may be little the wifer for reading the Dialogue, fince it nether fets foorth what this *Plangus* is, nor what *Erona* is, nor what the caufe fhould be which threatens her with death, and him with forow: therefore I woulde humbly craue to vnderftand the particular difcourfe thereof: becaufe (I muft confeffe) fome thing in my trauaile I haue heard of this ftrange matter, which I would be glad to find by fo fweet an authoritie confirmed. The trueth is (anfwered *Philoclea*) that after he knew my father to be Prince of this countrie·, while he hoped to preuaile fomething with him in a great requeft he made vnto him, he was content to open fully vnto him the eftate both of himfelfe, and of that Ladie; which with my fifters help (faid fhe) who remembers it better then I, I will declare vnto you: and firft of *Erona*, (being the chiefe Subiect of this difcourfe) this ftorie (with more teares and exclamations then I lifte to fpende about it) he recounted.

CHAP. 13.

Erona [1] *irreligious gainft Loue,* [2] *muft loue the bafe* Antiphilus, [3] *is loued, purfued, and beleaguered by the great* Tiridates. [4] *The two Greeke Princes ayde her.* [5] *They combatte with two Kings;* Antiphilus *with* Plangus; *they conquerors, he prifoner.* [6] Eronas *hard-choice to redeeme him.* [7] Tiridates *flaine,* Antiphilus *deliuered,* Artaxia *chafed by the two Princes,* [8] *and her hate to them.*

Of

1 F late there raigned a King in *Lycia*, who had for the bleſſing of his mariage, this onely daughter of his, *Erona* ; a Princeſſe worthie for her beautie, as much praiſe, as beautie may be praiſe-worthy. This Princeſſe *Erona*, being 19. yeres of age, ſeeing the countrie of *Lycia* ſo much deuoted to *Cupid*, as that in euery place his naked pictures & images were ſuperſtitiouſly adored (ether moued theruto, by the eſteeming that could be no Godhead, which could breed wickednes, or the ſhamefaſt conſideration of ſuch nakednes) procured ſo much of her father, as vtterly to pull downe, and deface all thoſe ſtatues and pictures. Which how terriblie he puniſhed (for to that the *Lycians* impute it) quickly after appeared.

2 For ſhe had not liued a yeare longer, when ſhe was ſtriken with moſt obſtinate Loue, to a yong man but of mean parentage, in her fathers court, named *Antiphilus*: ſo meane, as that he was but the ſonne of her Nurſe, & by that meanes (without other deſert) became knowen of her. Now ſo euill could ſhe conceale her fire, and ſo wilfully perſeuered ſhe in it, that her father offering her the mariage of the great *Tiridates*, king of *Armenia* (who deſired her more then the ioyes of heauen) ſhe for *Antiphilus* ſake refuſed it. Many wayes her father ſought to withdrawe her from it ; ſometimes perſwaſions, ſometimes threatnings; once hiding *Antiphilus*, & giuing her to vnderſtand that he was fled the countrie: Laſtly, making a ſolemne execution to be done of another, vnder the name of *Antiphilus*, whom he kept in priſon. But nether ſhe liked perſwaſions, nor feared threateninges, nor changed for abſence : and when ſhe thought him dead,

dead, she sought all meanes (as well by poyson as by
knife) to send her soule, at least, to be maried in the eternall church with him. This so brake the tender fathers
hart, that (leauing things as he found them) he shortly
after died. Then foorthwith *Erona* (being seazed of the
crowne, and arming her will with authoritie) sought to
aduance her affection to the holy title of matrimonie.

But before she could accoplish all the solenities, she 3
was ouertake with a war the King *Tiridates* made vpon
her, only for her person; towards whom (for her ruine)
Loue had kindled his cruel hart; indeed cruell & tyrannous: for (being far too strog in the field) he spared not
man, woman, and child, but (as though there could be
found no foile to set foorth the extremitie of his loue,
but extremity of hatred) wrote (as it were) the sonets of
his Loue, in the bloud, & tuned the in the cries of her
subiects; although his fair sister *Artaxia* (who would ac-
copany him in the army) sought all meanes to appease
his fury : till lastly, he besieged *Erona* in her best citie,
vowing to winne her, or lose his life. And now had he
brought her to the point ether of a wofull consent, or a
ruinous deniall; whe there came thether (following the
course which Vertue & Fortune led the) two excellent
youg Princes, *Pyrocles* and *Musidorus*, the one Prince of
Macedo, the other of *Thessalia*: two princes, as *Plagus* said,
(and he witnessed his saying with sighes & teares) the
most accnoplished both in body & mind, that the Sun
euer lookt vpon. While *Philoclea* spake those words, O
sweete wordes (thought *Zelmane* to her self) which are
not onely a praise to me, but a praise to praise it selfe,
which out of that mouth issueth.

These 2. princes (said *Philoclea*) aswel to help the weaker 4
(espe-

(especially being a Ladie) as to saue a Greeke people from being ruined by such, whom we call and count Barbarous, gathering together such of the honestest *Lycians*, as woulde venture their liues to succour their Princeße: giuing order by a secreat meßage they sent into the Citie, that they should ißue with all force at an appointed time; they set vpon *Tiridates* campe, with so well-guided a fiercenes, that being of both sides aßaulted, he was like to be ouerthrowen: but that this *Plangus* (being Generall of *Tiridates* horf-men) especially ayded by the two mightie men, *Euardes* and *Barzanes*, rescued the foot-men, euen almost defeated : but yet could not barre the Princes (with their succoures both of men and victuall)to enter the Citie.

Which when *Tiridates* found would make the war long, (which length seemed to him worse then a languishing consumption) he made a challenge of three Princes in his retinue, against those two Princes and *Antiphilus*: and that thereupon the quarrell should be decided; with compact, that neither side should helpe his felow:but of whose side the more ouercame, with him the victorie should remaine. *Antiphilus*(though *Erona* chose rather to bide the brunt of warre, then venture him,yet)could not for shame refuse the offer,especially since the two strangers that had no intereßt in it, did willingly accept it : besides that, he sawe it like enough,that the people(werie of the miseries of war) would rather giue him vp,if they saw him shrinke,then for his sake venture their ruine : considering that the challengers were farre of greater worthineße then him selfe. So it was agreed vpon ; and against *Pyrocles* was *Euardes*,King of *Bithinia*; *Barzanes* of *Hircania*, against

Mufi-

Muſidorus, two men, that thought the world ſcarſe able to reſiſt them: & againſt *Antiphilus* he placed this ſame *Plangus*, being his own couſin germain, & ſonne to the King of *Iberia*. Now ſo it fell out that *Muſidorus* ſlewe *Barzanes*, & *Pyrocles Euardes*; which victory thoſe Princes eſteemed aboue all that euer they had: but of the other ſide *Plagus* tooke *Antiphilus* priſoner: vnder which colour (as if the matter had bene equal, though indeed it was not, the greater part being ouercome of his ſide) *Tiridates* continued his war: & to bring *Erona* to a cõpelled yeelding, ſent her word, that he would the third morrow after, before the walles of the towne ſtrike of *Antiphilus* head; without his ſuite in that ſpace were graunted: adding withall (becauſe he had heard of her deſperate affectiõ) that if in the meane time ſhe did her ſelfe any hurt, what tortures could be deuiſed ſhould be layed vpon *Antiphilus*.

Then lo if *Cupid* be a God, or that the tyranny of our 6 own thoughts ſeeme as a God vnto vs. But whatſoeuer it was, then it did ſet foorth the miſerablenes of his effects: ſhe being drawne to two contraries by one cauſe. For the loue of him cõmaunded her to yeeld to no other: the loue of him cõmaunded him to preſerue his life: which knot might well be cut, but vntied it could not be. So that Loue in her paſſions (like a right makebate) whiſpered to both ſides arguments of quarrell. What (ſaid he of the one ſide) dooſt thou loue *Antiphilus*, ô *Erona*? and ſhal *Tiridates* enioy thy bodie? with what eyes wilt thou looke vpon *Antiphilus*, when he ſhall know that another poſſeſſeth thee? But if thou wilt do it, canſt thou do it? canſt thou force thy hart? Thinke with thy ſelfe, if this man haue thee, thou ſhalt neuer haue more part of *Antiphilus* thẽ if he were dead.

Y   But

But thus much more, that the affectió ſhalbe gnawing, & the remorſe ſtill preſent. Death perhaps will coole the rage of thy affection : where thus, thou ſhalt euer loue, and euer lacke. Thinke this beſidé, if thou marrie *Tiridates*, *Antiphilus* is ſo excellent a man, that long he cannot be from being in ſome high place maried: canſt thou ſuffer that too? If an other kill him, he doth him the wrong: if thou abuſe thy body, thou dooſt him the wrong. His death is a worke of nature, and either now, or at another time he ſhall die. But it ſhalbe thy worke, thy ſhamefull worke, which is in thy power to ſhun, to make him liue to ſee thy faith falſified, and his bed defiled. But when Loue had well kindled that parte of her thoughts, then went he to the other ſide. What (ſaid he) O *Erona*, and is thy Loue of *Antiphilus* come to that point, as thou dooſt now make it a queſtion, whether he ſhall die, or no? O excellent affection, which for too much loue, will ſee his head of. Marke well the reaſons of the other ſide, and thou ſhalt ſee, it is but loue of thy ſelfe which ſo diſputeth. Thou canſt not abide *Tiridates*: this is but loue of thy ſelfe: thou ſhalt be aſhamed to looke vpó him afterward; this is but feare of ſhame, & loue of thy ſelfe: thou ſhalt want him as much then; this is but loue of thy ſelfe: he ſhalbe married; if he be well, why ſhould that grieue thee, but for loue of thy ſelfe? No, no, pronounce theſe wordes if thou canſt, let *Antiphilus* die. Then the images of each ſide ſtood before her vnderſtanding; one time ſhe thought ſhe ſaw *Antiphilus* dying: an other time ſhe thought *Antiphilus* ſaw her by *Tiridates* enioyed: twenty times calling for a ſeruaunt to carry meſſage of yeelding, but before he came the minde was altered. She bluſht when ſhe conſidered the effect of granting; ſhe was pale, whé

ſhe

she remēbred the fruits of denial.As for weeping,sigh-
ing,wringing her hāds,& tearing her haire, were indif-
ferēt ofboth sides.Easily she wold haue agreed to haue
broken al disputatiōs with her owne death,but that the
feare of *Antiphilus* furder torments staied her.At lēgth,
euē the euening before the day apointed of his death,
the determinatiō of yeelding preuailed,especially,gro-
wing vpō a message of *Antiphilus;*who with all the coniuring termes he could deuise,besought her to saue his
life,vpon any cōdition. But she had no sooner sent her
messenger to *Tiridates*, but her mind changed , and she
went to the two yong ·Princes, *Pyrocles* & *Musidorus*, &
falling downe at their feet,desired thē to trie some way
for her deliuerance ; shewing her selfe resolued , not to
ouer-liue *Antiphilus*, nor yet to yeeld to *Tiridates.*

They that knew not what she had done in priuate, 7
prepared that night accordingly:& as sometimes it fals
out, that what is incōstancy, seemes cūning;so did this
chāge indeed stand in as good steed as a witty dissimu-
latiō. For it made the King as reckles , as them diligēt:
so that in the dead time of the night, the Princes issued
out of the towne;with whō she would needs go,either
to die her self, or reskew *Antiphilus*,hauing no armour,
nor weapon,but affection.And I cannot tell you how,
by what deuise (though *Plangus* at large described it)
the conclusion was, the wonderfull valour of the two
Princes so preuailed , that *Antiphilus* was succoured,
and the King slaine . *Plangus* was then the chiefe man
left in the campe; and therefore seeing no other remedie, coueied in safety into her country *Artaxia*,now
Queene of *Armenia;*who with truelamētations , made 8
known to the world,that her new greatnes did no way

eôfort her in refpeﬅ of her brothers loﬀe, whô ﬂhe ﬅu-
died all meanes poﬃble to reuenge vpon euery one of
the occaﬁoners, hauing (as ﬂhe thought) ouerthrowne
her brother by a moﬅ abominable treaﬂon. In ﬂomuch,
that being at home, ﬂhe proclaimed great rewards to a-
ny priuate man, and her ﬂelfe in mariage to any Prince,
that would deﬅroy *Pyrocles* and *Muſidorus*. But thus
was *Antiphilus* redeemed, and (though againﬅ the con-
ﬂent of all her nobility) married to *Erona*; in which caﬂe
the two Greeke Princes (being called away by an o-
ther aduenture) left them.

CHAP. 14.

¹ Philocleas *narration broken of by* Miﬂo. ² *Her old-wiues
tale,* ³ *and ballad againﬅ* Cupid. ⁴ *Their drawing cuts
for tales.* ⁵ Mopﬂas *tale of the old cut:* ⁶ *cut of by the Ladies to returne to their ﬅories.*

I   Vt now me thinkes as I haue read
ﬂome *P*oets, who when they intêd
to tell ﬂome horrible matter, they
bid men ﬂhun the hearing of it: ﬂo
if I do not deﬁre you to ﬅop your
eares frô me, yet may I well deﬁre
a breathing time, before I am to
tell the execrable treaﬂon of *Anti-*
philus, that brought her tô this miﬂery; and withall wiﬂh
you al, that frô al mankind indeed you ﬅop your eares.
O moﬅ happy were we, if we did ﬂet our loues one vpon another. (And as ﬂhe ﬂpake that worde, her cheekes
in red letters writ more, then her tongue did ﬂpeake.)
And therefore ﬁnce I haue named *Plangus,* I pray you
ﬁﬅer

fifter (faid fhe) helpe me with the reft, for I haue helde
the ftage long inough ; and if it pleafe you to make his
fortune knowne,as I haue done *Eronas*,I will after take
hart againe to go on with his falfhood; & fo betweene
vs both, my Ladie *Zelmane* fhall vnderftand both the
caufe and partics of this Lamentation. Nay I befhrow
me then(faid *Mifo*) I wil none of that,I promife you,as
lóg as I haue the gouernmét,I will firft haue my tale, &
thé my Lady *Pamela*,my Lady *Zelmane*,& my daughter
Mopfa(for *Mopfa* was then returned frô *Amphialus*) may
draw cuts,& the fhorteft cut fpeake firft. For I tell you,
and this may be fuffred, when you are married you wil
haue firft,and laft word of your husbands.The Ladies
laughed to fee with what an eger earneftneffe fhe looked,hauing threatning not onely in her Ferret eies,but
while fhe fpake,her nofe feeming to threaten her chin,
& her fhaking lims one to threaten another. But there
was no remedy,they muft obey : & *Mifo*(fitting on the
groûd with her knees vp,& her hands vpon her knees)
tuning her voice with many a quauering cough , thus
difcourfed vnto thé.I tel you true(faid fhe)whatfoeuer 2
you thinke of me,you will one day be as I am; & I,fim-
ple though I fit here,thought once my pénnie as good
filuer,as fome of you do:and if my father had not plaid
the hafty foole (it is no lie I tell you)I might haue had
an other-gaines husbâd,thé *Dametas*.But let that paffe,
God amend him:and yet I fpeake it not without good
caufe.You are ful of your tittle tattling of *Cupid*:here is
Cupid,& there is *Cupid*.I will tell you now,what a good
old womã told me,what an old wife mã told her, what
a great learned clerke told him, and gaue it him in writing; and here I haue it in my praier booke . I pray you

(faid

(said *Philoclea*)let vs see it,& read it . No haſt but good (said *Miſo*)you ſhal firſt know how I came by it. I was a young girle of a ſeuen and twenty yeare old,& I could not go thorow the ſtreate of our village , but I might heare the young mē talke;O the pretie little eies of *Mi-ſo*; O the fine thin lips of *Miſo* ; O the goodly fat hands of *Miſo* : beſides,how well a certaine wrying I had of my necke,became me . Then the one would wincke with one eye,& the other caſt daiſeys at me: I muſt cō-feſſe,ſeing ſo many amorous,it made me ſet vp my pea-cocks tayle with the hieſt .Which when this good old womā perceiued(O the good wold woman, well may the bones reſt of the good wold womā)ſhe cald me to her into her houſe.I remember full well it ſtood in the lane as you go to the Barbers ſhop,all the towne knew her,there was a great loſſe of her : ſhe called me to her, and taking firſt a ſoppe of wine to comfort her hart (it was of the ſame wine that comes out of *Candia*, which we pay ſo deere for now a daies , and in that good worlde was very good cheape) ſhe cald me to her;Mi-nion ſaid ſhe, (indeed I was a pretie one in thoſe daies thongh I ſay it)I ſee a nūber of lads that loue you; Wel (ſaid ſhe) I ſay no more:doo you know what Loue is? With that ſhe broght me into a corner,where ther was painted a foule fiēd I trow:for he had a paire of hornes like a Bull,his feete clouen, as many eyes vpon his bo-die,as my gray-mare hath dappels , & for all the world ſo placed. This mōſter ſat like a hāgman vpō a paire of gallowes , in his right hand he was painted holding a crowne of Laurell, in his left hand a purſe of mony,& out of his mouth honge a lace of two faire pictures,of a mā & a womā,& ſuch a coūtenance he ſhewed,as if he
would

would perſwade folks by thoſe aluremēts to come thither & be hanged. I, like a tēder harted wench, skriked
out for feare of the diuell. Well (ſayd ſhe) this ſame is
euen Loue: therefore do what thou liſt with all thoſe
fellowes, one after another; & it recks not much what
they do to thee,ſo it be in ſecreat; but vpon my charge,
neuer loue none of them. Why mother (ſaid I) could
ſuch a thing come frō the belly of thē faire *Venus?* for a
few dayes before,our (prieſt betweene him & me) had
tolde me the whole ſtoric of *Venus.* Tuſh(ſaid ſhe)they
are all deceaued: and therewith gaue me this Booke,
which ſhe ſaid a great maker of ballets had giuen to an
old painter,who for a litle pleaſure, had beſtowed both
booke and picture of her. Reade there(ſaid ſhe)& thou
ſhalt ſee that his mother was a cowe, and the falſe *Ar-*
gus his father. And ſo ſhe gaue me this Booke, & there
now you may reade it. With that the remembrance of
the good old woman, made her make ſuch a face to
weepe, as if it were not ſorrow, it was the carkaſſe of
ſorrow that appeared there. But while her teares came
out, like raine falling vpon durtie furrowes, the latter
end of her praier booke was read among theſe Ladies,
which contained this.

POore Painters oft with ſilly Poets ioyne,
  To fill the world with ſtrange but vaine conceits:
One brings the ſtuffe, the other ſtamps the coine,
Which breeds nought elſe but gloſes of deceits.
  Thus Painters Cupid paint, thus Poets do
  A naked god, young blind, with arrowes two.
Is he a God, that euer flies the light?
Or naked he, diſguis'd in all vntruth?

If

If he be blind, how hitteth he ſo right ?
How is he young, that tam'de old Phœbus *youth ?*
   But arrowes two, and tipt with gold or leade :
   Some hurt accuſe a third with horny head.
No, nothing ſo; an old falſe knaue he is
By Argus *got on* Io, *then a cow :*
What time for her Iuno *her* Ioue *did miſſe,*
And charge of her to Argus *did allow.*
   Mercury *kill'd his falſe ſire for this act,*
   His damme a beaſt was pardon'd beaſtly fact.
With fathers death, and mothers guiltie ſhame,
With Ioues *diſdaine at ſuch a riuals ſeed,*
The wretch compell'd a runnagate became,
And learn'd what ill a miſer ſtate doth breed,
   To lye, faine, gloze, to ſteale, pry, and accuſe,
   Naught in himſelfe ech other to abuſe.
Yet beares he ſtill his parents ſtately gifts,
A horned head, clouen foote, and thouſand eyes,
Some gazing ſtill, ſome winking wilye ſhiftes,
With long large eares where neuer rumour dyes.
   His horned head doth ſeeme the heauen to ſpight ·
   His clouen foote doth neuer treade aright.
Thus halfe a man, with man he dayly haunts,
Cloth'd in the ſhape which ſooneſt may deceaue :
Thus halfe a beaſt, ech beaſtly vice he plants,
In thoſe weake harts that his aduice receaue.
   He proules ech place ſtil in new colours deckt,
   Sucking ones ill, another to infect.
To narrow breſts he comes all wrapt in gaine :
To ſwelling harts he ſhines in honours fire :
To open eyes all beauties he doth raine ;
Creeping to ech with flattering of deſire.

But

But for that Loues defire moft rules the eyes,
Therein his name, there his chiefe triumph lyes.
Millions of yeares th` old driuell Cupid *liues ;*
While ftill more wretch, more wicked he doth proue :
Till now at length that Ioue *him office giues,*
(At Iunos *fuite who much did* Argus *loue)*
In this our world a hang-man for to be,
Of all thofe fooles that will haue all they fee.

Thefe Ladies made fport at the defcription and fto- 4
rie of *Cupid.* But *Zelmane* could fcarce fuffer thofe blafphemies (as fhe tooke them) to be read, but humbly befought *Pamela* fhe would perfourme her fifters requeft
of the other part of the ftorie. Noble Lady (anfwered
fhe, beautifying her face with a fweete fmiling, and the
fweetnes of her fmiling with the beautie of her face)
fince I am borne a Princes daughter, let me not giue
example of difobedience. My gouerneffe will haue vs
draw cuts, and therefore I pray you let vs do fo: and fo
perhaps it will light vpon you to entertaine this company with fome ftorie of your owne ; and it is reafon
our eares fhould be willinger to heare, as your tongue
is abler to deliuer. I will thinke (anfwered *Zelmane*) excellent Princeffe my tongue of fome value, if it can
procure your tongue thus much to fauour me. But *Pa-*
mela pleafantly perfifting to haue fortune their iudge,
they fet hands, and *Mopfa* (though at the firft for fqueca-
mifhnes going vp & downe, with her head like a boate
in a ftorme) put to her golden gols among them, and
blind Fortune (that faw not the coulor of them) gaue
her the preheminence : and fo being her time to fpeake
(wiping her mouth, as there was good caufe) fhe thus
tumbled

tumbled into her matter. In time paſt (ſayd ſhe) there was a King, the mightieſt man in all his country, that had by his wife, the faireſt daughter that euer did eate pappe. Now this King did keepe a great houſe, that euery body might come and take their meat freely. So one day, as his daughter was ſitting in her window, playing vpon a harpe, as ſweete as any Roſe; and combing her head with a combe all of precious ſtones, there came in a Knight into the court, vpó a goodly horſe, one haire of gold, & the other of ſiluer; *and ſo* the Knight caſting vp his eyes to the window, did fall into ſuch loue with her, that he grew not worth the bread he eate; till many a ſorry day going ouer his head, with Dayly Diligence and Griſly Grones, he wan her affection, ſo that they agreed to run away togither. *And ſo in May, when all true hartes reioyce*, they ſtale out of the Caſtel, without ſtaying ſo much as for their breakfaſt. Now forſooth, as they went togither, often all to kiſſing one another, the Knight told her, he was brought vp among the water Nymphes, who had ſo bewitched him, that if he were euer askt his name, he muſt preſently vaniſh away: and therefore charged her vpon his bleſſing, that ſhe neuer aſke him what he was, nor whether he would. *And ſo* a great while ſhe kept his commandement, til once, paſſing through a cruell wildernes, as darke as pitch; her mouth ſo watred, that ſhe could not chooſe but aſke him the queſtion. And then, he making the greeuouſeſt cóplaints that would haue melted a tree to haue heard them, vaniſht quite away: & ſhe lay down, caſting forth as pitifull cries as any ſhrich-owle. But hauing laien ſo, (wet by the raine, and burnt by the Sun) fiue dayes, & fiue nights, ſhe gat vp and went ouer many a high hil, &

many

many a deepe riuer; till ſhe came to an Aunts houſe of
hers;and came,& cried to her for helpe:and ſhe for pittie gaue her a Nut,and bad her neuer open her Nut, til
ſhe was come to the extremeſt miſery that euer tongue
could ſpeake of. *And ſo* ſhe went, & ſhe went,& neuer
reſted the euening,wher ſhe wét in the morning;til ſhe
came to a ſecond Aunt; and ſhe gaue her another Nut.

Now good *Mopſa* (ſaid the ſweete *Philoclea*) I pray
thee at my requeſt keepe this tale, till my marriage day,
& I promiſe thee that the beſt gowne I weare that day
ſhalbe thine. *Mopſa* was very glad of the bargaine,eſpe-
cially that it ſhuld grow a feſtiual Tale:ſo that *Zelmane*,
who deſired to finde the vttermoſt what theſe Ladies
vnderſtood touching her ſelfe,and hauing vnderſtood
the danger of *Erona* (of which before ſhe had neuer
heard)purpoſing with her ſelfe(as ſoone as this purſuit
ſhe now was in, was brought to any effect) to ſuccour
her, entreated againe, that ſhe might know as well the
ſtory of *Plangus*, as of *Erona*. *Philoclea* referred it to her
ſiſters perfecter remébrace, who with ſo ſweet a voice,
and ſo winning a grace, as in themſelues were of moſt
forcible eloquence to procure attention, in this maner
to their earneſt requeſt ſoone condiſcended.

CHAP. 15.

The

He father of this Prince *Plangus* as yet liues, and is King of *Iberia* : a man (if the iudgement of *Plangus* may be accepted) of no wicked nature, nor willingly doing euill, without himſelfe miſtake the euill, ſeeing it diſguiſed vnder ſome forme of goodneſſe. This Prince, being married at the firſt to a Princeſſe(who both from her auncesters, and in her ſelfe was worthy of him) by her had this ſon, *Plangus*. Not long after whoſe birth, the Queene (as though ſhe had perfourmed the meſſage for which ſhe was ſent into the world) returned again vnto her maker. The King(ſealing vp al thoughts of loue vnder the image of her memorie) remained a widdower many yeares after; recompencing the griefe of that disioyning from her, in conioyning in himſelfe both a fatherly and a motherly care toward her onely child,*Plangus*. Who being growne to mans age, as our owne eies may iudge, could not but fertilly requite his fathers fatherly education.

This Prince (while yet the errors in his nature were excuſed by the greenenes of his youth, which tooke all the fault vpon it ſelfe) loued a priuate mans wife of the principal Citie of that Kingdome, if that may be called loue, which he rather did take into himſelfe willingly. then by which he was take forcibly. It ſufficeth, that the yong man perſwaded himſelf he loued her: ſhe being a woman beautiful enough, if it be poſſible, that the outſide onely can iuſtly entitle a beauty. But finding ſuch a chaſe as onely fledde to be caught, the young Prince broght his affectiõ with her to that point, which ought to engraue remorſe in her harte,& to paint ſhame vpon

her

her face. And so possest he his desire without any in-
terruption;he constantly fauouring her, and she thinking,that the enameling of a Princes name,might hide
the spots of a broken wedlock. But as I haue seene one
that was sick of a sleeping disease, could not be made
wake, but with pinching of him : so out of his sinfull
sleepe his minde (vnworthie so to be loste) was not to
be cald to it selfe,but by a sharpe accident.

It fell out,that his many-times leauing of the court **3**
(in vndue times) began to be noted ; and (as Princes
eares be manifolde) from one to another came vnto
the King;who(carefull of his onely sonne)sought,and
found by his spies (the necessarie euill seruauntes to a
King)what it was,whereby he was from his better delights so diuerted.

Whereupon,the King(to giue his fault the greater **4**
blow)vsed such meanes, by disguising himselfe,that he
found them (her husband being absent) in her house
together: which he did,to make him the more feelingly ashamed of it. And that way he tooke,laying threatnings vpon her, and vpon him reproaches. But the
poore young Prince(deceiued with that young opinion,that if it be euer lawfull to lie,it is for ones Louer,)
employed all his witte to bring his father to a better o-
pinion. And because he might bende him from that
(as he counted it) crooked conceit of her, he wrested
him, as much as he coulde possiblie,to the other side:
not sticking with prodigall protestations to set foorth
her chastitie;not denying his own attempts, but thereby the more extolling her vertue. His Sophistrie preuayled, his father beleeued ; and so beleeued,that ere
long (though he were alredy stept into the winter of
his

his age) he founde himſelfe warme in thoſe deſires,
which were in his ſonne farre more excuſable . To be
ſhort, he gaue himſelfe ouer vnto it; and (becauſe he
would auoide the odious compariſon of a yong riuall)
ſent away his ſonne with an armie, to the ſubduing of a
Prouince lately rebelled againſt him, which he knewe
could not be a leſſe worke, thē of three or foure yeares.
Wherein he behaued him ſo worthilie , as euen to this
countrythe fame therof came, long before his own cōming: while yet his father had a ſpeedier ſucces, but in a
far vnnobler conqueſt. For while *Plangus* was away, the
old man (growing onely in age & affectiō) folowed his
ſuite with all meanes of vnhoneſt ſeruants, large promiſes, and each thing els that might help to counteruaile
his owne vnlouelines.

  And ſhe (whoſe huſband about that time died) forgetting the abſent *Plangus*, or at leſt not hoping of him
to obtaine ſo aſpiring a purpoſe , leſte no arte vnuſed,
which might keepe the line from breaking, wherat the
time was alredy taken; not drawing him violently, but
letting him play himſelf vpon the hooke, which he had
greedely ſwalowed. For, accompanying her mourning
with a dolefull countenaunce, yet neither forgetting
hanſomnes in her mourning garments, nor ſweetenes
in her dolefull countenance; her wordes were euer ſea-
ſoned with ſighes; and any fauour ſhe ſhewed , bathed
in teares, that affection might ſee cauſe of pity; and pity
might perſwade cauſe of affection . And being growen
ſkilfull in his humors, ſhe was no leſſe ſkilfull in applying his humors: neuer ſuffering his feare to fall to a deſpaire, nor his hope to haſten to an aſſurance : ſhe was
content he ſhould thinke that ſhe loued him; and a certaine

taine ftolne looke fhould fometimes (as though it were
againft her will) bewray it: But if thereupon he grewe
bolde, he ftraight was encountred with a mafke of vertue. And that which feemeth moft impoffible vnto me,
(for as neere as I can I repeate it as *Plangus* tolde it) fhe
could not onely figh when fhe would, as all can doo; &
weep when fhe would, as (they fay) fome can doo; but
(being moft impudent in her hart) fhe could, when fhe
would, teach her chekes blufhing, and make fhamefaftnes the cloake of fhamelefnes. In fumme, to leaue out
many particularities which he recited, fhe did not onely vfe fo the fpurre, that his Defire ran on, but fo the bit,
that it ran on, euē in fuch a careere as fhe would haue it:
that within a while, the king, feeing with no other eyes
but fuch as fhe gaue him, & thinking no other thoghts
but fuch as fhe taught him; hauing at the firft liberall
meafure of fauors, then fhortned of thē, when moft his
Defire was inflamed, he faw no other way but mariage
to fatisfie his longing, and her mind (as he thought) louing, but chaftly louing. So that by the time *Plangus* returned from being notably victorious of the Rebels, he
foūd his father, not only maried, but alredy a father of a
fonne & a daughter by this womā. Which though *Plāgus* (as he had euery way iuft caufe) was grieued at; yet
did his grief neuer bring forth ether cōtemning of her,
or repining at his father. But fhe (who befides fhe was   6
growen a mother, and a ftepmother, did read in his eies
her owne fault, and made his confcience her guiltines)
thought ftill that his prefence caried her condénation:
fo much the more, as that fhe (vnchaftly attempting his
wōted facies) foūd (for the reuerēce of his fathers bed)
a bitter refufall: which breeding rather fpite then fhame
                                                        in

in her, or if it were a shame, a shame not of the fault, but of the repulse, she did not onely (as hating him) thirst for a reuenge, but (as fearing harm from him) endeuoured to doo harme vnto him . Therefore did she rie the vttermost of her wicked wit, how to ouerthrow nim in the foundation of his strength , which was, in the fauour of his father : which because she saw strong both in nature and desert, it required the more cūning ow to vndermine it . And therfore (shunning the ordinary trade of hireling sycophants) she made her praises of him, to be accusations; and her aduauncing him, to be his ruine. For first with words (necrer admiration then liking) she would extoll his excellécies, the goodlines of his shape, the power of his witte, the valiantnes of his courage, the fortunatenes of his successes : so as the father might finde in her a singular loue towardes him: nay, she shunned not to kindle some fewe sparkes of ielousie in him . Thus hauing gotten an opinion in his father, that she was farre from meaning mischiefe to the sonne; then fell she to praise him with no lesse vehemencie of affection, but with much more cunning of malice. For then she sets forth the liberty of his mind, the high flying of his thoughts , the fitnesse in him to beare rule, the singular loue the Subiects bare him; that it was doubtfull , whether his wit were greater in winning their fauors, or his courage in employing their fauours: that he was not borne to liue a subiect-life, each action of his bearing in it Maiestie, such a Kingly entertainement, such a Kingly magnificence , such a Kingly harte for enterprises: especially remembring those vertues, which in a successor are no more honoured by the subiects, then suspected of the Princes. Then would she
by

by putting-of obiectiõs,bring in obiectiõs to her huf-
bands head,alredy infected with fufpitiõ. Nay (would
fhe fay)I dare take it vpon my death, that he is no fuch
fonne, as many of like might haue bene, who loued
greatnes fo well, as to build their greatnes vpon their
fathers ruine. Indeed Ambition, like Loue, can abide
no lingring,& euer vrgeth on his own fucceffes;hating
nothing,but what may ftop thē. But the Gods forbid,
we fhould euer once dreame of any fuch thing in him,
who perhaps might be content, that you & the world
fhould know,what he can do : but the more power he
hath to hurte, the more admirable is his praife, that he
wil not hurt. Then euer remembring to ftrengthen the
fufpition of his eftate with priuate ieloufie of her loue,
doing him exceffiue honour when he was in prefence,
and repeating his pretie fpeaches and graces in his abfence;befides,caufing him to be imployed in all fuch
dangerous matters, as ether he fhould perifh in them,
or if he preuailed,they fhould increafe his glory:which
fhe made a weapon to woūd him,vntill fhe found that
fufpition began already to fpeake for it felfe, and that
her husbands eares were growne hungry of rumours,
and his eies prying into euery accident.

Then tooke fhe help to her of a feruant neere about 7
her husband,whom fhe knew to be of a hafty ambitiõ,
and fuch a one,who wanting true fufficiencie to raife
him,would make a ladder of any mifchiefe. Him fhe v-
feth to deale more plainely in alleaging caufes of iealoufie, making him know the fitteft times when her
husband already was ftirred that way. And fo they
two, with diuers wayes,nourifhed one humour, like
Mufitians,that finging diuers parts,make one muficke.
He fometime with fearefull countenaunce would de-

fire the King to looke to himſelfe; for that all the court and Cittie were full of whiſperings, and expectation of ſome ſuddaine change, vpon what ground himſelfe knew not. Another time he would counſell the King to make much of his ſonne, and holde his fauour, for that it was too late now to keepe him vnder. Now ſeeming to feare himſelfe, becauſe (he ſaid) *Plangus* loued none of them that were great about his father. Laſtly, breaking with him directly (making a ſorrowful countenance, & an humble geſture beare falſe witneſſe for his true meaning) that he foũd, not only ſouldiery, but people weary of his gouernment, & al their affections bent vpon *Plangus*. Both he and the Queene concurring in ſtrange dreames, & each thing elſe, that in a mind (already perplexed) might breed aſtoniſhment: ſo that within a while, all *Plangus* actions began to be tranſlated into the language of ſuſpition.

8   Which though *Plangus* foũd, yet could he not auoid, euen cõtraries being driuen to draw one yoke of argumẽt: if he were magnificẽt, he ſpent much with an aſpiring intent: if he ſpared, he heaped much with an aſpiring intent: if he ſpake curteouſly, he angled the peoples harts: if he were ſilent, he muſed vpon ſome daungerous plot. In ſumme, if he could haue turned himſelf to as many formes as *Proteus*, euery forme ſhould haue bene made tedious.

9   But ſo it fell out, that a meere trifle gaue the occaſion of further proceeding. The King one morning, going to a vineyard that lay a long the hill where his caſtle ſtood, he ſaw a vine-labourer, that finding a bowe broken, tooke a branch of the ſame bowe for want of another thing, and tied it about the place broken. The King asking the fellow what he did, Marry (ſaid he) I make

make the fonne binde the father . This word (finding the King alredy fuperfticious through fufpitiō)amazed him ftreight, as a prefage of his owne fortune : fo that, returning , and breaking with his wife how much he mifdoubted his eftate , fhe made fuch gaine-faying an-fweres , as while they ftraue , ftraue to be ouercome. But euen while the doubtes moft boiled,fhe thus nou-rifhed them.

She vnder-hand dealt with the principall mē of that coūtry, that at the great Parliamēt (which was then to be held) they fhould in the name of all the eftates per-fwade the King (being now ftept deeply into old age) to make *Plangus*,his affociate in gouernmēt with him : affuring thē,that not only fhe would ioine with them, but that the father himfelf would take it kindly; charge-ing thē not to acquaint *Plangus* withal;for that perhaps it might be harmeful vnto him,if the King fhould find, that he wer a party.They (who thought they might do it,not only willingly,becaufe they loued him, & truly, becaufe fuch indeed was the minde of the people , but fafely,becaufe fhe who ruled the King was agreed ther-to)accōplifhed her coūfell:fhe indeed keeping promife of vehement perfwading the fame:which the more fhe & they did,the more fhe knew her husbād would fear, & hate the caufe of his feare.*Plangus* foūd this, & hūbly protefted againft fuch defire, or wil to accept . But the more he protefted , the more his father thought he dif-fēbled, accoūting his integritie to be but a cūning face of falfhood:and therfore delaying the defire of his fub-iects, attended fome fit occafion tō lay hands vpon his fonne:which his wife thus brought to paffe.

She caufed that fame minifter of hers to go vnto *Plā-*

gus,&(enabling his words with great ſhew of faith , & endearing them with deſire of ſecreſie) to tell him, that he found his ruine conſpired by his ſtepmother, with certain of the noble men of that coũtry, the King himſelfe giuing his conſent , and that few daies ſhould paſſe,before the putting it in practize: with all diſcouering the very truth indeed,with what cunning his ſtepmother had proceeded. This agreing with *Plangus* his owne opiniõ,made him giue him the better credit:yet not ſo far,as to flie out of his country (according to the naughty fellowes perſuaſion) but to attend , and to ſee further.Wherupon the fellow (by the direction of his miſtreſſe)told him one day, that the ſame night, about one of the clocke , the King had appointed to haue his wife,& thoſe noble mẽ together, to deliberate of their manner of proceeding againſt *Plangus*: & therfore offered him,that if himſelfe would agree ,he would bring him into a place where he ſhould heare all that paſſed; & ſo haue the more reaſon both to himſelfe, and to the world,to ſeeke his ſafetie. The poore *Plagus* (being ſubiect to that only diſaduantage of honeſt harts,credulitie)was perſwaded by him: & arming himſelf (becauſe of his late going) was cloſely conueied into the place appointed . In the meane time his ſtepmother making all her geſtures cunningly counterfait a miſerable afflictiõ,ſhe lay almoſt groueling on the flower of her chãber, not ſuffering any body to comfort her ; vntill they calling for her husband, and he held of with long enquiry, at length, ſhe told him (euen almoſt crying out euery word)that ſhe was wery of her life,ſince ſhe was brought to that plunge,either to conceale her husbãds murther,or accuſe her ſonne,who had euer bene more
deare.

deare, then a ſonne vnto her. Then with many inter-
ruptions and exclamations ſhe told him, that her ſonne
Plangus (ſolliciting her in the old affection betweene
them) had beſought her to put her helping hand to the
death of the King; aſſuring her, that though all the
lawes in the world were againſt it, he would marrie her
when he were King.

She had not fully ſaid thus much, with many pitifull 12
digreſſiõs, whẽ in comes the ſame fellow, that brought
Plãgus: & runing himſelf out of breath, fell at the Kings
feet, beſeeching him to ſaue himſelf, for that there was a
man with ſword drawen in the next roome. The King
affrighted, wẽt ont, & called his gard, who entring the
place, foũd indeed *Plangus* with his ſword in his hand,
but not naked, but ſtãding ſuſpiciouſly inough to one
already ſuſpicious. The King (thinking he had put vp
his ſworde becauſe of the noiſe) neuer tooke leaſure to
heare his anſwer, but made him priſoner, meaning the
next morning to put him to death in the market place.

But the day had no ſooner opened the eies & eares 13
of his friends & followers, but that there was a little army of them, who came, and by force deliuered him; although nũbers on the other ſide (abuſed with the fine
framing of their report) tooke armes for the King. But
Plangus, though he might haue vſed the force of his
friends to reuenge his wrong, and get the crowne; yet
the naturall loue of his father, and hate to make their
ſuſpition ſeeme iuſt, cauſed him rather to chooſe a vo-
lũtarie exile, thẽ to make his fathers death the purchaſe
of his life: & therefore went he to *Tiridates*, whoſe mother was his fathers ſiſter, liuing in his Court eleuen or
twelue yeares, euer hoping by his interceſſion, and his

owne

owne defert, to recouer his fathers grace. At the end of
which time the warre of *Erona* happened, which my
fifter with the caufe thereof difcourfed vnto you.

14   But his father had fo deeply engraued the fufpicion
in his hart, that he thought his flight rather to proceed
of a fearefull guiltines, then of an humble faithfulnes;
& therfore continued his hate, with fuch vehemencie,
that he did euer hate his Nephew *Tiridates*, and afterwards his neece *Artaxia*, becaufe in their Court he receiued countenance, leauing no meanes vnattēpted of
deftroying his fon; among other, employing that wicked feruant of his, who vndertooke to empoyfon him.
But his cūning difguifed him not fo well, but that the
watchful feruāts of *Plāgus* did difcouer him. Wherupō
the wretch was taken, & (before his wel-deferued execution) by torture forced to confeffe the particularities
of this, which in generall I haue told you.

15   Which cōfeffion autentically fet downe (though *Ti-*
ridates with folemne Embaffage fent it to the King)
wrought no effect. For the King hauing put the reines
of the gouernment into his wiues hande, neuer did fo
much as reade it; but fent it ftreight by her to be confidered. So as they rather heaped more hatred vpon
Plangus, for the death of their feruaunt. And now finding, that his abfence, and their reportes had much
diminifhed the wauering peoples affection towardes
Plangus, with aduauncing fit perfons for faction, and
graunting great immunities to the commons, they
preuailed fo farre, as to caufe the fonne of the fecond
wife, called *Palladius*, to be proclaymed fucceffour,
and *Plangus* quite excluded: fo that *Plangus* was driuen to continue his feruing *Tiridates*, as he did in the
warre

warre againſt *Erona* and brought home *Artaxia*,
as my ſiſter tolde you; when *Erona* by the treaſon of
Antiphilus, But at that word ſhe ſtopped. For *Baſilius*
(not able longer to abide their abſence) came ſodainly
among them, and with ſmiling countenance (telling
Zelmane he was affraid ſhe had ſtollen away his daughters) inuited them to follow the Sunnes counſel in going then to their lodging; for indeed the Sun was readie to ſet. They yeelded, *Zelmane* meaning ſome other
time to vnderſtand the ſtorie of *Antiphilus* treaſon, and
Eronas daunger, whoſe caſe ſhe greatly tendred. But
Miſo had no ſooner eſpied *Baſilius*,but that as ſpitefully,
as her rotten voice could vtter it, ſhe ſet forth the ſaw-
cineſſe of *Amphialus*. But *Baſilius* onely attended what
Zelmanes opinion was, who though ſhe hated *Amphia-*
lus, yet the nobilitie of her courage preuailed ouer it,
and ſhe deſired he might be pardoned that youthfull
error; conſidering the reputation he had, to be one of
the beſt knights in the world; ſo as hereafter he gouerned himſelfe, as one remembring his fault. *Baſilius* giuing the infinite tearmes of praiſes to *Zelmanes* both
valour in conquering, and pittifulneſſe in pardoning,
commanded no more words to be made of it, ſince
ſuch he thought was her pleaſure.

CHAP. 16.

¹*The cumber of* Zelmanes *loue and louers.* ²Gynecias *loue-*
lamentations. ³Zelmanes *paſsions* ⁴*& ſonet.* ⁵Baſilius *his*
wooing, and Zelmanes *anſweres.* ⁶ Philoclea *feed attur-*
ney to plead her fathers cauſe.

1

S O brought he them vp to viſite his wife, where betweene her, & him, the poore *Zelmane* receaued a tedious entertainemēt; oppreſſed with being loued, almoſt as much, as with louing. *Baſilius* not ſo wiſe in couering his paſſion, could make his toong go almoſt no other pace, but to runne into thoſe immoderate praiſes, which the fooliſh Louer thinkes ſhort of his Miſtres, though they reach farre beyond the heauens. But *Gynecia* (whome womanly modeſtie did more outwardly bridle) yet did oftentimes vſe the aduantage of her ſexe in kiſſing *Zelmane*, as ſhe ſate vpon her bedde-ſide by her; which was but ſtill more and more ſweete incenſe, to caſt vpon the fire wherein her harte was ſacrificed : Once *Zelmane* could not ſtirre, but that, (as if they had bene poppets, whoſe motion ſtoode onely vpon her pleaſure) *Baſilius* with ſeruiceable ſteppes, *Gynecia* with greedie eyes would follow her. *Baſilius* mind *Gynecia* well knew, and could haue found in her hart to laugh at, if mirth could haue borne any proportion with her fortune. But all *Gynecias* actions were interpreted by *Baſilius*, as proceeding from iealouſie of his amorouſneſſe. *Zelmane* betwixt both (like the poore childe, whoſe father while he beates him, will make him beleeue it is for loue; or like the ſicke man, to whom the Phiſition ſweares, the ill-taſting wallowiſh medicine he profers, is of a good taſte) their loue was hatefull, their courteſie troubleſome, their preſence cauſe of her abſence thence, where not onely her light, but her life conſiſted. Alas (thought ſhe to her ſelfe) deare

Dorus

Dorus, what ods is there betweene thy deſtiny & mine? For thou haſt to doo in thy purſuite but with ſhepher-diſh folkes, who trouble thee with a little enuious care, and affected diligence. But I (beſides that I haue now *Miſo*, the worſt of thy diuels, let looſe vpon me) am wai-ted on by Princes, and watched by the two wakefull eyes of Loue and Ieolouſie. Alas, incomparable *Philo-clea*, thou euer ſeeſt me, but doſt neuer ſee me as I am: thou heareſt willingly all that I dare ſay, and I dare not ſay that which were moſt fit for thee to heare. Alas who euer but I was impriſoned in libertie, and baniſhed be-ing ſtill preſent? To whom but me haue louers bene iailours, and honour a captiuitie.

But the night comming on with her ſilent ſteps vp-on thē, they parted ech from other (if at leſt they could be parted, of whom euery one did liue in another) and went about to flatter ſleepe with their beds, that diſdai-ned to beſtow it ſelfe liberally vpon ſuch eies which by their will would euer be looking: and in leſt meaſure vpon *Gynecia*, who (when *Baſilius* after long toſſing was gotten a ſleepe, and the cheereful comfort of the lights remoued from her) kneeling vp in her bed, began with a ſoft voice, and ſwolne hart, to renue the curſes of her birth; & thē in a maner embracing her bed; Ah chaſteſt bed of mine (ſaid ſhe) which neuer heretofore couldſt accuſe me of one defiled thought, how canſt thou now receaue this deſaſtred changeling? Happie, happie be they onely which be not: and thy bleſſednes onely in this reſpect thou maiſt feele, that thou haſt no feeling. With that ſhe furiouſly tare off great part of her faire haire: Take here ô forgotten vertue (ſaid ſhe) this miſe-rable ſacrifice; while my ſoule was clothed with mode-

ſtie.

stie,that was a comely ornament : now why should nature erowne that head,which is so wicked,as her onely
despaire is ; she cannot be enough wicked? More she
would haue said, but that *Basilius* (awaked with the
noise)tooke her in his armes, & begā to cōfort her; the
good-man thinking,it was all for a iealous loue of him:
which humor if she would a litle haue maintained, perchance it might haue weakned his new conceaued fan-
cies.But he finding her answeres wandring frō the purpose, left her to her selfe(glad the next morning to take
the aduātage of a sleepe,which a little before day,ouer-
watched with sorow,her teares had as it were sealed vp
in her eyes)to haue the more conference with *Zelmane*,
who baited on this fashion by these two louers, & euer
kept from any meane to declare herselfe, found in her
selfe a dayly encreafe of her violent desires ; like a riuer
the more swelling, the more his current is stopped.

3   The chiefe recreation she could find in her anguish,
was somtime to visite that place, where first she was so
happy as to see the cause of her vnhap.There would she
kisse the ground,and thanke the trees, blisse the aier, &
do dutifull reuerence to euery thing that she thought
did accompany her at their first meeting : then returne
again to her inward thoughts; somtimes despaire dark-
ning all her imaginations,sometimes the actiue passion
of Loue cheering and cleering her inuention, how to
vnbar that comberfome hinderance of her two ill-mat-
ched louers. But this morning *Basilius* himself gaue her
good occasion to go beyond them.For hauing combd
and trickt himself more curiously, then any time fortie
winters before,comming where *Zelmane* was,he found
her giuen ouer to her musicall muses,to the great pleasure

sure of the good old *Basilius*, who retired himselfe behinde a tree, while she with a most sweete voice did vtter these passionate verses.

L Oued I am, and yet complaine of Loue :
As louing not, accus'd, in Loue I die.   4
When pittie most I craue, I cruell proue :
Still seeking Loue, loue found as much I flie.
   Burnt in my selfe, I muse at others fire :
What I call wrong, I doo the same, and more :
Bard of my will, I haue beyond desire :
I waile for want, and yet am chokte with store.
   This is thy worke, thou God for euer blinde :
Though thousands old, a Boy entit'led still.
Thus children doo the silly birds they finde,
With stroking hurt, and too much cramming kill.
   Yet thus much Loue, O Loue, I craue of thee :
Let me be lou'd, or els not loued be.

Basilius made no great haste from behind the tree, till 5
he perceaued she had fully ended her musick. But then
loth to loose the pretious fruite of time, he presented
himselfe vnto her, falling downe vpon both his knees,
and holding vp his hands, as the old gouernesse of *Da-*
nae is painted, when she sodainly saw the goldē shoure,
O heauēly womā, or earthly Goddesse (said he) let not
my presence be odious vnto you, nor my humble suit
seeme of small weight in your eares. Vouchsafe your
eies to descend vpon this miserable old-mā, whose life
hath hitherto bene maintained but to serue as an encrease of your beautiful triumphs. You only haue ouerthrowne me, & in my bondage cosists my glory. Suffer
not

not your owne worke to be defpifed of you: but looke
vpon him with pittie, whofe life ferues for your praife.
Zelmane (keeping a coutenace afcanfes fhe vnderftood
him not) told him, It became her euil to fuffer fuch exceffiue reuerence of him, but that it worfe became her
to correct him, to whom fhe owed duetie: that the
opinion fhe had of his wifedome was fuch, as made
her efteeme greatly of his words; but that the words
themfelues founded fo, as fhe could not imagine what
they might intend. Intend? (faid *Bafilius*, proud that
that was brought in queftion) what may they intend,
but a refrefhing of my foule, and a fwaging of my heat,
and enioying thofe your excellencies, wherein my life
is vpheld, and my death threatned? *Zelmane* lifting vp
her face as if fhe had receaued a mortall iniurie of him,
And is this the deuotion your ceremonies haue bene
bent vnto? faid fhe: Is it the difdaine of my eftate, or
the opinion of my lightneffe, that haue emboldned
fuch bafe fancies towards me? enioying quoth you?
now little ioy come to them that yeeld to fuch enioying. Poore *Bafilius* was fo appalled, that his
legges bowed vnder him; his eyes lookt as though he
would gladly hide himfelf; and his old blood going to
his hart, a generall fhaking all ouer his bodie poffeffed
him. At length with a wanne mouth; he was about to
giue a ftammering anfwere, when it came into *Zelmanes*
head by this deuife to make her profite of his folly; and
therefore with a relented countenance, thus faid vnto him. Your words (mightie Prince) were vnfit either
for me to heare, or you to fpeake: but yet the large
teftimonie I fee of your affection makes me willing to
fuppreffe a great number of errors. Onely thus-much
I thinke

I thinke good to fay, that the fame words in my Ladie *Philoclea* mouth, as from one woman to another (fo as there were no other bodie by) might haue had a better grace; and perchance haue found a gentler receipt.

Bafilius (whofe fenfes by Defire were held open, and conceipt was by Loue quickned) heard fcarcely halfe her anfwere out, but that (as if fpeedie flight might faue his life) he turned away, and ran with all the fpeede his bodie would fuffer him, towardes his daughter *Philoclea*: whom he found at that time duetifully watching by her mother, and *Mifo* curiouflie watching her; hauing left *Mopfa* to doo the like feruice to *Pamela*. *Bafilius* foorthwith calling *Philoclea* afide, (with all the coniuring words which Defire could endite, and authoritie vtter) befought her fhe would preferue his life, in whô her life was begonne; fhe would faue his graye haires from rebuke, and his aged mind from defpaire; that if fhe were not cloyed with his companie, and that fhe thought not the earth ouer-burdened with him, fhe would coole his fierie griefe, which was to be done but by her breath. That in fine, whatfoeuer he was, he was nothing but what it pleafed *Zelmane*; all the powers of his fpirite depending of her : that if fhe continued cruell, he could no more fuftaine his life, then the earth remaine fruitefull in the Sunnes continuall abfence. He concluded, fhe fhould in one payment requite all his deferts : and that fhe needed not difdaine any feruice (though neuer fo meane) which was warranted by the facred name of a father. *Philoclea* more glad then euer fhe had knowen her felfe, that fhe might by this occafion, enioy the priuate conference of *Zelmane*, yet

had

had so sweete a feeling of vertue in her minde, that she would not suffer a vile colour to be cast ouer her faire thoughts; but with humble grace answered her father: That there needed nether promise nor perswasion to her, to make her doo her vttermost for her fathers seruice. That for *Zelmanes* fauour, she would in all vertuous sort seeke it towards him: and that as she woulde not pearce further into his meaning, then himselfe should declare, so would she interprete all his doinges to be accomplished in goodnes: and therfore desired, (if otherwise it were) that he woulde not imparte it to her, who then should be forced to beginne (by true obedience) a shew of disobedience: rather perfourming his generall commandement, which had euer beene, to embrace vertue, then any new particular, sprong out of passion, and contrarie to the former. *Basilius* content to take that, since he could haue no more (thinking it a great point, if by her meanes, he could get but a more free accesse vnto *Zelmane*) allowed her reasons, & took her proffer thākfully, desiring onely a speedy returne of comfort. *Philoclea* was parting, and *Miso* streight behind her, like *Alecto* following *Proserpina*. But *Basilius* forced her to stay, though with much a doo, she being sharp-set vpon the fulfilling of a shrewde office, in ouer-looking *Philoclea:* and so said to *Basilius*, that she did as she was comanded, and could not answere it to *Gynecia*, if she were any whitte from *Philoclea:* telling him true, that he did euill to take her charge from her. But *Basilius*, (swearing he would put out her eyes, if she stird a foote to trouble his daughter) gaue her a stoppe for that while.

CHAP.

CHAP. 17.

¹ Zelmanes *teares*, ² *and tearefull dittie.* ³ Philoclea *enters conference with her.* ⁴ *She ſhues, and ſhewes her ſelfe Prince* Pyrocles. ⁵ Philoclea *feares much, but loues more.* ⁶ *Their conclusion,* ⁷ *with reentrie to their intermitted hiſtoriologie.*

 O away departed *Philoclea*, with a new field of fancies for her trauayling mind. For well ſhe ſawe, her father was growen her aduerſe partie, and yet her fortune ſuch, as ſhe muſt fauour her Riuall; and the fortune of that fortune ſuch, as neither that did hurt her, nor any contrarie meane helpe her.

But ſhe walkt but a little on, before ſhe ſaw *Zelmane* lying vpon a banke, with her face ſo bent ouer *Ladon*, that (her teares falling into the water) one might haue thought, that ſhe began meltingly to be metamorphoſed to the vnder-running riuer. But by and by, with ſpeech ſhe made knowen, as well that ſhe liued, as that ſhe ſorrowed. Faire ſtreames (ſaid ſhe) that do vouchſafe in your cleerenes to repreſent vnto me my blubbered face, let the tribute-offer of my teares vnto you, procure your ſtay a while with me, that I may beginne yet at laſt, to finde ſome thing that pities me : and that all thinges of comfort and pleaſure doo not flie away from me. But if the violence of your ſpring commaund you to haſte away, to pay your dueties to your great prince, the Sea, yet carrie with you theſe fewe wordes, and let the yttermoſt ends of the world know them. A

Loue

Loue more cleer then your selues, dedicated to a Loue
(I feare) more cold then your selues, with the cleerenes
layes a night of sorow vpon me; and with the coldenes
enflames a worlde of fire within me. With that she
tooke a willowe stick, and wrote in a sandie banke these
fewe verses.

2

O*Ver these brooke. trusting to ease mine eyes,*
(Mine eyes euen great in labour with their teares)
I layde my face; my face wherein there lyes
Clusters of clowdes, which no Sunne euer cleares.
  In watry glasse my watrie eyes I see:
  Sorrowes ill easde, where sorrowes painted be.

My thoughts imprisonde in my secreat woes,
With flamie breathes doo issue oft in sound:
The sound to this strange aier no sooner goes,
But that it dooth with Echoes *force rebound.*
  And make me heare the plaints I would refraine:
  Thus outward helps my inward griefes maintaine.

Now in this sande I would discharge my minde,
And cast from me part of my burdnous cares:
But in the sand my tales foretolde I finde,
And see therein how well the writer fares.
  Since streame, aier, sand, mine eyes and eares conspire:
  What hope to quench, where each thing blowes the fire?

3

And assoon as she had written them (a new swarme
of thoughts stinging her mind) she was ready with her
foot to giue the new-borne letters both death and buriall. But *Philoclea* (to whom delight of hearing and seeing

ing was before a ftay from interrupting her) gaue her
felf to be feen vnto her, with fuch a lightning of Beauty
vpō *Zelmane*, that nether fhe could looke on, nor would
looke of. At laft *Philoclea* (hauing a little mufed how
to cut the threede euen, betweene her owne hopeleffe
affection, and her fathers vnbridled hope) with eyes,
cheekes, and lippes, (whereof each fange their parte, to
make vp the harmonie of bafhfulneffe) began to fay,
My Father to whom I owe my felf, & therefore, When
Zelmane (making a womanifh habite to be the Armour
of her boldneffe, giuing vp her life to the lippes of *Philoclea*, and taking it againe by the fweeteneffe of thofe
kiffes) humbly befought her to keepe her fpeach for a
while within the Paradife of her minde. For well fhe
knew herf athers errād, who fhould foon receiue a fufficient anfwere. But now fhe demaunded leaue not
to loofe this long fought-for commoditie of time, to
cafe her harte thus farre, that if in her agonies her deftinie was to be condemned by *Philocleas* mouth, at
left *Philoclea* might know, whom fhe had condemned.
Philoclea eafily yeelded to graunt her owne defire: and
fo making the greene banke the fituation, and the riuer the profpect of the moft beautiful buildings of Nature, *Zelmane* doubting how to beginne, though her
thoughts already had runne to the ende, with a minde
fearing the vnworthineffe of euery worde that fhould
be prefented to her eares, at length brought it forth in
this manner.

Moft beloued Ladie, the incomparable excellen- 4
cies of your felfe, (waited-on by the greatneffe of your
eftate) and the importaunce of the thing (whereon
my life confifteth) doth require both many ceremo-

nies before the beginning, and many circumſtaunces in the vttering my ſpeech, both bolde, and fearefull. But the ſmall opportunitie of enuious occaſion (by the malicious eie hateful Loue doth caſt vpon me) and the extreme bent of my affection (which will eyther breake out in wordes, or breake my harte) compell me, not onely to embrace the ſmalleſt time, but to paſſe by reſpects due vnto you, in reſpect of your poore caitifes life, who is now, or neuer to be preſerued. I doo therefore vowe vnto you, hereafter neuer more to omit all dutifull forme: doo you onely now vouchſafe to heare the matter of a minde moſt perplexed. If euer the ſound of Loue haue come to your eares, or if euer you haue vnderſtood, what force it hath had to conquere the ſtrongeſt hartes, and change the moſt ſetled eſtates: receiue here an example of thoſe ſtraunge Tragedies; one, that in him ſelfe conteineth the particularities of all thoſe misfortunes: and from hencefoorth beleeue that ſuch a thing may be, ſince you ſhall ſee it is. You ſhall ſee (I ſay) a liuing image, and a preſent ſtorie of what Loue can doo, when he is bent to ruine.

But alas, whether goeſt thou my tongue? or how doth my harte conſent to aduenture the reuealing his neereſt touching ſecrete? But peace Feare, thou commeſt too late, when already the harme is taken. Therefore I ſay againe, O onely Princeſſe, attend here a miſerable miracle of affection. Behold here before your eyes *Pyrocles*, Prince of *Macedon*, whome you onely haue brought to this game of Fortune, and vnuſed *Metamorphoſis*: whome you onely haue made neglect his countrie, forget his Father, and laſtly, forſake

to

'o be *Pyrocles* : the fame *Pyrocles*,who (you heard) was betrayed by being put in a fhip , which being burned, *Pyrocles* was drowned. O moft true prefage : for thefe traytors , my eyes , putting me in a fhippe of Defire, which dayly burneth,thofe eyes(I fay)which betraied me , will neuer leaue till they haue drowned me. But be not,be not,(moft excellent Lady) you that Nature hath made to be the Load-ftarre of comfort, be not the Rocke of fhipwracke : you whome vertue hath made the Princeffe of felicitie , be not the minifter of ruine : you, whom my choyfe hath made the Goddeffe of my fafetie, O let not,let not,from you be powred vpon me deftruction. Your faire face hath manie tokens in it of amazement at my wordes : thinke then what his amazement is,from whence they come:fince no wordes can carry with them the life of the inward feeling.I defire;that my defire may be waied in the ballances of Honour,and let Vertue hold them.For if the higheft Loue in no bafe perfon may afpire to grace, then may I hope your beautie will not be without pittie . If otherwife you be (alas but let it neuer be fo) refolued, yet fhall not my death be comfortles,receiuing it by your fentence.

The ioy which wrought into *Pygmalions* mind, while he found his beloued image was fofter, & warmer in his folded armes , till at length it accopplifhed his gladnes with a perfect womans fhape (ftill beautified with the former perfections) was euen fuch, as by each degree of *Zelmanes* wordes creepingly entred into *Philoclea* : till her pleafure was fully made vp with the manifefting of his being; which was fuch as in hope did ouer-come Hope. Yet Doubt would faine haue playd

Aa 2   his

his parte in her minde, and cald in queſtion, how ſhe
ſhould be aſſured that *Zelmane* was *Pyrocles*. But Loue
ſtreight ſtood vp & depoſed, that a lie could not come
from the mouth of *Zelmane*. Beſides, a certain ſparke of
honour, which roſe in her well-diſpoſed minde, made
her feare to be alone with him, with whom alone ſhe
deſired to be (with all the other côtradictions growing
in thoſe minds, which nether abſolutly clime the rocke
of Vertue, nor freely ſinke into the ſea of Vanitie) but
that ſparke ſoone gaue place, or at left gaue no more
light in her mind, then a câdle doth in the Sunnes preſence. But euen ſicke with a ſurfet of ioy, and fearefull
of ſhe knewe not what (as he that newly findes huge
treaſures, doubtes whether he ſleepe or no; or like a
fearfull Deere, which then lookes moſt about, when
he comes to the beſt feede) with a ſhrugging kinde of
tremor through all her principall partes, ſhe gaue theſe
affectionate wordes for anſwere. Alas, how painefull
a thing it is to a deuided minde to make a wel-ioyned
anſwere? how harde it is to bring inwarde ſhame to
outward confeſſion? and what handſomnes trow you
can be obſerued in that ſpeeche, which is made one
knowes not to whom? Shall I ſay ô *Zelmane?* Alas your
wordes be againſt it. Shall I ſay Prince *Pyrocles?* wretch
that I am, your ſhew is manifeſt againſt it. But this, this
I may well ſay; If I had continued as I ought, *Philoclea,*
you had either neuer bene, or euer bene *Zelmane:* you
had either neuer attempted this change, ſet on with
hope, or neuer diſcouered it, ſtopt with deſpaire. But I
feare me, my behauiour ill gouerncd, gaue you the firſt
comfort: I feare me, my affection ill Hid, hath giué you
this laſt aſſurance: I feare indeed, the weakeneſſe of my
gouern-

gouernment before, made you thinke such a maske would be gratefull vnto me : & my weaker gouernmēt since, makes you to pull of the visar . What shall I doo then? shal I seeke far fetched inuentions? shall I labour to lay marble coulours ouer my ruinous thoughts? or rather, though the purenes of my virgin-minde be stained, let me keepe the true simplicitie of my word. True it is, alas, too true it is, ô *Zelmane* (for so I loue to call thee, since in that name my loue first began, and in the shade of that name my loue shall best lie hidden,) that euen while so thou wert, (what eye bewitched me I know not) my passions were fitter to desire, then to be desired. Shall I say then, I am sory, or that my loue must be turned to hate, since thou art turned to *Pyrocles?* how may that wel be, since when thou wert *Zelmane*, the despaire thou mightest not be thus, did most torment me. Thou hast then the victorie : vse it with vertue . Thy vertue wan me ; with vertue preserue me . Doost thou loue me? keepe me then still worthy to be belouec

Then held she her tongue, and cast downe a self-ac- **6** cusing looke, finding, that in her selfe she had (as it were) shot out of the bow of her affectió, a more quick opening of her minde, then she minded to haue done. But *Pyrocles* so caried vp with ioy, that he did not enuy the Gods felicitie, presented her with some iewels of right princely value, as some litle tokens of his loue, & qualitie: and withall shewed her letters from his father King *Euarchus*, vnto him, which euen in the Sea had amongst his iewels bene preserued . But little needed those proofes to one, who would haue fallen out with her selfe, rather then make any contrarie coniectures to *Zelmanes* speeches; so that with such imbracements, as it seemed their soules desired to meete, and their harts to kisse, as their mouthes did : which faine *Pyrocles* would haue sealed with the chiefe armes of his desire, but *Philoclea* commaunded the contrary; and yet they passed the promise of mariage.

7   And then at *Philocleas* entreaty, who was willing to purloine all occasions of remayning with *Zelmane*, she tolde her the storie of her life, from the time of their departing from *Erona*, for the rest she had already vnderstood of her sister. For (saide she) I haue vnderstood, how you first in the companie of your Noble cousin *Musidorus* parted from *Thessalia*, and of diuers aduentures, which with no more daunger then glory you passed through, till your comming to the succour of the Queene *Erona*; and the ende of that warre (you might perceiue by my selfe) I had vnderstood of the Prince *Plangus*. But what since was the course of your doings, vntill you came, after so many victories, to make a conquest of poore me, that I know not, the fame thereof hauing rather shewed it by pieces; then deliuered any full forme of it. Therefore, deere *Pyrocles* (for what can mine eares be so sweetly fed with as to heare you of you) be liberall vnto me of those things which haue made you indeede pretious to the worlde, and now doubt not to tell of your perils; for since I haue you here out of them, euen the remembraunce of them is pleasaunt. *Pyrocles* easily perceiued she was content with kindnesse, to put of occasion of further kindnesse; wherein Loue shewed himselfe a cowardly boy, that durst not attempt for feare of offending. But rather Loue prooued him selfe valiant, that durst with the sworde of reuerent dutie gaine-stand the force

force of so many enraged desires. But so it was, that though he knewe this discourse was to entertaine him from a more streight parley, yet he durst not but kisse his rod, and gladly make much of the entertainement which she allotted vnto him : and therefore with a desirous sigh chastning his brest for too much desiring, Sweete Princesse of my life (said he) what Trophees, what Triumph, what Monuments, what Histories may euer make my fame yeeld so sweete a Musicke to my eares, as that it pleaseth you to lend your minde to the knowledge of any thing touching *Pyrocles*, onely therefore of value, because he is your *Pyrocles?* And therefore grow I now so proud, as to thinke it worth the hearing, since you vouchsafe to giue it hearing. Therefore (onely height of my hope) vouchsafe to know, that after the death of *Tiridates*, and setling *Eroma* in her gouernement; for setled we left her, howsoeuer since (as I perceiued by your speech the last day) the vngrateful treason of her ill-chosen husband ouerthrew her (a thing in trueth neuer till this time by me either heard, or suspected) for who could thinke without hauing such a minde as *Antiphilus*, that so great a beautie as *Eronas* (indeed excellent) could not haue held his affection? so great goodnes could not haue bound gratefulnesse? and so high aduancement could not haue satisfied his ambition? But therefore true it is, that wickednesse may well be compared to a bottomlesse pit, into which it is farre easier to keepe ones selfe from falling, then being fallen, to giue ones selfe any stay from falling infinitely. But for my Cosen, and me, vpon this cause we parted from *Erona*.

Aa 4 CHAP.

CHAP. 18.

¹Anaxius-*his ſurcuidrie*; ²*and challenge to* Pyrocles, *accepted.* ³ *The execution of Ladies done on a Light-of-loue.* ⁴ Pyrocles-*his intercesſion in the cauſe.* ⁵ *The lewd parts of that light lecher.* ⁶ *His ſcoffing excuſes.* ⁷Didos *reuenge on him ſtopped,* ⁸ *and his reuenge on her ſtayed by* Pyrocles.

Vardes (the braue & mighty Prince, whom it was my fortune to kill in the cōbat for *Erona*) had three Nephewes, ſonnes to a ſiſter of his; all three ſet among the foremoſt racks of Fame for great minds to attēpt, and great force to perfourme what they did attempt; eſpecially the eldeſt, by name *Anaxius*; to whom al men would willingly haue yeelded the height of praiſe, but that his nature was ſuch, as to beſtow it vpon himſelfe, before any could giue it. For of ſo vnſupportable a pride he was, that where his deede might well ſtirre enuie, his demeanor did rather breed diſdain. And if it be true that the *Gyants* euer made war againſt heauen, he had bene a fit enſigne-bearer for that company. For nothing ſeemed hard to him, though impoſſible; and nothing vniuſt, while his liking was his iuſtice. Now he in theſe wars had flatly refuſed his aid; becauſe he could not brooke, that the worthy Prince *Pligus* was by his coſen *Tiridates* preferred before him. For allowing no other weights, but the ſword & ſpeare in iudging of deſert, how much he eſteemed himſelfe

before

before *Plangus* in that, fo much would he haue had his allowance in his feruice.

But now that he vnderftood that his vncle was flaine by me, I thinke rather fcorne that any fhould kil his vncle, then any kindneffe (an vn-vfed gueft to an arrogant foule) made him feeke his reuenge; I muft confeffe in manner gallant enough. For he fent a challenge to me to meete him at a place appointed, in the confines of the kingdome of *Lycia*; where he would proue vpon me, that I had by fome trecherie ouercome his vncle, whom els many hundreds fuch as I, could not haue withftood. Youth & fucceffe made me willing enough to accept any fuch bargaine; efpecially, becaufe I had heard that your cofen *Amphialus* (who for fome yeares hath vniuerfally borne the name of the beft Knight in the world) had diuers times fought with him, & neuer bene able to mafter him; but fo had left him, that euery man thought *Anaxius* in that one vertue of curtefie far fhort of him, in al other his match; *Anaxius* ftil deeming himfelfe for his fuperiour. Therefore to him I would goe, and I would needs goe alone, becaufe fo I vnderftood for certaine, he was; and (I muft confeffe) defirous to do fomething without the company of the incomparable Prince *Mufidorus*, becaufe in my hart I acknowledge that I owed more to his prefence, then to any thing in my felf, whatfoeuer before I had done. For of him indeed (as of any worldly caufe) I muft grant, as receiued, whateuer there is, or may be good in me. He taught me by word, and beft by example, giuing me in him fo liuely an Image of vertue, as ignorance could not caft fuch mift ouer mine eyes, as not to fee, and to loue it, and all with fuch deare friendfhip and care, as (3 heauens)

heauens)how cã my life euer requite vnto him? which
made me indeed fina in my selfe such a kind of depending vpon him, as without him I found a weakenesse,
and a mistrustfulnes of my selfe,as one strayed from his
best strength,when at any time I mist him. Which humour perceiuing to ouer-rule me,I straue against it;not
that I was vnwilling to depend vpon him in iudgemẽt,
but by weakenesse I would not; which though it held
me to him, made me vnworthy of him. Therfore I desired his leaue, and obtained it : such confidence he
had in me, preferring my reputation before his owne
tendernesse; and so priuately went from him, he determining (as after I knew) in secreat maner,not to be far
from the place, where we appointed to meete, to preuent any foule play that might be offered vnto me.Full
loth was *Erona* to let vs depart from her, (as it were)
foreseeling the harmes which after fell to her. But I,
(ridde fully from those combers of kindnesse,and halfe
a dayes iourney in my way toward *Anaxius*) met an
aduenture, (though in it selfe of small importance) I
will tell you at large, because by the occasion thereof I
was brought to as great comber and danger, as lightly
any might escape.

3   As I past through a Laund (ech side whereof was so
bordred both with high tymber trees, and copses of
farre more humble growth, that it might easily bring a
solitarie minde to looke for no other companions then
the wild burgesses of the forrest) I heard certaine cries,
which comming by pawses to mine eares from within
the wood of the right hand, made me well assured by
the greatnesse of the crie, it was the voice of a man,
though it were a verie vnmanlike voice, so to crie. But
making

making mine eare my guide, I left not many trees behind me, before I faw at the bottome of one of them
a gentle-man bound (with many garters) hand & foot,
fo as well he might tomble and toffe, but neither runne
nor refift he could. Vpō him (like fo many Eagles vpon
an Oxe) were nine Gentle-women; truely fuch, as one
might well enough fay, they were hanfome. Each of
them helde bodkins in their handes, wherewith they
continually pricked him, hauing bene before-hand
vnarmed of any defence from the waft vpward, but
onely of his fhirte : fo as the poore man wept and
bled, cryed and prayed, while they fported themfelues
in his paine, and delighted in his prayers, as the arguments of their victorie.

I was moued to compaffion, and fo much the more ₄
that he ftraight cald to me for fuccour, defiring me at
left to kill him, to deliuer him from thofe tormenters.
But before my-felf could refolue, much leffe any other
tell what I would refolue, there came in cholericke haft
towards me about feuē or eight knights; the foremoft
of which willed me to get me away, and not to trouble
the Ladies, while they were taking their due reuenge,
but with fo ouer-maftring a maner of pride, as truly my
hart could not brooke it: & therfore (anfwering them,
that how I would haue defended him from the Ladies
I knew not, but from them I would) I began a combate
firft with him particularly, and after his death with the
others (that had leffe good maners) ioyntly. But fuch
was the end of it, that I kept the fielde with the death
of fome, and flight of others. In fo much as the women
(afraid, what angrie victorie would bring forth) ranne
away; fauing onely one; who was fo flefht in malice,
that

that neither during, nor after the fight, she gaue any truce to her crueltie, but still vsed the little instrument of her great spight, to the well-witnest paine of the impatient patient: and was now about to put out his eies, which all this while were spared, becaufe they should do him the difcomfort of feeing who preuailed ouer him. When I came in, and after much ado, brought her to fome conference, (for fome time it was before she would harken, more before she would speake; & most, before she would in her speech leaue off that remembrance of her bodkin) but at length whē I puld off my head-peece, and humbly entreated her pardon, or knowledge why she was cruell; out of breath more with choller(which increafed in his owne exercife)thē with the paine she tooke, much to this purpofe she gaue her griefe vnto my knowledge. Gentleman (faid she) much it is againſt my will to forbeare any time the executing of my iuſt reuēge vpon this naughtie creature, a man in nothing, but in deceauing women; But becaufe I fee you are young, and like enough to haue the power(if you would haue the mind)to do much more mifchiefe, then he, I am content vpon this bad fubiect to reade a lecture to your vertue.

5　This man called *Pamphilus*, in birth I muſt confeſſe is noble(but what is that to him, if it shalbe a ſtaine to his deade aunceſtors to haue left fuch an offpring?) in shape as you fee not vncomely (indeed the fit maſke of his difguifed falfhood) in conuerfation wittily pleafant, and pleafantly gamefome; his eyes full of meric fimplicitie, his words of hartie companableneſſe; and fuch a one, whofe head one would not think fo ſtayed, as to thinke mifchieuoufly: delighted in al fuch things,

which

which by imparting their delight to others, makes the
vſer therof welcome;as,Muſicke, Daunſing, Hunting,
Feaſting,Riding,& ſuch like. And to conclude, ſuch a
one;as who can keepe him at armes ende, neede neuer
wiſh a better cõpaniõ.But vnder theſe qualities lies ſuch
a poyſonous addar as I will tell you. For by thoſe gifts
of Nature and Fortune (being in all places acceptable)
he creepes, nay (to ſay truely) he flies ſo into the fauour
of poore ſillie women,that I would be too much aſhamed to confeſſe, if I had not reuenge in my hande, as
well as ſhame in my cheekes.For his hart being wholy
delighted in deceiuing vs, we could neuer be warned,
but rather, one bird caught, ſerued for a ſtale to bring
in more. For the more he gat,the more ſtill he ſhewed,
that he (as it were) gaue away to his nẽw miſtreſſe,whẽ
he betrayed his promiſes to the former. The cunning
of his flatterie,the readines of his teares,the infinitenes
of his vowes,were but among the weakeſt threedes of
his nette.But the ſtirring our owne paſſions,and by the
entrance of them,to make himſelfe Lord of our forces;
there lay his Maſters part of cunning, making vs now
iealous,now enuious,now proud of what we had, deſirous of more;now giuing one the triumph,to ſee him
that was Prince of many, Subiect to her; now with an
eſtranged looke, making her feare the loſſe of that
minde, which indeede could neuer be had:neuer ceaſing humblenes and diligence, till he had imbarked vs
in ſome ſuch diſaduantage,as we could not return dry-
ſhod; and then ſuddenly a tyrant, but a craftie tyrant.
For ſo would he vſe his imperiouſnes, that we had a
delightfull feare, and an awe which made vs loath to
loſe our hope. And, which is ſtrangeſt (when ſometimes

times with late repentance I thinke of it) I muſt confeſſe, euen in the greateſt tempeſt of my iudgemẽt was
I neuer driuen to think him excellent,and yet ſo could
ſet my minde,both to gette and keepe him, as though
herein had laien my felicitie : like them I haue ſeene
play at the ball, growe extremely earneſt, who ſhoulde
haue the ball, and yet euery one knew it was but a ball.
But in the end,the bitter ſauce of the ſport was,that we
had ether our hartes broken with ſorrow,or our eſtates
ſpoyled with being at his direction,or our honours for
euer loſt, partly by our owne faults, but principally by
his faultie vſing of our faults. For neuer was there man
that could with more ſcornefull eyes beholde her, at
whoſe feete he had lately laine, nor with a more vnmanlike brauerie vſe his tongue to her diſgrace, which
lately had ſong Sonets of her praiſes : being ſo naturally inconſtant, as I maruell his ſoule findes not ſome
way to kill his bodie, whereto it had beene ſo long v-
nited. For ſo hath he dealt with vs (vnhappie fooles,)
as we could neuer tell, whether he made greater haſte
after he once liked, to enioy, or after he once enioyed, to forſake. But making a glorie of his own ſhame,
it delighted him to be challenged of vnkindneſſe : it
was a triumph vnto him to haue his mercie called for:
and he thought the freſh colours of his beautie were
painted in nothing ſo well, as in the ruines of his Louers : yet ſo farre had we engaged our ſelues, (vnfortunate ſoules) that we liſted not complaine, ſince our
complaintes could not but carrie the greateſt accuſation to our ſelues. But euerie of vs(each for her ſelfe,)
laboured all meanes how to recouer him, while he
rather daily ſent vs companions of our deceipt, then
euer

euer returned in any found and faithfull manner. Till
at length he concluded all his wronges with betro-
thing himfelfe to one (I muſt confeſſe) worthie to be
liked, if any worthineſſe might excuſe ſo vnworthie a
changeableneſſe ; leauing vs nothing but remorſe for
what was paſt, and deſpaire of what might followe.
Then indeede, the common iniurie made vs all ioyne
in friendſhippe, who till that time, had employed our
endeuours one againſt the other. For, we thought
nothing was a more condemning of vs, then the iu-
ſtifying of his loue to her by mariage : then Deſpaire
made Feare valiant, and Reuenge gaue Shame countenance : whereupon, we (that you ſaw here) deuiſed
how to get him among vs alone: which he (ſuſpecting
no ſuch matter of them, whom he had by often abuſes
he thought made tame to be ſtill abuſed) eaſilie gaue
vs opportunitie to doo.

　　And a man may ſee, euen in this, how ſoone Ru- **6**
lers growe proude, and in their pride fooliſh. : he came
with ſuch an authoritie among vs, as if the Planets had
done inough for vs, that by vs once he had beene delighted. And when we began in courteous manner,
one after the other, to lay his vnkindneſſe vnto him,
he ſeeing himſelfe confronted by ſo many (like a reſolute Orator,) went not to deniall, but to iuſtifie his
cruell falſhoode, and all with ſuch ieſtes, and diſdainfull paſſages, that if the iniurie could not be made greater, yet were our conceiptes made the apter to appre-
hende it.

　　Among other of his anſweres (forſooth) I ſhall neuer forgette, how he woulde prooue it was no in-
conſtancie to chaunge from one Loue to an other,
　　　　　　　　　　　　　　　　　　　　　but

but a great conftancie; and contrarie, that which we call conftancie, to be moft changeable. For (faid he) I euer loued my Delight., & delighted alwayes in what was Louely : and where-foeuer I founde occafion to obtaine that, I conftantly folowed it. But thefe conftant fooles you fpeak of, though their Miftres grow by ficknes foule, or by fortune miferable, yet ftil will loue her, and fo committe the abfurdeft inconftancie that may be, in changing their loue from fairenes to fouleneffe, and from louelines to his contrarie; like one not content to leaue a friend, but will ftreight giue ouer himfelf to his mortall enemie : where I (whom you call inconftant) am euer conftant, to Beautie, in others; and Delight in my felf. And fo in this iollie fcoffing brauerie he went ouer vs all, faying, He left one, becaufe fhe was ouer-waiwarde; another, becaufe fhe was too foone woon; a third., becaufe fhe was not merie inough; a fourth, becaufe fhe was ouer-gamefome; the fifth, becaufe fhe was growen with griefe fubiect to fickneffe; the fixt, becaufe fhe was fo foolifh, as to be ielous of him; the feuenth, becaufe fhe had refufed to carie a letter for him, to another that he loued; the eight, becaufe fhe was not fecrete; the ninth, becaufe fhe was not liberall : but to me, who am named *Dido*, (and indeede haue mette with a falfe *Æneas*) to me, I fay, (ô the vngratefull villaine) he could finde no other fault to obiect, but that (perdie) he met with many fayrer.

7   But when he had thus plaide the careleffe Prince, we (hauing thofe feruants of ours in readines, whom you lately fo manfully ouercame) laide holde of him; beginning at firft but that trifling reuenge, in which you found vs bufie; but meaning afterwarwardes to

haue

haue mangled him fo,as fhould haue loft his credit for
euer abufing more. But as you haue made my fellowes
flie away,fo for my part the greatneffe of his wrong o-
uerfhadowes in my iudgement the greatneffe of any
daunger.For was it not inough for him,to haue deceiued me, & through the deceipt abufed me, & after the
abufe forfaken me,but that he muft now,of al the company,& before all the company lay want of beautie to
my charge? Many fairer? I trow euē in your iudgemēt,
Sir,(if your eies do not beguile me)not many fairer; &
now (whofoeuer faies the cōtrary)there are not many fairer. And of whom fhould I receiue this reproch,
but of him, who hath beft caufe to know there are not
many fairer? And therefore how foeuer my fellowes
pardon his iniuries,for my parte I will euer remember,
& remember to reuenge this fcorne of al fcornes.With
that fhe to him afrefh; & furely would haue put out his
eies (who lay muet for fhame, if he did not fometimes
crie for feare)if I had not lept from my horfe, & mingling force with intreaty,ftaied her furie.

But,while I was perfwading her to meekenes,comes **8**
a number of his friends, to whom he forthwith cried,
that they fhould kill that womā, that had thus betraied
and difgraced him. But then I was faine to forfake the
enfigne,vnder which I had before ferued,and to fpend
my vttermoft force in the protecting of the Ladie;
which fo well preuailed for her, that in the ende there
was a faithfull peace promifed of all fides.And fo I leauing her in a place of fecuritie (as fhe thought) went
on my iourney towards *Anaxius,*for whom I was faine
to ftay two daies in the apointed place, he difdaining
to waite for me,till he was fure I were there.

Bb   CHAP.

CHAP. 19.

The monomachie betweene Anaxius *and* Pyrocles; * *ad-iourned by* Pyrocles *to reſuccour* Dido. ² *The courſe of* Dido *daunger.* ⁴ *The miſerableneſſe of her father.* ⁵ *His carliſh entertainement to* Pyrocles; ⁶ *and his treaſon a-gainſt him.* ⁷ Pyrocles *hard beſtead.* ⁸ *ſuccoured by* Mu-ſidorus : ⁹ *both ſaued by the King of* Iberia. ¹⁰ *The exe-cution of the traitors, and death of* Dido.

I

Did patientlie abide his angrie pleaſure, till about that ſpace of time he came (indeede, according to promiſe) alone : and (that I may not ſay too little, becauſe he is wont to ſay too much) like a man whoſe courage was apt to clime o-uer any daunger. And aſſoone as euer he came neere me, in fit diſtaunce for his purpoſe, he with much fury, (but with fury skilfully guided) ran vpon me; which I (in the beſt ſort I could) reſiſted, ha-uing kept my ſelfe ready for him, becauſe I had vnder-ſtood, that he obſerued but few complements in mat-ters of armes, but ſuch as a proud anger did indite vnto him. And ſo putting our horſes into a full careere, we hit ech other vpon the head with our Launces: I think he felte my blowe; for my parte (I muſt confeſſe) I ne-uer receiued the like : but I thinke though my ſenſes were aſtoniſhed, my minde forced them to quicken themſelues, becauſe I had learned of him, how little fa-uour he is woont to ſhow in any matter of aduantage

And

And indeede he was turned, and comming vpon me
with his fworde drawne, both our ftaues hauing bene
broken at that encounter. But I was fo ready to anfwere him, that truely I know not who gaue the firft
blowe. But whofoeuer gaue the firft, it was quickly fe-
conded by the fecond. And indeed (excellenteft Ladie) I muft fay truely, for a time it was well fought betweene vs; he vndoubtedly being of fingular valour,
(I would to God, it were not abafed by his too much
loftineffe) but as by the occafion of the combate, winning and loofing ground, we chaunged places, his
horfe happened to come vpon the point of the broken fpeare, which fallen to the ground chaunced to
ftand vpward; fo as it lighting vpon his hart, the horfe
died. He driuen to difmount, threatned, if I did not
the like, to doo as much for my horfe, as Fortune had
done for his. But whether for that, or becaufe I would
not be beholding to Fortune for any part of the victorie, I defcended.

So began our foote-fight in fuch fort, that we were
well entred to bloud of both fides, when there comes
by, that vnconftant *Pamphilus*, whom I had deliuered
(eafie to be knowne, for he was bare faced) with a dofen armed men after him; but before him he had *Dido*
(that Ladie, who had moft fharpely punifhed him)
riding vpon a palfrey, he following her with moft vnmanlike crueltie; beating her with wandes he had in
his hande, fhe crying for fenfe of payne, or hope of
fuccour: which was fo pittifull a fight vnto me, that
it mooued me to require *Anaxius* to deferre our
combate, till an other day, and now to perfourme the
duties of Knighthood in helping this diftreffed Ladie.

But he that disdaines to obey any thing but his paffion (which he cals his mind) bad me leaue of that thought, but when he had killed me, he would then (perhaps) go to her fuccour. But I well finding the fight would belong betweene vs (longing in my hart to deliuer the poore *Dido*) giuing him fo great a blowe, as fomewhat ftaied him, (to terme it a right) I flatly ran away from him toward my horfe, who trotting after the côpanie, in mine armour I was put to fome paine, but that vfe made me nimble vnto it. But as I followed my horfe, *Anaxius* followed me: but his prowde harte did fo difdaine that exercife, that I had quickly ouer-run him, & ouer-taken my horfe; being (I muft côfeffe) afhamed to fee a number of country folks, who happened to paffe thereby, who hallowed & howted after me as at the arranteft coward, that euer fhewed his fhoulders to his enemie. But when I had leapt on my horfe (with fuch fpeedy agility, that they all cried, O fee how feare giues him wings) I turned to *Anaxius*, & aloud promifed him to returne thether again, as foone as I had relieued the iniuried Ladie. But he railing at me, with all the bafe wordes angry contempt could endite; I faid no more, but, *Anaxius*, affure thy felf, I nether feare thy force, nor thy opinion. And fo vfing no weapon of a Knight as at that time, but my fpurres, I ranne in my knowledge after *Pamphilus*, but in al their conceipts from *Anaxius*, which as far as I could heare, I might well heare teftified with fuch laughters and games, that I was fome few times moued to turne backe againe.

3   But the Ladies mifery ouer-balanced my reputation fo that after her I went, & with fix houres hard riding (through fo wild places, as it was rather the cunning of

my

my horſe ſometimes,then of my ſelfe, ſo rightly to hit
the way)I ouergat thē a little before night, neere to an
old il-fauoured caſtle,the place where I perceiued they
meant to perfourme their vnknightly errand.For there
they began to ſtrip her of her clothes, when I came in
among them,& running through the firſt with a lauce,
the iuſtneſſe of the cauſe ſo enhabled me againſt the
reſt (falſharted in their owne wrong doing) that I had,
in as ſhort time almoſt as I had bene fighting with only *Anaxius*, deliuered her from thoſe iniurious wret-
ches:moſt of whom carried newes to the other world
that amongſt men ſecret wronges are not alwaies left
vnpuniſhed.As for *Pamphilus*,he hauing once ſeene,&
(as it ſhould ſeeme) remembred me,euen from the beginning began to be in the rereward, and before they
had left fighting,he was too far of to giue them thanks
for their paines. But when I had deliuered to the Ladie a ful libertie,both in effect,& in opinion,(for ſome
time it was before ſhe could aſſure her ſelfe ſhe was
out of their handes,who had layd ſo vehement apprehenſion of death vpon her) ſhe then tolde me, how as
ſhe was returning toward her fathers, weakely accompanied (as too ſoone truſting to the falſhood of recon-
cilement) *Pamphilus* had ſet vpon her,and killing thoſe
that were with her, carried her ſelfe by ſuch force, and
with ſuch māner as I had ſeene, to this place, where he
meant in cruell and ſhamefull manner to kill her,in the
ſight of her owne Father;to whom he had already ſent
worde of it,that out of his caſtle windowe (for this caſtle, ſhe ſaid, was his) he might haue the proſpect of
his onely childes deſtruction, if my comming , whom
(ſhe ſaid) he feared (as ſoone as he knew me by the

Bb 3 armour)

armour) had not warraunted her from that neere ap-
proching crueltie. I was glad I had done ſo good a
deede for a Gentlewoman not vnhandſome, whome
before I had in like ſorte helped. But the night beginning to perſwade ſome retiring place, the Gentlewoman, euen out of countenaunce before ſhe began her
ſpeach, much after this manner inuited me to lodge
that night with her father.

4   Sir (ſaid ſhe) how much I owe you, can be but a-
baſed by wordes, ſince the life I haue, I holde it now
the ſecond time of you: and therefore neede not offer ſeruice vnto you, but onely to remember you, that
I am your ſeruaunt: and I would, my being ſo, might
any way yeeld any ſmall contentment vnto you. Now
onely I can but deſire you to harbour your ſelfe this
night in this caſtle; becauſe the time requires it; and in
truth this countrie is very daungerous for murthering
theeues, to truſt a ſleeping life among them. And yet I
muſt confeſſe, that as the loue I beare you makes me
thus inuite you, ſo the ſame loue makes me aſhamed to
bring you to a place, where you ſhalbe ſo (not ſpokē by
ceremonie but by truth) miſerably entertained. With
that ſhe tolde me, that though ſhe ſpake of her father
(whom ſhe named *Chremes*) ſhe would hide no truth
from me, which was in ſumme, that as he was of all
that region the man of greateſt poſſeſſions, and riches,
ſo was he either by nature, or an euill receiued opinion, giuen to ſparing, in ſo vnmeaſurable a ſorte, that
he did not onely barre him ſelfe from the delightfull, but almoſt from the neceſſarie vſe thereof; ſcarſely allowing him ſelfe fitte ſuſtenaunce of life, rather
then he would ſpende of thoſe goods, for whoſe ſake

onely

onely he feemed to ioye in life . Which extreame
dealing (defcending from himfelfe vpon her) had driuen her to put her felfe with a great Lady of that countrie, by which occafion fhe had ftumbled vpon fuch
mifchance, as were little for the honour either of her,
or her familie. But fo wife had he fhewed himfelfe
therein, as while he found his daughter maintained
without his coft, he was content to be deafe to any
noife of infamie : which though it had wronged her
much more then fhe deferued, yet fhe could not denie,
but fhe was driuen thereby to receaue more then de-
cent fauours. She concluded, that there at left I fhould
be free from iniuries, & fhould be affured to her-wards
to abound as much in the true caufes of welcomes, as
I fhould want of the effects thereof.

I, who had acquainted my felfe to meafure the de- 5
licacie of foode and reft, by hunger and wearineffe, at
that time well ftored of both, did not abide long entreatie; but went with her to the Caftle: which I found
of good ftrength, hauing a great mote rounde about it;
the worke of a noble Gentleman, of whofe vnthrif-
tie fonne he had bought it. The bridge drawne vp,
where we were faine to crie a good while before we
coulde haue anfweare, and to difpute a good while
before anfweare would bee brought to acceptance.
At length a willingneffe, rather then a ioy to receaue
his daughter, whome hee had lately feene fo neere
death, and an opinion rather brought into his heade
by courfe, becaufe he heard himfelfe called a father; rather then any kindneffe that hee found in his owne
harte, made him take vs in; for my part by that time
growne fo wearie of fuch entertainement, that no

regard

regard of my felfe, but onely the importunitie of his
daughter made me enter. Where I was met with this
Chremes, a driueling old fellow, leane, fhaking both of
head and hands, alredie halfe earth, and yet then moft
greedie of Earth: who fcarcely would giue me thankes
for that I had done, for feare I fuppofe, that thankeful-
neffe might haue an introduction of reward. But with
a hollow voice, giuing me a falfe welcome, I might
perceaue in his eye to his daughter, that it was hard to
fay, whether the difpleafure of her company did not
ouer-way the pleafure of her owne comming. But on
he brought me, into fo bare a houfe, that it was the
picture of miferable happineffe, and rich beggerie (ferued onely by a company of rufticall villaines, full of
fweate and duft, not one of them other, then a labou-
rer) in fumme (as he counted it) profitable drudgerie:
and all preparations both for foode and lodging fuch,
as would make one deteft nigardneffe, it is fo fluttifh a
vice. His talke nothing but of his pouertie, for feare
belike left I fhould haue proued a young borrower. In
fumme, fuch a man, as any enemy could not wifh him
worfe, then to be himfelfe. But there that night bidde
I the burthen of being a tedious gueft to a loathfome
hoft; ouer-hearing him fometimes bitterly warne his
daughter of bringing fuch coftly mates vnder his
roofe: which fhe grieuing at, defired much to know
my name, I thinke partly of kindneffe to remember
who had done fome-thing for her, and partly becaufe
fhe affured her felfe I was fuch a one as would make
euen his mifer-minde contented, with what he had
done. And accordingly fhe demaunded my name, and
eftate, with fuch earneftneffe, that I whom Loue had
n[ot]

not as then so robbed me of my selfe, as to be another then I am, told her directly my name and condition: whereof she was no more gladde then her father, as I might well perceaue by some ill-fauoured cheerefulnesse; which then first began to wrinckle it selfe in his face.

But the causes of their ioyes were farre different, for 6 as the shepheard and the butcher both may looke vpon one sheepe with pleasing conceipts, but the shepheard with minde to profite himselfe by preseruing, the butcher with killing him : So she reioyced to finde that mine owne benefits had tyed me to be her friend, who was a Prince of such greatnesse, and louingly reioyced: but his ioy grew, (as I to my danger after perceiued) by the occasion of the Queene *Artaxias* setting my head to sale, for hauing slaine her brother *Tiridates*; which being the summe of an hundreth thousand crownes (to whosoeuer brought me aliue into her hands) that old wretch, (who had ouer-liued all good nature) though he had lying idly by him much more then that, yet aboue all things louing money, for monies owne sake determined to betray me, so well deseruing of him, for to haue that which he was determined neuer to vse. And so knowing that the next morning I was resolued to go to the place where I had left *Anaxius*, he sent in all speed to a Captaine of a Garrison hard by; which though it belonged to the King of *Iberia*, (yet knowing theCaptaines humor to delight so in riotous spending; as he cared not how he came by the meanes to maintaine it) doubted not, that to be halfe with him in the gaine, he would play his quarters part in the treason. And therefore that night agreeing

of

of the fitteſt places where they might ſurpriſe me in the morning, the old caitiffe was growne ſo ceremonious, as he would needs accompanie me ſome myles in my way; a ſufficient token to me, if Nature had made me apte to ſuſpect; ſince a churles curteſie rathely comes but either for gaine, or falſhood. But I ſuffered him to ſtumble into that point of good manner: to which purpoſe he came out with all his clownes, horſt vpon ſuch cart-iades, and ſo furniſhed, as in good faith I thought with my ſelfe, if that were thrift, I wiſht none of my friends or ſubiectes euer to thriue. As for his daughter (the gentle *Dido*) ſhe would alſo (but in my conſcience with a farre better minde) prolong the time of farewell, as long as he.

7   So we went on togither: he ſo old in wickednes, that he could looke me in the face, and freely talke with me, whoſe life he had alreadie contracted for: till comming into the falling of a way which ledde vs into a place, of each-ſide whereof men might eaſily keepe themſelues vndiſcouered, I was encompaſſed ſodainly by a great troupe of enimies, both of horſe and foote, who willed me to yeelde my ſelfe to the Queene *Artaxia*. But they coulde not haue vſed worſe eloquence to haue perſwaded my yeelding, then that; I knowing the little good will *Artaxia* bare me. And therefore making neceſſitie and iuſtice my beſt ſword and ſhield, I vſed the other weapons I had as well as I could; I am ſure to the little eaſe of a good number, who truſting to their number more then to their valure, and valewing money higher then equitie, felt, that guiltleſneſſe is not alwayes with eaſe oppreſſed. As for *Chremes*, he withdrew himſelfe, yet ſo guilding

his

his wicked conceipts with his hope of gaine, that he was content to be a beholder, how I should be taken to make his pray.

But I was growne so wearie, that I supported my **8** selfe more with anger then strength, when the most excellent *Musidorus* came to my succour; who hauing followed my trace as well as he could, after he had found I had left the fight with *Anaxius*, came to the niggards Castell, where he found all burnd and spoiled by the countrie people, who bare mortall hatred to that couetous man, and now tooke the time, when the castell was left almost without garde, to come in, and leaue monuments of their malice therein: which *Musidorus* not staying either to further, or impeach, came vpon the spurre after me (becaufe with one voice many told him, that if I were in his company, it was for no good meant vnto me) and in this extremitie found me. But when I saw that Cosen of mine, me thought my life was doubled, and where before I thought of a noble death, I now thought of a noble victorie. For who can feare that hath *Musidorus* by him? who, what he did there for me, how many he killed, not straunger for the number, then for the straunge blowes wherwith he sent them to a wel-deserued death, might well delight me to speake off, but I should so holde you too long in euery particular. But in trueth, there if euer, and euer, if euer any man, did *Musidorus* shew himselfe second to none in able valour.

Yet what the vnmeasurable excesse of their num- **9** ber woulde haue done in the ende I knowe not, but the triall thereof was cutte off by the chaunceable

com-

comming thither of the King of *Iberia*, that fame father of that worthy *Plangus*, whom it hath pleafed you fomtimes to mention : who, (not yeelding ouer to old age his country delights, efpecially of hauking) was at that time (following a Merline) brought to fee this iniurie offred vnto vs : and hauing great numbers of Courtiers waiting vpon him, was ftraight known by the fouldiers that affaulted vs, to be their King, and fo moft of them with-drew themfelues.

10   He by his authoritie knowing of the Captaines owne conftrained confeffion, what was the motiue of this mifchieuous practife; miffiking much fuch violéce fhould be offred in his countrie to men of our ranke: but chiefely difdaining it fhould be done in refpect of his Niece, whom (I muft confeffe wrongfully) he hated, becaufe he interpreted that her brother and fhe had maintained his fonne *Plangus* againft him, caufed the Captaines head prefently to be ftriken off, and the old bad *Chremes* to be hanged : though truely for my part, I earneftly laboured for his life, becaufe I had eaten of his bread. But one thing was notable for a conclufion of his miferable life, that neither the death of his daughter, who (alas the poore Gentlewoman) was by chaunce flaine among his clownes, while fhe ouerboldly for her weake fex fought to hold thé from me, nor yet his owne fhamefull ende was fo much in his mouth as he was ledde to execution, as the loffe of his goods, and burning of his houfe : which often, with more laughter then teares of the hearers, he made pittifull exclamations vpon.

CHAP.

CHAP. 20.

¹ *The two Princes paſſage to the* Iberian *Court.* ² Andromanas *omniregencie.* ³ *Her parti-loue to them both.* ⁴ *Her
faire and foule meanes to inueigle them.* ⁵ Palladius *loue
to* Zelmane. ⁶ Zelmanes *loue to* Pyrocles, *and practiſe
with her Louer to releaſe her beloued.*

His iuſtice thus done, and we deliuered, the King indeede in royall
ſorte inuited vs to his Court, not
farre thence: in all points entertaining vs ſo, as truely I muſt euer acknowledge a beholdingneſſe vnto
him: although the ſtreame of it fell
outnot to be ſo ſweet as the ſpring.
For after ſome dayes being there (curing our ſelues of
ſuch wounds as we had receiued, while I, cauſing diligent ſearch to be made of *Anaxius*, could learne nothing, but that he was gone out of the countrie, boa-
ſting in euerie place, how he had made me run away)
we were brought to receiue the fauour of acquaintāce
with this Queene *Andromana*, whom the Princeſſe *Pamela* did in ſo liuely colours deſcribe the laſt day, as ſtill
me-thinkes the figure therof poſſeſſeth mine eyes, confirmed by the knowledge my ſelfe had.

And therefore I ſhall neede the leſſe to make you
know what kinde of woman ſhe was ; but this onely,
that firſt with the rarenes of affection, and after with
the very vſe of directing, ſhe had made her ſelfe ſo abſolute a maiſter of her huſbands minde, that a-while he
would

would not,and after,he could not tell how to gouern, without being gouerned by her: but finding an eaſe in not vnderſtanding, let looſe his thoughtes wholly to pleaſure, entruſting to her the entire conduct of all his royall affaires. A thing that may luckely fall out to him that hath the bleſſing, to match with ſome Heroicall minded Ladie.But in him it was nether guided by wiſdome,nor followed by Fortune,but thereby was ſlipte inſenſibiie into ſuch an eſtate, that he liued at her vndiſcreete diſcretion : all his ſubiectes hauing by ſome yeares learned,ſo to hope for good, and feare of harm, onely frō her,that it ſhould haue neded a ſtronger vertue thē his, to haue vnwound ſo deeply an entred vice. So that either not ſtriuing (becauſe he was contented) or contented (becauſe he would not ſtriue) he ſcarcelie knewe what was done in his owne chamber, but as it pleaſed her Inſtrumentes to frame the relation.

3   Now we being brought knowen vnto her(the time that we ſpent in curing ſome very dangerous wounds) after once we were acquainted, (and acquainted we were ſooner then our ſelues expected)ſhe continuallie almoſt haunted vs,till(and it was not long a doing)we diſcouered a moſt violent bent of affection:and that ſo ſtrangely,that we might well ſee,an euill minde in au-
    " thoritie,dooth not onely folow the ſway of the deſires
    " alreadie within it,but frames to it ſelfe new deſires,not before thought of. For,with equall ardour ſhe affected vs both: and ſo did her greatnes diſdaine ſhamefaſtnes, that ſhe was content to acknowledge it to both . For, (hauing many times torne the vaile of modeſtie)it ſeemed , for a laſte delight, that ſhe delighted in infamy: which often ſhe had vſed to her huſbands ſhame,filling
all

all mens eares (but his)with reproch;while he (hood-
winkt with kindnes)left of al mē knew who ftrake him.
But her firſt degree was,by ſetting foorth her beauties,
(truely in nature not to be miſliked, but as much aduā-
ced to the eye,as abaſed to the iudgemēt by arte)there-
by to bring vs(as willingly-caught fiſhes) to bite at her
baite.And thereto had ſhe that ſcutchion of her deſires
ſupported by certain badly-diligēt miniſters, who oftē
cloyed our eares with her praiſes,& would needs teach
vs a way of felicitie by ſeeking her fauor. But when ſhe
found,that we were as deaf to thē,as dumb to her;then
ſhe liſted no lōger ſtay in the ſuburbs of her fooliſh deſires,but directly entred vpō thē;making her ſelf an impudent ſuter,authorizing her ſelfe very much with making vs ſee that all fauor & power in that realm,ſo'depē-
ded vpon her, that now (being in her hands) we were
ether to keep,or loſe our liberty,at her diſcretiō; which
yet ſhe ſo tēpred,as that we might rather ſuſpect,thē ſhe
threatē . But whē our woūds grew ſo,as that they gaue
vs leaue to trauell , & that ſhe found we were purpoſed
to vſe all meanes we could to depart thence, ſhe (with
more & more importunatnes) craued that, which in all
good maners was ether of vs to be deſired,or not gran-
ted.Truely (moſt faire & euery way excellēt Lady) you
would haue wondred to haue ſeene,how before vs ſhe
would confes the contentiō in her own mind,between
that louely (indeed moſt louely) broūnes of *Muſidorus*
his face,& this colour of mine, which ſhe(in the decei-
uable ſtile of affection) would intitle beautifull : how
her eyes wandered (like a glutton at a feaſt) from the
one to the other; and how her wordes would beginne
halfe of the ſentence to *Muſidorus*,& end the other half

to

to *Pyrocles:* not aſhamed (ſeeing the friendſhippe betweene vs) to deſire either of vs to be a mediator to the
other; as if we ſhould haue played a requeſt at Tennis
betweene vs: and often wiſhing, that ſhe might be the
angle, where the lines of our friendſhippe might meet;
and be the knotte which might tie our hartes together.
Which proceeding of hers I doo the more largely ſet
before you (moſt deare Lady) that by the foyle therof,
you may ſee the noblenes of my deſire to you, & the
warrantablenes of your fauour to me.

4   At that *Philoclea* ſmiled, with a little nod. But (ſaide
Pyrocles) when ſhe perceiued no hope by ſuite to preuaile, then (perſwaded by the rage of affection, and encouraged by daring to doo any thing) ſhe founde
meanes to haue vs accuſed to the King, as though we
went about ſome practiſe to ouerthrowe him in his
owne eſtate. Which, becauſe of the ſtraunge ſucceſſes
we had in the kingdomes of *Phrigia*, *Pontus* & *Galatia*)
ſeemed not vnlikely to him, who (but ſkimming any
thing that came before him) was diſciplined to leaue
the through-handling of all, to his gentle wife : who
foorthwith cauſed vs to be put in priſon, hauing (while
we ſlept) depriued vs of our armour : a priſon, indeede
iniurious, becauſe a priſon, but els well teſtifying affection, becauſe in all reſpectes as commodious, as a priſon might be : and indeede ſo placed, as ſhe might at
all houres, (not ſeene by many, though ſhe cared not
much how many had ſeene her) come vnto vs. Then
fell ſhe to ſauſe her deſires with threatnings, ſo that we
were in a great perplexitie, reſtrained to ſo vnworthie a
bondage, and yet reſtrained by Loue, which (I cannot
tell how) in noble mindes, by a certain duety, claimes
                         an

an anſwering. And how much that loue might mooue
vs,ſo much,and more that faultines of her mind remoued vs;her beautie being balanced by her ſhamelesnes.
But that which did(as it were) tie vs in captiuitie,was,
that to graunt,had ben wickedly iniurious to him,that
ſaued our liues : and to accuſe a Ladie that loued vs,of
her loue vnto vs, we eſteemed almoſt as diſhonorable:
& but by one of thoſe waies we ſawe no likelihood of
going out of that place,where the words would be iniurious to your eares, which ſhould expreſſe the manner of her ſuite : while yet many times earneſtnes died
her cheekes with the colour of ſhamefaſtnes;anu wanton languiſhing borrowed of her eies the downe-caſt
looke of modeſtie . But we in the meane time far from
louing her, and often aſſuring her, that we would not
ſo recompence her husbandes ſauing of our liues ; to
ſuch a ridiculous degree of truſting her , ſhe had
brought him, that ſhe cauſed him ſende vs worde,that
vpon our liues, we ſhould doo whatſoeuer ſhe commaunded vs: good man , not knowing any other, but
that all her pleaſures bent to the preſeruation of his e-
ſtate . But when that made vs rather pittie,then obey
his folly,then fel ſhe to ſeruile entreating vs,as though
force could haue bene the ſchoole of Loue, or that an
honeſt courage would not rather ſtriue againſt , then
yeelde to iniurie . All which yet could not make vs accuſe her , though it made vs almoſt pine awaie for
ſpight, to looſe any of our time in ſo troubleſome an i-
dleneſſe.

But while we were thus full of wearineſſe of what
was paſt,and doubt of what was to follow,Loue(that I
thinke in the courſe of my life hath a ſporte ſometimes

to poifon me with rofes , fometimes to heale me with wormewood)brought forth a remedy vnto vs : which though it helped me out of that diftres, alas the cõclufion was fuch, as I muft euer while I liue,think it worfe then a wracke,fo to haue bene preferued.This King by this Queene had a fonne of tender age,but of great expectation, brought vp in the hope of themfelues, & already acceptation of the inconftant people, as fucceffour of his fathers crowne:whereof he was as worthy, confidering his partes, as vnworthie, in refpect of the wrong was therby done againft the moft worthy *Plangus :* whofe great defertes now either forgotten,or vngratefully remembred, all men fet their fayles with the fauourable winde, which blewe on the fortune of this young Prince,perchaunce not in their harts,but furely not in their mouths , now giuing *Plangus* (who fome veares before was their only chãpion)the poore cõfort of calamitie, pittie . This youth therefore accounted Prince of that regiõ, by name *Palladius*,did with vehement affection loue a young Ladie,brought vp in his fathers court,called *Zelmane*, daughter to that mifchieuoufly vnhappie Prince *Plexirtus* (of whom already I haue, and fometimes muft make, but neuer honorable mention) left there by her father , becaufe of the intricate changeablenes of his eftate; he by the motherfide being halfe brother to this Queene *Andromana* , and therefore the willinger committing her to her care. But as Loue (alas) doth not alwaies reflect it felfe , fo fel it out that this *Zelmane*, (though truely reafon there was inough to loue *Palladius*) yet could not euer perfiwade her hartê to yeelde thereunto : with that paine to *Palladius* , as they feele , that feele an vnloued loue .

Yet

Yet louing indeede, and therefore conftant, he vfed ftill the interceffion of diligéce and faith, euer hoping, becaufe he would not put him felfe into that hell, to be hopeleffe : vntill the time of our being come, and captiued there, brought foorth this ende, whiche truely deferues of me a further degree of forrow then teares.

Such was therein my ill deftinie, that this young 6 Ladie *Zelmane* (like fome vnwifely liberall, that more delight to giue prefentes, then pay debtes) fhe chofe (alas for the pittie) rather to beftowe her loue (fo much vndeferued, as not defired) vpon me, then to re-cópence him, whofe loue (befides many other things) might feeme (euen in the court of Honour) iuftly to claime it of her. But fo it was (alas that fo it was) where-by it came to paffe, that (as nothing doth more natural-ly follow his caufe, then care to preferue, and benefite doth follow vnfained affection) fhe felt with me, what I felte of my captiuitie, and ftreight laboured to re-dreffe my paine, which was her paine: which fhe could do by no better meanes, then by vfing the helpe there-in of *Palladius* : who (true Louer) confidering what, and not why, in all her commaundements; and indeed fhe concealing from him her affection (which fhe in-tituled compaffion,) immediatly obeyed to imploy his vttermoft credite to relieue vs : which though as great, as a beloued fon with a mother, faulty otherwife, but not hard harted toward him, yet it could not pre-uaile to procure vs libertie. Wherefore he fought to haue that by practife, which he could not by praier. And fo being allowed often to vifit vs (for indeed our reftraints were more, or leffe, according as the ague of

her

her paſſion was either in the fit, or intermiſſion) he vſed the opportunitie of a fit time thus to deliuer vs.

CHAP. 21.

[1] He time of the maryinge that Queene was euery year, by the extreame loue of her husband, & the ſeruiceable loue of the Courtiers, made notable by ſome publike honours, which indeede (as it were) proclaymed to the worlde, how deare ſhe was to the people. Among other, none was either more gratefull to the beholders, or more noble in it ſelfe, then iuſts, both with ſword and launce, mainteined for a ſeuen-night together: wherein that Nation dooth ſo excell, bothe for comelines and hablenes, that from neighbour-countries they ordinarily come, ſome to ſtriue, ſome to learne, and ſome to behold.

[2] This day it happened that diuers famous Knights came thither frō the court of *Helen*, Queene of *Corinth*; a Ladie, whom Fame at that time was ſo deſirous to honor, that ſhe borrowed all mens mouthes to ioyne

with

with the founde of her Trumpet. For as her beautie
hath wonne the prize from all women, that ftande in
degree of comparifon (for as for the two fifters of
Arcadia, they are farre beyond all conceipt of comparifon) fo hath her gouernment bene fuch, as hath bene
no leffe beautifull to mens iudgements, then her beautie to the eiefight. For being brought by right of birth,
a woman, a yong woman, a faire woman, to gouerne a
people, in nature mutinoufly prowde, and alwaies before fo vfed to hard gouernours, as they knew not how
to obey without the fworde were drawne. Ye could
fhe for fome yeares, fo carry her felfe among them, that
they found caufe in the delicacie of her fex, of admiration, not of cótempt: & which was notable, euen in the
time that many countries were full of wars (which for
old grudges to *Corinth* were thought ftill would conclude there) yet fo hadled fhe the matter, that the threatens euer fmarted in the threatners; fhe vfing fo ftrauge,
and yet fo well-fucceeding a temper, that fhe made her
people by peace, warlike; her courtiers by fports, learned; her Ladies by Loue, chaft. For by continuall martiall exercifes without bloud, fhe made them perfect in
that bloudy art. Her fportes were fuch as caried riches
of Knowledge vpó the ftreame of Delight: & fuch the
behauiour both of her felfe, and her Ladies, as builded
their chaftitie, not vpon waywardnes, but by choice of
worthines: So as it feemed, that court to haue bene the
mariage place of Loue and Vertue, & that her felfe was
a *Diana* apparelled in the garments of *Venus*. And this
which Fame onely deliuered vnto me, (for yet I haue
neuer feene her) I am the willinger to fpeake of to you,
who (I knowe) knowe her better, being your neere

neigh-

neighbour, becaufe you may fee by her example (in her felfe wife,and of others beloued)that neither follie is the caufe of vehement Loue, nor reproch the effect. For neuer (I thinke) was there any woman, that with more vnremoueable determinatiō gaue her felf to the coūcell of Loue,after fhe had once fet before her mind the worthines of your coufin *Amphialus*;& yet is nether her wifedome doubted of,nor honour blemifhed. For (O God) what doth better become wifdome, then to difcerne,what is worthy the louing? what more agreable to goodnes,then to loue it fo difcerned?and what to greatneffe of hart,then to be conftant in it once loued? But at that time, that Loue of hers was not fo publikely knowne, as the death of *Philoxenus*, and her fearch of *Amphialus* hath made it : but then feemed to haue fuch leafure to fende thither diuerfe choyfe Knights of her court,becaufe they might bring her, at left the knowledge, perchaunce the honour, of that Triumph.

3   Wherein fo they behaued themfelues as for three daies they caried the prize; which being come from fo farre a place to difgrace her feruaunts, *Palladius* (who himfelfe had neuer vfed armes)perfuaded the Queene *Andromana* to be content (for the honour fake of her court) to fuffer vs two to haue our horfe and armour, that he with vs might vndertake the recouerie of their loft honour : which fhe graunted ; taking our oth to go no further then her fonne, and neuer to abandon him.Which fhe did not more for fauing him,then keeping vs: and yet not fatisfied with our oth,appointed a band of horfemen to haue eye, that we fhould not go beyond appointed limits. We were willing to gratifie
                 the

the young Prince, who (we faw) loued vs. And fo the
fourth day of that exercife, we came into the fielde:
where (I remember) the manner was, that the fore-
noone they fhould run at tilt, one after the other: the
afternoone in a broad field, in manner of a battell, till
either the ftrangers, or that countrie Knights wan the
field.

The firft that ran was a braue Knight, whofe deuife 4
was to come in, all chayned with a Nymph leading
him: his *Imprefa* was

        Againft him came forth an *Ibe-
rian* whofe manner of entring was, with bagpipes in
fteed of trumpets; a fhepheards boy before him for a
Page, and by him a dofen apparelled like fhepherds for
the fafhion, though rich in ftuffe, who caried his launces, which though ftrong to giue a launcely blow indeed, yet fo were they couloured with hooks neere the
mourn, that they pretily reprefeted fhephooks. His own
furniture was dreft ouer with wooll, fo enriched with
Iewels artificially placed, that one would haue thought
it a mariage betweene the loweft and the higheft. His
Imprefa was a fheepe marked with pitch, with this word
Spotted to be knowne. And becaufe I may tell you out his
conceipt (though that were not done, till the running
for that time was ended) before the Ladies departed
from the windowes, among them there was one (they
fay) that was the *Star*, wherby his courfe was only directed. The fhepherds attending vpõ *PHILISIDES* went
amõg thẽ, & fãg an eclogue; one of thẽ anfwering another, while the other fhepheards pulling out recorders
(which poffeft the place of pipes) accorded their mufick to the others voice. The Eclogue had great praife:

                Cc 4   I onely

I onely remember sixe verses, while hauing questioned one with the other, of their fellow-shepheards sodaine growing a man of armes, and the cause of his so doing, they thus said.

ME thought some staues he mist : if so, not much amisse:
For where he most would hit, he euer yet did misse.
One said he brake acrosse ; full well it so might be :
For neuer was there man more crossely crost then he.
But most cryed, O well broke : O foole full gaily blest:
Where failing is a shame, and breaking is his best.

Thus I haue digrest, becaufe his maner liked me wel: But when he began to run against *LElius*, it had neere growne (though great loue had euer bene betwixt them) to a quarrell. For *Philisides* breaking his staues with great commendation, *Lelius* (who was knowne to be second to none in the perfection of that Art) ranne euer ouer his head, but so finely to the skilfull eyes, that one might well see, he shewed more knowledge in missing, then others did in hitting. For with so gallant a grace his staffe came swimming close ouer the crest of the Helmet, as if he would represent the kisse, and not the stroke of *Mars*. But *Philisides* was much moued with it, while he thought *Lelius* would shew a contempt of his youth: till *Lelius* (who therefore would satiffie him, becaufe he was his friend) made him know, that to such bondage he was for so many courses tyed by her, whose disgraces to him were graced by her excellency, and whose iniuries he could neuer otherwise returne, then honours.

But so by *Lelius* willing-missing was the odds of the

Iberian fide, and continued fo in the next by the excellent rūning of a Knight, though foftred fo by the *Mufes*, as many times the verie ruftick people left both their delights and profites to harken to his fongs; yet could he fo well perfourme all armed fports, as if he had neuer had any other pen, then a Launce in his hand. He came in like a wild man; but fuch a wildnes, as fhewed his eye-fight had tamed him, full of withered leaues, which though they fell not, ftill threatned falling. His *Imprefa* was, a mill-horfe ftill bound to goe in one circle; with this word, *Data fata fequutus.* But after him the *Corinthian* Knights abfolutely preuailed, efpecially a greatnoble man of *Corinth*; whofe deuife was to come without any deuife, all in white like a new knight, as indeed he was; but fo new, as his newnes fhamed moft of the others long exercife. Then another from whofe tent I remember a birde was made flie, with fuch art to carry a written embaffage among the Ladies, that one might fay, If a liue bird, how fo taught? if a dead bird, how fo made? Then he, who hidden, man and horfe in a great figure liuely reprefenting the *Phœnix* : the fire tooke fo artificially, as it confumed the birde, and left him to rife as it were, out of the afhes thereof. Againft whom was the fine frofen Knight, frofen in defpaire; but his armor fo naturally reprefenting Ice, and all his furniture fo liuely anfwering therto, as yet did I neuer fee any thing that pleafed me better.

But the delight of thofe pleafing fights haue carried 5 me too farre in an vnneceffary difcourfe. Let it then fuffice (moft excellent Ladie) that you know the *Corinthians* that morning in the exercife (as they had done the dayes beto. e) had the better; *Palladius* neither fuffring

rs, nor himselfe to take in hand that partie till the afternoone; when we were to fight in troopes, not differing
otherwise from earnest, but that the sharpenesse of the
weapons was taken away. But in the triall *Palladius* (e-
specially led by *Musidorus*, and somewhat aided by me)
himselfe truely behauing himselfe nothing like a be-
ginner, brought the honor to rest it selfe that night of
the *Iberian* side: And the next day, both morning, and
after-noone being kept by our party, He (that saw the
time fitte for that deliuerie he intended) called vnto vs
to follow him; which we both bound by oth, and willing by good-wil, obeyed: and so the gard not daring
to interrupt vs (he commanding passage) we went after
him vpon the spur to a little house in a forrest neere by:
which he thought would be the fittest resting place, till
we might go further from his mothers fury, whereat he
was no lesse angry, & ashamed, then desirous to obay
Zelmane.

6 But his mother (as I learned since) vnderstanding by
the gard her sonnes conuaying vs away (forgetting her
greatnes, & resining modesty to more quiet thoughts)
flew out from her place, and cried to be accompanied,
for she her-selfe would follow vs. But what she did (being rather with vehemency of passion, then conduct of
reason) made her stumble while she ran, & by her owne
confusion hinder her owne desires. For so impatiently
she commanded, as a good while no body knew what
she commanded; so as we had gotten so far the start, as to
be alredy past the confines of her kingdome before she
ouertooke vs: and ouertake vs she did in the kingdome
of *Bythinia*, not regarding shame, or daunger of hauing
entred into anothers dominions: but (hauing with her
                                                    about

about a three score horſ-men)ſtreight commaunded to
take vs aliue, and not to regard her ſonnes threatening
therein: which they attempted to do,firſt by ſpeach, &
then by force. But neither liking their eloquence, nor
fearing their might, we eſteemed few ſwordes in a iuſt
defence,able to reſiſt any vniuſt aſſaulters. And ſo *Mu-*
ſidorus incredible valour (beating downe all lets) made
both me, and *Palladius,*ſo good way, that we had little
to doo to ouercome weake wrong.

And now had the victorie in effect without bloud, 7
when *Palladius* (heated with the fight, and angrie with
his mothers fault)ſo purſued our aſſaylers, that one of
them (who as I heard ſince had before our comming
bene a ſpeciall minion of *Andromanas*, and hated vs for
hauing diſpoſſeſt him of her hart) taking him to be one
of vs,with a traiterous blow ſlew his youg Prince: who
falling downe before our eyes, whom he ſpecially had
deliuered, iudge(ſweeteſt Lady) whether anger might
not be called iuſtice in ſuch a caſe: once, ſo it wroght in
vs, that many of his ſubiects bodies we left there dead,
to wait on him more faithfully to the other world.

All this while diſdaine, ſtrengthened by the furie of 8
a furious loue,made *Andromana* ſtay to the laſt of the
combat:& whe ſhe ſaw vs light down,to ſee what help
we might do to the helpleſſe *Palladius,*ſhe came runing
madly vnto vs, then no leſſe threatning, when ſhe had
no more power to hurt. But when ſhe perceiued it was
her onely ſonne that lay hurt, and that his hurt was ſo
deadly, as that alredy his life had loſte the vſe of the
reaſonable, and almoſt ſenſible part; then onely did
misfortune lay his owne ouglineſſe vpon his faulte,
and make her ſee what ſhe had done, and to what ſhe
was come : eſpeciallie, finding in vs rather deteſtation
then

then pittie (considering the losse of that young Prince)
and resolution presently to depart, which stil she laboured to stay. But depriued of all comfort, with eyes full
of death, she ranne to her sonnes dagger, and before we
were aware of it (who else could haue stayed it) strake
her selfe a mortall wound. But then her loue, though
not her person, awaked pittie in vs, and I went to her,
while *Musidorus* labored about *Palladius*. But the wound
was past the cure of a better surgeon then my selfe, so as
I could but receaue some few of her dying words;
which were cursings of her ill set affection, and wishing
vnto me many crosses & mischances in my loue, whensoeuer I should loue, wherin I feare, and only feare that
her prayer is from aboue granted. But the noise of this
fight, & issue thereof being blazed by the country people to some noble-mé there-abouts, they came thither,
and finding the wrong offered vs, let vs go on our iourney, we hauing recommended those royal bodies vnto
thé to be conueyed to the King of *Iberia*. With that *Philoclea*, seeing the teares stand in his eyes with remembrance of *Palladius*, but much more of that which thervpon grew, she would needs drinke a kisse from those
eyes, and he sucke another from her lippes; whereat she
blushed, & yet kissed him againe to hide her blushing.
Which had almost brought *Pyrocles* into another discourse, but that she with so sweete a rigor forbad him,
that he durst not rebell, though he found it a great war
to keepe that peace, but was faine to go on his storie:
for so she absolutely badde him, and he durst not know
how to disobey.

CHAP.

CHAP. 22.

¹ A new complaint of Pamphilus *new change,* ² *to a grace-*
leſſe curtiſan. ³ Zelmane *loues, and as a Page ſerues* Pyrocles. ⁴ *The two Princes policie to reconcile two warring*
brothers ⁵ *The vnbrotherly braue combat of* Tydeus *and*
Telenor. ⁶ Plexirtus *his viperine vnkindnes to the kin-*
deſt Leonatus. ⁷ *His conqueſt by the two brothers,* ⁸ *and*
his dogtrick to deſtroy them by themſelues. ⁹ *The regrecte*
of the dying brothers

S O (ſaid he) parting from that place
before the Sunne had much abaſed
himſelfe of his greateſt height, we
ſawe ſitting vpon the drie ſandes
(which yeelded at that time a verie
hotte reflection) a faire Gentlewoman, whoſe geſture accuſed her of
much ſorow; & euery way ſhewed
ſhe cared not what paine ſhe put her body to, ſince the
better parte (her minde) was laide vnder ſo much agonie: and ſo was ſhe dulled withall, that we could come
ſo neare, as to heare her ſpeeches, and yet ſhe not perceiue the hearers of her lamentation. But wel we might
vnderſtand her at times, ſay, Thou dooſt kill me with
thy vnkind falſhood: and, It greeues me not to die, but
it greeues me that thou art the murtherer: neither doth
mine owne paine ſo much vexe me, as thy errour. For
God knowes, it would not trouble me to be ſlaine for
thee, but much it tormêts me to be ſlain by thee. Thou
art vntrue, *Pamphilus*, thou art vntrue, and woe is me
thete-

therefore . How oft didſt thou ſweare vnto me , that
the Sun ſhould looſe his light,and the rocks runne vp
and down like little kiddes,before thou wouldſt falſifie
thy faith to me?Sunne therefore put out thy ſhining,&
rockes runne mad for ſorrow,for *Pamphilus* is falſe.But
alas,the Sun keepes his light,though thy faith be darck-
ned;the rockes ſtand ſtill, though thou change like the
wethercocke. O foole that I am, that thought I coulde
graſpe water, and binde the winde . I might well haue
knowē thee by others,but I would not;&rather wiſhed
to learne poiſon by drinking it my ſelfe, while my loue
helped thy wordes to deceiue me . Well , yet I would
thou hadſt made a better choiſe , when thou didſt forſake thy vnfortunate *Leucippe*.But it is no matter,*Baccha*
(thy new miſtres)will reuenge my wrongs. But do not
Baccha,let *Pamphilus* liue happie,though I die

2   And much more to ſuch like phraſe ſhe ſpake , but
that I(who had occaſion to know ſome-thing of that
Pamphilus)ſtept to comfort her : & though I could not
doo that,yet I gotte thus much knowledge of her, that
this being the ſame *Leucippe*, to whom the vnconſtante
Pāphilus had betrothed himſelfe,which had moued the
other Ladies to ſuch indignation as I tolde you:nether
her woorthineſſe (which in truthe was great) nor his
owne ſuffering for her (which is woont to endeare affection)could fetter his ficklenes , but that before his
mariage-day appointed, he had taken to wife that *Baccha*, of whom ſhe complayned; one,that in diuers places I had heard before blazed,as the moſt impudentlie
vnchaſte woman of all *Aſia* ; and withall,of ſuch an imperiouſnes therein, that ſhe would not ſtick to employ
them (whom ſhe made vnhappie with her fauour) to
                                                    draw

draw more companions of their follie : in the multitude of whom she did no lesse glorie, then a Captaine
would doo, of being followed by braue souldiers: wai-
wardly proud; and therefore bold, becaufe extreamely
faultie: and yet hauing no good thing to redeeme both
thefe, and other vnlouely parts, but a little beautie, difgraced with wandring eyes, and vnwaied speeches; yet
had *Pamphilus* (for her) left *Leucippe*, and withall, left his
faith: *Leucippe*, of whom one looke (in a cleere iudgement) would haue bene more acceptable, then all her
kindeneffes fo prodigallie beftowed . For my felfe, the
remembrance of his crueltie to *Dido*, ioyned to this,
ftirred me to feeke fome reuenge vpon him, but that
I thought, it fhoulde be a gayne to him to lofe his life,
being fo matched : and therefore (leauing him to be
punifhed by his owne election) we conueyed *Leucippe* to a houfe thereby, dedicated to *Veftall* Nunnes,
where fhe refolued to fpende all her yeares (which her
youth promifed fhoulde be many) in bewayling the
wrong, and yet praying for the wrong-dooer.

But the next morning, we (hauing ftriuen with the   3
Sunnes earlines) were fcarcely beyond the profpect of
the high turrets of that building, when there ouertoke
vs a young Gentleman, for fo he feemed to vs, but indeede (fweete Ladie) it was the faire *Zelmane*, *Plexirtus*
daughter; whom vnconfulting affection (vnfortunate-
ly borne to me-wards) had made borrowe fo much of
her naturall modeftie, as to leaue her more-decent rayments, and taking occafion of *Andromanas* tumultuous
purfuing vs, had apparrelled her felfe like a Page, with a
pittifull crueltie cutting of her golden haire, leauing
nothing, but the fhort curles, to couer that noble head,
but

but that she ware vpon it a faire head-peece, a shielde at
her back, and a launce in her hand, els disarmed. Her
apparrell of white, wrought vpon with broken knots,
her horse, faire & lustie, which she rid so, as might shew
a fearefull boldnes, daring to doo that, which she knew
that she knew not how to doo: and the sweetnes of her
countenance did giue such a grace to what she did, that
it did make hansome the vnhansomnes, and make the
eye force the minde to beleeue, that there was a praise
in that vnskilfulnesse. But she straight approached me,
and with fewe words (which borowed the help of her
countenance to make themselues vnderstood) she desired me to accept her in my seruice; telling me, she was a
noble-mans sonne of *Iberia*, her name *Daiphantus*, who
hauing seene what I had done in that court, had stolne
from her father, to follow me. I enquired the particularities of the maner of *Andromana* following me, which
by her I vnderstood, she hiding nothing (but her sexe)
from me. And still me thought I had seen that face, but
the great alteration of her fortune, made her far distant
from my memorie: but liking very well the yong Gentleman, (such I tooke her to be) admitted this *Daiphah-
tus* about me: who well shewed, there is no seruice like
his, that serues because he loues. For, though borne of
Princes bloud, brought vp with tenderest education,
vnapt to seruice (because a woman) & full of thoughts
(because in a strange estate;) yet Loue enioyned such
diligence, that no apprentise, no, no bondslaue could e-
uer be by feare more readie at all commaundementes,
then that yong Princesse was. How often (alas) did her
eyes say vnto me, that they loued? and yet, I (not looking for such a matter) had not my conceipt open, to
vnder-

vnderſtand them. How ofté would ſhe come creeping
to me, betweene gladnes to be neere me, & feare to offend me ᶜ Truly I remember, that then I maruailing, to
ſee her receiue my cōmandements with ſighes, & yet
do them with cheerefulnes : ſometimes anſwering me
in ſuch riddles, as I then thought childiſh in experiéce:
but ſince returning to my remébrance, they haue come
more neere vnto my knowledge : & pardon me (onely
deare Lady) that I vſe many words: for her affection to
me deſerues of me an affectionate ſpeach.

In ſuch ſort did ſhe ſerue me in that kingdom of *Bythi-* 4
nia, for two moneths ſpace. In which time we brought
to good end, a cruell warre long maintained betweene
the King of *Bythinia* and his brother. For my excellent
couſin, and I (diuiding our ſelues to either ſide) found
meanes (after ſome triall we had made of our ſelues) to
get ſuch credite with them, as we brought them to as
great peace betweene théſelues, as loue towards vs, for
hauing made the peace. Which done, we intended to
returne through the Kingdome of *Galatia*, towarde
Thrace, to eaſe the care of our father and mother, who
(we were ſure) firſt with the ſhipwracke; and then with
the other daungers we dayly paſt, ſhould haue litle reſt
in their thoughts, till they ſaw vs.

But we were not entred into that Kingdome, whé by 5
the noiſe of a great fight, we were guided to a pleaſaunt
valey, which like one of thoſe Circuſſes, which in great
ᴄities ſome-where doth giue a pleaſant ſpectacle of rūning horſes; ſo of either ſide ſtretching it ſelfe in a narrow length was it hemd in by wooddy hilles; as if in
deed Nature had meant therein to make a place for beholders. And there we behelde one of the cruelleſt

fights

fights betweene two Knights, that euer hath adorned
the martial ftorie. So as I muft côfeffe, a while we ftood
wondring, another while delighted with the rare brauery therof, till feing fuch ftreames of bloud, as threatned a drowning of life, we galloped towarde them to
part them. But we were preuented by a dofen armed
Knights, or rather villains, who vfing this time of their
extreame feeblenesse, all together fet vpon them. But
common daunger brake of particular difcorde, fo that
(though with a dying weakenes) with a liuely courage
they refifted, and by our help draue away, or flue thofe
murdering attempters : among whom we hapt to take
aliue the principall. But going to difarme thofe two
excellent Knights, we found with no leffe wonder to
vs, then aftonifhment to themfelues, that they were
the two valiaunt, and indeede famous Brothers, *Tydeus* and *Telenor*; whofe aduenture (as afterwarde we
made that vngratious wretch confeffe) had thus fallen out.

6   After the noble Prince *Leonatus* had by his fathers
death fucceeded in the kingdome of *Galatia*, he (forgetting all former iniuries) had receiued that naughtie *Plexirtus* into a ftreight degree of fauour, his goodneffe being as apt to be deceiued, as the others crafte
was to deceiue. Till by plaine proofe finding, that the
vngratefull man went about to poyfon him, yet would
not fuffer his kindneffe to be ouercome, not by iuftice
it felfe: but calling him to him, vfed wordes to this purpofe. *Plexirtus* (faid he) this wickedneffe is founde
by thee. No good deedes of mine haue bene able to
keepe it downe in thee. All men counfell me to take a-
way thy life, likely to bring foorth nothing, but as
daunge-

daungerous, as wicked effects. But I cannot finde it in my harte, remembring what fathers sonne thou arte. But since it is the violence of ambition, which perchaunce puls thee from thine owne iudgement, I will see, whether the satisfying that, may quiet the ill working of thy spirites. Not farre hence is the great cittie of *Trebisonde*; which, with the territorie about it, aunciently pertained vnto this crowne, now vniustly possessed, and as vniustly abused by those, who haue neither title to holde it, nor vertue to vse it. To the conquest of that for thy selfe I will lende thee force, and giue thee my right. Go therfore, and with lesse vnnaturalnesse glut thy ambition there; and that done, if it be possible, learne vertue.

Plexirtus; mingling forsworne excuses with false-meant promises, gladly embraced the offer: and hastilie sending backe for those two Brothers (who at that time were with vs succouring the gratious Queen *Erona*) by their vertue chiefly (if not onely) obteyned the conquest of that goodly dominion. Which indeede done by them, gaue them such an authoritie, that though he raigned, they in effect ruled, most men honouring them, becaufe they onely deserued honour; and many, thinking therein to pleafe *Plexirtus*, considering how much he was bound vnto them: while they likewise (with a certaine sincere boldenesse of selfe-warranting friendship) accepted all openly and plainely, thinking nothing should euer by *Plexirtus* be thought too much in them, since all they were, was his.

But he(who by the rules of his own mind, could construe no other end of mēs doings, but self seeking)sodély

feared,

feared what they could doo ; and as fodainely fufpe-
&ted, what they would doo, and as fodainely hated
them, as hauing both might, and minde to doo. But
dreading their power, ftanding fo ftrongly in their
owne valour,& others affection,he durft not take open
way againft them: and as harde it was to take a fecrete,
they being fo continually followed by the beft, & euery way hableft of that region:and therfore vfed this di-
uelifh fleight(which I wil tel you) not doubting(moft
wicked man)to turne their owne friédfhip toward him
to their owne deftruction. He,(knowing that they wel
knew, there was no friendfhip betweene him and the
new King of *Pontus*, neuer fince he fuccoured *Lema-
tus* and vs,to his ouerthrow) gaue them to vnderftand
that of late there had paffed fecrete defiance betweene
them, to meete priuately at a place apointed. Which
though not fo fit a thing for men of their greatnes, yet
was his honour fo engaged, as he could not go backe.
Yet faining to find himfelf weake by fome counterfait
infirmitie,the day drawing neere,hé requefted each of
them to go in his ftead; making either of thé fweare,to
keep the matter fecret,euer ech frö other,deliuering the
felfe fame particularities to both, but that he told *Tydeus*,the King would meet him in a blew armour; & *Telenor*,that it was a black armour: & with wicked fubtiltie
(as if it had bene fo apointed) caufed *Tydeus* to take a
black armour,&*Telenor* a blew;appointing them waies
how to go,fo as he knew they fhould not meet,til they
came to the place appointed, where each had promifed to keep filence, left the King fhould difcouer it was
not *Plexirtus*:and there in await had he laied thefe murtherers, that who ouerliued the other,fhould by them
                                                    be

be difpatched : he not daring truft more then thofe, with that enterprife,and yet thinking them too few,till themfelues by themfelues were weakened.

This we learned chiefly, by the chiefe of thofe way-beaters, after the death of thofe worthie brothers, whofe loue was no leffe,then their valour : but well we might finde much thereof by their pitifull lamentation, when they knew their mifmeeting, and faw each other (in defpite of the Surgerie we could doo vnto them)ftriuing who fhould runne fafteft to the goale of death : each bewailing the other, and more dying in the other, then in himfelfe : curfing their owne hands for doing, and their breaftes for not fooner fuffering : detefting their vnfortunately-fpent time in hauing ferued fo vngrateful a Tyraunt:and accufing their folly in hauing beleeued,he could faithfully loue,who did not loue faithfulnes: wifhing vs to take heed, how we placed our good wil vpon any other ground, then proofe of vertue : fince length of acquaintance,mutuall fecrecies, nor height of benefits could binde a fauage harte; no man being good to other, that is not good in himfelf. Then(while any hope was)befeeching vs to leaue the cure of him that befought, and onely looke to the other. But when they found by themfelues,and vs, no poffibilitie,they defired to be ioined;and fo embracing and crauing that pardon each of other, which they denied to themfelues, they gaue vs a moft forrowfull fpectacle of their death; leauing fewe in the world behind them, their matches in any thing, if they had foone inough knowne the ground and limits of friendfhip. But with wofull hartes, we caufed thofe bodies to be conueyed to the nexte towne of *Bythinia,* where we

learning

9

learning thus much (as I haue tolde you) caused the
wicked Historian to cóclude his history, with his owne
well-deserued death.

CHAP. 23.

1 *Zelmanes griefe for* Plexirtus *fault.* 2 *Otaues , and his
Gyants warre on* Pontus. 3 Plexirtus *endaungered ,
needes helpe of the dead brothers.* 4 *Zelmane thought-
sicke, vnmaskes her selfe.* 5 *Her dying teares* 6 *and last
requestes.* 7 Musidorus *to* Pontus , Pyrocles *hardly
partes to saue* Plexirtus. 8 *The sourse and course of his
deaths-doome,* 9 *stayed by* Pyrocles. 10 *The combat of*
Pontus *well ended.* 11 *The* Asian *Princes meeting, to
honour the two* Greekes.

1   Vt then (I must tell you) I found
such wofull countenances in *Daiphantus,* that I could not but much
maruaile (finding them continew
beyond the first assault of pittie)
how the cause of strangers (for further I did not conceiue) could so
deepely pearce . But the truth in-
deed is, that partly with the shame & sorrow she tooke
of her fathers faultinesse , partly with the feare, that the
hate I cóceiued against him, would vtterly disgrace her
in my opinion , whensoeuer I should know her, so vehemently perplexed her, that her fayre colour decaied;
and dayly, and hastily grew into the very extreme working of sorowfulnesse : which oft I sought to learne, &
helpe . But she, as fearefull as louing, still concealed it,
and

and fo decaying ftill more and more, in the excellencie of her faireneffe, but that whatfoeuer weakeneffe
took away, pitie feemed to adde: yet ftill fhe forced her
felfe to waite on me, with fuch care and diligence, as
might well fhew had bene taught in no other fchoole,
but Loue.

While we returning againe to embarke our felues for
Greece, vnderftood that the mighty *Otaues* (brother to
Barzanes flaine by *Mufidorus*, in the battaile of the fix
Princes) had entred vpõ the kingdome of *Pontus*, partly vpon the pretences he had to the crowne, but principally, becaufe he would reuenge vpon him (whom he
knew we loued)the loffe of his brother : thincking (as
indeede he had caufe) that wherefoeuer we were, hearing of his extremitie, we would come to reliue him ;
in fpite whereof he doubted not to preuaile, not onely
vpon the confidence of his owne vertue and power,
but efpecially becaufe he had in his cõpany two mighty *Giants*, fonnes to a couple whom we flue in the fame
realme: they hauing bene abfent at their fathers death,
and now returned, willingly entered into his feruice,
hating (more then he) both vs, and that King of *Pontus*. We therefore withall fpeede went thetherwarde,
but by the way this fell out, which whenfoeuer I remember without forrow, I muft forget withall, all humanitie.

Poore *Daiphantus* fell extreme fick, yet would needs
conquere the delicacie of her conftitution, and force
her felfe to waite on me : till one day going towarde
Pontus, we met one, who in great haft went feeking for
Tydeus & *Telenor*, whofe death as yet was not knowne
vnto the meffenger ; who (being their feruaunt and

Dd 4   knowing.

knowing how deerely they loued *Plexirtus*) brought
them word, how since their departing, *Plexirtus* was
in prent daunger of a cruel death, if by the valiantnesse
of one of the best Knightes of the world, he were not
reskewed: we enquired no further of the matter (being glad he should now to his losse finde what an vn-
profitable treason it had bene vnto him, to dismember
himselfe of two such friendes) and so let the messenger
part, not sticking to make him know his masters destruction, by the falshood of *Plexirtus*.

4　　But the griefe of that (finding a bodie alreadie
brought to the last degree of weakenesse) so ouerwhel-
med the little remnant of the spirits left in *Daiphantus*,
that she fell sodainely into deadly soundings; neuer
comming to her selfe, but that withall she returned to
make most pittifull lamentatiõs; most straunge vnto vs, becaufe we were farre from gheffing the ground
thereof. But finding her sicknesse such, as beganne to
print death in her eyes, we made al hast possible to conuey her to the next towne: but before we could lay
her on a bed, both we, & she might find in herselfe, that
the harbinger of ouer-haftie death, had prepared his
lodging in that daintie body, which she vndoubtedly
feeling, with a weake chearefulnes, shewed cõfort therin; and then desiring vs both to come neere her, & that
no bodie els might be present; with pale, and yet (euen
in palenes) louely lippes, Now or neuer, and neuer indeed, but now it is time for me (said she) to speake: and
I thanke death which gaue me leaue to difcouer that,
the suppressing whereof perchance hath bene the sharpest spur, that hath hafted my race to this end. Know
then my Lords, and especially you my Lord and master,

fter,*Pyrocles*,that your page *Daiphantus* is the vnfortunat
Zelmane, who for your fake caufed my(as vnfortunate)
louer,and cofen,*Palladius*,to leaue his fathers court,and
côfequently,both him & my Aunt his mother,to loofe
their liues. For your fake my felfe haue become, of a
Princeffe a Page: and for your fake haue put off the
apparell of a woman, & (if you iudge not more merci-
fully)modeftie.We were amazed at her fpeach,and thê
had(as it were)new eyes giuê vs to perceue that which
before had bene a prefent ftrâger to our minds. For indeed, we forthwith knew it to be the face of *Zelmane*,
whô before we had knowen in the court of *Iberia*. And
forrow and pittie laying her paine vpon me, I comforted her the beft I could by the tendernes of good-will,
pretending indeed better hope then I had of her recouery.

But fhe that had inward ambaffadors from the tyrât 5
that fhould fhortly oppreffe her. No, my deere mafter
(faid fhe) I neither hope nor defire to liue. I know you
would neuer haue loued me(&with that fhe wept)nor,
alas,had it bene reafon you fhould, confidering manie
wayes my vnworthines. It fufficeth me that the ftrange
courfe I haue takê,fhall to your remembrance,witneffe
my loue : and yet this breaking of my harte, before I
would difcouer my paine,will make you(I hope)think
I was not altogether vnmodeft.Thinke of me fo, deare
Mafter,and that thought fhal be my life:and with that,
languifhingly looking vpon me; And I pray you (faid
fhe) euen by thefe dying eies of mine(which are onely
forrie to dye,becaufe they fhall lofe your fight) and by
thefe pouled lockes of mine (which while they were
long, were the ornament of my fex, now in their fhort
                                                    curles

curles, the teftimonie of my feruitude) and by the feruice I haue done you(which God knowes hath beene
full of loue) thinke of me after my death with kindnes,
though ye cannot with loue. And whenfoeuer ye fhall
make any other Ladie happie with your placed affectiō,
if you tell her my folly,I pray you fpeake of it, not with
fcorne,but with pitie.I affure you(deare Princeffe of my
life, for how could it be otherwife?) her words and her
manners, with the liuely confideration of her loue, fo
pearced me,that I, though I had diuerfe griefes before,
yet me thought I neuer felt till then, how much forow
enfeebleth all refolution. For I coulde not chufe, but
yeeld to the weakenes of abundant weeping; in trueth
with fuch griefe,that I could willingly at that time haue
chaunged liues with her.

6   But when fhe faw my teares, O God(faid fhe)howe
largely am I recompenced for my loffes?why then(faid
fhee) I may take boldneffe to make fome requefts vnto
you. I befought her to doo, vowing the performance,
though my life were the price therof.She fhewed great
ioy: The firft(faid fhe) is this,that you will pardon my
father the difpleafure you haue iuftly conceiued againft
him, and for this once fuccour, him out of the daunger
wherin he is : I hope he will amende : and I pray you,
whenfoeuer you remember him to be the faultie *Plexir-*
tus,remember withall that he is *Zelmanes* father.The fecond is,that when you come into *Greece*, you will take
vnto your felfe this name(though vnlucky)of *Daiphan-*
tus,and vouchfafe to be called by it:for fo fhal I be fure,
you fhall haue caufe to remember me : and let it pleafe
your noble coufin to be called *Palladius*, that I doo that
right to that poore Prince, that his name may yet liue
                                                    vpon

vpon the earth in so excellent a person: and so betwene
you, I trust sometimes your vnluckie page shall be (perhaps with a sigh) mencioned. Lastly, let me be buried
here obscurely, not suffering my friends to knowe my
fortune, till (when you are safely returned to your own
countrie) you cause my bones to be conueied thither,
and laid (I beseech you) in some place, where your selfe
vouchsafe sometimes to resort. Alas, small petitions for
such a suter; which yet she so earnestly craued, that I was
faine to sweare the accomplishment. And then kissing
me, & often desiring me not to condemne her of light-
nesse, in mine armes she deliuered her pure soule to the
purest place: leauing me as full of agonie, as kindnes, pitie, and sorow could make an honest harte. For I must
confesse for true, that if my starres had not wholy reserued me for you, there els perhaps I might haue loued,
& (which had bene most strange) begun my loue after
death: whereof let it be the lesse maruaile, because somwhat shee did resemble you: though as farre short of
your perfectió, as her selfe dying, was of her flourishing:
yet somthing there was, which (when I saw a picture of
yours) brought againe her figure into my remébrance,
and made my harte as apte to receiue the wounde, as
the power of your beauty with vnresistable force to
pearce.

But we in wofull (& yet priuat) manner burying her, **7**
performed her commandement: & then enquiring of
her fathers estate, certainly learned that he was present-
lie to be succoured, or by death to passe the neede of
succour. Therfore we determined to diuide our selues;
I, according to my vowe, to helpe him, and *Musidorus*
toward the King of *Pontus*, who stood in no lesse need
then

then immediate fuccour, and euen readie to depart one from the other, there came a meffenger from him, who after fome enquirie found vs, giuing vs to vnderftand, that he trufting vpon vs two, had apointed the combat betweene him & vs, againft *Otaues*, and the two *Gyants*. Now the day was fo accorded, as it was impoffible for me both to fuccour *Plexirtus*, & be there, where my honour was not onely gaged fo far, but (by the ftraunge working of vniuft fortune) I was to leaue the ftanding by *Mufidorus*, whom better then my felfe I loued, to go faue him whom for iuft caufes I hated. But my promife giuen, & giuen to *Zelmane*, & to *Zelmane* dying, preuailed more with me, then my friendfhip to *Mufidorus*: though certainely I may affirme, nothing had fo great rule in my thoughts as that. But my promife caried me the eafier, becaufe *Mufidorus* himfelfe would not fuffer me to breake it. And fo with heauy mindes (more carefull each of others fucceffe, the of our owne) we parted; I towarde the place, where I vnderftood *Plexirtus* was prifoner to an auncient Knight, abfolutely gouerning a goodly Caftle, with a large territory about it, whereof he acknowledged no other foueraigne, but himfelfe: whofe hate to *Plexirtus*, grew for a kinfman of his, who he malitioufly had murdered, becaufe in the time that he raigned in *Galatia*, he foũd him apt to practife for the reftoring of his vertuous brother *Leonatus*. This old Knight, ftill thirfting for reuenge, vfed (as the way to it) a pollicie, which this occafion I will tell you, prepared for him. *Plexirtus* in his youth had maried *Zelmanes* mother, who dying of that only child-birth, he a widdower, and not yet a King, haunted the Court of *Armenia*; where (as he was comming to winne fauour)

uour)he obteined great good liking of *Artaxia*, which
he purſued, till (being called home by his father) hc
falſly got his fathers kingdome; and then neglected his
former loue: till throwen out of that (by our meanes)
before he was deeply rooted in it, and by and by again
placed in *Trebiſonde*, vnderſtanding that *Artaxia* by her
brothers death was become Queen of *Armenia*, he was
hotter then euer, in that purſuit, which being vnderſtood by this olde Knight, he forged ſuch a letter, as
might be written from *Artaxia*, entreating his preſent
(but very priuie) repaire thether, giuing him faithfull
promiſe of preſente mariage : a thing farre from her
thought, hauing faithfully, and publiquely proteſted,
that ſhe would neuer marrie any, but ſome ſuch Prince
who woulde giue ſure proofe, that by his meanes we
were deſtroyed. But he(no more wittie to frame, then
blinde to iudge hopes)bitte haſtely at the baite, and in
priuate maner poaſted toward her, but by the way he
was met by this Knight, far better accompanied, who
quickly laid holde of him, & condemned him to death,
cruell inough, if any thing may be both cruell and iuſt.
For he cauſed him to be kept in a miſerable priſon, till a
day appointed, at which time he would deliuer him to
be deuoured by a monſtrous beaſt, of moſt vgly ſhape,
armed like a *Rhinoceros*, as ſtrong as an Elephant, as
fierce as a Lion, as nimble as a Leopard, and as cruell as
a Tigre : whom he hauing kept in a ſtrong place, from
the firſt youth of it, now thought no fitter match, then
ſuch a beaſtly monſter with a monſtrous Tyrant : pro-
claiming yet withall, that if any ſo well loued him, as to
venture their liues againſt this beaſt, for him, if they o-
uercame, he ſhould be ſaued : not caring how many
                                                        they

they were (such confidence he had in the monsters strength) but especially hoping to entrappe therby the great courages of *Tydeus* and *Telenor*,whom he no lesse hated,because they had bene principall instruments of the others power.

9   I dare say, if *Zelmane* had knowen what daunger I should haue passed, she would rather haue let her father perishe, then me to haue bidden that aduenture. But my word was past, and truely,the hardnes of the enterprise,was not so much a bitte,as a spurre vnto me; " knowing well,that the iorney of high honor lies not in plaine wayes. Therefore, going thether, and taking sufficient securitie, that *Plexirtus* should be deliuered if I were victorious,I vndertooke the combatte : and (to make shorte, excellent Ladie, and not trouble your eares with recounting a terrible matter) so was my weakenes blessed from aboue, that without dangerous wounds I slewe that monster, which hundreds durste not attempt : to so great admiration of many (who from a safe place might looke on) that there was order giuen to haue the fight, both by sculpture and picture, celebrated in most parts of *Asia*. And the olde nobleman so well liked me,that he loued me; onely bewayling, my vertue had beene imployed to saue a worse monster then I killed:whom yet(according to faith giuen)he deliuered, and accompanied me to the kingdome of *Pontus*, whether I would needes in all speede go, to see whether it were possible for me(if perchance the day had bene delaied)to come to the combat . But that(before I came) had bene thus finished.

10   The vertuous *Leonatus* vnderstanding two so good friends of his were to be in that danger,would perforce

be

be one him felfe: where he did valiantly and fo did the
King of *Pontus*. But the truthe is, that both they being
fore hurt, the incomparable *Mufidorus* finifhed the
combat by the death of both the Giants, and the taking of *Otaues* prifoner. To whom as he gaue his life, fo
he gotte a noble friend: for fo he gaue his worde to be,
and he is well knowen to thinke him felfe greater in being fubiect to that, then in the greatnes of his principalitie.

But thither (vnderftanding of our being there) 11
flocked great multitudes of many great perfons, and e-
uen of Princes; efpecially thofe, whom we had made
beholding vnto vs: as, the Kings of *Phrygia, Bythinia,*
with thofe two hurte, of *Pontus* and *Galatia*, and *Otaues*
the prifoner, by *Mufidorus* fet free; and thither came
Plexirtus of *Trebifonde*, and *Antiphilus*, then King of
Lycia; with as many mo great Princes, drawen ether by
our reputation, or by willingnes to acknowledge them
felues obliged vnto vs, for what we had done for tho
others. So as in thofe partes of the world, I thinke, in
many hundreds of yeares, there was not feene fo royall
an affemblie: where nothing was let paffe to doo vs the
higheft honors, which fuch perfons (who might commaund both purfes and inuentions) could perfourme.
All from all fides bringing vnto vs right royall prefents
(which we to auoide both vnkindnes, and importunitie, liberally receiued,) & not content therewith, would
needes accept, as from vs, their crownes, and acknowledge to hold them of vs: with many other exceffiue
honors, which would not fuffer the meafure of this
fhort leifure to defcribe vnto you.

                                                    CHAP.

CHAP. 24.

¹ *The cauſes and prouiſions of the Princes embarking for* Arcadia. ² Plexirtus *his treaſon againſt them diſcloſed by
one,* ³ *attempted by another of his miniſters.* ⁴ *Sedition and
ſlaughter in the ſhippe about it.* ⁵ *Their ſhipwrack by fire.*
⁶ Pyrocles *fight with the Captaine, and eſcape from ſea.*
⁷ *The amarous concluding the olde, and beginning a newe
ſtorie, both broken of by* Miſo.

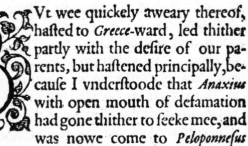

Vt wee quickely aweary thereof,
haſted to *Greece*-ward, led thither
partly with the deſire of our parents, but haſtened principally, becauſe I vnderſtoode that *Anaxius*
with open mouth of defamation
had gone thither to ſeeke mee, and
was nowe come to *Peloponneſus*
where from Court to Court he made enquyrie of me,
doing yet himſelfe ſo noble deedes, as might hap to
aucthorize an ill opinion of me. We therefore ſuffred
but ſhort delayes, deſiring to take this countrey in our
way, ſo renowmed ouer the worlde, that no Prince
coulde pretend height, nor begger lowneſſe, to barre
him from the ſound thereof: renowmed indeede, not
ſo much for the ancient prayſes attributed thereunto,
as for the hauing in it *Argalus* and *Amphialus* (two
knights of ſuch rare prowes, as we deſired eſpecially to
know) and yet by farre, not ſo much for that, as without ſuffering of compariſon for the beautie of you and
your ſiſter, which makes all indifferent iudges, that
speake

ſpeake thereof, account this countrie as a temple of
deities. But theſe cauſes indeed mouing vs to come
by this land, we embarked our ſelues in the next porte,
whether all thoſe Princes (ſauing *Antiphilus*, who returned, as he pretended, not able to tarry long from *Ero-*
na) conueied vs. And there found we a ſhip moſt royal-
ly furniſhed by *Plexirtus*, who made all thinges ſo proper (as well for our defence, as eaſe) that all the other
Princes greatly commended him for it: who (ſeeming
a quite altered man) had nothing but repetance in his
eies, friendſhip in his geſture, & vertue in his mouth: ſo
that we who had promiſed the ſweete *Zelmane* to pardon him, now not onely forgaue, but began to fauour;
perſwading our ſelues with a youthfull credulitie, that
perchance things were not ſo euil as we tooke them, &
as it were deſiring our owne memorie, that it might be
ſo. But ſo were we licenſed from thoſe Princes, truly
not without teares, eſpecially of the vertuous *Leonatus*,
who with the king of *Potus*, would haue come with vs,
but that we (in reſpect of the ones young wife, & both
their new ſettled kingdomes) would not ſuffer it. Then
would they haue ſent whole fleets to guard vs: but we,
that deſired to paſſe ſecretely into *Greece*, made them
leaue that motion, when they found that more ſhips,
then one, would be diſpleaſing vnto vs. But ſo comit-
ting our ſelues to the vncertaine diſcretió of the wind,
we (then determining as ſoone as we came to *Greece*,
to take the names of *Daiphantus* and *Palladius*, as well
for our owne promiſe to *Zelmane*, as becauſe we deſired to come vnknowne into *Greece*) left the *Aſian*
ſhore full of Princely perſons, who euen vpon their
knees, recommended our ſafeties to the deuotion of

E e   their

their chiefe defires : among whom none had bene fo
officious (though I dare affirme, all quite contrarie to
his vnfaithfulnes) as *Plexirtus*.

So hauing failed almoft two daies, looking for nothing but when we might looke vpon the land, a graue
man (whom we had feene of great truft with *Plexirtus*, and was fent as our principall guide) came vnto vs,
and with a certaine kinde manner, mixt with fhame,
and repentaunce, began to tell vs, that he had taken
fuch a loue vnto vs (confidering our youth and fame)
that though he were a feruaunt, and a feruaunt of fuch
truft about *Plexirtus*, as that he had committed vnto
him euen thofe fecretes of his hart, which abhorde all
other knowledge ; yet he rather chofe to reueale at
this time a moft pernitious counfell, then by concealing it bring to ruin thofe, whom he could not choofe
but honour. So went he on, and tolde vs, that *Plexirtus* (in hope thereby to haue *Artaxia*, endowed with
the great Kingdome of *Armenia*, to his wife) had giuen him order, when we were neere *Greece*, to finde
fome opportunitie to murder vs, bidding him to take
vs a fleepe, becaufe he had feene what we could do waking. Now firs (faid he) I would rather a thoufand
times loofe my life, then haue my remembrance (while
I liued) poyfoned with fuch a mifchiefe : and therefore if it were onely I, that knewe herein the Kings
order, then fhould my difobedience be a warrant of
your fafetie. But to one more (faid he) namely the
Captaine of the fhippe, *Plexirtus* hath opened fo much
touching the effect of murdering you, though I think,
laying the caufe rather vpon old grudge, then his hope
of *Artaxia*. And my felfe, (before the confideration

of

of your excellencies had drawne loue and pittie into
minde) imparted it to fuch, as I thought fitteft for
fuch a mifchiefe. Therefore,I wifhe you to ftand vpon
your garde, affuring you, that what I can doo for your
fafetie,you fhall fee (if it come to the pufhe) by me
perfoufmed. We thanked him, as the matter indeed
deferued, and from that time would no more difarme
our felues, nor the one fleepe without his friendes
eyes waked for him : fo that it delaied the going forwarde of their bad enterprize, while they thought it
rather chaunce,then prouidence,which made vs fo behaue our felues.

But when we came within halfe a daies fayling of 3
the fhore, foone they faw it was fpeedily, or not at all
to be done. Then (and I remember it was about the
firft watch in the night) came the Captaine and whifpered thé Councellour in the eare:But he (as it fhould
feem) diffwading him from it, the Captaine(who had
bene a pyrate from his youth,and often blouded in it)
with a lowde voice fware, that if *Plexirtus* bad him, he
would not fticke to kill God him felfe. And therewith
cald his mates, and in the Kings name willed them to
take vs,aliue or dead; encouraging thé with the fpoile
of vs,which he faid, (& indeed was true) would yeeld
many exceeding rich iewels. But the Councellour(according to his promife)commandedthem they fhould
not cómit fuch a villany, protefting that he would ftád
betweene them and the Kings anger therein. Wherewith the Captaine enraged:Nay (faid he)thé we muft
begin with this traitor him felfe : and therewith gaue
him a fore blow vpon the head, who honeftly did the
beft he could to reuenge himfelfe.

Ee 2   But

4   But then we knew it time rather to encounter, then waite for miſchiefe. And ſo againſt the Captaine we went, who ſtraight was enuironned with moſt parte of the Souldiers and Mariners. And yet the truth is, there were ſome, whom either the authoritie of the councellour, doubt of the Kings minde, or liking of vs, made draw their ſwor ls of our ſide : ſo that quickly it grew a moſt confuſed fight. For the narrowneſſe of the place, the darkeneſſe of the time, and the vncertainty in ſuch a tumult how to know friēds from foes, made the rage of ſwordes rather guide, then be guided by their maiſters. For my couſin and me, truly I thinke we neuer perfourmed leſſe in any place, doing no other hurte, then the defence of our ſelues, and ſuccouring them who came for it, draue vs to : for not diſcerning perfectlie, who were for, or againſt ys, we thought it leſſe euill to ſpare a foe, then ſpoyle a friend. But from the hieſt to the loweſt parte of the ſhippe there was no place lefte, without cries of murdring, and murdred perſons. The Captaine I hapt a while to fight withall, but was driuen to parte with him, by hearing the crie of the Councellour, who receiued a mortall wounde, miſtaken of one of his owne ſide. Some of the wiſer would call to parley, & wiſh peace, but while the wordes of peace were in their mouthes, ſome of their auditours gaue them death for their hire. So that no man almoſt could conceiue hope of liuing, but being lefte aliue : and therefore euery one was willing to make him ſelfe roome, by diſpatching almoſt any other : ſo that the great number in the ſhip was reduced to exceeding few, when of thoſe few the moſt part weary of thoſe troubles leapt into the boate,
which

which was faft to the fhip : but while they that were firft, were cutting of the rope that tied it, others came leaping in, fo diforderly, that they drowned both the boate, and themfelues.

But while euen in that little remnant (like the children of *Cadmus*) we continued ftill to flay one another, a fire, which (whether by the defperate malice of fome, or intention to feparate, or accidentally while all things were caft vp and downe) it fhould feeme had taken a good while before, but neuer heeded of vs, (who onely thought to preferue, or reuenge) now violently burft out in many places, and began to maifter the principall partes of the fhip. Then neceffitie made vs fee, that, a common enimy fets at one a ciuill warre: for that little all we were (as if we had bene waged by one man to quench a fire) ftreight went to refift that furious enimie by all art and labour : but it was too late, for already it did embrace and deuoure from the fterne, to the waft of the fhip: fo as labouring in vaine, we were driuen to get vp to the prowe of the fhip, by the worke of nature feeking to preferue life, as long as we could : while truely it was a ftraunge and ougly fight, to fee fo huge a fire, as it quickly grew to be, in the Sea, and in the night, as if it had come to light vs to death. And by and by it had burned off the mafte, which all this while had prowdly borne the fayle (the winde, as might feeme, delighted to carrie fire and bloud in his mouth) but now it fell ouer boord, and the fire growing neerer vs, it was not onely terrible in refpect of what we were to attend, but infupportable through the heat of it.

So that we were conftrained to bide it no longer,

but

but difarming and ftripping our felues, and laying our felues vpon fuch things, as we thought might help our fwimming to the lande (too far for our owne ftrength to beare vs) my coufin and I threw our felues into the Sea. But I had fwomme a very little way, when I felt (by reafon of a wound I had) that I fhould not be able to bide the trauaile, and therefore feeing the mafte (whofe tackling had bene burnt of) flote cleare from the fhip, I fwamme vnto it; and getting on it, I found mine owne fworde, which by chaunce, when I threw it away (caught by a peece of canuas) had honge to the mafte. I was glad, becaufe I loued it well; but gladder, when I faw at the other end, the Captaine of the fhip, and of all this mifchiefe; who hauing a long pike, be-like had borne him felfe vp with that, till he had fet him felfe vpon the maft. But when I perceiued him, Villaine (faid I) dooft thou thinke to ouerliue fo many honeft men, whom thy falfehood hath brought to de-ftruction? with that beftriding the maft, I gat by little and little towards him, after fuch a manner as boies are wont (if euer you faw that fport) when they ride the wild mare. And he perceiuing my intention, like a fel-low that had much more courage then honeftie, fet him felfe to refift. But I had in fhort fpace gotten with-in him, and (giuing him a found blowe) fent him to feede fifhes. But there my felfe remainde, vntill by py-rates I was taken vp, and among them againe taken pri-foner, and brought into *Laconia*.

7   But what (faid *Philoclea*) became of your coufin *Mufi-dorus?* Loft faid *Pyrocles*. Ah my *Pyrocles*, faid *Philoclea*, I am glad I haue take you. I perceiue you louers do not alwaies fay truely: as though I know not your coufin

Dorus,

Dorus,the fheepeheard? Life of my defires (faide *Pyro-cles*) what is mine,euen to my foule is yours: but the fe-cret of my friend is not mine.But if you know fo much, then I may truely fay,he is loft, fince he is no more his owne.But I perceiue, your noble fifter & you are great friends,and well doth it become you fo to be. But go forward deare *Pyrocles*, I lóg to heare out till your mee-ting me:for there to me-warde is the beft part of your ftorie.Ah fweet *Philoclea*(faid *Pyrocles*) do you thinke I can thinke fo precious leyfure as this well fpent in tal-king.Are your eyes a fit booke (thinke you) to reade a tale vpon? Is my loue quiet inough to be an hiftori-an? Deare Princeffe,be gracious vnto me.And then he faine would haue remembred to haue forgot himfelfe. But fhe, with a fweetly difobeying grace, defired that her defire (once for euer) might ferue, that no fpotte might difgrace that loue which fhortly fhe hoped fhold be to the world warrantable. Faine he would not haue heard,til fhe threatned anger.And then the poore louer durft not,becaufe he durft not. Nay I pray thee,deare *Pyrocles*(faid fhe)let me haue my ftory.Sweet Princeffe (faid he)giue my thoughts a litle refpite:and if it pleafe you,fince this time muft fo be fpoiled, yet it fhall fuffer the leffe harme,if you vouchfafe to beftow your voice, and let me k...ow,how the good Queene *Erona* was be-traied into fuch dáger,and why *Plangus* fought me.For in deede,I fhould pitie greatly any mifchance fallen to that Princeffe. I will, faid *Philoclea* fmiling,fo you giue me your worde,your handes fhall be quiet auditours. They fhal,faid he,becaufe fubiect. Then began fhe to fpeake, but with fo prettie and delightfull a maieftie, when fhe fet her countenaunce to tell the matter, that *Pyrocles* could not chufe but rebell fo far, as to kiffe her.

She

She would haue puld her head away, and speake, but while she spake he kist, and it seemed he fedde vpon her wordes: but shee gate away. Howe will you haue your discourse (said she) without you let my lips alone? He yeelded and tooke her hand. On this (said he) will I reuenge my wrong: and so began to make much of that hand, when her tale, & his delight were interrupted by *Miso*: who taking her time, while *Basilius* backe was turned, came vnto them: and told *Philoclea*, she deserued she knewe what, for leauing her mother, being euill at ease, to keepe companie with straungers. But *Philoclea* telling her, that she was there by her fathers commandemēt, she went away muttering, that though her back, and her shoulders, and her necke were broken, yet as long as her tongue would wagge, it should do her errand to her mother.

CHAP. 25.

¹ *Gynecias diuining dreame.* ² *Her passionate ielousie in actions,* ³ *speach, and* ⁴ *song described* ⁵ *Her troubling* Philoclea *and* Zelmane, ⁶ *The rebels troubling her.* ⁷ *Rebels resisted by* Zelmane. ⁸ Zelmane *assisted by* Dorus. ⁹ Dorus *and* Zelmanes *fiue memorable strokes.*

¹ O went vp *Miso* to *Gynecia*, who was at that time miserably vexed with this manner of dreame. It seemed vnto her to be in a place full of thornes, which so molested her, as she could neither abide standing still, nor treade safely going forward. In this case she thought *Zel-*

mane,

mane,being vpon a faire hill,delightfull to the eye, and
eatie in apparance, called her thither: whither with
much anguish being come, *Zelmane* was vanished,
and she found nothing but a dead bodie like vnto her
husband, which seeming at the first with a strange smell
to infect her, as she was redie likewise within a while to
die,the dead bodie,she thought,tooke her in his armes,
and said,*Gynecia*,leaue all;for here is thy onely rest.

With that she awaked, crying very loud,*Zelmane*,*Zel*-
mane.But remembring her selfe, and seeing *Basilius* by,
(her guiltie conscience more suspecting, then being suspected)she turned her call,and called for *Philoclea*.*Miso*
forthwith like a valiant shrew, (looking at *Basilius*, as
though she would speake though she died for it) tolde
Gynecia,that her daughter had bene a whole houre togither in secrete talke with *Zelmane*: And (sayes she) for
my part I coulde not be heard (your daughters are
brought vp in such awe) though I tolde her of your
pleasure sufficiently. *Gynecia*, as if she had heard her
last doome pronounced agaynst her, with a side-looke
and chaunged countenance, O my Lorde (said she)
what meane you to suffer these yong folkes together?
Basilius (that aymed nothing at the marke of her suspition) smilingly tooke her in his armes, sweete wife
(said he) I thanke you for your care of your childe:but
they must be youthes of other mettall, then *Zel*-
mane, that can endaunger her. O but; cryed *Gyne*-
cia,and therewith she stayed: for then indeede she did
suffer a right conflict, betwixt the force of loue, and
rage of iealousie. Manie times was she about to satiffie the spite of her minde, and tell *Basilius*, how
she knewe *Zelmane* to be farre otherwise then the outward

warde appearance . But thoſe many times were all put
backe, by the manifolde obiections of her vehement
loue.Faine ſhe would haue barde her daughters happe,
but loth ſhe was to cut off her owne hope. But now,
as if her life had bene ſet vppon a wager of quicke ry-
ſing, as weake as ſhe was, ſhe gat vp; though *Baſilius*,
(with a kindneſſe flowing onely from the fountaine of
vnkindneſſe , being in deede deſirous to winne his
daughter as much time as might be) was loth to ſuffer it, ſwearing he ſawe ſickeneſſe in her face, and therefore was loath ſhe ſhould aduenture the ayre.

3　　But the great and wretched Ladie *Gynecia*, poſſeſſed
with thoſe deuils of Loue and Iealouſie, did rid herſelf
from her tedious husbande : and taking no body with
her, going toward the; O Iealouſie(ſaid ſhe) the phren-
ſie of wiſe folkes, the well-wiſhing ſpite, and vnkinde
carefulneſſe, the ſelfe-puniſhment for others faults, and
ſelfe-miſerie in others happineſſe, the couſin of enuie,
daughter of loue,& mother of ha.e, how couldeſt thou
ſo quietly get thee a ſeate in the vnquiet hart of *Gynecia*,
Gynecia(ſaid ſhe ſighing) thought wiſe, and once vertuous? Alas it is thy breeders power which plantes thee
there : it is the flaming agonie of affection, that works
the chilling acceſſe of thy feuer,in ſuch ſort, that nature
giues place ; the growing of my daughter ſeemes the
decay of my ſelfe; the bleſſings of a mother turne to the
curſes of a copetitor; and the faire face of *Philoclea*, appeares more horrible in my ſight, then the image of
death. Then remembred ſhe this ſong , which ſhe
thought tooke a right meaſure of her preſent mind.

With

VV *Yth two strange fires of equall heate possest,*
  The one of Loue, the other Iealousie,
Both still do worke, in neither finde I rest :
For both, alas, their strengthes together tie:
The one aloft doth holde, the other hie
   Loue wakes the iealous eye least thence it moues .
   The iealous eye, the more it lookes, it loues.

These fires increase: in these I dayly burne :   4
They feede on me, and with my wings do flie :
My louely ioyes to dolefull ashes turne :
Their flames mount vp, my powers prostrate lie :
They liue in force, I quite consumed die.
   One wonder yet farre passeth my conceate :
   The fuell small : how be the fires so great ?

But her vnleasured thoughtes ran not ouer the ten 5
firſt wordes; but going with a pace, not ſo much too faſt
for her bodie, as ſlowe for her minde, ſhe found them
together, who after *Miſos* departure, had left their
tale, and determined what to ſay to *Baſilius*. But full
abaſhed was poore *Philoclea*, (whoſe conſcience
nowe began to knowe cauſe of bluſhing) for firſt ſalutation, receyuing an eye from her mother, full of
the ſame diſdainefull ſcorne, which *Pallas* ſhewed to
poore *Arachne*, that durſt contende with her for
the prize of well weauing : yet did the force of loue
ſo much rule her, that though for *Zelmanes* ſake ſhe did
deteſt her, yet for *Zelmanes* ſake ſhe vſed no harder
words to her, then to bid her go home, and accompany
her ſolitarie father.

                                        Then

6   Then began fhe to difplay to *Zelmane* the ftorehoufe
of her deadly defires , when fodainly the confufed ru-
mor of a mutinous multitude gaue iuft occafion to
Zelmane to breake of any fuch conference, (for well fhe
found, they were not friendly voices they heard) and
to retire with as much diligence as conueniently they
could, towards the lodge. Yet before they could winne
the lodge by twentie paces, they were ouertaken by an
vnruly fort of clownes , and other rebels, which like a
violent floud, were caried, they themfelues knewe not
whether. But affoone as they came within perfect difcerning thefe Ladies , like enraged beaftes , without
refpect of their eftates, or pitie of their fexe, they began
to runne againft them, as right villaines, thinking abilitie to doo hurt, to be a great aduancement : yet fo many as they were, fo many almoft were their mindes , all
knitte together onely in madnes . Some cried, Take;
fome, Kill; fome, Saue : but euen they that cried faue,
ran for companie with them that meant to kill . Euerie
one commaunded, none obeyed, he only feemed chief
Captain, that was moft ragefull.

7   *Zelmane* (whofe vertuous courage was euer awake)
drew out her fword, which vpon thofe il-armed churls
giuing as many wounds as blowes, & as many deathes
almoft as wounds (lightning courage, and thundering
fmart vpon them) kept them at a bay , while the two
Ladies got thefelues into the lodge: out of the which,
Bafilius (hauing put on an armour long vntried) came
to proue his authoritie among his fubiects, or at left, to
aduenture his life with his deare miftreffe , to whô
he brought a fhield, while the Ladies tremblingly attended the iffue of this dangerous aduenture. But *Zel-*
mane

maine made them perceiue the ods betweene an Eagle
and a Kight, with fuch a nimble ftayednes, and fuch an
affured nimblenes, that while one was running backe
for feare, his fellow had her fword in his guts.

And by and by was both her harte and helpe well
encreafed by the comming of *Dorus*, who hauing been
making of hurdles for his mafters fheepe, hearde the
horrible cries of this madde multitude; and hauing
ftreight reprefented before the eies of his carefull loue,
the perill wherein the foule of his foule might be, he
went to *Pamelas* lodge, but found her in a caue hard by,
with *Mopfa* and *Dametas*, who at that time would not
haue opened the entrie to his father. And therfore leauing them there (as in a place fafe, both for being
ftrong, and vnknowen) he ranne as the noife guyded
him. But when he faw his friend in fuch danger among
them, anger and contempt (afking no counfell but of
courage) made him roome among them, with no other
weapon but his fheephooke, and with that ouerthrowing one of the villaines, took away a two-hand fword
from him, and withall, helpt him from euer being afhamed of lofing it. Then lifting vp his braue head, and
flafhing terror into their faces, he made armes & legs
goe complaine to the earth, how euill their mafters had
kept them. Yet the multitude ftill growing, and the
verie killing wearying them (fearing, left in long fight
they fhould be conquered with cõquering) they drew
back toward the lodge; but drew back in fuch fort, that
ftill their terror went forwarde: like a valiant maftiffe,
whom when his mafter pulles backe by the taile from
the beare (with whom he hath alreadie interchanged a
hatefull imbracement) though his pace be backwarde,
his

his gesture is foreward, his teeth and eyes threatening more in the retiring, then they did in the aduancing: so guided they themselues homeward, neuer stepping steppe backward, but that they proued themselues masters of the ground where they stept.

9 Yet among the rebels there was a dapper fellowe, a tayler by occupation, who fetching his courage onelie from their going back, began to bow his knees, & very fencer-like to draw neere to *Zelmane*. But as he came within her distáce, turning his swerd very nicely about his crown, *Basilius*, with a side blow, strake of his nose. He (being a suiter to a seimsters daughter, and therfore not a little grieued for such a disgrace) stouped downe, becaufe he had hard, that if it were fresh put to, it would cleaue on againe. But as his hand was on the grounde to bring his nose to his head, *Zelmane* with a blow, sent his head to his nose. That saw a butcher, a butcherlie chuffe indeed (who that day was sworn brother to him in a cup of wine) & lifted vp a great leauer, calling *Zelmane* all the vile names of a butcherly eloquence. But she (letting slippe the blowe of the leauer) hitte him so surely on the side of his face, that she lefte nothing but the nether iawe, where the tongue still wagged, as willing to say more, if his masters remébrance had serued. O (said a miller that was halfe dronke) see the lucke of a good fellow, and with that word, ran with a pitchforke at *Dorus*: but the nimblenes of the wine caried his head so fast, that it made it ouer-runne his feet, so that he fell withall, iust betwene the legs of *Dorus*: who setting his foote on his neck (though he offered two milche kine, and foure fatte hogs for his life) thrust his sword quite through, from one eare to the other; which toke it very

vn-

vnkindlie, to feele fuch newes before they heard of them, in ftead of hearing, to be put to fuch feeling. But *Dorus* (leauing the miller to vomit his foul out in wine and bloud) with his two-hand fword ftrake of another quite by the wafte, who the night before had dreamed he was growen a couple, and (interpreting it he fhould be maried) had bragd of his dreame that morning among his neighbors. But that blow aftonifhed quite a poore painter, who ftood by with a pike in his handes. This painter was to counterfette the fkirmifhing betwene the *Centaures* and *Lapithes*, and had bene very defirous to fee fome notable wounds, to be able the more liuely to expreffe them, and this morning (being caried by the ftreame of this companie) the foolifh felow was euen delighted to fee the effect of blowes. But this laft, (hapning neere him) fo amazed him, that he ftood ftill, while *Dorus* (with a turne of his fword) ftrake of both his hands. And fo the painter returned, well fkilled in wounds, but with neuer a hand to performe his fkill.

CHAP. 26.

Zelmanes confident attempt to appeafe the mutinie. ² *A bone of diuifion caft by her,* ³ *and caught by them.* ⁴ *Her pacificatorie oration.* ⁵ *The acceptation and iffue of it.*

N this manner they recouered the lodge, and gaue the rebels a face of wood of the out-fide. But they then (though no more furious, yet more couragious when they faw no refifter) went about with pickaxe to the wall, and fire to the gate, to gette themfelues entrance.

trance. Then did the two Ladies mixe feare with loue, eſpecially *Philoclea*, who euer caught hold of *Zelmane*, ſo (by the follie of loue) hindering the help which ſhe deſired. But *Zelmane* ſeeing no way of defence, nor time to deliberate (the number of thoſe villaines ſtill encreaſing, and their madneſſe ſtill encreaſing with their number) thought it onely the meanes to goe beyond their expectation with an vnuſed boldeneſſe, and with danger to auoide danger : and therfore opened againe the gate, and (*Dorus* and *Baſilius* ſtanding redie for her defence). ſhe iſſued againe among them. The blowes ſhe had dealt before (though all in generall were haſtie) made each of them in particular take breath, before they brought them ſodainly ouer-neere her, ſo that ſhe had time to gette vp to the iudgementſeate of the Prince, which (according to the guiſe of that countrie) was before the gate. There ſhe pauſed a while, making ſigne with her hand vnto them, & withall, ſpeaking aloud, that ſhe had ſomething to ſay vnto them, that would pleaſe them. But ſhe was anſwered a while with nothing but ſhouts and cries; and ſome beginning to throw ſtones at her, not daring to approach her. But at length, a young farmer (who might do moſt among the countrie ſort, and was caught in a little affection towardes *Zelmane*) hoping by this kindeneſſe to haue ſome good of her, deſired them, if they were honeſt men, to heare the woman ſpeake. Fie fellowes, fie, (ſaid he) what will all the maides in our towne ſay, if ſo many tall men ſhall be afraide to heare a faire wench? I ſweare vnto you by no little ones, I had rather giue my teeme of oxen, then we ſhould ſhewe our ſelues ſo vnciuill wights. Beſides, I tell you true, I haue heard it

of

of old men counted wifdome, to heare much,& fay little. His fententious fpeech fo preuailed, that the moft
parte began to liften. Then fhe, with fuch efficacie
of gracefulnes, & fuch a quiet magnanimitie reprefented in her face in this vttermoft perill, as the more the
barbarous people looked, the more it fixed their looks
vpon her, in this forte began vnto them.

It is no fmall comfort vnto me (faid fhe) hauing to
fpeake fomething vnto you for your owne behoofs, to
find that I haue to deale with fuch a people, who fhew
indeed in thefelues the right nature of valure, which as
it leaues no violence vnattempted, while the choller is
nourifhed with refiftance; fo when the fubiect of their
wrath, doth of it felf vnloked-for offer it felf into their
hands, it makes thé at left take a paufe before they determine cruelty. Now then firft (before I come to the
principall matter) haue I to fay vnto you; that your
Prince *Bafilius* himfelfe in perfon is within this Lodge,
& was one of the three, whó a few of you went about
to fight withall: (& this fhe faid, not doubting but they
knew it well inough; but becaufe fhe would haue them
imagine, that the Prince might think that they did not
know it) by him am I fent vnto you, as fró a Prince to
his well approoued fubiects, nay as from a father to beloued children, to know what it is that hath bred iuft
quarrell among you, or who they be that haue any way
wróged you? what it is with which you are difpleafed,
or of which you are defirous? This he requires: and indeed (for he knowes your faithfulnes) he commaunds
you prefently to fet downe, & to choofe among your
felues fome one, who may relate your griefes or de-
maundes vnto him.

Ff　　　　This

3   This (being more then they hoped for from their
Prince)aſſwaged well their furie,& many of them conſented (eſpecially the young farmer helping on, who
meant to make one of the demaũds that he might haue
Zelmane for his wife) but when they began to talke of
their grieues,neuer Bees made ſuch a cõfuſed hũming:
the towne dwellers demanding putting downe of im-
poſts:the country felowes laying out of cõmons:ſome
would haue the Prince keepe his Court in one place,
ſome in another.Al cried out to haue new coũcellors:
but when they ſhould think of any new,they liked thẽ
as well as any other,that they could remẽber, eſpecially they would haue the treaſure ſo looked vnto , as that
he ſhould neuer neede to take any more ſubſidies . At
length they fel to direct contrarieties.For the Artiſans,
they would haue corne & wine ſet at a lower price,and
bound to be kept ſo ſtil:the plowmen,vine-laborers,&
farmers would none of that . The coũtrimen demaunded that euery man might be free in the chief townes:
that could not the Burgeſſes like of.The peaſãts would
haue the Gentlemẽ deſtroied, the Citizens (eſpecially
ſuch as Cookes,Barbers,& thoſe other that liued moſt
on Gentlemen)would but haue them refourmed.And
of ech ſide were like diuiſions,one neighbourhood beginning to find fault with another . But no confuſion
was greater then of particular mens likings and diſli-
kings:one diſpraiſing ſuch a one, whõ another praiſed,
& demanding ſuch a one to be puniſhed,whom the o-
ther would haue exalted.No leſſe ado was there about
chooſing him,who ſhould be their ſpokes-man.The fi-
ner ſort of Burgeſſes,as Marchants Prentiſes,& Cloth-
workers, becauſe of their riches , diſdaining the baſer
occupations , & they becauſe of their number as much
                                        diſdaining

diſdaining them: all they ſcorning the countrimens ignoraunce, & the countrymen ſuſpecting as much their
cūning: So that *Zelmane* (finding that their vnited rage
was now growne, not only to a diuiding, but to a croſſing one of another, & that the miſlike growne among
theſelues did wel allay the heat againſt her) made tokēs
againe vnto thē (as though ſhe tooke great care of their
wel doing, and were afraid of their falling out) that ſhe
would ſpeake vnto thē. They now growne iealous one
of another (the ſtay hauing ingēdred diuiſiō, & diuiſiō
hauing manifeſted their weaknes) were willing inough
to heare, thē moſt part ſtriuing to ſhow themſelues willinger then their fellowes : which *Zelmane* (by the acquaintaunce ſhe had had with ſuch kinde of humors)
ſoone perceiuing, with an angerles brauery, & an vna-
baſhed mildnes, in this manner ſpake vnto them.

An vnuſed thing it is, & I think not heretofore ſeene,
ô *Arcadians,* that a womā ſhould giue publike coūſel to
men, a ſtrāger to the coūtry people, & that laſtly iñ ſuch
a preſence by a priuate perſon, the regãll throne ſhould
be poſſeſſed. But the ſtraungenes of your action makes
that vſed for vertue, which your violent neceſſitie im-
poſeth For certainely, a woman may well ſpeake to
ſuch men, who haue forgottē a manlike gouernment:
a ſtraunger may with reaſon inſtruct ſuch ſubiects, that
neglect due points of ſubiection : and is it maruaile
this place is entred into by another, ſince your owne
Prince (after thirtie yeares gouerment) dare not ſhew
his face vnto his faithfull people? Heare therfore ô *Arcadians,* & be aſhamed: againſt whō hath this rage bene
ſtirred? whether haue bene bent theſe māfull weapons
of yours? In this quiet harmles lodge are harbourd no

Argians your ancient enimies, nor *Laconians* your now
feared neighbours. Here be nether hard landlords, nor
biting vſurers. Here lodge none, but ſuch as either you
haue great cauſe to loue, or no cauſe to haue: here being
none, beſides your Prince, Princeſſe, and their children,
but my ſelf. Is it I then, ô *Arcadians*, againſt whom your
anger is armed? Am I the marke of your vehemēt quarrell? if it be ſo, that innocencie ſhall not be a ſtop for furie; if it be ſo, that the law of hoſpitalitie (ſo long & holily obſerued among you) may not defend a ſtraunger
fled to your armes for ſuccour: if in fine it be ſo, that ſo
many valiaunt mens courages can be enflamed to the
miſchiefe of one ſilly woman; I refuſe not to make my
life a ſacrifice to your wrath. Exerciſe in me your indig-
natiō, ſo it go no further, I am content to pay the great
fauours I haue receiued amōg you, with my life, not ill
deſeruing I preſent it here vnto you, ô *Arcadians*, if that
may ſatisfie you; rather thē you(called ouer the world
the wiſe and quiet *Arcadians*) ſhould be ſo vaine, as to
attempt that alone, which all the reſt of your countrie
wil abhor; thē you ſhould ſhew your ſelues ſo vngratefull, as to forget the fruite of ſo many yeares peaceable
gouernment; or ſo vnnaturall, as not to haue with the
holy name of your naturall Prince, any furie ouer-mai-
ſtred. For ſuch a helliſh madnes (I know) did neuer
enter into your harts, as to attēpt any thing againſt his
perſon; which no ſucceſſor, though neuer ſo hatefull,
wil euer leaue(for his owne ſake)vnreuenged. Neither
can your wonted valour be turned to ſuch a baſenes, as
in ſtead of a Prince, deliuered vnto you by ſo many roiall anceſtors, to take the tyrannous yoke of your fellow
ſubiect, in whom the innate meanes will bring forth rauenous

uenous couetousnes,and the newnes of his eftate, fuf-
pectfull cruelty. Imagine, what could your enimies
more wifh vnto you,then to fee your owne eftate with
your owne handes vndermined? O what would your
fore-fathers fay,if they lined at this time,& faw their offpring defacing fuch an excellent principalitie, which
they with fo much labour & bloud fo wifely haue efta-
blifht? Do you thinke them fooles,that faw you fhould
not enioy your vines, your cattell, no not your wiues
& children,without gouernment; and that there could
be no gouernment without a Magiftrate,and no Magiftrate without obedience,and no obediēce where euery one vpon his owne priuate paffion, may interprete
the doings of the rulers? Let your wits make your prefent exāple to you.What fweetnes (in good faith) find
you in your prefent condition? what choife of choife
finde you,if you had loft *Bafilius*? vnder whofe enfigne
would you go, if your enimies fhould inuade you? If
you cannot agree vpon one to fpeake for you, how wil
you agree vpō one to fight for you? But with this feare
of I cannot tel what,one is troubled,and with that paffed wrong another is grieued. And I pray you did the
Sunne euer bring you a fruitfull harueft,but that it was
more hote then pleafant? Haue any of you childrē,that
be not fometimes cumberfome? Haue any of you fathers, that be not fometime weerifh? What, fhall we
curfe the Sonne,hate our children,or difobey our fathers? But what need I vfe thefe wordes, fince I fee in
your countenances (now vertuoufly fettled) nothing
els but loue and dutie to him, by whom for your only
fakes the gouernmēt is embraced. For al what is done,
he doth not only pardon you,but thanke you; iudging
the action by the minds,& not the minds by the actiō.

Your

Your grieues, and defires, whatfoeuer,& whenfoeuer you lift,he wil confider of,and to his confideration it is reafon you fhould refer them. So then,to cōclude; the vncertainty of his eftate made you take armes ; now you fee him well, with the fame loue lay them downe. If now you end (as I know you will) he will make no other account of this matter , but as of a vehement, I muft cōfeffe ouer-vehement affection : the only conti-ᵘaunce might proue a wickednes.But it is not fo,I fee very wel,you begā with zeale,&wil end with reuerēce.

5   The action *Zelmane* vfed , being beautified by na-ture and apparelled with skill , her geftures beyng fuch , that as her wordes did paint out her minde , fo they ferued as a fhadow,to make the picture more liue-ly and fenfible,with the fweete cleernesse of her voice, rifing & falling kindly as the nature of the worde, and efficacie of the matter required , altogether in fuch ad-mirable perfon , whofe incomparable valour they had well felte,whofe beautie did pearce through the thicke dulnes of their fenfes,gaue fuch a way vnto her fpeach through the rugged wildernesse of their imaginations, who (befides they were ftriken in admiration of her, as of more then a humane creature) were coold with taking breath , and had learned doubts out of leafure, that in fteed of roaring cries, there was now heard no-thing,but a cōfufed muttring,whether her faying were to be followed,betwixt feare to purfue , & lothnesse to leaue:moft of them could haue bene cōtent, it had ne-uer bene begun , but how to end it (each afraid of his companion,)they knew not , finding it far eafier to tie then to loofe knots.But *Zelmane* thinking it no euil way in fuch mutinies,to giue the mutinous fome occafiō of fuch feruice,as they might thinke (in their own iudge-ment)

ment would counteruaile their trefpaffe, withal, to take
the more affured poffeffion of their mindes, which fhe
feared might begin to wauer, Loiall *Arcadians* (faid fhe)
now do I offer vnto you the manifefting of your duties: all thofe that haue taken armes for the Princes fafetie, let the turne their backs to the gate, with their weapons bent againft fuch as would hurt his facred perfon.
O weak truft of the many-headed multitude, whom inconftancie onely doth guide to well doing: who can fet
confidence there, where company takes away fhame,
and ech may lay the fault of his fellow? So faid a craftie
felow among them, named *Clinias*, to himfelfe, when he
faw the worde no fooner out of *Zelmanes* mouth, but
that there were fome fhouts of ioy, with, God faue *Bafilius*, and diuers of them with much iollity growne to be
his guard, that but litle before met to be his murderers.

CHAP. 27.

A verball craftie coward purtrayed in Clinias. • *His firft
raifing, and with the firft, relenting in this mutinie,* ³ *punifhed by the farmer.* ⁴*The vprore reenforced, & weakned by themfelues.* ⁵ Clinias-*his* Sinon-*like narration
of this drüken rebellions original.* ⁶*The kings order in it.*

His *Clinias* in his youth had bene a
fcholler fo farre, as to learne rather
wordes then maners, and of words
rather plentie then order; and oft
had vfed to be an actor in Tragedies, where he had learned, befides
a flidingneffe of language, acquain-

tance

tance with many paſſions, and to frame his face to beare
the figure of them: long vſed to the eyes and eares of
men, and to recken no fault, but ſhamefaſtneſſe; in nature, a moſt notable Coward, and yet more ſtrangely
then rarely venturous in priuie practiſes.

2   This fellowe was become of neere truſt to *Cecropia,*
Amphialus-his mother, ſo that he was priuy to al the miſchieuous deuiſes, wherewith ſhe went about to ruine
Baſilius, and his children, for the aduauncing of her
ſonne : and though his education had made him full
of tongue, yet his loue to be doing, taught him in any
euill to be ſecret; and had by his miſtreſſe bene vſed (e-
uer ſince the ſtrange retiring of *Baſilius*) to whiſper rumors into the peoples eares: and this time (finding great
aptnes in the multitude) was one of the chiefe that ſet
them in the vprore (though quite without the cõſent of
Amphialus, who would not for all the Kingdoms of the
world ſo haue aduétured the life of *Philoclea.*) But now
perceiuing the flood of their furie began to ebbe, he
thought it policie to take the firſt of the tide, ſo that no
mã cried lowder then he, vpon *Baſilius*. And ſom of the
luſtieſt rebels not yet agreeing to the reſt, he cauſed two
or three of his mates that were at his cõmandement to
lift him vp, & then as if he had had a prologue to vtter,
he began with a nice grauitie to demand audience. But
few attending what he ſaid, with vehement geſture, as
if he would teare the ſtars from the skies, he fell to crying out ſo lowde, that not onely *Zelmane*, but *Baſilius*
might heare him. O vnhappie men, more madde
then the Giants that would haue plucked *Iupiter* out of
heauen, how long ſhal this rage continue? why do you
not all throw downe your weapons, and ſubmit your
ſelues

felues to our good Prince, our good *Bafilius*, the *Pelops* of wifdom,& *Minos* of all good gouernmēt?when will you begin to beleue me,and other honeſt and faithfull fubiects,that haue done all we could to ſtop your furie?

The farmer that loued *Zelmane* could abide him no 3 longer.For as at the firſt he was willing to ſpeake of cō- ditions,hoping to haue gotten great foueraınties, & a- mong the reſt *Zelmane*:fo now perceiuing,that the peo- ple, once any thing downe the hill from their furie, would neuer ſtop till they came to the bottom of abſo- lute yeelding,and fo that he ſhould be nearer feares of puniſhment,then hopes of fuch aduancement, he was one of them that ſtood moſt againſt the agreement:and to begin withall, difdaining this fellow ſhould play the preacher,who had bin one of the chiefeſt make-bates, ſtrake him a great wound vpon the face with his ſword. The cowardly wretch fell down,crying for fuccour, & (fcrambling through the legs of them that were about him)gat to the throne, where *Zelmane* tooke him, and comforted him,bleeding for that was paſt,and quaking for feare of more.

But as foone as that blow was giuen(as if *Æolus* had 4 broke open the doore to let all his winds out) no hand was idle,ech one killing him that was next, for feare he ſhould do as much to him.For being diuided in minds & not diuided in cōpanies,they that would yeeld to *Ba-filius* were intermingled with thē that would not yeeld. Thefe men thinking their ruine ſtood vpō it,thofe men to get fauor of their Prince,conuerted their vngracious motion into their owne bowels,& by a true iudgement grew their owne puniſhers.None was fooner killed thē thofe that had bene leaders in the difobedience : who by

by being ∫o, had taught them, that they did leade di∫-
obediēce to the ∫ame leaders. And many times it fel out
that they killed them that were of their owne fa&ion,
anger whetting, and doubt ha∫tening their fingers. But
then came downe *Zelmane*; and *Ba∫ilius* with *Dorus* i∫-
∫ued, and ∫omtimes ∫eeking to draw together tho∫e of
their party, ∫omtimes laying indifferently among them,
made ∫uch hauocke (amōg the re∫t *Zel-mane* ∫triking the
farmer to the hart with her ∫worde, as before ∫he had
done with her eyes) that in a while all they of the contrary ∫ide were put to flight, and fled to certaine woods
vpon the frontiers; where feeding coldly, and drinking
onely water, they were di∫ciplined for their dronken ri-
ots; many of them being ∫laine in that cha∫e, about a
∫core onely e∫caping. But when the∫e late rebels, nowe
∫ouldiers, were returned from the cha∫e, *Ba∫ilius* calling
them togither, partly for policy ∫ake, but principally be-
cau∫e *Zelmane* before had ∫poken it (which was to him
more thē a diuine ordinance) he pronounced their generall pardon, willing them to returne to their hou∫es,
and therafter be more circū∫pe& in their proceedings:
which they did mo∫t of them with ∫hare-marks of their
folly. But imagining *Clinias* to be one of the chiefe that
had bred this good alteration, he gaue him particular
thanks, and withall willed him to make him know, how
this frenzie had entred into the people.

5   *Clinias* purpo∫ing indeede to tell him the trueth of al,
∫auing what did touch him∫elf, or *Cecropia*, fir∫t, dipping
his hand in the blood of his woūd, Now by this blood
(∫aid he) which is more deare to me, then al the re∫t that
is in my body, ∫ince it is ∫pent for your ∫afety: this tōgue
(perchance vnfortunate, but neuer fal∫e) ∫hall not now
begin to lie vnto my Prince, of me mo∫t beloued. Then
                                                        ∫tret-

ſtretching out his hand, and making vehement counte-
naces the vſhers to his ſpeches, in ſuch maner of tearms
recounted this accident. Yeſterday (ſaid he) being your
birth-day, in the goodly greene two mile hence before
the city of *Eniſpus*, to do honour to the day, were a four
or fiue thouſand people (of all conditions, as I thinke)
gathered together, ſpending al the day in dancings and
other exercifes: and when night came, vnder tents and
bowes making great cheare, and meaning to obſerue a
waſſaling watch all that night for your ſake. *Bacchus* (the
lcarned ſay) was begot with thunder: I think, that made
him euer ſince ſo full of ſtur & debate. *Bacchus* indeed it
was which ſoūded the firſt trūpet to this rude alarū. For
that barbarous opinion being generally amongthem, to
thinke with vice to do honor, & with actiuitie in beaſt-
lines to ſhew abundāce of loue, made moſt of thē ſeeke
to ſhew the depth of their affectiō in the depth of their
draught. But being once wel chafed with wine (hauing
ſpent al the night, & ſome peece of the morning in ſuch
reuelling) & imboldned by your abſented maner of liuing, there was no matter their eares had euer heard of
that grew not to be a ſubiect of their winie conference.
I ſpeake it by proofe: for I take witnes of the gods (who
neuer leaue periuries vnpuniſhed) that I oftē cried out
againſt their impudency, & (whē that would not ſerue)
ſtopt mine eares, becaufe I wold not be partakeroftheir
blaſphemies, till with buffets they forced me to haue
mine eares & eies defiled. Publike affairs were minlegd
with priuate grudges, neither was any man thought of
wit, that did not pretende ſome caufe of miſlike. Ray-
ling was counted the fruite of freedome, and ſaying
nothing had his vttermoſte prayſe in ignoraunce.
At the length, your ſacred perſon (alas why did I
liue

liue to heare it?alas how do I breath to vtter it?But your
cōmandement doth not onely enioine obedience,but
giue me force:your sacred person (I say) fell to be their
table-talke:a proud word swelling in their stomacks , &
disdainfull reproches against so great a greatnes,hauing
put on the shew of greatnes in their little mindes: till at
length the very vnbrideled vse of words hauing increased fire in their mindes (which God knowes thought
their knowledge notable , becaufe they had at all no
knowledge to cōdemne their own want of knowledge)
they descended(O neuer to be forgotten presumption)
to a direct mislike of your liuing from among them.
Whereupon it were tedious to remember their far-fet-
ched constructions.But the summe was, you disdained
them : and what were the pompes of your estate, if
their armes mainteyned you not? Who woulde call
you a Prince, if you had not a people? When certaine of them of wretched estates , and worse mindes
(whose fortunes,change could not impaire) began to
say,that your gouernment was to be looked into; how
the great treasures (you had leuied amōg thē)had bene
spent; why none but great men & gentlemen could be
admitted into counsel,that the cōmons(forsooth)were
to plain headed to say their opiniōs:but yet their blood
& sweat must maintain all.Who could tell whether you
were not betraied in this place, where you liued? nay
whether you did liue or no? Therefore that it was time
to come & see;and if you were here,to know(if *Arca-*
dia were growne lothsome in your sight) why you did
not ridde your selfe of the trouble? There would not
want those that would take so faire a cumber in good
part. Since the Countrie was theirs,and the gouerne-

ment

ment an adherent to the countrie, why fhould they not
confider of the one, as well as inhabite the other? Nay
rather (faid they) let vs beginne that, which all *Arcadia*
will followe. Let vs deliuer our Prince from daunger
of practifes, and our felues from want of a Prince. Let
vs doo that, which all the reft thinke. Let it be faid, that
we onely are not aftonifhed with vaine titles, which
haue their force but in our force. Laftly, to haue faide
& heard fo much, was as dägerous, as to haue attëpted:
& to attëpt they had the name of glorious liberty with
them. Thefe words being fpoke (like a furious ftorme)
prefently caried away their wel inclined braines. What
I, and fome other of the honefter fort could do, was no
more, then if with a puffe of breath, one fhould goe a-
bout to make a faile goe againft a mightie winde: or,
with one hand, ftay the ruine of a mightie wall. So generall grewe this madnes among them, there needed
no drumme, where each man cried, each fpake to other
that fpake as faft to him, and the difagreeing founde of
fo many voices, was the chiefe token of their vnmeete
agreement. Thus was their banquette turned to a battaile, their winie mirthes to bloudie rages, and the happie prayers for your life, to monftrous threatning of
your eftate; the folemnizing your birth-day, tended to
haue been the caufe of your funerals. But as a dronken
rage hath (befides his wickednes) that follie, that the
more it feekes to hurt, the leffe it confiders how to be
able to hurt: they neuer weyed how to arme thëfelues,
but tooke vp euery thing for a weapon, that furie
offered to their handes. Many fwordes, pikes, and
billes there were: others tooke pitchforkes and rakes,
conuerting hufbandrie to fouldierie: fome caught hold

of

of spittes (thinges seruiceable for life) to be the instruments of death. And there was some such one, who held the same pot wherein he drank to your health, to vse it (as he could) to your mischiefe. Thus armed, thus gouerned, forcing the vnwilling, and hartening the willing, adding furie to furie, and encreasing rage with running, they came headlong towarde this lodge: no man (I dare say) resolued in his own hart, what was the vttermost he would doo when he came hether. But as mischief is of such nature, that it cannot stand but with strengthning one euill by an other, and so multiplie in it selfe, till it come to the highest, and then fall with his owne weight: so to their mindes (once passed the bounds of obedience) more and more wickednes opened it selfe, so that they who first pretended to preserue you, then to reforme you, (I speak it in my conscience, and with a bleeding hart) now thought no safetie for them, without murdering you. So as if the Gods (who preserue you for the preseruation of *Arcadia*) had not shewed their miraculous power, and that they had not vsed for instruments, both your owne valour (not fit to be spoken of by so meane a mouth as mine) and some (I must confesse) honest minds, (whō alas why should I mention, since what we did, reached not the hundred part of our duetie?) our hands (I tremble to think of it) had destroyed all that, for which we haue cause to reioyce that we are *Arcadians*.

6   With that the fellow did wring his hands, & wrang out teares: so as *Basilius*, that was not the sharpest pearcer into masked minds, toke a good liking to him; & so much the more as he had tickled him with praise in the hearing of his mistres. And therfore pitying his woūd,
willed

willed him to get him home, and looke well vnto it, & make the beſt ſearch he could, to know if there were a-ny further depth in this matter, for which he ſhould be well rewarded. But before he went away, certain of the ſhepheards being come (for that day was appointed for their paſtorals) he ſent one of them to *Philanax*, and an other to other principal noble-men, and cities there abouts, to make through-inquirie of this vprore, and withall, to place ſuch garriſons in all the townes & vil-lages neere vnto him, that he might thereafter keep his ſolitary lodge in more ſecurity, vpõ the making of a fire, or ringing of a bell, hauing them in a redines for him.

CHAP. 28.

[1] *The praiſes of* Zelmanes *act.* [2] Dametas *his caroll for ſa-uing himſelf, and his charge.* [3] Baſilius *his conference with* Philanax *of the* Oracle *(the ground of all this ſtorie.)* [4] *His wrong-conſtruction of it.* [5] *His hymne to* Apollo. [6] *His cour-ting turnde ouer to tale-telling.*

His, *Clinias* (hauing his eare one way   1
when his eye was an other) had perceiued, & therefore haſted away, with mind
to tell *Cecropia* that ſhe was to take ſome
ſpeedie reſolution, or els it were daunger
thoſe examinations would both diſcouer, & ruine her:
and ſo went his way, leauing that little companie with
embracements, and praiſing of *Zelmanes* excellent proceeding, to ſhew, that no decking ſets foorth any thing „
ſo much, as affection. For as, while ſhe ſtoode at
the diſcretion of thoſe indiſcreete rebelles, euerie
angry

angrie countenance any of them made,ſeemed a knife
layde vpon their owne throates; ſo vnſpeakable was
now their ioy.that they ſaw(beſides her ſafetie & their
owne) the ſame wrought, and ſafely wrought by her
meanes, in whom they had placed all their delightes.
What examples *Greece* could euer alledge of witte and
fortitude,were ſet in the ranke of trifles, being compared to this action.

2   But as they were in the midſt of thoſe vnfained ceremonies,a Gitterne,ill-played on, accompanied with
a hoarce voice(who ſeemed to ſing maugre the Muſes,
and to be merie in ſpite of Fortune) made them looke
the way of the ill-noyſed ſong. The ſong was this.

A *Hatefull cure with hate to heale :*
  A blooddy helpe with blood to ſaue :
A fooliſh thing with fooles to deale :
Let him be bold that bobs will haue.
    But who by meanes of wiſdome hie
    Hath ſau'd his charge? it is euen I.

Let other deck their pride with skarres,
And of their wounds make braue lame ſhowes :
Firſt let them die,then paſſe the ſtarres,
When rotten Fame will tell their blowes .
    But eye from blade,and eare from crie :
    Who hath ſau'd all? it is euen I.

They had ſoone found it was *Dametas* , who came
with no leſſe lifted vp countenance,then if he had paſſed ouer the bellies of all his enemies : ſo wiſe a point
he thought he had perfourmed, in vſing the naturall
ſtrength

ftrength of a caue.But neuer was it his dooing to come
fo foone thence, till the coaft were more affuredly
cleare: for it was a rule with him, that after a great
ftorme there euer fell a fewe droppes before it be fully
finifhed.But *Pamela* (who had now experienced how ,,
much care doth follicite a Louers hart) vfed this occafion of going to her parents and fifter,indeed afwel for
that caufe, as being vnquiet, till her eye might be affured, how her fhepheard had gone through the.daun-
ger. But *Bafilius* with the fight of *Pamela* (of whom almoft his head otherwife occupied,had left the wonted
remembrance) was fodainly ftriken into a deuout kind
of admiration, remembring the oracle, which (according to the fauning humour of falfe hope) he interpreted now his owne to his owne beft, and with the
willing blindneffe of affection (becaufe his minde ran
wholly vpon *Zelmane)*he thought the Gods in their o-
racles did principally minde her.

But as he was deepely thinking of the matter,one of 3
the fhepheards tolde him, that *Philanax* was already
come with a hundred horfe in his company. For hauing by chaunce rid not farre of the little defert, he
had heard of this vprore, and fo was come vpon the
fpurre (gathering a company of Gentlemen as faft as
he could)to the fuccour of his Mafter.*Bafilius* was glad
of it;but(not willing to haue him,nor any other of the
Noble men, fee his Miftreffe)he himfelfe went out of
the Lodge, and fo giuing order vnto him of placing
garrifons, and examining thefe matters; and *Philanax*
with humble earneftneffe beginning to entreate him
to leaue of his folitarie courfe(which already had bene
fo daungerous vnto him)Well(faid *Bafilius*) it may be
Gg   ere

ere long I wil códiscend vnto your desire. In the meane
time, take you the best order you can to keepe me safe
in my solitarinesse. But, (said he) doo you remember,
how earnestly you wrote vnto me, that I should not be
moued by that Oracles authoritie, which brought me
to this resolution? Full well Sir (answered *Philanax*) for
though it pleased you not as then to let me knowe,
what the Oracles words were, yet all Oracles holding
(in my conceipt) one degree of reputatió, it suffised me
to know, it was but an Oracle, which led you fró your
owne course. Well (said *Basilius*) I will now tell you the
wordes; which before I thought not good to doo; because when al the euents fall out (as some already haue
done) I may charge you with your incredulitie. So he
repeated them in this forte.

THy elder care shall from thy carefull face
By princely meane be stolne, and yet not lost.
Thy yonger shall with Natures blisse embrace
An vncouth loue, which Nature hateth most.
Both they themselues vnto such two shall wed,
Who at thy beer, as at a barre, shall plead;
Why thee (a liuing man) they had made dead.
In thy owne seate a forraine state shall sit.
And ere that all these blowes thy head doo hit,
Thou, with thy wife, adultry shall commit.

For you forsooth (said he) when I told you, that some
supernaturall cause sent me strange visiós, which being
cófirmed with presagious chaunces, I had gone to *Del-*
phos,

phos,& there receiued this anfwere: you replied to me,
that the onely fupernaturall caufes were the humors of
my body, which bred fuch melancholy dreames; and
that both they framed a mind full of conceipts, apt to
make prefages of things, which in thefelues were meerly chaungeable : & with all as I fay, you remeber what
you wrot vnto me, touching authoritie of the Oracle :
but now I haue fome notable triall of the truth therof,
which herafter I wil more largly cōmunicate vnto you.
Only now, know that the thing I moft feared is alredy
performed; I mean that a forraine ftate fhould poffeffe
my throne. For that hath ben done by *Zelmane,*but not
as I feared, to my ruine, but to my preferuatiō. But whē
he had once named *Zelmane,*that name was as good as
a pully, to make the clocke of his praifes run on in fuch
fort, that(*Philanax* found) was more exquifite then the
only admiration of vertue breedeth: which his faithful
hart inwardly repining at made him fhrinke away as
foone as he could, to go about the other matters of importance, which *Bafilius* had enioyned vnto him.

Bafilius returned into the Lodge, thus by him felfe 4
conftruing the oracle, that in that he faid, his elder care
fhould by Princely meane be ftolne away from him,
and yet not loft, it was now perfourmed, fince *Zelmane* had as it were robd from him the care of his firft
begotten childe, yet was it not loft, fince in his harte
the ground of it remained. That his younger fhould
with Natures bliffe embrace the loue of *Zelmane,* becaufe he had fo commaunded her for his fake to doo;
yet fhoulde it be with as much hate of Nature, for
being fo hatefull an oppofite to the iealoufie hee
thought her mother had of him. The fitting in his

feate he deemed by her already perfourmed : but that
which moſt cóforted him,was his interpretation of the
adulterie, which he thought he ſhould commit with
Zelmane, whom afterwards he ſhould haue to his wife.
The point of his daughters marriage, becauſe it threatned his death withall, he determined to preuent,with
keeping them vnmaried while he liued . But hauing as
he thought,gotten thus much vnderſtanding of the O-
racie,he determined for three daies after to perfourme
certaine rites to *Apollo* : and euen then began with
hiᴜ wife and daughters to ſinge this Hymne ,by them
yearely vſed.

5   A Pollo *great, whoſe beames the greater world do light,*
     And in our little world do cleare our inward ſight,
 Which euer ſhine, though hid from earth by earthly ſhade,
 Whoſe lights do euer liue , but in our darkeneſſe fade;
 Thou God,whoſe youth was deckt with ſpoiles of Pythōs *skin:*
" *(So humble knowledge can throw downe the ſnakiſh kinne)*
 Latonas *ſonne,whoſe birth in paine and trauaile long*
 Doth teach,to learne the good what trauailes do belong :
" *In trauaile of our life.(a ſhort but tedious ſpace)*
 While brickle houreglas runnes, guide thou our panting pace :
 Giue vs foreſightfull mindes : giue vs minds to obaye
 What foreſight tels;our thoughts vpon thy knowledge ſtaye.
 Let ſo our fruites grow vp,that nature be maintainde :
 But ſo our hartes keepe downe,with vice they be not ſtainde.
 Let this aſſured holde our iudgements oucrtake,
" *That nothing winnes the heauen,but what doth earth forſake.*

6   Aſſone as he had ended his deuotion (all the priuiledged ſhepheards being now come) knowing well
                      inough

inough he might lay all his care vpon *Philanax*, he was willing to fweeten the taft of this paffed tumult, with fome rurall paftimes. For which while the fhepheards prepared themfelues in their beft māner, *Bafilius* tooke his daughter *Philoclea* afide, and with fuch haft, as if his eares hunted for wordes, defired to know how fhe had found *Zelmane*. She humbly anfwered him, according to the agreement betwixt them, that thus much for her fake *Zelmane* was content to defcend from her former refolutiō, as to heare him, whēfoeuer he would fpeake; & further then that (fhe faid) as *Zelmane* had not graunted, fo fhe nether did, nor euer would defire. *Bafilius* kift her with more then fatherly thanks, and ftraight (like a hard-kept warde new come to his lands) would faine haue vfed the benefite of that graunt, in laying his ficknes before his onely phyfition. But *Zelmane* (that had not yet fully determined with her felfe, how to beare her felfe toward him) made him in a few words vnderftand, that the time in refpect of the cōpanie was vnfit for fuch a parley, & therfore to keep his braines the bufier, letting him vnderftand what fhe had learned of his daughters, touching *Eronas* diftreffe (whom in her trauaile fhe had knowne, and bene greatly beholding to) fhe defired him to finifh the.reft, for fo far as *Plagus* had told him; Becaufe fhe faid (& fhe faid truly) fhe was full of care for that Ladie, whofe defart (onely except an o-uer-bafe choife) was nothing agreable to misfortune. *Bafilius* glad that fhe would commaund him any thing, but more glad, that in excufing the vnfitneffe of that time, fhe argued an intention to graunt a fitter, obeyed her in this manner.

Gg 3 CHAP.

CHAP. 29.

Adame (said he) it is very true, that since yeares enhabled me to iudge what is, or is not to be pitied, I ne-uer saw any thing that more moued me to iustifie a vehemēt compassi-on in my self, then the estate of that Prince, whom strong against al his owne afflictions (which yet were great, as I perceaue you haue heard) yet true and no-ble loue had so pulled downe, as to lie vnder sorrow for another. In so much as I could not temper my long idle pen in that subiect, which I perceiue you haue seene. But then to leaue that vnrepeated, which I finde my daughters haue told you, It may please you to vn-derstād, since it pleaseth you to demaūd, that *Antiphilus* being crowned, & so left by the famous Princes *Musi-dorus* & *Pyrocles* (led thēce by the challenge of *Anaxius*, who is now in these prouinces of *Greece*, making a dis-honorable

honorable enquirie after that excellent prince *Pyrocles*
alreadie perifhed) *Antiphilus* (I fay) being crowned, and
deliuered from the prefence of thofe two, whofe vertues (while they were prefent, good fchoolmafters) fup-
preffed his vanities, he had not ftrēgth of mind enough
in him to make long delay, of difcouering what maner
of man he was. But ftreight like one caried vp to fo hie
a place, that he loofeth the difcerning of the ground o-
uer which he is; fo was his mind lifted fo far beyōd the
leuell of his owne difcourfe, that remembring only that
himfelfe was in the high feate of a King, he coulde not
perceiue that he was a king of reafonable creatures, who
would quickly fcorne follies, and repine at iniuries. But
imagining no fo true propertie of fouereigntie, as to do
what he lifted, and to lift whatfoeuer pleafed his fanfie,
he quickly made his kingdome a Tenifcourt, where his
fubiects fhould be the balles; not in truth cruelly, but
licencioufly abufing them, prefuming fo far vpon himfelfe, that what he did was liked of euery bodie : nay,
that his difgraces were fauours, and all becaufe he was
a King. For in Nature not able to conceyue the bonds
of great matters (fuddenly borne into an vnknowne
Ocean of abfolute power) he was fwayed withall (he
knewe not howe) as euerie winde of paffions puffed
him. Whereto nothing helped him better, then that
poyfonous fugar of flatterie: which fome vfed, out of
the innate bafeneffe of their hart, ftraight like dogges
fawning vppon the greateft; others fecretely hating
him, and difdayning his great rifing fo fuddenly, fo
vndeferuedly (finding his humour) bent their exalting him only to his ouerthrow; like the bird that caries
the fhell-fifh high, to breake him the eafier with his fall.

But

But his minde (being an apt matter to receiue what forme their amplifying fpeeches woulde lay vpon it) daunced fo prettie a muficke to their falfe meafure, that he thought himfelfe the wyfeft, the woorthyeft, and beft beloued, that euer gaue honour to a royall tytle. And being but obfcurely borne, he had found out vnblufhing pedegrees, that made him not onely of the blood royall, but true heyre, vniuftly difpoffeft by *Eronas* aunceftours. And like the foolifh birde, that when it fo hides the heade that it fees not it felfe, thinkes no bodie elfe fees it : fo did he imagine, that no bodie knew his bafeneffe, while he himfelfe turned his eyes from it.

2   Then vaineneffe (a meager friend to gratefulneffe) brought him fo to defpife *Erona,* as of whom he had receiued no benefit, that within halfe a yeeres mariage he began to pretend barrenneffe : and making firft an vnlawfull law of hauing mo wiues then one, he ftill keeping *Erona,* vnder-hãd, by meffage fought *Artaxia,* who no leffe hating him, then louing (as vnluckie a choife) the naughtie King *Plexirtus,* yet to bring to paffe what he purpofed, was content to train him into falfe hopes, till alreadie his imagination had crowned him King of *Armenia,* & had made that, but the foundation of more, and more monarchies; as if fortune had only gottẽ eies to cherifh him. In which time a great affembly of moft part of al the Princes of *Afia* being to do honour to the neuer fufficiently praifed *Pyrocles* & *Mufidorus,* he would be one not to acknowledge his obligation (which was as great as any of the others,) but looking to haue bene yong mafter among thofe great eftates, as he was amõg his abufing vnderlings. But fo many valorous Princes,

in-deed farre neerer to difdaine him then otherwife, he
was quickly (as ftanding vpon no true ground, inwardly) out of countenance with himfelfe, till his feldom-cō-
fortleffe flatterers (perfwading him, it was enuie & feare
of his expected greatnes) made him haft away frō that
company, & without further delay appointed the meeting with *Artaxia*; fo incredibly blinded with the ouer-
bright fhining of his roialty, that he could thinke fuch a
Queene could be content to be ioined-patent with an
other to haue fuch an husband. Poore *Erona* to all this
obeied, either vehemecy of affection making her ftoop
to fo ouerbale a feruitude, or aftonifhed with an vnlooked-for fortune, dull to any behoofeful refolutiō, or (as
many times it falles out euen in great harts when they
can accufe none but thēfelues) defperatly bent to maintaine it. For fo went fhe on in that way of her loue, that
(poore Lady) to be beyond all other examples of ill-fet
affection, fhe was brought to write to *Artaxia,* that fhe
was content, for the publike good, to be a fecond wife,
and yeeld the firft place to her : nay to extoll him, and
euen woo *Artaxia* for him.

But *Artaxia* (mortally hating them both for her brothers fake) was content to hide her hate, til fhe had time
to fhewe it : and pretending that all her grudge was a-
gainft the two paragons of vertue, *Mufidorus* & *Pyrocles,*
euen met them halfe way in excufing her brothers murder, as not being principall actors; and of the other-fide,
driuen to what they did by the euer-pardonable neceffitie : and fo well handled the matter, as, though fhe
promifed nothing, yet *Antiphilus* promifed himfelfe all
that fhe woulde haue him thinke. And fo a folemne
enteruiew was appointed. But (as the Poets fay) *Hymen*

had.

had not there his faffron-coloured cote. For *Artaxia*
laying men fecretly (and eafily they might be fecret,
fince *Antiphilus* thought fhe ouerran him in loue)when
he came euen readie to embrace her, fhewing rather a
countenaunce of accepting then offering, they came
forth, and (hauing much aduauntage both in number,
valure, and fore-preparation) put all his companie to
the fword; but fuch as could flie away. As for *Antiphilus* fhe caufed him and *Erona* both to be put in irons, ha-
fting backe toward her brothers tombe, vpõ which fhe
ment to facrifice them, making the loue of her brother
ftand betwene her and all other motions of grace, from
which by nature fhe was alienated.

4   But great diuerfitie in them two quickely difcouered
it felfe for the bearing of that affliction. For *Antiphilus*
that had no greatnelfe but outwarde, that taken away,
was readie to fall fafter then calamitie could thruft him;
with fruitlefle begging (where reafon might well affure
him his death was refolued) and weake bemoning his
fortune, to giue his enemies a moft pleafing mufique,
with manie promifes, and proteftations, to as little purpofe, as from a little minde. But *Erona* fadde in-deede,
yet like one rather vfed, then new fallen to fadnelle (as
who had the ioyes of her hart alreadie broken) feemed
rather to welcome then to fhunne that ende of miferie,
fpeaking little, but what fhe fpake was for *Antiphilus*,
remembring his guiltlefnelle, being at that time prifoner to *Tiridates*, when the valiant princes flue him : to
the difgrace of men, fhewing that there are women
more wife to iudge what is to be expected, and more
conftant to beare it when it is happened.

5   But her witte endeared by her youth, her affliction
by

by her birth, and her sadnesse by her beautie, made
this noble prince *Plangus*, who (neuer almost from his
coufin *Artaxia*) was nowe prefent at *Eronaes* taking, to
perceyue the shape of louelinesse more perfectly in wo,
then in ioyfulnesse (as in a picture which receiues
greater life by the darkenesse of shadowes, then by
more glittering colours) and feeing to like; and liking
to loue; and louing ftraight to feele the moft incident
effects of loue, to ferue and preferue. So borne by the
haftie tide of fhort leyfure, he did haftily deliuer together his affection, and affectionate care. But fhe (as if he
had fpoken of a fmall matter, when he mencioned her
life, to which fhe had not leifure to attend)defired him
if he loued her, to fhew it, in finding fome way to faue
Antiphilus. For her, fhe found the world but a wearifom
ftage vnto her, where fhe played a part againft her will:
and therefore befought him, not to caft his loue in fo
vnfruitfull a place, as could not loue it felfe: but for a
teftimonie of conftancie, and a futablenes to his word,
to do fo much comfort to her minde, as that for her
fake *Antiphilus* were faued. He tolde me how much he
argued againft her tendering him, who had fo vngratefully betraied her, and foolifhly caft away himfelfe. But
perceiuing fhe did not only bend her very goodwits to
fpeake for him againft her-felfe, but when fuch a caufe
could be allied to no reafo, yet loue would needs make
it-felf a caufe, & barre her rather fró hearing, then yeeld
that fhe fhould yeeld to fuch arguments: he likewife in
whó the power of Loue (as they fay of fpirits) was fubiect to the loue in her, with griefe confented, & (though
backwardly) was diligét to labor the help of *Antiphilus:*
a man whom he not onely hated, as a traitour to *Erona*,
but

but enuied as a poſſeſſor of *Erona*. Yet Loue ſware, his hart, in ſpite of his hart, ſhould make him become a ſeruant to his riuall. And ſo did he, ſeeking all the meanes of perſwading *Artaxia*, which the authority of ſo neere, and ſo vertuous a kinſmã would giue vnto him. But ſhe to whom the eloquence of hatred had giuen reuenge the face of delight, reiected all ſuch motions; but rather the more cloſely impriſoning them in her chiefe citie, where ſhe kept them with intention at the birth-day of *Tiridates* (which was very nere) to execute *Antiphilus*, & at the day of his death (which was about halfe a yeere after) to vſe the ſame rigor towars *Erona*. *Plangus* much grieued (becauſe much louing) attempted the humors of the *Lycians*, to ſee, whether they would come in with forces to ſuccor their Princeſſe. But there the next inheritor to the crowne (with the true play that is vſed in the gamę of kingdõs) had no ſooner his miſtres in captiuity, but he had vſurped her place, & making her odious to her people, becauſe of the vnfit electiõ ſhe had made, had ſo left no hope there: but which is worſe, had ſent to *Artaxia*, perſwading the ſuſticing her, becauſe that vniuſtice might giue his title the namc of iuſtice. Wãting that way, *Plangus* practiſed with ſome deere friends of his, to ſaue *Antiphilus* out of priſon, whoſe day becauſe it was much neerer then *Eronaes*, & that he wel found, ſhe had twiſted her life vpõ the ſame threed with his, he determined firſt to get him out of priſon: & to that end hauing prepared al matters as wel as in ſuch caſe he could, where *Artaxia* had ſet many of *Tiridates* old ſeruants to haue well-marking eyes, he cõferred with *Antiphilus*, as (by the aucthoritie he had) he found meanes to do; & agreed with him of the time and maner, how he ſhould

by

by the death of fome of his iaylors efcape.

But all being well ordered, and *Plangus* willinglie 6
putting himfelfe into the greateft danger, *Antiphilus*
(who, like a bladder, fweld redie to breake, while it was
full of the winde of profperitie, that being out, was fo
abiected, as apt to be trode on by euery bodie) when it
came to the point, that with fome hazard, he might be
in apparaæ likelihoode to auoide the vttermoft harm,
his harte fainted, and (weake foole, neither hoping, nor
fearing as he fhould) gat a conceite, that with bewraying his practife, he might obtaine pardon: and therefore, euen a little before *Plangus* fhould haue come vnto him, opened the whole practife to him that had the
charge, with vnpittyed teares idly protefting, he had
rather die by *Artaxias* commaundement, then againft
her will efcape: yet begging life vpon any the hardeft,
and wretchedeft conditions that fhe woulde lay vpon
him. His keeper prouided accordingly, fo that when
Plangus came, he was like, himfelf to haue bene entrap-
pud: but that finding (with a luckie in-fight) that it
was difcouered, he retired; and (calling his friendes a-
bout him) ftood vpon his guard, as he had good caufe.
For, *Artaxia* (accounting him moft vngrateful confidering that her brother and fhe, had not onely preferued
him againft the malice of his father, but euer vfed him
much liker his birth, then his fortune) fent forces to apprehend him. But he among the martiall men had gotten fo great loue, that he could not onely keep himfelf
from the malice, but worke in their mindes a compaffion of *Eronas* aduerfitie.

But for the fuccour of *Antiphilus* he could gette no
bodie to ioyne with him, the contempt of him hauing

uing not bene able to qualifie the hatred ; so that *Arta-*
xia might easilie vpon him perfourme her will ; which
was (at humble suite of all the women of that citie) to
deliuer him to their censure, who mortally hating him
for hauing made a lawe of *Polygamie*, after many tortures, forste him to throwe himselfe from a high *Pyra-*
mis, which was built ouer *Tiridates* tombe, and so to
end his faillse-harted life, which had planted no strong
thought in him, but that he could be vnkinde.

8 But *Plangus* well perceiuing that *Artaxia* staied onely for the appointed day, that the faire *Eronas* bodie,
(consumed to ashes) should make a notorious testimo-
nie, how deepely her brothers death was engrauen in
her brest, he assembled good numbers of friendes, whõ
his vertue (though a stranger) had tied vnto him, by
force to giue her libertie. Contrariwise, *Artaxia*, to
whom Anger gaue more courage then her sexe did
feare, vsed her regall authoritie (the most she could) to
suppresse that sedition, and haue her will : which (she
thought) is the most princely thing that may be . But
Plangus, who indeede (as all men witnes) is one of the
best captains (both for policie and valour) that are trained in the schoole of *Mars*, in a conflict ouerthrew *Ar-*
taxias power, though of far greater number : and there
toke prisoner a base sonne of her brothers, whom she
deerly affected, & then sent her word that he should run
the same race of fortune (whatsoeuer it was) that *Erona*
did : & happy was that threatning for her; for els *Artaxia*
had hastened the day of her death , in respecte of those
tumults.

9 But now (some principal noble-mẽ of that countrie
interposing theselues) it was agreed, that all persons els
fullie

fullie pardoned, and all prisoners (except *Erona*) deliuered, she should be put into the hands of a principall nobleman, who had a castle of great strength, vpon oath,
that if by the day two yeare fró *Tiridates* death, *Pyrocles*
and *Musidorus* did not in person combat, & ouercome
two knights, whó she appointed to maintain henquar-
rell against *Erona* and them, of hauing by treason destroyed her brother, that thé *Erona* should be that same
day burned to ashes: but if they came, and had the victorie, she should be deliuered; but vpon no occasion,
neither freed, nor executed, till that day. And hereto of
both sides, all toke solemne oath, and so the peace was
concluded; they of *Plangus* partie forcing him to agree,
though he himselfe the sooner condiscended, knowing
the courtesie of those two excellent Princes, not to refuse so noble a quarrell, and their power such, as two
more (like the other two) were not able to resist. But *Artaxia* was more, and vpon better ground, pleased with
this action; for she had euen newly receiued newes fró
Plexirtus, that vpon the sea he had caused them both to
perish, and therefore she held her self sure of the match.

But poore *Plangus* knew not so much, and therefore 10
seeing his partie (as most times it falles out in like case)
hungry of conditions of peace, accepted them, & then
obteined leaue of the Lord, that indifferently kept her,
to visite *Erona*, whom he founde full of desperate sorowe, not suffering, neither his vnwoorthinesse, nor
his wronges, nor his death (which is the naturall conclusion of all worldly acts) either to couer with forgetfulnes, or diminish with consideration, the affection
she had borne him: but euen glorying in affliction,
and shunning all comforte, she seemed to haue no
delight, but in making her selfe the picture of miserie.

So

So that when *Plangus* came to her, ſhe fell in deadlie traunces, as if in him ſhe had ſeene the death of *Anti-philus*, becauſe he had not ſuccoured him : and yet (her vertue ſtriuing) ſhe did at one time acknowledge her ſelfe bound, and profeſſe her ſelfe iniured ; in ſteede of allowing the concluſion they had made, or writing to the Princes (as he wiſht her to doo) crauing nothing but ſome ſpeedie death to followe, her (in ſpite of iuſt hate) beloued *Antiphilus*.

So that *Plangus* hauing nothing but a rauiſht kiſſe from her hande at their parting, went away towarde *Greece*, whetherward he vnderſtoode the Princes were embarked. But by the way it was his fortune to inter-cept letters, written by *Artaxia* to *Plexirtus*: wherein ſhe ſignified her accepting him to her huſband, whom ſhe had euer fauoured, ſo much the rather, as he had per-fourmed the conditions of her mariage, in bringing to their deſerued end, her greateſt enemies: withall, than-king the ſea, in ſuch tearmes, as he might well perceiue, it was by ſome treaſon wrought in *Plexirtus* ſhippe. Whereupon (to make more diligent ſearch) he tooke ſhippe himſelfe, and came into *Laconia*, enquiring, and by his enquirie finding, that ſuch a ſhippe was indeede with fight, and fire, periſhed, none (almoſt) eſcaping. But for *Pyrocles* and *Muſidorus*, it was aſſuredly determi-ned that they were caſt away : for the name of ſuch Princes (eſpecially in *Greece*) would quickly els haue bene a large witneſſe to the contrarie. Full of griefe with that, for the loſſe of ſuch, who left the world poor of perfection: but more ſorie for *Eronas* ſake, who now by them could not be relieued. A new aduertiſement from *Armenia* ouertooke him, which multiplied the

force

force of his anguish. It was a message from the Nobleman who had *Erona* in ward, giuing him to vnderstad,
that since his departure, *Artaxia* (vsing the benefite of
time) had besieged him in his castell, demaunding present deliuery of her, whom yet for his faith giuen, he
would not, before the day appointed, if possibly he
could resist, which he foresaw, lóg he should not do for
want of victuall, which he had not so wisely prouided,
because he trusted vpon the generall oth taken for two
yeares space: & therfore willed him to make hast to his
succour, & come with no small forces; for all they that
were of his side in *Armenia*, were consumed, & *Artaxia*
had encreased her might by mariage of *Plexirtus*, who
now crowned King there, stickt not to glory in the
murder of *Pyrocles* and *Musidorus*, as hauing iust cause
thereto, in respect of the deaths of his sister *Andromana*,
her sonne his nephew, and his own daughter *Zelmane*,
all whose losse he vniustly charged them withal, & now
openly stickt not to cófesse, what a reuenge his wit had
brought forth. *Plangus* much astonished herewith, bethought himselfe what to doo. For to returne to *Armenia* was vaine, since his friends there were vtterly ouerthrowne. The thought he of going to his father but he
had already (euen since the death of his stepmother, &
brother) attempted the recouering his fauour, & all in
vaine. For they, that had before ioined with *Andromana*
to do him the wrong, thought now no life for thē if he
returned, & therfore kept him stil (with new forged suspicions) odious to his father. So that *Plangus* reseruing
that for a worke of longer time, then the sauing of *Erona* could beare, determined to go to the mighty and
good King *Euarchus*: who lately hauing (to his eternall
fame) fully, not onely conquered his enimies, but esta-

blished

blifhed good gouernment in their countries, he hoped he might haue prefent fuccour of him, both for the
iuftnes of the caufe, & reuenge of his childrens death,
by fo hainous a treafon murthered. Therefore with diligence he went to him; & by the way (paffing through
my country) it was my hap to find him, the moft ouerthrowne mã with griefe, that euer I hope to fee againe.
For ftil it feemed he had *Erona* at a ftake before his eies;
fuch an apprehenfion he had taken of her daunger;
which in defpite of all the comfort I could giue him,
he poured out in fuch lamentations, that I was moued
not to let him paffe, till he had made full declaration,
which by peeces my daughters & I haue deliuered vnto you. Fayne he would haue had fuccour of my felfe,
but the courfe of my life being otherwife bent, I onely
accompanied him with fome that might fafely guide
him to the great *Euarchus*: for my parte hauing had
fome of his fpeeches fo feelingly in my memory, that
at an idle time (as I tolde you) I fet them downe Dia-
logue-wife, in fuch manner as you haue feene. And
thus, excellent Ladie, I haue obeyed you in this ftorie;
wherein if it well pleafe you to confider, what is the
ftraunge power of Loue, and what is due to his authoritie, you fhall exercife therein the true nobleneffe of
your iudgement, and doo the more right to the vnfortunate Hiftorian. *Zelmane* (fighing for *Eronaes* fake, yet
inwardly comforted in that fhe affured her felfe, *Euar-*
chus would not fpare to take in hande the iuft deliuering of her, ioyned with the iuft reuenge of his childrens loffe) hauing now what fhe defired of *Bafilius*,
to auoide his further difcourfes of affection, encouraged the fhepheards to begin, whom fhe faw all ready
for them.

The

The second Eclogues.

He rude tumulte of the *Enispians* gaue occasion to the honest shepheards to beginne their pastorals this day with a daūce, which they called the skirmish betwixt *Reason* and *Passion.* For seuen shepheards (which were named the Reasonable shepheards) ioined theselues; foure of them making a square, and the other two going a litle wide of either side, like winges for the maine battell; and the seuenth man formost, like the forlorne hope to begin the skirmish. In like order came out the seuen appassionated shepheards; all keeping the pase of their foote by their voice, and sundry consorted instrumēts they held in their armes. And first, the formost of Reasonable side began to sing.

R.	*Thou Rebell vile, come, to thy master yelde.*
	And the other that met with him answered.
P.	*No, Tyrant, no: mine, mine shall be the fielde.*
Reason.	*Can* Reason *then a Tyraunt counted be?*
Passion.	*If* Reason *will, that* Passions *be not free.*
R.	*But* Reason *will, that* Reason *gouerne most.*
P.	*And* Passion *will, that* Passion *rule the rost.*
R.	*Your will is will; but* Reason *reason is.*
P.	*Will hath his will, when* Reasons *will doth misse.*
R.	*Whom* Passion *leades vnto his death is bent.*
P.	*And let him die, so that he die content.*
R.	*By nature you to* Reason *faith haue sworne.*

Hh 2   P.   Not

P,   *Not so,but fellowlike together borne.*

R.   *Who* Paſſion *doth enſue,liues in annoy.*

P.   *Who* Paſſion *doth forſake,liues void of ioy.*

R.   Paſſion *is blinde,and treades an vnknowne trace*

P.   R eaſon *hath eyes to ſee his owne ill caſe.*

Then as they approched neerer, the two of *Reaſons* ſides,as if they ſhot at the other, thus ſange.

R.   *Dare* Paſſions *then abide in*Reaſons *light?*

P.   *And is not* R eaſon *dimde with* Paſſions *might?*

R.   *O fooliſh thing,which glory doth deſtroye.*

P.   *O glorious title of a fooliſh toye.*

R.   *Weakenes you are,dare you with our ſtrength fight?*

P.   *Becauſe our weaknes weakeneth all your might.*

R.   *O ſacred* R eaſon, *helpe our vertuous toiles.*

P.   *O* Paſſion,*paſſe on feeble* Reaſons *ſpoiles.*

R.   *We with ourſelues abide a daily ſtrife.*

P.   *We gladly vſe the ſweetnes of our life.*

R.   *But yet our ſtrife ſure peace in end doth breede.*

P.   *We now haue peace,your peace we doo not neede.*

Then did the two ſquare battailes meete, & in ſteed of fighting embrace one another,ſinging thus.

R.   *We are too ſtrong : but* R eaſon *ſeekes no blood.*

P.   *Who be too weake,do feigne they be too good.*

R.   *Though we cannot orecome, our cauſe is iuſt.*

P.   *Let vs orecome,and let vs be vniuſt.*

R.   *Yet* Paſſion, *yeeld at length to* R eaſons *ſtroke.*

P.   *What ſhall we winne by taking* Reaſons *yoke?*

R.   *The ioyes you haue ſhall be made permanent.*

P.   *But ſo we ſhall with griefe learne to repent.*

R.   *Repent indeed,but that ſhall be your bliſſe.*

P,   *How know we that, ſince preſent ioyes we miſſe?*

R.   *You know it not : of* Reaſon *therefore know it.*

P.   *No* Reaſon *yet had euer skill to ſhow it.*
R. P.   *Then let vs both to heauenly rules giue place,*
    Which Paſſions *skill, and* Reaſon *do deface.*

THen embraced they one another, and came to the
King, who framed his praiſes of thē according to
Zelmanes liking; whoſe vnreſtrained parts, the minde &
eie, had their free courſe to the delicate *Philoclea*, whoſe
looke was not ſhort in well requiting it, although ſhe
knew it was a hatefull ſight to her iealous mother. But
Dicus (that had in this time taken a great liking of *Dorus* for the good partes he found aboue his age in him)
had a delight to taſte the fruites of his wit, though in a
ſubiect which he him ſelfe moſt of all other deſpiſed:
and ſo entred to ſpeach with him in the manner of this
following Eclogue.

Dicus.   Dorus.

DOrus, *tell me, where is thy wonted motion*   Dicus
  To make theſe woods reſounde thy lamentation?
Thy ſainte is dead, or dead is thy deuotion.
  For who doth holde his loue in eſtimation,
To witnes, that he thinkes his thoughts delicious,
Thinks to make ech thing badge of his ſweet paſſion.

  But what doth make thee Dicus *ſo ſuſpicious*   Dorus
Of my due faith, which needs muſt be immutable?
Who others vertue doubt, themſelues are vicious.
  Not ſo; although my mettall were moſt mutable,
Her beames haue wrought therin moſt faire impreſſion:
To ſuch a force ſome chaunge were nothing ſutable.

Dicus. *The harte well ſet doth neuer ſhunne confeſſion :*
If noble be thy bandes, make them notorious:
Silence doth ſeeme the maske of baſe oppreſſion.

Who glories in his loue, doth make Loue glorious :
But who doth feare, or bideth muet wilfully,
Showes, guilty harte doth deeme his ſtate opprobrious.

Thou then, that framſte both words & voice moſt skilfully,
Yeeld to our eares a ſweet and ſound relation,
If Loue tooke thee by force, or caught thee guilefully

Dorus. *If Sunnie beames ſhame heau'nly habitation ;*
If three-leau'd graſſe ſeeme to the ſheepe vnſauorie,
Then baſe and ſower is Loues moſt high vocation.

Or if ſheepes cries can helpe the Sunnes owne brauerie,
Then may I hope, my pipe may haue abilitie,
To helpe her praiſe, who decks me in her ſlauerie.

No, no: no wordes ennoble ſelfe-nobilitie.
As for your doubts ; her voice was it deceaued me,
Her eye the force beyond all poſſibilitie.

Dicus *Thy words well voic'd, well graſte had almoſt heaued me*
Quite from my ſelfe to loue Loues contemplation ;
Till of theſe thoughts thy ſodaine ende bereaued me.

Goe on therefore, and tell vs, by what faſhion
In thy owne proofe he gets ſo ſtraunge poſſeſſion,
And how poſſeſt he ſtrengthens his inuaſion ?

Dorus. *Sight is his roote, in thought is his progreſſion,*
His childhood woonder, prenticeſhip attention,
His youth delight, his age the ſoules oppreſſion :
Doubte is his ſleepe, he waketh in inuention;
Fancie his foode, his clothing is of carefulnes;

Beautie

Beautie his boote, his play louers diſſention:
 His eyes are curious ſearch, but vailde with warefulneſſe:
His wings deſire oft clipt with deſperation :
Largeſſe his hands could neuer skill of ſparefulneſſe.
 But how he doth by might, or by perſuaſion
To conquere, and his conqneſt how to ratifie,
Experience doubts, and ſchooles holde diſputation,

 But ſo thy ſheepe may thy good wiſhes ſatisfie   Dicus.
With large encreaſe, and wooll of fine perfection,
So ſhe thy loue, her eyes thy eyes may gratifie,
 As thou wilt giue our ſoules a deare refection,
By telling how ſhe was, how now ſhe framed is
To helpe, or hurt in thee her owne infection.

 Bleſt be the name, wherewith my miſtres named is: Dorus.
Whoſe wounds are ſalues, whoſe yokes pleaſe more then pleaſure
Her ſtaines are beames; vertue the fault ſhe blamed is. *(doth:*
 The hart, eye, eare here onely find his treaſure doth:
All numbring artes her endleſſe graces number not:
Time, place, life, wit ſcarcely her rare gifts meaſure doth.
 Is ſhe in rage? ſo is the Sunne in ſommer hot,
Yet harueſt brings. Doth ſhe alas abſent herſelfe ?
The Sunne is hid; his kindly ſhadows cumber not.
 But when to giue ſome grace ſhe doth content herſelfe,
O then it ſhines; then are the heau'ns diſtributed,
And Venus ſeemes, to make vp her, ſhe ſpent herſelfe.
 Thus then (I ſay) my miſchiefes haue contributed
A greater good by her diuine reflection;
My harmes to me, my bliſſe to her attributed,
 Thus ſhe is framde: her eyes are my direction;
Her loue my life; her anger my deſtruction.

Laſtly what ſo ſhe is, that's my protection.

Dicus. *Thy ſafetie ſure is wrapped in deſtruction:*
For that conſtruction thine owne wordes do beare.
A man to feare a womans moodie eye,
Makes Reaſon lie a ſlaue to ſeruile Senſe.
A weake defence where weakeneſſe is thy force :
So is remorſe in follie dearely bought.

Dorus. *If I had thought to heare blaſphemous wordes,*
My breſt to ſwords, my ſoule to hell haue ſolde
I rather would, then thus mine eares defile
With words ſo vile, which viler breath doth breed.
O heards take heed; for I a woolfe haue found;
Who hunting round the ſtrongeſt for to kill,
His breaſt doth fill with earth of others ioyes,
And loden ſo puls downe, puld downe deſtroyes.
O ſheepheards boyes, eſchue theſe tongues of venome,
Which do enuenome both the ſoule and ſenſes.
Our beſt defenſes are to flie theſe adders.
O tongues like ladders made to clime diſhonour,
Who iudge that honour, which hath ſcope to ſlander.

Dicus. *Dorus you wander farre in great reproches;*
So loue encroches on your charmed reaſon,
But it is ſeaſon for to end our ſinging.
Such anger bringing : as for me, my fancie
In ſicke-mans frenzie rather takes compaſsion,
Then rage for rage : rather my wiſh I ſend to thee,
Thou ſoone may haue ſome helpe, or change of paſsion.
She oft her lookes, the ſtarres her fauour bend to thee:
Fortune ſtore, Nature health, Loue grant perſwaſion.

A quiet

A quiet mind none but thy selfe can lend to thee,
Thus I commend to thee all our former loue,

Well do I proue, errour lies oft in zeale,   „ Dorus
Yet it is seale, though errour, of true hart.   „
Nought could impart such heates to friendly mind.
But for to find thy words did her disgrace,
Whose onely face the little heauen is,
Which who doth misse his eyes are but delusions,
Barr'd from their chiefest obiect of delightfulnesse,
Throwne on this earth the Chaos of confusions.
As for thy wish to my enraged spitefulnesse,   ✲
The louely blowne with rare reward, my prayer is
Thou mayest loue her that I may see thy sightfulnesse.
The quiet mind (whereof my selfe empairer is,
As thou doest thinke) should most of all disquiet me
Without her loue, then any mind who fairer is.
Her onely cure from surfet-woes can diet me :
She holdes the ballance of my contentation:
Her cleared eyes, nought els in stormes can quiet me.
Nay rather then my ease discontentation
Should breed to her, let me for aye deiected be
From any ioy, which might her griefe occasion.
With so sweete plagues my happie harmes infected be :
Paine willes me die, yet will of death I mortifie:
For though life irkes, in life my loues protected be.
Thus for ech change my changelesse hart I fortifie.

VVHen they had ended to the good pleasing of the
assistants, especially of *Zelmane*, who neuer forgat
to giue due commendations to her friend *Dorus*, the more
to aduance him in his pursute (although therein he had
brought

brought his matters to a more wished conclusion then
yet she knew of) out starte a iolly yonker, his name was
Nico, whose tongue had borne a very itching silence all
this while. And hauing spied one *Pas,* a mate of his, as
mad as himselfe (both indeed lads to clime any tree in
the world) he bestowed this maner of salutation vpon
him, and was with like reuerence requited.

Nico.   Dorus.

Nico.

    ANd are you there old Pas *? in troth I euer thought,*
    Among vs all we should find out some thing of nought.

Pas.

    And I am here the same, so mote I thriue and thee,
    Despairde in all this flocke to find a knaue, but thee.

Nico.

    Ah now I see, why thou art in thy selfe so blind :
    Thy gray-hood hides the thing, that thou despairst to find.

Pas.

    My gray-hood is mine owne, all be it be but gray,
    Not like the scrippe thou stol'ste, while Dorcas *sleeping lay.*

Nico.

    Mine was the scrippe: but thou, that seeming raid with loue,
    Didst snatch from Cosmas *hand her greeny wroughte gloue.*

Pas.

    Ah foole: so Courtiers do. But who did liuely skippe,
    When for a treene-dish stolne, thy father did thee whippe ?

Nico.

    In deed the witch thy dam her crouch from shoulder spred,
    For pilfring Lalus *lambe, with crouch to blesse thy head.*

Pas.

    My voice the lambe did winne, Menalcas *was our iudge:*
    Of singing match was made, whence he with shame did trudge.
                               Couldst

Couldſt thou make Lalus *flie? ſo nightingales auoide,*　　Nico
When with the kawing crowes their muſicke is annoide.

Nay like to nightingales the other birds giue eare:　　Pas.
My pipe and ſong made him both pipe and ſang forſweare.

I thinke it well : ſuch voice would make one muſicke hate:　　Nico.
But if I had bene there,th'adſt met another mate.

Another ſure as is a gander from a gooſe :　　Pas.
But ſtill when thou doſt ſing,me thinkes a colt is looſe.

Well aimed by my hat : for as thou ſang ſt laſt day;　　Nico.
The neighhours all did crie,alas what aſſe doth bray ?

But here is Dicus *old;let him then ſpeake the woord,*　　Pas.
To whether with beſt cauſe the Nymphes faire flowers affoord.

Content : but I will lay a wager hercunto,　　Nico.
That profit may enſue to him that beſt can do.
I haue (and long ſhall haue) a white great nimble cat,
A king vpon a mouſe,a ſtrong foe to the rat,
Fine eares,long taile he hath, with Lions curbed clawe,
Which oft he lifteth vp, and ſtayes his lifted pawe,
Deepe muſing to himſelfe,which after-mewing ſhowes,
Till with lickt beard, his eye of fire eſpie his foes.
If thou(alas poore if)do winne,then winne thou this,
And if I better ſing,let me thy Coſma *kiſſe.*

Kiſſe her? now mayſt thou kiſſe.I haue a better match;　　Pas.
A prettie curre it is; his name iwis is Catch,
No eare nor taile he hath,leaſt they ſhould him diſgrace,
A ruddie

A ruddie haire his cote, with fine long ſpeckled face:
He neuer muſing ſtandes, but with himſelfe will play
Leaping at euery flie, and angrie with a flea:
He eft would kill a mouſe, but he diſdaines to fight,
And makes our home good ſport with dauncing bolt vpright.
This is my pawne, the price let Dicus *iudgement ſhow:*
Such oddes I willing lay, for him and you I know.

Dicus.   *Sing then my lads, but ſing with better vaine then yet,*
Or elſe who ſingeth worſt, my skill will hardly hit.

Nico.   *Who doubts but* Pas *fine pipe againe will bring*
The auncient prayſe to Arcad *ſhepheards skill ?*
Pan *is not dead, ſince* Pas *beginnes to ſing.*

Pas.   *Who euermore will loue* Apollos *quill,*
Since Nico *doth to ſing ſo widely gape ?*
Nico *his place farre better furniſh will.*

Nico.   *Was not this he, who did for* Syrinx *ſcape*
Raging in woes teach paſtors firſt to plaine ?
Do you not heare his voice, and ſee his ſhape ?

Pas.   *This is not he that failed her to gaine,*
Which made a Bay, made Bay a holy tree :
But this is one that doth his muſicke ſtaine.

Nico.   *O* Faunes, *O* Fairies *all, and do you ſee,*
And ſuffer ſuch a wrong ? a wrong I trowe,
That Nico *muſt with* Pas *compared be ?*

Pas.   *O* Nymphes, *I tell you newes, for* Pas *you knowe :*

While

While I was warbling out your woonted praise,
Nico *would needes with* Pas *his bagpipe blowe.*

If neuer I did faile your holy-dayes,
With daunces, carols, or with barlybreake:
Let Pas *now know, how* Nico *makes the layes.*

If each day hath bene holy for your sake,
Vnto my pipe, O Nimphes, helpe now my pipe,
For Pas *well knowes what layes can* Nico *make.*

Alas how oft I looke on cherries ripe,
Me thinkes I see the lippes my Leuca *hath,*
And wanting her, my weeping eyes I wipe.

Alas, when I in spring meete roses rathe,
And thinke from Cosmas *sweet red lips I liue,*
I leaue mine eyes vnwipte my cheekes to bathe.

As I of late, neer bushes vsde my siue,
I spied a thrush where she did make her nest,
That will I take, and to my Leuca *giue.*

But long haue I a sparrow gailie drest,
As white as milke, and comming to the call,
To put it with my hand in Cosmas *brest.*

I oft doo sue, and Leuca *saith, I shall,*
But when I did come neere with heate and hope,
She ranne away, and threw at me a ball.

Cosma *once said, she left the wicket ope,*

For

For me to come, and so she did: I came,
But in the place found nothing but a rope.

Nico. When Leuca dooth appeare, the Sunne for shame
Dooth hide himselfe: for to himselfe he sayes,
If Leuca liue, she darken will my fame.

Pas. When Cosma doth come forth, the Sun displaies
His vtmost light: for well his witte doth know,
Cosmas faire beames emblemish much his raies.

Nico. Leuca to me did yester-morning showe
In perfect light, which could not me deceaue,
Her naked legge, more white then whitest snowe.

Pas. But yesternight by light I did receaue
From Cosmas eyes, which full in darkenes shine,
I sawe her arme, where purest Lillies cleaue.

Nico. She once starke nak'd did bathe a little tine;
But still (me thought) with beauties from her fell,
She did the waters wash, and make more fine.

Pas. She once, to coole her selfe, stood in a well,
But euer since that well is well besought,
And for Rose-water sould of rarest smeli.

Nico. To riuers banke, being on walking brought,
She bad me spie her babie in the brooke,
Alas (said I) this babe dooth nurce my thought.

Pas. As in a glasse I held she once did looke,

I said,

I said, my hands well paide her for mine eyes,
Since in my hands selfe goodly sight she tooke.

   O if I had a ladder for the skies,   Nico.
I would climbe vp, and bring a prettie starre,
To weare vpon her neck, that open lies.

   O if I had Apollos golden carre,   Pas.
I would come downe, and yeeld to her my place,
That (shining now) she then might shine more farre.

   Nothing (O Leuca) shall thy fame deface,   Nico.
While shepheards tunes be heard, or rimes be read,
Or while that shepheards loue a louely face.

   Thy name (O Cosma) shall with praise be spread,   Pas.
As farre as any shepheards piping be :
As farre as Loue possesseth any head.

   Thy monument is layd in many a tree,   Nico.
With name engrau'd: so though thy bodie die
The after-folkes shall wonder still at thee.

   So oft these woods haue heard me Cosma crie,   Pas.
That after death, to heau'n in woods resound,
With Echoes help, shall Cosma, Cosma flie.

  Peace, peace good Pas, thou weeriest euen the ground Nico
With sluttish song: I pray thee learne to blea,
For good thou mayst yet prooue in sheepish sound.

  My father hath at home a prettie Iay,   Pas.

                         Goe

Goe winne of him (for chattering) praiſe or ſhame:
For ſo yet of a conqueſt ſpeake thou may.

Nico.　　*Tell me (and be my Pan) the monſters name,*
That hath foure legs, and with two onely goes,
That hath foure eyes, and onely two can frame.

Pas.　　*Tell me (and Phœbus be) what monſter growes*
With ſo ſtrong liues, that bodie cannot reſt
In eaſe, vntill that bodie life forgoes.

Dicus.　　*Enough, enough: ſo ill hath done the beſt,*
That ſince the hauing them to neither's due,
Let cat and dog fight which ſhall haue both you.

SOme ſpeech there ſtreight grew among the hearers, what they ſhould meane by the riddles of the two monſters. But *Zelmane*, whoſe harte better delighted in wailefull ditties, as more according to her fortune, ſhe deſired *Lamon*, he would againe repeate ſome other lamentation of the ſtill-abſent *Strephon* and *Klaius*. *Baſilius* (as ſoone as he vnderſtood *Zelmanes* pleaſure) commaunded *Lamon* vpon paine of his life (as though euery thing were a matter of life and death, that pertained to his miſtreſſe ſeruice) immediately to ſing it: who with great cunning, varying his voice according to the diuerſitie of the perſons, began this Dizaine, anſwered in that kinde of verſe, which is called the Crowne.

　　　　Strephon.　　Klaius.

Strephon. I *ioye in griefe, and doo deteſt all ioyes:*
Deſpiſe delight, and tyrde with thought of eaſe

　　　　　　　　　　　　　　　　　I turne

I turne my minde to all formes of annoyes,
And with the chaunge of them my fancie please.
I studie that which may me most displease;
And in despite of that displeasures might,
Embrace that most, that most my soule destroyes.
Blinded with beames, fell darkenes is my sight :
Dole on my ruine feedes, with sucking smarte,
I thinke from me, not from my woes to parte.

I thinke from me, not from my woes to parte,   Klaius.
And loth this time, calld life, nay thinke, that life
Nature to me for torment did emparte ;
Thinke, my harde haps haue blunted deaths sharpe knife,
Not sparing me, in whom his workes be rise :
And thinking this, thinke Nature, Life, and Death
Place Sorrowes triumph on my conquered brest:
Whereto I yeeld, and seeke none other breath,
But from the sent of some infectious graue :
Nor of my fortune ought, but mischiese craue.

Nor of my fortune ought but mischiese craue,   Strephon
And seeke to nourish that, which now contaynes
All what I am : if I my selfe will saue,
Then must I saue, what in me chiefly raignes.
Which is the hatefull web of Sorowes paines.
Sorow then cherish me, for I am sorowe :
No being now, but sorowe I can haue :
Then decke me as thine owne, thy helpe I borowe,
Since thou my riches arte, and that thou haste
Enough to make a fertill minde lie waste.

Enough to make a fertill minde lie waste   Klaius.
                        Ii   Is

Is that huge ſtorme, which powres it ſelfe on me:
Haileſtones of teares, of ſighes a monſtrous blaſt,
Thunders of cries; lightnings my wilde lookes be,
The darkened heau'n my ſoule which nought can ſee;
The flying ſprites which trees by rootes vp teare
Be thoſe deſpaires, which haue my hopes quite waſt.
The diffrence is; all folkes thoſe ſtormes forbeare:
But I cannot; who then my ſelfe ſhould flie
So cloſe vnto my ſelfe my wrackes doo lie.

Strephon.
   So cloſe vnto my ſelfe my wrackes doo lie;
   Both cauſe, effect, beginning, and the ende
   Are all in me : what helpe then can I trie?
   My ſhip, my ſelfe; whoſe courſe to loue *doth bende,*
   Sore beaten doth her maſt of Comforte *ſpende :*
   Her cable, Reaſon, *breakes from anchor,* Hope *:*
   Fancie, her tackling, torne away doth flie :
   Ruine, the winde, hath blowne her from her ſcope:
   Bruſed with waues of Cares, *but broken is*
   On rocke, Deſpaire, *the buriall of my bliſſe.*

Klaius.
   On rocke, Deſpaire, *the buriall of my bliſſe*
   I long doo plowe with plough of deepe Deſire:
   The ſeed Faſt-meaning *is, no truth to miſſe :*
   I harowe it with Thoughts, *which all conſpire*
   Fauour *to make my chiefe and onely hire:*
   But, woe is me, the yeare is gone about,
   And now I faine would reape, I reape but this,
   Hate *fully growne,* Abſence *new ſprongen out.*
   So that I ſee, although my ſight empaire,
   Vaine is their paine, who labour in Deſpaire.

Vaine is their paine, who Labour in Despaire.
For so did I, when with my angle, Will,
I sought to catch the fish Torpedo *faire.*
Eu'n then Despaire *did* Hope *already kill:*
Yet Fancie *would perforce employ his skill,*
And this hath got; the catcher now is caught,
Lamde with the angle, which it selfe did beare,
And vnto death, quite drownde in Dolours, *brought*
To death, as then disguisde in her faire face.
Thus, thus I had, alas, my losse in chase.

Strephon.

Thus, thus I had, alas, my losse in chase,
When first that crowned Basiliske *I knewe,*
Whose footesteps I with kisses oft did trace,
Till by such hap, as I must euer rewe,
Mine eyes did light vpon her shining hewe,
And hers on me, astonisht with that sight.
Since then my harte did loose his wonted place,
Infected so with her sweet poysons might,
That, leauing me for dead, to her it went:
But ah her flight hath my dead reliques spent.

Klaius.

But ah her flight hath my dead reliques spent,
Her flight from me, from me, though dead to me,
Yet liuing still in her, while her beames lent
Such vitall sparke, that her mine eyes might see.
But now those liuing lights absented be,
Full dead before, I now to dust should fall;
But that eternall paines my soule should hent,
And keepe it still within this body thrall:
That thus I must, while in this death I dwell,
In earthly fetters feele a lasting hell.

Strephon.

Klaius.   *In earthly fetters feele a laſting hell*
Alas I doo ; from which to finde releaſe,
I would the earth, I would the heauens fell.
But vaine it is to thinke theſe paines ſhould ceaſe,
Where life is death, and death cannot breed peace.
O faire, ô onely faire, from thee, alas;
Theſe foule, moſt foule, diſtreſſes to me fell;
Since thou from me (ô me) ô Sunne didſt paſſe.
Therefore eſteeming all good bleſſings toyes
I ioy in griefe, and doo deteſt all ioyes.

Strephon.   *I ioye in griefe, and doo deteſt all ioyes.*
And now an ende, (ô Claius) *now an ende*
For euen the hearbes our mournefull muſique ſtroyes,
And from our burning breath the trees doo bende.

SO wel did *Lamons* voice expreſſe the paſſiôs of thoſe
ſhepheards, that all the Princely beholders were ſtriken in a ſilent côſideration of them ; indeed euery one
making, that he heard of another the balâce of his own
troubles . And *Baſilius* perceiuing ſuch melancholique
muſique beſt conſorted to the humor of his miſtreſſe,
entreated againe the young melancholy ſhepheard,
that he would emparte ſome part of the ſorow his coûtenaunce ſo well witneſſed vnto them . Which he in
parte to ſatisfie, began an Eclogue betwixt himſelf and
the *Echo :* framing his voice in thoſe deſerte places, as
what words he would haue the *Echo* replie, vnto thoſe
he would ſinge higher then the reſt, and ſo kindly framed a diſputation betwixt himſelfe and it. Which with
theſe *Hexameters* in the following order he vttered.

                                                    Faire

Echo

*F*Aire rocks, goodly riuers, sweet woods, when shall I see peace? Peace.
 Peace? who debars me my tongue? who is it that comes me so nie? I.
O I doo know what guest I doo meete : it is Echo.   'T is Echo
Well mett Echo ; aproch, and tell me thy will too.   I will too
Echo, what doo I get yeelding my sprite to my grieues?   Grieues.
What medicine may I finde for a paine that drawes me to death? Death.
O poif'nous medicine : what worse to me can be then it?   It.
In what state was I then, when I tooke this deadly diseafe?   Eafe.
And what maner a minde, which had to that humor a vaine?   Vaine.
Hath not reafon enough vehemence the desire to reproue?   Proue.
Oft proue I : but what falue, when Reafon feeks to be gone?   One.
O what is it? what is it, that may be a falue to my loue?   Loue.
What doo louers feeke for, long feeking for t'enioye?   Ioye.
What be the ioyes, for which i enioye they went to the paines? Paines.
Then to an earnest loue what doth best victorie lende?   Ende.
Ende? but I can neuer ende : Loue will not giue me the leaue. Leaue.
How be the mindes difpofde, that cannot tafte the Phyficke? Sicke.
Yet fay againe th'aduice for th'ils that I tolde thee.   I told th
Doth th'infected wretch of his ill th'extremitie know?   No.
But if he know not his harmes, what guids hath he whilst he be blind? Blinde.
What blinde guides can he haue that leades to a fancie?   A fancie
Can fancies wante eyes? or he fall that fteppeth aloft?   Oft.
What caufes first made these torments on me to light?   Light.
Can then a caufe be fo light, that forceth a man to goe die? I.
Yet tell, what light thing I had in me to drawe me to die?   Eye.
Eie-fight made me to yeeld : but what first pearst to my eyes? Eyes.
Eyes hurters? eyes hurte? but what from them to me falls?   Falls.
But when I first did fall, what brought moft fall to my harte? Arte.
Arte? what can be that arte, which thou dooft meane by thy fpeach? Spæach
What be the fruites of fpeaking arte, what growes by the wordes? Wordes.
O much more then wordes : those wordes feru'd more me to blofse. Lefse

Ii 3   O

O when ſhall I be knowne, where moſt to be known I doo long ?	*Longe.*
Long be thy woes for ſuch bad newes : how recks ſhe my thoughts ?	*Oughts.*
Then, then what doo I gayne, ſince vnt' her will I doo winde?	*Winde.*
Winde, tempeſts, and ſtormes : yet in ende what giues ſhe deſire ?	*Ire.*
Silly rewarde : yet aboue women hath ſhe a title.	*A titile.*
What great name may I giue to ſo heau'nly a woman ?	*A wo-man.*
Woe, but ſeems to me ioye, that agrees to my thought ſo.	*I thought ſo.*
Thinke ſo : for of my deſired bliſſe it is onely the courſe.	*Courſe.*
Curſt be thy ſelfe for curſing that, which leades me to ioyes.	*T'oyes.*
What be the ſweete creatures where lowly demaundes be not harde ?	*Harde.*
Harde to be gott, but got conſtant, to be helde very ſteeles.	*Eeles.*
How be they helde vnkinde? ſpeake, for th'haſt narrowly pry de.	*Pride.*
How can pride come there ſince ſprings of beautie be thence ?	*Thence.*
Horrible is this blaſphemie vnto the moſt holie.	*O lye.*
Thou liſt, falſe Echo; their mindes, as vertue, be iuſte.	*Iuſte.*
Mockſt thou thoſe Diamonds, which onely bematcht by the Godds?	*Odds.*
Odds ? what an odds is there, ſince them to the heau'ns I preferre ?	*Erre.*
Tell yet againe, how name ye the goodly made euill ?	*A deuill.*
Deuill ? in hell where ſuch Deuili is, to that hell I doo goe.	*Goe.*

AFter this well placed *Echo,* the other ſhepheards were offring them-ſelues to haue continued the ſports : But the night had ſo quietly ſpent moſt part of her ſelfe, that the King for that time licenſed them : & ſo bringing *Zelmane* to her lodging, who would much rather haue done the ſame for *Philoclea,* of all ſides they went to counterfait a ſleep in their beds, for a true one their agonies could not afoord them. Yet there lay they (for ſo might they be moſt ſolitarie) for the foode of their thoughts, till it was neere noone the next day. After which *Baſilius* was to continue his *Apollo* deuotions, and the other to meditate vpon their priuate deſires.

The end of the ſecond Booke.

THE THIRDE BOOKE
OF THE COVNTESSE OF
PEMBROKES ARCADIA.

CHAP. I.

*Dorus—his ¹ faire and ² foule weather in his loue. ³ His for-
lorne agonies. ⁴ His doubts to write, ⁵ and Pamelaes
to reade, ⁶ his elegie.*

His laſt dayes daunger, ¹
hauing made *Pamelaes*
loue diſcerne, what a
loſſe it ſhould haue ſuf-
fered, if *Dorus* had bene
deſtroyed, bredde ſuch
tenderneſſe of kindnes
in her toward him: that
ſhe coulde no longer
keepe Loue from loo-
king through her eyes,
and going forth in her words ; whom before as a cloſe
priſoner ſhe had to her hart onely committed; ſo as finding not only by his ſpeeches & letters, but by the pitifull oratiõ of a languiſhing behauior, & the eaſily diſcy-
phered character of a ſorowful face, that Deſpair began
nowe to threaten him deſtruction, ſhe grewe content both to pitie him , and let him ſee ſhe pityed
him : as well by making her owne beautifull beames
thawe away the former icineſſe of her behauiour, as
Ii 4   by

by entertaining his difcourfes (whenfoeuer he did vfe
them)in the third perfon of *Mufidorus* ; to fo farre a degree,that in the ende fhe faid, that if fhe had bene the
Princeffe,whom that difguifed Prince had vertuoufly
,, loued,fhe would haue requited his faith with faithfull
affection:finding in her hart,that nothing could fo hartily loue as vertue : with many mo words to the fame
fenfe of noble fauour,& chaft plainneffe. Which when
at the firft it made that expected bliffe fhine vpon *Do-*
rus;he was like one frozen with extremitie of colde, o-
uer-haftily brought to agreat fire,rather oppreffed,then
relieued with fuch a lightning of felicitie. But after the
ftrength of nature had made him able to feel the fweetneffe of ioyfulnes,that again being a child of Paffion,&
neuer acquainted with mediocrity,could not fet boûds
vpon his happines,nor be côtent to giue Defire a kingdome,but that it muft be an vnlimited Monarchy. So
that the ground he ftood vpon being ouer-high in happines,& flipperie through affection, he could not hold
himfelfe frô falling into fuch an error,which with fighs
blew all côfort out of his breft, & wafht away all cheerfulnes of his cheere, with teares. For this fauour filling
him with hope,Hope encouraging his defire, & Defire
confidering nothing,but oportunitie: one time (*Mopfa*
being called away by her mother, & he left alone with
Pamela)the fudden occafion called Loue, & that neuer
ftaid to aske Reafons leaue; but made the too-much louing *Dorus* take her in his armes, offering to kiffe her,
and, as it were, to eftablifh a trophee of his victorie.
    But fhe,as if fhe had bin ready to drinke a wine of ex-
cellent taft & colour,which fuddenly fhe perceiued had
poifon in it,fo did fhe put him away frô her: loking firft
vnto

vnto heauen,as amazed to find herſelfe ſo beguiled in him;then laying the cruel puniſhment vpon him of an-gry Loue,and lowring beautie,ſhewing diſdain,& a de-ſpiſing diſdain, Away(ſaid ſhe)vnworthy man to loue, or to be loued.Aſſure thy ſelfe,I hate my ſelfe for being ſo deceiued;iudge then what I doo thee,for deceiuing me.Let me ſee thee no more,the only fall of my iudge-ment,and ſtaine of my conſcience.With that ſhe called *Mopſa*,not ſtaying for any anſwer(which was no other, but a flood of tears,which ſhe ſemed not to mark(much leſſe to pity)& chid her for hauing ſo left her alone.

It was not an amazement, it was not a ſorrow,but it was euen a death,which then laid hold of *Dorus*:which certainly at that inſtant would haue killed him, but that the feare to tary longer in her preſence(contrary to her cõmandement)gaue him life to cary himſelfe away frõ her ſight, and to run into the woods, where,throwing himſelfe downe at the foot of a tree, he did not fall to lamentation (for that proceeded of pitying) or grie-uing for himſelfe (which he did no way) but to curſes of his life, as one that deteſted himſelfe. For finding himſelfe not onely vnhappy,but vnhappie after being falne from all happineſſe : and to be falne from all hap-pines,not by any miſconceiuing, but by his own fault, and his fault to be done to no other but to *Pamela :* he did not tender his owne eſtate, but deſpiſed it; greedi-ly drawing into his minde, all conceipts which might more and more torment him. And ſo remained he two dayes in the woods,diſdaining to giue his bodie food, or his mind comfort,louing in himſelfe nothing, but the loue of her.And indeed that loue onely ſtraue with the fury of his anguiſh,telling it,that if it deſtroyed *Do-*

3

rus

rus,it fhould alfo deftroy the image of her that liued in *Dorus.* and when the thought of that was crept in vnto him,it begã to win of him fome cõpaffion to the fhrine of the image,& to bewaile not for himfelfe(whõ he ha-ted)but that fo notable a loue fhould perifh.Thẽ began he onely fo farre to wifh his owne good,as that *Pamela* might pardon him the fault, though not the punifh-ment:& the vttermoft height hc afpired vnto,was, that after his death,fhe might yet pittie his error, and know that it proceeded of loue,and not of boldneffe.

4   That conceipt found fuch friendfhip in his thoughts, that at laft he yelded,fince he was banifhed her prefẽce, to feeke fome meanes by writing to fhew his forrow,& teftifie his repentance.Therfore getting him the necef-farie inftruments of writing,he thought beft to coũter-faite his hand(fearing that as alreadie fhe knew his, fhe would caft it away as foone as fhe faw it)and to put it in verf,hoping,that would draw her on to read the more, chufing the *Elegiac* as fitteft for mourning. But pen did neuer more quakingly performe his office ; neuer was paper more double moiftned with inke & teares; neuer words more flowly maried together,& neuer the *Mufes* more tired,then now with changes & rechanges of his deuifes:fearing howe to ende, before he had refolued how to begin,miftrufting ech word,condemning eche fentence.This word was not fignificant, that word was too plain:this would not be cõceiued;the other would be il conceiued.Here Sorow was not inoughexpreffed; there he feemed too much for his owne fake to be fory. This fentence rather fhewed art,then paffion; that fen-tence rather foolifhly paffionate,then forcibly mouing. At laft,marring with mending, and putting out better, then

then he left,he made an end of it;& being ended, & diuerse times ready to teare it:till his reason assuring him,
the more he studied, the worse it grew,he folded it vp,
deuoutly inuoking good acceptation vnto it; and watching his time, when they were all gone one day to
dinner(sauing *Mopsa*)t·· the other lodge, stale vp into
Pamelaes chamber,and in her stādish (which first he kissed; and craued of it a safe and friendly keeping) left it
there,to be seene at her next vsing her inke (himselfe returning againe to be true prisoner to desperate sorrow)
leauing her standish vpon her beds head,to giue her the
more occasion to marke it:which also fell out.

For she finding it at her after noone-returne,in ano-   5
ther place then she left it, opened it. But when she saw
the letter, her hart gaue her from whence it came.And
therefore clapping it to againe, she went away from it,
as if it had bin a contagious garment of an infected person: and yet was not long away, but that she wished
she had read it,though she were loth to reade it. Shall
I (said she) second his boldnesse so farre, as to reade his
presumptuous letters? And yet (said she) he sees me
not to growe the bolder thereby : And how can I tell,
whether they be presumptuous? The paper came from
him, and therefore not worthie to be receyued; and
yet the paper (she thought) was not guiltie. At last,she
concluded, it were not much amisse to looke it ouer,
that she might out of his wordes picke some further
quarrell against him. Then she opened it, and threwe it
away, and tooke it vp againe, till (ere she were aware)
her eyes woulde needes reade it, conteining this
matter.

Vnto

6 VNto a caitife wretch, whom long affliction holdeth,
and now fully beleeues helpe to be quite perished;
Grant yet, grant yet a looke, to the laſt monumēt of his anguiſh;
O you (alas ſo I find) cauſe of his onely ruine.

Dread not a whit (O goodly cruell) that pittie may enter
into thy hart by the ſight of this Epiſtle I ſend:
And ſo refuſe to behold of theſe ſtrange wounds the recitall,
leaſt it might th'allure home to thy ſelfe to returne.

(Vnto thy ſelfe I do meane thoſe graces dwell ſo within thee,
gratefulnes, ſweetnes, holy loue, hartie regard)
Such thing cannot I ſeeke (Deſpaire hath giu'n me my anſwer
deſpaire moſt tragicall clauſe to a deadly requeſt)
Such thing canot he hope, that knowes thy determinat hardnes;
hard like a rich marble: hard, but a faire Diamond.

Can thoſe eyes that of eyes drownd in moſt harty flowing teares,
(teares and teares of a man) had no returne to remorſe;
Can thoſe eyes now yeeld to the kind conceit of a ſorow,
which inke onely relates, but ne laments ne replies?

Ah, that, that I do I not conceiue (though that to my bliſſe were)
more then Neſtors yeares, more then a Kings diademe.
Ah, that, that I do not cōceiue; to the heaue when a mouſe climes
then may I hope t'atchieue grace of a heauenly tiger.

But, but alas, like a man cōdemn'd doth craue to be heard ſpeake
not that he hopes for amends of the deſaſter he feeles,
But finding th'approch of death with an ougly relenting,
giues an adieu to the world, as to his onely delight:

Right ſo my boiling hart, enflam'de with fire of a faire eye,
bubling out doth breath ſignes of his hugie dolcurs:
Now that he finds to what end his life and loue be reſerued,
and that he hence muſt part where to liue onely he lou'd.

O faire, O faireſt, are ſuch thy triumphs to thy fairneſſe?
can death beautie become? muſt be ſuch a monument?

Muſt

Muſt I be onely the marke,ſhall proue that Vertue is angrie?
ſhall proue that fiercenes can with a white doue abide?
Shall to the world appeare that faith and loue be rewarded
with mortall diſdaine,bent to vnendly reuenge?
Vnto reuenge? O ſweete,on a wretch wilt thou be reuenged?
ſhall ſuch high Plannets ende to the loſſe of a worme?
And to reuenge who doo bend,would in that kind be reuenged,
as th'offence was done,and goe beyond if he can.
All my offence was Loue:with Loue then muſt I be chaſtned,
and with more,by the lawes that to Reuenge doo belong.
If that loue be a fault,more fault in you to be louely :
Loue neuer had me oppreſt,but that I ſaw to be lou'd.
You be the cauſe that I lou'd:what Reaſon blameth a ſhadowe,
that with a body't goes? ſince by a body it is.
If that Loue you did hate,you ſhould your beautie haue hidden:
you ſhould thoſe faire eyes haue with a veile couered.
But foole,foole that I am,thoſe eyes would ſhine frō a dark caue.
what veiles then doo preuaile,but to a more miracle?
Or thoſe golden lockes,thoſe lockes which lock me to bondage,
torne you ſhould diſperſe vnto the blaſts of a winde.
But foole,foole that I am,tho I had but a hair of her head foūd,
eu'n as I am,ſo I ſhould vnto that haire be a thrall.
Or with fair hāds-nailes (ò hād which nailes me to this death)
you ſhould haue your face(ſince Loue is ill)blemiſhed.
O wretch,what do I ſay? ſhould that faire face be defaced?
ſhould my too-much ſight cauſe ſo true a Sunne to be loſt ?
Firſt let Cimmerian *darknes be my onel habitacion:*
firſt be mine eyes pulde out,firſt be my braine periſhed;
Ere that I ſhould conſent to doo ſuch exceſſiue a dammage
vnto the earth,by the hurt of this her heauenly iewell.
O no:but ſuch loue you ſay you could haue afoorded,
as might learne Temprance voyde of a rages euents.

                                             O ſweete

O sweet simplicitie: from whence should Loue so be learned?
vnto Cupid *that boy shall a Pedante be found?*
Well: but faultie I was: Reason to my Passion yeelded,
Passion vnto my rage, Rage to a hastie reuenge.
But what's this for a fault, for which such fault is abolisht,
such faith, so staineles, inuiolate, violent?
Shall I not? ô may I not thus yet refresh the remembrance,
what sweete ioyes I had once, and what a place I did hold?
Shall I not once obiect, that you, you graunted a fauour
vnto the man, whom now such miseries you awarde? (were:
Bēd your thoghts to the dear sweet words which thē to me giu'n
think what a world is now, think who hath altred her hart.
What? was I then worthie such good, now worthie such euill?
now fled, then cherished? then so nie, now so remote?
Did not a rosed breath, from lips more rosie proceeding,
say, that I should well finde in what a care I was had?
With much more: now what doo I finde, but Care to abhor me,
Care that I sinke in griefe, Care that I liue banished?
And banished doo I liue, nor now will seeke a recou'rie,
since so she will, whose will is to me more then a lawe.
If then a man in most ill case may giue you a farewell;
farewell, long farewell, all my woe, all my delight.

CHAP. 2.

[1] *The young Ladies mette:* [2] *inuited to the countrie-wenches sports,* [3] *goe thether,* [4] *there are taken, and thence caried to* Amphialus *castle.* [5] *Their entertainement there.* [6] Cecropias *auricular confession of her proud cariage in prosperitie,* [7] *and ambitious practises in aduersitie.* [8] Amphialus *his affection in these actions.*

What

W Hat this would haue wrought in her, fhe her felfe could not tell: for, before her Reafon could moderate the difputation betwene Fauour & Faultines, her fifter, and *Mifo*, called her downe to entertaine *Zelmane*, who was come to vifite the two fifters; about whom, as about two Poles, the Skie of Beautie was turned : while *Gynecia* wearied her bed with her melancholie ficknes, and made *Mifos* fhrewdneffe (who like a fprite, fette to keep a treafure, barde *Zelmane* from any further conference) to be the Lieutenant of her iealoufie: Both fhe and her hufband, driuing *Zelmane* to fuch a ftreit of refolution, either of impoffible graunting, or dangerous refufing, as the beft efcape fhe had, was (as much as fhe coulde) to auoyde their companie. So as, this day, being the fourth day after the vprore, (*Bafilius* being with his ficke wife, conferring vpon fuch examinations, as *Philanax*, and other of his noble-men had made of this late feditiõ, all touching *Cecropia* with vehemẽt fufpition of giuing either flame or fuell vnto it) *Zelmane* came with her bodie, to find her mind, which was gone long before her, & had gotten his feate in *Philoclea*: who now with a bafhfull cheerefulneffe (as though fhe were afhamed, that fhe could not choofe but be glad) ioyned with her fifter, in making much of *Zelmane*.

And fo as they fate deuifing how to giue more feathers to the winges of Time, there came to the lodge dore, fixe maides, all in one liuerie of fkarlette petti cotes, which were tuckt vp almofte to their knees, the petticoates them felues beinge in many places garni-

garnished with leaues, their legges naked, sauing that a-
boue the anckles they had little black silke laces, vpon
which did hang a few siluer belles: like which they had
a little aboue their elbowes, vpon their bare armes. Vpon their haire they ware garlands of roses and gilliflo-
wers; and the haire was so drest, as that came againe a-
boue the garlandes; enterchaunging a mutuall couering: so as it was doubtfull, whether the haire drest
the garlandes, or the garlandes drest the haire. Their
breasts liberall to the eye: the face of the formoste of
of them, in excellencie faire; and of the rest louely, if
not beautifull: and beautifull would haue bene, if they
had not suffered greedy *Phæbus*, ouer-often, and harde,
to kisse them. Their countenaunces full of a gracefull
grauitie; so as the gesture matcht with the apparrell, it
might seem a wanton modestie, and an entising sobernes. Each of them had an instrument of musick in their
hands, which consorting their wel-pleasing tunes, did
charge each eare with vnsensiblenes, that did not lende
it selfe vnto them. The Musicke entring alone into the
lodge, the Ladies were all desirous to see from whence
so pleasant a guest was come: and therefore went out
together; where, before they coulde take the paines to
doubt, much lesse to aske the question of their qualitie,
the fairest of them (with a gay, but yet discreete demeanour) in this sort spake vnto them. Most excellent Ladies, (whose excellencies haue power to make cities
enuie these woods, and solitarines to be accounted the
sweetest companie) vouchsafe our message your gracious hearing, which as it comes from Loue, so comes it
from louely persons. The maides of all this coast of
Arcadia, vnderstanding the often accesse that certaine
shep-

shepheards of these quarters, are allowed to haue in this forbidden place;and that their rurall sports are not disdained of you, haue bene stird with emulation to them,and affection to you, to bring forth some thing, which might as well breede your contentment: and therefore hoping that the goodnes of their intention, & the hurtlesnes of their sex shall excuse the breach of the commandemét in cóming to this place vnsent for, they chose out vs,to inuite both your princely parents, & your selues,to a place in the woods about halfe a mile hence:where they haue prouided some such sports, as they trust your gratious acceptatiós will interpret to be deliteful. We haue bene at the other lodge,but finding them there,busied in weightier affaires,our trust is,that you yet will not denie the shining of your eies vpó vs.

The Ladies stood in some doubte, whether they should goe or not, lest *Basilius* might be angry withall. But *Miso* (that had bene at none of the pastorals, and had a great desire to lead her old senses abroad to some pleasure) told them plainely, they should nor will nor choose, but go thether, and make the honest countrie people know,that they were not so squeamish as folkes thought of them. The Ladies glad to be warranted by her authoritie;with a smiling humblenesse obeied her: *Pamela* only casting a seeking looke,whether she could see *Dorus* (who poore wretch wandred halfe mad for sorrow in the woods, crying for pardon of her,who could not heare him) but indeed was grieued for his absence, hauing giuen the wound to him through her owne harte. But so the three Ladies & *Miso* went with those six *Nymphes*, conquering the length of the way with the force of musique, leauing only *Mopsa* behind;

who difgraced weeping with her countenaunce, becaufe her mother would not fuffer her to fhewe her
newskoured face among them. But the place apointed
(as they thought)met them halfe in their way, fo well
were they pleafed with the fweete tunes and prettie
connerfation of their inuiters. There founde they in
the midft of the thickeft part of the wood,a litle fquare
place,not burdened with trees,but with a boord couered,& beautified with the pleafanteft fruites, that Sun-
burnd *Autumne* could deliuer vnto thē. The maids befought the Ladies to fit downe,and taft of the fwelling
grapes,which feemed great with child of *Bacchus:* & of
the diuers coloured plums , which gaue the eye a pleafant taft before they came to the mouth. The Ladies
would not fhew to fcorne their prouifion, but eat, and
dranke a little of their coole wine, which feemed to
laugh for ioy to come to fuch lips.

4   But after the collation was ended,and that they looked for the cōming foorth of fuch deuifes,as were prepared for them, there rufht out of the woods twentie
armed men, who round about enuironed them,& laying hold of *Zelmane* before fhe could draw her fword,
and taking it from her, put hoods ouer the heads of all
fower,and fo muffled,by force fet them on horfebacke
and carried them away; the fifters in vaine crying for
fuccour, while *Zelmanes* harte was rent in peeces with
rage of the iniurie, and difdaine of her fortune. But
when they had caried them a foure or fiue mile further, they lefte *Mifo* with a gagge in her mouth, and
bound hande and foote, fo to take her fortune : and
brought the three Ladies (by that time that the Night
feemed with her filence to confpire to their treafon)

to a caftle about ten mile of from the Lodges : where they were fayne to take a boate whiche wayted for them. For the caftle ftood in the midft of a great lake, vppon a high rocke, where partly by Arte, but principallie by Nature, it was by all men efteemed impregnable.

But at the Caftle gate their faces were difcouered, and there were mett with a great number of torches, after whome the fifters knewe their aunt in lawe, *Cecropia*. But that fight increafed the deadly terrour of the Princeffes, looking for nothing but death, fince they were in the power of the wicked *Cecropia*: who yet came vnto them, making curtefie the outfide of mifchiefe, and defiring them not to be difcomforted: for they were in a place dedicated to their feruice. *Philoclea* (with a looke where Loue fhined through the mifte of Feare) befought her to be good vnto them, hauing neuer deferued euill of her. But *Pamelas* high harte difdayning humbleneffe to iniurie, Aunt, (faid fhe) what you haue determined of vs I pray you doo it fpeedily : for my part I looke for no feruice, where I finde violence.

But *Cecropia* (vfing no more wordes with them) conueyed them all three to feuerall lodgings (*Zelmanes* harte fo fwelling with fpite, that fhe coulde not bring foorth a worde) and fo lefte them : firft taking from them their kniues, becaufe they fhould do themfelues no hurte, before fhe had determined of them : and then giuing fuch order that they wanted nothing but libertie, & comfort, fhe went to her fonne, who yet kept his bed, becaufe of his wound he had receiued of *Zelmane*, & told him, whom now he had in his power.

Amphia-

Amphialus was but euen then returned from far countries, where he had wonne immortall fame, both of
courage & curtesie, when he met with the Princesses,
and was hurt by *Zelmane*, so as he was vtterly ignorant
of all his mothers wicked deuises; to which he would
neuer haue consented, being (like a rose out of a brier)
an excellent sonne of an euill mother : and now when
he heard of this, was as much amazed, as if he had seen
the Sunne fall to the earth. And therefore desired his
mother that she would tell him the whole discourse,
how all these matters had happened.

6   Sonne (said she) I will doo it willingly, and since all
is done for you, I will hide nothing from you. And
howsoeuer I might be ashamed to tell it strangers, who
would thinke it wickednesse, yet what is done for your
sake (how euill soeuer to others) to you is vertue To
begin then euen with the beginning, this doting foole
Basilius that now raignes, hauing liued vnmarried till
he was nigh threescore yeares old (and in all his speaches affirming, and in all his dooings assuring, that he
neuer would marrie) made all the eyes of the country
to be bent vpon your father, his onely brother (but
then younger by thirty yeares) as vpon the vndoubted
successour : being indeed a man worthy to raigne, thinking nothing enough for himselfe : where this goose
(you see) puts downe his head, before there be any
thing neere to touch him. So that he holding place
and estimation as heyre of *Arcadia*, obteyned me of
my father the King of *Argos*, his brother helping to
the conclusion, with protesting his bachelerly intention : for else you may be sure the King of *Argos*, nor
his daughter would haue suffered their Royall bloud
to

to be ftained with the bafe name of .fubiection . So
that I came into this countrie as apparant Princeffe
therof, and accordingly was courted, and followed of
all the Ladies of this countrie. My porte and pompe
did well become a King of *Argos* daughter : in my
prefence their tongues were turned into eares , & their
eares were captiues vnto my tongue . Their eyes admired my Maieftie, & happy was he or fhe, on whom
I would fuffer the beames thereof to fall.Did I goe to
church ? it feemed the very Gods wayted for me, their
deuotions not being folemnized till I was ready . Did
I walke abroad to fee any delight? **Nay , my walking
was the delight it felfe:** for to it was the concourfe,one
thrufting vpon another, who might fhewe him felfe
moft diligent and feruiceable towardes me:my fleepes
were inquired after, and my wakings neuer vnfaluted:
the very gate of my houfe full of principall perfons,
who were glad , if their prefents had receaued a gratefull acceptation. And in this felicitie wert thou borne,
the very earth fubmitting it felfe vnto thee to be troden on as by his Prince ; and to that paffe had my huf-
bandes vertue (by my good helpe) within fhort time
brought it with a plot we laide, as we fhould not haue
needed to haue waited the tedious worke of a naturall
end of *Bafilius*;when the heaués (I thinke enuying my
great felicity)thé ftopt thy fathers breath,whé he breathed nothing but power and foueraigntie.Yet did not
thy orphancie, or my widdowhood, depriue vs of the
delightfull profpect , which the hill of honour dooth
yeeld,while expectation of thy fucceffion did bind de-
pendencies vnto vs.

But before , (my fonne) thou wert come to the age 7

to feele the sweetnesse of authoritie, this beast (whom I can neuer name with patience) falsely and foolishly married this *Gynecia*, then a young girle, and brought her to sit aboue me in al feasts, to turne her shoulder to me-ward in all our solemnities. It is certaine, it is not so
" great a spite to be surmounted by straungers, as by ones owne allies. Thinke then what my minde was, since withall there is no queStion: The fall is greater from the first to the second, then from the second to the vndermost. The rage did swell in my harte, so much the more as it was faine to be suppressed in silence, & disguised with humblenes. But aboue al the rest, the griefe of grieues was, whē with these daughters (now thy prisoners) she cut of al hope of thy successiō. It was a tedious thing to me, that my eies should looke lower then any bodies, that (my selfe being by) anothers voice then mine, should be more respected: But it was insupportable vnto me, to think that not only I, but thou shouldSt spend al thy time in such misery, & that the Sun should see my eldeSt son lesse then a Prince. And though I had ben a sainct I could not choose, finding the chaūge this chaūge of fortune bred vnto me, for now frō the multitude of followers, silēce grew to be at my gate, & abfēce in my presence. The guesse of my mind could preuaile more before, then now many of my earneSt requeSts. And thou (my deare sonne) by the fickle multitude no more then any ordinary person (borne of the mud of
" the people) regarded. But I (remēbring that in all mise-
" ries weeping becomes fooles, and practize wise folks) haue tried diuers meanes to pull vs out of the mire of subiectiō. And though many times Fortune failed me, yet did I neuer faile my self. Wild beaSts I kept in a caue

hard

hard by the lodges, which I caused by night to be fed in the place of their paftorals, I as then liuing in my houfe hard by the place, and againft the houre they were to meete (hauing kept the beafts without meate) then let them loofe, knowing that they would feeke their food there, and deuoure what they founde. But blind Fortune hating fharpe-fighted inuentions, made them vnluckily to be killed. After, I vfed my feruant *Clinias* to ftir a notable tumult of country people: but thofe louts were too groffe inftruments for delicate conceits. Now laftly, finding *Philanax*-his examinations grow daungerous, I thought to play double or quit; & with a fleight I vfed of my fine-witted wēch *Artefia*, with other maids of mine, would haue fent thefe good inheritrixes of *Arcadia*, to haue pleaded their caufe before *Pluto*, but that ouer-fortunatly for thē, you made me know the laft day how vehemently this childifh paffion of loue doth torment you. Therfore I haue brought them vnto you, yet wifhing rather hate thē loue in you. For Hate often begetteth victory; Loue commonly is the inftrument of " fubiection. It is true, that I would alfo by the fame practife haue entrapped the parents, but my maids failed of it, not daring to tary long about it. But this fufficeth, fince (thefe being taken away) you are the vndoubted inheritor, and *Bafilius* will not long ouer-liue this loffe.

O mother (faid *Amphialus*) fpeake not of doing them **8** hurt, no more then to mine eies, or my hart, or if I haue any thing more deare then eyes, or hart vnto me. Let others finde what fweetneffe they will in euer fearing, becaufe they are euer feared : for my part, I will thinke my felfe highly intitled, if I may be once by *Philoclea* accepted for a feruant. Well (faid *Cecropia*) I would I had borne you of my minde, as well as of my body :

then

then fhould you not haue funcke vnder bafe weakenef-
fes.But fince you haue tied your thoughts in fo wilfull
a knot, it is happie I haue brought matters to fuch a
paffe,as you may both enioy affection, and vppon that
build your foueraigntie. Alas (faid *Amphialus*) my hart
would faine yeeld you thanks for fetting me in the way
of felicitie,but that feare killes them in me, before they
are fully borne.For if *Philoclea* be difpleafed, how can I
be pleafed? if fhe count it vnkindnes, fhal I giue tokens
of kindnes? perchance fhe códemnes me of this action,
and fhall I triumph? perchance fhe drownes nowe the
beauties I loue with forrowful teares,and where is then
my reioicing? You haue reafon (faid *Cecropia* with a fei-
ned grauitie) I will therefore fend her away prefently,
that her contentment may be recouered.No good mother (faid *Amphialus*) fince fhe is here, I would not for
my life conftraine prefence,but rather would I die then
cófent to abfence.Prety intricat follies (faid *Cecropia*) but
get you vp,& fee how you can preuaile with her, while
I go to the other fifter.For after we fhal haue our hands
full to defend our felues,if *Bafilius* hap to befiege vs.But
remembring herfelf,fhe turned back,& asked him what
he woulde haue done with *Zelmane*, fince nowe he
might be reuenged of his hurt. Nothing but honorably,anfwered *Amphialus*, hauing deferued no other of
me,efpecially being (as I heare) greatly cherifhed of
Philoclea.And therefore I could wifh they were lodged
„ together.O no(faid *Cecropia*)company confirmes refo-
„ lutiós,& lonelines breeds a werines of ones thoughts,
„ and fo a fooner confenting to reafonable profers.

CHAP.

CHAP. 3.

Amphialus *addressing him to* Philoclea. ² *Her melan-*
cholie habit. ³ *His humble sute.* ⁴ *Her pitifull answere :*
⁵ *and his compassionate replie.* ⁶*Their parting with cold*
comfort.

Vt *Amphialus* (taking of his mother   1
Philocleas kniues, which he kept as
a relique, since she had worne
them) gat vp, and calling for his ri-
chest apparell, nothing seemed
sumptuous inough for his mistresses eyes : and that which was costly, he feared were not daintie : and
though the inuention were delicat, he misdoubted the
making. As carefull he was too of the colour; lest if gay,
he might seeme to glorie in his iniury, and her wrong;
if mourning, it might strike some euill presage vnto her
of her fortune. At length he tooke a garment more rich
then glaring, the ground being black veluet, richly em-
brodered with great pearle, & precious stones, but they
set so among certaine tuffes of cypres, that the cypres
was like blacke clowds, through which the starrs might
yeeld a darke luster. About his necke he ware a brode &
gorgeous coller ; whereof the pieces enterchangeably
answering; the one was of Diamonds and pearle, set
with a white enamell, so as by the cunning of the work-
man it seemed like a shining ice, and the other piece being of Rubies, and Opalles, had a fierie glistring, which
he thought pictured the two passions of Feare and
Desire,

Defire,wherein he was enchayned . His hurt (not yet fully well) made him a little halt , but he ftraue to giue the beft grace he could vnto his halting.

2   And in that fort he went to *Philocleas* chamber : whome he found (becaufe her chamber was ouer-lightfome) fitting of that fide of her bedde which was from the windowe;which did caft fuch a fhadow vpon her, as a good Painter woulde beftowe vppon *Venus*, when vnder the trees fhe bewayled the murther of *Adonis* : her handes and fingers (as it were) indented one within the other: her fhoulder leaning to her beds head,and ouer.her head a fcarfe, which did eclipfe al-moft halfe her eyes,which vnder it fixed their beames vpon the wall by,with fo fteddic a maner, as if in that place they might well chaunge , but not mende their obiect : and fo remayned they a good while after his comming in, he not daring to trouble her, nor fhe perceyuing him, till that (a little varying her thoughts fomething quickening her fenfes) fhe heard him as he happed to ftirre his vpper garment : and perceyuing him, rofe vp, with a demeanure, where in the booke of Beautie there was nothing to be read but Sorrow : for Kindneffe was blotted out, and Anger was neuer there.

3   But *Amphialus* that had entrufted his memorie with long and forcible fpeeches , found it fo locked vp in a-mazement,that he could pike nothing out of it,but the befeeching her to take what was don in good part, and to affure herfelfe there was nothing but honour meant vnto her perfon. But fhe making no other aunfivere, but letting her handes fall one from the other , which

before

before were ioyned (with eyes fomething caſt afide,
and a filent figh) gaue him to vnderſtande, that conſidering his dooings, ſhe thought his fpeech as full of
incongruitie, as her aunſwere would be voyde of purpoſe : wherevppon he knēeling downe, and kiſſing her
hande, (which ſhe ſuffered with a countenaunce witneſſing captiuitie, but not kindneſſe) he befought her
to haue pitie of him, whoſe loue went beyonde the
boundes of conceite, much more of vttering : that in
her handes the ballance of his life or death did ſtande;
whereto the leaſt motion of hers woulde ſerue to determine, ſhe being indeede the miſtreſſe of his life, and
he her eternall ſlaue ; and with true vehemencie befought her that he might heare her ſpeake, wherevpon
ſhe ſuffered her ſweete breath to turne it ſelfe into theſe
kind of words.

Alas coufin, (ſaide ſhe) what ſhall my tongue be   4
able to doo, which is infourmed by the eares one way,
and by the eyes another? You call for pittie, and vſe
crueltie; you ſay, you loue me, and yet do the effectes
of enmitie. You affirme your death is in my handes,
but you haue brought me to ſo neere a degree to
death, as when you will, you may lay death vpon me :
fo that while you ſay I am miſtreſſe of your life, I am
not miſtreſſe of mine owne . You entitle your ſelfe
my ſlaue, but I am ſure I am yours . If then violence,
iniurie, terror, and depriuing of that which is more dear
then life it ſelfe, libertie, be fit orators for affection, you
may expect that I will be eafily perſwaded. But if the
neareneſſe of our kinred breede any remorſe in you, or
there be any ſuch thing in you, which you call loue
toward

towarde me, then let not my fortune be difgraced with the name of imprifonment : let not my hart waite it felfe by being vexed with feeling euill, and fearing worfe. Let not me be a caufe of my parents wofull deftruction; but reftore me to my felfe; and fo doing I fhall account I haue receyued my feife of you. And what I fay for my felfe, I fay for my deare fifter, and my friend *Zelmane:* for I defire no wel being, without they may be partakers. With that her teares rained downe from her heauenly eyes, and feemed to water the fweet and beautifull flowers of her face.

5   But *Amphialus* was like the poore woman, who louing a tame Doe fhe had, aboue all earthly things, hauing long played withall, and made it feede at her hand and lappe, is conftrained at length by famine (all her flocke being fpent, and fhe fallen into extreeme pouertie) to kill the Deare, to fuftaine her life. Manie a pitifull looke doth fhe caft vpon it, and many a time doth fhe draw backe her hand before fhe can giue the ftroke. For euen fo *Amphialus* by a hunger-fterued affection, was compelled to offer this iniurie, and yet the fame affection made him with a tormenting griefe, thinke vnkindneffe in himfelfe, that he could finde in his hart any way to reftraine her freedome. But at length, neither able to grant, nor denie, he thus anfwered her. Deare ladie (faid he) I will not fay vnto you (how iuftly foeuer I may do it) that I am neither author, nor accefsarie vnto this your withholding. For fince I do not redres it, I am as faulty as if I had begun it. But this I proteft vnto you (and this proteftation of mine, let the heauens heare, and if I lie, let them anfwer me with a deadly thunderbolt) that in my foule I wifh I had neuer

feene

feene the light, or rather, that I had neuer had a father to beget fuch a child, the that by my meanes thofe
eyes fhould ouerflow their owne beauties, then by my
meanes the fkie of your vertue fhould be ouerclowded
with forrow. But woe is me, moft excellent Ladie, I
finde my felfe moft willing to obey you: neither truely
doo mine eares receaue the leaft word you fpeak, with
any leffe reuerence, then as abfolute, and vnrefiftable
commaundements.But alas,that Tyrant Loue,(which
now poffeffeth the holde of all my life and reafon)will
no way fuffer it. It is Loue, it is Loue,not I,which difobey you. What then fhall I fay? but that I,who am redie to lie vnder your feete,to venture, nay to loofe my
life at your leaft commandement:I am not the ftaye of
your freedome, but Loue, Loue, which ties you in
your owne knots. It is you your felfe, that imprifon
your felfe : it is your beautie which makes thefe caftle-
walles embrace you : it is your owne eyes, which reflect vpon themfelues this iniurie: Then is there no
other remedie, but that you fome way vouchfafe
to fatisfie this Loues vehemencie ; which (fince it
grewe in your felfe) without queftion you fhall finde it
(far more then I) tractable.

　　But with thefe wordes *Philoclea* fell to fo extreame
a quaking, and her liuely whiteneffe did degenerate
to fo dead a paleneffe, that *Amphialus* feared fome
daungerous traunce : fo that taking her hande, and
feelinge that it (which was woonte to be one of the
chiefe firebrands of *Cupid*) nad all the fenfe of it wrapt
vp in coldnes, he began humblie to befeech her to put
away all feare, and to affure herfelfe vpon the vowe he
made thereof vnto God, and her felfe, that the vtter-
　　　　　　　　　　　　　　　　　　moft

moſt forces he would euer employ to conquere her affection, ſhould be Deſire,and Deſert. That promiſe
brought *Philoclea* againe to her ſelfe, ſo that ſlowiy lifting vp her eyes vpon him, with a countenaunce euer
courteous,but then languiſhing,ſhe tolde him, that he
ſhould doo well to do ſo, if indeede he had euer taſted
what true loue was : for that where now ſhe did beare
him good will, ſhe ſhould(if he tooke any other way)
hate, and abhor the very thought of him:offering him
withall, that though his mother had taken away her
kniues, yet the houſe of Death had ſo many doores,as
ſhe would eaſilie flie into it, if euer ſhe founde her honor endaungered.

6   *Amphialus* hauing the colde aſhes of Care caſt vpon the coales of Deſire, leauing ſome of his mothers
Gentlewomen to waite vpon *Philoclea*, himſelfe indeede a priſoner to his priſoner, and making all his
authoritie to be but a footeſtoole to Humblenes,went
from her to his mother. To whom with words which
Affection endited, but Amazement vttered,he deliuered what had paſſed betwene him and *Philoclea* : beſeeching her to trie what her perſwaſions could doo with
her, while he gaue order for all ſuch things as were neceſſarie againſt ſuch forces, as he looked dayly *Baſilius*
would bring before his câſtle. His mother bade him
quiette him ſelfe, for ſhe doubted not to take fitte
times. But that the beſt way was, firſt to let her owne
Paſſion a little tire it ſelfe.

CHAP.

CHAP. 4.

[1] Amphiälus *warlike preparations.* [2] *His iuſtification.* [3] *His
fortifications.* [4] *His Arte of men.* [5] *His Loue-paſsions, and
paſsionate complaints.*

SO they calling *Clinias*, and ſome o- [1]
ther of their counſell, aduiſed vpon their preſent affaires. Firſt, he
diſpatched priuat letters to al thoſe
principall Lords and gentlemen of
the country, whō he thought ether
alliance, or friendſhip to himſelfe
might drawe; with ſpeciall moti-
ons from the generall conſideration of duetie : not o-
mitting all ſuch, whom either youthfull age, or youth-
like mindes did fill with vnlimited deſires : beſides
ſuch, whom any diſcontentment made hungry of
change, or an ouer-ſpended wante, made want a ciuill
warre : to each (according to the counſell of his mother) conforming himſelfe after their humors. To his
friends, friendlines; to the ambitious, great expectations; to the diſpleaſed, reuenge; to the greedie, ſpoyle:
wrapping their hopes with ſuch cunning, as they rather ſeemed giuen ouer vnto them as partakers : then
promiſes ſprong of neceſſitie. Then ſent he to his mothers brother, the King of *Argos* : but he was as then
ſo ouer-laide with warre himſelfe, as from thence he
could attend ſmall ſuccour.

But becauſe he knewe, how violently rumors doo [2]
blow the ſailes of popular iudgemēts, & how few there
be

be,that can difcerne betweene trueth and truthlikenes,
betweene fhowes and fubftance;he caufed a iuftificati-
on of this his action to be written, wherof were fowed
abroad many copies, which with fome gloffes of pro-
babilitie, might hide indeede the foulenes of his treafon ; and from true common-places,fetch downe moft
falfe applications. For, beginning how much the duetie which is owed to the countrie, goes beyond all o-
ther dueties, fince in it felfe it conteines them all, and
that for the refpect therof, not onely all tender refpects
of kinred,or whatfoeuer other friendfhippes, are to be
laide afide,but that euen long-helde opinions (rather
builded vpon a fecreate of gouernement, then any
groūd of truthe) are to be forfaken. He fell by degrees
to fhew, that fince the ende whereto any thing is directed, is euer to be of more noble reckning, then the
thing thereto directed : that therefore, the weale-pub-
licke was more to be regarded,then any perfon or magiftrate that thereunto was ordeined. The feeling confideration whereof,had moued him(though as nere of
kinne to *Bafilius* as could be, yet) to fet principally before his eyes,the good eftate of fo many thoufands, o-
uer whom *Bafilius* raigned : rather then fo to hood-
winke himfelfe with affection,as to fuffer the realme to
runne to manifeft ruine. The care whereof, did kindly
appertaine to thofe, who being fubalterne magiftrates
and officers of the crowne,were to be employed as frō
the Prince,fo for the people;and of all other,efpeciallie
himfelfe,who being defcended of the R oyall race, and
next heire male,Nature had no foner opened his eyes,
but that the foyle where-upon they did looke, was to
looke for at his hands a continuall carefulnes:which as
from

frõ his childhood he had euer caried ; ſo now finding that his vncle had not only giuē ouer al care of gouernment,but had put it into the hands of *Philanax,* (a man neither in birth comparable to many , nor for his corrupt,prowde,and partiall dealing,liked of any)but beſide,had ſet his daughters (in whom the whole eſtate, as next heires thereunto, had no leſſe intereſt thē himſelfe) in ſo vnfit & il-guarded a place,as it was not only dãgerous for their perſons,but (if they ſhould be conueied to any forraine country)to the whole commonwealth pernicious:that therfore he had brought them into this ſtrõg caſtle of his,which way , if it might ſeem ſtrange, they were to conſider, that new neceſſities re „ quire new remedies:but there they ſhould be ſerued & honored as belonged to their greatnes,vntil by the generall aſſembly of the eſtates, it ſhould be determined how they ſhould to their beſt (both priuate , and publique)aduantage be matched;vowing all faith & duty both to the father & children , neuer by him to be violated.But if in the meane time,before the eſtates could be aſſēbled,he were aſſailed, he would thē for his own defence take armes:deſiring all, that either tendred the dangerous caſe of their country,or in their harts loued iuſtice,to defēd him in this iuſt actio.And if the Prince ſhould commaund them otherwiſe , yet to know , that therein he was no more to be obeied,then if he ſhould call for poiſon to hurt himſelf withall:ſince all that was done , was done for his ſeruice, howſoeuer he might (ſeduced by *Philanax*) interprete of it : he proteſting, that whatſoeuer he ſhould doo for his owne defence, ſhould be againſt *Philanax,*& no way againſt *Baſilius.*

To this effect,amplified with arguments and exam- 3

ples, and painted with rhetoricall colours, did he ſow abroad many diſcourſes : which as they preuayled with ſome of more quicke then ſounde conceipte,to runne his fortune with him; ſo in many did it breed a cooleneſſe,to deale violently againſt him, and a falſe-minded neutralitie to expect the iſſue. But beſides the waies he vſed to weaken the aduerſe partie, he omitted nothing for the ſtrengthning of his owne. The chiefe truſt whereof (becauſe he wanted men to keepe the field)he repoſed in the ſuretie of his caſtle;which at leſt would winne him much time, the mother of many mutations.To that therfore he bent his outward & inward eyes, ſtriuing to make Art ſtriue with Nature, to whether of them two that fortification ſhould be moſt beholding. The ſeat Nature beſtowed, but Arte gaue the building : which as his rocky hardneſſe would not yeeld to vndermining force,ſo to opé aſſaults he tooke counſell of skill, how to make all approches, if not im-poſſible, yet difficult; as well at the foot of the caſtle,as round about the lake, to giue vnquiet lodgings to thé, whom onely enmitie would make neighbors. Then o-mitted he nothing of defence,as wel ſimple defence,as that which did defend by offending, fitting inſtruméts of miſchiefe to places, whence the miſchiefe might be moſt liberally beſtowed. Nether was his ſmalleſt care for victuals,as wel for the prouiding that which ſhould ſuffice both in ſtore & goodneſſe,as in well preſeruing it, ahd wary diſtributing it, both in quantitie, and qua-litie; ſpending that firſt which would keepe leſt.

4   But wherein he ſharpned his wits to the pearcingeſt point,was touching his men (knowing them to be the weapon of weapons,& maſter-ſpring(as it were)which

makes

makes all the reſt to ſtir; and that therefore in the Arte
of man ſtood the quinteſſence, & ruling skill of all proſperous gouernement, either peaceable, or military) he
choſe in number as many as without peſtring (and ſo
daunger of infection) his victuall would ſeem for two
yeare to maintaine; all of hable bodies, and ſome few
of able mindes to direct, not ſeeking many commaun-
ders, but contenting himſelfe, that the multitude
ſhould haue obeying wills, euery one knowing whom
he ſhould commaund, and whom he ſhould obey, the
place where, and the matter wherein; diſtributing each
office as neere as he could, to the diſpoſition of the perſon that ſhould exerciſe it : knowing no loue, daunger,
nor diſcipline can ſodainly alter an habite in nature.
Therfore would he not employ the ſtil mã to a ſhifting
practiſe, nor the liberall man to be a diſpenſer of his victuals, nor the kind-harted man to be a puniſher : but
would exerciſe their vertues in ſorts, where they might
be profitable, employing his chief care to know thē all
particularly, & throughly, regarding alſo the cõſtitutiõ
of their bodies; ſome being able better to abide watching, ſome hūger, ſome labour, making his benefit of ech
hability & not forcing beyond power. Time to euery
thing by iuſt proportiõ he allotted, & as well in that, as
in euery thing els, no ſmall errour winckt at, leſt greater
ſhould be animated. Euen of vices he made his profite, making the cowardly *Clinias* to haue care of the
watch, which he knew his own feare would make him
very wakefully performe. And before the ſiege began,
he himſelfe cauſed rumors to be ſowed, and libels to be
ſpread againſt himſelfe, fuller of mallice, then witty perſuaſion : partly, to knowe thoſe that would be apt to

ftumble at fuch motions, that he might cull them from the faithfuller band; but principally, becaufe in neceffitie they fhould not know when any fuch thing were in earneft attempted, whether it were, or not, of his owne inuention. But euen then (before the enemies face came neere to breed any terrour) did he exercife his men dayly in all their charges, as if Daunger had prefently prefented his moft hideous prefence : him felfe rather inftructing by example, then precept; being neither more fparing in trauaile, nor fpēding in diet, then the meaneft fouldier: his hand and body difdaining no oafe matters, nor fhrinking from the heauy.

5   The onely ods was, that when others tooke breath, he fighed; and when others refted, he croft his armes. For Loue paffing thorow the pikes of Daūger, & tumbling it felfe in the duft of Labour, yet ftill made him remember his fweete defire, and beautifull image. Often when he had begun to commaund one, fomewhat before halfe the fentence were ended, his inward gueft did fo entertaine him, that he would breake it of, and a prettie while after end it, when he had (to the maruaile of the ftanders by) fent himfelf in to talke with his own thoughts. Sometimes when his hand was lifted vp to fome thing, as if with the fight of *Gorgons* head he had bene fodainely turned into a ftone, fo would he there abide with his eyes planted, and handes lifted, till at length, comming to the vfe of himfelf, he would looke about whether any had perceiued him ; then would he accufe, and in himfelfe condemne all thofe wits, that durft affirme Idleneffe to be the well-fpring of Loue. O, would he fay, al you that affect the title of wifdome, by vngratefull fcorning the ornaments of Nature, am

I

I now piping in a fhaddow? or doo flouthfull feathers
now enwrap me? Is not hate before me, and doubte
behinde me? is not daunger of the one fide,and fhame
of the other? And doo I not ftande vpon paine, and
trauaile, and yet ouer all,my affection triumphes? The
more I ftirre about vrgent affaires, the more me thinks
the very ftirring breeds a breath to blow the coales of
my loue : the more I exercife my thoughts, the more
they encreafe the appetite of my defires . O fweet *Philoclea* (with that he would caft vp his eies wherin fome
water did appeare, as if they would wafh themfelues a-
gainft they fhould fee her) thy heauenly face is my A-
ftronomie;thy fweet vertue,my fweet Philofophie : let
me profite therein, and farewell all other cogitations.
But alas,my mind mifgiues me, for your planets beare
a contrarie afpect vnto me.Woe,woe is me,they threaten my deftruction: and whom doo they threaten this
deftruction? euen him that loues them ; and by what
means will they deftroy,but by louing them? O deare
(though killing) eyes, fhall death head his darte with
the golde of *Cupids* arrowe? Shall death take his ayme
from the reft of Beautie? O beloued (though hating)
Philoclea, how if thou beeft mercifull, hath crueltie
ftolne into thee? Or how if thou beeft cruell,doth crueltie looke more mercifull then euer Mercie did? Or
alas, is it my deftinie that makes Mercie cruell? Like
an euill veffell which turnes fweete licour to fowernes;
fo when thy grace fals vpon me, my wretched conftitution makes it become fierceneffe. Thus would he
exercife his eloquence,when fhe could not heare him,
and be dumbe-ftriken, when her prefence gaue him fit
occafion of fpeaking : fo that his witte could finde out

no other refuge, but the comfort and counfell of his mother, defiring her (whofe thoughts were vnperplexed) to vfe for his fake the moft preuailing manners of interceffion.

CHAP. 5.

¹ Suttle Cecropia *vifites fad* Philoclea. *² The fhamel--ße Aunts fhrewd temptations to loue and mariage : The modeft neeces maidenly refiftance.*

Ecropia feing her fonnes fafetie depende thereon, (though her pride much difdained the name of a defire) tooke the charge vpon her, not doubting the eafie conqueft of an vnexpert virgin, who had alreadie with fubtiltie and impudencie begun to vndermine a monarchy. Therfore, waighing *Philocleas* refolutions by the counterpeafe of her own youthful thoughts, which fhe then called to minde, fhe doubted not at leaft to make *Philoclea* receiue the poyfon diftilled in fweete liquour, which fhe with little difguifing had drunke vp thirftily. Therefore fhe went foftly to *Philocleas* chamber, & peeping through the fide of the doore, then being a little open, fhe fawe *Philoclea* fitting lowe vpon a cufhion, in fuch a giuen-ouer manner, that one would haue thought, filence, folitarineffe, and melancholie were come there, vnder the enfigne of mifhap, to conquere delight, and driue him from his naturall feate of beautie: her teares came dropping downe like raine in Sunfhine, shine, and she not taking heede to wipe the teares, they ranne downe vpon her cheekes, and lips, as vpon cherries which the dropping tree bedeweth. In the dressing of her haire and apparell, she might see neither a careful arte, nor an arte of carelesnesse, but euen left to a neglected chaunce, which yet coulde no more vnperfect her perfections, then a Die anie way cast, could loose his squarenesse.

Cecropia (stirred with no other pitie, but for her son) came in, and haling kindnesse into her countenance, What ayres this sweete Ladie, (said she) will you marre so good eyes with weeping? shall teares take away the beautie of that complexion, which the women of *Arcadia* wish for, and the men long after? Fie of this peeuish sadnesse; in sooth it is vntimely for your age. Looke vpon your owne bodie, and see whether it deserue to pine away with sorrow: see whether you will haue these hands (with that she tooke one of her hands and kissing it, looked vppon it as if she were enamoured with it) fade from their whitenesse, which makes one desire to touch them; & their softnesse, which rebounds againe a desire to looke on them, and become drie, leane and yellowe, and make euerie bodie woonder at the chaunge, and say, that sure you had vsed some arte before, which nowe you had left? for if the beauties had beene naturall, they woulde neuer so soone haue beene blemished. Take a glasse, and see whether these tears become your eies: although, I must confesse, those eies are able to make tears comely. Alas Madame (answered *Philoclea*) I know not whether my teares become mine eyes, but I am sure mine eies thus beteared, become my fortune. Your fortune (saide *Cecropia*)

ifshe

if she could see to attire herselfe, would put on her best raiments. For I see, and I see it with griefe, and (to tell you true) vnkindnes: you misconster euery thing, that only for your sake is attempted. You thinke you are offended, and are indeed defended: you esteeme your selfe a prisoner, and are in truth a mistres: you feare hate, and shall find loue. And truely, I had a thing to say to you, but it is no matter, since I find you are so obstinatly melancholy, as that you woo his felowship: I will spare my paines, and hold my peace: And so staied indeede, thinking *Philoclea* would haue had a female inquisitiue-nesse of the matter. But she, who rather wished to vn-knowe what she knewe, then to burden her hart with more hopeles knowledge, only desired her to haue pity of her, and if indeed she did meane her no hurt, then to grant her liberty: for else the very griefe & feare, would proue her vnappointed executioners. For that (said *Cecropia*) beleue me vpō the faith of a kings daughter, you shall be free, so soone as your freedome may be free of mortal dāger, being brought hither for no other cause, but to preuent such mischiefes as you know not of. But if you thinke indeed to winne me to haue care of you, euen as of mine owne daughter, then lend your eares vnto me, & let not your mind arme it selfe with a wilful-nesse to be flexible to nothing. But if I speake reason, let Reason haue his due reward, persuasion. Then sweet neece (said she) I pray vou presuppose, that now, euē in the midst of your agonies, which you paint vnto your selfe most horrible, wishing with sighes, & praying with vowes, for a soone & safe deliuerie. Imagin neece (I say) that some heauenly spirit should appeare vnto you, and bid you follow him through the doore, that goes into

the

the garden,affuring you, that you fhould therby return
to your deare mother, and what other delights foeuer
your mind efteemes delights:would you(fweet neece)
would you refufe to folow him,& fay,that if he led you
not through the chiefe gate,you would not enioy your
ouer-defired liberty? Would you not drinke the wine
you thirft for, without it were in fuch a glaffe, as you e-
fpecially fancied? tel me(deare neece:)but I wil anfwer
for you,becaufe I know your reafon and will is fuch, as
muft needs conclude, that fuch niceneffe can no more
be in you,to difgrace fuch a mind,then difgracefulneffe
can haue any place in fo faultles a beauty.Your wifdom
would affuredly determin,how the marke were hit,not
whether the bow were of Ewe or no,wherein you fhot.
If this be fo,and thus fure(my deare neece) it is,then (I
pray you)imagin,that I am that fame good Angel,who
grieuing in your griefe, and in truth not able to fuffer,
that bitter fighs fhould be fent foorth with fo fweete a
breath,am come to lead you, not only to your defired,
and imagined happines,but to a true and effentiall happines;not only to liberty,but to libertie with comman-
dement.The way I will fhew you(which if it be not the
gate builded hitherto in your priuate choife, yet fhall it
be a doore to bring you through a garden of pleafures,
as fweet as this life can bring foorth ; nay rather, which
makes this life to be a life:(My fon,)let it be no blemifh
to him that I name him my fon, who was your fathers
own nephew:for you know I am no fmal kings daughter,)my fonne(I fay) farre paffing the neerneffe of his
kinred,with the neerneffe of good-will, and ftriuing to
match your matchleffe beautie with a matchleffe affection,doth by me prefent vnto you the full enioying of
your

your liberty,ſo as with this gift you wil accept a greater, which is, this caſtell,with all the reſt which you knowe he hath,in honorable quantitie ; and will confirme his gift, and your receipt of both, with accepting him to be yours.I might ſay much both for the perſon and the matter;but who will crie out the Sun ſhines:It is ſo manifeſt a profit vnto you,as the meaneſt iudgement muſt ſtraight apprehend it:ſo farre is it from the ſharpeneſſe of yours,therof to be ignorant. Therfore (ſweet neece) let your gratefulnes be my interceſſion, & your gentleneſſe my eloquence, and let me cary comfort to a hart which greatly needs it.*Philoclea* ooked vpon her,& caſt downe her eie again.Aunt(ſaid ſhe)I would I could be ſo much a miſtres of my owne mind,as to yeelde to my couſins vertuous requeſt:for ſo I conſtrue of it. But my hart is already ſet(and ſtaying a while on that word,ſhe brought foorth afterwards) to lead a virgins life to my death:for ſuch a vow I haue in my ſelfe deuoutly made. The heauens preuent ſuch a miſchiefe (ſaid *Cecropia*.) A vowe,quoth you? no, no, my deere neece, Nature, when you were firſt borne,vowed you a womã,& as ſhe made you child of a mother, ſo to do your beſt to be mother of a child:ſhe gaue you beautie to moue loue; ſhe gaue you wit to know loue;ſhe gaue you an excellẽt body to reward loue : which kind of liberall rewarding is crowned with vnſpeakable felicitie.For this,as it bindeth the receiuer,ſo it makes happy the beſtower : this doth not impoueriſh,but enrich the giuer. O the ſweet name of a mother:O the cõfort of cõforts, to ſee your childrẽ grow vp,in whõ you are(as it were)eternized:if you could conceiue what a hart-tickling ioy it is to ſee your own litle ones, with awfull loue come running to your lap,and like litle models of your ſelfe,ſtill cary you
                                                                about

about them,you would thinke vnkindnes in your own
thoughts,that euer they did rebell againſt the mean vnto it.But perchāce I ſet this bleſſednes before your eies,
as Captains do victorie before their ſouldiers,to which
they might come through many paines,grieues & dan-
gers.No,I am cōtent you ſhrinke from this my counſel,
if the way to come vnto it,be not moſt of all pleaſant. I
know not (anſwered the ſweet *Philoclea*,fearing leaſt ſilence would offend her ſullennes) what contentment
you ſpeake of:but I am ſure the beſt you can make of it,
(which is mariage)is a burdenous yoke.Ah,deer neece
(ſaid *Cecropia*)how much you are deceiued? A yoke indeed we all beare,laid vpō vs in our creation, which by
mariage is not increaſed,but thus farre eaſed, that you
haue a yoke-fellow to help to draw through the cloddy
cumbers of this world. O widow-nights,beare witnes
with me of the difference.How often alas do I embrace
the orfan-ſide of my bed, which was wōt to be imprinted by the body of my deare husband,& with teares acknowledge, that I now enioy ſuch a liberty as the baniſhed mā hath;who may,if he liſt,wāder ouer the world,
but is euer reſtrained frō his moſt delightful home:that
I haue now ſuch a liberty as the ſeeled dou hath, which
being firſt depriued of eies, is then by the falconer caſt
off?For beleue me,neece,beleue me, mans experiēce is
womās beſt eie-ſight.Haue you euer ſeene a pure Roſe-
water kept in a chriſtal glas;how fine it lokes,how ſweet
it ſmels,while that beautifull glaſſe impriſons it? Breake
the priſon,and let the water take his owne courſe, doth
it not imbrace duſt , and looſe all his former ſweete-
neſſe,and faireneſſe?Truly ſo are we,if we haue not the
ſtay , rather then the reſtraine of Criſtalline mariage.
My hart meltes to thinke of the ſweete comfortes,

I in

I in that happie time receiued, when I had neuer cauſe
to care, but the care was doubled: whē I neuer reioiced,
but that I ſaw my ioy ſhine in anothers eies. What ſhall
I ſay of the free delight, which the hart might embrace,
without the accuſing of the inward conſcience, or feare
of outward ſhame: and is a ſolitary life as good as this?
then can one ſtring make as good muſicke as a conſort:
thē can one colour ſet forth a beautie. But it may be, the
generall conſideration of mariage dooth not ſo much
miſlike you, as the applying of it to him. He is my ſone,
I muſt confeſſe, I ſee him with a mothers eyes, which
if they doo not much deceiue me, he is no ſuch one, o-
uer whom Contempt may make any iuſt chalenge. He
is comely, he is noble, he is rich; but that which in it
ſelfe ſhould carie all comelineſſe, nobilitie, and riches,
he loues you; and he loues you, who is beloued of o-
thers. Driue not away his affection (ſweete Ladie) and
make no other Ladie hereafter proudly bragge, that ſhe
hath robbed you of ſo faithfull and notable a ſeruant.
Philoclea heard ſome pieces of her ſpeches, no otherwiſe
then one doth when a tedious pratler cōbers the hearing of a delightful muſicke. For her thoughts had left
her eares in that captiuitie, and conueied thēſelues to
behold (with ſuch eies as imagination could lend thē)
the eſtate of her *Zelmane*: for whō how wel ſhe thought
many of thoſe ſayings might haue ben vſed with a farre
more gratefull acceptation. Therefore liſting not to diſ-
pute in a matter whereof her ſelfe was reſolute, and deſired not to enforme the other, ſhe onely told her, that
whileſt ſhe was ſo captiued, ſhe could not conceiue of
any ſuch perſuaſions (though neuer ſo reaſonable) any
otherwiſe, then as conſtraints : and as conſtraints muſt
needs

needs euẽ in nature abhor thẽ, which at her libertie, in
their owne force of reaſon, might more preuaile with
her: and ſo faine would haue returned the ſtrength of
Cecropias perſwaſions, to haue procured freedome.

CHAP. 6.

¹ *Freſh motiues to* Philoclea. ² Cecropias *new fetch to at-
tempt* Pamela. ³ Pamelas *prayer,* ⁴ *and Sainct-like gra-
.ces in it.* ⁵ *Her Auntes fruiteles argumentes.*

Vt neither her wittie wordes in an   1
enemie, nor thoſe wordes, made
more then eloquent with paſſing
through ſuch lips, could preuaile
in *Cecropia*, no more then her perſwaſions coulde winne *Philoclea*
to diſauowe her former vowe, or
to leaue the priſoner *Zelmane*, for
the commaunding *Amphialus*. So that both ſides
being deſirous, and neither graunters, they brake of
conference. *Cecropia* ſucking vp more and more ſpite
out of her deniall, which yet for her ſonnes ſake, ſhe
diſguiſed with a viſarde of kindnes, leauing no office
vnperfourmed, which might either witnes, or endeare
her ſonnes affection. Whatſoeuer could be imagined
likely to pleaſe her, was with liberall diligence perfourmed: Muſickes at her windowe, & eſpecially ſuch Muſickes, as might (with dolefull embaſſage) call the mind
to thinke of ſorow, and thinke of it with ſweetnes; with
ditties ſo ſenſiblie expreſſing *Amphialus* caſe, that euerie worde ſeemed to be but a diuerſifying of the name
of

of *Amphialus*. Daily presents, as it were oblations, to pacifie an angrie Deitie, sent vnto her : wherein, if the workmanship of the forme, had striuen with the sumptuousnes of the matter, as much did the inuention in the application, contende to haue the chiefe excellencie:for they were as so many stories of his disgraces,& her perfections;where the richnes did inuite the eyes, the fashion did entertaine the eyes, and the deuice did teach the eyes the present miserie of the presenter himselfe awefully seruiceable : which was the more notable,as his authoritie was manifest. And for the bondage wherein she liued, all meanes vsed to make knowen, that if it were a bondage, it was a bondage onely knitte in loue-knots. But in harte alreadie vnderstanding no language but one, the Musicke wrought indeede a dolefulnes, but it was a dolefulnes to be in his power : the dittie intended for *Amphialus*, she translated to *Zelmane*: the presents seemed so many tedious clogs of a thralled obligation : and his seruice, the more diligent it was,the more it did exprobrate (as she thought)vnto her,her vnworthie estate : that euen he that did her seruice,had authoritie of commanding her, onely construing her seruitude in his own nature, esteeming it a right,and a right bitter seruitude : so that all their shots(how well soeuer leuelled) being carried awrie from the marke,by the storme of her mislike, the Prince *Amphialus* affectionately languished , & *Cecropia* spitefullie cunning,disdained at the barrennes of their successe.

2 　　Which willingly *Cecropia* woulde haue reuenged, but that she sawe,her hurte could not be diuided from her sonnes mischiefe:wherefore,she bethought her self

to

to attempt *Pamela*,whofe beautie being equall, fhe hoped, if fhe might be woon, that her fonnes thoughtes
would rather reft on a beautifull gratefulnes, then ftill
be tormented with a difdaining beautie. Wherfore,gi-
uing new courage to her wicked inuentions, and vfing
the more induftry,becaufe fhe had mift in this,& taking
euen precepts of preuailing in *Pamela*, by her fayling in
Philoclea, fhe went to her chamber,& (according to her
own vngratious method of a fubtile proceeding)ftood
liftning at the dore, becaufe that out of the circuftance
of her prefent behauiour,there might kindly arife a fitte
beginning of her intended difcourfe.

And fo fhe might perceaue that *Pamela* did walke vp
and down,full of deep(though patient)thoughts . For
her look and countenance was fetled,her pace foft,and
almoft ftill of one meafure,without any paffionate gefture, or violent motion:till at length (as it were) awa-
king, & ftrengthning her felfe,Well(faid fhe)yet this is
the beft,& of this I am fure,that how foeuer they wrõg
me,they cannot ouer-mafter God . No darknes blinds
his eyes,no Iayle barres him out. To whome then elfe
fhould I flie, but to him for fuccoure ? And therewith
kneeling down,euẽ in the fame place where fhe ftood,
fhe thus faid . O all-feeing Light,and eternal Life or all
things,to whom nothing is either fo great, that it may,
refift;or fo fmall, that it is contemned : looke vpon my
miferie with thine eye of mercie, and let thine infinite
power vouchfafe to limite out fome proportion of deliuerance vnto me,as to thee fhall feem moft conuenient . Let not iniurie, ô Lord, triumphe ouer me, and
let my faultes by thy handes be correðed, and make
not mine vniufte enemie the minifter of thy Iuftice.
But

But yet, my God, if in thy wisdome, this be the aptest chastizement for my inexcusable follie; if this low bondage be fittest for my ouer-hie desires ; if the pride of my not-inough humble harte, be thus to be broken, O Lord, I yeeld vnto thy will, and ioyfully embrace what sorrow thou wilt haue me suffer. Onely thus much let me craue of thee, (let my crauing, ô Lord, be accepted of thee, since euen that proceedes from thee) let me craue, euen by the noblest title, which in my greatest affliction I may giue my selfe, that I am thy creature, & by thy goodnes (which is thy self) that thou wilt suffer some beame of thy Maiestie so to shine into my mind, that it may still depende confidently vpon thee. Let calamitie be the exercise, but not the ouerthrowe of my vertue : let their power preuaile, but preuaile not to destruction : let my greatnes be their praie : let my paine be the sweetnes of their reuenge : let them (if so it seem good vnto thee) vexe me with more and more punishment. But, ô Lord, let neuer their wickednes haue such a hand, but that I may carie a pure minde in a pure bodie. (And pausing a while) And ô most gracious Lord (said she) what euer become of me, preserue the vertuous *Musidorus*.

4　　　The other parte *Cecropia* might well heare, but this latter prayer for *Musidorus*, her hart helde it, as so iewel-like a treasure, that it would scarce trust her owne lippes withall. But this prayer, sent to heauen, from so heauenly a creature, with such a feruent grace, as if Deuotion had borowed her bodie, to make of it selfe a most beautifull representation; with her eyes so lifted to the skie-ward, that one would haue thought they had begunne to flie thetherward, to take their place amõg their felow

starres,

ſtars;her naked hands raiſing vp their whole length, &
as it were kiſſing one another, as if the right had bene
the picture of *Zeale*,and the left, of *Humbleneſſe*, which
both vnited themſelues to make their ſuites more acceptable. Laſtly, all her ſenſes being rather tokens then
inſtruments of her inwarde motions,altogether had ſo
ſtraunge a working power, that euen the harde-harted
wickedneſſe of *Cecropia*, if it founde not a loue of that
goodnes,yet it felt an abaſhment at that goodnes; & if
ſhe had not a kindly remorſe, yet had ſhe an yrkſome
accuſation of her owne naughtines,ſo that ſhe was put
frõ the biaſſe of her fore-intended leſſon. For well ſhe
found there was no way at that time to take that mind,
but with ſome,at leſt,image of Vertue,and what the figure thereof was her hart knew not.

Yet did ſhe prodigally ſpende her vttermoſt eloquence,leauing no argument vnproued, which might
with any force inuade her excellent iudgement : the
iuſtnes of the requeſt being, but for marriage;the worthineſſe of the ſuiter : then her owne preſent fortune,
if ſhe would not onely haue amendment, but felicitie:
beſides falſely making her belieue,that her ſiſter would
thinke her ſelfe happie, if now ſhe might haue his
loue which before ſhe contemned : and obliquely touching, what daunger it ſhould be for her, if her ſonne
ſhould accept *Philoclea* in marriage, and ſo match the
next heire apparant, ſhe being in his powre : yet plentifully periuring,how extreamely her ſonne loued her,
and excuſing the little ſhewes he made of it, with the
dutifull reſpect he bare vnto her, & taking vpõ her ſelfe
that ſhe reſtrayned him,ſince ſhe found ſhe could ſet
no limits to his paſſions. And as ſhe did to *Philoclea*, ſo

Mm   did

did she to her, with the tribute of gifts, seeke to bring her minde into seruitude: and all other meanes, that might either establish a beholdingnesse, or at the left awake a kindnes; doing it so, as by reason of their imprisonment, one sister knew not how the other was wooed, but each might thinke, that onely she was sought. But if *Philoclea* with sweete and humble dealing did auoid their assaults, she with the Maiestie of Vertue did beate them of.

CHAP. 7.

1 *An Allarme to the* Amphialians. 2 *Base cowardise in* Clinias; 3 *braue courage imaged in* Amphialus. 4 *His onset with the death of two friendes his foes.* 5 *The horrour of* Mars-*his game.* 6 *Two deaths taken where they were not lookt for, the third delayed where it was expected.*

1 BVt this day their speach was the sooner broken of, by reason that he, who stood as watche vpon the top of the keepe, did not onely see a great dust arise (which the earth sent vp, as if it would striue to haue clowdes as well as the aire) but might spie sometimes, especially when the dust (wherein the naked winde did apparaile it self) was caried aside frō them, the shining of armour, like flashing of lightning, wherwith the clowdes did seeme to be with child; which the Sunne guilding with his beames, it gaue a sight delightfull to any, but

to

to them that were to abide the terrour . But the watch
gaue a quick Alarum to the fouldiers within , whome
practife already hauing prepared , began each , with
vnabafhed hartes , or at left countenaunces , to looke
to their charge, or obedience, which was allotted vnto
them.

Onely *Clinias* and *Amphialus* did exceed the bounds 2
of mediocrity : the one in his naturall coldneffe of co-
wardife, the other in heate of courage. For *Clinias* (who
was bold onely in bufie whifperings ; and euen in that
whifperingnes rather indeed confident in his cunning,
that it fhould not be bewraied , then any way bolde , if
euer it fhould be bewrayed) now that the enemy gaue
a dreadful afpect vnto the caftle, his eyes faw no terror,
nor eare heard any martiall founde, but that they multiplied the hideoufneffe of it to his mated minde . Before their comming he had many times felt a dreadfull
expectation, but yet his minde (that was willing to eafe
it felfe of the burden of feare) did fomtimes feine vnto
it felfe poffibility of let; as the death of *Bafilius*, the difcord of the nobility, & (when other caufe fayled him)
the nature of chaunce ferued as a caufe vnto him : and
fometimes the hearing other men fpeake ;valiantly ,
and the quietneffe of his vnaffailed fenfes, would make
himfelfe beleue, that he durft do fomething. But now,
that prefent daunger did difplay it felfe vnto his eye, &
that a daungerous dooing muft be the onely meane to
preuet the dager of fuffering, one that had marked him
would haue iudged , that his eies would haue run into
him,& his foule out of him; fo vnkindly did either take
a fent of danger. He thought the lake was too fhallow,
& the walles too thin: he mifdouted ech mans treafon,

and coniectured euery possibilitie of misfortune, not onely fore-casting likely perils, but such as all the planets together could scarce haue conspired : & already began to arme him selfe, though it was determined he should tarrie within doores; and while he armed himselfe, imagined in what part of the vault he might hide himself if the enimies wonne the castle. Desirous he was that euery body should do valiantly, but himselfe; and therefore was afraid to shew his feare,but for very feare would haue hid his feare ; lest it should discōfort others: but the more he sought to disguize it, the more the vnsutablenes of a weake broke voice to high braue wordes,and of a pale shaking countenance to a gesture of animating, did discouer him.

3   But quite contrarily *Amphialus*,who before the enimies came was carefull, prouidently diligent, and not somtimes without doubting of the issue; now the nearer danger approched(like the light of a glow-worme) the lesse still it seemed : and now his courage began to boile in choler, and with such impatience to desire to powre out both vpō the enimie, that he issued presently into certaine boates he had of purpose, and carying with him some choise men, went to the fortresse he had vpō the edge of the lake, which he thought would be the first thing, that the enimy would attempt; because it was a passage, which cōmanding all that side of of that country, & being lost would stop victuall, or other supply, that might be brought into the castle:& in that fortresse hauing some force of horsemen, he issued out with two hundred horse, & fiue hūdred footmen, embushed his footmē in the falling of a hill, which was ouer shadowed with a wood, he with his horsmē went

a quarter of a mile further,afide had of which he might
perceaue the many troupes of the enimie, who came
but to take view where beft to encampe themfelues.

But as if the fight of the enimie had bene a Magnes
ftone to his courage he could not côtaine himfelf, but   4
fhewing his face to the enimie, & his backe to his fouldiers,vfed that action,as his onely oration,both of de-
nouncing warre to the one,and perfuading help of the
other.Who faithfully folowing an example of fuch authoritie,they made the earth to grone vnder their furious burden,and the enimies to begin to be angry with
thê,whom in particular they knew not.Among whom
there was a young man, youngeft brother to *Philanax*,
whofe face as yet did not bewray his fex,with fo much
as fhew of haire; of a minde hauing no limits of hope,
nor knowing why to feare ; full of iollitie in conuerfation,and lately growne a Louer.His name was *Agenor*,
of all that armie the moft beautifull : who hauing rid-
den in fportfull conuerfatiô among the foremoft,all armed fauing that his beauer was vp , to haue his breath
in more freedome, feing *Amphialus* come a pretty way
before his côpany,neither ftaying the cômaundement
of the captaine , nor recking whether his face were armed, or no,fet fpurs to his horfe,& with youthfull brauery cafting his ftaffe about his head , put it then in his
reft,as carefull of comely carying it,as if the marke had
ben but a ring,& the lookers on Ladies. But *Amphialus*
launce was already come to the laft of his defcending
line , and began to make the full point of death againft
the head of this young Gentleman , when *Amphia-*
lus perceyuing his youth and beautie, Compaffion fo
rebated the edge of Choller, that he fpared that faire

Mm 3   naked-

nakedneſſe, and let his ſtaffe fall to *Agenors* vamplat:
ſo as both with braue breaking ſhould hurtleſlie haue
perfourmed that match, but that the pittileſſe launce
of *Amphialus* (angry with being broken) with an vnlucky counterbuffe full of vnſparing ſplinters, lighted
vpon that face farre fitter for the combats of *Venus*; geuing not onely a ſuddaine, but a fowle death, leauing
ſcarſely any tokens of his former beautie: but his hãds
abandoning the reynes, and his thighes the ſaddle, he
fell ſidewarde from the horſe. Which ſight comming
to *Leontius*, a deere friende of his, who in vayne had lamentably cried vnto him to ſtay, when he ſaw him beginne his careere, it was harde to ſay, whether pittie of
the one, or reuenge of the other, helde as then the ſoueraigntie in his paſſions. But while he directed his
eye to his friende, and his hande to his enimie, ſo
wrongly-conſorted a power could not reſiſt the ready
minded force of *Amphialus*: who perceyuing his il-di-
rected direction againſt him, ſo paide him his debt
before it was lent, that he alſo fell to the earth, onely
happy that one place, & one time, did finiſh both their
loues and liues together.

5   But by this time there had bene a furious meeting
of either ſide: where after the terrible ſalutation of
warlike noyſe, the ſhaking of handes was with ſharpe
weapons: ſome launces according to the mettall they
mett, and skill of the guider, did ſtaine themſelues in
bloud; ſome flew vp in pieces, as if they would threaten heauen, becauſe they fayled on earth. But their office was quickly inherited, either by (the Prince of
weapons) the ſworde, or by ſome heauy maſe, or biting axe; which hunting ſtill the weakeſt chaſe, ſought
euer

euer to light there, where smallest resistãce might worse
preuent mischief. The clashing of armour, and crushing
of staues; the iustling of bodies, the resounding of
blowes, was the first part of that ill-agreeing musicke,
which was beautified with the griselinesse of wounds,
the rising of dust, the hideous falles, and grones of the
dying. The verie horses angrie in their maisters anger,
with loue and obedience brought foorth the effects
of hate and resistance, and with minds of seruitude, did
as if they affected glorie. Some lay deade vnder their
dead maisters, whome vnknightly wounds had vniustly punished for a faithfull dutie. Some lay vppon their
Lordes by like accidents, and in death had the honour
to be borne by them, whõ in life they had borne. Some
hauing lost their commaunding burthens, ranne scattered about the field, abashed with the madnesse of mankinde. The earth it selfe (woont to be a buriall of men)
was nowe (as it were) buried with men: so·was the
face thereof hidden with deade bodies, to whome
Death had come masked in diuerse manners. In one
place lay disinherited heades, dispossessed of their naturall seignories: in an other, whole bodies to see to,
but that their harts wont to be bound all ouer so close,
were nowe with deadly violence opened: in others,
fowler deaths had ouglily displayed their trayling
guttes. There lay armes, whose fingers yet.mooued,
as if they woulde feele for him that made them feele:
and legges, which contrarie to common nature, by being discharged of their burthen, were growne heauier.
But no sworde payed so large a tribute of soules to
the eternall Kingdome, as that of *Amphialus,* who like
a Tigre, from whome a companie of Woolues did

seeke,

feeke to rauifh a newe gotten pray ; fo he (remembring
they came to take away *Philoclea*) did labour to make
valure,ftrength,hatred, and choller to anfwere the proportion of his loue,which was infinit.

6   There died of his handes the olde knight *Æfchylus*,
who though by yeares might well haue beene allowed
to vfe rather the exercife of wifedome,then of courage;
yet hauing a luftie bodie & a merrie hart,he euer tooke
the fummons of Time in ieft, or elfe it had fo creepingly ftollen vpon him,that he had heard fcarcely the noife
of his feete,and therefore was as frefh in apparell, and
as forwarde in enterprifes , as a farre yonger man : but
nothing made him bolder , then a certaine prophecie
had beene tolde him , that he fhoulde die in the armes
of his fonne;and therefore feared the leffe the arme of
an enemie. But nowe, when *Amphialus* fworde was
paffed through his throate, he thought himfelfe abufed ; but that before he died,his fonne,indeede,feeing
his father beginne to fall, helde him vp in his armes,
till a pitileffe fouldier of the other fide,with a mace brai-
ned him, making father and fonne become twinnes in
their neuer againe dying birth. As for *Drialus*, *Mem-*
non, *Nifus* and *Policrates*;the firft had his eyes cut out fo,
as he could not fee to bid the neare following death
welcome : the feconde had met with the fame Prophet
that olde *Æfchylus* had, and hauing founde manie of
his fpeeches true, beleeued this to, that he fhould neuer be killed,but by his owne companions : and therefore no man was more valiant then he againft an enemie , no man more fufpicious of his friends : fo as he
feemed to fleepe in fecuritie,when he went to a battell,
and to enter into a battaile , when he began to fleepe,

fuch.

such guards he would set about his person ; yet mistru-
sting the verie guardes, that they would murther him.
But nowe *Amphialus* helped to vnriddle his doubts; for
he ouerthrowing him from his horse, his owne companions comming with a fresh supplie, pressed him to
death. *Nisus* grasping with *Amphialus*, was with a short
dagger slaine. And for *Policrates*, while he shunned as
much as he could, keeping onely his place for feare of
punishment, *Amphialus* with a memorable blowe strake
of his head, where, with the conuulsions of death setting his spurres to his horse, he gaue so braue a charge
vpon the enemie, as it grewe a prouerbe, that *Policrates*
was onely valiant, after his head was off. But no man
escaped so well his handes as *Phebilus* did : for he hauing long loued *Philoclea*, though for the meannesse of
his estate he neuer durst reueale it, nowe knowing
Amphialus, setting the edge of a riuall vpon the sworde
of an enemie, he helde strong fight with him. But *Amphialus* had alreadie in the daungeroussest places disarmed him, and was lifting vp his sworde to sende him
away from him, when he thinking indeede to die, O
Philoclea (said he) yet this ioyes me, that I die for thy
sake. The name of *Philoclea* first staied his sworde, and
when he heard him out, though he abhorde him much
worse then before, yet could he not vouchsafe him the
honour of dying for *Philoclea*, but turned his sword a-
nother way, doing him no hurt for ouer-much hatred.
But what good did that to poore *Phebilus*, if escaping a
valiant hand, he was slaine by a base souldiour, who seeing him so disarmed, thrust him through .

CHAP.

CHAP. 8.

The Basilians reembattelled [1] *first by* Philanax, [2] *then by the blacke Knight.* [3] Ismenus *slaine by* Philanax. [4] Philanax *captiued by* Amphialus. [5] *The blacke Knights exploits.* [6] *His encounter with* Amphialus, *parted by a by-blow.* [7] *The Amphialians retrait, and departure of the blacke Knight.*

1 Hus with the well-followed valure of *Amphialus* were the other almoſt ouerthrowne, when *Philanax* (who was the marſhal of the army) came in, with newe force renuing the almoſt decayed courage of his ſouldiers. For, crying to them (and asking them whether their backes or their armes were better fighters) he himſelfe thruſt into the preſſe, and making force and furie waite vppon diſcretion and gouernement, he might ſeeme a braue Lion, who taught his yong Lionets, how in taking of a pray, to ioine courage with cunning. The Fortune (as if ſhe had made chaſes inow of the one ſide of that bloody Teniſcourt) went of the other ſide the line, making as many fall downe of *Amphialus* followers, as before had done of *Philanaxis*; they looſing the ground, as faſt as before they had woon it, only leauing them to keepe it, who had loſt themſelues in keeping it. Then thoſe that had kille'd, inherited the lot of thoſe that had bene killed; and cruel Death made the lie quietly togither, who moſt in their liues had ſought to diſquiet ech other; and

many

many of thofe firſt ouerthrowne, had the comfort to fee
the murtherers ouerrun them to *Charons* ferrie.

Codrus,Cteſiphon, and *Milo,* loſt their liues vpon *Phila-*　2
nax. his fword:but no bodies cafe was more pitied, then
of a yong efquire of *Amphialus,* called *Iſmenus,* who neuer abandoning his maifter, and making his tender age
afpire to actes of the ſtrongeſt manhoode, in this time
that his fide was put to the worſt, and that *Amphialus-*
his valure was the onely ſtay of them from deliuering
themfelues ouer to a ſhamefull flight, he fawe his maſters horfe killed vnder him. Whereupon, asking no aduife of no thought, but of faithfulnes and courage, he
prefently lighted from his owne horfe, and with the
helpe of fome choife and faithfull feruants, gat his maſter vp. But in the multitude that came of either fide,
fome to fuccour, fome to faue *Amphialus,* he came vnder the hande of *Philanax* : and the youth perceyuing
he was the man that did moſt hurt to his partie, (defirous euē to change his life for glorie) ſtrake at him, as
he rode by him, and gaue him a hurt vpon the leg, that
made *Philanax* turn towards him; but feing him fo yōg,
& of a moſt louely prefence, he rather toke pity of him;
meaning to make him prifoner, & thē to giue him to his
brother *Agenor* to be his companion, becaufe they were
not much vnlike, neither in yeeres, nor countenance.
But as he loked down vpon him with that thought, he
fpied wher his brother lay dead, & his friend *Leontius* by
him, euē almoſt vnder the fquiers feet. Thē foroing not
only his owne forow, but the paſt-cōfort forow, which
he fore-knew his mother would take, (who with many
teares, & mifgiuing fighs had fuffred him to go with his
elder brother *Philanax*) blotted out all figures of pitie
　　　　　　　　　　　　　　　　　　　　　　out

out of his minde, and putting foorth his horfe (while
Ifmenus doubled two or three more valiant, then well
fet blowes) faying to himfelfe, Let other mothers bewaile an vntimely death as well as mine; he thruft him
through. And the boy fearce though beautiful, & beautifull, though dying, not able to keepe his failing feete,
fel downe to the earth, which he bit for anger, repining
at his Fortune, and as long as he could refifting Death,
which might feeme vnwilling to; fo long he was in taking away his yong ftruggling foule.

3   *Philanax* himfelfe could haue wifhed the blow vngi-
uen, when he faw him fall like a faire apple, which fome
vncourteous bodie (breaking his bowe) fhould throwe
downe before it were ripe. But the cafe of his brother
made him forget both that, and himfelfe : fo as ouerha-
ftily preffing vppon the retiring enemies, he was (ere he
was aware) further engaged then his owne fouldiers
could relieue him; were being ouerthrowne by *Amphialus*, *Amphialus* glad of him, kept head aginft his enemies
while fome of his men caried away *Philanax*.

4   But *Philanax*-his men as if with the loffe of *Philanax*
they had loft the fountaine of their valure, had their
courages fo dried vp in feare, that they began to fet honour at their backes, and to vfe the vertue of pacience in
an vntimely time: when into the preffe comes (as hard
as his horfe, more afraied of the fpurre, then the fword
could carie him) a Knight in armor as darke as blacknes
coulde make it, followed by none, and adorned by
nothing; fo far without authoritie that he was without
knowledge. But vertue quickly made him knowne, and
admiration bred him fuch authoritie, that though they
of whofe fide he came knew him not, yet they all knew
                                                                it was

it was fitte to obey him : and while he was followed by
the valianteſt, he made way for the vileſt. For, taking
part with the beſiegers, he made the *Amphialians* bloud
ſerue for a capariſon to his horſe, and a decking to his
armour. His arme no oftner gaue blowes, then the
blowes gaue wounds, then the wounds gaue deathes:
ſo terrible was his force, and yet was his quicknes more
forcible then his force, and his iudgement more quick
then his quicknes. For though the ſword went faſter
then eyeſight could follow it, yet his owne iudgement
went ſtill before it. There died of his hand, *Sarpedon*,
Pliſtonax, *Strophilus*, and *Hippolitus*, men of great proofe
in warres, and who had that day vndertaken the guard
of *Amphialus*. But while they ſought to ſaue him, they
loſt the fortreſſes that Nature had placed them in. The
ſlew he *Megalus*, who was a little before proude, to ſee
himſelfe ſtained in the bloud of his enemies: but when
his owne bloud came to be married to theirs, he then
felt, that Crueltie dooth neuer enioy a good cheape „
glorie. After him ſent he *Palemon*, who had that daye
vowed (with fooliſh brauerie) to be the death of tenne:
and nine already he had killed, and was carefull to performe his (almoſt performed) vowe, when the Blacke
Knight helpt him to make vp the tenth himſelfe.

And now the often-changing Fortune began alſo 5
to chaunge the hewe of the battailes. For at the firſt,
though it were terrible, yet Terror was deckt ſo braue-
lie with rich furniture, guilte ſwords, ſhining armours,
pleaſant penſils, that the eye with delight had ſcarce
leaſure to be afraide : But now all vniuerſally defiled
with duſt, bloud, broken armours, mangled bodies,
tooke away the maſke, and ſette foorth Horror in his
                                                owne

owne horrible manner . But neither could danger be
dreadfull to *Amphialus* his vndifmayable courage,
nor yet feeme ougly to him , whofe truely-affected
minde, did ftill paint it ouer with the beautie of *Philoclea* . And therefore he, rather enfiamed then troubled
with the encreafe of dangers,and glad to finde a woorthie fubiect to exercife his courage , fought out this
newe Knight , whom he might eafilie finde : for he,
like a wanton rich man, that throwes down his neighbours houfes , to make himfelfe the better profpecte,
fo had his fworde made him fo fpatious a roome , that
Amphialus had more caufe to wonder at the finding,
then labour for the feeking : which, if it ftirred hate in
him , to feehow much harme he did to the one fide,
it prouoked as much æmulation in him, to perceaue
how much good he did to the other fide . Therefore,
they approaching one to the other, as in two beautifull folkes , Loue naturally ftirres a defire of ioyning,
fo in their two courages Hate ftirred a defire of triall.
Then began there a combatte betweene them,worthy
to haue had more large liftes , and more quiet beholders : for with the fpurre of Courage , and the bitte of
Refpect, each fo guided himfelfe , that one might well
fee,the defire to ouercome,made them not forget how
to ouercome : in fuch time & proportion they did employ their blowes, that none of *Ceres* feruaunts coulde
more cunningly place his flaile : while the lefte foote
fpurre fet forwarde his owne horfe,the right fette backward the contrarie horfe , euen fometimes by the aduauntage of the enemies legge , while the lefte hande
(like him that helde the fterne) guyded the horfes obedient courage : All done in fuch order , that it might
                                                    feeme

feeme,the minde was a right Prince indeede, who fent wife and diligent Lieutenants into each of thofe well gouerned partes. But the more they fought, the more they defired to fight; and the more they fmarted, the lefle they felte the fmaite: and now were like to make a quicke proofe, to whom Fortune or Valour woulde feeme moft friendly, when in comes an olde Gouernour of *Amphialus*, alwayes a good Knight,and carefull of his charge; who giuing a fore wounde to the blacke Knights thigh, while he thought not of him, with an other blowe flewe his horfe vnde him. *Amphialus* cried to him,that he difhonoured him: You fay well (anfwered the olde Knight) to ftande now like a priuate fouldier, fetting your credite vpon particular fighting, while you may fee *Bafilius* with all his hofte, is getting betweene you and your towne.

He looked that way, and found that true indeede, 6 that the enemie was beginning to encompafle him about, and ftoppe his returne: and therefore caufing the retreite to be founded, his Gouernour ledde his men homewarde, while he kepte him felfe ftill hindmofte, as if hee had ftoode at the gate of a flufe, to lette the ftreame goe, with fuch proportion, as fhoulde feeme good vnto him: and with fo manfull difcretion perfourmed it, that (though with loffe of many of his men) he returned in him felfe fafe, and content, that his enemies had felte, how fharpe the fworde coulde bite of *Philoclea* Louer. The other partie being forie for the loffe of *Philanax*, was yet forrier when the blacke Knight could not be found. For he hauing gotten on a horfe, whom his dying mafter had bequeathed to the world,finding himfelfe

fore

ſore hurt, and not deſirous to be knowen, had in the time of the enemies retiring, retired away alſo : his thigh not bleeding bloud ſo faſt, as his harte bledde re-uenge. But *Baſilius* hauing attempted in vaine to barre the ſafe returne of *Amphialus*, encamped himſelfe as ſtrongly as he could, while he (to his grief) might heare the ioy was made in the towne by his owne ſubiectes, that he had that day ſped no better. For *Amphialus* (be-ing well beloued of that people) when they ſawe him not vanquiſhed, they eſteemed him as victorious, his youth ſetting a flouriſhing ſhew vpon his worthineſſe, and his great nobilitie ennobling his dangers.

CHAP. 9.

¹ *The Loue-diuining dreame of* Amphialus *ſong to* Philo-clea. ² *Philanax* *his captiuitie, and deaths-doome*, ³ *for* Philocleas *ſake turnde to life and libertie.* ⁴ *His loyall an-ſwere of his Lords intents.* ⁵ Cecropias *artes to perſwade the ſiſters.*

Vt the firſt thing *Amphialus* did, be-ing returned, was to viſite *Philoclea*, and firſt preſuming to cauſe his dreame to be ſong vnto her (which he had ſeen the night before he fell in loue with her) making a fine boy he had, accorde a prettie dolefulnes vnto it. The ſong was this.

NOw was our heau'nly vaulte depriued of the light
With Sunnes depart : and now the darkenes of the night
Did

Did light thofe beamye ftars which greater light did darke :
Now each thing that enioy'd that firie quickning fparke
(Which life is cald) were mou'd their fpirits to repofe,
And wanting vfe of eyes their eyes began to clofe :
A filence fweet each where with one confent embrafte
(A mufique fweet to one in carefull mufing plafte)
And mother Earth, now clad in mourning weeds, did breath
A dull defire to kiffe the image of our death :
When i, difgraced wretch, not wretched then, did giue
My fenfes fuch reliefe, as they which quiet liue,
Whofe braines broile not in woes, nor brefts with beatings ake,
With natures praife are wont in fafeft home to take.
Far from my thoughts was ought, whereto their minds afpire,
Who vnder courtly pompes doo hatch a bafe defire.
Free all my powers were from thofe captiuing fnares,
Which heau'nly pureft gifts defile in muddy cares.
Ne could my foule it felfe accufe of fuch a faulte,
As tender confcience might with furious panges affaulte.
But like the feeble flower (whofe ftalke cannot fuftaine
His weighty top) his top doth downeward drooping leane:
Or as the filly birde in well acquainted neft
Doth hide his head with cares but onely how to reft :
So I in fimple courfe, and vnentangled minde
Did fuffer droufie lids mine eyes then cleare to blinde;
And laying downe my head, did natures rule obferue,
Which fenfes vp doth fhut the fenfes to preferue.
They firft their vfe forgot, then fancies loft their force ;
Till deadly fleepe at length poffeft my liuing coarfe.
A liuing coarfe I lay : but ah, my wakefull minde
(Which made of heau'nly ftuffe no mortal chauge doth blind)
Flew vp with freer wings of flefhly bondage free;
And hauing plafte my thoughts, my thoughts thus placed me.

N n

Me

Me thought,nay sure I was, I was in fairest wood
Of Samothea *lande;a lande,which whilom stood*
An honour to the world,while Honour was their ende,
And while their line of yeares they did in vertue spende.
But there I was,and there my calmie thoughts I fedd
On Natures sweet repast,as healthfull senses ledd..
Her giftes my study was,her beauties were my sporte :
My worke her workes to know,her dwelling my resorte .
Those lampes of heau'nly fire to fixed motion bound,
The euer-turning spheares,the neuer-mouing ground;
What essence dest'nie hath; if fortune be or no;
Whence our immortall soules to mortall earth doo flowe;
What life it is,and how that all these liues doo gather,
With outward makers force,or like an inward father. (mind
Such thoughts,me thought,I thought, and straind my single
Then void of neerer cares,the depth of things to find.
When lo with hugest noise (such noise a tower makes
When it blowne downe with winde a fall of ruine takes)
(Or such a noise it was,as highest thunders sende,
Or canons thunder-like, all shot togither,lende)
The Moone a sunder rent; whereout with sodaine fall
(More swift then falcons stoope to feeding Falconers call)
There came a chariot faire by doues and sparrowes guided:
Whose stormelike course staid not till hard by me it bided.
I wretch astonisht was,and thought the deathfull doome
Of heauen,of earth,of hell,of time and place was come.
But streight there issued forth two Ladies (Ladies sure
They seemd to me)on whom did waite a Virgin pure :
Straunge were the Ladies weeds; yet more vnfit then strange.
The first with cloth s tuckt vp as Nymphes in woods do range;
Tuckt vp euen with the knees, with bowe and arrowes prest:
Her right arme naked was, discouered was her brest.

But

But heauy was her pace,and such a meagre cheere,
As little hunting minde(God knowes)did there appeere.
The other had with arte(more then our women knowe,
As stuffe meant for the sale set out to glaring showe)
A wanton womans face,and with curld knots had twinde
Her haire,which by the helpe of painters cunning,shinde.
When I such guests did see come out of such a house, (*mouse.*
The mountaines great with childe I thought brought foorth a
But walking forth,the first thus to the second saide,
Venus come on : said she, Diane *you are obaide.*
Those names abasht me much, whē those great names I hard:
Although their fame(me seemd)from truth had greatly iard.
As I thus musing stood, Diana *cald to her*
The waiting Nymphe,a Nymphe that did excell as farr
All things that earst I sawe,as orient pearles exceed,
That which their mother hight, or els their silly seed.
Indeed a perfect hewe,indeed a sweet consent
Of all those Graces giftes the heauens haue euer lent.
And so she was attirde,as one that did not prize
Too much her peerles parts,nor yet could them despise.
But cald,she came apace; a pace wherein did moue
The bande of beauties all,the little world of Loue.
And bending humbled eyes (ò eyes the Sunne of sight)
She waited mistresse will: who thus disclosd her spright.
Sweet Mira *mine(quoth she)the pleasure of my minde,*
In whom of all my rules the perfect proofe I finde,
To onely thee thou seest we graunt this speciall grace
Vs to attend,in this most priuate time and place.
Be silent therefore now,and so be silent still
Of that thou seest : close vp in secrete knot thy will.
She answer'd was with looke,and well perj..rm'd behest :
And Mira *I admirde : her shape sonke in my brest.*

But thus with irefull eyes, and face that shooke with spite
Diana *did begin.* What mou'd me to inuite
Your presence (sister deare) first to my Moony sphaere,
And hither now, vouchsafe to take with willing eare.
I know full well you know, what discord long hath raign'd
Betwixt vs two; how much that discord foule hath stain'd
Both our estates, while each the other did depraue,
Proofe speakes too much to vs that feeling triall haue.
Our names are quite forgot, our temples are defac'd:
Our offrings spoil'd, our priest from priesthood are displac'd
Is this the fruite of strife? those thousand churches hie,
Those thousand altars faire now in the dust to lie?
In mortall mindes our mindes but planets names preserue:
No knees once bowed, forsooth, for them they say we serue.
Are we their seruants growne? no doubt a noble staye:
Celestiall powers to wormes, Ioues children serue to claye.
But such they say we be: this praise our discord bred,
While we for mutuall spight a striuing passion fed.
But let vs wiser be; and what foule discorde brake,
So much more strong againe let fastest concorde make.
Our yeares doo it require: you see we both doo feele
The weakning worke of Times for euer-whirling wheele.
Although we be diuine, our grandsire Saturne *is*
With ages force decay'd, yet once the heauen was his.
And now before we seeke by wise Apollos skill
Our young yeares to renew (for so he saith he will)
Let vs a perfect peace betweene vs two resolue:
Which lest the ruinous want of gouernment dissolue;
Let one the Princesse be, to her the other yeeld:
For vaine equalitie is but contentions field.
And let her haue the giftes that should in both remaine:
In her let beautie both, and chastnesse fully raigne.

So as if I preuaile, you giue your giftes to me:
If you, on you I lay what in my office be.
Now resteth onely this, which of vs two is she,
To whom precedence shall of both accorded be.
For that (so that you like) hereby doth lie a youth
(She beckned vnto me) as yet of spotlesse truth,
Who may this doubt discerne : for better, witt, then lot
Becommeth vs: in vs fortune determines not.
This crowne of amber faire (an amber crowne she held)
To worthiest let him giue, when both he hath beheld :
And be it as he saith . Venus *was glad to heare*
Such proffer made, which she well showd with smiling cheere
As though she were the same, as when by Paris *doome*
She had chiefe Goddesses in beautie ouercome.
And smirkly thus gan say . I neuer sought debate
Diana *deare: my minde to loue and not to hate*
Was euer apt : but you my pastimes did despise.
I neuer spited you, but thought you ouerwise.
Now kindnesse profred is, none kinder is then I :
And so most ready am this meane of peace to trie .
And let him be our iudge : the lad doth please me well.
Thus both did come to me, and both began to tell
(For both togither spake, each loth to be behinde)
That they by solemne oth their Deities would binde
To stand vnto my will : their will they made me know.
I that was first agast, when first I saw their showe:
Now bolder waxt, waxt prowde, that I such sway must beare:
For neere acquaintance dooth diminish reuerent feare.
And hauing bound them fast by Styx, *they should obaye*
To all what I decreed, did thus my verdict saye.
How ill both you can rule, well hath your discord taught :
Ne yet for ought I see, your beauties merite ought .

To

To yonder Nymphe therefore(to Mira *I did point)*
The crowne aboue.you both for euer I appoint.
I would haue spoken out:but out they both did crie;
Fie, fie, what haue,we done? vngodly rebell fie.
But now we needs must yeelde,to that our othes require.
Yet thou shalt not go free(quoth Venus*) such a fire*
Her beautie kindle shall within thy foolish minde,
That thou full oft shalt wish thy iudging eyes were blinde.
*Nay then(*Diana *said) the chastnesse I will giue*
In ashes of despaire (though burnt) shall make thee liue.
Nay thou (said both) shalt see such beames shine in her face
That thou shalt neuer dare seeke helpe of wretched case.
And with that cursed curse away to heauen they fled,
First hauing all their giftes vpon faire Mira *spred.*
The rest I cannot tell, for therewithall I wak'd
And found with deadly feare that all my sinewes shak'd.
Was it a dreame? O dreame, how hast thou wrought in me,
That I things erst vnseene should first in dreaming see?
And thou ò traytour Sleepe,made for to be our rest,
How hast thou framde the paine wherewith I am opprest?
O cowarde Cupid *thus doost thou thy honour keepe,*
Vnarmde (alas) vnwares to take a man asleepe?

Laying not onely the conquests,but the hart of the cóquerour at her feet. *** But she receiuing him after her woonted sorrowfull(but otherwise vnmoued) má- ner, it made him thinke, his good succeffe was but a pleafant monument of a dolefull buriall : Ioy it felfe feeming bitter vnto him, since it agreed not to her tafte.

2   Therefore, ftill crauing his mothers helpe to per- fuade her,he himfelf fent for *Philanax* vnto him,whom he

he had not onely long hated, but nowe had his hate greatly encreafed by the death of his Squire *Ifmenus.* Befides he had made him as one of the chiefe caufes that mooued him to this rebellion, and therefore was enclined (to colour the better his action, and the more to embrewe the handes of his accomplices by making them guiltie of fuch a trefpaffe) in fome formall fort to caufe him to be executed : being alfo greatly egged thereunto by his mother, and fome other, who long had hated *Philanax*, onely becaufe he was more worthy to be loued then they.

But while that deliberation was handeled, accor- 3 ding rather to the humour then the reafon of ech fpea- ker, *Philoclea* comming to knowledge of the hard plight wherein *Philanax* ftood, fhe defired one of the gentle- women appoynted to waite vpon her, to goe in her name, and befeech *Amphialus*, that if the loue of her had any power of perfwafion in his minde, he would lay no further punifhment, then imprifonment, vppon *Philanax.* This meffage was deliuered euen as *Phi- lanax* was entring to the prefence of *Amphialus*, com- ming (according to the warning was giuen him) to receyue a iudgement of death. But when he with manfull refolution attended the fruite of fuch a ty- rannicall fentence, thinking it wrong, but no harme to him that fhoulde die in fo good a caufe; *Amphi- alus* turned quite the fourme of his pretended fpeech, and yeelded him humble thankes, that by his meanes he had come to that happineffe, as to receiue a com- maundement of his Ladie: and therefore he willingly gaue him libertie to returne in fafetye whither he would;

would; quitting him, not onely of all former grudge, but aſſuring him that he would be willing to do him a-ny friendſhip, and ſeruice: onely deſiring thus much of him, that he would let him know the diſcourſe and in-tent of *Baſilius*-his proceeding.

4   Truely my Lorde (anſwered *Philanax*) if there were any ſuch knowne to me, ſecrete in my maiſters coun-ſaile, as that the reuealing thereof might hinder his good ſucceſſe, I ſhoulde loath the keeping of my blood, with the loſſe of my faith; and woulde thinke the iuſt name of a traitour a harde purchaſe of a fewe yeares liuing. But ſince it is ſo, that my maiſter hath indeede no way of priuie practiſe, but meanes openly and forcibly to deale againſt you, I will not ſticke in fewe wordes to make your required declaration. Then tolde he him in what amaze of amazement, both *Baſi-lius* and *Gynecia* were, when they miſt their children and *Zelmane*. Sometimes apt to ſuſpect ſome practiſe of *Zelmane*, becauſe ſhe was a ſtraunger; ſometimes doub-ting ſome reliques of the late mutinie, which doubt was rather encreaſed, then any way ſatisfied, by *Miſo*: who (being founde, almoſt deade for hunger, by cer-taine Countrey-people) brought home worde, with what cunning they were trayned out, and with what violence they were caried away. But that within a fewe dayes they came to knowledge where they were, with *Amphialus*-his owne letters ſent abroade to pro-cure confederates in his attemptes. That *Baſilius* his purpoſe was neuer to leaue the ſiege of this towne, till he had taken it, and reuenged the iniurie done vn-to him. That he meant rather to winne it by time, and famine, then by force of aſſault: knowing howe
valiant

valiaunt men he had to deale withall in the towne: that he had sent order, that supplyes of souldiours, pioners, and all things else necessarie, shoulde dayly be brought vnto him: so as, my Lorde (sayde *Philanax*) let me nowe, hauing receyued my life bv your grace. let me giue you your life and honour by my counsaile; protesting vnto you, that I cannot choose but loue you, being my maister-his nephewe; and that I wish you well in all causes: but this, you knowe his nature is as apte to forgiue, as his power is able to conquere. Your fault passed is excusable, in that Loue perswaded, and youth was perswaded. Do not vrge the effects of angrie victorie, but rather seeke to obtaine that constantly by courtesie, which you can neuer assuredly enioy by violence. One might easily haue seene in the cheare of *Amphialus*, that disdainfull choller woulde faine haue made the aunswere for him, but the remembraunce of *Philoclea* serued for forcibie barriers betweene Anger, and angry effects: so as he saide no more, but that he woulde not put him to the trouble to giue him any further counsaile: But that he might returne, if he listed, presently. *Philanax* glad to receyue an vncorrupted libertie, humbly accepted his fauourable conuoy out of the towne; and so departed, not hauing visited the Princesses, thinking it might be offensiue to *Amphialus*, and no way fruitfull to them, who were no way but by force to be relieued.

The poore Ladies indeede, not suffered either to meet together, or to haue cóference with anv other, but such as *Cecropia* had alreadie framed to sing all her songs to her tune, she herselfe omitting no day, and catching

ching holde of euerie occaſion to mooue forwarde
her ſonnes deſire, and remoue their knowne reſolutions : vſing the ſame arguments to the one ſiſter, as to
the other; determining that whome ſhe coulde winne
firſt, the other ſhoulde (without her ſonnes knowledge) by poyſon be made away. But though the
reaſons were the ſame to both, yet the handeling was
diuerſe, according as ſhe ſawe their humours to preferre a more or leſſe aptneſſe of apprehenſion : this
day hauing vſed long ſpeech to *Philoclea*, amplifying
not a little the great duetifulneſſe her ſonne had ſhewed in deliuering *Philanax* : of whome ſhe coulde get
no aunſwere, but a ſilence ſealed vp in vertue, and ſo
ſweetly graced, as that in one inſtant it caried with it
both reſiſtance, and humbleneſſe.

CHAP. 10.

[1] Pamelas *exerciſe.* Cecropias *talke with her* [2] *of Beautie*
[3] *and the vſe thereof.* [4] *The Auntes Atheiſme* [5] *refu-*
ted by the Neeces Diuinitie.

[1] Ecropia threatning in her ſelfe to
runne a more ragged race with her,
went to her ſiſter *Pamela* : who that
day hauing wearied her ſelfe with
reading, and with the height of her
hart diſdaining to keepe companie
with any of the Gentlewomen appointed to attende her, whome ſhe
accounted her iaylours, was woorking vppon a purſe
certaine Roſes and Lillies, as by the fineneſſe of the
worke

worke, one might see she had borowed her wittes of the sorow that owed them, & lent them wholy to that exereise. For the flowers she had wrought, caried such life in them, that the cuningest painter might haue learned of her needle : which with so prety a maner made his careers to & fro through the cloth, as if the needle it selfe would haue bene loth to haue gone froward such a mistres, but that it hoped to return the ceward very quickly againe : the cloth loking with many eies vpon her, & louingly embracing the wounds she gaue it: the sheares also were at hand to behead the silke, tha was growne to short. And if at any time she put her mouth to bite it off, it seemed, that where she had beene long in making of a Rose with her hand, she would in an instant make Roses with her lips; as the Lillies seemed to haue their whitenesse, rather of the hande that made them, then of the matter whereof they were made; and that they grew there by the Sunes of her eyes, & were refreshed by the most in discomfort comfortable ayre, which an vnwares sigh might bestow vpon them. But the colours for the grounde were so well chosen, neither sullenly darke, nor glaringly lightsome, and so well proportioned, as that, though much cunning were in it, yet it was but to serue for an ornament of the principall woorke; that it was not without maruaile to see, howe a minde which could cast a carelesse semblant vppon the greatest conflictes of Fortune, coulde commaunde it selfe to take care for so small matters. Neither had she neglected the daintie dressing of her selfe : but as it had ben her mariage time to Affliction, she rather semed to remember her owne worthinesse, then the vnworthinesse of her husband. For well one might perceyue

she

ſhe had not reiected the counſaile of a glaſſe, and
that her handes had pleaſed themſelues, in paying
the tribute of vndeceyuing skill, to ſo high perfections
of Nature.

The ſight whereof ſo diuerſe from her ſiſter, (who
rather ſuffered ſorrow to diſtreſſe it ſelfe in her beautie,
then that ſhe would beſtow any intertainment of ſo vnwelcome a gueſt) made *Cecropia* take a ſuddaine aſſu-
redneſſe of hope,that ſhe ſhould obtaine ſomewhat of
Pamela : thinking (according to the ſquaring out of her
own good nature)that beauty, carefully ſet forth,wold
ſoone proue a ſigne of an vnrefuſing harborough. Animated wherewith, ſhe ſate downe by *Pamela:* and taking the purſe,and with affected curioſitie looking vpon the worke,Full happie is he (ſaide ſhe) at leaſt if he
knew his owne happineſſe,to whom a purſe in this maner,and by this hand wrought,is dedicated.In faith he
ſhall haue cauſe to account it,not as a purſe for treaſure,
but as a treaſure it ſelfe, worthie to be purſed vp in the
purſe of his owne hart. And thinke you ſo indeed (ſaid
Pamela halfe ſmiling) I promiſe you I wrought it, but
to make ſome tedious houres beleeue, that I thought
not of them : for elſe I valued it, but euen as a verie
purſe. It is the right nature (ſaide *Cecropia*) of Beautie, to woorke vnwitting effectes of wonder. Truely
(ſaide *Pamela*) I neuer thought till nowe,that this outward glaſſe, intitled Beautie, which it pleaſeth you to
lay to my(as I thinke) vnguiltie charge,was but a pleaſaunt mixture of naturall colours, delightfull to the
eye, as muſicke is to the eare, without any further conſequence : ſince it is a thing, which not
onely beaſtes haue; but euen ſtones and trees many of
them

them doo greatly excell in it. That other thinges (anfwered *Cecropia*) haue fome portion of it, takes not a-
way the excellencie of it, where indeede it doth excell:
fince we fee, that euen thofe beaftes, trees, & ftones, are
in the name of Beauty only highly praifed. But that the
beautie of humaine perfons be beyond all other things
there is great likelihood of reafon, fince to them onely is giuen the iudgement to difcerne Beautie; and a-
mong reafonable wights, as it feemes, that our fex hath
the preheminence, fo that in that preheminence, Nature counteruailes all other liberalities, wherin fhe may
be thought to haue dealte more fauourably towarde
mankind. How doo men crowne (thinke you) themfelues with glorie, for hauing either by force brought
others to yeeld to their minde, or with long ftudie, and
premeditated orations, perfwaded what they woulde
haue perfwaded? and fee, a faire woman fhall not onely commaund without authoritie, but perfwade without fpeaking. She fhall not neede to procure attention, for their owne eyes will chaine their eares vnto it.
Men venture liues to conquere; fhe conqueres liues
without venturing. She is ferued, and obeyed, which
is the moft notable, not becaufe the lawes fo commaund it, but becaufe they become lawes to thefelues
to obey her; not for her parents fake, but for her owne
fake. She neede not difpute, whether to gouerne by
Feare, or by Loue, fince without her thinking thereof,
their loue will bring foorth feare, and their feare will
fortifie their loue: and fhe neede not feeke offenfiue,
or defenfiue force, fince her lippes may ftande for ten
thoufand fhieldes, and tenne thoufand vneuitable fhot
goe from her eyes. Beautie, Beautie (deare Neece) is

the

the crowne of the feminine greatnes; which gifte, on whom'soeuer the heauens (therein most nigardly) do bestowe, without question, she is bound to vse it to the noble purpose, for which it is created: not onely winning, but preseruing; since that indeede is the right happines, which is not onely in it selfe happie, but can also deriue the happines to another. Certainly Aunt (said *Pamela*) I feare me you will make me not onely thinke my selfe fairer then euer I did, but think my fairnes a matter of greater valew then heretofore I coulde imagine it. For I euer (till now) conceaued these conquests you spake of, rather to proceed from the weakenes of the conquered, then from the strength of the cōquering power: as they say, the Cranes ouerthrowe whole battailes of *Pygmees*, not so much of their Cranish courage, as because the other are *Pygmees*: and that we see, young babes think babies of woonderful excellencie, and yet the babies are but babies. But since your elder yeares, and abler iudgement, finde Beautie to be worthy of so incomparable estimation, certainly me thinks, it ought to be held in dearnes, according to the e:cellencie, and (no more then we would do of things which we accoūt pretious) euer to suffer it to be defiled.

3   Defiled? (said *Cecropia*) Mary God forbid that my speech should tend to any such purpose, as should deserue so foul a title. My meaning is to ioyn your beauty to loue; your youth to delight.. For truely, as colours should be as good as nothing, if there were no eyes to behold them: so is Beauty nothing, without the eye of Loue behold it. and therfore, so far is it from defiling it, that it is the only honoring of it, the only preseruing of it: for Beauty goes away, deuoured by Time, but where

remaines

remaines it euer flourifhing, but in the hart of a true louer? And fuch a one (if euer there were any) is my fon:
whofe loue is fo fubiected vnto you, that rather then
breed any offence vnto you, it will not delight it felfe
in beholding you. Ther is no effect of his loue (anfwered *Pamela*) better pleafeth me then that: but as I haue
ofté anfwered you, fo, refolutely I fay vnto you, that he
muft get my parents confent, & then he fhall know further of my mind; for, without that, I know I fhould offend God. O fweet youth (faid *Cecropia*) how vntimely
fubiect it is to deuotion? No, no fweet neece, let vs old
folks think of fuch precife confideratiós, do you enioy
the heauen of your age, whereof you are fure : and like
good houfholders, which fpend thofe thinges that will
not be kept, fo do you pleafantly enioy that, which clfe
will bring an ouer-late repentance, whé your glas fhall
accufe you to your face, what a change there is in you.
Do you fee how the fpring-time is ful of flowers, decking it felf with them, & not afpiring to the fruits of *Au-*
tumn? what leffon is that vnto you, but that in the april
of your age, you fhould be like *April*? Let not fome of
thé, for whom alredy the graue gapeth, & perhaps enuy
the felicity in you, which théfelues cannot enioy, perfwade you to lofe the hold of occafió, while it may not
only be taken, but offers, nay fues to be také: which if it
be not now taken, will neuer hereafter be ouertaken.
Your felf know, how your father hath refufed all offers
made by the greateft Princes about you, & wil you fuffer your beauty to be hid in the wrinckles of his peuifh
thoughts? If he be peuifh (faid *Pamela*) yet is he my father, & how beautiful foeuer I be, I am his daughter: fo
as God claimes at my hands obedience, and makes me
no iudge of his imperfections.

                                                    Thefe

4

These often replies vpon conscience in *Pamela*, made *Cecropia* thinke, that there was no righter waye for her, then as she had (in her opinion) set her in liking of Beautie, with perswasion not to suffer it to be voide of purpose, so if she coulde make her lesse feeling of those heauenly conceipts, that then she might easilie winde her to her croked bias. Therefore, employing the vttermost of her mischieuous witte, and speaking the more earnestly, because she spake as she thought, she thus dealt with her. Deare neece, or rather, deare daughter (if my affection and wishe might preuaile therein) how much dooth it increase (trowe you) the earnest desire I haue of this blessed match, to see these vertues of yours knit fast with such zeale of Deuotion, indeede the best bonde, which the most politicke wittes haue found, to holde mans witte in well doing? For, as children must first by feare be induced to know that, which after (when they doo know) they are most glad of: So are these bugbeares of opinions brought by great Clearkes into the world, to serue as shewelles to keepe them from those faults, whereto els the vanitie of the worlde, and weakenes of senses might pull them. But in you (Neece) whose excellencie is such, as it neede not to be helde vp by the staffe of vulgar opinions, I would not you should loue Vertue seruillie, for feare of I know not what, which you see not: but euen for the good effects of vertue which you see. Feare, and indeede, foolish feare, and fearefull ignorance, was the first inuenter of those conceates. For, when they heard it thunder, not knowing the naturall cause, they thought there was some angrie body aboue, that spake so lowde: and euer the lesse they did

per-

perceiue, the more they did conceiue. Whereof they knew no caufe that grewe ftreight a miracle : foolifh folks, not marking that the alterations be but vpon particular accidents, the vniuerfalitie being alwaies one. Yefterday was but as to day, and to morrow will tread the fame footfteps of his foregoers : fo as it is manifeft inough, that all things follow but the courfe of their own nature, fauing only Man, who while by the pregnancie of his imagination he ftriues to things fupernaturall, meane-while he loofeth his owne naturall felicitie. Be wife, and that wifedome fhalbe a God vnto thee; be contented, and that is thy heauen : for els to thinke that thofe powers (if there be any fuch) aboue, are moued either by the eloquence of our prayers, or in a chafe by the folly of our actions; caries afmuch reafon as if flies fhould thinke, that men take great care which of them hums fweeteft, and which of them flies nimbleft.

　She would haue fpoken further to haue enlarged & côfirmed her difcourfe: but *Pamela* (whofe cheeks were died in the beautifulleft graine of vertuous anger, with eies which gliftered forth beames of difdaine) thus interrupted her. Peace (wicked woman) peace, vnworthy to breathe, that doeft not acknowledge the breath-giuer; moft vnworthy to haue a tongue, which fpeakeft againft him, through whom thou fpeakeft: keepe your affection to your felf, which like a bemired dog, would defile with fauning. You fay yefterday was as to day. O foolifh woman, and moft miferably foolifh, fince wit makes you foolifh. What dooth that argue, but that there is a conftancie in the euerlafting gouernoui ∙ Would you haue an inconftant God, fince we count a

O o 　　man

man foolifh that is inconftant? He is not feene you fay, and would you thinke him a God, who might be feene by fo wicked eyes, as yours? which yet might fee enough if they were not like fuch, who for fport-fake willingly hood-wincke themfelues to receaue blowes the eafier. But though I fpeake to you without any hope of fruite in fo rotten a harte, and there be no bodie elfe here to iudge of my fpeeches, yet be thou my witneffe, O captiuitie, that my eares fhall not be willingly guiltie of my Creators blafphemie. You faie, becaufe we know not the caufes of things, therefore feare was the mother of fuperftition : nay, becaufe we know that each effect hath a caufe, that hath engendred a true & liuely deuotion. For this goodly worke of which we are, and in which we liue, hath not his being by Chaunce; on which opinion it is beyond meruaile by what chaunce any braine could ftumble. For if it be eternall (as you would feeme to conceiue of it) Eternity, & Chaunce are things vnfufferable together. For that is chaunceable which happeneth; & if it happen, there was a time before it hapned, when it might not haue happened; or els it did not happen; and fo of chaunceable, not eternall, as now being, the not being. And as abfurd it is to thinke that if it had a beginning, his beginning was deriued fro Chaunce: for Chaunce could neuer make all thinges of nothing : and if there were fubftaunces before, which by chaunce fhoulde meete to make vp this worke, thereon followes another bottomleffe pitt of abfurdities. For then thofe fubftaunces muft needes haue bene from euer, and fo eternall : and that eternall caufes fhould bring forth chaunceable effects, is as fenfible, as that the Sunne

fhould

should be the author of darkenesse. Againe, if it were chaunceable, then was it not necessarie; whereby you take away all consequents. But we see in all thinges, in some respect or other, necessitie of consequence: therfore in reason we must needs know that the causes were necessarie.

Lastly, Chaunce is variable, or els it is not to be called Chaunce: but we see this worke is steady and permanent. If nothing but Chaunce had glewed those pieces of this All, the heauie partes would haue gone infinitely downewarde, the light infinitely vpwarde, and so neuer haue mett to haue made vp this goodly bodie. For before there was a heauen, or a earth, there was neyther a heauen to stay the height of the rising, nor an earth, which (in respect of the round walles of heauen) should become a centre. Lastly, perfect order, perfect beautie, perfect constancie, if these be the children of Chaunce, or Fortune the efficient of these, let Wisedome be counted the roote of wickednesse, and eternitie the fruite of her inconstancie. But you will say it is so by nature, as much as if you said it is so, becaufe it is so: if you meane of many natures conspiring together, as in a popular gouernement to establish this fayre estate; as if the Elementishe and ethereall partes should in their towne-house set downe the boundes of each ones office; then consider what followes: that there must needes haue bene a wisedome which made them concurre: for their natures beyng absolute contrarie, in nature rather woulde haue sought each others ruine, then haue serued as well consorted partes to such an vnexpress-

able

able harmonie. For that contrary things fhould meete to make vp a perfectió without a force and Wifedome aboue their powers, is abfolutely impoffible; vnles you will flie to that hiffed-out opinion of Chaunce againe. But you may perhaps affirme, that one vniuerfall Nature (which hath bene for euer) is the knitting together of thefe many partes to fuch an excellent vnitie. If you meane a Nature of wifdome, goodnes, & prouidence, which knowes what it doth, then fay you that, which I feeke of you, and cannot conclude thófe blafphemies, with which you defiled your mouth, & mine eares. But if you meane a Nature, as we fpeake of the fire, which goeth vpward, it knowes not why: and of the nature of the Sea which in ebbing and flowing feemes to obferue fo iuft a daunce, and yet vnderftands no muficke, it is but ftill the fame abfurditie fubfcribed with another title. For this worde, one, being attributed to that which is All, is but one mingling of many, and many ones; as in a leffe matter, when we fay one kingdome which conteines many citties; or one cittie which conteines many perfons, wherein the vnder ones (if there be not a fuperiour power and wifedome) cannot by nature regarde to any preferuation but of themfelues: no more we fee they doo, fince the water willingly quenches the fire, and drownes the earth; fo farre are they from a confpired vnitie : but that a right heauenly Nature indeed, as it were vnnaturing them, doth fo bridle them.

Againe, it is as abfurde in nature that from an vnitie many contraries fhould proceede ftill kept in an vnitie : as that from the number of contrarieties an vnitie

tie fhould arife . I fay ftill, if you banifh both a fingu-
laritie,and pluralitie of iudgement from among them,
then (if fo earthly a minde can lift it felfe vp fo hie)
doo but conceaue , how a thing whereto you giue the
higheft, and moft excellent kinde of being (which is
eternitie)can be of the bafe and vileft degree of being,
and next to a not-being;which is fo to be,as not to enioy his owne being? I will not here call all your fenfes to witnes,which can heare , nor fee nothing, which
yeeldes not moft euident euidence of the vnfpeake-
ablenefle of that Wifedome : each thing being directed to an ende , and an ende of preferuation : fo proper effects of iudgement, as fpeaking,and laughing are
of mankind.

But what madd furie can euer fo enueagle any conceipte , as to fee our mortall and corruptible felues to
haue a reafon , and that this vniuerfalitie (whereof
we are but the left pieces) fhould be vtterly deuoide
thereof? as if one fhould faie , that ones foote might
be wife , and him felfe foolifh . This hearde I once alledged againft fuch a godlefle minde as yours , who
being driuen to acknowledge thefe beaftly abfurdities , that our bodies fhould be better then the whole
worlde , if it had the knowledge , whereof the other
were voide ; he fought (not able to anfwere directly)
to fhifte it of in this forte:that if that reafon were true,
then muft it followe alfo , that the worlde muft haue
in it a fpirite,that could write and reade to, and be learned ; fince that was in vs fo commendable : wretched
foole , not confidering that Bookes be but fupplies
of defects; and fo are prayfed , becaufe they helpe our

want, and therefore cannot be incident to the eternall intelligence, which needes no recording of opinions to confirme his knowledge, no more then the Sunne wants waxe to be the fewell of his glorious lightfulnesse. This worlde therefore cannot otherwise consist but by a minde of Wisedome, whiche gouernes it, which whether you wil allow to be the Creator thereof, as vndoubtedly he is, or the soule and gouernour thereof, most certaine it is that whether he gouerne all, or make all, his power is aboue either his creatures, or his gouernement. And if his power be aboue all thinges, then consequently it must needes be infinite, since there is nothing aboue it to limit it. For beyond which there is nothing, must needes be boundlesse, and infinite: if his power be infinite, then likewise must his knowledge be infinite : for else there should be an infinite proportion of power which he shoulde not know how to vse; the vnsensiblenesse whereof I thinke euen you can conceaue : and if infinite, then must nothing, no not the estate of flies (which you with so vnsauerie skorne did iest at) be vnknowne vnto him. For if it were, then there were his knowledge bounded, and so not infinite : if knowledge and power be infinite, then must needs his goodnesse and iustice march in the same rancke : for infinitenes of power, & knowledge, without like measure of goodnesse, must necessarily bring foorth destruction and ruine, and not ornament and preseruation. Since then there is a God, and an all-knowing God, so as he sees into the darkest of all naturall secretes, which is the harte of Man; and sees therein the deepest dissembled thoughts, nay

sees

fees the thoughts before they be thought : fince he is
iuft to exercife his might, and mightie to performe his
iuftice, affure thy felfe, moft wicked woman (that haft fo
plaguily a corrupted minde, as thou canft not keepe thy
fickeneffe to thy felfe, but muft moft wickedly infect o-
thers) affure thy felfe, I fay, (for what I fay dependes of
euerlafting and vnremooueable caufes) that the time
will come, when thou fhalt knowe that power by feeling it, when thou fhalt fee his wifedome in the manifefting thy ougly fhamelefneffe, and fhalt onely perceiue him to haue bene a Creator in thy deftruction.

CHAP. 11.

* Cecropia *malcontent, ftill practifeth.* ' *The befiegers difci-*
pline, and attempts of the befieged. ' Phalantus *chá-*
lengeth ' by Letter Amphialus : ' *who by Letter ac-*
cepteth it. ' Amphialus ' *and* Phalantus *militar ac-*
couftrements. ' *Their fo-like combate,* ' *but friendly*
conclufion.

Hus fhe faide, thus fhe ended, with
fo faire a maieftie of vnconquered
vertue, that captiuitie might feeme
to haue authoritie ouer tyrannie :
fo fowly was the filthineffe of im-
pietie difcouered by the fhining
of her vnftayned goodnes, fo farre,
as either *Cecropia* faw indeed, or elfe
the guilty amazement of her felfe-accufing confcience,
made her eies vntrue iudges of their natural obiect, that

there

there was a light more then humaine, which gaue a lu-
ſtre to her perfectiens. But *Cecropia*, like a Batte(which
though it haue eyes to diſcerne that there is a Sunne,
yet hath ſo euill eyes, that it cannot delight in the
Sunne) found a trueth, but could not loue it. But as
great perſons are woont to make the wrong they haue
done, to be a cauſe to doo the more wrong, her knowledge roſe to no higher point, but to enuie a worthier, and her will was no otherwiſe bent, but the more
to hate, the more ſhe founde her enemie prouided a-
gainſt her. Yet all the while ſhe ſpake (though with
eyes caſt like a horſe that woulde ſtrike at the ſtirrop,
and with colour which bluſhed through yellowneſſe)
ſhe ſate rather ſtill then quiet, and after her ſpeech rather
muttered, then replied: for the warre of wickedneſſe in
her ſelfe, brought forth diſdainefull pride to reſiſt cunning diſſimulation; ſo as, ſaying little more vnto her,
but that ſhe ſhoulde haue leyſure inough. better to bethinke her ſelfe; ſhe went away repining, but not repenting: condemning greatly (as ſhe thought) her ſonnes
ouer-feeble humbleneſſe, and purpoſing to egge him
forward to a courſe of violence. For her ſelfe, determining to deale with neither of them both any more in
maner of a ſuter : for what maieſtie of vertue did in the
one, that did ſilent humbleneſſe in the other. But finding her ſonne ouer-apt to lay both condemnation,
and execution of ſorrowe vppon himſelfe, ſhe ſought
to mitigate his minde with feigned delayes of comforte, who (hauing this inward ouerthrow in himſelfe)
was the more vexed, that he coulde not vtter the rage
thereof vpon his outward enemies.

2   For *Baſilius* taught by the laſt dayes triall, what
                                                    daungerous

daungerous effectes chosen courages can bring forth,
rather vsed the spade, then the sworde ; or the sworde,
but to defende the spade ; girding aboute the whole
towne with trenches; which beginning a good way
of from the towne, with a number of well directed
Pioners, he still caryed before him till they came to a
neere distance, where he builded Fortes, one answering the other, in such sort, as it was a prettie consideration in the discipline of warre, to see building vsed
for the instrument of ruine, and the assayler entren-
ched as if he were besieged . But many sallies did
Amphialus make to hinder their woorking. But they
(exercising more melancholie, then choller in their
resolution) made him finde, that if by the aduauntage of place, fewe are able to defende themselues
from manie, that manie must needes haue power,
(making themselues strong in seate) to repell fewe ;
referring the reuenge rather to the ende, then a present requitall . Yet oftentimes they dealt some
blowes in light skirmishes, eche side hauing a strong
retyring place, and rather fighting with manie alarums,
to vexe the enemie, then for anie hope of great successe.

Which euerie way was a tedious comber to the im- 3
pacient courage of *Amphialus* : till the fame of this
warre, bringing thither diuerse, both straungers, and
subiects, as well of princely, as noble houses, the gallant *Phalantus*, who restrayned his sportfull delightes
as then, to serue *Basilius*, (whome he honoured for receyued honours) when he had spent some time in
considering the *Arcadian* manner in marching, en-
camping, and fighting, and had learned in what points
of

of gouernement, and obedience their difcipline differed from others, and had fatiffied his minde in the
knowledge , both for the cutting off the enemies
helpes, and furnifhing ones felfe , which *Bafilius* orders coulde deliuer vnto him, his yong fpirites (wearie of wanting caufe to be wearie) defired to keepe
his valûre in knowledge, by fome priuate acte , fince
the publique policie reftrayned him ; the rather, becaufe his olde miftreffe *Artefia* might fee , whome fhe
had fo lightly forfaken : and therefore demaunding
and obteyning leaue of *Bafilius* ; he caufed a Heraulde
to be furnifhed with apparell of his office , and tokens of a peaceable meffage , and fo fent him to the
gate of the towne to demaunde audience of *Amphia-*
lus : who vnderftanding thereof, caufed him both
fafely , and courteoufly to be brought into his prefence : who making lowly reuerence vnto him, prefented his Letters , defiring *Amphialus* that whatfoeuer they conteyned , he woulde confider that he
was onely the bearer, but not the inditer. *Amphialus*
with noble gentleneffe affured him both , by honourable fpeeches , and a demeanure which aunfwered
for him, that his reuenge, whenfoeuer, fhould fort vnto it felfe a higher fubiect. But opening the Letters, he
found them to fpeake in this maner.

4 PHalantus of *Corintht*, to *Amphialus* of *Arcadia*, fen-
deth the greeting of a hateleffe enemie. The liking of martiall matters without anie miflike of your
perfon, hath brought me rather to the companie,
then to the minde of your befiegers : where languifhing

shing in idleneſſe, I deſire to refreſh my minde with
ſome exerciſe of armes, which might make knowne
the dooers, with delight of the beholders. Therefore, if there be any Gentleman in your Towne, that
eyther for the loue of Honour, or honour of his
Loue, well armed, on horſebacke, with launce, and
ſworde, will winne another, or looſe himſelfe, to be a
priſoner at diſcretion of the conquerour, I will to morrowe morning by Sunne riſing, with a trumpet and a
Squire onely, attende him in like order furniſhed. The
place I thinke fitteſt, the Iland within the Lake, becauſe it ſtandes ſo well in the view of your Caſtell, as
that the Ladies may haue the pleaſure of ſeeing the
combate: which though it be within the commaundement of your Caſtell, I deſire no better ſecuritie,
then the promiſe I make to my ſelfe of your vertue.
I attende your aunſwere, and wiſh you ſuch ſucceſſe
as may be to your honour, rather in yeelding to that
which is iuſt, then in mainteyning wrong by much
violence.

Mphialus read it with cheerefull countenance, and
thinking but a little with himſelfe, called for inke
and paper, and wrote this aunſwere.

Mphialus of *Arcadia*, to *Phalantus* of *Corinthe*, wiſheth all his owne wiſhes, ſauing thoſe which
may be hurtful to another. The matter of your letters ſo
fit for a worthy minde, and the maner ſo ſutable to the
nobleneſſe of the matter, giue me cauſe to thinke
howe happie I might accounte my ſelfe, if I coulde
get

get fuch a friende,who esteeme it no fmall happineſſe to haue mette with ſo noble an enemie. Your chalenge ſhall be aunfwered , and both time , place, and weapon accepted . For your fecuritie for any treacherie (hauing no hoſtage woorthie to counteruaile you) take my woorde , which I eſteeme aboue all reſpectes. Prepare therefore your armes to fight, but not your hart to malice;ſince true valure needes no other whetſtone,then deſire of honour.

6   HAuing writte and fealed his letter , he deliuered it to the Heraulde, and withall tooke a faire chaine from off his owne necke, and gaue it him. And ſo with fafe conuoy ſent him away fromout his Citie:and he being gone, *Amphialus* fhewed vnto his mother, and fome other of his chiefe Counfailours, what he had receyued, and howe he had aunfwered : telling them withall, that he was determined to aunfwere the chalenge in his owne perfon. His mother with prayers authorized by motherly commaundement ; his olde gouernour with perfwaſions mingled with reprehenſions, (that he would rather affect the glorie of a priuate fighter, then of a wife Generall) *Clinias* with falling downe at his feete, and befeeching him to remember, that all their liues depended vppon his fafetie,fought all to diſſuade him. But *Amphialus* (whofe hart was enflamed with courage, and courage enflamed with affection) made an imperious refolution cutte off the tedioufneffe of replyes, giuing them in charge , what they ſhoulde doo vppon all occaſions, and particularly to deliuer the Ladies, if otherwife then well happened vnto him : onely defiring
his

his mother, that fhe woulde bring *Philoclea* to a window, where fhe might with eafe perfectly difcerne the
combat. And fo, as foone as the morning beganne to
draw dewe from the faireft greenes, to wafh her face
withall, againft the approach of the burning Sunne, he
went to his ftable, where himfelfe chofe out a horfe,
whom (though he was neere twentie yeere olde) he
preferred for a peece of fure feruice, before a great nuber of yonger. His colour was of a browne bay, dapled
thick with black fpots; his forhead marked with a white
ftarre; to which, in all his bodie there was no part futable, but the left foote before; his mane and taile black,
and thick, of goodly, and well proportioned greatnes.
He caufed him to be trimmed with a fumptuous
faddle of tawnie, and golde ennamell, enriched with
pretious ftones: his furniture was made into the fafhio
of the branches of a tree, from which the leaues were
falling: and fo artificiallie were the leaues made, that as
the horfe moued, it feemed indeed that the leaues wagged, as when the winde plaies with them; and being
made of a pale cloath of gold, they did beare the ftraw-
coloured liuerie of ruine. His armour was alfo of tawnie and golde, but formed into the figure of flames
darckened, as when they newelie breake the prifon
of a fmoakie furnace. In his fhielde he had painted
the *Torpedo* fifh. And fo appointed, he caufed himfelfe,
with his trumpet and fquire (whom he had taken fince
the death of *Ifmenus*) to be ferried ouer into the Iland:
a place well chofen for fuch a purpofe. For, it was fo
plaine, as there was fcarcely any bufh, or hillock, either
to vnleuell, or fhadowe it: of length and breadth e-
nough, to trie the vttermoft both of launce and fword
and

and the one end of it facing of the caftle, the other ex-
tending it felfe toward the campe, and no accefle to
it, butby water : there coulde no fecreate trecherie be
wrought, and for manifeft violence, ether fide might
haue time inough to fuccour their party.

7 But there he found *Phalantus*,alredy waiting for him
vpon a horfe, milke white, but that vpon his fhoulder
and withers,he was fretned with red ftaines,as when a
few ftrawberies are fcattered into a difh of creame. He
had caufed his mane and taile to be died in carnation;
his reines were vine branches, which ingendring one
with the other, at the end, when it came to the bitte,
there,for the boffe, brought foorth a clufter of grapes,
by the workeman made fo liuely, that it feemed, as
the horfe champed on his bitte, he chopped for them,
and that it did make his mouth water, to fee the grapes
fo neere him.His furniture behind was of vines,fo artificially made,as it femed the horfe ftood in the fhadow
of the vine, fo pretily were clufters of rubie grapes dif-
perfed among the trappers which embraced his fides.
His armour was blew,like the heauen,which a Sun did
with his rayes (proportionately deliuered) guilde in
moft places. His fhield was beautified with this deuice;
A greyhound,which ouerrunning his fellow, and taking the hare,yet hurts it not whē it takes it . The word
was,*The glorie,not the pray.*

8 But as foone as *Amphialus* landed,he fent his fquire to
Phalantus,to tel him, that there was the Knight,redy to
know whether he had any thing to him . *Phalantus* anfwered,that his anfwere now muft be in the laguage of
launces;& fo each attended the warning of the trupets,
which were to found at the appointment of foure iudges,

ges,who with confideration of the fame, had deuided
the ground. *Phalantus*-his horfe young,and feeling the
youth of his mafter, ftoode coruetting ; which being
wel gouerned by *Phalatus*,gaue fuch a glittering grace,
as when the Sunne fhines vpon a wauing water. *Am-*
phialus-horfe ftood panting vpon the ground, with his
further foot before,as if he would for his mafters caufe
begin to make himfelfe angry: till the trumpet founded
together. Together they fet fpurres to their horfes , together took their launces from their thighes,conueied
them vp into their reftes together, together let them
finke downward;fo as it was a deleƈtable fight,in a dangerous effeƈt; and a pleafant confideration , that there
was fo perfeƈt agreement, in fo mortall difagreement:
like a mufick, made of cunning difcords.But their horfes keeping an euen line their mafters had fkilfully allotted vnto them paffed one by another without encountring, although either might feel the angry breath
of other . But the ftaues being come to a iuft defcent,
but euen when the mark was ready to meet them, *Am-*
phialus was runne through the vamplate,and vnder the
arme:fo as the ftaffe appearing behind him, it femed to
the beholders he had bene in danger. But he ftrake *Pha*
lantus iuft vpon the gorget,fo as he battred the lamms
therof,and made his head almoft touch the back of his
horfe.But either fide hauing ftaied the fpur, & vfed the
bit to ftop their horfes fury,cafting away the trôcheons
of their ftaues , & drawing their fwords, they attended
the fecond fummons of the death threatning trumpet,
which quickly folowed;and they affoone making their
horfes anfwer their hâds,with a gêtle galop,fet the one
toward the other;til being come in the neernes of litle
more

more then a staues length. *Amphialus* trusting more
to the strength, then to the nimblenes of his horse, put
him foorth with speedie violence, and making his head
ioyne to the others flanke, guiding his blow with discretion, and strengthning it with the course of his
horse, strake *Phalantus* vpon the head, in such sort, that
his feeling sense did both dazell his sight, and astonish
his hearing. But *Phalantus* (not accustomed to be vngratefull to such benefites) strake him vpon the side of
his face, with such a force, that he thought his iawe had
bene cut asunder: though the faithfulnes of his armour indeede garded him from further damage. And
so remayned they awhile, rather angry with fighting,
then fighting for anger, till *Amphialus*-his horse, leaning harde vpon the other, and winning ground, the
other horse feeling himselfe prest, began to rise a little
before, as he was woont to doo in his coruette: which
aduantage *Amphialus* taking, set forward his own horse
with the further spurre, so as *Phalantus*-his horse came
ouer with his master vnder him. Which *Amphialus* seeing, lighted, with intention to help *Phalantus*. But his
horse that had faulted, rather with vntimely arte, then
want of force, gatte vp from burdning his burden, so
as *Phalantus* (in the fall hauing gotten his feete free of
& the stirrop) could (though something bruised)arise,
seeing *Amphialus* neere him, he asked him, Whether he
had giue him any help in remouing his horse. *Amphia-*
lus said No. Truely sayd *Phalantus*, I asked it, because I
would not willingly haue fought with him, that had
had my life in his mercie. But now(said *Phalantus*) before we procced further, let me know who you are, because neuer yet did any man bring me to the like fortune.

tune. *Amphialus* lifting to keepe him felfe vnknowne,
told him he was a Gentlemā, to whom *Amphialus* that
day had giuen armour and horfe to trie his valour, hauing neuer before bene in any combat worthy remembrance. Ah, (faid *Phalantus* in a rage) And muft I be the
exercife of your prentif-age? & with that, choler tooke
away either the brufe, or the feeling of the brufe, fo as
he entred a frefh into the cōbat, & boiling in his armes
the difdaine of his harte, ftrake fo thicke vpon *Amphia-*
lus, as if euery blow would faine haue bene foremoft.
But *Amphialus* (that many like trials had taught, great
fpending to leaue fmall remnants) let paffe the ftorme
with ftrong wardes, and nimble auoidings : till feeing
his time fit, both for diftaunce and nakednes, he ftrake
him fo cruell a blow on the knee, that the poore Gentleman fell downe withall in a fowne.

But *Amphialus*, pittying approued valoure, made pretious by naturall curtefie, went to him; & taking of his
head-piece to giue him aire, the young Knight (difdained to buy life with yeelding) bad him vfe his fortune:
for he was refolued neuer to yeeld. No more you fhall
(faid *Amphialus*) if it be not to my requeft, that you will
account your felf to haue great intereft in me. *Phalantus*
more ouercome by his kindnes, thē by his fortune, defired yet once againe to know his name, who in his firft
beginning had fhewed fuch furie in his force, and yet
fuch ftay in his furie. *Amphialus*, then named himfelfe,
telling him withal, he would think his name much bet-
tred, if it might be honored by the title of his friēd. But
no Baulme could be more comfortable to his wound,
then the knowledge thereof was to his mind, when he
knew his mifhap fhould be excufed by the renowmed

valoure

valour of the other. And so promising each to other as-
surednes of good will, *Phalantus*, (of whom *Amphialus*
would haue no other raunsome, but his word of fried-
ship) was conueyed into the campe, where he would
but litle remaine among the enimies of *Amphialus:* but
went to seeke his aduentures other-where.

CHAP. 12.

* Philocleas *il-taking* Amphialus *wel.meaning.* [2] *His challenge and conquests continued for Loue, & his loue.* [3] Argalus *sent for to this challenge.* [4] *The coniugall happines
of him and his wife.* [5] *The passions stirred by this message.*
[6] *Their sorrow-sounding farewell.* [7] Argalusis *defie.*
[8] Amphialusis *answere.* [9] Argalusis *furniture.* [10] *Their
combat, bloudy to both, deadly to* Argalus. [11] *Parthenia
comes to the end of it, and him.* [12] *Her* [13] *and his lamentations.* [14] *The funerals.*

S for *Amphialus* he was receaued
with triumph into the castle; although one might see by his eyes
(humbly lifted vp to the window
where *Philoclea* stood) that he was
rather suppliaunt, then victorious:
whiche occasion *Cecropia* taking,
(who as then stoode by *Philoclea*, and had lately lefte
Pamela in another roome, whence also she might see
the combate) Sweet Lady (said she) now you may see,
whether you haue cause to loue my sonne, who then
lies vnder your feete, when he standes vpon the necke
of his braueft enemies. Alas said *Philoclea*, a simple seruice

nice to me,me thinkes it is,to haue thofe,who come to fuccour me,deſtroied : If it be my dutie to call it loue, be it ſo : but the effeſts it brings foorth I confeſſe I account hatefull. *Cecropia* grew ſo angry with this vnkind anſwere, that ſhe eould not abſtayne from telling her, that ſhe was like them that could not ſleepe,when they were ſoftly layed . but that if her ſonne would follow her counſell, he ſhould take another courſe with her : and ſo flange away from her.

Yet (knowing the deſperate melancholy of *Amphia-* 2 *lus* in like caſes) framed to him a very thankefull meſ-ſage,poudring it with ſome hope-giuingphraſes,which were of ſuch ioy to *Amphialus*, that he (though againſt publike reſpeſt,& importunity of diſſuaders)preſently cauſed it to be made knowne to the campe, that what-ſoeuer Knight would trie the like fortune as *Phalantus* did,he ſhould in like ſorte be anſwered : ſo as diuers of the valianteſt, partly of themſelues, partly at the inſti-gation of *Baſilius*,attempted the combat with him:and according to euery ones humour,ſo were the cauſes of the challêge groûded:one laying treaſon to his charge; another preferring himſelfe in the worthines to ſerue *Philoclea*; a third,exalting ſome Ladies beautie beyond ether of the ſiſters ; a fourth, laying diſgraces to Loue it ſelfe, naming it the bewitcher of the witt, the re-bell to Reaſon, the betrayer of reſolution, the defiler of thoughts, the vnderminer of magnanimitie, the flatterer of vice, the ſlaue to weakeneſſe, the infeſti on of youth, the madneſſe of age; the curſe of life, and reproch of deathe ; a fifth, diſdayning to caſte at leſſe then at all, woulde make the cauſe of his quar-rell the cauſers of loue , and proclayme his blaſ-phemies againſt womankinde ; that namely that ſex,

was the ouerfight of Nature, the difgrace of reafona-
blenes,the obftinate cowards, the flaue-borne tyrants,
the fhops of vanities,the guilded wethercocks;in whō
confcience is but peeuifhnes, chaftitie waywardnes,&
gratefulnes a miracle.But all thefe challenges(how wel
fo euer endited) were fo well anfwered, that fome by
death taught others, though paſt learning themfelues;
& fome by yeelding gaue themfelues the lie for hauing
blafphemed; to the great griefe of *Bafilius*, fo to fee his
Rebell preuaile, and in his own fight to crowne himfelfe with deferued honour.

3   Wherupon thirfting for reuenge,& elfe not hoping
to preuaile, the beft of his campe being already ouerthrowne; he fent a meſſenger to *Argalus*, in whofe approued courage and force,he had (and had caufe) to
haue great confidence, with a letter; requiring him, to
take this quarrell in hand,from which he had hetherto
fpared him in refpeſt of his late mariage. But now his
honour,and (as he efteemed it) felicitie ftanding vpon
it,he could no longer forbeare to chalenge of him his
faithfull feruice.

   The meſſenger made fpeede, and found *Argalus* at a
4 caftle of his owne, fitting in a parler with the faire *Parthenia*,he reading in a booke the ftories of *Hercules*, fhe
by him,as to heare him reade; but while his eyes looked on the booke,fhe looked on his eies, & fometimes
ftaying him with fome prety queftion, notfo much to
be refolued of the doubte; as to giue him occáfion to
looke vpon her. A happy couple, he ioying in her, fhe
ioying in her felfe, but in her felfe, becaufe fhe enioyed
him : both encreafing their riches by giuing to each o-
ther;each making one life double,becaufe they made a
double life; one,where defire neuer wanted fatisfactió,

nor

nor fatisfaction neuer bred facietie; he ruling, becaufe
fhe would obey: or rather becaufe fhe would obey, fhe
therein ruling.

But when the meffenger came in with letters in his
hand, & haft in his countenance, though fhe knew not
what to feare, yet fhe feared, becaufe fhe knew not; but
fhe rofe, and went afide, while he deliuered his letters
and meffage; yet a far of fhe looked, now at the meffenger, & then at her husband: the fame feare, which made
her loth to haue caufe of feare, yet making her feeke
caufe to nourifh her feare. And wel fhe foũd there was
fome ferious matter; for her husbands countenance figured fome refolution betweene lothneffe and neceffitie: and once his eie caft vpon her, & finding hers vpon him, he blufhed; & fhe blufhed, becaufe he blufhed;
and yet ftreight grew paler, becaufe fhe knew not why
he had blufhed. But when he had read, & heard, & difpatched away the meffenger (like a man in whom Honour could not be rocked on fleepe by Affection) with
promife quickly to follow; he came to *Parthenia,* and as
forie as might be for parting, and yet more forie for her
forrow, he gaue her the letter to reade. She with fearful
flownes tooke it, and with fearefull quickneffe read it;
and hauing read it, *Ah* my *Argalus* (faid fhe) and haue
you made fuch haft to anfwere? and are you fo foone
refolued to leaue me? But he difcourfing vnto her, how
much it imparted his honour (which fince it was deare
to him, he knew it would be deare vnto her) her reafon
ouerclowded with forow, fuffered her not prefently to
replie, but left the charge thereof to teares, and fighes;
which he not able to beare, left her alone, and went to
giue order for his prefent departure.

By that time he was armde, and readie to go, fhe had 6
recoue-

recouered a little strength of spirite againe, & cōming out, & seing him armed, & wanting nothing for his departure but her farewell, she ran to him, tooke him by the arme, and kneeling downe without regard, who either heard her speach, or saw her demeanour, My *Argalus*, my *Argalus* (said she) doo not thus forsake me. Remember, alas, Remember that I haue interest in you, which I will neuer yeeld shalbe thus aduentured. Your valour is already sufficiently knowne : sufficiently haue you already done for your country : ennow, ennow there are besides you to loose lesse worthie liues. Woe is me, what shall become of me, if you thus abandon me? Then was it time for you to follow these aduentures, when you aduentured no body but your selfe, and were no bodies but your owne. But now pardon me, that now, or neuer, I claime mine owne; mine you are, & without me you can vndertake no dāger: & will you endager *Parthenia? Parthenia* shalbe in the battle of your fight : *Parthenia* shall smart in your paine, & your blood must be bled by *Parthenia.* Deare *Parthenia* (said he) this is the first time, that euer you resisted my will : I thanke you for it; but perseuer not in it; & let not the teares of those most beloued eies be a presage vnto me of that, which you would not should happen. I shal liue, doubte not : for so great a blessing, as you are, was not giuen vnto me, so soone to be depriued of it. Looke for me therefore shortly, and victorious; and prepare a ioyfull welcome, and I will wish for no other triumph. She answered not, but stood as it were thunder-striken with amazement : for true Loue made obedience stande vp against all other passions. But when he tooke her in his armes, and sought to printe his harte in her sweete lippes, she fell in a sounde, so

as he was faine to leaue her to her Gentlewomen:
and caried away by the tyrannie of Honour, though
with manie a backe-caſt looke, and hartie grone, went
to the campe. When vnderſtanding the notable victories of *Amphialus*, he thought to giue him ſome dayes
reſpite of reſt, becauſe he woulde not haue his victorie
diſgraced by the others wearineſſe. In which dayes, he
ſought by all meanes (hauing leaue to parley with him)
to diſſuade him from his enterpriſe: and then imparting
his mind to *Baſilius*, becauſe he found *Amphialus* was in-
flexible, wrote his defie vnto him in this maner.

Ight famous *Amphialus*, if my perſuaſion in reaſon, 7
or praier in good wil, might preuaile with you, you
ſhould by better meanes be like to obteine your deſire.
You ſhoulde make many braue enemies become your
faithful ſeruāts, & make your honor flie vp to the heauē,
being caried vp by both the wings of valure & iuſtice;
whereof now it wants the latter. But ſince my ſuite, nor
counſel can get no place in you, diſdaine not to receiue
a mortall chalenge, from a man ſo farre inferiour vnto
you in vertue, as that I do not ſo much miſlike of the
deed, as I haue the doer in admiration Prepare therfore
your ſelf, according to the noble maner you haue vſed,
and think not lightly of neuer ſo weake an arme, which
ſtrikes with the ſword of iuſtice.

To this quickely he receiued this anſwere.

Vch more famous *Argalus*, I, whom neuer threat- 8
nings could make afraid, am now terrified by your
noble curteſie. For wel I knowe, from what height of
vertue it doth proceed, and what cauſe I haue to doubt
ſuch vertue bent to my ruine: but Loue, which iuſtifieth
the vniuſtice you lay vnto me, dooth alſo animate me

Pp 4　　　　　againſt

againſt all daungers, ſince I come full of him by whom your ſelfe haue beene (if I be not deceiued) ſometimes conquered. I will therfore attend your appearaunce in the Ile, carying this aduantage with me, that as it ſhal be a ſingular honour if I get the victorie, ſo there can be no diſhonour in being ouercome by *Argalus*.

9   The chalenge thus denounced, and accepted, *Argalus* was armed in a white armour, which was guilded ouer with knots of womans haire, which came downe from the creſt of his head-peece, and ſpred it ſelfe in rich quã-titie ouer all his armour: his furniture was cut out into the faſhion of an Eagle, whereof the beake (made into a rich iewell) was faſtened to the ſaddle, the taile coue-red the crooper of the horſe, and the wings ſerued for trappers; which falling of ech ſide, as the horſe ſtirred, the bird ſeemed to flie. His pettrell and reines, were em-brodered with feathers ſutable vnto it: vpon his right arme he ware a ſleeue, which his deare *Parthenia* had made for him, to be worne in a iuſtes, in the time that ſucceſſe was vngratefull to their well-deſerued loue: It was full of bleeding hartes, though neuer intended to any blooddie enterpriſe. In this ſhield (as his owne de-uice) he had two Palme trees, neere one another, with a worde ſignifying, *In that ſort flouriſhing.* His horſe was of a firie ſorrell, with blacke feete, and blacke liſt on his back, who with open noſtrels breathed warre, before he could ſee an enemy: and now vp with one legge, and then with another, ſeemed to complain of Nature, that ſhe had made him any whit earthie.

10   But he had ſcarcely viewed the grounde of the I-lande, and conſidered the aduauntages (if any were) therof, before the Caſtel boat had deliuered *Amphialus*,

in

in al points prouided to giue a hard entertainmēt. And then sending ech to other their Squires in honourable maner, to knowe whether they should attende any further ceremony; the trumpets sounding, the horses with smooth running, their staues with vnshaked motion, o-bediently performed their cholericke cōmandements. But when they drew nere, *Argalus*-his horse being hot, prest in with his head: which *Amphialus* perceiuing, knowing if he gaue him his side, it should be to his disaduauntage, prest in also with him, so as both the horses & men met shoulder to shoulder, so as the horses (hurt as much with the striking, as being striken) tumbled downe to the earth, daungerously to their maister, but that they by strength nimble, and by vse skilfull, in the falling shunned the harme of the fall, and without more respite, drewe out their swordes with a gallant brauerie, eche striuing to shewe himselfe the lesse endamaged, and to make knowne that they were glad, they had nowe nothing else to trust to, but their owne vertue. True it is, that *Amphialus* was the sooner vp; but *Argalus* had his sworde out the sooner: and then fell they to the cruellest combate, that any present eye had seene. Their swordes first, like Canons, battering downe the walles of their armour, making breaches almost in euerie place for troupes of woundes to enter. Among the rest, *Argalus* gaue a great wound to *Amphialus*-his disarmed face; though part of the force of it *Amphialus* warded vpon his shielde, and with-all (first casting his eye vp to *Philoclea* Window, as if he had fetched his courage thence) feyning to entend the same sort of blowes, turned his sword, and with a mightie reuerse, gaue a cruell wounde to the

right

right arme of *Argalus*, the vnfaythfull armour yeelding to the fwoordes ftrong-guided fharpeneffe. But
though the blood accufed the hurt of *Argalus*, yet
woulde he in no action of his confeffe it : but keeping
himfelfe in a lower warde, ftoode watching with timely thruftes to repaire his loffe ; which quickly he did .
For *Amphialus* (following his fawning fortune) laid on
fo thicke vpon *Argalus*, that his fhield had almoft fallen
peece-meale to the earth, when *Argalus* comming in
with his right foote, and fomething ftowping to come
vnder his armour, thruft him into the belly daunge-
roufly, and mortally it would haue beene, but that with
the blowe before, *Amphialus* had ouerthrowne himfelfe fo, as he fell fide-warde downe, and with falling
faued himfelfe from ruine. The fworde by that meanes
flipping afide, and not pearcing more deepely, *Argalus* feeing him fall, threatning with voyce and fworde,
bad him yeelde. But he ftriuing without aunfwere to
rife, *Argalus* ftrake with all his might vpon his head.
But his hurte arme not able to maifter fo founde a
force, let the fwoorde fall fo, as *Amphialus*, though
aftonifhed with the blowe, could arife : which *Argalus* confidering, ranne in to grafpe with him, and fo
clofed together ; falling fo to the grounde, nowe one
getting aboue, and then the other ; at length, both
wearie of fo vnlouely embracements, with a diffenting
confent gate vp, and went to their fwordes : but happened eche of his enemies : where *Argalus* finding
his foes fworde garnifhed in his blood, his hart rafe
with the fame fwoorde to reuenge it, and on that
blade to allie their bloods together . But his minde
was euill wayted-on by his lamed force , fo as he receyued

ceyued ftill more and more woundes, which made all his armour feeme to blufh, that it had defended his maſter no better. But *Amphialus* perceiuing it, & waying the ſmall hatefulneſſe of their quarrell, with the worthineſſe of the Knight, defired him to take pitie of himſelfe. But *Argalus*, the more repining, the more he founde himſelfe in difaduauntage, filling his veynes with ſpite in ſteade of blood, and making courage a-riſe agaynſt faintneſſe, (like a Candle, which a little before it goes out, giues then the greateſt blaze) ſo did he vnite all his force, that caſting away the little remnaunt of his ſhielde, and taking his ſwoorde in both handes, he ſtroke ſuch a notable blowe, that he cleft his ſhielde, armour, and arme almoſt to the bone.

But then *Amphialus* forgat all ceremonies, and with cruell blowes made more of his blood ſucceed the reſt; til his hand being ſtaied by his care, his eare filled with a pitifull crie, the crie guided his ſight to an excellent faire Ladie, who came running as faſt as ſhe could, and yet becauſe ſhe coulde not as faſt as ſhe would, ſhe ſent her lamentable voyce before her: and being come, and being knowne to them both, to be the beautifull *Parthenia*, (who had that night dreamed ſhee ſawe her husbande in ſuch eſtate, as ſhe then founde him, which made her make ſuch haſte thither) they both maruailed. But *Parthenia* ranne betweene them (feare of loue making her forget the feare of Nature) and then fell downe at their feete, determining ſo to part them, till ſhe coulde get breathe to ſigh out her doolefull ſpeeches: and when her breath (which running had ſpent, and difmayedneſſe made

made ſlowe to returne) had by ſobbes gotten into her ſorow-cloſed breaſt, for a while ſhe coulde ſay nothing, but, O wretched eyes of mine, O wailefull ſight, O day of darkeneſſe: at length turning her eyes (wherein ſorrowe ſwamme) to *Amphialus*, My Lorde (ſaide ſhe) it is ſaide you loue; in the power of that loue, I beſeech you to leaue of this combate, as euen your harte may finde comfort in his affection, euen for her ſake, I craue it : or if you be mortally determined, be ſo pitifull vnto me, as firſt to kill me, that I may not ſee the death of *Argalus*. *Amphialus* was aboute to haue aunſwered, when *Argalus*, vexed with his Fortune, but moſt vexed that ſhe ſhoulde ſee him in that fortune, Ah *Parthenia* (ſaide he) neuer till nowe vnwelcome vnto me, do you come to get my life by requeſt? And can not *Argalus* liue but by requeſt? Is it a life? With that he went aſide, for feare of hurting her, and woulde haue begunne the combate afreſh. But *Amphialus* not onely coniured by that which helde the Monarchie of his mind, but euen in his noble hart melting with compaſſion at ſo paſſionate a ſight, deſired him to withholde his handes, for that he ſhoulde ſtrike one, who ſought his fauour, and woulde not make reſiſtaunce. A notable example of the woonderfull effectes of Vertue, where the conquerour, ſought for friendſhip of the conquered, and the conquered woulde not pardon the conquerour : both indeede being of that minde to loue eche other for accepting, but not for giuing mercie ; and neyther affected to ouer-liue a diſhonour : ſo that *Argalus* not ſo much ſtriuing with *Amphialus* (for if he had had him in the like ſorte,

in

In like fort he would haue dealt with him) as labouring
againſt his owne power (which he chiefly deſpiſed) ſet
himſelfe forward, ſtretching his ſtrength to the vttermoſt. But the fire of that ſtrife, blowen with his inward
rage, boyled out his bloud in ſuch aboundance, that he
was driuen to reſt him vpon the pommel of his ſword:
and then each thing beginning to turne rounde in the
daunce of Death before his eyes, his ſight both daz-
led, and dimmed, till (thinking to ſit downe) he fell in a
ſowne. *Parthenia*, and *Amphialus* both haſtely went
vnto him: *Amphialus* tooke of his helmet, and *Parthenia*
laid his head in her lap, tearing of her linnen ſleeues &
partlet, to ſerue about his wounds; to bind which, ſhe
tooke of her hair-lace, and would haue cut of her faire
haire herſelfe, but that the ſquires and iudges came in
with fitter things for the purpoſe: while ſhe bewayled
her ſelfe with ſo lamentable ſweetnes, as was inough to
haue taught ſorrow to the gladdeſt thoughts, and haue
engraued it in the mindes of hardeſt mettall.

O *Parthenia*, no more *Parthenia* (ſaid ſhe) What art 12
thou? what ſeeſt thou? how is thy bliſſe in a moment
fallen? how art thou, euen-now before all Ladies the
example of perfect happines, and now the gaſing-ſtock
of endles miſerie? O God, what hath bene my deſert
to be thus puniſhed? or if ſuch haue bene my deſert,
why was I not in my ſelfe puniſhed? O wandring life,
to what wildernes wouldſt thou lead one? But Sorow,
I hope thou art ſharp inough to ſaue my labour from
other remedies. *Argalus*, *Argalus*, I will folow thee, I wil
folow thee.

But with that *Argalus* came out of his ſowne, and
lifting vp his languiſhing eyes (which a painefull reſt, 13
and

and iron sleepe did seeke to lock vp) seeing her, in whō
(euen dying) he liued, and him selfe seated in so beloued a place, it seemed a little cheerefull bloud came vp
to his cheekes, like a burning cole, almost dead, if some
breath a little reuiue it: & forcing vp (the best he could)
his feeble voice, My deare, my deare, my better halfe
(said he) I finde I must now leaue thee: and by that
sweet hand, and faire eyes of thine I sweare, that Death
bringes nothing with it to grieue me, but that I must
leaue thee, and cannot remaine to answere part of thy
infinit deserts, with being some comfort vnto thee. But
since so it pleaseth him, whose wisdome and goodnesse
guideth all, put thy confidence in him, and one day
we shall blessedly meet againe, neuer to depart: meane
while liue happily, deare *Parthenia*, and I perswade my
selfe, it will increase the blessednes of my soule, so to see
thee. Loue well the remembrance of thy louing, and
truely louing, *Argalus* : and let not (with that worde
he sighed) this disgrace of mine, make thee one day
thinke, thou hadst an vnwoorthie husband. They
could scarcely vnderstand the last wordes : for Death
began to seaze him selfe of his harte, neither coulde
Parthenia make answere, so full was her breast of anguish. But while the other sought to stanch his remediles wounds, she with her kisses made him happie: for
his last breath was deliuered into her mouth.

14   But when indeede she found his ghost was gone,
then Sorrowe lost the witte of vtterance, and grewe
ragefull, and madde, so that she tare her beautifull face,
and rent her haire, as though they could serue for nothing, since *Argalus* was gone; till *Amphialus* (so moued with pittie of that sight, as that he honoured his
ad-

aduerſaries death with teares) cauſed her (with the helpe of her women that came with her) partelie by force,to be conueyed into boate, with the dead body of *Argalus*, from which ſhe could not depart. And being come of the other ſide, there ſhe was receaued by *Baſilius* him ſelfe; with all the funerall pompe of militarie diſcipline, trayling all their Enſignes vpon the ground, making his warlike inſtruments ſound dolefull notes, and *Baſilius* (with comfort in his mouth, and woe in his face) ſou_ght to perſwade ſome eaſe into *Parthenias* minde: but all was as eaſefull to her, as the handling of ſore woundes: all the honour done, being to her but the triumph of her ruine, ſhe finding no comfort, but in deſperate yeelding to Sorrow:and rather determined to hate her ſelfe, if euer ſhe ſhould finde eaſe thereof. And well might ſhe heare as ſhe paſt through the Campe, the great prayſes ſpoken of her husbande, which all were recordes of her loſſe. But the more excellent he was (being indeede accounted ſeconde to none in all Greece) the more did the breath of thoſe praiſes, beare vp the winges of *Amphialus*-his fame: to whom yet (ſuch was his caſe) that Trophe vpon Trophe,ſtill did but builde vp the monumēt of his thraldome; he euer finding himſelfe in ſuch fauour of *Philoclea*, that ſhe was moſt abſent,when he was preſent with her; and euer ſorrieſt, when he had beſt ſucceſſe: which would haue made him renounce all comfort,but that his mother,with diuerſity of deuiſes, kept vp his hart.

But while he allayed thus his outward glorie,with inward diſcomfort,he was like to haue bene ouertaken

with

with a notable treaſon, the beginning wherof (though meerely ridiculous) had like to haue brought forth vnto him a weeping effect.

CHAP. 13.

[1] Dametas *put in harte* [2] *to defie* Clinias. [3] Clinias *out of harte to ſee the vie*. [4] Dametas *brauerie, adoubements, and impreſe*. [5] Clinias *drawne* [6] *to anſwere him*. [7] *Their paſsions in comming to the field*. [8] *Their actions in it, not ſo doubty, as their fortune doubtfull*. [9] Clinias *yeelding to triumphant* Dametas.

A Mong other that attended *Baſilius* in this expedition, *Dametas* was one; whether to be preſent with him, or abſent from *Miſo:* once, certaine it was without any minde to make his ſworde curſed by any widow. Nowe, being in the campe, while each talke ſeemed iniurious, which did not acknowledge ſome duety to the fame of *Amphialus*, it fell out ſometimes in communication, that as the ſpeech of heauen doth often beget the mention of hell, ſo the admirable prowes of *Amphialus* (by a cōtrarie) brought forth the remembrance of the cowardiſe of *Clinias*: in ſo much, as it grew almoſt to a prouerb, *As very a coward, as Clinias*. Deſcribing him in ſuch ſort, that in the end, *Dametas* began to thinke with himſelfe, that if he made a chalenge vnto him, he would neuer anſwere it; and that then he ſhould greatly encreaſe the fauourable conceite of *Baſilius*. This fancie of his he vttered to a young a young Gentleman, that waited vpon *Philanax*, in whofe friendſhip he had eſpeciall cõfidence, becauſe he haunted his company, laughing often merely at his ſpeeches, and not a little extolling the goodly *dotes* of *Mopfa*. The young Gentleman as glad, as if he had found a Hare ſitting, egd him on, breaking the matter with *Philanax*, and then (for feare the humour ſhould quayle in him) wrote a challenge him ſelfe for *Damætas*, and brought it to him. But when *Damætas* read it, putting his head on his ſhoulder, and ſomewhat ſmiling, he ſaid, it was prettie indeed; but that it had not a loftie ſtile enough : and ſo would needes indite it in this ſort.

O Clinias, *thou* Clinias, *the wickedeſt worme that euer* 2
went vpon two legges ; the very fritter of fraude, and ſee-
thing pot of iniquitie: I Damætas, *chiefe gouernour of all*
the royall cattell, and alſo of Pamela (*whom thy* Maiſter
moſt perniciouſly hath ſuggeſted out of my dominion) *doo de-*
fie thee, in a mortall affray from the bodkin to the pike vp-
warde. Which if thou dooſt preſume to take in hande, I will
out of that ſuperfluous bodie of thine make thy ſoule to be eua-
cuated.

The young Gentleman ſeemed dumbe-ſtriken with
admiration, and preſently tooke vpon him to be the 3
bearer thereof, while the heate of the fit laſted : and
hauing gotten leaue of *Baſilius* (euery one helping on,
to eaſe his minde ouercharged with melancholy) he
went into the towne according to the manner before
time vſed, and in the preſence of *Amphialus* deliuered
this letter to *Clinias*; deſiring to haue an anſwere, which

Q q   might

might be fit for his reputation. *Clinias* opened it, and read it; and in the reading, his bloud not daring to be in so daungerous a place, went out of his face, and hid it selfe more inwardly : and his very wordes (as if they vere afraid of blowes) came very slowly out of his mouth : but, aswell as his painting breath would vtter it, he bad him tell the lowte that sent him, that he disdained to haue any thing to doo with him. But *Amphialus*, perceauing the matter, tooke him aside, and very earnestly dealt with him not to shame himselfe; *Amphialus* not onely desirous to bring it to passe to make some sport to *Philoclea*, but not being able to perswade with him, *Amphialus* licenced the Gentleman, telling him, by the next morning he should haue answere.

4　The yong Gentlemā (sory he had sped no better) returned to *Damætas*, who had fetched many a sowerbreathed sigh, for fear *Clinias* would accept the chalēge. But whē he perceiued by his trusty messenger, that this delay was in effect a denial, there being no dispositiō in him to accept it; then lo, *Damætas* began to speake his lowd voice, to looke big, to march vp & down, & in his march to lift his legs higher thē he was wont, swearing by no meane deuotiōs, that the wals should not keepe the coward frō him, but he would fetch him out of his connie-berrie: & then was hotter then euer to prouide himselfe of horse & armour, saying, he would go to the Iland brauely addoubed, & shew himself to his charge *Pamela*. To this purpose many willing hāds were about him, letting him haue reynes, pettrell, with the rest of the furniture, and very braue bases; but all comming from diuers houses, nether in coulour or fashion, shewing any kinred one with another; but that liked *Damæ-*

tas

tas the better: for that he thought would argue,that he was maifter of many braue furnitures. Then gaue he order to a painter for his deuice; which was, a plowe with the oxen lewfed from it, a fword with a great many armes and legges cut of; and laftly a great armie of pen and inke-hornes,and bookes. Nether did he fticke to tell the fecrete of his intent, which was, that he had lefte of the plowe,to doo fuch bloudy deedes with his fwoorde, as many inkehornes and bookes fhould be employed about the hiftorifying of them : and being asked, why he fet no worde vnto it,he faid,that was indeede like the painter, that fayeth in his picture , Here is the dog, and here is the Hare: & with that he laughed fo perfectly , as was great confolation to the beholders. Yet remembring,that *Mifo* would not take it well at his returne , if he forgat his dutie to her,he caufed about in a border to be written :

Mifo *mine own pigfnie,thou fhalt heare news o'* Damætas.

Thus all things being condignely ordered, with an ill fauoured impatiencie he waited,vntil the next morning, that he might make a mufter of him felfe in the Iland; often asking them that very diligently wayted vpon him , whether it were not pittie, that fuch a coward, as *Clinias,* fhould fet his runaway feete vpon the face of the earth?

But as he was by diuers principal yong Gentlemen, to his no fmall glory, lifted vp on horfebacke, comes me a page of *Amphialus,* who with humble fmiling reuerence deliuered a letter vnto him from *Clinias:* whom *Amphialus* had brought to this, firft with perfwafions (that for certaine,if he did accept the combat,

Damætas would neuer dare to appeare, and that then the honour ſhould be his) but principally threatning him, that if he refuſed it, he would turne him out of the towne to be put to death for a traitour by *Baſilius:* ſo as the preſent feare (euer to a coward moſt terrible) of being turned out of the towne, made him, though full vnwillingly, vndertake the other feare, wherein he had ſome ſhewe of hope, that *Damætas* might hap either to be ſick, or not to haue the courage to performe the matter. But when *Damætas* heard the name of *Clinias*, very aptly ſuſpecting what the matter might be, he bad the page carry backe his letter, like a naughty boy as he was: for he was in no humour, he tolde him, of reading letters. But *Damætas*-his frièd, firſt perſuading him, that for certaine it was ſome ſubmiſſion, tooke vpon him ſo much boldneſſe, as to open his letter, and to reade it alowd in this ſort.

6 FIlthy driuell, *vnworthy to haue thy name ſet in any letter by a ſouldiers hande written: could thy wretched harte thinke it was timorouſneſſe, that made* Clinias *ſuſpende a while his anſwere? No caitiffe, no: it was but as a Ramme, which goes backe to returne with the greater force. Know therefore that thou ſhalt no ſooner appeare (appeare now if thou dareſt) I ſay thou ſhalt no ſooner appeare in the Ilande (O happy thou, if thou doo not appeare) but that I will come vpon thee withall my force; and cut thee in pieces (marke, what I ſaie) ioynte after ioynte, to the eternall terrour of all preſumptuous villaynes. Therefore looke what thou dooſt: for I tell thee, horrible ſmarte, and paine ſhalbe thy lot, if thou wilt needes be ſo fooliſh (I hauing giuen thee no ſuch cauſe) as to meete with me.*

Theſe

These terrible wordes *Clinias* vſed, hoping they 7 would giue a cooling to the heate of *Dametas*-his courage : and ſo indeede they did, that he did grone to heare the thundring of thoſe threatnings. And when the Gentleman had ended the reading of them, *Dametas* tolde them, that in his opinion he thought his anſwere came too late, and that therefore he might very well go, and diſarme him ſelfe : eſpecially conſidering, the other had in curteous maner warned him not to come. But they (hauing him now on horſebacke) led him vnto the ferrie, and ſo into the Iland ; the claſhing of his owne armour ſtriking miſerable feare into him, and in his minde thinking greate vnkindneſſe in his friende, that he had brought him to a matter ſo contrarie to his complexion. There ſtayed he but a little (the Gentlemen that came with him teaching him how to vſe his ſworde and launce, while he caſt his eye about, to ſee which way he might runne away, curſing all Ilands in being euill ſcituated) when *Clinias* with a braue ſounde of trumpets landed at the other ende : who came all the way debating with himſelfe, what he had deſerued of *Amphialus* to driue him to thoſe inconueniences. Sometimes his witte made him bethinke him ſelfe what was beſte to be done : but feare did ſo corrupt his witt, that whatſoeuer he thought was beſt, he ſtill found daunger therein ; fearefulneſſe (contrarie to all other vices) making him thinke the better of another, the worſe he found him ſelfe ; rather imagining in him ſelfe, what wordes he would vſe (if he were ouercome) to get his life of *Dametas*, then how to ouercome, whereof he could thinke with no patience. But oftentimes looking to the

Earth

Earth pittifully complayning, that a man of such suffi-
eiencie (as he thought him selfe) shoulde in his best
yeares be swallowed vp by so base an element. Faine
he would haue prayed, but he had not harte inough to
haue confidence in praier; the glittering of the armour,
and sounding of the trumpets giuing such an assault
to the weake-breache of his false senses, that he grewe
from the degrae of feare to an amazement, not almost
to know what he did; till two iudges (chosen for the
purpose) making the trumpets cease, and taking the
oth of those champions, that they came without guile
or witchcraft, set them at wonted distaunce; one from
the other.

8   Then the trumpets sounding, *Dametas*-his horse (v-
sed to such causes) when he thought lest of the matter,
started out so lustely, that *Damatas* was iogde back with
head, and bodie, and pulling withall his bridle-hande,
the horse (that was tender of mouth) made halfe a stop,
and fell to bounding, so that *Damatas* threw away his
launce, and with both his hands held by the pummell:
the horse, halfe running, halfe leaping, till he met with
Clinias: who fearing he should misse his reste, had put
his staffe therein before he began his careere: neither
would he then haue begun, but that at the trumpets
warning, one (that stood behinde) strake on his horse,
who running swiftly, the winde tooke such holde of
his staffe, that it croft quite ouer his breast, and in that
sorte gaue a flat bastonado to *Damatas:* who, halfe out
of his sadle, went neere to his olde occupation of dig-
ging the earth, but with the creste of his helmet. *Clinias* when he was paste him, not knowing what he
had done, but fearing lest *Damatas* were at his backe,
turned

turned with a wide turne; & feeing him on the ground,
he thought then was his time, or neuer, to treade him
vnder his horfes feete; & withall (if he could) hurt him
with his launce,which had not broken, the encounter
was fo eafie.But putting forth his horfe , what with the
falling of the ftaffe to low before the legs of the horfe,&
the cōming vpon *Damætas*,who was then fcrābling vp,
the horfe fell ouer & ouer,and lay vpon *Clinias.* Which
Damætas (who was gotten vp) perceiuing, drew out his
fword,prying which way he might beft come to kil *Clinias* behind. But the horfe that lay vpon him,kept fuch
a pawing with his feet,that *Damætas* durft not approch,
but verie leyfurely; fo as the horfe (being luftie) gat vp,
and withall fell to ftrike,and leape,that *Damætas* ftarted
vp a good way,and gaue *Clinias* time to rife,but fo brui-
fed in bodie,and broken in hart, that he meant to yeeld
himfelfe to mercie : and with that intent drew out his
fworde,entending when he came nearer,to prefent the
pommell of it to *Damætas.* But *Damætas,* when he fawe
him come with his fword drawne,nothing conceiuing
of any fuch intent, went backe as faft as his backe and
heeles woulde leade him. But as *Clinias* founde that,
he beganne to thinke a poffibilitie in the victorie, and
therefore followed with the cruell hafte of a preuailing cowarde; laying vpon *Damætas*,who did nothing
but crie out to him to holde his hand : fometimes that
he was dead , fometimes that he woulde complaine to
Bafilius : but ftill bare the blowes vngratefully, going
backe, till at length he came into the water with one of
his feete.

But then a new feare of drowning tocke him,fo that 9
ot daring to go back,nor to deliberat(the blows ftil fo
Q q 4 lighted

lighted on him) nor to yeelde (becauſe of the cruell
threatnings of *Clinias*) feare being come to the extremitie, fell to a madneſſe of deſpaire: ſo that (winking as
hard as euer he could) he began to deale ſome blowes,
and his arme (being vſed to a flaile in his youth) laid the
on ſo thick, that *Clinias* now began with lamētable eies
to ſee his owne blood come out in many places, and
before he had loſt halfe an ounce, finding in himſelfe
that he fainted, cried out aloud to *Damætas*, that he yeelded. Throw away thy ſword then (ſaid *Damætas*) and I
will ſaue thee; but ſtill laying on, as faſt as he could. *Clinias* ſtraight obeyed, and humbly craued mercie, telling him, his ſworde was gone. Then *Damætas* firſt opened his eyes, and ſeeing him indeed vnweapened,
made him ſtande a good way of from it; and then willed him to lie downe vpon the earth as flat as he could.
Clinias obeyed; and *Damætas* (who neuer could thinke
himſelfe ſafe, till *Clinias* were deade) began to thinke
with himſelfe, that if he ſtrake at him with his ſworde,
if he did not kill him at the firſt blowe, that then *Clinias*
might happe to ariſe, and reuenge himſelfe. Therefore he thought beſt to kneele downe vpon him, and
with a great whittle he had (hauing diſarmed his
heade) to cut his throate, which he had vſed ſo with
Calues, as he had no ſmall dexteritie in it. But while
he ſought for his Knife, which vnder his armour he
coulde not well finde out, and that *Clinias* lay with ſo
ſheepiſh a countenaunce, as if he would haue beene
glad to haue his throate cut for feare of more paine,
the Iudges came in, and tooke *Damætas* from off him,
telling him he did againſt the lawe of Armes, hauing
promiſed life, if he threwe away his ſworde. *Damætas*
was

was loath to confent, till they fware, they woulde not
fuffer him to fight any more,when he was vp:and then
more forced,then perfwaded, he let him rife, crowing
ouer him,and warning him to take heede how he dealt
any more with any that came of his fathers kinred. But
thus this *combate of cowardes* being finifhed, *Damœtas*
was with much mirth and melodie receiued into the
campe as victorious,neuer a Page there failing to waite
vpon this Triumph.

CHAP. 14.

V T *Clinias*, though he wanted ¹
hart to preuent fhame, yet he
wanted not witte to feele fhame;
not fo much repining at it for the
abhorring of fhame,as for the dif-
commodities, that to them that
are fhamed, enfue. For well he
deemed,it would be a great barre
to practize,and a pulling on of iniuries,when men needed not care,how they vfed him.Infomuch,that *Clinias*
(finding himfelfe the fcorning-ftocke of euery companie)fell with repining to hate the caufe thereof; & hate
in a cowards hart, could fet it felfe no other limites,but
death. Which purpofe was well egged on by reprefenting vnto himfelfe , what daunger he lately was
in;

in; which ſtill kept no leſſe ougly figure in his minde, then when it was preſent : and quickly (euen in his diſſembling countenance) might be diſcerned a concealed grudge. For though he forced in himſelfe a farre more diligent officiouſneſſe towarde *Amphialus*, then euer before, yet a leering eye vpon the one ſide at him, a countenance ſtill framed to ſmiling before him (how little cauſe ſoeuer there was of ſmiling) and grombling behind him, at any of his commaundements, with an vncertaine manner of behauiour: his words comming out, though full of flatterie, yet ſlowly, and hoarcely pronounced, might well haue blazed, what armes his falſe hart bare. But deſpiſed, becauſe of his cowardlineſſe, and not marked, becauſe deſpiſed, he had the freer ſcope of practize. Which he did the more deſperately enter into, becauſe the dayly dangers *Amphialus* did ſubmit himſelfe into, made *Clinias* aſſuredly looke for his ouerthrow, and for his owne conſequently, if he did not redeme his former treaſon to *Baſilius*, with a more treaſonable falſhood toward *Amphialus*.

2   His chiefe care therefore was, to find out among all ſorts of *Amphialus*, whom either like feare, tediouſnes of the ſiege, or diſcontentment of ſome vnſatiſfied ambitió would make apt to dig in the ſame mine that he did: & ſome alredy of welthy weary folks, & vnconſtát youths (who had not found ſuch ſudden ſucceſſe as they had promiſed theſelues) he had made ſtoupe to the lure. But of none he made ſo good account as of *Arteſia*, ſiſter to the late ſlain *Iſmenus*, & the chiefe of ſix maids, who had trained out the Princeſſes to their banket of miſerie : ſo much did the ſharpnes of her wit counteruaile (as he thought) any other defects of her ſex : for ſhe had vndertaken

dertaken that dangerous practife by the perfuafion of *Cecropia*;who affured her that the two princeffes fhould be made away;& thē *Amphialus* wold marry her:which fhe was the apter to beleue, by fome falfe perfuafiō her glas had giuē her of her own incōparable excellencies, & by the great fauor fhe knew he bare to her brother *If-menus*,which (like a felf-flattering womā) fhe conceiued was done for her fake.But when fhe had atchieued her attempt,& that fhe found the Princeffes were fo far frō their intended death,as that the one of them was like to be her fouereigne,& that neither her feruice had woon of *Amphialus* much more thē ordinary fauor,nor her o-uer-large offring herfelf to a mind otherwife owed,had obteined a loked-for acceptatiō; difdain to be difdained fpite of a fruftrate hope, & perchaūce vnquenched luft-growne rage,made her vnquiet thoughts find no other reft, but malice ∙ which was increafed by the death of her brother, whō fhe iudged neither fuccoured againft *Philanax*,nor reuēged vpon *Philanax*.But all thefe coles were wel blowneby the cōpany fhe efpecially kept with *Zelmane*, all this time of her imprifonment. For finding her prefence vncheerfull to the mourning *Philoclea*,and contemned of the hie harted *Pamela*,fhe fpent her time moft with *Zelmane*.Who though at the firft hardly bro-king the inftrument of their miferie, learning cunning in the fchoole of aduerfitie, in time framed her felfe to yeeld her acceptable intertainment.

For *Zelmane*, when fhe had by that vnexpected mif-chief her bodie imprifoned,her valure ouermaftred,her wit beguiled,her defires barred, her loue eclipfed; affu-red of euill,fearing worfe, able to knowe *Philocleas* mif-fortune, and not able to fuccour her , fhe was a great while,before the greatnes of her hart could defcend to
  forowe,

forow, but rather rofe boyling vp in fpight and difdain, Reafon hardly. making Courage beleeue, that it was diftreffed: but as if the walles would be afraid of her, fo woulde her lookes fhoote out threatning vpon them. But the fetters of feruitude (growing heauier with wearing) made her feele her cafe, and the little preuailing of repining : and then griefe gat feate in her foftned minde, making fweetenefle of paffed comfortes by due title claime teares of prefent difcomfort : and fince her fortune made her able to helpe as litle as any bodie, yet to be able to waile as much as any bodie ; folitarie Scrrowe, with a continuall circle in her felfe, going out at her owne mouth, to come in againe at her owne eares. Then was the name of *Philoclea* graued in the glas windowes, and by the foolifh idolatrie of affection, no fooner written, theadored; & no fooner adored, the pitied: al the woted praifes (fhe was wont to giue vnto her) being now but figures of rethorick to amplifie the iniuries of misfortune; againft which being alone, fhe woulde often make inuective declamations, methodized onely by raging forow.

4   But whe *Artefia* did infinuat herfelf into her acquaintance, fhe gaue the gouernment of her courage to wit, & was cotent to familiarize herfelfe with her. fo much the rather, as that fhe perceiued in her certaine flawes of il-cocealed difcontentmet. Infomuch that whe *Zelmane* would fweete her mouth with the praifes of the fifters, efpecially fetting forth their noble gratefulnes, in neuer forgetting wel-intended feruices, & inuokingthe iuftice of the gods, not to fuffer fuch treafures to be wrogfully hidde, & fomtimes with a kind vnkindnes, charging *Artefia* that fhe had ben abufed to abufe fo worthy perfos:

Artefia

Artesia (though falſly)woldproteſt.that ſhe had bin beguiled in it, neuer meaning other matter thē recreatiō:
& yet withall (by alleaging how vngratefully ſhe was
dealt with) it was eaſie to be ſeene,it was the vnrewar-
ding,& not the euil employing herſeruice,which grieued her.But *Zelmane*(vſing her own bias to bowle neer
the miſtreſſe of her owne thoughtes) was content to
lende her beleefe,and withall,to magnifie her deſert, if
willingly ſhe would deliuer, whom vnwillingly ſhe
had impriſoned; leauing no argument which might
tickle ambition, or flatter reuenge. So that *Arteſia,*
(puſht forward by *Clinias,*and drawne onward by *Zelmane*)bound her ſelfe to that practiſe; wherin *Zelmane*
(for her part)deſired no more,but to haue armour and
weapons brought into her chamber, not doubting,
therewith to perfourm any thing, how impoſſible ſoeuer,which longing Loue can perſwade, and inuincible
Valour dare promiſe.

But *Clinias*(whoſefaith could neuer comprehende 5
the miſteries of Courage)perſwaded *Arteſia*, while he
by corruptiō had drawn the guard ofone gate,to open
it (when he would appoint the time) to the enemie:
that ſheſhould impoyſon *Amphialus,* which ſhe might
the eaſier do,becauſe ſhe her ſelfe had vſed to make the
broaths,when *Amphialus*(either wearied or wounded)
did vſe ſuch diet.And al things alredy were ready to be
put in executiō , when they thought beſt to breake the
matterwith the two excellent ſiſters , not doubting of
their cōſent in a thing ſo behoofefull to thēſelues:their
reaſons being, that the Princeſſes knowing their ſeruice,might be ſure to preſerue them from the fury of
the entring ſouldiers: whereof *Clinias* (euen ſo) could
ſcarcely

scarcely be sufficiently certaine : and withall, making
them priuie to their action, to binde them afterwardes
to acknowledg gratefulnes towards them. They went
therefore at one time, when they knewe them to be a-
lone, *Clinias* to *Philoclea*, and *Artesia* to *Pamela* : and *Clinias*, with no fewe words, did set forth what an exploite
was intended for her seruice. But *Philoclea* (in whose
cleere minde treason could finde no hiding place) told
him, that she would be glad, if he could perswade her
cosin to deliuer her, and that she would neuer forgett
his seruice therin: but that she desired him to lay down
any such way of mischiefe, for that (for her part) she
would rather yeeld to perpetuall imprisonment, then
consent to the destroying her cosin, who (she knewe)
loued her, though wronged her. This vnlooked-for answere amazed *Clinias*, so that he had no other remedie
in his minde, but to kneele downe to *Philoclea*, and beseech her to keep it secrete, considering that the intention was for her seruice: and vowing (since she misliked
it) to proceed no further therin. She comforted him
with promise of silence, which she perfourmed.

6   But that little auayled : for *Artesia* hauing in like
sort opened this deuice to *Pamela*, she (in whose mind
Vertue gouerned with the scepter of Knowledge) hating so horrible a wickednes, and streight iudging what
was fitte to doo, Wicked woman (said she) whose vn-
repenting harte can find no way to amend treason, but
by treason : nowe the time is come, that thy wicked
wiles haue caught thy selfe in thine owne nette : as for
me, let the Gods dispose of me as shall please them; but
sure it shall be no such way, nor way-leader, by which
I will come to libertie. This she spake something with a
louder

lowder voice then fhe was woont to vfe, fo as *Cecropia*
heard the noife; who was (fooner then *Artefia* imagined fhe would)come vp, to bring *Pamela* to a window,
where fhe might fee a notable fkirmifh happened in the
Campe, as fhe thought, among themfelues : and being
a cunning fifher in troubled waters, ftreight found by
their voices and geftures, there was fome matter of
confequence, which fhe defired *Pamela* to tell her. Alke
of her (faid *Pamela*) & learne to know, that who do falfhoode to their fuperiours ; teach falfhoode to their in-
feriours. More fhe would not fay. But *Cecropia* taking
away the each-way guiltie *Artefia*, with feare of torture,
gat of her the whole-practife : fo as *Zelmane* was the
more clofely imprifoned, and *Clinias* (with the reft
of his corrupted mates, according to their merites) executed : For, as for *Artefia*, fhe was but lockt vp in
her chamber, *Amphialus* not confenting (for the
loue he bare *Ifmenus*) that further punifhment fhould
be laide vpon her.

CHAP. 15.

[1] *Proude* Anaxius *breaketh through the befiegers.* [2] *His
welcome by* Amphialus. [3] *The Muficke,* [4] *and loue-
fong made to* Philoclea. [5] *The fallie of* Anaxius
and his on the Bafilians, [6] *backt by* Amphialus,
[7] *beaten backe by three vnknowen Knightes.* [8] *The
Retraite of both fides.*

But

I

BVt the noyse they hearde in the campe, was occasioned by the famous Prince *Anaxius*, nephewe to the Giant *Euardes* whom *Pyrocles* flew: A Prince, of body excedingly strong; in armes so skilfull and fortunate, as no man was thought to excel him; of courage that knew not how to feare: partes worthie praise, if they had not bene guyded by pride, and followed by vniustice. For, by a strange composition of minde, there was no man more tenderly sensible in any thing offred to himselfe, which in the farthest-fette construction, might be wrested to the name of wróg; no man, that in his own actions could worse distinguish betwene Valour and Violence: So proud, as he could not abstaine from a *Thraso*-like boasting, and yet (so vnluckie a lodging his vertues had gotten) he would neuer boast more then he would accomplish: falsly accounting an vnflexible anger, a couragious constancie: esteeming feare, and astonishment, righter causes of admiration, then Loue and Honour. This man had foure sundrie times fought with *Amphialus*, but *Mars* had bene so vnpartiall an arbiter, that neither side gate aduauntage of the other. But in the end it hapned, that *Anaxius* found *Amphialus* (vnknowen) in a great danger, and saued his life: wherupon (louing his owne benefite) began to fauour him, so much the more, as, thinking so well of himselfe, he coulde not choose but like him, whom he founde a match for himselfe: which at last grewe to as much friendship towardes him, as could by a proud harte be
con-

conceiued. So as in this trauaile (seeking *Pyrocles* to be reuenged of his vncles death) hearing of this siege, neuer taking paines to examine the quarrell (like a man whose will was his God, and his hand his lawe) taking with him his two brothers (men accounted little inferiour to him selfe in martiall matters) and two hundred chosen horsemen (with whome he thought him selfe able to conquere the world) yet commaunding the rest of his forces to follow, he him selfe vpon such an vnexpected suddaineneffe entred in vpon the backe of *Basilius*, that many with great vnkindneffe tooke their death, not knowing why, nor how they were so murdred. There, if euer, did he make knowne the wonderfulnes of his force. But the valiant, & faithfull *Philanax*, with wel gouerned speed made such head againft him, as would haue shewed, how soone Courage falles in „ the ditch which hath not the eie of Wisdome: but that „ *Amphialus* at the same time issued out, & winning with an abondaunce of courage one of the sconses, which *Basilius* had builded, made waie for his friend *Anaxius* with great losse of both sides, but especially of the *Basilians*; such notable monuments had those two swords especially lefte of their Maisters redoubted worthyneffe.

There with the respect fit to his estate, the honour dewe to his worthineffe, and the kindneffe which accompanies friendship (made fast by enterchaunged benefites) did *Amphialus* enforce him selfe (as much as in a besieged towne he could) to make *Anaxius* know, that his succour was not so needefull, as his presence gratefull. For causing the streates and houses of the towne to witnes his welcome (making both souldiers

R r   and

and Magiſtrates in their countenaunces to ſhewe their
gladneſſe of him) he led him to his mother, whom he
beſought to entertain him with no leſſe loue and kindneſſe, then as one, who once had ſaued her ſonnes life,
and now came to ſaue both life and honour. Tuſh (ſaid
Anaxius, ſpeaking alowde, looking vpon his brothers)
I am onely ſorie there are not halfe a dozen Kinges
more about you: that what *Anaxius* can doo, might be
the better manifeſted. His brothers ſmiled, as though
he had ouer-modeſtly ſpoken farre vnderneath the
pitch of his power. Then was he diſarmed at the earneſt requeſt of *Amphialus :* for *Anaxius* boiled with
deſire to iſſue out vppon the enemies , perſwading
himſelfe, that the Sunne ſhoulde not be ſette, before
he had ouerthrowne them. And hauing repoſed himſelfe, *Amphialus* asked him , whether he woulde viſite the yong Princeſſes . But *Anaxius* whiſpered
him in the eare : In trueth (ſaide he) deare friende
Amphialus, though I am none of thoſe, that loue to
ſpeake of themſelues, I neuer came yet in companie
of Ladies, but that they fell in loue with me. And I
that in my hart ſcorne them as a peeuiſh paltrie ſexe,
not woorthie to communicate with my vertues, would
not do you the wrong : ſince (as I heare) you doo de-
baſe your ſelfe ſo much as to affect them. The curteous *Amphialus* could haue beene angrie with him for
thoſe wordes ; but knowing his humour, ſuffered him
to daunce to his owne muſicke : and gaue himſelfe to
entertaine both him and his brothers, with as cheerefull a maner, as coulde iſſue from a minde whome
vnluckie loue had filled with melancholie . For to
Anaxius he yeelded the direction of all . He gaue
the

the watchwoorde, and if any grace were graunted, the meanes were to be made to *Anaxius.* And that night when fupper was ended, wherein *Amphialus* woulde needes himfelfe waite vpon him, he caufed in Boates vpon the Lake an excellent muficke to be ordered : which, though *Anaxius* might conceiue was for his honour, yet indeede he was but the Bricke-wall to conuey it to the eares of the beloued *Philoclea.*

The muficke was of Cornets, whereof one aunfwe- 3 ring the other, with a fweete emulation, ftriuing for the glorie of muficke, and ftriking vpon the fmooth face of the quiet Lake, was then deliuered vp to the caftell walles, which with a proude reuerberation, fpreading it into the aire; it feemed before the harmonie came to the eare, that it had enriched it felfe in trauaile, the nature of thofe places adding melodie to that melodious inftrument. And when a while that inftrument had made a braue proclamation to all vnpoffeffed mindes of attention, an excellent confort ftreight followed of fiue Violles, and as manie voyces; which all being but Oratours of their maifters paffions, beftowed this fong vppon her, that thought vppon another matter.

T He Fire to fee my woes for anger burneth: 4
 The Aire in raine for my affliction weepeth :
  The Sea to ebbe for griefe his flowing turneth :
 The Earth with pitie dull his center turneth.
  Fame is with wonder blazed :
  Time runnes away for forrow :

Place ſtandeth ſtill amazed,
To ſee my night of ils,which hath no morrowe.
Alas all onely ſhe no pitie taketh
To know my miſeries , but chaſte and cruell
My fall her glory maketh ;
Yet ſtill her eyes giue to my flames their fuell.

Fire, burne me quite till ſenſe of burning leaue me .
Aire, let me drawe thy breath no more in anguiſh :
Sea, drown'd in thee of tedious life bereaue me :
Earth, take this earth wherein my ſpirits languiſh.
Fame , ſay I was not borne :
Time, haſt my dying hower :
Place, ſee my graue vptorne :
Fire, aire, ſea, earth, fame, time, place ſhow your power.
Alas from all their helpe I am exiled :
For hers am I, and Death feares her diſpleaſure.
Fie Death thou art beguiled :
Though I be hers, ſhe ſets by me no treaſure.

5 But *Anaxius* (ſeeming a weary before it was ended)
told *Amphialus*, that for his part he liked no muſick, but
the neighing of horſes, the ſound of trumpets, and the
cries of yeelding perſons : and therefore deſired , that
the next morning they ſhoulde iſſue vpon the ſame
place , where they had entred that day, not doubting
to make them quickly a wearie of being the beſiegers
of *Anaxius*. *Amphialus*, who had no whit leſſe courage,
though nothing blowne vp with pride, willingly condiſcended : and ſo the next morning (giuing falſe alarum to the other ſide of the campe) *Amphialus* at *A-*
naxius earneſt requeſt, ſtaying within the towne to ſee

it

it garded, *Anaxius* and his brethren, *Lycurgus*, and *Zoilus*, sallied out with the best chosen men. But *Basilius* (hauing bene the last day somewhat vnprouided) now had better fortified the ouerthrowne sconse; and so well had prepared euery thing for defence, that it was impossible for any valour from within, to preuaile. Yet things were perfourmed by *Anaxius* beyonde the credite of the credulous. For thrise (valiantly followed by his brothers) did he set vp his banner vpon the rampire of the enemie: though thrise againe by the multitude, and aduauntage of the place, but especially by the comming of three valiant Knights, he were driuen downe againe. Nũbers there were that day, whose deathes and ouerthrowes were executed by the well knowen sworde of *Anaxius:* but the rest, by the length of time and iniurie of Historians, haue bene wrapped vp in darke forgetfulnesse : onely *Tressennius* is spoken of, becaufe when all abandoned the place, hee onely made head to *Anaxius*; till hauing lost one of his legs, yet not lost the harte of fighting, *Lycurgus* (second brother to *Anaxius*) cruellie murthered him; *Anaxius* him selfe disdayning any further to deale with him.

But so farre had *Anaxius* at the thirde time preuayled, that now the *Basilians* began to let their courage descende to their feete, *Basilius*, and *Philanax* in vaine striuing, with reuerence of authoritie to bridle the flight of aftonishment, and to teach-Feare discretion : fo that *Amphialus*, feeing Victorie shew fuch a flattering countenaunce to him, came out with all his force; hoping that day to end the fiege.

But that fancie altered quicklie by the fuddaine

comming to the other side of three Knights, whereof
the one was in white armour, the other in greene,
and the thirde by his blacke armour , and deuice
streight knowne to be the notable Knight , who
the first day had giuen Fortune so short a stoppe with
his notable deedes, and fighting hand to hand with the
deemed inuincible *Amphialus*. For the very cowardes
no sooner saw him, but as borrowing some of his spirit,
they went like yong Eagles to the pray, vnder the wing
of their damme. For the three aduenturers, not content to keepe them from their rampier , leapt downe a-
mong them, and entered into a braue combate with
the three valiaunt brothers. But to whether side Fortune woulde haue beene partiall, could not be determined. For the *Basilians*, lightened with the beames
of these straungers valure, followed so thicke, that the
Amphialians were glad with some haste to retire to the
walles warde : though *Anaxius* neither reason, feare,
nor example , coulde make him asswage the furie of
his fight : vntill one of the *Basilians* (vnwoorthie to
haue his name regiftred, since he did it cowardly, side-
warde, when he leaft looked that way) almost cut off
one of his legges : so as he fell downe, blaspheming
heauen , that all the influences thereof had power to
ouerthrow him; and there death would haue seazed of
his proude hart , but that *Amphialus* tooke in hand the
blacke knight, while some of his souldiers conueied a-
way *Anaxius*, so requiting life for life vnto him.

3   And for the loue and example of *Amphialus*, the fight
began to enter into a new fitte of heate : when *Basilius*
(that thought inough to be done for that day) caused
                                                  retraite

retraite to be founded; fearing leaſt his men following ouer-haſtily, might bee the loſſe of thoſe excellent Knights whom he deſired to knowe. The Knights as ſoone as they heard the retraite (though they were eagerly ſet, knowing that courage without diſcipline is „ nearer beaſtlineſſe then manhood) drew backe their „ ſwords, though hungrie of more blood: eſpecially the blacke Knight, who, knowing *Amphialus*, could not refraine to tell him, that this was the ſecond time he eſcaped out of his hands, but that he would ſhortly bring him a bill of all the former accounts. *Amphialus* ſeing it fit to retire alſo (moſt of his people being hurt, both in bodies and harts) withdrew himſelfe, with ſo well ſeated a reſolution, that it was as farre from anger, as from diſmayedneſſe; anſwering no other to the blacke Knights threats, but that when he brought him his account, he ſhould finde a good pay-maſter.

CHAP. 16.

¹ The vnknowne Knights will not be knowne. ² The Knight of the Tombes ſhew, ³ and challenge accepted by Amphialus. *⁴ Their fight, with the death of the Tombe-knight. ⁵ Who that Knight was. ⁶ The dying ſpeeches, and ⁷ the lamentable funerals.*

He fight being ceaſed, and ech ſide withdrawne within their ſtrengthes, *Baſilius* ſent *Philanax* to entertaine the ſtraunge Knights, and to bring them vnto him, that he might acknowledge what honour was due to their vertue. But they excused themselues, desiring to be knowne first by their deedes, before their names should accuse their vnworthinesse: and though the other replied according as they deserued, yet (finding that vnwelcome curtesie is a degree of iniury) " he suffered them to retire themselues to a tent of their owne without the campe, where they kept themselues secrete: *Philanax* himselfe being called away to another straunge Knight; straunge not onely by the vnlooked-fornesse of his comming, but by the straunge maner of his comming.

For he had before him foure damosels, and so many behind him, all vpon palfreys, & all appareled in mourning weedes; ech of them seruants of ech side, with like liueries of sorrow. Himselfe in an armour, all painted ouer with such a cunning of shadow, that it represented a gaping sepulchre, the furniture of his horse was all of Cypresse braunches; wherwith in olde time they were woont to dresse graues. His Bases (which he ware so long, as they came almost to his ankle) were imbrodered onely with blacke wormes, which seemed to crawle vp and downe, as readie alreadie to deuoure him. In his shielde for *Impresa*, he had a beautifull childe, but hauing two heades; whereof the one shewed, that it was alreadie dead : the other aliue, but in that case, necessarily looking for death. The word was, *No way to be rid from death, but by death.*

3   This Knight of the tombe (for so the souldiours termed him) sent to *Basilius*, to demaund leaue to send in a damosel into the towne, to cal out *Amphialus*, according as before time some others had done. Which being grated (as glad any would vndertake the charge, which

no bodie elſe in that campe was knowne willing to do)
the damoſell went in, and hauing with tears ſobbed out
a braue chalenge to *Amphialus*, from the Knight of the
Tombe, *Amphialus*, honourably enterteining the gentlewoman, & deſiring to know the Knights name (which
the doolefull Gentlewoman would not diſcouer) accepted the chalenge, onely deſiring the Gentlewoman
to ſay thus much to the ſtrange Knight, from him; that
if his minde were like to his title, there were more cauſe
of affinitie, then enmitie betweene them. And therefore preſently (according as he was woont) as ſoone
as he perceyued the Knight of the Tombe, with his
Damoſels and Iudge, was come into the Iland, he alſo
went ouer in accuſtomed maner: and yet for the curteſie of his nature, deſired to ſpeake with him.

But the Knight of the Tombe, with ſilence, and   4
drawing his horſe backe , ſhewed no will to heare,
nor ſpeake : but with Launce on thigh, made him
knowe, it was fitte for him to go to the other ende
of the Career, whence wayting the ſtarte of the
vnknowne Knight , he likewiſe made his ſpurres
claime haſte of his horſe . But when his ſtaffe was
in his reſt, comming downe to meete with the Knight,
nowe verie neere him , he perceyued the Knight had
miſt his reſt : wherefore the curteous *Amphialus*
woulde not let his Launce deſcende, but with a gallant grace, ranne ouer the heade of his there-in frien-
ded enemie : and hauing ſtopped his horſe, and with
the turning of him, bleſſed his ſight with the Windowe where he thought *Philoclea* might ſtand, he perceyued the Knight had lighted from his horſe, and
throwne away his ſtaffe, angrie with his misfortune,

as

as hauing mift his reft, and drawne his fworde to make that fupply his fellowes fault. He alfo lighted, and » drew his fworde, efteeming victorie by aduantage, rather robbed then purchafed: and fo the other comming eagerly toward him, he with his fhield out, and fword aloft, with more brauerie then anger, drew vnto him; and ftraight made their fwords fpeake for them a pretie-while with equall fearcenes. But *Amphialus* (to whom the earth brought forth few matches) hauing both much more skill to choofe the places, and more force to worke vpon the chofen, had already made many windowes in his armour for death to come in at; whē (the noblenes of his nature abhorring to make the punifhment ouergoe the offence) he ftept a little backe, and withal, Sir Knight (faid he) you may eafely fee, that it pleafeth God to fauour my caufe; employ your valour againft them that wifh you hurte: for my part, I haue not deferued hate of you. Thou lyeft falfe traytor, faide the other, with an angrie, but weake voyce. But *Amphialus*, in whome abufed kindnefle became fpitefull rage, Ah barbarous wretch (faid hee) onely couragious in difcourtefie; thou fhalt foone fee whether thy toonge hath betrayed thy harte, or no: and with that, redoubling his blowes, gaue him, a great wounde vpon his necke, and clofing with him ouerthrew him, and with the fall thruft him mortally into the bodie: and with that went to pull off his helmet, with intention to make him giue himfelfe the lye, for hauing fo faide, or to cut off his head.

But the head-peece was no fooner off, but that there fell about the fhoulders of the ouercome Knight the treafure of faire golden haire, which with the face

face (foone knowne by the badge of excellencie)
witneffed that it was *Parthenia* , the vnfortunatelie
vertuous wife of *Argalus* : her beautie then euen in
defpight of the paffed forrow, or comming death, affuring all beholders, that it was nothing fhort of perfection. For her exceeding faire eyes, hauing with continuall weeping gotten a little redneffe about them;
her roundy fweetly fwelling lippes a little trembling,
as though they kiffed their neighbour death; in her
cheekes the whiteneffe ftriuing by little and little to get
vpon the rofineffe of them; her necke, a necke indeed
of Alablafter, difplaying the wounde,which with moft
daintie blood laboured to drowne his owne beauties;
fo as here was a riuer of pureft redde, there an Iland of
perfitteft white,each giuing luftre to the other;with the
fweete countenáce(God-knowes)full of an vnaffected
languifhing : though thefe thinges to a grofly conceau-
uing fenfe might feeme difgraces;yet indeed were they
but apparailing beautie in a new fafhion,which all loo-
ked-vpon thorough the fpectacles of pittie,did eué encreafe the lynes of her naturall fairenes,fo as *Amphialus*
was aftonifhed with griefe, compaffion,& fhame, detefting his fortune,that made him vnfortunate in victory.

Therfore,putting off his headpeece & gauntlet;knee- 6
ling down vnto her,& with teares teftifying his forow,
he offred his (by himfelfe accurfed)hands to helpe her:
protefting his life and power to be readie to doo her
honour.But *Parthenia* (who had inward meffingers of
the defired deathes approch) looking vpon him, and
ftreight turning away her feeble fight, as from a de-
lightleffe obiect, drawing out her wordes , which
her breath (loath to parte from fo fweete a bodie)
did

did faintly deliuer, Sir (faide fhe) I pray you (if prayers haue place in enemies) to let my maides take my body vntouched by you : the onely honour I now defire by your meanes, is, that I haue no honour of you. *Argalus* made no fuch bargaine with you, that the hands which killed him, fhoulde helpe me. I haue of them (and I doo not onely pardon you, but thanke you for it) the feruice which I defired. There refts nothing now, but that I go liue with him, fince whofe death I haue done nothing but die. Then pawfing, and a little fainting, and againe comming to herfelfe, O fweete life, welcome (faide fhe) nowe feele I the bandes vntied of the cruell death, which fo long hath helde me. And O life, O death, aunfwere for me, that my thoughts haue not fo much as in a dreame tafted any comfort; fince they were depriued of *Argalus*. I come, my *Argalus*, I come : And, O God hide my faultes in thy mercies, and graunt (as I feele thou dooft graunt) that in thy eternall loue, we may loue eche other eternally. And this O Lorde: But there *Atropos* cut off her fentence : for with that, cafting vp both eyes and hands to the skies, the noble foule departed (one might well affure himfelfe) to heauen, which left the bodie in fo heauenly a demeanure.

But *Amphialus* (with a hart oppreffed with griefe, becaufe of her requeft) withdrewe himfelfe, but the Iudges, as fullof pitie, had bene al this while difarming her, and her gentlewomen with lamentable cries, laboring to ftanch the remediles wounds: & a while fhe was dead before they perceiued it; death being able to diuide the foul, but not the beauty frõ that body. But whẽ the infallible tokens of death affured thẽ of their loffe, one of

of the women would haue killed her selfe, but that the
squire of *Amphialus* perceauing it, by force held her. O-
thers that had as strong passions, though weaker resolution, fell to cast dust vpon their heads, to teare their
garments: all falling vpon, and crying vpon their sweet
mistres; as if their cries could perswade the soul to leaue
the celestiall happines, to come again into the elemēts
of sorrow: one time calling to remembrance her vertue, chastnes, sweetnes, goodnes to them: another time
accursing themselucs, that they had obeyed her, they
hauing bene deceaued by her words, who assured thē,
that it was reuealed vnto her, that she should haue her
harts desire in the battaile against *Amphialus*, which
they wrongly vnderstood. Then kissing her cold hands
and feet, wearie of the world, since she was gone, who
was their world. The very heauens semed, with a clou-
die countenance, to loure at the losse, and Fame it selfe
(though by nature glad to tell rare accidents, yet)
could not choose but deliuer it in lamentable accents,
& in such sort went it quickly all ouer the Campe: &, as
if the aire had bene infected with sorow, no hart was so
hard, but was subiect to that contagion; the rarenes of
the accident, matching together (the rarely matched
together) pittie with admiration. *Basilius* himselfe came
foorth, and brought foorth the faire *Gynecia* with him,
who was gone into the campe vnder colour of visiting
her husband, and hearing of her daughters: but indeed
Zelmane was the Sainct, to which her pilgrimage was
entended: cursing, enuying, blessing, and in her harte
kissing the walles which imprisoned her. But both they
with *Philanax*, and the rest of the principall Nobilitie,
went out, to make Honour triumph ouer Death, con-
　　　　　　　　　　　　　　　　　　　ueying

ing that excellent body (wherto *Baſilius* himſelf would
needes bend his ſhoulder) to a church a mile from the
campe, where the valiant *Argalus* lay intombed; recommending to that ſepulchre, the bleſſed reliques of
faithfull and vertuous Loue : giuing order for the making of marble images, to repreſent them, & each way
enriching the tombe. Vpon which, *Baſilius* himſelf cauſed this Epitaphe to be written.

CHAP. 17.

[1] *The remorse of* Amphialus *for his last deede, and lasting destinie.* [2] *His reuerent respect in loue.* [3] *His mothers ghostly counsell to a rape.*

THen with eyes full of teares, and [1] mouthes full of her prayses, returned they to the campe, with more and more hate against *Amphialus:* who (poore Gentleman) had therfore greater portion of woe, then any of them. For that courteous harte, which would haue grieued but to haue heard the like aduenture, was rent with remembring himselfe to be the author: so that his wisdome could not so farre temper his passion, but that he tooke his sword, counted the best in the world (which with much bloud he had once conquered of a mightie Giant) and brake it into many peeces (which afterwardes he had good cause to repent) saying, that neither it was worthie to serue the noble exercise of chiualrie, nor any other worthie to feel that sword, which had stroken so excellent a Ladie: & withall, banishing all cheerfulnes of his countenance, he returned home. Where he gate him to his bed, not so much to rest his restles minde, as to auoyd all companie, the sight whereof was tedious vnto him. And then melancholie (onely riche in vnfortunate remembrances) brought before him all the mishappes, with which his life had wrestled: taking this, not onely as a confirming of the former,
but

but a presage of following miserie; and to his harte (alredie ouercome by sorrowrulnes)euen trifling misfortunes came,to fill vp the rolle of a grieued memorie,labouring onely his wittes to pearce farther and farther into his owne wretchednes.So all that night(in despite of darkenes)he held his eyes open ; and the morning when the light began to restore to each body his colour, then with curtaines barde he himselfe from the enioying of it : neither willing to feele the comfort of the day, nor the ease of the night : vntill his mother (who neuer knew what loue meant, but onely to himward)came to his bed side,and beginning with louing earnestnes to lay a kinde chiding vpon him, becaufe he would suffer the weakenesse of sorow,to conquere the strength of his vertues ; he did with a broaken peecemeale speach (as if the tempest of passion vnorderly blewe out his words) remember the mishappes of his youth,the euils he had bene cause of,his rebelling with Shame, and that shame increased with shamefull accidents , the deaths of *Philoxenus* and *Parthenia*, wherein he found himselfe hated of the euer-ruling powers,but especially (and so especially,as the rest seemed nothing when he came to that) his fatall loue to *Philoclea* : to whom he had so gouerned himselfe, as one that could neither conquere, nor yeeld ; being of the one side a slaue, and of the other a iaylor : and with all, almost vpbrayding vnto his mother the little successe of her large hoping promises,he in effect finding *Philoclea* nothing mollified , and now himselfe so cast downe,as he thought him vnworthy of better.

2   But his mother (as she had plentifull cause) making him see, that of his other griefes there was little or no fault

faulte in him selfe, and therefore there ought to be little or no griefe in him; when she came to the head of the sore, indeed seeing that she could not patch vp her former promises (he taking a desperate deafnesse to all delaying hopes) she confest plainly, that she could preuaile nothing: but the faulte was his owne, who had marred the yong Girle by seeking to haue that by praier, which he should haue taken by authoritie. That as it were an absurd cunning to make hie ladders to go in a plaine way; so was it an vntimely and foolish flattery, there to beseech, where one might commaund, puffing thé vp by being besought, with such a selfe-pride of superioritie, that it was not (forsooth) to be held out, but by a denial. O God (said *Amphialus*) how wel I thought my fortune would bring forth this end of your labors? assure your self, mother, I will sooner pull out these eies then they shal looke vpon the heauenly *Philoclea*, but as vpó a heaué, whence they haue their light, & to which they are subiect, if they will power down any influéces of cófort, O happy I: but if by the sacrifice of a faithfull hart, they will not be called vnto me, let me languish, & wither with languishing, & grieue with withering, but neuer so much as repine with neuer so much grieuing. Mother, ô Mother, lust may well be a tyrant, but true-,, loue where it is indeed, it is a seruant. Accursed more ,, then I am, may I be, if euer I did approch her, but that I friezed as much in a fearefull reuerence, as I burned in a vehement desire. Did euer mans eye looke thorough loue vpó the maiesty of vertue, shining through beauty, but that he became (as it wel became him) a captiue? & is it the stile of a captiue, to write, *Our will and pleasure?*

Tush, tush sonne (said *Cecropia*) if you say you loue,

Sf   but   3

but withall you feare;you feare left you fhould offend;
offend?& how know you,that you fhould offend? becaufe fhe doth denie: denie? Now by my truth;if your
fadnes would let me laugh,I could laugh hartily,to fee
that yet you are ignorant, that No, is no negatiue in a
,, womans mouth. My fonne,beleeue me,a womã, fpeaking of women : a louers modefty among vs is much
more praifed,then liked:or if we like it, fo well we like
it,that for marring of his modeftie , he fhall neuer proceed further.Each vertue hath his time:if you cõmand
your fouldier to march formoft , & he for curtefie put
others before him,would you praife his modefty?loue
is your Generall:he bids you dare:& will *Amphialus* be
a daftard? Let examples feruc: doo you thinke *Thefeus*
fhould euer haue gotten *Antiope* with fighing , & crof-
fing his armes? he rauifhed her, and rauifhed her that
was an *Amazon*, and therefore had gotten a habite of
ftoutnes aboue the nature of a woman; but hauing rauifhed her,he got a child of her.And I fay no more,but
that (they fay) is not gotten without confent of both
fides. *Iole* had her owne father killed by *Hercules*, & her
felfe rauifhed,by force rauifhed, & yet ere long this rauifhed,& vnfathered Lady could fportfully put on the
Lions skin vpon her owne faire fhoulders,& play with
the clubbe with her owne delicate hands:fo eafily had
fhe pardoned the rauifher, that fhe could not but delight in thofe weapõs of rauifhing.But aboue all, mark
Helen daughter to *Iupiter*, who could neuer brooke her
manerly-wooing *Menelaus*, but difdained his humblenes,& lothed his foftnes . But fo well fhe could like the
force of enforcing *Paris*, that for him fhe could abide
what might be abidden.But what? *Menelaus* takes hart;
he

he recouers her by force;by force carries her home; by
force inioies her;and she,who could neuer like him for
feruiceablenesse,euer after loued him for violence.For
what can be more agreable, then vpon force to lay the
fault of defire ,and in one inftant to ioyne a deare delight with a iuft excufe? or rather the true caufe is (pardon me ô woman-kinde for reuealing to mine owne
fonne the truth of this myftery) we thinke there wants
fire, where we find no fparkles at left of furie . Truly I
haue knowen a great Lady,long fought by moft great,
moft wife,moft beautifull, moft valiant perfons ; neuer
wonne ; becaufe they did ouer-fufpicioufly follicite
her: the fame Ladie brought vnder by an other;inferi-
our to all them in all thofe qualities, onely becaufe he
could vfe that imperious maifterfulneffe,which nature
giues to men aboue women. For indeede (fonne , I
confeffe vnto you) in our very creatió we are feruants :
and who prayfeth his feruaunts fhall neuer be well o-
beyed : but as a ready horfe ftreight yeeldes;when he
findes one that will haue him yeelde; the fame fals to
boundes when he feeles a fearefull horfeman . Awake
thy fpirits (good *Amphialus)* and affure thy felfe , that
though fhe refufeth , fhe refufeth but to endeere the
obtaining . If fhe weepe,and chide, and proteft,before
it be gotten,fhe can but weepe,and chide,and proteft,
when it is gotté . Thinke,fhe would not ftriue,but that
fhe meanes to trie thy force : and my *Amphialus,*know
thy felfe a man,and fhew thy felfe a man : and(beleeue
me vpon my word)a woman is a woman.

SF 2   CHAP.

CHAP. 18.

The forſaken Knights defie. [2] *Amphialus anſwere.* [3] *The one* [3] *and others armour and impreſe.* [5] *The iſſue of their quarrell.* [6] *Their heroicall monomachy on horſe,* [7] *and foot.* [8] *Their breathings,* [9] *& reencounters.* [10] *Amphialus reſcued by* Anaxius *brethren, the Blacke Knight by the greene and white.* [11] *The ſupply of both ſides to cary a-way the breathles Knights.* [12] *The Blackknights grieues.*

Mphialus was aboute to anſwere her, when a Gentlemā of his made him vnderſtande, that there was a meſſengericome, who had brought a letter vnto him from out of the campe: whom he preſently calling for, tooke, opened, and read the letter, importing this.

I   To thee Amphialus of Arcadia, the forſakē Knight wiſheth health, and courage, that by my hand thou maieſt receyue puniſhment for thy treaſon, according to thine owne offer, which wickedly occaſioned, thou haſte proudly begun, and accurſedly mainteyned. I will preſently (if thy minde faint thee not for his owne guiltineſſe) meete thee in thy Iland, in ſuch order, as hath by the former beene vſed: or if thou li-keſt not the time, place, or weapon, I am ready to take thine owne reaſonable choiſe in any of them; ſo as thou do perſourme the ſubſtaunce. Make me ſuch anſwere as may ſhew that thou haſt ſome taſte of honour: and ſo I leaue thee, to liue till I meete thee.

Amphialus

Amphialus read it, and with a deepe figh (according to the humour of inward affection) feemed euen to códemne him felfe, as though indeed his reproches were true. But howfoeuer the dulnes of Melancholy would haue languifhingly yeelded thereunto, his Courage (vnufed to fuch iniuries) defired helpe of Anger to make him this anfwere.

Orfaken Knight, though your namelesse challenge might 2 carry in it selfe excuse for a man of my birth and estate, yet herein set your harte at rest, you shall not be forsaken. I will without stay answere you in the woonted manner, and come both armed in your foolish threatnings, and yet the more fearelesse, expecting weake blowes, where I finde so strong wordes. You shall not therefore long attende me in the Ilande, before proofe teache you, that of my life you haue made your selfe too large a promise. In the meane time, Farewell.

This being written, and deliuered, the meffenger 3 tolde him, that his Lord would (if he liked the fame) bring two Knights with him to be his *Patrons*. Which *Amphialus* accepted, and withall fhaking of (with refolution) his mothers importunate diffwafions, he furnifhed him felfe for the fight: but not in his wonted furniture. For now (as if he would turne his infide outwarde) he would needes appeare all in blacke; his decking both for him felfe, and horfe, being cut out into the fafhion of very ragges: yet all fo dainty, ioyned together with pretious ftones, as it was a braue raggednesse, and a riche pouertie: and fo cunningly had a workeman followed his humour in his armour, that

he

he had giuen it a ruſtie ſhewe, and yet ſo, as any man might perceiue was by arte, and not negligence; carying at one inſtant a diſgraced handſomneſſe, and a new oldnes. In his ſhield he bare for his deuiſe, a Night, by an excellently painter, with a Sunne with a ſhadow, and vpon the ſhadow with a ſpeech ſignifying, that it *onely* was *barrd from inioying that, whereof it had his life*: or, *From whoſe I am banniſhed.* In his creſte he caried *Philoclea* kniues, the onely token of her forwarde fauour.

So paſt he ouer into the Iland, taking with him the two brothers of *Anaxius*; where he founde the forſaken Knight, attired in his owne liuerie, as blacke, as ſorrowe it ſelfe could ſee it ſelfe in the blackeſt glaſſe: his ornaments of the ſame hew, but formed in the figure of Rauens, which ſeemed to gape for carrion: onely his raynes were ſnakes, which finely wrapping themſelues one within the other, their heads came together to the cheekes and boſſes of the bit, where they mightſeeme to bite at the horſe, and the horſe (as he champte the bit) to bite at them; and that the white foame was ingendred by the poyſonous furie of the combatt. His *Impreſa* was a *Catoblepta*. which ſo long lies dead, as the Moone (whereto it hath ſo naturall a ſympathie) wants her light. The worde ſignified that *The Moone wanted not the light, but the poore beaſt wanted the Moones light*. He had in his headpiece, a whippe, to witneſſe a ſelfe-puniſhing repentaunce: Their very horſes were cole-blacke too, not hauing ſo much as one ſtarre to giue light to their night of blackeneſſe: ſo as one would haue thought they had bene the two ſonnes of Sorrow, and were come thether to fight for

their

their birth-right in that ſorie inheritance.

Which aliance of paſſions ſo moued *Amphialus* (al- 5
redy tender-minded by the afflictions of Loue) that
without ſtaffe or ſword drawne, he trotted fairely to
the forſaké Knight, willing to haue put off his combat,
to which his melancholy hart did (more then euer in
like occaſion)miſgiue him: and therefore ſaluting him,
Good Knight(ſaid he)becauſe we are men,and ſhould
knowe reaſon why we doo things; tell me the cauſe,
that makes you thus eager to fight with me. Becauſe I
affirme (anſwered the forſaken Knight) that thou doſt
moſt rebellious iniurie to thoſe Ladies, to whome all
men owe ſeruice. You ſhall not fight with me (ſaide
Amphialus) vpon that quarrell: for I confeſſe the ſame
too:but it proceeds from their owne beauty, to inforce
Loue to offer this force. I maintaine then(ſaid the forſaken Knight) that thou art not worthy ſo to loue.
And that confeſſe I too (ſaide *Amphialus*) ſince the
world is not ſo richly bleſſed, as to bring forth any
thing worthy thereof.But no more vnworthy then any
other, ſince in none can be a more worthy loue. Yes,
more vnworthy then my ſelf(ſaid the forſakenKnight)
for though I deſerue contempt, thou deſerueſt both
contempt,and hatred.

But *Amphialus* by that thinking (though wrongly, 6
each indeede miſtaking other) that he was his riuall,
forgat all minde of reconciliation, and hauing all his
thoughts boūd vp in choler,neuer ſtaying either iudge,
trūpet,or his owne laūce,drew out his ſword,& ſaying,
Thou lyeſt falſe villaine,vnto him,his words &blowes
came ſo quick togither,as the one ſeemed a lightning of
the others thūder. But he foūd no barre groūd of ſuch

feede : for it yeelded him his owne with such encrease, that though Reason and Amazement go rarely togither, yet the most reasonable eies that saw it, founde reason to be amazed at the fury of their combat. Neuer game of death better plaid;neuer fury set it self forth in greater brauerie. The curteous *Vulcan*, whē he wrought at his nowe more curteous wiues request, *Æneas* an armour, made not his hammer beget a greater sounde; then the swordes of those noble Knights did; they needed no fire to their forge;for they made the fire to shine at the meeting of their swords, & armours; ech side fetching new spirit from the castle window, and careful of keeping their sight,it was a matter of greater.consideration in their combat, then either the aduantage of Sun or winde : which Sunne and wind (if the astonished eies of the beholders were not by the astonishment deceiued) did both stand still to be beholders of this rare match. For neither could their amazed eies discerne motion in the Sunne, and no breath of wind stirred, as if either for feare it would not come amōg such blows, or with delight had his eies so busie, as it had forgot to open his mouth. This fight being the more cruell, since both Loue and Hatred conspired to sharpen their humours, that hard it was to say, whether Loue with one trumpet, or Hatred with another, gaue the lowder alarum to their courages. Spite, rage, disdaine, shame, reuenge, came waighting vpon Hatred : of the other side came with loue-longing Desire, both inuincible Hope, and fearelesse Despaire, with riuallike Iealousie, which (although brought vp within doores in the schoole of *Cupid*) woulde shewe themselues no lesse forwarde, then the other dustie bande of *Mars*, to make themselues themfelues notable in the notablenes of this combat. Of eyther fide Confidence, vnacquainted with Loffe, but affured truft to ouercome, and good experience howe to ouercome : nowe feconding their terrible blowes with cunning labouring the horfes, to winne ground of the enimie ; now vnlooked-for parting one from the other, to win aduantage by an aduantageous retourne. But force againft force, fkill againft fkill, fo enterchangeably encountred, that it was not eafie to determine, whether enterprifing, or preuenting came former : both, fometimes at one inftant, doing and fuffring wrong, and choller no leffe rifing of the doing, then of the fuffring. But as the fire, the more fuell is put to it, the more hungrie ftill it is to deuoure more : fo the more they ftrake, the more vnfatiffied they were with ftriking. Their verie armour by piece-meale fell away from them : and yet their flefh abode the wounds conftantly, as though it were leffe fenfible of fmarte, then the fenfeleffe armour : their blood in moft places ftayning the blacke, as if it would giue a more liuely coulour of mourning, then blacke can doo. And fo a long fpace they fought, while neither vertue, nor fortune feemed partiall of either fide: which fo tormented the vnquiet hart of *Amphialus*, that he refolued to fee a quicke ende : and therefore with the violence of courage, adding ftrength to his blow, he ftrake in fuch wife vpon the fide of the others heade, that his remembrance left that battered lodging : fo as he was quite from himfelfe, cafting his armes abroade, and redie to fall downe ; his fword likewife went out of his hande ; but that being faft by a chaine to his arme, he could not loofe. And *Amphialus* vfed the fa-

uour

uour of occasion, redoubling his blowes: but the horse
(weary to be beaten, as well as the master) carried his
master away, till he came vnto himselfe: But then who
could haue seene him, might wel haue discerned shame
in his cheekes, and reuenge in his eyes: so as setting his
teeth togither with rage, he came running vpon *Amphialus*, reaching out his arme, which had gathered vp
the sword, meaning with that blow to haue cleaued
Amphialus in two. But *Amphialus* seeing the blow comming, shunned it with nimble turning his horse aside;
wherwith the forsaken Knight ouer-strake himself so, as
almost he came downe with his owne strength. But
the more hungrie he was of his purpose, the more he
was bard the food of it: disdaining the resistance, both
of force, and fortune, he returned vpon the spurre a-
gaine, and ranne with such violence vpon *Amphialus*,
that his horse with the force of the shocke rose vp before, almost ouerturned: which *Amphialus* perceauing,
with rayne and spurre put forth his horse; and withall
gaue a mightie blow in the descent of his horse, vpon
the shoulder of the forsaken Knight; from whence sli-
ding, it fell vpon the necke of his horse, so as horse and
man fell to the ground: but he was scarce downe before he was vpon his feete againe, with braue gesture shewing rising of corage, in the falling of fortune.

7   But the curteous *Amphialus* excused himselfe, for hauing (against his will) kild his horse. Excuse thy selfe
for viler faults (answered the forsaken Knight) and vse
this poore aduantage the best thou canst; for thou
shalt quickely finde thou hast neede of more. Thy folly
(said *Amphialus*) shall not make me forget my selfe: and
therewith (trotting a little aside) alighted from his
horse

horfe, becaufe he would not haue fortune come to claime any part of the victory. Which curteous act would haue mollified the noble harte of the forfaken Knight, if any other had done it, befides the Iaylor of his miftres : but that was a fufficient defeazaunce for the firmeft bonde of good nature; and therfore he was no fooner alighted, but that he ranne vnto him, re-en-tring into as cruel a fight, as eye did euer fee, or thought could reafonably imagine; farre beyond the reach of weak words to be able to expreffe it. For what they had done on horfebacke, was but as a morfell to keep their ftomakes in appetite, in comparifon of that, which now (being themfelues) they did. Nor euer glutton by the châge of daintie diet could be brought to fetch feeding (when he might haue bene fatiffied before) with more earneftnes, then thofe (by the change of their maner of fight) fell cleane to a new fight, though any elfe would haue thought they had had their fill alredy. *Amphialus* being the taller man, for the moft part ftood with his right legge before, his fhield at the vttermoft length of his arme; his fword hie, but with the point toward his enemy. But whê he ftrake, which came fo thick, as if eue-ry blow would ftriue to be foremoft, his arme feemed ftill a poftillion of death. The forfaken Knight fhewed with like skil, vnlike gefture, keeping himfelfe in conti-nual motion, proportioning the diftance betweene thê to any thing that *Amphialus* attempted : his eye guided his foote, and his foote conueighed his hand; and fince nature had made him fomething the lower of the two, he made art follow, and not ftriue with nature: fhunning rather thê warding his blowes; like a cûning maftiffe, who knowes the fharpnes of the horne, and ftrêgth of the Bul, fights low to get his proper aduâtage;

anfwering

anſwering mightines with nimblenes, and yet at times imploying his wonderfull force, wherein he was ſeconde to none. In ſumme, the blowes were ſtronge, the thruſts thicke, and the auoydings cunning. But the forſaken Knight (that thought it a degree of being cõquered to be long in conquering) ſtrake ſo mightie a blow, that he made *Amphialus* put knee to the ground, without any humblenes. But when he felt himſelfe ſtriken downe, and ſaw himſelfe ſtriken downe by his riuall, then ſhame ſeemed one arme, and diſdaine another; fury in his eyes, and reuenge in his hart; ſkill and force gaue place, & they tooke the place of ſkil & force: with ſo vnweariable a manner, that the forſakenKnight was alſo driuen to leaue the ſtreame of cunning, and giue himſelfe wholly to be guided by the ſtorme of fury: there being in both (becauſe hate would not ſuffer admiration) extreame diſdaine to finde themſelues ſo matched.

8   What (ſaid *Amphialus* to himſelfe) am I *Amphialus*, before whom ſo many monſters & Gyants haue falne dead, when I onely ſought cauſeleſſe aduentures? and can one Knight now withſtand me in the preſence of *Philoclea*, and fighting for *Philoclea*? or ſince I loſt my liberty, haue I loſt my courage? haue I gotten the hart of a ſlaue, as well as the fortune? If an armie were againſt me in the ſight of *Philoclea*, could it reſiſt me? O beaſt, one man reſiſtes thee; thy ryuall reſiſts thee? or am I indeed *Amphialus*? haue not paſſions kild him, and wretched I (I know not how) ſucceeded into his place? Of the other ſide the forſakenKnight with no leſſe ſpite, fel out with himſelf; Haſt thou brokē (ſaid he to himſelfe) the cõmãdemēt of thy only Princeſſe to come now into her

her preſéce,& in her preſéce to proue thy ſelf a coward?
Doth *Aſia* and *Ægypt* ſet vp Trophes vnto thee, to be
matched here by a traytor? O noble *Barſanes*,how ſhamed will thy ſoule be,that he that ſlew thee, ſhould be
reſiſted by this one man? O incomparable *Pyrocles*,
more grieued wilt thou be with thy friends ſhame, the
with thine owne impriſonment,when thou ſhalt know
how little I haue bene able to doo for the deliuerie of
thee,and thoſe heauenlie Princeſſes Am I worthie to
be friend to the moſt valourous Prince that euer was
entituled valourous, and ſhewe my ſelfe ſo weake a
wretch? No,ſhamed *Muſidorus*, worthie for nothing,
but to keepe ſheepe,get thee a ſheephooke again, ſince
thou canſt vſe a ſword no better.

Thus at times did they,now with one thought,then   9
with another, ſharpen their ouer-ſharpe humors ; like
the Lion, that beates himſelfe with his owne taile, to
make himſelfe the more angrie. Theſe thoughtes indeede not ſtaying, but whetting their angrie ſwordes,
which now had put on the apparraile of Crueltie:they
bleeding ſo aboundantly, that euery bodie that ſawe
them,fainted for them,& yet they fainted not in themſelues : their ſmart being more ſenſible to others eyes,
then to their owne feeling : Wrath and Courage barring the common ſenſe from bringing any meſſage of
their caſe to the minde : Paine, Wearines, and Weakenes,not daring to make knowen their caſe (though already in the limits of death) in the preſence of ſo violent furie: which filling the veines with rage,in ſtead of
bloud, and making the minde miniſter ſpirites to the
bodie, a great while held out their fight,like an arrowe
ſhotte vpward by the force of the bowe, though by his
owne

owne nature he would goe downward . The forsaken
Knight had the more wounds , but *Amphialus* had the
soarer;which the other(watchinge time and place)had
cōningly geuen vnto him. Who euer saw a well-mand
Galley fight with a tall ship , might make vnto himselfe
some kind of comparison of the difference of these two
Knights ; a better couple then which , the world could
not bragge of . *Amphialus* seemed to excell in strength,
the forsaken Knight in nimblenes;and yet did the ones
strength excel in nimblenes, and the others nimblenes
excell in strength : but now , strength and nimblenes
were both gone,and excesse of courage only maintay-
ned the fight . Three times had *Amphialus* with his
mightie blowes driuen the forsaken Knight to go stag-
gering backwarde , but euery one of those times he requited pain with smarte,and shame with repulse . And
now , whether he had cause, or that ouer-much confi-
dence(an ouer-forward scholer of vnconquered Courage)made him think he had cause,he begā to persuade
himself he had the aduātage of the combat,though the
aduantage he toke himselfe to haue , was onely that he
should be the later to die: which hopes,Hate (as vnse-
crete as Loue)could not conceale,but drawing himself
a little back frō him,brake out in these maner of words.

Ah *Amphialus*(said the forsakē knight)this third time
thou shalt not escape me,but thy death shall satisfie thy
iniury,& my malice;and pay for the cruelty thou shew-
edst in killing the noble *Argalus*,& the fair *Parthenia*. In
troth(said *Amphialus*) thou art the best knight that euer
I fought withal,which would make me willing to graut
thee thy life,if thy wit were as good as thy corage; that
(besides other follies)layest that to my charge , which
most

moſt againſt my will was committed . But whether my
death be in thy power,or no,let this tel thee;And vpon
the worde wayted a blow,which parted his ſhield into
two peeces ; & deſpiſing the weak reſiſtance of his alredie broke armor,made a great breach into his hart ſide,
as if he would make a paſſage for his loue to get out at.
But paine rather ſeemedto increaſe life,then to weaken life in thoſe champions . For, the forſaken Knight   9
comming in with his right leg,and making it guide the
force of the blow,ſtrake *Amphialus* vpon the bellie,ſo
horrible a woūd,that his guts came out withall.Which
Amphialus perceauing (fearing death, onely becauſe it
ſhould come with ouerthrow)he ſeemed to coniure all
his ſtrength for one moments ſeruice; and ſo,lifting vp
his ſword with both hands,hit the forſaken knight vpō
the head,a blow,wherewith his ſword brake . But(as if
it would do a notable ſeruice before it died) it preuayled ſo,euen in the inſtant of breaking,that the forſaken
Knight fell to the ground, quite for that inſtant forgetting both loue and hatred: and *Amphialus* (finding him
ſelf alſo in ſuch weaknes, as he loked for ſpeedy death)
glad of the victorie, though little hoping to enioy it,
puld vp his viſar,meaning with his dagger to giue him
death;but in ſtead of death , he gaue him life : for, the
aire ſo reuiued his ſpirits,that comming to himſelf, and
ſeeing hispreſent danger,with a life conquering death,
he tooke *Amphialus* by the thigh,& together roſe himſelfe, and ouerturned him.But *Amphialus* ſcrambled vp
againe,both now ſo weake indeede, as their motions
rather ſeemed the afterdrops to a ſtorme,then any matter of great furie.

But *Amphialus* might repent himſelfe of his wilfull
breaking

breaking his good sword : for, the forsaken Knight (hauing with the extremitie of iustly-conceiued hate, and
the vnpitifulnes of his owne neere-threatning death,
blotted out all complements of courtesie) let flie at him
so cruelly, that though the blowes were weake, yet
weaknes vpon a weakned subiect, proued such strégth,
that *Amphialus* hauing attempted in vaine, once or
twise to close with him, receauing wound vpó wound,
sent his whole burden to strike the earth with falling,
since he could strike his foe no better in standing : geuing no other tokens of himself, then as of a man euen
ready to take his oath to be Deathes true seruant.

10   Which when the hardie brothers of *Anaxius* perceaued, not recking law of armes, nor vse of chiualrie,
they flew in to defende their friende, or reuenge their
losse of him. But they were foorthwith encountred
with the two braue cópanions of the forsaken Knight;
whereof the one being all in greene, both armour and
furniture, it seemed a pleasant garden, wherein grewe
orange trees, which with their golden fruites, cunningly beaten in, & embrodered, greatly enriched the eye-
pleasing colour of greene. In his shield was a sheep, feeding in a pleasant field, with this word, *Without feare, or
enuie.* And therfore was called the Knight of the sheep.
The other Knight was all in milke white, his attiring
els, all cutte in starres, which made of cloath of siluer,
and siluer spangles, each way seemed to cast many aspects. His deuice was the very Pole it selfe, about
which many starres stirring, but the place it selfe lefte
voide. The word was, *The best place yet reserued.* But these
foure Knights, inheriting the hate of their friends, began a fierce combat: the forsaken Knight himselfe not
able

able to helpe his fide, but was driuen to fit him downe, with the extreame faintneſſe of his more & more fainting body. But thoſe valiant couples feeking honour by diſhonouring, and to build ſafety vpon ruine, gaue new appetites, to the almoſt glutted eies of the beholders : and now bloud began to put ſweat from the full poſſeſſion of theh outſides, no aduantage being yet to be feene ; onely the Knight of the ſheepe feeming moſt deliuer, and affecting moſt all that viewed him, when a company of ſouldiers fent by *Cecropia*, came out in boates to the Ilande : and all came running to the deſtruction of the three Knights, whereof the one was vtterly vnable to defend himſelfe.

But then did the other two Knights ſhewe their 11 wonderfull courage, and fidelitie. For turning backe to backe, and bothe beſtriding the blacke forſaken Knight (who had fainted ſo long till he had loſt the feeling of faintneſſe) they helde playe againſt the reſt, though the two brothers vnknightly helped them ; till *Philanax* (who watchfully attended ſuch traiterous practiſes) fent likewiſe ouer, both by boate and ſwimming, ſo choiſe a number as did put moſt of the other to the ſworde. Onely the two Brothers, with ſome of the braueſt of them, carrying away the body of *Amphialus*, which they would rather haue died, then haue left behind them.

So was the forſaken Knight (layed vpon clokes) 12 carried home to the campe. But his two friends knowing his earneſt deſire not to be knowen, couering him from any bodies eyes, conueyed him to their owne tente : *Baſilius* himſelfe conquering his earneſt deſire to fee him, with feare to diſpleaſe him, who had fought ſo notably in his quarrell. But Fame ſet the honour vpon his backe, which he would not ſuffer to ſhine in his face: no mans mouth being barrein of prayſes to the noble Knight, that had bettered the moſt eſteemed Knight in the world: euery bodie praying for his life, and thinking that therein they prayed for themſelues. But he himſelfe, when by the diligent care of friends, and well applied cunning of ſurgeons, he came to renewe againe the league betweene his minde and body, then fell he to a freſhe warre with his owne thoughts, wrongfully condemning his manhood, laying cowardiſe to himſelfe, whome the impudenteſt backbiter would not ſo haue wróged. For his courage (vſed to vſe victory as an inheritaunce) could brooke no reſiſtance at any time: but now that he had promiſed himſelfe, not onely the conqueſt of him, but the ſcaling of the walles, and deliuery of *Pamela*, though he had done beyond al others expectation, yet ſo ſhort was he of his owne; that he hated to looke vpon the Sunne, that had ſeene him do ſo weakely: and ſo much abhorred all viſitation or honour, whereof he thought himſelfe vnworthy, that he beſought his two noble friends to carrie him away to a caſtle not far of, where he might cure his wounds, and neuer be knowne till he made ſucceſſe excuſe this (as he thought) want in him. They louingly obeyed him, leauing *Baſilius* and all the campe very ſorrie for the parting of theſe three vnknowne Knights, in whoſe proweſſe they had repoſed greateſt truſt of victory.

CHAP.

CHAP. 19.

¹ *The ſtate of the leaguer, and beleaguered.* ² *The agonies of* Amphialus. ³ *The wit-craft of* Cecropia, *to threaten* Baſilius *with the three Ladies death.* ⁴ Kalanders *compaſſion.* ⁵ Philanax-*his counter-counſell.* ⁶ *The breaking vp the ſiege.*

Vt they being gone, *Baſilius* and ¹ *Philanax* gaue good order to the ſtrengthning of the ſiege, fortifying themſelues, ſo as they feared no more any ſuch ſuddaine onſet, as that of *Anaxius* . And they within (by reaſõ of *Anaxius* hurt, but eſpecially of *Amphialus*-his) gaue themſelues onely to diligent watch & ward, making no ſallies out, but committing the principall truſt to *Zoilus* and *Lycurgus.* For *Anaxius* was yet forced to keepe his chamber. And as for *Amphialus*, his body had ſuch wounds, and gaue ſuch wounds to his mind, as eaſily it coulde not be determined, whether death or he made the greater haſt one to the other: for when the diligent care of cunning ſurgeons, had brought life to the poſſeſſion of his owne right , Sorrowe and Shame (like two corrupted ſeruaunts) came waiting of it , perſwading nothing but the giuing ouer of it ſelfe to deſtruction . They laide before his eyes his preſent caſe, painting euery piece of it in moſte ougly colours : they ſhewed him his loue wrapped in deſpaire, his fame blotted by ouerthrow ; ſo that if before he languiſhed, becauſe he could not obtaine his

deſiring

desiring,he now lamented becaufe he durft not defire
the obtaining. Recreant *Amphialus*, (would he fay to
him felfe)how dareft thou intitle thy felfe the louer of
Philoclea,that haft neither fhewed thy felf a faithfull coward, nor a valiant rebell, but both rebellious and cowardly,which no law cã quite,nor grace haue pitie of?
Alas life,what little pleafure thou dooft me,to giue me
nothing but fenfe of reproach,and exercife of ruine? I
would fweete *Philoclea*, I had died,before thy eies had
feene my weaknes: & then perchaunce with fome figh
thou wouldeft haue cõfeffed, thou hadft loft a worthy
feruaunt. But now, caitife that I am, what euer I haue
done,ferues but to builde vp my riuals glory. To thefe
fpeeches he would couple fuch geftures of vexation,&
would fortifie the geftures with fuch effe(ts of furie,as
fometimes oftring to teare vp his woũds,fometimes to
refufe the fuftenance of meat, & counfell of phifitions,
that his perplexed mother was driuen to make him by
force to be tended,with extreame corfey to her felfe,&
annoiance to him: till in the end he was contented to
promife her, he would attempt no violence vpon himfelf,vpon condition he might be troubled by no body,
but onely his Phifitions: his melancholy detefting all
cõpany, fo as not the very furgeons nor feruants durft
fpeak vnto him in doing him feruice: only he had praied his mother,as fhe tendered his life, fhe would procure him grace;and that without that,fhe would neuer
come at him more.

3   His mother,who had cõfined all her loue only vnto
him,fet only fuch about him, as were abfolutely at her
cõmandement, whom fhe forbad to let him know any
thing that paffed in the caftle, till his wounds were cu-
                                                        red,

red, but as she from time to time should instruct them:
she (for her selfe) being resolued, now she had the gouernment of al things in her owne hands,to satisfie her
sonnes loue,by their yeelding, or satisfie her owne reuenge in their punishment. Yet first,becaufe he should
be the freer frō outward force, she sent a messenger to
the campe,to denounce vnto *Basilius*, that if he did not
presently raise his siege, she would cause the heads of
the three Ladies,prisoners,to be cut of before his eies.
And to make him the more feare a present performance, she caused his two daughters & *Zelmane* to be
led vnto the wals, where she had made a scaffold, easie
to be seene by *Basilius :* and there caused thē to be kept,
as ready for the slaughter, til answere came from *Basilius.* A sight full of pittie it was, to see those three(all excelling in all those excellencies, wherwith Nature can
beautifie any body: *Pamela* giuing sweetnes to maiesty,
Philoclea enriching noblenes with humblenes,*Zelmane*
setting in womanly beautie manlike valour) to be thus
subiected to the basest iniury of vniust Fortune. One
might see in *Pamela* a willingnesse to die,rather then to
haue life at others discretion , though sometimes a
princely disdaine would sparkle out of her Princely
eies ,that it should be in others power to force her to
die.In *Philoclea* a prety feare came vp,to endamaske her
rosie cheekes:but it was such a feare,as rather seemed a
kindly childe to her innate humblenes,then any other
dismaiednes : or if she were.dismaied, it was more for
Zelmane ,then for her selfe; or if more for her selfe,it
was becaufe *Zelmane* should loose her . As for *Zelmane*,
as she went with her hands bound (for they durst not
aduenture on her well knowne valour,especially amōg

people

people which perchāce might be moued by such a spectacle to some reuolte) she was the true image of ouer-
maistred courage,& of spite,that sees no remedie. For
her breast swelled withall, the bloud burst out at her
nose, and she looked paler then accustomed, with her
eies cast on the ground,with such a grace,as if she were
fallen out with the heauens, for suffering such an iniu-
ry.The lookers on were so moued withal,as they misliked what themselues did, and yet still did what themselues misliked.For some,glad to rid themselues of the
dangerous annoyaunce of this siege, some willing to
shorten the way to *Amphialus*-his succession (whereon
they were dependents)some, & the greatest some, doing because others did,and suffring because none durst
begin to hinder, did in this sort set their hands to this
(in their owne conscience)wicked enterprise.

4   But whē this message was brought to *Basilius*,& that
this pittifull preparation was a sufficient letter of credit
for him to beleeue it, he called vnto him his chief coū-
celors:amōg which,those he chiefly trusted were *Philanax* and *Kalander*(lately come to the campe at *Basilius*
cōmandement, & in him selfe wery of his solitary life,
wanting his sons presence, & neuer hauing heard him
his beloued guestes since they parted from him). Now
in this doubt what he should do, he willed *Kalander* to
giue him his aduise.: who spake much to this purpose.
You cōmaund me Sir(said he)to speake,rather because
you will keepe your wonted graue,& noble manner,to
do nothing o^f importāce without coūcell,then that in
this cause(which indeed hath but one way)your mind
needs to haue any counsell:so as my speech shall rather
be to cōfirme what you haue alredy determined,thē to

argue

argue againſt any poſſibilitie of other determination.
For what ſophiſtical ſcholler can finde any queſtion in
this, whether you will haue your incomparable daughters liue, or dye? whether ſince you be here to cauſe
their deliuerance, you will make your being here the
cauſe of their deſtruction? for nothing can be more vnſenſible, then to thinke what one doth, & to forget the "
end why it is done. Do therefore as I am ſure you meane
to doo, remoue the ſiege, and after ſeeke by practiſe, or
other getle meanes, to recouer that which by force you
cānot: & therof is indeed (whē it pleaſe you) more coūſel to be takē. Once, in extremities the winning of time "
is the purchaſe of life, & worſe by no meanes then their
deaths cā befal vnto you. A mā might vſe more words,
if it were to any purpoſe to guild gold, or that I had any
cauſe to doubt of your mind: But you are wiſe, & are a
father. He ſaid no more, for he durſt not attempt to perſwade the marrying of his daughter to *Amphialus*, but
left that to bring in at another conſultation But *Baſilius*
made ſigne to *Philanax*, who ſtāding a while in a maze
as inwardly perplexed, at laſt thus deliuered his opiniō.

If euer I could wiſh my faith vntried, & my counſell 5
vntruſted, it ſhould be at this time, whē in truth I muſt
cōfeſſe I would be cōtent to purchaſe ſiléce with diſcre-
dit. But ſince you cōmand, I obey: onely let me ſay thus
much, that I obey not to theſe excellent Ladies father,
but to my Prince: & a Prince it is to whō I giue coūſel.
Therefore as to a Prince I ſay, that the graue and (I well
know) true-minded counſell of my Lord *Kalander* had
come in good time whē you firſt tooke armes, before al
your ſubiects gate notice of your intention, before ſo
much blood was ſpēt, & before they were driuē to ſeek
this ſhift for their laſt remedy But if now, this force you

away, why did you take armes? since you might be sure
when euer they were in extremitie they would haue
recourse to this threatning? and for a wise man to take
in hand that which his enimie may with a word ouerthrow, hath in my conceit great incongruity, & as great
not to forethink what his enemy in reason wil doo. But
they threaten they wil kil your daughters. What if they
promised you if you remoued your siege, they would
honorably send home your daughters? would you be
angled by their promises? truly no more ought you be
,, terrified by their threatnings. For yet of the two, pro-
,, mise binds faith more then threatning. But indeede a
,, Prince of iudgemēt ought not to consider what his eni-
,, mies promise, or threaten, but what the promisers and
,, threatners in reasō wil do: & the neerest cōiecture thervnto, is what is best for their own behoose to do. They
threatē if you remoue not, they wil kil your daughters,
and if you doo remoue, what surety haue you, but that
they will kil thē, since if the purpose be to cut off al impediments of *Amphialus*-his ambitiō, the same cause wil
continue when you are away; & so much the more en-
coraged, as the reuenging power is absent, & they haue
the more oportunitie to draw their factious friends a-
bout them: but if it be for their security onely, the same
cause wil bring forth the same effect: & for their security
they wil preserue thē. But it may be said, no man knows
what desperate folkes will do: it is true, and as true that
no reason nor policie can preuent what desperate folks
,, wil do: & therfore they are amōg those dangers, which
,, wisdome is not to reckē. Only let it suffice to take away
their despaire, which may be by granting pardon for
what is past; so as the Ladies may be freely deliuered.
And

And let them that are your fubiects, truft you that are
their Prince : doo not you fubiect your ſelfe to truſt.
them, who are ſo vntruſty as to be manifeſt traitors. For
if they finde you ſo baſe-minded, as by their theatning
to remoue your force, what indignitie is it, that they
would not bring you vnto, ſtill by the ſame threatning?
ſince then if Loue ſtir them, loue will keep them from
murthering what they loue; and if Ambition prouoke
them, ambitious they will be, when you are away, as
well as while you are here : take not away your force,
which bars not the one, & bridels the other. For as for
their ſhewes and words they are but to feare babes, not
worthy once to moue a worthy mans conceit; which
muſt ſtill cōſider what in reaſō they are like to do. Their
deſpaire I grant you ſhall do wel to preuent, which as it
is the laſt of all reſolutions, ſo no man fals into it, while „
ſo good a way as you may offer, is open vnto thē. In ſū, „
you are a Prince, & a father of people, who ought with „
the eye of wiſdome, the hand of fortitude, and the hart „
of iuſtice to ſet downe all priuate conceits, in compari- „
ſon of what for the publike is profitable. „

He would haue proceeded on, whē *Gynecia* came rū- 6
ning in amazed for her daughter *Pamela*, but mad for
Zelmane; & falling at *Baſilius* feet, beſought him to make
no delay: vſing ſuch geſtures of cōpaſſiō inſteed of ſtopped words, that *Baſilius*, otherwiſe enough tender minded, eaſily granted to raiſe the ſiege, which he ſaw dangerous to his daughters : but indeed more carefull for
Zelmane, by whoſe beſieged perſon, the poore old man
was ſtreightly beſieged: ſo as to rid him of the famine of
his minde, he went in ſpeed away; diſcharging his ſoul-
diors: only leauing the authority, as before, in *Philanax*
his

his hands, he himselfe went with *Gynecia* to a strong
Castle of his, where he took couseli how first to deliuer
Zelmane, whom he called the poore stranger, as though
onely Law of hospitalitie moued him; and for that purpose sent diuers messengers to trafficke with *Cecropia*.

CHAP. 20.

he sweete resistance of the true sisters ¹ *to the sower assaultes
of their false Aunt. The whipping of* ³Philoclea ⁵ *and* Pamela. ⁴*The patience of both* ⁶*and passions for their louers.*

Ecropia by this meanes rid of the
present daunger of the siege (desiring *Zoilus* and *Lycurgus* to take the
care, till their brother recouered, of
reuictualling, and furnishing the
Citie, both with men and what els
wanted, against any new occasion
should vrge them, she her selfe dis-
daining to harken to *Basilius*, without he would grant
his daughter in mariage to her son, which by no means
he would be brought vnto) bent all the sharpenesse of
her malicious wit, how to bring a comfortable graunt
to her sonne; whereupon she well found no lesse then
his life depended. Therfore for a while shie attēpted all
meanes of eloquent praying, and flattering perswasion,
mingling sometimes gifts, somtimes threatnings, as she
had cause to hope, that either open force, or vndermining, would best winn the castle of their Resolu tion And euer as much as she did to *Philoclea*, so much
did she to *Pamela*, though in manner sometimes differing

ring, as she found fit to leuell at the ones noble height,
and the others sweet lowlinesse. For though she knew
her sonnes harte had wholly giuen it selfe to *Philoclea*,
yet seeing the equall gifts in *Pamela*, she hoped, a faire
grant would recouer the sorrow of a faire refusal: cruelly entēding the present impoysoning the one, as soone
as the others affection were purchased.

But in vaine was all her vaine oratory employed.
Pamelaes determination was built vpō so braue a Rock,
that no shot of hers could reach vnto it : and *Philoclea*
(though humbly seated) was so inuironed with sweete
riuers of cleere vertue, as could neither be battred, nor
vndermined: her witty perswasions had wise answeres;
her eloquence recompenced with sweetnes;her threatnings repelled with disdaine in the one, & patience in
the other ; her gifts either not accepted, or accepted to
obey, but not to bind. So as *Cecropia* in nature violent;
cruel,because ambitious;hateful,for old rooted grudge
to their mother, & now spitefull because she could not
preuaile with girles,as she counted them;lastly,drawne
on by her loue to her son,& held vp by a tyrannical authoritie,forthwith followed the byas of her own crooked disposition,& doubling and redoubling her threatnings,fel to cōfirme some of her threatned effects : first
withdrawing al cōfort, both of seruāts, & seruice from
thē.But that those excellēt Ladies had bene vsed vnto,
cuē at home,& thē foūd in thēselues how much good
he hardnes of educatiō doth to the resistāce of misery.
Then dishonorably vsing them both in dyet,and lodging, by a contempt to pull downe their thoughts to
yeelding. But as before, the consideration of a prison
had disgraced al ornamēts,so now the same cōsideratiō
made

made thē attend al diſeaſetulnes. Then ſtil, as ſhe found thoſe not preuaile, would ſhe go forward with giuing them terrors, ſometimes with nōices of horror, ſometimes with ſuddaine frightings in the night, when the ſolitary darkeneſſe thereof might eaſier aſtoniſh the diſarmed ſenſes. But to all Vertue, and Loue reſiſted, ſtrengthned one by the other, when each found it ſelfe ouer-vehemently aſſaulted. *Cecropia* ſtill ſweetning her fierceneſſes with faire promiſes, if they would promiſe faire; that feeling euill, and ſeing a way far better, their minds might the ſooner be mollified. But they that could not taſte her behauiour, when it was pleaſing, indeed could worſe now, when they had loſt al taſte by her iniuries.

3　　She reſoluing all extremities, rather then faile of cō-queſt, purſued on her rugged way : letting no day paſſe, without new and new perplexing the poore Ladies minds, and troubling their bodies : and ſtill ſwelling, the more ſhe was ſtopped, and growing hot with her owne doings, at length, abhominable rage carried her to abſolute tyrānies, ſo that taking with her certaine olde women (of wicked diſpoſitions, and apt for enuie-ſake to be cruel to youth and beautie) with a countenācce impoyſoned with malice, flew to the ſweet *Phi*-*ſoclea*, as if ſo many Kites ſhould come about a white Doue, & matching violent geſtures with miſchieuous threatnings, ſhe hauing a rod in her hād (like a fury that ſhould carry wood to the burning of *Dianas* temple) fel to ſcourge that moſt beautifull body: Loue in vaine holding the ſhield of Beautie againſt her blind cruelty. The Son drew clouds vp to hide his face from ſo pitiful a ſight & the very ſtone wals did yeeld drops of ſweate

for

for agonie of such a mischiefe: each senselesse thing had
sense of pittie; onely they that had sense, were senseles.
Vertue rarely found her worldly weakenes more, then
by the oppression of that day: and weeping *Cupid* told
his weeping mother, that he was sorie he was not deaf,
as well as blind, that he might neuer know so lamentable a worke. *Philoclea*, with tearefull eyes, and sobbing
breast (as soon as her wearines rather then compassion,
gaue her respite) kneeled dowe to *Cecropia*, and making
pittie in her face honourable, and torment delightfull,
besought her, since she hated her (for what cause she
tooke God to witnesse she knew not) that she would at
once take away her life, and not please her self with the
tormenting of a poore Gentlewoman. If (said she) the
common course of humanitie cannot moue you, nor
the hauing me in your owne walles, cannot claime pittie: nor womanly mercie, nor neere alliance, nor remēbrance (how miserable so euer now) that I am a Princes
daughter; yet let the loue (you haue often tolde me)
your sonne beares me, so much procure, that for his
sake, one death may be thought inough for me; I haue
not liued so many yeares, but that one death may be a-
ble to conclude them: neither haue my faults, I hope,
bene so many, but that one death may satisfie them. It
is no great suite to an enemie, when but death is desired. I craue but that, and as for the graunting your request, know for certaine you lose your labours, being
euery day further of-minded from becōming his wife,
who vseth me like a slaue. But that in stead of getting
grace renued againe *Cecropias*, fury: so that (excellent
creature) she was newly again tormented by those hellish monsters: *Cecropia* vsing no other words, but that
she

she was a proud and vngratefull wench: and that she would teach her to know her owne good, since of her selfe she would not conceaue it.

4   So with silence and patience (like a faire gorgeous armour, hammered vpon by an ilfauoured Smith) she abode their pittiles dealing with her: till, rather reseruing her for more, then meaning to end, they left her to an vncomfortable leysure, to consider with her selfe her fortune; both helplesse her selfe, being a prisoner, and hopeles, since *Zelmane* was a prisoner: who therein onely was short of the bottome of miserie, that she knew not how vnworthilie her Angell, by these deuils was abused: but wanted (God wot) no stings of griefe, when those words did but strike vpon her hart, that *Philoclea* was a captiue, and she not able to succour her. For well she knew the confidence *Philoclea* had in her, and well she knew, *Philoclea* had cause to haue confidence: and all troden vnder foot by the wheele of

6   senseleffe Fortune. Yet if there be that imperious power in the soule, as it can deliuer knowledge to another, without bodilie organs; so vehement were the workings of their spirites, as one mette with other, though themselues perceaued it not, but only thought it to be the doubling of their owne louing fancies. And that was the onely worldly thing, whereon *Philoclea* rested her minde, that she knewe she should die beloued of *Zelmane*, and shoulde die, rather then be false to *Zelmane*. And so this most daintie Nimphe, easing the paine of her minde with thinking of anothers paine; and almost forgetting the paine of her bodie, through the paine of her minde, she wasted, euen longing for the conclusion of her tedious tra-

            ge-

gedie.

But for a while fhe was vnuifited, *Cecropia* employ-   5
ing her time in vfing the like crueltie vpon *Pamela*, her
harte growing not onely to defire the fruite of punifhing them, but euen to delight in the punifhing them.
But if euer the beames of perfection fhined through
the clowdes of affliction, if euer Vertue tooke a bodie to fhewe his (els vnconceaueable) beautie, it was
in *Pamela*. For when Reafon taught her there was no
refiftance, (for to iuft refiftance firft her harte was enclined) then with fo heauenly a quietnes, and fo gracefull a calmenes, did fhe fuffer the diuers kindes of torments they vfed to her, that while they vexed her
faire bodie, it feemed, that fhe rather directed, then
obeyed the vexation. And when *Cecropia* ended,
and asked whether her harte woulde yeelde: fhe a
little fmiled, but fuch a fmiling as fhewed no loue,
and yet coulde not but be louelie. And then, Beaftly woman (faide fhe) followe on, doo what thou
wilt, and canft vpon me: for I know thy power is
not vnlimited. Thou maift well wracke this fillie
bodie, but me thou canft neuer ouerthrowe. For
my part, I will not doo thee the pleafure to defire death
of thee : but affure thy felf, both my life and death, fhall
triumph with honour, laying fhame vpon thy detefta-
ble tyranny.

And fo; in effect, conquering their doing with her   4
fuffering, while *Cecropia* tried as many forts of paines,
as might rather vexe them, then fpoyle them (for that
fhe would not do while fhe were in any hope to winne
either of them for her fonne) *Pamela* remained almoft
as much content with triall in her felfe, what vertue
could

could doo, as grieued with the miserie wherein she found her selfe plunged: only sometimes her thoughts softned in her, when with open wings they flew to *Musidorus*. For then she would thinke with her selfe, how grieuously *Musidorus* would take this her miserie; and she, that wept not for her selfe, wept yet *Musidorus*-his teares, which he would weep for her. For gentle Loue did eaßier yeeld to lamentation, then the constancy of vertue would els admitte. Then would she remember the case wherein she had left her poore shepheard, and she that wished death for her self, feared death for him; and she that condemned in her selfe the feeblenes of sorrow, yet thought it great reason to be sory for his sorow: & she that long had prayed for the vertuous ioyning themselues together, now thinking to die herself, hartely prayed, that long time their fortunes might be seperated. Liue long my *Musidorus* (would she say) and let my name liue in thy mouth; in thy harte my memorie. Liue long, that thou mayst loue long the chast loue of thy dead *Pamela*. Then would she wish to her selfe, that no other woman might euer possesse his harte: and yet scarcely the wish was made a wish, when her selfe would finde fault with it, as being too vniust, that so excellent a man should be banished from the comfort of life. Then would she fortifie her resolution, with bethinking the worste, taking the counsell of vertue, and comfort of loue.

CHAP. 21.

1 Cecropias *indurate tyrannies.* 2 *Her deuise with the death of one to threaten another.* 3 Philoclea *threatned, persisteth.* 4 *The execution done in sight of* Philoclea *&* Zelmane. 5 Philocleas *sorrow for her sister.*

So

S O thefe diamonds of the worlde r whom Nature had made to be pre-cioufly fet in the eyes of her crea-tures, to be the chiefe workes of her workemanfhip, the chiefe or-naments of the worlde, and Prin-ceffes of felicitie, by rebellious in-iury were brought to the ytter-moft diftres that an enemies hart could wifh, or a wo-mans fpite inuent: *Cecropia* dayly in one or other forte punifhing thē, ftill with her euill torments giuing them feare of worfe, making the feare it felfe the forrieft tor-ment of all; that in the end wearie of their bodies they fhould be content to beftow them at her appointmēt. But as in labour, the more one doth exercife it, the more by the doing one is enabled to doo; ftrength growing vpō the worke, fo as what at firft would haue feemed impoffible, after growes eafie: fo thefe Prin-ceffes fecond to none, and far from any fecond, only to be matched by thēfelues, with the vfe of fuffering their minds gat the habit of fuffring fo, as all feares & terrors were to them but fummons to a battaile, whereof they knew before hād they would be victorious, & which in the fuffering was painfull, being fuffered, was a trophe to it felf: whereby *Cecropia* found her felf ftill farder of: for where at firft fhe might perchance haue perfwaded them to haue vifited her fonne, and haue giuen him fome comforte in his fickneffe, drawing neere to the cōfines of Deaths kingdome, now they protefted, that they would neuer otherwife fpeake to him, then as to the enemy, of moft vniuft cruelty towards them, that a-ny time or place could euer make them know.

This made the poifon fwell in her cankred breft, perceiuing that (as in water) the more fhe grafped the leffe fhe held: but yet now hauing run fo long the way of rigour, it was too late in reafon, and too contrary to her paffion, to returne to a courfe of meekeneffe. And therefore (taking counfell of one of her olde affociates who fo far excelled in wickedneffe as that fhe had not onely loft all feeling of confcience, but had gotten a very glory in euill) in the ende they determined, that beating, and other fuch fharp dealing did not fo much pull downe a womans harte, as it bred anger, and that nothing was more enemy to yeelding, then anger; making their téder harts take on the armour of obftinacy: (for thus did their wicked mindes blind to the light of vertue, & owly eied in the night of wickednes interpret of it) & that therfore that was no more to be tried. And for feare of death (which no queftion would doo moft with them) they had bene fo often threatened, as they began to be familiarly acquainted with it, and learned to efteeme threatning wordes to be but words. Therefore the laft, but beft way now was, that the one feing indeede the others death, fhould perceiue, there was no dallying meant: and then there was no doubt, that a womans foule would do much, rather then leaue fo beautifull a body.

This being concluded, *Cecropia* went to *Philoclea*, and tolde her, that now fhe was to come to the laft parte of the play: for her part, though fhe found her hard harted obftinacie fuch, that neither the fweetneffe of louing meanes, nor the force of harde meancs could preuaile with her, yet before fhe would paffe to a further degree of extremity; fhe had fought to win her fifter; in hope, that

that her ſonne might be with time ſatisfied with the
loue of ſo faire a Lady: but finding her alſo rather more
then leſſe wilful,ſhe was now minded that one of their
deathes ſhould ſerue for an example to the other, that
deſpiſing worthy folks was more hurtfull to the deſpi-
ſer,then the deſpiſed: that yet becauſe her ſonne eſpeci- ”
ally affected her,& that in her owne ſelfe ſhe was more
inclinable to pittie her,thē ſhe had deſerued,ſhe would
begin with her ſiſter;who that afternoone ſhould haue
her head cut of before her face;if in the mean time one
of them,did not pull out their il-wrought ſtiches of vnkindnes,ſhe bad her looke for no other, nor lōger time
thē ſhe told her. There was no aſſault giuē to the ſweet
Philoclea mind, that entered ſo far,as this: for where to
all paines and daungers of her ſelfe,foreſight with (his
Lieutenant Reſolution)had made ready defence; now
with the loue ſhe bare her ſiſter, ſhe was driuen to a
ſtay, before ſhe determined : but long ſhe ſtaied not,
before this reaſon did ſhine vnto her, that ſince in her
ſelfe ſhe preferred death-before ſuch a baſe ſeruitude,
loue did teach her to wiſh the ſame to her ſiſter. Therefore croſſing her armes, & looking ſideward vpon the
groūd,Do what you wil(ſaid ſhe)with vs:for my part,
heauen ſhall melt before I be remoued. But if you will
follow my counſell,for your owne ſake(for as for praiers for my ſake I haue felt how little they preuaile) let
my death firſt ſerue for example to win her, who perchaunce is not ſo reſolued againſt *Amphialus*, and ſo
ſhall you not onely iuſtly puniſh me (who indeede
doo hate both you and your ſonne) but , if that may
mooue you, you ſhall doo more vertuouſly in preſeruing one moſt worthy of life, and killing an other

Vu 2   moſt

moſt deſirous of death : laſtly in winning her, in ſteed
of a peeuiſh vnhappie creature, that I am, you ſhall
bleſſe your ſonne with the moſt excellent woman in
all praiſe - worthy thinges, that the worlde holdeth.
But *Cecropia*, (who had already ſet downe to her ſelfe
what ſhe would do) with bitter both termes, & countenaunce, told her, that ſhe ſhould not neede to woo
death ouer-egerly: for if her ſiſter going before her did
not teach her witt, herſelfe ſhould quickly follow. For
ſince they were not to be gotten, there was no way
for her ſonnes quiet, but to know, that they were paſt
getting. And ſo ſince no intreating, nor threatning
might preuayle, ſhe bad her prepare her eies for a new
play, which ſhe ſhould ſee within fewe houres in the
hall of that caſtle.

4   A place indeed ouerfit for ſo vnfit a matter: for being ſo ſtately made that the bottome of it being euen
with the grounde, the roofe reached as hie as any part
of the caſtle, at either ende it had conuenient lodge-
ings. In the one end was (one ſtorie from the ground)
Philoclea abode, in the other of euen height, *Pamelas*,
and *Zelmanes* in a chamber aboue her: but all ſo vaulted
of ſtrong, and thickly built ſtone, as one could no way
heare the other: each of theſe chambers had a litle windowe to looke into the hall, but becauſe the ſiſters
ſhould not haue ſo much comforte, as to looke out to
one another, there was (of the outſides) curtaynes
drawne, which they could not reach with their hands,
ſo barring the reach of their ſight. But when the houre
came that the Tragedie ſhould beginne, the curtaynes
were withdrawen from before the windowes of *Zel-*
mane, and of *Philoclea*: a ſufficient challenge to call their
eyes

eyes to defende themſelues in ſuch an incounter. And by and by came in at one ende of the hall, with about a dozen armed ſouldiers a Ladie, led by a couple, with her handes bounde before her: from aboue her eyes to her lippes muffled with a faire kerchiefe, but from her mouth to the ſhoulders all bare: and ſo was led on to a ſcaffold raiſed a good deale from the floore, and all couered with crimſin veluet. But neither *Zelmane*, nor *Philoclea* needed to be tolde, who ſhe was: for the apparell ſhe ware made them too well aſſured, that it was the admirable *Pamela*. Whereunto the rare whiteneſſe of her naked necke gaue ſufficient teſtimonie to their aſtonniſhed ſenſes. But the fayre Ladie being come to the ſcaffold, and then made to kneele downe, and ſo lefte by her vnkinde ſupporters, as it ſeemed that ſhe was about to ſpeake ſomewhat (whereunto *Philoclea*, poore ſoule, earneſtly liſtned, according to her ſpeach euen minded to frame her minde, her harte neuer till then almoſt wauering to ſaue her ſiſters life) before the vnfortunate Ladie could pronounce three wordes, the executioner cutt of the ones ſpeech, and the others attention, with making his ſworde doo his cruell office vpon that beautifull necke. Yet the pittileſſe ſworde had ſuch pittie of ſo pretious an obiect, that at firſt it did but hitte flat long. But litle auailed that, ſince the Ladie falling downe aſtonniſhed withall, the cruell villayne forced the ſworde with another blowe to diuorce the faire marriage of the head and body.

And this was done ſo in an inſtant, that the very act did ouerrun *Philocleas* ſorrow (ſorrow not being able ſo quickly to thunderbolte her harte thorough her

ſenſes

senses, but firſt onely oppreſt her with a ſtorme of a-
mazement)but when her eies ſaw that they did ſee, as
condemning themſelues to haue ſeene it,they became
weary of their owne power of ſeing : & her ſoule then
drinking vp woe with great draughts, ſhe fel downe to
deadly traüces:but her waiting iaylors with cruell pitty
brought lothed life vnto her; which yet many times
tooke his leaue as though he would indeed depart:but
when he was ſtaied by force, he kept with him deadly
Sorrow, which thus exerciſed her mourning ſpeech.
Pamela my ſiſter, my ſiſter *Pamela*,woe is me for thee,I
would I had died for thee. *Pamela* neuer more ſhall I
ſee thee:neuer more ſhall I enioy thy ſweet companie,
and wiſe counſell. Alas, thou arte gone to beautifie
heauen, and haſte thou lefte me here, who haue nothing good in me, but that I did euer loue thee, and
euer will lament thee? Let this day be noted of all
vertuous folkes for moſt vnfortunate : let it neuer be
mentioned,but among curſes; and curſed be they that
did this miſchiefe, and moſt accurſed be mine eyes
that behelde it. Sweete *Pamela*;that head is ſtriken of,
where onely wiſedome might be ſpoken withall; that
bodie is deſtroied,which was the liuing booke of vertue. Deare *Pamela*, how haſte thou lefte me to all
wretchedneſſe, and miſerie? Yet while thou liuedſt,
in thee I breathed, of thee I hoped. O *Pamela*,how
much did I for thy excellencie honour thee,more then
my mother, and loue thee more then my ſelfe? Neuer more ſhall I lie with thee : neuer more ſhall we
bathe in the pleaſant riuer together : neuer more ſhall
I ſee thee in thy ſhephearde apparell. But thou arte
gone,and where am I? *Pamela* is dead;and liue I? My
God

God, And with that fhe fell againe in a foune, fo as it
was a great while before they could bring her to her
felfe againe; but being come to her-felfe, Alas (faid
fhe) vnkind women,fince you haue giuen me fo many
deathes, torment me not now with life: for Gods fake
let me goe,and excufe your hands of more blood. Let
me follow my *Pamela*, whom euer I fought to follow.
Alas *Pamela*, they will not let me come to thee. But if
they keepe promife, I fhall treade thine owne fteppes
after thee. For to what am I borne (miferable foule)
but to be moft vnhappie in my felfe, and yet more vnhappie in others? But ô that a thoufand more miferies had happened vnto me, fo thou haddeft not dyed:
Pamela, my fifter *Pamela*. And fo, like lamentable *Philomela*, complained fhe the horrible wrong done to her
fifter, which if it ftird not in the wickedly clofed minds
of her tormentors,a pittie of her forrow, yet bredde it
a wearineffe of her forrow : fo as onely leauing one to
preuent any harme fhe fhould doo her felfe, the reft
went away, confulting againe with *Cecropia*, how to
make profite of this their late bloodie act.

CHAP. 22.

Cecropias *pollicie to vfe* Zelmanes *interceſsion.* [2] Zelmanes *felfe-conflict.* [3] *Her motion to* Philoclea *rather to diffemble then dye.* [4] Philocleas *refolution rather to dye then
diffemble.* [5] *At fight of* Philocleas *head* Zelmanes *ex-
tafies,* [7] *defperate defeignes,* [8] *and comfortleffe complaints.*

IN the ende, that woman that vſed moſt to keep company with *Zelmane*, told *Cecropia*, that ſhe founde by many moſt ſenſible proofes in *Zelmane*, that there was neuer woman ſo loued another, as ſhe loued *Philoclea*: which was the cauſe that ſhe (further then the commandement of *Cecropia*) had cauſed *Zelmanes* curtaines to be alſo drawne: becauſe hauing the ſame ſpectacle that *Philoclea* had, ſhe might ſtand in the greater feare for her, whom ſhe loued ſo wel: and that indeed ſhe had hit the needle in that deuiſe: for neuer ſaw ſhe creature ſo aſtoniſhed as *Zelmane*, exceedingly ſory for *Pamela*, but exceedingly exceeding that exceedingnes in feare for *Philoclea*. Therefore her aduice was, ſhe ſhould cauſe *Zelmane* to come and ſpeake with *Philoclea*. For there being ſuch vehemencie of friendſhip between them, it was both likely to moue *Zelmane* to perſwade, and *Philoclea* to be perſwaded. *Cecropia* liked wel of the counſell, and gaue order to the ſame woman to go deale therein with *Zelmane*, and to aſſure her with othe, that *Cecropia* was determined *Philoclea* ſhould paſſe the ſame way that *Pamela* had done, without ſhe did yeeld to ſatiſſie the extremitie of her ſonnes affection: which the woman did, adding thervnto many (as ſhe thought) good reaſons to make *Zelmane* thinke *Amphialus* a fit match for *Philoclea*.

But *Zelmane* (who had from time to time vnderſtood the cruell dealing they had vſed to the ſiſters, & now had her own eies wounded with the ſight of ones death) was ſo confuſed withall (her courage ſtill rebelling againſt her wit, deſiring ſtill with force to doo impoſſible

poſſible matters) that as her deſire was ſtopped with power, ſo her cōceit was darkned with a miſt of deſire. For blind Loue,& inuincible valure ſtil would cry out, that it could not be, *Philoclea* ſhould be in ſo miſerable eſtate, and ſhe not relieue her : and ſo while ſhe haled her wit to her courage, ſhe drew it from his owne limits. But now *Philocleas* death (a word able to marſhall al his thoughts in order) being come to ſo ſhort a point either with ſmal delay to be ſuffred,or by the giuing her ſelfe to another to be preuented,ſhe was driué to think, and to deſire ſome leaſure of thinking : which the woman granted for that night vnto her. A night that was not halfe ſo blacke, as her mind; not halfe ſo ſilent, as was fit for her muſing thoughts. At laſt, he that would faine haue deſperatly loſt a thouſand liues for her ſake, could not finde in his harte, that ſhe ſhould looſe any life for her owne ſake; and he that deſpiſed his owne death in reſpect of honour, yet could well nye diſpenſe with honor it ſelf in reſpect of *Philocleas* death:for once the thought could not enter into his harte, nor the breath iſſue out of his mouth, which could conſent to *Philocleas* death for any bargaine.Then how to preuent the next degree to death (which was her being poſſeſt by another) was the point of his minds labour : and in that he found no other way, but that *Philoclea* ſhould pretend a yeelding vnto *Cecropias* requeſt;& ſo by ſpeaking with *Amphialus*, and making faire(but delaying) promiſes,procure libertie for *Zelmane*, who onely wiſht but to come by a ſword, not doubting then to deſtroy them all,and deliuer *Philoclea*:ſo little did both the mē, and their forces ſeeme in her eyes, looking downe vpon them from the hye toppe of affections tower.

With

3 With that minde therefore(but firſt wel bound)ſhe was brought to *Philoclea*, hauing alredy plotted out in her cōceite, how ſhe would deale with her:& ſo came ſhe with hart and eyes, which did each ſacrifice either to Loue vpon the aultar of Sorrow : and there had ſhe the pleaſing diſpleaſing ſight of *Philoclea:Philoclea*,who alredie the extreame ſenſe of ſorrow had brought to a dulneſſe therin, her face not without tokens that beautie had bene by many miſeries cruelly battered,& yet ſhewed it moſt the perfection of the beautie, which could remaine vnouerthrowne by ſuch enimies. But whē *Zelmane* was ſet downe by her,& the womē gone away (becauſe ſhe might be the better perſwaded whē no body was by, that had heard her ſay ſhe would not be perſwaded) then began firſt the eyes to ſpeake, and the harts to crie out : Sorrow a while would needes ſpeake his owne language without vſing their tongues to be his interpreters. At laſt *Zelmane* brake ſilence, but ſpake with the onely eloquence of amazement : for all her long methodized oration was inherited onely by ſuch kinde of ſpeeches. Deare Ladie, in extreame neceſſities we muſt not. But alas vnfortunate wretch that I am, that I liue to ſee this day. And I take heauen and earth to witneſſe,that nothing : and with that her breſt ſwelled ſo with ſpite and griefe,that her breath had not leaſure to turne her ſelfe into words.But the ſweet *Philoclea* that had alredie dyed in *Pamela*, and of the other ſide had the heauines of her hart ſomthing quickned in the moſt beloued ſight of *Zelmane*, gheſſed ſomewhat at *Zelmanes* minde; and therefore ſpake vnto her in this ſort. My *Pyrocles* (ſaid ſhe) I know this exceeding comfort of your preſence, is not brought vnto me for any

good

good-will that is owed vnto me : but (as I suppose) to make you perswade me to saue my life with the ransome of mine honour:although no bodie should be so vnfit a pleader in that cause,as your selfe,yet perchance you would haue me liue. Your honour? God forbid (said *Zelmane*)that euer,for any cause,I should yeeld to any touch of it. But a while to pretend some affection, til time, or my libertie might worke somthing for your seruice : this, if my astonished senses would giue me leaue, I would faine haue perswaded you.

To what purpose my *Pyrocles?* (said *Philoclea*) of a miserable time what gaine is there? hath *Pamelaes* example wrought no more in me? is a captiue life so much worth? cā euer it goe out of these lips,that I loue any other but *Pyrocles?* shal my tongue be so false a traitor to my hart, as to say I loue any other but *Pyrocles?* And why should I do all this? to liue? O *Pamela*, sister *Pamela*, why should I liue? onely for thy sake *Pyrocles* I would liue : but to thee I know too well I shal not liue; and if not to thee, hath thy loue so base allay, my *Pyrocles*,as to wish me to liue?for dissimulation,my *Pyrocles*, my simplicitie is such , that I haue hardly bene able to keepe a straight way; what shall I doo in a crooked? But in this case there is no meane of dissimulation, not for the cunningest : present answere is required, and present performance vpon the answere. Art thou so terrible,ô Death? No my *Pyrocles* ; and for that I doo thanke thee, and in my soule thanke thee ; for I confesse the loue of thee is heerein my chiefest vertue. Trouble me not therefore, deare *Pyrocles*, nor double not my death by tormenting my resolution:since I cannot liue with thee, I wil dye for thee.

Onely

Onely remember me deare *Pyrocles* ; and loue the remembrance of me : and if I may craue ſo much of thee, let me be thy laſt loue, for though I be not worthy of thee (who indeed art the worthieſt creature liuing) yet remember that my loue was a worthy loue. But *Pyrocles* was ſo ouercome with ſorrow (which wiſdome & vertue made iuſt in ſo excellent a Ladies caſe, ful of ſo excellēt kindnes) that words were aſhamed to come forth knowing how weake they were to expreſſe his mind, & her merit : and therfore ſo ſtayed in a deadly ſilence, forſaken of hope, & forſaking comfort : till the appointed gardians came in, to ſee the fruits of *Zelmanes* labour : & then *Zelmane* warned by their preſence, fel againe to perſwade, though ſcarcely her ſelfe could tell what ; but in ſum, deſirous of delayes. But *Philoclea* ſweetly continuing cōſtant, & in the end puniſhing her importunity with ſilence, *Zelmane* was faine to ende. Yet crauing another times cōference, ſhe obtained it, & diuers others ; till at the laſt *Cecropia* found it was to no purpoſe, and therfore determined to follow her owne way. *Zelmane* yet ſtil deſirous to win (by any meanes) reſpit, euen waſted with ſorrow, & vncertaine, whether in worſe caſe in her preſēce, or abſence, being able to do nothing for *Philocleas* ſuccour, but by ſubmitting the greateſt corage of the earth to fall at the feete of *Cecropia*, and craue ſtay of their ſentence till the vttermoſt was ſeene, what her perſwaſions might doo.

5   *Cecropia* ſeemed much to be moued by her importunitie, ſo as diuers dayes were wonne of painefull life to the excellent *Philoclea* : while *Zelmane* ſuffred ſome hope to cherriſh her mind, eſpecially truſting vpon the helpe of *Muſidorus*, who (ſhe knew) would not be idle in this matter :

matter,till one morning a noife awaked *Zelmane*,from
whofe ouer-watchfull mind,the tired body had ftolne
a little fleep : and ftreight with the firft opening of her
eyes , Care taking the woonted place,fhe ranne to the
window which looked into the hall (for that way the
noife guided her,)and there might fhe fee (the curtaine
being lett open euer fince the laft execution) feuen or
eight perfons in a clufter vpon the fcaffold : who by &
by retiring themfelues, nothing was to be feene there-
vpon, but a bafon of golde, pitifully enameled with
bloud, and in the midft of it,the head of the moft beautifull *Philoclea*. The horriblenes of the mifchiefe was
fuch , as *Pyrocles* could not at firft beleeue his own fenfes, but bent his woful eyes to difcerne it better:where
too well he might fee it was *Philocleas* felfe , hauing no
veile,but beautie, ouer the face,which ftill appeared to
be aliue : fo did thofe eyes fhine , euen as they were
wont,and they were woont more then any other : and
fometimes as they moued , it might well make the beholder think,that death therin had borowed their beutie, and not they any way difgraced by death : fo fweet
and pearfing a grace they caried with them.

It was not a pitie, it was not an amazement , it was
not a forow which then laid holde on *Pyrocles* , but a
wilde furie of defperate agonie, fo that he cried out, O
tyraunt heauen, traytor earth , blinde prouidence; no
iuftice, how is this done? how is this fuffered? hath
this world a gouernment? If it haue,let it poure out all
his mifchiefes vpon me,and fee whether it haue power
to make me more wretched then I am . Did fhe excell
for this? haue I prayed for this? abhominable hande
that did it;deteftable deuil that commaunded it;curfed
light

light that beheld it: and if the light be curſed, what are then mine eyes that haue ſeene it? And haue I ſeen *Philoclea* dead, and doo I liue? and haue I liued, not to help her, but to talke of her? and ſtande I ſtill talking? And with that (caried with the madnes of anguiſh, not hauing a redier way to kill himſelfe) he rannc as hard as euer he could, with his head againſt the wall, with intention to braine himſelf: but the haſte to doo it, made the doing the ſlower. For, as he came to giue the blow, his foot tript, ſo as it came not with the full force: yet forcible inough to ſtrike him downe, and withall, to depriue him of his ſenſe, ſo that he lay a while, comforted by the hurt, in that he felte not his diſcomfort.

7 And when he came againe to himſelfe, he heard, or he thought he heard a voice, which cried, Reuége, Reuenge; whether indeed it were his good Angell, which vſed that voice to ſtay him from vnnaturall murdering of him ſelfe; or that his wandering ſpirites lighted vpon that conceite, and by their weakenes (ſubiect to apprehenſions) ſuppoſed they heard it. But that indeed, helped with Vertue, and her valiant ſeruant Anger, ſtopped him from preſent deſtroying him ſelfe: yeelding, in reaſon and manhoode, firſt to deſtroy, man, woman, and childe, that were any way of kinne to them that were acceſſarie to this crueltie; then to raze the Caſtle, and to builde a ſumptuous monument for her ſiſter, and a moſt ſumptuous for her ſelfe; and then, himſelfe to die vpon her tomb. This determining in himſelfe to do, and to ſeeke all meanes how (for that purpoſe) to get out of priſon: he was content a while to beare the thirſt of death: and yet went he againe to the windowe, to kiſſe the beloued head

with

with his eies, but there saw he nothing but the scaffold,
all couered ouer with skarlet, and nothing but solitarie
silence, to mourn this mischiefe. But then, Sorrow hauing disperste it selfe from his harte, in all his noble
partes, it proclaimed his authoritie, in cries, and teares,
and with a more gentle dolefulnes, could poure out his
inward euill.

Alas (said he) and is that head taken away too, so   **8**
soone from mine eyes ? What, mine eyes, perhappes
they enuie the excellencie of your sorrow ? Indeede,
there is nothing now left to become the eyes of all mākind, but teares: and wo be to me, if any exceede me in
wofulnes. I do coniure you all, my senses, to accept no
obiect, but of Sorow: be ashamed, nay, abhor to thinke
of comfort. Vnhappie eyes, you haue seene too much,
that euer the light should be welcome to you : vnhappie eares, you shall neuer heare the musicke of Musicke
in her voice: vnhappie harte, that hast liued to feel these
pangues. Thou hast done thy worst, World, & curfed
be thou, and cursed art thou, since to thine owne selfe
thou hast done the worst thou couldest doo. Exiled
Beautie, let onely now thy beautie be blubbered faces.
Widowed Musick, let now thy tunes be rorings, and
lamentations. Orphane Vertue, get thee winges, and
flie after her into heauen ; here is no dwelling place for
thee. Why liued I, alas? Alas why loued I ? to die wretched, and to be the example of the heauens hate? And
hate, & spare not, for your worst blow is striken. Sweet
Philoclea, thou art gone, and hast caried with thee my
loue ; & hast thy loue in me, & I wretched mā do liue; I
liue, to die cōtinually, till thy reuenge do giue me leaue
to dy: & then dy I will, my *Philoclea*, my hart willinglie
                                                    makes

makes this promise to it selfe . Surely he did not looke vpon thee, that gaue the cruell blow:for no eye coulde haue abidden to see such beautie ouerthrowen by such mischiefe. Alas, why should they diuide such a head from such a bodie ？ no other bodye is worthy of that head; no other head is woorthie of that body : O yet, if I had taken my last leaue, if I might haue taken a holie kisse from that dying mouth . Where art thou Hope which promisest neuer to leaue a mã while he liueth ？ Tell me , what canst thow hope for ？ nay tel me , what is there which I would willingly hope after？ Wishing power (which is accounted infinite) what now is left to wish for ？ She is gone,and gone with her all my hope , all my wishing . Loue,be ashamed to be called Loue: cruell Hate , vnspeakeable Hate is victori-ous ouer thee . Who is there now left, that can iustifie thy tyrannie , and giue reason to thy passion ？ O cruell diuorce of the sweetest mariage that euer was in Na-ture : *Philoclea* is dead , and dead is with her all good-nesse , all sweetnesse , all excellencie . *Philoclea* is dead, and yet Life is not ashamed to cõtinue vpon the earth. *Philoclea* is dead: O deadly word; which containeth in it selfe the vttermost of all misfortunes . But happie worde when thou shalt be said of me , and long it shall not be,before it be said.

CHAP. 17.

[1] *A Ladies kinde comforts to* Pyrocles *comfortlesse vnkind-nesse.* [2] *His hardly knowing her.* [3] *Her vnmasking of* Cecropias *fruitlesse sophistrie.* [4] *Their medley of so-lace and sorowe.*

Then

Hen ſtopping his woordes with ſighes, drowning his ſighes in teares, & drying againe his teares in rage, he would ſitte a while in a wandring muſe, which repreſented nothing but vexations vnto him: then throwing himſelfe ſomtimes vpon the floore, and ſometimes vpon the bedde: then vp againe, till walking was weariſome, and reſt loathſome: and ſo neither ſuffering foode, nor ſleepe to helpe his afflicted nature, all that day and night he did nothing, but weepe *Philoclea*, ſigh *Philoclea*, and crie out *Philoclea*: till as it happened (at that time vpon his bed) towarde the dawning of the day, he heard one ſtirre in his chamber, by the motion of garméts; and he with an angry voice asked, Who was there? A poore Gentlewoman (anſwered the partie) that wiſh long life vnto you. And I ſoone death to you (ſaid he) for the horrible cnrſe you haue giuen me. Certainely (ſaid ſhe) an vnkinde anſwere, and far vnworthy the excellencie of your mind; but not vnſutable to the reſt of your behauiour. For moſt parte of this night I haue hearde you (being let into your chamber, you neuer perceiuing it, ſo was your minde eſtraunged from your ſenſes) and haue hearde nothing of *Zelmane*, in *Zelmane*, nothing but weake waylings, fitter for ſome nurſe of a village, then ſo famous a creature as you are. O God (cried out *Pyrocles*) that thou wert a man that vſeſt theſe wordes vnto me. I tell thee I am ſory: I tell thee I will be ſory in deſpite of thee, and all them that would haue me ioyfull. And yet (replied ſhe) perchaunce *Philoclea* is not

X x   dead,

dead, whom you so much bemone. I would we were both dead of that condition, said *Pyrocles*. See the folly of your passion (said she) as though you should be neerer to her, you being dead, and she aliue; then she being dead, & you aliue: & if she be dead, was she not borne to die? what then do you crie out for? not for her, who must haue died one time or other; but for some fewe yeares: so as it is time, & this world that seeme so louely things, and not *Philoclea* vnto you. O noble Sisters (cried *Pyrocles*) now you be gone (who were the onely exalters of all womankind) what is left in that sex, but babling, and businesse? And truly (said she) I will yet a little longer trouble you. Nay, I pray you doo (said *Pyrocles*) for I wishe for nothing in my shorte life, but mischiefes, and combers: and I am content you shall be one of them. In truth (said she) you would thinke your selfe a greatly priuiledged person, if since the strongest buildings, and lastingest monarchies are subiect to end, onely your *Philoclea* (becaufe she is yours) should be exempted. But indeede you bemone your selfe, who haue lost a friende: you cannot her, who hath in one act both preferued her honour, and lefte the miseries of this worlde. O womans philosophie, childish follie (said *Pyrocles*) as though if I do bemone my selfe, I haue not reason to doo so, hauing lost more then any Monarchie, nay then my life can be wooth vnto me. Alas (said she) comforte your selfe, Nature did not forget her skill, when she had made them: you shall find many their superiours, and perchaunce such, as (when your eyes shall looke abroad) your selfe will like better.

2 But that speech put all good maners out of the conceit

ceit of *Pyrocles*;in so much, that leaping out of his bed,
he ran to haue striken her: but comming neere her(the
morning then winning the field of darkenesse)he saw,
or he thought he sawe, indeede, the very face of *Philoclea*; the same sweetenesse, the same grace, the same
beautie : with which carried into a diuine astonishment, he fell downe at her feete. Most blessed Angell
(said he) well haste thou done to take that shape, since
thou wouldest submit thy selfe to mortall sense; for a
a more Angelicall forme could not haue bene created
for thee. Alas, euen by that excellent beautie, so beloued of me, let it be lawfull for me to aske of thee,
what is the cause, that she, that heauenly creature,
whose forme you haue taken, should by the heauens
be destined to so vnripe an ende? Why should vniustice so preuaile? Why was she seene to the world, so
soone to be rauished from vs? Why was she not suffered to liue,to teach the world perfection? Doo not deceiue thy selfe (answered she) I am no Angell; I am
Philoclea, the same *Philoclea*, so truely louing you, so
truly beloued of you. If it be so (said he) that you are
indeede the soule of *Philoclea.*, you haue done well to
keepe your owne figure: for no heauen could haue giuen you a better. Then alas, why haue you taken the
paines to leaue your blisfull seat to come to this place
most wretched, to me, who am wretchednes it selfe,&
not rather obtain for me,that I might come where you
are,there eternally to behold, & eternally to loue your
beauties? you know (I know) that I desire nothing but
death, which I only stay, to be iustly reuenged of your
vniust murtherers.Deare *Pyrocles*(said she)I am thy *Philoclea*,and as yet liuing: not murdred, as you supposed,

and therefore to be comforted. And with that gaue
him her hand. But the sweet touch of that hande, seemed to his astraied powers so heauenly a thing, that it
rather for a while confirmed him in his former beliefe:
till she, with vehement protestations (and desire that
it might be so, helping to perswade that it was so)
brought him to yeeld; yet doubtfully to yeelde to this
height of al comfort, that *Philoclea* liued: which witnes-
sing with the teares of ioy, Alas (said he) how shall I
beleeue mine eies any more? or doo you yet but appeare thus vnto me, to stay me from some desperate
end? For alas I sawe the excellent *Pamela* beheaded: I
saw your head (the head indeede, and chiefe parte of
all natures workes) standing in a dishe of golde, too
meane a shrine (God wote) for such a relike. How can
this be, my onely deare, and you liue? or if this be not
so, how can I beleeue mine owne senses? and if I can
not beleeue the, why should I now beleeue these blessed tidings they bring me?

3   The truth is (said she) my *Pyrocles*, that nether I (as you
finde) nor yet my deare sister is dead: although the mis-
chieuously suttle *Cecropia* vsed slightes to make either
of vs thinke so of other. For, hauing in vaine attempted the fardest of her wicked eloquence, to make eyther of vs yeeld to her sonne, and seeing that neither it,
accompanied with great flatteries, and riche presents,
could get any grounde of vs, nor yet the violent way
she fell into of crueltie, tormenting our bodies, could
preuayle with vs; at last, she made either of vs thinke
the other dead, and so hoped to haue wrested our
mindes to the forgetting of vertue: and first she gaue
to mine eyes the miserable spectacle of my sisters (as

I

I thought) death : but indeede not my fifter : it was onely *Artefia*, fhe who fo cunningly brought vs to this mifery. Truly I am fory for the poore Gentlewoman, though iuftly fhe be punifhed for her double falfhood : but *Artefia* muffled fo, as you could not eafily difcerne her ; and in my fifters apparell (which they had taken from her vnder colour of giuing her other) did they execute : And when I (for thy fake efpecially deare *Pyrocles*) could by no force, nor feare be won, they affayed the like with my fifter, by bringing me downe vnder the fcaffolde, and (making me thruft my head vp through a hole they had made therin) they did put about my poore necke a difhe of gold, whereout they had beaten the bottome, fo as hauing fet bloud in it, you fawe how I played the parte of death (God knowes euen willing to haue done it in earneft) and fo had they fet me, that I reached but on tiptoes to the grounde, fo as fcarcely I could breathe, much leffe fpeake : And truely if they had kepte me there any whit longer, they had ftrangled me, in fteed of beheading me : but then they tooke me away, and feeking to fee their iffue of this practife, they found my noble fifter (for the deare loue fhe vouchfafeth to beare me) fo grieued withall, that fhe willed them to doo their vttermoft crueltie vnto her : for fhe vowed, neuer to receiue fuftenaunce of them, that had bene the caufers of my murther : and finding both of vs, euen giuen ouer, not like to liue many houres longer, and my fifter *Pamela*, rather worfe then my felfe, (the ftrength of her harte worfe bearing thofe indignities) the good woman *Cecropia* (with the fame pittie as folkes keepe foule, when they are not fatte inough for

their

their eating)made vs know her deceipt, & let vs come
one to another; with what ioye you can well imagine,
who I know feele the like, sauing that we only thought
our selues reserued to miseries, and therefore fitter for
condoling, then congratulating. For my parte, I am
fully perswaded, it is but with a little respite, to haue a
more feeling sense of the tormentes she prepares for
vs. True it is, that one of my guardians would haue
me to beleeue, that this proceedes of my gentle cousin
Amphialus: who hauing hearde some inckling that
we were euill entreated, had called his mother to his
bedside, from whence he neuer rose since his last combat, and besought, & charged her vpon all the loue she
bare him, to vse vs with all kindnesse: vowing, with all
the imprecations he could imagine, that if euer he vnderstood for his sake, that I receiued further hurt then
the want of my libertie, he woulde not liue an houre
longer. And the good woman sware to me that he
would kill his mother, if he knewe how I had bene
dealte with; but that *Cecropia* keepes him from vnderstanding thinges how they passe, onely hauing heard
a whispering, and my selfe named, he had (of aboun-
daunce, forsooth, of honorable loue) giuen this charge
for vs. Whereupon this enlargement of mine was
growne: for my parte I know too well their cunning
(who leaue no mony vnoffered that may buy mine
honour) to beleeue any worde they say, but (my
deare *Pyrocles*) euen looke for the worste, and prepare
my selfe for the same. Yet I must confesse, I was content to robbe from death, and borrowe of my misery
the sweet comfort of-seeing my sweet sister, and moste
sweete comforte of thee my *Pyrocles*. And so hauing
leaue,

leaue, I came ftealing into your chamber : where
(O Lord) what a ioy it was vnto me, to heare you fo-
lemnife the funerals of the poore *Philoclea*? That I
my felfe might liue to heare my death bewailed? and
by whom? by my deere *Pyrocles*. That I faw death
was not ftrong enough to diuide thy loue from me?
O my *Pyrocles*, I am too well paide for my paines I
haue fuffred : ioyfull is my woe for fo noble a caufe;
and welcome be all miferies, fince to thee I am fo
welcome. Alas how I pittied to heare thy pittie of me;
and yet a great while I could not finde in my hart to interrupt thee, but often had euen pleafure to weepe
with thee : and fo kindly came forth thy lamentations,
that they inforced me to lament to, as if indeed I had
beene a looker on, to fee poore *Philoclea* dye. Til at laft I
fpake with you, to try whether I could remoue thee fró
forrow, till I had almoft procured my felfe a beating.

And with that fhe pretily fmiled, which, mingled 4
with her teares, one could not tell whether it were a
mourning pleafure, or a delightful forrow: but like whé
a few Aprill drops are fcattered by a gentle *Zephyrus* a-
mong fine coloured flowers. But *Pyrocles*, who had felt
(with fo fmal diftáce of time) in himfelf the ouerthrow
both of hope and defpaire, knew not to what key he
fhould tune his mind, either of ioy, or forrow. But finding perfite reafon in neither, fuffred himfelfe to be caried by the tide of his imagination, & his imaginations
to be raifed euen by the fway, which hearing or feing,
might giue vnto thé: he faw her aliue, he was glad to fee
her aliue: he faw her weep, he was fory to fee her weep:
he heard her cófortable fpeeches, nothing more glad-
fome: he hard her prognofticating her own deftrució,
nothing

nothing more dolefull. But when he had a little taken breath from the panting motion of such contrarietie in paffions, he fell to confider with her of her prefent eftate, both comforting her, that certainely the worft of this ftorme was paft, fince alreadie they had done the worft, which mans wit could imagine: and that if they had determined to haue killed her, they would haue now done it: and alfo earneftly counfelling her, and inhabling his counfels with vehement prayers, that fhe would fo far fecond the hopes of *Amphialus*, as that fhe might but procure him liberty;promifing then as much to her, as the liberalitie of louing corage durft promife to himfelfe.

CHAP. 24.

[1] *Amphialus excufeth.* [2] *The Princeffes accufe.* [3] Cecropia *feeking their death* [4] *findeth her owne.* [5] *Amphialus-his death-pangcs and felfe-killing.* [6] *The wofull knowledge of it.*

Vt who would liuely defcribe the manner of thefe fpeeches, fhould paint out the lightfome coulours of affection, fhaded with the deepeft fhadowes of forrow, finding them betweene hope and feare, a kind of fweetenes in teares: til *Philoclea* content to receaue a kiffe,and but a kiffe of *Pyrocles*,fealed vp with mouing lippes,and clofed them vp in comfort: and her-felfe (for the paffage was left betweene them open) went to her fifter:

with

with whom she had stayed but a while, fortifying one
another (while *Philoclea* tempered *Pamelas* iust difdaine, and *Pamela* ennobled *Philocleas* sweete humblenesse) when *Amphialus* came vnto them : who neuer
since he had heard *Philoclea* named, coulde bee quiet
in himselfe, although none of them about him (fearing more his mothers violence thē his power) would
discouer what had passed : and many messages he sent
to know her estate, which brought answere backe, according as it pleased *Cecropia* to indite them, till his
hart full of vnfortunate affliction, more and more mis-
giuing him, hauing impatiently borne the delay of the
nights vnfitnesse, this morning he gat vp, and though
full of wounds (which not without daunger could suffer such exercise) he apparelled himselfe, and with a
countenance, that shewed strength in nothing but in
griefe, he came where the sisters were; and weakely
kneeling downe, he besought them to pardon him, if
they had not bene vsed in that castle according to their
worthines, and his duetie; beginning to excuse small
matters, poore Gentleman, not knowing in what sort
they had bene handled.

But *Pamelaes* hye hart (hauing conceiued mortall
hate for the iniurie offred to her and her sister) coulde
scarcely abide his sight, much lesse heare out his excuses; but interrupted him with these words. Traitor (said
she) to thine owne blood, and false to the profession of
so much loue as thou hast vowed, doo not defile our
eares with thy excuses; but pursue on thy crueltie, that
thou and thy godly mother haue vsed towards vs : for
my part, assure thy self, and so do I answere for my sister
(whose mind I know) I do not more desire mine owne
safeue

safetie then thy destruction. Amazed with this speech, he turned his eye, ful of humble sorrowfulnesse, to *Philoclea*. And is this (most excellent Ladie) your doome of me also? She, sweete Ladie, sate weeping: for as her most noble kinsman she had euer fauoured him, & loued his loue, though she could not be in loue with his person; and now partly vnkindnes of his wrong, partly pittie of his case, made her sweete minde yeelde some teares, before she could answere; and her answere was no other, but that she had the same cause as her sister had. He replyed no further, but deliuering from his hart two or three (vntaught) sighes, rose, and with most low reuerence went out of their chamber: and streight by threatning torture, learned of one of the women, in what terrible manner those Princesses had bene vsed. But when he heard it, crying out, O God; and then not able to say any more (for his speech went backe to rebounde woe vpon his hart) he needed no iudge to goe vpon him: for no man could euer thinke any otherworthy of greater punishmēt, thē he thought himselfe.

3   Ful therefore of the horriblest despaire, which a most guiltie conscience could breed, with wild lookes promising some terrible issue, vnderstanding his mother was on the toppe of the leades, he caught one of his seruants swords from him, and none of them daring to stay him, he went vp, carried by furie, in steede of strength; where she was at that time, musing how to goe thorough with this matter, and resoluing to make much of her Neeces in shew, and secreatly to impoison them; thinking since they were not to be wonne, her sonnes loue woulde no otherwise be

mitiga-

mitigated.

But when she sawe him come in with a sworde 4 drawne, and a looke more terrible then the sworde, she streight was stricke with the guiltines of her own conscience: yet the wel known humblenes of her son somwhat animated her, till he, comming nearer her, and crying to her, Thou damnable creature, onely fit to bring forth such a monster of vnhappines as I am; she fearing he would haue stricken her (though indeed he meant it not, but onely intended to kill himselfe in her presence) went backe so far, til ere she were aware, she ouerthrew her selfe from ouer the Leades, to receaue her deathes kisse at the ground: and yet was she not so happie as presently to dye, but that she had time with hellish agonie to see her sonnes mischiefe (whom she loued so well) before her end; when she confest (with most desperate, but not repeting mind) the purpose she had to impoison the princesses, & would then haue had them murthred. But euerie bodie seing, and glad to see her end, had left obedience to her tyranny.

And (if it could be) her ruine increased woe in the 5 noble hart of *Amphialus*, who when he saw her fal, had his owne rage stayed a little with the soddennes of her destruction. And was I not enough miserable before (said he) but that before my end I must be the death of my mother? who how wicked so euer, yet I would she had receaued her punishmēt by some other. O *Amphialus*, wretched *Amphialus*; thou hast liued to be the death of thy most deere cōpanion & friend *Philoxenus*, and of his father, thy most carefull fosterfather. Thou hast liued to kill a Ladie with thine owne handes, and so excellent, and vertuous a Lady, as the faire *Parthenia* was

was : thou haſt liued to ſee thy faithfull *Iſmenus* ſlaine
in ſuccouring thee, and thou not able to defende him:
thou haſt liued to ſhew thy ſelfe ſuch a coward, as that
one vnknowne Knight could ouercome thee in thy
Ladies preſence: thou haſt liued to beare armes againſt
thy rightfull Prince, thine owne vnckle : Thou haſt
liued to be accounted, and iuſtly accounted, a traitor,
by the moſt excellent perſons, that this world holdeth : Thou haſt liued to bee the death of her, that
gaue thee life. But ah wretched *Amphialus*, thou haſt
liued for thy ſake, and by thy authoritie, to haue *Philoclea* tormented : O heauens, in *Amphialus* caſtle,
where *Amphialus* commaunded, tormented, tormented? torment of my ſoule, *Philoclea* tormented : and
thou haſt had ſuch comfort in thy life, as to liue all
this while. Perchance this hande (vſed onely to miſchieuous actes) thinkes it were too good a deede to
kill me; or elſe filthy hande, onely woorthy to kill
women, thou art afraide to ſtrike a man. Feare not
cowardly hand, for thou ſhalt kill but a cowardly traitor : and doo it gladlie; for thou ſhalt kill him,
whome *Philoclea* hateth. With that, furiouſly he tare
open his doublet, and ſetting the pommell of the
ſworde to the grounde, and the point to his breſt,
hee fell vpon it. But the ſworde more mercifull
then hee to himſelfe, with the ſlipping of the pommell, the point ſwarued, and razed him but vpon
the ſide : yet with the fall, his other wounds opened ſo, as hee bledde in ſuch extremitie, that *Charons* boate might verie well be carried in that flood:
which yet he ſought to haſten by this meanes. As
he opened his dublet, and fell, there fell out *Phi-*
loclea

locleas kniues, which *Cecropia* at the firſt had taken from her, and deliuered to her ſonne; and he had euer worne them next his hart, as the only relique he had of his Saint: now ſeeing them by him, (his ſword being ſo, as weakenes could not well draw it out from his doublette) he tooke the kniues, and pulling one of them out, and many times kiſſing it and then, firſt with the paſſions of kindnes, and ynkindnes, melting in teares, O deare kniues, you are come in a good time, to reuenge the wrong I haue done you all this while, in keeping you from her bleſſed ſide, and wearing you without your miſtreſſe leaue. Alas, be witnes with me, yet before I die, (and well you may, for you haue layn next my hart) that by my conſent, your excellent miſtreſſe ſhould haue had as much honour, as this poore place could haue brought foorth, for ſo high an excellencie; and now I am condemned to die by her mouth. Alas, other, far other hope would my deſire often haue giuen me: but other euent it hath pleaſed her to lay vpon me. Ah *Philoclea* (with that his teares guſhed out, as though they would ſtriue to ouerflow his bloud) I would yet thou kneweſt how I loue thee. Vnworthie I am, vnhappie I am, falſe I am; but to thee, alas, I am not falſe. But what a traitor am I, any way to excuſe him, whom ſhe condemneth? Since there is nothing left me, wherein I may do her ſeruice, but in puniſhing him, who hath ſo offended her. Deare knife, then doo your noble miſtreſſes commaundement. With that, he ſtabbed himſelfe into diuers places of his breaſt, and throte, vntill thoſe wounds (with the old, freſhly bleeding) brought him to the ſenſeleſſe gate of Death.

By which time, his ſeruants hauing (with feare of 6
his

his furie) abſtained a while from comming vnto him, one of them (preferring duetifull affection before fearfull duetie) came in, and there found him ſwimming in his owne bloud, there giuing a pittiful ſpectacle, where the conqueſt was the conquerors ouerthrow, and ſelf-ruine the onely triumph of a battaile, fought betweene him, and himſelfe. The time full of danger, the perſon full of worthines, the maner full of horror, did greatlie aſtoniſh all the beholders; ſo as by and by, all the town was full of it, and then of all ages came running vp to ſee the beloued body ; euery body thinking, their ſafetie bledde in his woundes, and their honor died in his deſtruction.

CHAP. 25.

[1] Anaxius-*his rages for the death* [2], *Queen* Helens *comming for the cure of* Amphialus. [3] *Her complaints ouer him.* [4] *Her paſport and ſafeconduct, to carrie him to her Chirurgion.* [5] *The peoples ſorow,* [6] *ſet downe in a ſong.*

I ꜱVt when it came, (and quickly it came) to the eares of his proude friende *Anaxius*, (who by that time was growē well of his woūd, but neuer had come abroad, diſdayning to abaſe himſelfe to the companie of any other but of *Amphialus*) he was exceedingly vexed, either with kindnes, or (if a proud hart be not capable therof) with diſdaine, that he, who had the honor to be called the frend of *Anaxius*, ſhould come to ſuch an vnexpected ruine. Therfore, then comming abroad, with a face red in anger, and engrained in pride, with liddes
ray-

rayſed vp, and eyes leuelling from toppe to the toe of
them that met him , treading,as though he thought to
make the earth ſhake vnder him , with his hande vpon
his ſword;ſhort ſpeeches,and diſdainfull anſweres , giuing ſtreight order to his two brothers,to goe take the
oath of obedience,in his name,of all the ſouldiers,and
Citizens in the towne : and withall, to ſweare them to
reuenge the death of *Amphialus*,vpon *Baſilius*. He himſelf went to ſee him, calling for all the ſurgeons & phy-
ſicions there; ſpending ſome time in vewing the body,
and threatning them all to be hanged , if they did not
heale him. But they (taking view of his woundes , and
falling down at *Anaxius* feete) aſſured him , that they
were mortall,& no poſſible meanes to keep him aboue
two dayes aliue: and he ſtood partly in doubt,to kil,or
ſaue them,betweene his own furie,and their humblenes . But vowing,with his owne hands to kill the two
ſiſters , as cauſers of his friends death:when his brothers came to him,& told him they had done his commaundement , in hauing receaued the oath of allege-
ance,with no great difficultie:the moſt part terrified by
their valure,& force of their ſeruants, & many that had
bene forward actors in the rebellion, willing to do any
thing,rather then come vnder the ſubiection of *Baſilius*
againe;and ſuch fewe as durſt gaineſay,being cut of by
preſent ſlaughter.

But withall(as the chiefe matter of their comming to
him)they told *Anaxius* , that the faire Queen *Helen* was
come,with an honorable retinue,to the towne:hublie
deſiring leaue to ſee *Amphialus* , whō ſhe had ſought in
many places of the world,& laſtly,being returned into
her owne countrie, ſhe heard together of the late ſiege
and

and of his combat with the ſtrange Knight, who had dangerouſly hurt him. Wherupon, full of louing care (which ſhe was content euen to publiſh to the world, how vngratefully ſoeuer he dealt with her) ſhe had gotten leaue of *Baſilius*, to come by his frontiers, to cary away *Amphialus* with her, to the excellenteſt ſurgeon then knowen, whom ſhe had in her Countrey, but ſo olde, as not able to trauaile: but had giuen her ſoueraigne annointments, to preſerue his body withal, till he might be brought vnto him: and that *Baſilius* had graunted leaue: either naturall kindnes preuailing ouer all the offences done, or rather glad to make any paſſage, which might leade him out of his countrie, and from his daughters. This diſcourſe *Lycurgus* vnderſtanding of *Helene*, deliuered to his brother, with her vehement deſire to ſee the body, and take her laſt farewell of him. *Anaxius*, though he were fallen out with all womankind (in reſpect of the hate he bare the ſiſters, whom he accounted murtherers of *Amphialus*) yet at his brothers requeſt, graunted her leaue. And ſhe (poore Lady) with grieuous expectation, and languiſhing deſire, caried her faint legs to the place where he lay, ether not breathing, or in all appearance breathing but death.

3   In which pittious plight when ſhe ſaw him, though Sorow had ſet before her minde the pittifulleſt conceit thereof that it could paint, yet the preſent ſight went beyonde all former apprehenſions: ſo that beginning to kneele by the bodie, her ſight ranne from her ſeruice, rather then abide ſuch a ſight, and ſhe fell in a ſoune vpon him, as if ſhe could not chooſe but die of his wounds. But when her breath (aweary to be cloſed

vp

vp in woe) broke the prifon of her faire lippes, and
brought memorie (with his feruaunt fenfes) to his
naturall office, fhe yet made the breath conuey thefe
dolefull wordes with it. Alas (faid fhe) *Amphialus*,
what ftrange difeafes be thefe, that hauing fought thee
fo long, I fhould be now forie to finde thee? that thefe
eyes fhould looke vpon *Amphialus*, and be grieued
withall? that I fhould haue thee in my power without
glory, and embrace thee without comfort? How often
haue I bleft the means that might bring me neer thee?
Now, woe worth the caufe that brings me fo neer thee.
Often, alas, often haft thou difdained my teares : but
now, my deare *Amphialus*, receiue them : thefe eies can
ferue for nothing elfe, but weepe for thee; fince thou
wouldeft neuer vouchfafe them thy comforte, yet difdaine not them thy forrowe. I would they had bene
more deare vnto thee; for then hadft thou liued. Woe
is me that thy noble harte could loue who hated thee,
and hate who loued thee. Alas, why fhould not my
faith to thee couer my other defects, who only fought
to make my Crowne thy foote-ftoole, my felfe thy feruaunt? that was all my ambition; and alas thou dif-
dainedft it to ferue them, by whom thy incomparable
felfe were difdained. Yet (ô *Philoclea*) wherefoeuer you
are, pardon me, if I fpeake in the bitternes of my foule,
excellent may you be in all other things (and excellent
fure you are fince he loued you) your want of pittie,
where the fault onely was infinitenefle of defert, cannot be excufed. I would, O God, I would that you
had graunted his deferued fuite of marrying you, and
that I had bene your feruing-maide, to haue made my
eftate the foile of your felicitie, fo he had liued. How

Yy   many

many weary steps haue I trodden after thee , while my
onely complaint was, that thou werte vnkinde? Alas I
would now thou werte, to be vnkind. Alas why wouldest thou not cómaund my seruice, in perfuading *Philoclea* to loue thee? who could, or(if euery one could)
who would haue recounted thy perfections so well, as
I? who with such kindly passions could haue stirred
pittie for thee as I? who should haue deliuered not
onely the wordes but the teares I had of thee? and so
shouldest thou haue exercised thy disdaine in me, and
yet vsed my seruice for thee.

4   With that the body mouing somewhat, and giuing
a grone full of deaths musicke, she fell ypon his face , &
kist him, and with all cried out. O miserable I, that haue
onely fauour by miserie : and then, would she haue returned to a fresh careere of complaints , when an aged
and wise Gentleman came to her, and besought her, to
remember what was fit for her greatnesse, wisdome, &
honour: and with al, that it was fitter to shew her loue,
in carying the body to her excellent Surgeon , first applying such excellent medicines as she had receiued of
him for that purpose, rather then onely shew her selfe a
woman-louer in fruitles lamétations. She was streight
warned with the obedience of an ouerthrowen mind,
and therefore leauing some surgeons of her owne to
dresse the body, went her selfe to *Anaxius*,& humbling
her selfe to him, as lowe as his owne pride could wish,
besought him , that since the surgeons there had vtterly giuen him ouer , that he would let her carrie him a-
way in her litter with her , since the worst he could
haue should be to die, and to die in her armes that loued him aboue al things;& where he should haue such
monu-

monuments erected ouer-him, as were fit for her loue, & his worthines: befeeching him withall, fince fhe was in a country of enemies (where fhe trufted more to *A-naxius* valour, then *Bafilius* promife) that he would con-uey them fafely out of thofe territories. Her reafons fomething moued him, but nothing thoroughly per-fwaded him, but the laft requeft of his helpe: which he ftreight promifed, warrating all fecuritie, as long as that fword had his mafter aliue. She as happy therein as vn-happines could be (hauing receiued as fmall cofort of her owne furgeons as of the others) caufed yet the bo-dy to be eafily conueyed into the litter: all the people then beginning to roare and crie, as though neuer till then they had loft their Lorde. And if the terrour of *Anaxius* had not kept them vnder, they would haue mutinied, rather then fuffered his bodie to be caried a-way.

But *Anaxius* him felfe riding before the litter, with the choyce men of that place, they were affraid euen to crie, though they were readie to crie for feare: but (becaufe that they might doo) euery bodie forced (e-uen with harming themfelues) to doo honour to him: fome throwing themfelues vpon the grounde; fome tearing their clothes, and cafting dufte vpon their heades, and fome euen wounding themfelues, and fprinkling their owne bloud in the aire. Among the reft, one accounted good in that kinde, and made the better by the true feeling of forrowe, roared out a fong of Lamentation, which (as well as might be) was ga-thered vp in this forme.

6 SInce that to death is gone the ſhepheard hie,
    Whom moſt the ſilly ſhepheards pipe did pryſe,
    Your dolefull tunes ſweete Muſes now applie.

And you ò trees (if any life there lies
    In trees) now through your porous barkes receaue
    The ſtraunge reſounde of theſe my cauſefull cries :
And let my breath vpon your braunches leaue,
    My breath diſtinguiſh'd into wordes of woe,
    That ſo I may ſignes of my ſorrowe leaue.
But if among your ſelues ſome one tree growe,
    That apteſt is to figure miſerie,
    Let it embaſſage beare your grieues to ſhowe.
The weeping Myrrhe I thinke will not denie
    Her helpe to this, this iuſteſt cauſe of plaint.
    Your dolefull tunes ſweet Muſes now applie.

And thou poore Earth, whom fortune doth attaint
    In Natures name to ſuffer ſuch a harme,
    As for to looſe thy gemme, and ſuch a Sainct,
Vpon thy face let coaly Rauens ſwarme :
    Let all the Sea thy teares accounted be :
    Thy bowels with all killing mettals arme.
Let golde now ruſt, let Diamonds waſte in thee :
    Let pearls be wan with woe their damme doth beare :
    Thy ſelfe henceforth the light doo neuer ſee.
And you, ò flowers, which ſometimes Princes were,
    Till theſe ſtraunge altrings-you did hap to trie,
    Of Princes loſſe your ſelues for tokens reare.
Lilly in mourning blacke thy whitenes die :
    O Hiacinthe let Ai be on thee ſtill.
    Your dolefull tunes ſweet Muſes now applie.

                        O Echo

O Echo, *all these woods with roaring fill,*
  And doo not oncly marke the accents last,
  But all, for all reach out my wailefull will :
One Echo *to another* Echo *cast*
  Sounde of my griefes, and let it neuer ende,
  Till that it hath all woods and waters past.
Nay to the heau'ns *your iust complaining sende,*
  And stay the starrs inconstant constant racc,
  Till that they doo vnto our dolours bende:
And aske the reason of that speciall grace,
  That they, which haue no liues, should liue so long,
  And vertuous soules so soone should loose their place?
Aske, if in great men good men doo so thronge,
  That he for want of elbowe roome must die ?
  Or if that they be skante, if this be wronge ?
Did Wisedome *this our wretched time espie*
  In one true chest to rob all Vertues *treasure ?*
  Your dolefull tunes sweete Muses *now applie.*

And if that any counsell you to measure
  Your dolefull tunes, to them still playning say,
  To well felte griefe, plainte is the onely pleasure.   ,,
O light of Sunne, *which is entit'led day,*
  O well thou doost that thou no longer bidest ;
  For mourning light her blacke weedes may display.
O Phœbus *with good cause thy face thou hidest,*
  Rather then haue thy all-beholding eye
  Fould with this sight, while thou thy chariot guidest.
And well (me thinks) becomes this vaultie skie
  A stately tombe to couer him deceased.
  Your dolefull tunes sweet Muses *now applie.*

O Philomela *with thy breſt oppreſſed*
  By ſhame and griefe, helpe, helpe me to lament
  Such curſed harmes as cannot be redreſſed.
Or if thy mourning notes be fully ſpent,
  Then giue a quiet eare vnto my playning:
  For I to teach the world complainte am bent.
You dimmy clowdes, which well employ your ſtayning
  This cheereſull aire with your obſcured cheere,.
  Witneſſe your woſull teares with daily rayning.
And if, ô Sunne, thou euer didſt appeare,
  In ſhape, which by mans eye might be perceiued,
  Vertue is dead, now ſet thy triumph here.
Now ſet thy triumph in this world, bereaued
  Of what was good, where now no good doth lie ;
  And by thy pompe our loſſe will be conceaued.
O notes of mine your ſelues together tie :
  With too much griefe me thinkes you are diſſolued.
  Your doleſull tunes ſweete Muſes *now applie.*

Time euer old, and yonge is ſtill reuolued
  Within it ſelfe, and neuer taſteth ende :
  But mankind is for aye to nought reſolued.
The filthy ſnake her aged coate can mende,
  And getting youth againe, in youth doth flouriſh :
  But vnto Man, age euer death doth ſende.
The very trees with graſting we can cheriſh,
  So that we can long time produce their time:
  But Man which helpeth them, helpleſſe muſt periſh.
Thus, thus the mindes, which ouer all doo clime,
  When they by yeares experience get beſt graces,
  Muſt finiſh then by deaths deteſted crime.

We

We laſt ſhort while, and build long laſting places:
Ah let vs all againſt foule Nature crie :
We Natures workes doo helpe, ſhe vs defaces.
For how can Nature vnto this reply ?
That ſhe her child, I ſay, her beſt child killeth ?
Your dolefull tunes ſweete Muſes now apply.

Alas, me thinkes, my weakned voice but ſpilleth,
The vehement courſe of this iuſt lamentation :
Me thinkes, my ſound no place with ſorrow filleth.
I know not I, but once in deteſtation
I haue my ſelfe, and all what life containeth,
Since Death on Vertues fort hath made inuaſion.
One word of woe another after traineth :
Ne doo I care how rude be my inuention,
So it be ſeene what ſorrow in me raigneth.
O Elements, by whoſe (men ſay) contention,
Our bodies be in liuing power maintained,
Was this mans death the fruite of your diſſention?
O Phiſickes power, which (ſome ſay) hath reſtrained
Approch of death, alas thou helpeſt meagerly,
When once one is for Atropos diſtrained.
Great be Phyſitions brags, but aid is beggerly,
When rooted moiſture failes, or groweth drie,
They leaue off al, and ſay, death comes too eagerlie.
They are but words therefore that men do buy,
Of any ſince God AEſculapius ceaſed.
Your dolefull tunes ſweete Muſes now applie.

Iuſtice, iuſtice is now (alas) oppreſſed:
Bountifulnes hath made his laſt concluſion:
Goodnes for beſt attire in duſt is dreſſed.

Y y 4   Shepheards

Shepheards bewaile your vttermoſt confuſion;
  And ſee by this picture to you preſented,
,, *Death is our home, life is but a deluſion.*
For ſee alas, who is from you abſented?
  Abſented? nay I ſay for euer baniſhed
  From ſuch as were to dye for him contented?
Out of our ſight in turne of hand is vaniſhed
  Shepherd of ſhepherds, whoſe well ſetled order
  Priuate with welth, publike with quiet garniſhed.
While he did liue, farre, farre was all diſorder;
  Example more preuailing then direction,
  Far was homeſtrife, and far was foe from border.
His life a law, his looke a full correction:
  As in his health we healthfull were preſerued,
  So in his ſickneſſe grew our ſure infection.
His death our death. But ah; my Muſe hath ſwarued,
  From ſuch deepe plaint as ſhould ſuch woes deſcrie;
  Which he of vs for euer hath deſerued.
The ſtile of heauie hart can neuer flie
  So high, as ſhould make ſuch a paine notorious :
  Ceaſe Muſe therfore : thy dart ô Death applie;
And farewell Prince, whom goodneſſe hath made glorious.

CHAP.

CHAP. 26.

[1] The publike griefe amplified. [2] Anaxius death-threatning to the Princesses. [3] Their resolutenes in it. [4] His returne, and stop. [5] Zelmanes braue challenge vnto him [6] scorned by him. [7] His loue to Pamela scorned by her. [8] His brothers braue loues haue as meane successe.

He general consort of al such num- [1] bers mourning, perfourmed so the naturall times of sorrow; that euen to them (if any such were) that felt not the losse, yet others grief taught them griefe; hauing before their compassionate sense so passionate a spectacle, of a young man, of great beautie, beautified with great honour, honored by great valure, made of inestimable valure, by the noble vsing of it, to lye there languishing, vnder the arrest of death, and a death, where the manner could be no comfort to the discomfortablenes of the matter. But when the bodie was carried thorough the gate, and the people (sauing such as were appointed) not suffred to goe further, then was such an vniuersal crie, as if they had all had but one life, and all receaued but one blow.

Which so moued *Anaxius* to consider the losse of [2] his friend, that (his minde apter to reuenge, then tendernesse) he presently giuing order to his brother to keepe the prisoners safe, and vnuisited, till his retourne from coueying *Helen*, he sent a messenger to the sisters, to tel them this curteous message : that at his retourne,
with

with his owne hands, he would cut off their heads, and send them for tokens to their father.

3　This meſſage was brought vnto the ſiſters, as they ſate at that time together with *Zelmane*, conferring how to carrie themſelues, hauing heard of the death of " *Amphialus*. And as no expectation of death is ſo pain-" full, as where the reſolution is hindred by the intermixing of hopes, ſo did this new alarum, though not remoue, yet moue ſomwhat the côſtancy of their minds, which were ſo vnconſtantly dealt with. But within a while, the excellent *Pamela* had brought her minde againe to his old acquaintance: and then, as carefull for her ſiſter (whom moſt deerely ſhe loued) Siſter (ſaid ſhe) you ſee how many acts our Tragedy hath: Fortune is not yet a wearie of vexing vs : but what? A ſhippe is not counted ſtrong for byding one ſtorme? It is but the ſame trumpet of death, which now perhaps giues the laſt ſounde : and let vs make that profite of our former miſeries, that in them we learned to dye willingly. Truely ſaid *Philoclea*, deare ſiſter, I was ſo beaten with the euils of life, that though I had not vertue enough to deſpiſe the ſweetneſſe of it, yet my weakneſſe bredde that ſtrength, to be wearie of the paines of it: onely I muſt confeſſe, that little hope, which by theſe late accidents was awaked in me, was at the firſt angrie withall. But euen in the darkeneſſe of that horrour, I ſee a light of comfort appeare ; and how can I treade amiſſe, that ſee *Pamelas* ſteppes? I would onely (O that my wiſh might take place) that my ſchoole-Miſtres might liue, to ſee me ſay my leſſon truely. Were that a life, my *Philoclea*? ſaid *Pamela*. No, no, (ſaid ſhe) let it come, and put on his worſt face : for at the worſt it is

but

but a bug-beare. Ioy is it to me to fee you fo well refolued; and fince the world will not haue vs, let it lofe vs.
Onely (with that fhe ftayed a little, and fight) onely my
Philoclea, (then fhe bowed downe, and whifpered in
her eare) onely *Mufidorus*, my fhepheard, comes betweene me and death, and makes me thinke I fhould
not dye, becaufe I know he would not I fhould dye.
With that *Philoclea* fighed alfo, faying no more, but
looking vpon *Zelmane*: who was walking vp & downe
the chamber, hauing heard this meffage from *Anaxius*,
and hauing in times paft heard of his nature, thought
him like enough to performe it, which winded her a-
gaine into the former maze of perplexitie Yet debating with her felfe of the manner how to preuent it, fhe
continued her mufing humour, little faying, or indeed,
little finding in her hart to fay, in a cafe of fuch extremitie, where peremptorily death was threatned: and fo
ftayed they; hauing yet that comfort, that they might
tarrie togither. *Pamela* nobly, *Philoclea* fweetly, and
Zelmane fadly, and defperately none of them entertaining fleepe, which they thought fhould fhortly begin,
neuer to awake.

But *Anaxius* came home, hauing fafely conducted 4
Helen: and fafely he might wel do it: For though many
of *Bafilius* Knights would haue attempted fomething
vpon *Anaxius*, by that meanes to deliuer the Ladies, yet
Philanax, hauing receiued his mafters commadement,
& knowing his word was giue, would not cofent vnto
it. And the black-Knight (who by the was aole to carie
abroad his wouds) did not know therof; but was bringing forces, by force to deliuer his Lady. So as *Anaxius*,
interpreting it rather feare, then faith, and making
euen

euen chance an argument of his vertue, returned: and
as foone as he was returned, with a felon hart calling
his brothers vp with him, he went into the chamber,
where they were all three togither; with full intention
to kill the sifters with his owne hands, and send their
heads for tokens to their father: Though his brothers
(who were otherwise inclined) diffwaded him: but his
reuerence stayed their perswasions. But when he was
come into the chamber, with the very words of cholerike threatning climing vp his throate, his eies first lighted vpon *Pamela*; who hearing he was comming, and
looking for death, thought she would keepe her owne
maiestie in welcomming it; but the beames thereof so
strake his eyes, with such a counterbuffe vnto his pride,
that if his anger could not so quickly loue, nor his pride
so easily honor, yet both were forced to finde a worthinesse.

Which while it bred a pause in him, *Zelmane* (who
had ready in her mind both what and how to say) stept
out vnto him, & with a resolute stayednes (void either
of anger, kindnes, disdaine, or humblenesse) spake in
this sort. *Anaxius* (said she) if *Fame* haue not bene ouer-
partiall to thee, thou art a man of exceeding valour.
Therefore I doo call thee euen before that vertue, and
will make it the iudge betweene vs. And now I doo affirme, that to the eternall blot of all the faire actes that
thou hast done, thou doest weakly, in seeking without
daunger to reuenge his death, whose life with daunger thou mightst perhaps haue preserued: thou doost
cowardly, in going about by the death of these excellent Ladies, to preuent the iust punishmēt, that hereafter they by the powers, which they better then their fa-

ther

ther, or any other could make, might lay vpon thee; and dooſt moſt baſely, in once preſenting thy ſelfe as an executioner; a vile office vpon men, and in a iuſt cauſe: beyond the degree of any vile worde, in ſo vn-iuſt a cauſe, and vpon Ladies, and ſuch Ladies. And therefore, as a hangman, I ſay, thou art vnworthy to be counted a Knight, or to be admitted into the compa-nie of Knights. Neither for what, I ſay, will I alleadge other reaſons, of wiſdome, or iuſtice, to prooue my ſpeech, becauſe I know thou dooſt diſdaine to be tied to their rules: but euen in thine owne vertue (whereof thou ſo much glorieſt) I will make my triall: and there-fore defie thee, by the death of one of vs two, to proue, or diſproue theſe reproaches. Chooſe thee what armes thou likeſt, I onely demaund, that theſe Ladies (whom I defend) may in liberty ſee the combat.

When *Zelmane* began her ſpeech, the excellency of her beautie, and grace, made him a little content to heare. Beſides that, a new leſſon he had read in *Pamela*, had already taught him ſome regard. But when ſhe en-tered into brauerie of ſpeech, he thought at firſt, a mad, and railing humor poſſeſt her; till, finding the ſpeeches hold well together, and at length come to flatte chal-lenge of combat; he ſtood leaning back with his bodie and head, ſometimes with bent browes looking vpon the one ſide of her, ſometimes of the other, beyonde maruell maruailing, that he, who had neuer heard ſuch ſpeeches from any Knight, ſhould be thus rebuffed by a woman; and that maruell made him heare out her ſpeech: which ended, he turned his head to his bro-ther *Zoilus*, and ſaid nothing, but onely lifting vp his eyes, ſmiled. But *Zelmane* finding his minde, *Anaxius*
(ſaid

(ſaid ſhe) perchaunce thou diſdayneſt to anſwere me, becauſe, as a woman, thou thinkeſt me not fitte to be fought withall. But I tell thee, that I haue bene trayned vp in martial matters, with ſo good ſucceſſe, that I haue many times ouercome better Knightes then thy ſelfe: and am well knowen to be equall in feates of armes, to the famous *Pyrocles*, who ſlewe thy valiaunt Vncle, the Giant *Euardes*. The remembraunce of his Vncles death ſomething netled him, ſo as he anſwered thus.

Indeed (ſaide he) any woman may be as valiaunt as that coward, and traytorly boy, who ſlewe my Vncle trayterouſlie, and after ranne from me in the plaine field. Fiue thouſand ſuch could not haue ouercome *Euardes*, but by falſhood. But I ſought him all ouer *Aſia*, following him ſtill from one of his cony-holes to another: till, comming into this Countrie, I heard of my friendes being beſieged, and ſo came to blowe away the wretches that troubled him. But whereſoeuer the miſerable boy flie, heauen, nor hell, ſhall keep his harte from being torne by theſe handes. Thou lyeſt in thy throate (ſaid *Zelmane*) that boye, where euer he went, did ſo noble actes, as thy harte (as proude as it is) dares not thinke of, much leſſe perfourme. But to pleaſe thee the better with my preſence, I tell thee, no creature can be neerer of kinne to him, then my ſelfe: and ſo well we loue, that he woulde not be ſorrier for his owne death, then for mine: I being begotten by his father, of an Amazon Ladie. And therefore, thou canſt not deuiſe to reuenge thy ſelfe more vpon him, then by killing me: which, if thou dareſt doo manfullie, doo it; otherwiſe, if thou harme theſe incomparable Ladies, or

my

my felfe, without daring to fight with me, I proteft before thefe Knightes, and before heauen, and earth, (that will reueale thy fhame) that thou art the beggerlieft daftardly villaine, that difhonoureth the earth with his fteppes: and if thou letteft me ouer-liue them, fo will I blaze thee. But all this could not moue *Anaxius*, but that he onely faid, Euill fhould it become the terror of the world, to fight, much leffe to fkolde with thee.

But (faid he)for the death of thefe fame (pointing to the Princeffes) of my grace, I giue them life. And withall, going to *Pamela*, and offring to take her by the chin, And as for you, Minion(faid he)yeeld but gently to my will, and you fhall not only liue, but liue fo happely. He would haue faid further, whē *Pamela*, difpleafed both with words, matter, and maner, putting him away with her faire hand, Proud beaft(faid fhe)yet thou plaieft worfe thy Comedy, then thy Tragedy. For my part, affure thy felfe, fince my deftiny is fuch, that at ech moment my life & death ftand in equall balance, I had rather haue thee,& think thee far fitter to be my hangman, then my hufband. Pride & anger, would faine haue cruelly reuēged fo bitter an anfwer, but alredy *Cupia* had begun to make it his fport, to pull his plumes: fo that, vnufed to a way of courtefie, and put out of his byas of pride, he haftily went away, grumbling to himfelfe, betwene threatning & wifhing; leauing his brothers with thē: the elder of whom, *Lycurgus*, liked *Philoclea*,& *Zoilus* would nedes loue *Zelmane*; or at left, entertain themfelues with making thē beleue fo. *Lycurgus* more braggard,& nere his brothers humor, begā, with fetting foorth their bloud, their deedes, how many

they

7

8

they had defpifed, of moft excellent womē; how much
they were boūd to them, that would feek that of them.
In fumme, in all his fpeeches, more like the beftower,
then the defirer of felicitie. Whom it was an excellent
paftime (to thofe that would delight in the play of vertue) to fee, with what a wittie ignorance fhe would not
vnderftand: and how, acknowledging his perfections,
fhe would make, that one of his perfections, not to be
iniurions to Ladies. But when he knew not how to replie, then would he fall to touching and toying, ftill
vewing his graces in no glaffe but felf-likin To which,
Philocleas fhamefaftnes, and humblenes, were as ftrong
refifters, as choller, and difdaine. For though fhe yeelded not, he thought fhe was to be ouercome: and that
thought a while ftayed him from further violence. But
Zelmane had eye to his behauiour, and fet in her memorie, vpon the fcore of Reuenge, while fhe her felfe
was no leffe attempted by *Zoilus*; who leffe full of
bragges, was forwardeft in offering (indeed) difhonou-
rable violence.

CHAP. 27.

But

Vt when after their fruitleſſe labours they had gone away, called by their brother, (who began to be perplexed betweene new conceaued deſires, and diſdaine, to be diſdained) *Zelmane* (who with moſt aſſured quietneſſe of iudgement looked into their preſent eſtate) earneſtly perſwaded the two ſiſters, that to auoide the miſchiefes of prowde outrage, they would onely ſo farre ſute their behauiour to their eſtates, as they might winne time; which as it could not bring them to worſe caſe then they were, ſo it might bring forth inexpected relief. And why (ſaid *Pamela*)ſhal we any longer flatter aduerſity? Why ſhould we delight to make our ſelues any longer balls to iniurious *Fortune*, ſince our owne kinne are content traitorouſly to abuſe vs? Certainely, in miſhap it may be ſome comforte to vs, that we are lighted in theſe fellowes handes, who yet will keepe vs from hauing cauſe of being miſerable by our friends meanes. Nothing grieues me more, then that you, noble Ladie *Zelmane* (to whome the worlde might haue made vs able to doo honour)ſhoulde receaue onely hurte by the contagion of our miſerie. As for me, and my ſiſter, vndoubtedly it becomes our birth to thinke of dying nobly, while we haue done, or ſuffered nothing, which might make our ſoule aſhamed at the parture from theſe bodies. Hope is the fawning traitour of „ the minde, while vnder colour of friendſhip, it robbes „ it of his chiefe force of reſolution. Vertuous and faire

Z z   Ladie

Ladie (said *Zelmane*) what you say is true; and that truth may well make vp a part in the harmonie of your noble thoughts. But yet the time (which ought alwaies to be one) is not tuned for it; while that may bring foorth any good, doo not barre your selfe there-
" of: for then would be the time to die nobly, when you cā not liue nobly. Then so earnestly she persuaded with them both, to referre themselues to their fathers consent (in obtayning whereof they knewe some while would be spent) and by that meanes to temper the mindes of their prowde woers; that in the ende *Pamela* yeelded to her, because she spake reason; and *Philoclea* yeelded to her reason, because she spake it.

2   And so when they were againe sollicited in that little pleasing petition, *Pamela* forced her selfe to make answere to *Anaxius*, that if her father gaue his consent she would make her selfe belieue, that such was the heauenly determination, since she had no meanes to auoide it. *Anaxius* (who was the most franke promiser to him selfe of successe) nothing doubted of *Basilius* consent, but rather assured him selfe, he would be his oratour in that matter: And therefore he chose out an officious seruaunt (whome he esteemed very wise, because he neuer found him but iust of his opinion) and willed him to be his embassadour to *Basilius*, and to make him knowe, that if he meant to haue his daughter both safe and happie, and desired him selfe to haue such a sonne in lawe, as would not onely protect him in his quiet course, but (if he listed to accept it) would giue him the monarchy of the worlde, that then he should receaue *Anaxius*, who neuer before knewe what it was to pray any thing. That if he did not,

not, he would make him know, that the power of *A-naxius* was in euery thing beyonde his will, and yet his will not to be refisted by any other power. His feruaunt with fmiling and cafte-vp looke, defired God to make his memorie able to containe the trea-fure of that wife fpeach: and therefore befought him to repeate it againe, that by the oftener hearing it, his mind might be the better acquainted with the diuine-neffe therof, and that being gratioufly granted, he then doubted not by carying with him in his conceit, the grace wherewith *Anaxius* fpake it, to perfuade rocky minds to their owne harme: fo little doubted he to win *Bafilius* to that, which he thought would make him thinke the heauens opened, when he harde but the proffer thereof. *Anaxius* grauely allowed the probabi-litie of his conie&ture, and therefore fent him away, promifing him he fhould haue the bringing vp of his fecond fonne by *Pamela*.

The meffenger with fpeede perfourmed his Lords commaundement to *Bafilius*, who by nature quiet, and by fuperftition made doubtfull, was lothe to take any matter of armes in hand, wherin already he had found fo flowe fucceffe; though *Philanax* vehemently vrged him therunto, making him fee that his retiring back did encourage iniuries. But *Bafilius* betwixt the feare of *A-naxius* might, the paffió of his loue, & iealoufie of his e-ftate, was fo perplexed, that not able to determine, he tooke the cómon courfe of mé, to flie only thé to deuo-tió, whé they want refolutió: fo detaining the mefséger with delaies, he deferred the dire&ing of his courfe to the coúfell of *Apollo*, which becaufe himfelf at that time

could not well go to require, he entrusted the matter to his best trusted *Philanax :* who (as one in whom obedience was a sufficient reason vnto him) wente with diligence to *Delphos,* where being entred into the secrete place of the temple, and hauing performed the sacrifices vsuall, the spirite that possest the prohesying woman, with a sacred fury, attended not his demaund, but as if it would argue him of incredulitie, tolde him, not in darke wonted speeches, but plainely to be vnderstood, what he came for, and that he should returne to *Basilius,* and will him to denie his daughters to *Anaxius* and his brothers, for that they were reserued for such as were better beloued of the gods. That he should not doubte, for they should returne vnto him safely and speedily. And that he should keepe on his solitary course, till bothe *Philanax* and *Basilius* fully agreed in the vnderstanding of the former pro-
,, phecie : withall, commaunding *Philanax* from thence forward to giue tribute, but not oblation, to humane wisedome.

4   *Philanax* then finding that reason cannot shewe it
,, selfe more reasonable, then to leaue reasoning in things aboue reason, returnes to his Lorde, and like one that preferred truth before the maintaining of an opinion, hidde nothing from him, nor from thence foorth durste any more disswade him, from that which he founde by the celestiall prouidence directed; but he him selfe looking to repayre the gouernment as much as in so broken an estate by ciuill dissention he might, and fortifying with notable arte, bothe the lodges, so as they were almost made vnaprochable, he lefte *Ba-*

                                                    silius

filius to bemone the abſence of his daughters, and to bewayle the impriſonment of *Zelmane*: yet wholy giuen holily to obey the Oracle, he gaue a reſolute negatiue vnto the meſſenger of *Anaxius*, who all this while had waited for it, yet in good termes deſiring him to ſhewe him ſelfe, in reſpect of his birth and profeſſion, ſo Princely a Knight, as without forcing him to ſeeke the way of force, to deliuer in noble ſorte thoſe Ladies vnto him, and ſo ſhould the iniurie haue bene in *Amphialus*, and the benefite in him.

The meſſenger went backe with this anſwere, yet hauing euer vſed to ſugre any thing which his Maiſter was to receaue, he tolde him, that when *Baſilius* firſt vnderſtood his deſires, he did ouerreach ſo farre all his moſt hopefull expectations, that he thought it were too great a boldneſſe to harken to ſuch a man, in whome the heauens had ſuch intereſt, without asking the Gods counſell, and therefore had ſent his principall counſailour to *Delphos*, who although he kepte the matter neuer ſo ſecrete, yet his diligence, inſpired by *Anaxius* his priuiledge ouer all worldly thinges, had founde out the ſecrete, which was, that he ſhould not preſume to marrie his daughters, to one who already was enrolled among the demie-Gods, and yet much leſſe he ſhould dare the attempting to take them out of his hands.

Anaxius, who till then had made Fortune his creator, and Force his God, nowe beganne to finde an other wiſedome to be aboue, that iudged ſo rightly of him: and where in this time of his ſeruauntes wayting for *Baſilius* reſolution, he and his brothers had

Z z 3   courted

courted their Ladies , as whome they vouchſafed to haue for their wiues , he reſolued now to dally no longer in delayes , but to make violence his Oratour, ſince he had found perſuaſions had gotten nothing but anſweres. Which intention he opened to his bro-thers, who hauing all this while wanted nothing to take that way, but his authoritie , gaue ſpurres to his running, and , vnworthy men , neither feeling vertue in themſelues, nor tendring it in others , they were head-long to make that euill conſorte of loue and force, when *Anaxius* had worde , that from the Tower there were deſcried ſome companies of armed men, marching towardes the towne ; wherefore he gaue preſente order to his ſeruauntes, and ſouldiers, to goe to the gates and walles , leauing none within but him-ſelfe, and his brothers : his thoughts then ſo full of their intended pray , that *Mars*-his lowdeſt trumpet could ſcarcely haue awaked him.

CHAP. 28.

Zoilus the meſſenger, [1] *and firſt offerer of force,* [2] *is for-ced to flie, and die.* [4] Lycurgus *pointed to kill,* [5] *is fought withal,* [6] *foiled,* [7] *& killed.* [8] Anaxius *the* Reuenger *with* Pyrocles *the* Puniſher *braue, and brauely combatted.*

I Vt while he was directing what he would haue done, his yongeſt brother *Zoilus*, glad that he had the commiſſion , went in the name of *Anaxius*, to tel the ſiſters, that ſince he had anſwere from their father, that he

and

and his brother *Licurgus,* should haue them in what fort
it pleafed them, that they would now graunt them no
longer time, but prefently to determine, whether they
thought it more honorable comfort to be compelled,
or perfwaded. *Pamela* made him anfwere, that in a matter whereon the whole ftate of her life depended, and
wherin fhe had euer anfwered, fhe would not lead, but
follow her parents pleafure; fhe thought it reafon fhe
fhould, either by letter, or particular meffeger vnderftad
fomthing from thefelucs, & not haue her beleef bound
to the report of their partiall feruants, & therefore, as to
their words, fhe & her fifter, had euer a fimple & true refolution, fo againft their vniuft force, God, they hoped,
would either arme their liues, or take away their liues.

Wel Ladies (faid he) I wil leaue my brothers, who by
& by wil come vnto you, to be their own embaffadors,
for my parte, I muft now do my felf feruice. And with
that turning vp his muftachoes, and marching as if he
would begin a pauen, he went toward *Zelmane.* But *Zelmane* (hauing had all this while of the meffengers being with *Bafilius*, much to do to keepe thofe excellent
Ladies from feeking by the pafport of death, to efcape
thofe bafe dangers wherevnto they found themfelues
fubiect) ftill hoping that *Mufidorus* would finde fome
meanes to deliuer them; and therefore had often both
by her owne example, & comfortable reafons, perfwaded the to ouerpaffe many infolent indignities of their
proud futers, who thought it was a fufficient fauour
not to doo the vttermoft iniurie, now come againe to
the ftreight fhe moft feared for them; either of death
or difhonor, if heroicall courage would haue let her,
fhe had beene beyonde herfelfe amazed: but that

Zz 4 yet

yet held vp her wit, to attend the vttermoſt occaſion, which euē then brought his hairie forehead vnto her: for *Zoilus* ſmacking his lippes, as for the Prologue of a kiſſe, and ſomething aduancing himſelfe, Darling (ſaid he) let thy hart be full of ioy, and let thy faire eies be of counſel with it, for this day thou ſhalt haue *Zoilus*, whō many haue lōged for, but none ſhall haue him, but *Zelmane*. And oh, how much glory I haue to think what a race will be betwene vs. The world, by the heauens, the world will be too litle for them. And with that, he would haue put his arme about her necke, but ſhe, withdrawing her ſelfe from him, My Lord (ſaid ſhe) much good may your thoughts do you, but that I may not diſſemble with you, my natiuitie being caſt by one that neuer failed in any of his prognoſticatiōs, I haue bene aſſured, that I ſhould neuer be apt to beare children. But ſince you wil honor me with ſo hie fauor, I muſt onely deſire that I may performe a vow which I made among my coūtriwomen, the famous *Amazons*, that I would neuer marrie none, but ſuch one as was able to withſtand me in Armes: therfore, before I make mine own deſire ſeruiceable to yours, you muſt vouchſafe to lend me armor and weapons, that at leaſt, with a blow or two of the ſword, I may not finde my ſelfe periured to my ſelfe. But *Zoilus* (but laughing with a hartie lowdnes) went by force to embrace her; making no other anſwere, but ſince ſhe had a minde to trie his Knighthood, ſhe ſhould quickly know what a man of armes he was: and ſo, without reuerence to the Ladies, began to ſtruggle with her.

But in *Zelmane* then Diſdaine became wiſdome, & Anger gaue occaſion. For abiding no longer aboad in

the

the matter, she that had not put off, though she had dif-
guised, *Pyrocles,* being farre fuller of strong nimblenes,
tript vp his feete, so that he fel down at hers. And withall (meaning to pursue what she had begun) puld out
his sword, which he ware about him : but before she
could strike him withall, he gat vp, and ranne to a faire
chamber, where he had left his two brethrē, preparing
themselues to come downe to their mistresses. But she
followed at his heeles, & euē as he came to throw himselfe into their arms for succor, she hit him with his own
sword, such a blow vpō the wast, that she almost cut him
a sūder: once, she sundred his soule frō his body, sēding
it to *Proserpina,* an angry Goddesse against rauishers.

But *Anaxius,* seing before his eyes the miserable end   4.
of his brother, fuller of despite thē wrath, & yet fuller of
wrath then sorow, looking with a wofull eye vpon his
brother *Lycurgus,* Brother, said he, chastice this vile creature, while I go down, & take order left further mischief
arise: & so went down to the Ladies, whom he visited,
doubting there had bene some further practise thē yet
he conceiued. But finding thē only strong in pacience,
he went & lockt a great Iron gate, by which onely any
body might mounte to that part of the Castle, rather to
conceale the shame of his brother, slaine by a woman,
then for doubt of any other anoyance, and thē went vp
to receaue some comfort of the execution, he was sure
his brother had done of *Zelmane.*

But *Zelmane* no sooner saw those brothers, of whom   5
Reasō assured her she was to expect reuēge, but that she
lept to a target, as one that well knew the first marke of   ,,
valure to be defence. And thē accepting the oportunitie of *Anaxius* going away, she waited not the pleasure
of

of *Lycurgus*, but without any words (which ſhe euer thought vaine, whē reſolutiō tooke the place of perſwaſion) gaue her owne hart the contentment to be the aſſailer. *Lycurgus*, who was in the diſpoſitiō of his nature hazardouſe, & by the luckie paſſing through many dangers, growne confident in himſelfe, went toward her, rather as to ſpoile, then to fight, ſo farre from feare, that his aſſurednesse diſdained to hope. But whē her ſword made demonſtrations aboue al flattery of argumēts, & that he found ſhe preſt ſo vpon him, as ſhewed that her courage ſprang not from blind deſpair, but was garded both with cunning & ſtrength: ſelf-loue thē firſt in him diuided it ſelfe frō vain-glory, & made him find that the world of worthines had not his whole globe cōpriſed in his breſt, but that it was neceſſary to haue ſtrong reſiſtāce againſt ſo ſtrong aſſailing. And ſo between thē, for a few blowes, *Mars* himſelf might haue bin delighted to looke on. But *Zelmane*, who knew that in her caſe, ſlowneſſe of victory was little better thē ruine, with the bellowes of hate, blew the fire of courage, and he ſtriking a maine blow at her head, ſhe warded it with the ſhield, but ſo warded, that the ſhield was cut in two pieces, while it protected her, & withall ſhe ran in to him, and thruſting at his breſt, which he put by with his target, as he was lifting vp his ſword to ſtrike again, ſhe let fall the piece of her ſhield, and with her left hand catching his ſword of the inſide of the pōmel, with nimble & ſtrong ſleight, ſhe had gottē his ſword out of his hand before his ſence could cōuey to his imaginatiō, what was to be doubted. And hauing now two ſwords againſt one ſhield, meaning not fooliſhly to be vngratefull to good fortune, while he was no more amazed with his being vnweapned, then with the ſuddainnes therof, ſhe gaue him

him such a woūd vpō his head, in despite of the shields
ouer-weak resistāce,that withal he fel to the groūd,asto-
nished with the paine, & agast with feare.But seing *Zel-*
mane ready to cōclude her victory in his death,bowing
vp his head to her,with a countenance that had forgotten al pride,Enough excellent Lady,said he,the honor
is yours: Wherof you shall want the best witnes,if you
kil me.As you haue takē frō men the glory of māhood,
returne so now againe to your owne sex, for mercy. I
wil redeeme my life of you with no smal seruices, for I
will vndertake to make my brother obey all your com-
mādements:Grant life I beseech you,for your own honor,and for the persons sake that you loue best.

 Zelmane represt a while her great hart,either disdaining 7
to be cruell,or pitiful, & therfore not cruell:& now the
image of humane condition,begā to be an Orator vnto
her of compassiō, whē she saw, as he lifted vp his armes
with a suppliāts grace,about one of thē, vnhappily,tied
a garter with a Iewel,which(giue to *Pyrocles* by his aunt
of *Thessalia*,& greatly esteemed by him)he had preseted
to *Philoclea*, & with inward rage promising extream hatred,had seene *Lycurgus* with a proud force,& not with
out some hurt vnto her, pull away frō *Philoclea*, because
at entreatie she would not giue it him. But the sight of
that was like a cyphar, signifying all the iniuries which
Philoclea had of him suffred,& that remēbrance feeding
vpō wrath,trod down al cōceits of mercy.And therfore
saying no more,but,No villaine,dye:It is *Philoclea* that
feds thee this tokē for thy loue.With that she made her
sword drink the blood of his hart, though he wresting
his body, & with a coūtenāce prepared to excuse,wold
fain haue delaied the receiuing of deaths embassadors.

 But neither that staied *Zelmanes* hand,nor yet *Anaxius* 8
cric

crie vnto her, who hauing made faſt the Iron gate, euen
then came to the top of the ſtaires, when, contrarie to
all his imaginations, he ſaw his brother lie at *Zelmanes*
mercie. Therefore crying, promiſing, and threatning
to her to hold her hand: the laſt grone of his brother
was the onely anſwere he could get to his vnreſpected
eloquence. But then Pittie would faine haue drawne
teares, which Furie in their ſpring dried ; and Anger
would faine haue ſpoken, but that Diſdaine ſealed vp
his lippes ; but in his hart he blaſphemed heauen, that
it could haue ſuch a power ouer him ; no leſſe aſhamed
of the victorie he ſhould haue of her, then of his brothers ouerthrow: and no more ſpited, that it was yet vn-
reuenged, then that the reuenge ſhould be no greater,
then a womans deſtruction. Therefore with no ſpeach,
but ſuch a groning crie, as often is the language of ſo-
rowfull anger, he came running at *Zelmane*, vſe of fighting then ſeruing in ſteed of patient conſideration what
to doo. Guided wherewith, though he did not with
knowledge, yet did he according to knowledge, preſ-
ſing vpon *Zelmane* in ſuch a wel defended manner, that
in all the combats that euer ſhe had fought, ſhe had neuer more need of quicke ſenſes, & ready vertue. For being one of the greateſt men of ſtature then liuing, as he
did fully anſwere that ſtature in greatneſſe of might, ſo
did he exceed both in greatnes of courage, which with
a coūtenāce formed by the nature both of his mind &
body, to an almoſt horrible fiercenes, was able to haue
carried feare to any mind, that was not priuie to it ſelfe
of a true & cōſtant worthines. But *Pyrocles*, whoſe ſoule
might well be ſeparated frō his body, but neuer alienated frō the remembring what was comely, if at the firſt
he

he did a little apprehend the dangerousnes of his aduersarie, whom once before he had something tried, & now perfectly saw, as the very picture of forcible furie: yet was that apprehension quickly stayed in him, rather strengthning, then weakning his vertue by that wrestling; like wine, growing the stróger by being moued. So that they both, prepared in harts, and able in hands, did honor solitarines there with such a combat, as might haue demaunded, as a right of fortune, whole armies of beholders. But no beholders needed there, where manhood blew the trumpet, & satisfaction did whette, as much as glorie. There was strength against nimblenes; rage, against resolution, fury, against vertue; confidence, against courage; pride, against noblenesse: loue, in both, breeding mutual hatred, & desire of reuéging the iniurie of his brothers slaughter, to *Anaxius*, being like *Philocleas* captiuity to *Pyrocles*. Who had seen the one, would haue thought nothing could haue resisted; who had marked the other, would haue marueiled that the other had so long resisted. But like two contrarie tides, either of which are able to carry worldes of shippes, and men vpon them, with such swiftnes, as nothing seemes able to withstand them: yet meeting one another, with mingling their watrie forces, and strugling together, it is long to say whether streame gets the victorie: So betweene these, if *Pallas* had bene there, she could scarcely haue tolde, whether she had nurced better in the feates of armes. The Irish greyhound, against the English mastiffe; the sword-fish, against the whale; the Rhinoceros, against the elephãt, might be models, & but models of this cóbat. *Anaxius* was better armed defensiuely: for (beside a strong caske braue-

brauely couered,wherwith he couerd his head)he had
a huge fhield,fuch perchance,as *Achilles* fhewed to the
pale walles of Troy,wherewithall that body was coue-
red.But *Pyrocles*,vtterly vnarmed for defence,to offend
had the aduantage: for,in either hand he had a fword,
& with both hands nimbly performed that office.And
according.as they were diuerfly furnifhed, fo did they
differ in the manner of fighting . For *Anaxius* moft by
warding,and *Pyrocles* oftneft by auoyding , refifted the
aduerfaries affault . Both haftie to end , yet both often
ftaying for aduantage.Time,diftance,& motiõ cuftom
made them fo perfeð in,that as if they had bene felow
Counfellers, and not enemies, each knewe the others
minde, and knew how to preuent it. So as their ftrégth
fayled them fooner then their skill,and yet their breath
fayled them fooner then their ftrength. And breathles
indeed they grew, before either could complaine of a-
ny loffe of bloud.

CHAP. 29.

¹ The Combattants firſt breathing, ² reencounter,and

SO confenting by the mediation
of neceffitie, to a breathing time
of truce , being withdrawen a little
one from the other; *Anaxius* ſtood
leaning vpon his fworde , with his
grym eye, fo fetled vpon *Zelmane,*
as is wont to be the look of an ear-
neftthought.Which *Zelmane* marking,&,according to
the *Pyroclean* nature, fuller of gay brauerie in the midſt,
then.

then in the beginning of dāger; What is it(said she)*A-naxius;* that thou so deeply musest on? Dooth thy bro-thers exāple make thee thinke of thy fault past,or of thy cōming punishmēt? I think(said he)what spiteful God it should be, who,enuying my glory, hath brought me to such a waywarde case, that neither thy death can be a reuenge, nor thy ouerthrow a victorie. Thou doost well indeede (saide *Zelmane)* to impute thy case to the heauenly prouidence, which will haue thy pride find it selfe(euen in that whereof thou art most proud) puni-shed by the weake sex, which thou most contem-nest.

But then,hauing sufficiently rested themselues, they renewed againe their combatte, farre more terribly then before : like nimble vaulters, who at the first and second leape, doo but stirre,and(as it were) awake the fierie and aërie partes, which after in the other leapes, they doo with more excellencie exercise. For in this pausing,ech had brought to his thoughts the maner of the others fighting,and the aduantages,which by that, and by the qualitie of their weapons,they might work themselues ; and so againe repeated the lesson they had said before,more perfectly, by the vsing of it . *Anaxius* oftner vsed blowes, his huge force (as it were) more delighting therein, and the large protection of his shield,animating him vnto it . *Pyrocles,* of a more fine, and deliuer strength , watching his time when to giue fitte thrustes ; as , with the quick obeying of his bodie, to his eyes quicke commaundement, he shunned any harme *Anaxius* could do to him:so would he soon haue made an end of *Anaxius,*if he had not foūd him a mā of

WOR-

wonderful,& almoſt matchleſſe excellécy in matters of armes. *Pyrocles* vſcd diuers faynings,to bring *Anaxius* on, into ſome inconuenience. But *Anaxius* keeping a found maner of fighting,neuer offered,but ſeeing faire cauſe, & then followed it with wel-gouerned violence. Thus ſpent they a great time,ſtriuing to doo , and with ſtriuing to doo , wearying themſelues,more then with the very doing. *Anaxius* finding *Zelmane* ſo neere vnto him , that with little motion he might reach her , knitting all his ſtrength together , at that time mainly ſoyned at her face. But *Zelmane* ſtrongly putting it by with her right handc ſword, comming in with her left foote, and hand   woulde haue giuen him a ſharpe viſitation to his right ſide , but that he was faine to leape away. Whereat aſhamed, (as hauing neuer done ſo much before in his life)

❖ ❖ ❖